REGULATING REPRODUCTION

Regulating Reproduction
Law, Technology and Autonomy

EMILY JACKSON
London School of Economics

·HART·
PUBLISHING
OXFORD – PORTLAND OREGON
2001

Oxford and Portland, Oregon

Published in North America (US and Canada) by
Hart Publishing
c/o International Specialized Book Services
5804 NE Hassalo Street
Portland, Oregon
97213-3644
USA

Distributed in the Netherlands, Belgium and Luxembourg by
Intersentia, Churchillaan 108
B2900 Schoten
Antwerpen
Belgium

Hart Publishing Ltd is a specialist legal publisher based in Oxford, England.
To order further copies of this book or to request a list of other
publications please write to:

Hart Publishing Ltd, Salter's Boatyard, Folly Bridge, Abingdon Road,
Oxford OX1 4LB
Telephone: +44 (0)1865 245533 or Fax: +44 (0)1865 794882
e-mail: mail@hartpub.co.uk
WEBSITE: http://www.hartpub.co.uk

British Library Cataloguing in Publication Data
Data Available
ISBN 1–84113–054–0 (Hardback)
ISBN 1–84113–301–9 (Paperback)

Typeset by Hope Services (Abingdon) Ltd.
Printed and bound in Great Britain by
Biddles Ltd,
www.biddles.co.uk

In memory of my mother
Lesley Jackson

Acknowledgments

I would like to thank Richard Hart for his enthusiasm, patience and support over the past two years. Sabbatical leave from Birkbeck College Law Department and a grant from the British Academy enabled me to start the research for this book in New York, and I am grateful to NYU Law School, and particularly to Holly Maguigan, for the help I received during my stay. The students on my medical law course at LSE deserve thanks for their persistent and challenging interest in the subject, among them Aimée Shirin-Daruwala and Karen Stephens were diligent proof-readers.

Of the countless colleagues and friends who have provided me with inspiration, encouragement and welcome distractions during the writing of this book I should especially like to thank Hugh Collins, Nicola Lacey, Ellie Lee, Mavis Maclean, Ngaire Naffine, Katherine O'Donovan, Helen Reece, Sally Sheldon, Juliet Tizzard and Matthew Weait, all of whom made perceptive and invaluable comments on earlier drafts. For their wit, wisdom and love, I am grateful to my best and oldest friends: Jonathan Brenton, Alison Cox, Rebecca Mead, Ciarán O'Meara, Duncan Paterson and Monica Thurnauer. My father and brother have, as ever, been a constant source of support. But my greatest debt is undoubtedly to my husband, Paul Raffield, who continues to be indispensable.

Contents

Table of Cases

Table of Legislation

INTERNATIONAL

EUROPEAN

Directives

Protocols

Regulations

NATIONAL

Australia

Germany

India

Japan

South Africa

United Kingdom

Circulars

Notices

Statutory Instruments

United States

Regulations

1

In Defence of Reproductive Autonomy

THE RELATIONSHIP BETWEEN law and human reproduction is a complex and a fascinating one. When human beings could do little to control their fertility or infertility, law was of comparatively little importance. As the reproductive process has been opened up to more intensive scrutiny, and as the opportunities for its external manipulation multiply, law has assumed an ever greater significance. In addition to some important statutes and developments in the common law, there is also now an expanding body of diverse regulatory practices that are directed towards the government of human procreation.

Innovative technologies and advances in human genetics are forcing us to constantly rethink the boundaries of what might be humanly possible. Creating a regulatory framework capable of accommodating all of the ethical dilemmas thrown up by this rapidly shifting terrain undoubtedly represents one of the most important and difficult tasks for law in the twenty-first century. In addition to the speed with which law may inevitably become obsolete, the regulation of reproduction is further complicated by the existence of profound moral disagreement about the propriety of human intervention in the reproductive process. There will, for example, never be consensus about the moral status of a fetus. So in working out how to regulate abortion, pursuit of a compromise that reaches even a minimal level of universal acceptability is almost certainly futile.

The purpose of this book is to offer a critical and legal analysis of the regulation of five different aspects of reproduction: birth control, abortion, pregnancy and childbirth, reproductive technologies and surrogacy. Throughout these five chapters the overarching theme will be my argument that regulation should be concerned to promote autonomous reproductive decision-making. This means, for example, that I believe the decision to use contraception or to be sterilised cannot properly be made by anyone other than the individual whose fertility is to be controlled. Similarly, I argue that a pregnant woman should be allowed to decide for herself whether or not to have an abortion. Where a woman is carrying a pregnancy to term, her right to make decisions about her medical treatment and lifestyle should not be compromised by her pregnancy. If someone cannot reproduce without medical assistance, then I suggest that we should, as far as possible, offer them that assistance. And I argue that people who have freely entered into a surrogacy contract should not have their clearly expressed wishes ignored. In this introductory chapter, I want to briefly explain my enthusiasm for autonomy as an organising principle since some readers will find it surprising or believe it to be misguided.

At its most basic, the liberal concept of autonomy has its roots in the idea that, provided others are not harmed, each individual should be entitled to follow their own life plan in the light of their beliefs and convictions.[1] It would, however, be a mistake to imagine that the concept of autonomy within the liberal tradition has had a single, unitary meaning. On the contrary, a variety of different ideas concerning moral independence, self-government, freedom from external constraints, tolerance, pluralism and liberty have all crystallised around the notion that an individual's life may be enriched by her capacity to direct the course of her life according to her own values. My argument here will be that while liberalism's critics have tended to invoke a particularly narrow and impoverished conception of autonomy, a broader and richer understanding of reproductive autonomy may be both descriptively accurate and normatively desirable.

A certain strand of feminism has accused this liberal commitment to self-determination of excessive individualism and a lack of attentiveness to the importance of connections with others. Autonomy, it is sometimes argued, is principally a masculine trait and preoccupation, relying upon a (mis)conception of the self as unencumbered and emotionally detached. According to this critique, to prioritise autonomy is to value independence and self-sufficiency more highly than interdependence and connection. Reproductive autonomy, in the eyes of these critics, purports to treat pregnant women as isolated and primarily self-interested citizens, thus ignoring first the profound connection that exists between the pregnant woman and her fetus and second the network of relationships within which an individual's preferences are constructed.

The former objection to autonomy, namely that it inaccurately describes women's lived experience of maternity, assumes that being a woman is synonymous with possessing the capacity for pregnancy. Thus, for example, Robin West has said that

> "the experience of being human, for women, differentially from men, includes the counter-autonomous experience of a shared physical identity between woman and fetus, as well as the counter-autonomous experience of the emotional and psychological bond between mother and infant'.[2]

Elsewhere, West argues that women are "connected to life and to other human beings during at least four recurrent and critical material experiences", namely pregnancy, heterosexual penetrative sexual intercourse, menstruation and breastfeeding.[3] While a recognition of the political significance of sexuality, pregnancy and motherhood is undeniably important, it is plainly untrue that *all*

---

[1] See, for example, Kymlicka, 1989, pp. 9–19.
[2] West, 1992, p. 823.
[3] West, 1991, p. 204.

women have the "counter-autonomous experience" of pregnancy, or share these "material experiences" of connectedness. For women who are infertile, or who have infertile partners, the capacity for pregnancy and hence for breastfeeding and childbearing may be irrevocably absent. Not all women have sexual partners, and not all women menstruate regularly throughout their adult lives. Thus, by effectively conflating being female with being a fertile, heterosexual and sexually active woman, the critique of autonomy which is grounded in its inability to accurately describe women's lives may itself be fundamentally flawed.

Furthermore, acknowledging the unparalled intimacy of pregnancy does not necessarily render the concept of autonomy redundant or meaningless. On the contrary, I suggest that the uniqueness of the bond that exists between a pregnant woman and her fetus should alert us to her intrinsic interest in defining for herself the scope of her relationship with the fetus that is living inside her body. Thus, rather than ascribing some essential and separate moral status to the fetus, I argue that its interests can only be determined in conjunction with a consideration of the interests of the pregnant woman within whom it exists. Thus, we acknowledge the special bond of pregnancy precisely by treating the pregnant woman's moral agency with particular respect. In my discussion both of abortion, and of the regulation of pregnancy and childbirth, I shall suggest that the pregnant woman should be entitled to control the course of her pregnancy. In my view, the law's failure to endow her with ultimate decision-making authority during pregnancy is only not perceived to be an egregious violation of her right to make important decisions about her body and her life because of a network of dominant cultural assumptions about the instinctiveness of maternal self-abnegation.

The second feminist critique of autonomy is grounded in the communitarian insight that an individual's identity and desires are largely determined by their membership of various social groups or communities.[4] Alison Jaggar, for example has condemned:

> "the liberal assumption that human individuals are essentially solitary with needs and interests that are separate from if not in opposition to those of other individuals".[5]

It is undoubtedly true that individuals cannot exist in this sort of social and cultural vacuum, with needs and interests that emerge and can be satisfied without reference to the needs and interests of others. Reproductive decisions, in particular, will obviously be informed by the rich network of relationships and cultural expectations within which each individual is situated. But my argument in this book will be that acknowledging the significance of our social, economic and emotional context should not lead us to jettison the whole concept of autonomy. Rather we should perhaps think about how we might reconfigure autonomy in a way that is not predicated upon the isolation of the self-directed and self-sufficient subject.

[4] See for example, MacIntyre, 1981; Sandel, 1982; Taylor, 1985.
[5] Jaggar, 1983, p. 40.

The problem with the conventional feminist critique of autonomy is that it sets up a binary opposition between interdependence and autonomy, as if the two were inevitably mutually exclusive. Thus it assumes we can only give priority to the autonomous choosing self if we completely disregard the web of connections that have moulded her identity, and conversely, that the project of respecting an individual's choices necessarily disintegrates if we acknowledge human beings' social embeddedness. Yet is this perceived tension between autonomy and interdependence simply the ways things are? Do alienation and self-determination always come as an indissoluble package?

That an association has commonly been drawn between self-sufficiency and self-determination does not, in itself, establish their inseparability. A conception of autonomy that is effectively synonymous with "erecting a wall of rights around the individual"[6] is indubitably a thin and unsatisfactory one, relying on a wholly fictitious conception of the self as essentially insular. The "boundary metaphor"[7] may have had powerful symbolic resonance, allowing analogies to be drawn between the sovereignty of nation states and the sovereignty of the individual subject, but it has also proved to be manifestly inadequate in describing the "irreducibly mysterious . . . combination of individuality and 'enmeshedness', integrity and integration that constitutes the human being".[8]

Certainly many mainstream liberal philosophers acknowledge that it is impossible to think about ourselves without acknowledging the web of obligations that we acquire by virtue of our multiple connections with others.[9] Bernard Williams, for example, has argued that commitments, duties and relationships are precisely what give our lives meaning and character.[10] In fact few liberals believe that the capacity for autonomous choice is an innate attribute of humanness, rather most would argue that it emerges from the set of cultural traditions within which individuals learn to interact with each other, and to develop their sense of self. Thus, Will Kymlicka has suggested that in order to pursue their own conception of the good:

> "Individuals must . . . have the *resources* and liberties needed to live their lives in accordance with their beliefs about value . . . and individuals must have the *cultural conditions* conducive to acquiring an awareness of different views about the good life, and to acquiring an ability to intelligently examine and re-examine these views" (my emphasis).[11]

Within conventional liberal accounts of the self, it is not simply the existence of freedom of choice that matters, rather their habitual concern has been with the conditions and resources that may be necessary precursors of the capacity for

---

[6] Nedelsky, 1990, p. 167.
[7] *ibid*. p. 168.
[8] *ibid*. p. 182.
[9] Feinberg, 1986; Dworkin, 1988.
[10] Williams, 1973.
[11] Kymlicka, 1989, p. 13.

autonomy. It is therefore axiomatic that without socialisation within a strong network of relationships, an individual's right to self-determination would be both meaningless and irrelevant.

Possessing freedom of choice does not, without more, guarantee that an individual's life will be enriched by choosing between the options that are available to them. Even if we do have a degree of control over our reproductive lives, it is clear that we will sometimes have few realistic alternatives. In fact, as we see at several points during this book, the right to make procreative choices can coexist with the substantive incapacity to exercise any real control over one's reproductive life. The space within which autonomy may be exercised will always perhaps be comparatively small, but I would argue that possessing *some* control over the direction of one's life is a necessary constituent part of a "good" or agreeable existence. A commitment to autonomy may therefore emerge precisely from the recognition that many people's capacity to lead a self-authored life is profoundly limited.

Liberal theory does not necessarily presuppose that every individual *already has* the freedom to choose between a set of genuine and valuable alternatives, rather this may be a principal *goal* of theories of redistributive justice. In order to treat individuals with dignity and respect, we should therefore give them both the freedom to exercise reproductive choice, *and a set of realistic and valuable reproductive opportunities*. Here Joseph Raz's formulation of autonomy is useful:

> "To be autonomous a person must not only be given a choice but he must also be given an adequate range of choices".[12]

Thus, my point is not to argue that reproductive choices exist and can be satisfied in a social vacuum, instead I suggest that a community should be concerned to foster an environment in which the exercise of reproductive choice is both possible *and valuable*.

In order to establish its target's excessive and objectionable individualism, the conventional feminist critique of autonomy may therefore be relying upon a distorted and exaggerated version of the liberal conception of the self. The liberal tradition is a broad and varied one, and while there may be some liberals who believe that the self is intrinsically insular, there are others for whom a commitment to autonomy is synonymous with a rich and nuanced account of our inevitable interdependence.

In recent years there has been revived feminist interest in reworking the concept of autonomy so that the part relationships and community play in its realisation are properly acknowledged.[13] This feminist analysis has rejected the "pathological conception of autonomy as boundaries against others",[14] in order to understand that relationships and interdependence may be necessary

---

[12] Raz, 1986, p. 373.
[13] See further Meyers, 1989; Nedelsky, 1989; Huntington, 1995; Friedman, 1997.
[14] Nedelsky, 1989, p. 13.

preconditions for the productive exercise of meaningful choice. Iris Marion Young's participatory model of empowerment, for example, emphasises the social constraints upon the options from which an individual is able to choose.[15] Thus our preoccupation should not be with the essentially uncontentious insight that we are not self-sufficient, atomistic individuals relentlessly pursuing our own purely self-interested ends, but rather we should be thinking about what sort of laws, institutions and services might allow us to maximise our capacity to exercise control over reproduction given the network of social constraints that will always tend to limit our options.

A crucial initial step might be the recognition that reproductive autonomy is not something that an individual either has or does not have. It is not a static or innate quality, rather a person's capacity to make meaningful choices about their reproductive capacity may fluctuate according to a complex matrix of social, economic and psychological factors. Autonomy is, as Jennifer Nedelsky has explained

> "a capacity that requires ongoing relationships that help it flourish; it can wither or thrive throughout one's adult life".[16]

The willingness of the British courts to authorise the sterilisation of mentally ill women, for example, reveals their perception that possessing autonomy is a permanent and immutable function of one's status, as either competent or incompetent. This static conception of autonomy ignores both the future mutability of a diagnosis of incompetence, and the possibility that a woman's decision-making incapacity may in fact reflect a systematic failure to provide her with appropriate support. Thus, by addressing the nature of the care that is and will be available to the mentally incapacitated woman, her ability to make autonomous reproductive decisions might be enhanced.

Autonomy, then, is not just the right to pursue ends that one already has, but also to live in an environment which enables one to form one's own value system and to have it treated with respect. Acknowledging that our preferences do not spring unbidden from the inner depths of our self-constituting minds need not lead to the refusal to respect those preferences on the grounds that they are inevitably socially constructed. It is true that none of us chooses some of the crucial determinants of our values and beliefs, such as our parents, nationality, education, religion etc.. But the fact that we cannot choose *who we are* does not necessarily mean that we should not be allowed to choose *what we do*. Our reproductive choices are, of course, shaped by multiple external influences, but they are the only choices we have, and they are therefore of critical importance to our sense of self. The decision to have an abortion, for example, is made because, for a variety of reasons, this particular woman does not want to carry her pregnancy to term. That she is not in control of all of those reasons should

---

[15]   Young, 1997.
[16]   Nedelsky, 1993, p. 8.

not lead us to ignore her deeply felt preference. Even if we recognise that social
forces may shape and constrain our choices, our sense of being the author of
our own actions, especially when they pertain to something as personal as
reproduction, is profoundly valuable to us. We cannot believe that all of our
preferences are irredeemably "not ours" without our sense of self effectively col-
lapsing.

Human beings are not self-constituting subjects, with a set of pre-social
desires, but neither do they entirely lack the capacity for agency and self-
direction, otherwise it would be impossible to account for the different choices
made by similarly situated people.[17] We may be able to explain many of our
beliefs with reference to our circumstances, but our socially constructed value
system does not effectively predetermine *all* of the decisions that we take about
the course of our lives.[18] Replacing the caricatured version of the autonomous
self's endless capacity for unmediated, self-interested decision making with a
theoretical paradigm that leaves no room for an individual to make unexpected
or unorthodox choices is, I argue, equally unsatisfactory. Equivalent respect for
both surprising and predictable decisions is one of the most important features
of a commitment to autonomy, and I argue that this is especially necessary when
a person is making choices about reproduction.

When we disregard an individual's reproductive preferences, we undermine
their ability to control one of the most intimate spheres of their life. Our reproductive capacity or incapacity indubitably has a profound impact upon the
course of our lives, and decisions about whether or not to reproduce are
among the most momentous choices that we will ever make. Ronald Dworkin
has distinguished between our experiential preferences for various activities or
pastimes that might make our lives more pleasurable, but do not go to the
heart of what makes our lives worth living, and what he describes as "critical
interests".[19] I would argue that reproductive freedom is sufficiently integral to
a satisfying life that it should be recognised as a critical "conviction about
what helps to make a life good".[20] Insofar as it is now possible for individuals
to decide if, whether or when to reproduce, depriving them of this control significantly interferes with their capacity to live their life according to their own
beliefs and priorities. In relation to women, a lack of respect for their reproductive autonomy may even involve infringing their bodily integrity, as has
happened when the courts have authorised non-consensual surgical intervention in childbirth.

Moreover, proper respect for reproductive autonomy cannot be limited to
removing external constraints from an individual's capacity to follow preferences that are *already* fully formed and clearly articulated. Instead there may be
times when the positive provision of resources and services may be necessary in

[17] Bevir, 1999.
[18] Nedelsky, 1995, p. 159.
[19] Dworkin, 1993, pp. 200–2.
[20] *ibid.* p. 202.

order to assist people both to work out their own priorities and to realise them. Adopting Martha Nussbaum's idea of the citizen as "a free and dignified human being, a maker of choices",[21] simply having reproductive choices to make in the first place might be an essential precondition of a life that is, in some important sense, self-authored. Before the articulation of their preferences is even possible, mentally incapacitated women may first require a supportive environment that treats their sexuality and bodily integrity with appropriate seriousness. Similarly, without the provision of assisted conception services, infertile people may have no valuable reproductive options from which to choose. That the paucity of their opportunities is in some sense "natural" does not mean that it should be tolerated. Modern medicine is predicated on enabling people to avoid the disabling impact of natural phenomena. Insofar as infertile individuals' lives *can* be enriched by the provision of assisted conception services, we should strive to maximise their reproductive options. In sum, respect for reproductive autonomy may mean both fostering individuals' capacity to form their own conception of the good, and providing them with a range of life-enhancing procreative choices.

Most of this book will be arguing for *women's* rights to make reproductive choices for themselves. This is because reproductive choice commonly, but not exclusively, involves making intimate decisions about a woman's body. The decision to, for example, have an abortion or a caesarean section must, if each individual's bodily integrity is adequately protected, be made by the woman herself. If a man's interest in reproductive outcomes can only be respected at the expense of respect for the separate integrity of a woman's body, then it must be ignored. There are, however, some situations in which taking a man's reproductive preferences seriously will not jeopardise women's bodily autonomy. If a man chooses to undergo a vasectomy, for example, his desire for sterility should be respected. This means that if his partner subsequently becomes pregnant following negligent post-operative tests, he ought not to be advised that the operation's failure is treated by the law as a "blessing".

While writing this book, I have been aware that many strands of my argument could plausibly be framed in terms of rights. The Human Rights Act 1998, for example, contains a right to privacy and respect for one's family life,[22] and a right to "found a family".[23] Could we say that a woman's right to determine the course of her pregnancy is an aspect of her privacy right? Might we argue that the right to found a family requires universal access to infertility treatment? These are questions that will undoubtedly be addressed in subsequent case law, and it would be a mistake for me to underplay their significance. However, neither of these rights is absolute and the various qualifications undoubtedly offer multiple possible justifications for their denial. Moreover, reproduction has conventionally been treated as a subject in which individual member states'

---

[21] Nussbaum, 1999, p. 46.
[22] Article 8.
[23] Article 12.

margin of appreciation should be especially wide. Within Europe, for example, there is enormous variation in abortion law and in the regulations governing assisted conception.

Rights, in the narrow sense envisaged by the Human Rights Act 1998, are unlikely to transform the regulation of reproduction in the UK. Nevertheless, I would argue that a more broadly conceived right to respect for reproductive autonomy is demanded by basic principles of justice, liberty and moral tolerance. A commitment to autonomy should, in my opinion, inform the complex relationship between law and reproduction, leading to a strong predilection to give maximum possible respect to individuals' interest in making some of the most important decisions of their lives according to their own conception of the good. Of course there will be times when one person's procreative freedom might be incompatible with other more important social values, but the very intimacy of reproduction means that such circumstances are likely to be rare.

The right to reproductive self-determination that I defend in this book is not an absolute right to, for example, have a baby or an abortion, rather it is a right to have one's reproductive choices treated with respect. This means that the law should strive, as far as possible, to expand our procreative freedom, and protect our moral agency. Thus our capacity to make these critical choices about the course of our lives should be inhibited only where there are good and *relevant* reasons for interfering with our interest in directing the course of our reproductive lives. In practice, as I argue in chapter three, it may be difficult to find adequate reasons for refusing a woman's request for an abortion. But we might, for example, accept that unlimited access to infertility treatment would jeopardise the NHS's capacity to offer universal health care, and that resource-based considerations might legitimately inform a *just* rationing system.

A rich understanding of autonomy, as a capacity that is dependent upon the existence of strong social support and constructive networks of relationships, can help us to identify the law's task in regulating reproduction. We should, I argue, be alert to the web of constraints that may impoverish many people's reproductive lives, and think about ways in which we might be able to foster each individual's capacity to exercise meaningful and enriching reproductive choice.

2

Birth Control

1. INTRODUCTION

Birth CONTROL HAS been practised throughout history: Plato's laws, for example, referred to the "many devices available . . . to check propagation"[1] and Aristotle suggested that official endorsement of homosexuality in Crete was principally a population control strategy.[2] At the beginning of the second century, a comprehensive treatise of contraceptive techniques was published,[3] and while some contraceptive advice, such as "spitting into a frog's open mouth three times",[4] was obviously purely superstitious, modern research has indicated that other primitive birth control methods may have been effective.[5]

For hundreds of years, information about the natural contraceptive properties of various plants was passed down orally by generations of midwives.[6] The correlation that was commonly drawn between the practices of midwifery and witchcraft has even been attributed to the pro-natalist agenda of certain religious and political leaders.[7] In 1484, for example, Pope Innocent VIII issued a *summis desiderantes* against witchcraft, singling out as especially heinous the crimes:

> "to ruin and cause to perish the offspring of women and hinder men from begetting and women from conceiving".[8]

Thus, attempts to suppress the dissemination of information about birth control techniques through the persecution of witches might constitute an early example of the state seeking to control the fertility of its citizens.

[1] Quoted in Riddle, 1997, p. 14.
[2] Pollard, 1994, p. 275.
[3] Soranus's *Gynaecia* described vaginal plugs, astringent solutions and the use of fruit acids (Pollard, 1994, p. 275).
[4] *Qusta ibn Luqa*, a 10th century Arabic text (quoted in Riddle, 1997, p. 67).
[5] The Ebers papyrus, written around 1500 BC contained prescriptions in use from 2500 BC One of these, compounded acacia, produces lactic acid which is still used in many modern spermicides. Modern tests on rats suggest that ingestion of acacia Koa may reduce the frequency of litters by between 88–100%. Pomegranate seeds were recognised as antifertility agents in Greek medicine and are still used in India, East Africa and some Pacific areas. Tests on guinea pigs have shown reduction in fertility of up to 100% (Riddle 1997).
[6] Riddle, 1997, pp. 123–5.
[7] Heinsohn and Steiger, 1982.
[8] Quoted in Riddle, 1997, p. 124.

A recurring theme in this chapter will be the complex relationship between individuals' contraceptive behaviour and public policy.[9] Throughout the world, concern about rates of population growth has led to the adoption of either anti or pro-natalist policies.[10] As demographic shifts have become more minutely visible, population policies have been subject to increasingly rapid and dramatic change.[11] Given that it has become the received wisdom that there is a causal link between demography and development, it is probably unsurprising that there has been considerable public interest in what is also one of the most intimate of choices. Although it is undoubtedly true that demographic shifts are in part the cumulative result of millions of individual decisions about contraception, there is in fact little empirical evidence[12] to support the assumption that a country's economic prosperity depends upon its population's fertility.[13] Instead, a variety of often unarticulated fears tend to crystallise around the perception that the fertility of a particular population or social group is out of control.

A second ambiguity that emerges in relation to the regulation of birth control concerns its impact upon women's lives. On the one hand it could be argued that the freedom to have sexual intercourse without the burden of unwanted pregnancy is essentially liberating and empowering.[14] On the other hand, controlling a woman's fertility without her fully informed and freely given consent is intensely violatory and disempowering.[15] So while birth control may be an important adjunct of women's equality, it also has the potential to be used in discriminatory and oppressive ways.[16] This rather slippery

[9] Moskowitz *et al* argue that "sexuality and reproduction are never solely self-regarding and merely private. They always have both social consequences and social dimensions" (Moskowitz *et al*, 1996, p. 6).

[10] In Singapore, concern about falling birth rates has led to the Government's current promotion of 3 children per family as the ideal (Chamie, 1994, p. 42).

[11] In the UK, for example, fears of population decline were central to the active prosecution of abortionists after World War II, while a few years later, the perceived threat of a population explosion undoubtedly played an important role in campaigns for free access to safe legal abortion. In the US in November 1959 the US President Dwight Eisenhower said that "so long as I am president, this government will have nothing to do with birth control". While in August 1965, President Lyndon Johnson urged the American people to "face forthrightly the multiplying problems of our multiplying populations" (Chamie, 1994, pp. 42, 37). Malcolm Potts has suggested that "over the past 25 years population policies have swung back and forth like a pendulum" (Potts, 1999, p. 933).

[12] Furedi, 1997.

[13] The preamble to the European Council Regulation No. 1484/97 states that "the capacity of most developing countries to achieve sustainable human development is hampered by . . . the high rate of population growth".

[14] In addition, the American anarchist Emma Goldman regarded birth control as an important tactic in the fight against capitalism: "the struggle against capitalism would be more effective once the labourer was freed from the shackles of the overly large family" (Quoted in McLaren and McLaren, 1997, p. 75).

[15] This paradox was clearly visible in the change in Government policy that took place in the Philippines when President Marcos was replaced by Corazon Aquino. Under Marcos, women were coerced into accepting IUDs and sterilisation, while Aquino, a Catholic, banned the use of birth control. Ruth Macklin suggests that both policies violated women's reproductive rights (Macklin, 1996, p. 181).

[16] Dorothy Roberts has pointed out that "the first publicly funded birth control clinics in the United States were established in the South in the 1930s as a way of lowering the black birthrate" (Roberts, 1993, p. 1970).

distinction between freedom and its opposite is of particular importance given the development of new techniques which improve contraceptive efficacy by eliminating the need for user participation, and thus removing the possibility of user-failure. For some women, long-lasting protection against pregnancy will have considerable appeal, but taking control over their fertility out of the hands of individual women inevitably also facilitates the quasi-coercive use of birth control.

Law undoubtedly plays a significant role in facilitating the provision of safe and accessible birth control, through, for example, licensing requirements and rules governing the prescription of medicines. An important line must, however, be drawn between ensuring access to contraception and effectively mandating its use. While extreme cases in which the law is used to directly control an individual's fertility may now be rare, it is not always easy to distinguish policies that aim to encourage the use of birth control from those which subtly reduce individuals' reproductive freedom. The ability to exercise control over one's reproductive capacity is central to both sexual privacy and bodily autonomy, and throughout this chapter my argument will be that the decision to practise birth control ought properly to belong only to the individual citizen. As a result, I would confine the law's role to providing a regulatory framework for the licensing and distribution of a range of safe contraceptive options, and to ascribing responsibility when an individual has suffered harm as a result of defective birth control.

In this chapter, we consider three disparate ways in which the law has regulated the provision of birth control. First, the law has a role in managing access to various contraceptive techniques, both by licensing particular methods and by demarcating the circumstances in which they may be obtained. Second, the law of tort governs the availability of remedies when contraception or sterilisation proves defective. Third, the law has been used to authorise the involuntary use of birth control. Although different issues are raised by each of these three functions, the common thread will be my argument that the decision to exercise control over one's fertility is an essential adjunct of bodily autonomy, and should therefore be treated with appropriate respect.

2. REGULATING ACCESS TO BIRTH CONTROL

(a) United Kingdom

(i) Licensing

The rules governing the licensing of contraceptives in the UK consist of an amalgamation of British and European provisions. Contraceptives are medicinal products within the definition of Council Directive 65/65/EEC because their purpose is to "modify.. physiological functions". Various statutory instruments, such as the Medicines for Human Use (Authorisations Etc.) Regulations[17] incorporate the EU framework into British law so that, for example, every application for a license must be made in accordance with the relevant EU provisions.[18] Before any new contraceptive can be distributed, it must first have been licensed either by the Medicines Control Agency (MCA), or by the European Agency for the Evaluation of Medicinal Products (commonly known as the European Medicines Evaluation Agency or EMEA).[19] Applications to EMEA for a European marketing authorisation are relatively uncommon, and most contraceptives continue to be licensed by the MCA. Any application must contain full details of the research trials that have been carried out, on both animals and humans. Following evaluation by the Committee on the Safety of Medicines, a recommendation is then made to the Medicines Control Agency.

In deciding whether to grant a marketing authorisation, the Medicines Act 1968 requires the Agency to give particular consideration to the safety, efficacy and quality of the product.[20] The price of the product is not an adequate reason for rejecting an application.[21] Once granted, a marketing authorisation lasts for five years, during which time the MCA will monitor the medicine and keep a record of reported side-effects.[22] The producer of the product is also under a duty to record details of any adverse reactions reported to it. The MCA can immediately withdraw a marketing authorisation in the light of evidence it receives about a product's side effects.

In addition to the licensing procedure, medicinal products must also be classified according to whether they are prescription-only, available for sale only in pharmacies, or on general sale. A medicine should be available solely on prescription if it is likely to present some direct or indirect danger to human health.[23] Until recently, all hormonal contraception was classified as prescription-only. In 2000 both the Medicines Control Agency and the Committee on Safety of Medicines agreed that the risks presented by post-coital contraception did not justify its prescription-only status and from January 2001 it has been

---

[17] S.I 1994/3144. Also the Medicines Act 1968 (Amendment)(No.2) Regulations 1992 (S.I. 1992/3271).

[18] Regulation 4.

[19] Since January 1995 a new European system, offering two routes for authorising medicinal products has been in operation. First, there is a "centralised" procedure, established by Directive 93/41/EEC Council Regulation (EEC) No. 2309/93 with applications made directly to EMEA. This leads to the granting of a European marketing authorisation by the Commission. Use of this procedure is compulsory for products derived from biotechnology, and optional for other innovative medicinal products. Second, there is the "mutual recognition" procedure established by Directive 93/39/EEC through which member states agree to recognise other member states' national marketing authorisations. This is applicable to the majority of conventional medicinal products.

[20] S. 19.

[21] S. 20(2).

[22] Under the yellow card scheme, doctors must report to the MCA all suspected adverse reactions to a medicinal product during the first two years of its license. Thereafter only serious suspected adverse reactions must be reported.

[23] S. 58A of the Medicines Act 1968.

sold over the counter in pharmacies.[24] The existence of several contra-indications for taking the ordinary oral contraceptive pill means that it is unlikely to become available without medical supervision.

In 1999 a new body called the National Institute for Clinical Excellence (NICE) was set up in order to monitor the clinical and cost-effectiveness of both new and existing medical treatments, and issue guidance about their availability within the NHS. NICE has not yet appraised any contraceptives, and given that most methods are both effective and relatively inexpensive, birth control may be a comparatively low priority in NICE's rolling programme of clinical appraisals.

(ii) Public Policy

Although people have attempted to control their fertility for thousands of years, until relatively recently practising birth control was considered deviant and immoral.[25] In the United Kingdom, birth control was never directly prohibited by law, although people providing contraceptive information were prosecuted under the Obscene Publications Act 1857. In 1877, for example, Charles Bradlaugh and Annie Besant were initially convicted on the grounds that a book[26] describing and recommending methods of birth control was obscene.[27] In 1925 Marie Stopes failed in a libel action because the House of Lords decided that it was fair comment to suggest that birth control practices were "monstrous" and "revolting to the healthy instincts of human nature".[28] Using birth control against the wishes of one's spouse for many years represented grounds for divorce. In 1956, for example, a divorce petition was granted on the grounds of the wife's cruelty in insisting upon the use of a female contraceptive device which the husband found "repulsive".[29]

There are still some people who believe that using birth control is immoral, but this is undoubtedly now a minority view. Aside from the Vatican, there is a

---

[24] An amendment to the Prescription Only Medicines (Human Use) Order was laid before Parliament on 11 December 2000. The order came into effect on 1 January 2001 and reclassifed progestogen-only emergency contraception to "pharmacy availability" for women aged 16 and over. The pills cost £19.99.

[25] In some countries, decriminalisation has only taken place relatively recently. For example, until 1969 selling contraceptives was unlawful in Canada, and as recently as 1961 a Toronto pharmacist was jailed for selling condoms (McLaren and McLaren, 1997, p. 132).

[26] The book was written by Charles Knowlton in 1832, it was called *The Fruits of Philosophy: The Private Companion of Young Married People by a Physician*. It was published with pictures in England in 1876 and the publishers were fined for producing a "dirty, filthy book". Annie Besant and Charles Bradlaugh subsequently reprinted it as *A Dirty, Filthy Book*.

[27] Their convictions were quashed on appeal *Bradlaugh and Besant* v. *The Queen* [1877] LR3 QBD 607. In the United States the Comstock Law of 1873 made it illegal to transport obscene material through the mail. It specifically included anything "designed or intended for the prevention of conception", and was used to confiscate condoms and diaphragms. It was not repealed until 1936 (See further Powderly, 1996).

[28] *Sutherland* v. *Stopes* [1925] AC 45.

[29] In *Forbes* v. *Forbes* [1956] P. 16, Latey QC held that a wife who had insisted upon "the use of a female contraceptive device (which) in time became repulsive" to her husband, had treated him with cruelty.

broad consensus at the United Nations in favour of comprehensive access to birth control. And despite the Vatican's continued opposition, most Roman Catholics in the developed world practise contraception.[30] Within Europe, Italy and Spain, both predominantly Catholic countries, have the lowest and the second lowest birth rates respectively.[31]

In the UK, access to birth control is comparatively straightforward. Since 1974 all forms of contraception, from condoms to the oral contraceptive pill, have been obtainable free of charge from General Practitioners and family planning clinics.[32] Both male and female elective sterilisation is available within the NHS, although there is usually a waiting list. The House of Lords decision in *Gillick* v. *Norfolk and Wisbech AHA*[33] means that even children who are below the age at which they are lawfully able to consent to sexual intercourse may be given contraceptive advice without their parents' consent.

Yet despite birth control's relative accessibility in the UK, its widespread non-use, particularly among teenagers, is increasingly perceived to be a pressing social problem. The UK has the highest rate of teenage pregnancy in Europe, and a high incidence of teenage motherhood.[34] Responding to concern about the social consequences of high teenage pregnancy rates, in June 1999 the Government's Social Exclusion Unit published a programme designed to halve the rates of teenage pregnancy within ten years.[35]

It seems clear that teenage girls with low expectations of education or employment are more likely to become pregnant,[36] and less likely to terminate an unwanted pregnancy. So, for example, a fall of twelve per cent in teenage pregnancy rates in the US between 1991 and 1996 was attributed, in part, to the health of the economy and better job prospects.[37] In the UK conception rates among the under-sixteens in the poorest London boroughs of Lambeth, Southwark and Lewisham are three times the national average, and birth rates are five times the national average.[38] This correlation between social and economic disadvantage and early parenthood inevitably also has a disproportionate impact upon certain

---

[30] Sander, 1992.

[31] Kulczycki, 1999, p. 20.

[32] Health Service Circular (I.S.) 32 (1974).

[33] [1986] 1 AC 112.

[34] The UK's teenage pregnancy rate is twice as high as Germany, three times as high as France, and six times as high as the Netherlands (Social Exclusion Unit, 1999, p. 6) Rates of teenage pregnancy have been rising; from 8.4 per 1000 girls aged 13–15 in 1995, to 9.4 per 1000 in 1996 (Office for National Statistics, 1997).

[35] Social Exclusion Unit, 1999.

[36] "One reason why the UK has such high teenage pregnancy rates is that there are more young people who see no prospect of a job and fear they will end up on benefit one way or the other. Put simply, they see no reason not to get pregnant". (Social Exclusion Unit, 1999, p. 7). The risk of becoming a teenage mother is almost ten times higher for a girl whose family is in social class V (unskilled manual), than those in social class I (professional) (Botting *et al*, 1998). Low educational achievement is also a risk factor for teenage parenthood (Kiernan, 1995).

[37] Donovan, 1998.

[38] Mawer, 1999, p. 1714.

ethnic minority groups.[39] There also appears to be a connection between un-protected sexual intercourse and common adolescent psychiatric disorders such as substance abuse, anti-social behaviour and eating disorders.[40] Thus, early first intercourse, and the non-use of contraception seem to be most common among already disadvantaged teenagers.

It is at least arguable then that high rates of teenage pregnancy depend primarily upon the nature of the employment and training opportunities available to unskilled young women. Government policy has, however, tended to focus upon improving sex education.[41] It is, of course, true that there are some obvious defects in the provision of school-based sex education and studies have shown that many teenagers consider their sex education to have been almost entirely without utility.[42] Moreover, in the UK any parent who believes, despite overwhelming evidence to the contrary,[43] that sex education encourages premature sexual activity has the legal right to withdraw their children from sex education.[44] This right is currently exercised by around one per cent of parents.[45]

The Government's new strategy advocates sex education that addresses young people's "relationship and negotiation skills", rather than simply explaining the mechanics of conception.[46] Advertising campaigns have been devised to counter the peer pressure that emerges from the misperception that most young teenagers are having sexual intercourse. In addition, the Government is keen to promote schemes that emphasise how hard it is to be a parent. There has, for example, been considerable interest in programmes which enable teenagers to discover that looking after a new baby is extremely

[39] According to the Policy Studies Institute, Bangladeshis, African-Caribbeans and Pakistanis face an increased risk of teenage parenthood. (Policy Studies Institute, 1994). For some groups, the main reason will be early marriage, but others are disproportionately likely to be in the groups at particularly high risk of unplanned pregnancy, such as teenagers within the care system or those excluded from school (Social Exclusion Unit, 1999, 19).

[40] Ramrakha *et al*, 2000.

[41] Social Exclusion Unit, 1999.

[42] Yamey, 1999. Brent Miller and Roberta Paikoff have even suggested that "sex education has little or no relationship to adolescent sexual behaviour, contraceptive use or pregnancy" (Miller and Paikoff, 1997, p. 265).

[43] In their review of the literature, Grunseit and Kippax, 1994 conclude that "The overwhelming majority of articles reviewed here, despite the variety of methodologies, countries under investigation and year of publication, find no support for the contention that sex education encourages sexual experimentation or increased activity. If any effect is observed, it is in the direction of postponed initiation of sexual intercourse and/or effective use of contraception." The Government's report on teenage pregnancy states that "good, comprehensive sex and relationships education does not make young people more likely to start sex. Indeed it can help them delay starting sex and make them more likely to use contraceptives when they do" (Social Exclusion Unit, 1999 p. 37).

[44] Section 405 of the Education Act 1996 gives parents the right to withdraw their children from any or all parts of a school's programme of sex education, apart from those elements of health and sex education which are required by the National Curriculum Science Order.

[45] Social Exclusion Unit, 1999, p. 39.

[46] Wright *et al*, 2000.

disruptive and stressful,[47] and the Government also intends to target young men in order to draw their attention to the Child Support Act 1991, and the potentially drastic financial implications of unprotected sexual intercourse.

Commentators often cite the Netherlands as an example of effective sex education, and it is certainly true that taking responsibility for planning pregnancies is widely regarded as a civic duty and the abortion rate is low.[48] Dutch teenagers do seem better able to communicate about sex and its consequences than their British counterparts.[49] But an environment in which open communication about sexual relationships is the norm is the result of multiple social influences, not just direct sex education.[50] As a result, copying the way in which Dutch schoolchildren learn about birth control will not instantly reduce rates of unintended pregnancy.

And while access to contraception is in theory straightforward, teenage girls do not always find it easy to attend a GP's surgery or a family planning clinic. So although it is clear that girls under sixteen can obtain contraceptive treatment without parental consent, and have a right to confidentiality for their discussions with medical practitioners, many teenagers still fear seeking contraceptive advice.[51] Making contraception more accessible to teenagers might then be an important priority for public policy. Evidence from other countries appears to show that school-based provision significantly increases teenagers' use of contraception, without increasing sexual activity,[52] and pilot schemes in which school nurses have been trained to dispense the morning-after pill are currently underway in state schools in Kent, Oxfordshire, Derbyshire and South Yorkshire.[53]

[47] For example, there have been trials of a scheme in which schoolchildren take home a "virtual baby" for a weekend. The computerised "baby" asks for food at random intervals and constantly demands attention. All of the pupils concluded that a baby was more demanding than they had imagined and had an adverse effect on their social life. The health visitor who introduced the scheme suggested that the experience had "more impact than words of advice ever could" (Cramb, 1998).

[48] For every 1000 women, 6 will have an abortion each year in the Netherlands, compared with 14 in the United Kingdom (Hadley, 1997, p. 179). Sex education begins at an early age and tends to be non-judgmental. It is estimated that 85% of Dutch adolescents use contraception the first time they have sexual intercourse (David and Radenakers, 1996).

[49] One survey found that two and a half times more Dutch than English boys discuss contraception with their partners before sex (Social Exclusion Unit, 1999, p. 53).

[50] Deeply embedded attitudes to female promiscuity may make some women reluctant to equip themselves with contraception. Thus, Catharine MacKinnon has argued that "using contraception means acknowledging and planning the possibility of intercourse, accepting one's sexual availability and appearing non-spontaneous" (MacKinnon, 1987, p. 95).

[51] In a 1993 survey, 66% of pregnant teenagers said that they thought it was illegal to get contraception from a GP or a family planning clinic (Family Planning Association, 1993) It has been estimated that, on average, teenagers first visit a doctor or a clinic to obtain contraception 11 months after they start having sex. Those who started having sex before they were fifteen years old waited 23.5 months before seeking contraceptive advice (Zabin and Hayward, 1993 p. 57).

[52] Kirby and Wasbak, 1992, p. 206. Schuster *et al*, 1998, p. 67. And although the French Conseil Constitutionnel has ruled that it is illegal for nurses to distribute the post-coital contraceptive pill in schools, the French Government intends to introduce legislation that would authorise school-based provision (Dorozynski, 2000).

[53] Nathan, 2001. Dr Bill Reith, honorary secretary of the Royal College of Practitioners, has argued that although it was better for GPs to prescribe emergency contraception "many teenagers are unable to get to a phone, let alone make an appointment." (Illman, 1998).

Of course, it is not only schoolchildren who may find it difficult to gain immediate access to emergency birth control.[54] As we saw earlier the benefits in making emergency contraception more easily available have been judged to
outweigh any disadvantages in pharmacy dispensation of hormonal medicine,
and post-coital contraception can now be sold to women aged sixteen and over
in pharmacies.

In public policies designed to influence contraceptive behaviour, we have a
compelling example of the rather fuzzy distinction that exists between using the
law to improve the availability of birth control and excessively paternalistic
attempts to shape people's reproductive choices. Sexually active teenagers and
adults need to have straightforward access to a range of contraceptive methods.
Deregulation of certain prescription-only contraceptives, and the provision of
age-appropriate information about birth control are both then valuable public
policy objectives. But it might also be important to recognise the limits of "relationships" education, and to acknowledge instead the overwhelming significance
of an individual's perception of their future employment opportunities. If many
young women quite reasonably perceive that becoming a mother offers a more
valuable and fulfilling future than working in a demoralising and underpaid job,
rates of teenage motherhood are likely to remain high. Teenage pregnancy may
then be a *symptom* of various social problems rather than their cause.

(iii) New Techniques

Despite widespread dissatisfaction with the available means of contraception,[55]
research into new techniques is relatively poorly funded,[56] and sterilisation
remains the most commonly used method of birth control worldwide.[57] Both
male and female sterilisation is a simple procedure which has none of the side-
effects associated with hormonal contraception and offers almost one hundred
per cent reliability.[58] But sterilisation's defect is its permanence, and surveys
tend to indicate high levels of regret.[59] Rising divorce and remarriage rates are

---

[54] Indeed David Paintin has estimated that easier access to emergency contraception could reduce
the abortion rate by 70% (Boseley, 1998, 11). Experience of pharmacy distribution in the United States
has been positive (Webb, 1999.) In a monitored scheme in the United States in which pharmacists have
been selling emergency contraception, 50% of the women using the service said that if they had not
had direct access to the pills, they would have waited to see if they became pregnant (Illman, 1998).

[55] In a survey carried out in 7 countries, a substantial majority of women expressed dissatisfaction with all available methods of contraception (Snow *et al*, 1996, p. 8).

[56] It has been estimated that global expenditure on research and development represents less than
3% of global contraceptive sales (Fathalla, 1994).

[57] Blank, 1991, p. 16.

[58] Concerns about the risks associated with the pill and the IUD, combined with improvements
in surgical techniques have led to increased interest in sterilisation. Female tubal occlusion can now
be done by laparoscopy without the need for incision. It can be performed at an outpatient clinic
with minimal inconvenience (Blank, 1991 p. 24).

[59] In a US study, 26% of sterilised men and women said that they wanted more children. Of those
under 30 years old at the time of the operation, 42% wanted more children (Blank, 1991, p. 28). In
another study of Hispanic women who had been sterilised, 49% said that they wanted to have more
children (Henshaw and Singh, 1986, p. 240).

leading to increased demand for complicated and often unsuccessful reversal procedures.[60] The proportion of women seeking sterilisation would, it has been predicted, more than double if reversal was ninety-five per cent effective.[61]

The introduction of new long-acting birth control techniques are supposed to have the benefits of sterilisation without the disadvantage of permanence. By offering semi-permanent protection against conception, without any need for user-proficiency, these long-acting methods of birth control tend to subvert the distinction between contraception and sterilisation. Most scientific interest is now concentrated upon the development of contraceptives that remove the possibility of "user failure".[62] Norplant, for example, consists of six small, thin, flexible capsules which are inserted under the skin of the upper arm and continuously release a synthetic hormone which inhibits ovulation and fertilisation.[63] Norplant is ninety-nine point eight per cent effective for five years, and fertility can only be restored during those five years by its surgical removal. It is no longer available in the UK, and it is unclear whether the abandoned action by two hundred and seventy-five women who claimed to been injured by Norplant had any impact upon the manufacturer's decision to end its distribution.[64] Other long-acting techniques are, however, being developed. Within the next five years contraceptive vaginal rings and transdermal patches are likely to be licensed, and more sophisticated contraceptive implants will become available.[65] As we see later in this chapter, semi-permanent contraceptives may be more convenient for individual women, but they simultaneously make it possible to temporarily remove a woman's capacity to take decisions about her fertility.[66]

There has also been considerable interest in research into a contraceptive "vaccine". It would be cheap to administer, there would be no removal costs, and it would be easy to deliver via existing vaccination schemes.[67] Since immunisation

[60]   Vasovasostomy where the cut ends of the vas deferens are rejoined is, in contrast to the simple day surgery of vasectomy, a complex operation requiring general anaesthetic. Its success rate is between 55–76%. Reversal of female sterilisation is even more complicated, with a success rate of 40–75% and a significantly increased risk of ectopic pregnancy (Blank, 1991, pp. 31–33).

[61]   Blank, 1991, p. 41.

[62]   There is, however, some interest in the development of a new male contraceptive pill, the principal disadvantage of which would be the opportunities for "user failure" (Berger, 2000).

[63]   Each capsule is 34mm in length and 2.4mm in diameter, they contain levonogestrel which both suppresses ovulation and prevents the sperm from reaching and fertilising the egg by keeping the cervical mucus viscous (see further Spitz, 1993, p. 132).

[64]   Dyer, 1999.

[65]   Norplant-2, for example, involves a three-rod system, and Implanon is a single rod contraceptive implant, which can be inserted and removed much more quickly than Norplant . The mean time for insertion of Implanon is 1.1. minutes, and mean removal time was 2.6 minutes (Mascarenhas, 1998).

[66]   Interestingly, Snow *et al* found that women in developing countries expressed considerable interest in long-acting contraceptive techniques, while Western women, especially those described as upper middle-class, expressed a strong preference for flexible, user-controlled methods (Snow *et al*, 1996, p. 12).

[67]   The World Heath Organisation Task Force stated that "Immunization as a prophylactic measure is now so widely accepted that it has been suggested that one method of fertility regulation which would have wide appeal as well as great ease of service delivery would be an anti-fertility vaccine" (WHO, 1978).

programmes have achieved such immediate health benefits for populations in developing countries, it has been argued that a vaccine to protect against pregnancy might seem both attractive and acceptable to potential users.[68] However, there could be dangers in immunising women against conception. First, it would be difficult to ensure that consent to delivery during an existing immunisation programme was entirely free and fully informed. Second, conception is not a disease and "tricking" the body into producing an immune response to normal human cells or hormones creates the risk of auto-immunity. Third, given that individual's immunological responses differ, it would also be difficult to predict the precise duration of immunity without carrying out additional blood tests. Finally, once administered, the temporary infertility would be irreversible, even in the event of intolerable side-effects. While obviously some of these potential problems are surmountable, as we see in the next section, programmes designed to reduce the birth rates in developing countries have had a lamentable tendency to pay insufficient attention to individual women's preferences and safety.

(b) Developing Countries

During the 1960s, Western Governments became alarmed by high rates of population growth in developing countries.[69] Concern about a Malthusian[70] population "time-bomb" led to wide international interest in supplying birth control to the poorest nations of the world. In 1974 the World Population Conference drew up a World Population Plan promoting the adoption of population policies with the aim of controlling fertility in developing countries. Most poor nations have now implemented programmes directed towards reducing their birth rates,[71] and it is estimated that 50 per cent of couples in developing countries now practise contraception.[72] In the very poorest parts of the world, however, non-use of contraception continues to be prevalent, and population growth rates remain high.[73] Exacerbated by declining birth rates in the West, the proportion of the world's population living in poverty continues to rise, thus heightening anxieties about the long-term consequences of uneven

---

[68] Schrater, 1995, p. 664.

[69] In 1969 Alan Guttmacher argued that "civilisation is less threatened by cancer than by the present epidemic of human beings" (Guttmacher, 1969, p. 118).

[70] In 1798 Thomas Malthus published his first essay on population. His theory was that mankind was doomed because increased prosperity is accompanied by much greater increases in population. The population, he believed, increased geometrically, while subsistence could only increase arithmetically (Riddle, 1997, p. 217).

[71] Chamie, 1994, p. 47.

[72] Compared with 10% in the 1960s (Black, 1999, p. 932).

[73] In Africa, 18% of couples use contraception (Black, 1999, p. 932). Africa's population grows by 3% each year, which means that it will double every 20 years if not checked (Kokole, 1994, p. 73). India's population grows by one million more births than deaths every 23 days (Potts, 1999, p. 934). The world's population reached six billion in October 1999, and it is estimated that by 2011, there will be seven billion people in the world (Black, 1999).

fertility patterns. The prevalent assumption is that the world cannot support a constantly growing population, and that we may soon reach some sort of absolute limit to the world's "carrying capacity". If finite resources place an absolute ceiling upon population numbers, then famine and environmental disaster on a massive scale are predicted as the inevitable consequences of continuous population growth.

The correlation between financial prosperity in the West, and high rates of contraceptive use was for many years misunderstood as establishing that practising birth control inexorably leads to economic growth.[74] This misperception was superseded by the similarly erroneous assumption that development or modernisation inevitably leads people to want smaller families. In fact the relationship between development and fertility control is much more complex[75] and aid policies that provide contraception without addressing other basic needs, such as clean water, agrarian reform or adult literacy have been largely ineffectual. In many developing countries, a high birth rate is a necessary survival strategy.[76] For example, high rates of HIV infection in sub-Saharan Africa mean that

[74] Betsy Hartmann has argued that "the myth of overpopulation is one of the pervasive myths in Western society, so deeply ingrained in the culture that it profoundly shapes the culture's world view. The myth is compelling because of its simplicity. More people equal fewer resources and more hunger, poverty, environmental degradation and political instability." (Hartmann, 1995, p. 4). In the 19th century fertility declined later in England than in both the US and France, despite England being more advanced in terms of structural economic change. Michael Haines suggests that this may be due to the democratic political revolutions that had taken place in France and the United States which led to greater emphasis on individual choice and education (Haines, 1992, p. 225). Despite Pakistan being much more economically successful than Bangladesh, Bangladesh has a much higher rate of contraceptive use than Pakistan, 40% of Bangladeshi couples use birth control, compared with 12% in Pakistan. Cleland *et al* therefore suggest that cultural factors may be more significant than economic progress in promoting contraceptive use. (Cleland *et al*, 1994, p. 138).

[75] Gillis *et al* contradict the widely held misapprehension that industrialisation and urbanisation automatically lead to falling birth rates, instead they argue that "fertility decline was connected with the political and economic, as well as the social and cultural changes that make up the broad sweep of modern European history". (Gillis *et al*, 1992, p.3) Michael Hanagan suggests that increased job security and organised provision for the elderly may have been crucial in enabling workers to restrict their fertility (Hanagan, 1992, p. 144). Carlos Aramburu points out "in the West declining fertility happened in the absence of organised family planning policies and at a time when it was widely thought immoral and many governments were pro-natalist." (Aramburu, 1994, p. 159).

[76] Unlike in the West, children in developing countries are a financial asset not a burden. In addition to their labour, one's children often represent the only insurance in illness or old age. High mortality rates mean that it is necessary to give birth to many children in order to guarantee future security. Commenting on Nigeria, Tola Olu Pearce argues that "we must question the ethics of pressing for sterilization in an environment in which infant mortality rates remain unacceptably high" (Pearce, 1996, p. 195). Moreover, within some cultures, having many children confers social prestige and demonstrates divine or ancestral satisfaction (see further Kokole, 1994, pp. 74–6). Ruth Macklin points out that men in Mexico believe that having many children establishes their masculinity (Macklin, 1996, p. 180). Grace Osakue and Adriane Martin-Hilber suggest that widespread belief in reincarnation in Nigeria leads to a prevailing assumption that sterilised individuals will be childless in the next life (Osakue and Martin-Hilber, 1998, p.185). OA Ojo points out that male sterilisation is "almost totally unacceptable in the great majority of developing countries" because of a "generally held belief that vasectomy causes impotence". Female contraception is thought to encourage female infidelity and is similarly rejected (Ojo, 1995, pp. 41, 52). Ojo also suggests that in African culture a woman's place in the matrimonial home is secured by the birth of children. Barrenness is associated with witchcraft, and a childless woman will often be ostracised (Ojo, 1995, p. 52).

infant and child mortality is *increasing*, which in turn leads to higher birth rates.[77] Some of the inevitable side-effects of Westernisation may also increase fertility.[78] Traditional strategies of fertility control, such as prolonged abstention from sexual intercourse after childbirth, and extended periods of breast-feeding tend to be ignored by Western-style birth control programmes, and are eroded by the adoption of an increasingly Western lifestyle.[79]

Over the last fifty years, the provision of birth control to developing countries has been politically fraught. Many poor nations have regarded Western interest in third world fertility as either imperialist or corrupting.[80] For example, in Iraq a policy designed to *raise* the birth rate has been adopted primarily in order to facilitate independence from the West both by reducing dependency on foreign goods and labour, and by strengthening the army.[81] Within countries where there is conflict between different religious or political factions, minority groups commonly suspect that fertility control policies may be intended to reduce their status and leverage.[82] Thus, there may be an important but sometimes elusive difference between making safe and effective methods of birth control freely available to women throughout the world, and attempting to impose fertility control upon them against their will.

If international financial support is contingent upon the adoption of effective population control policies, it is probably unsurprising that some countries have

[77] Gottlieb, 2000. Ainsworth *et al* quote UN estimates that AIDS will increase the mortality of children under 5 by 7.8% by 2005. Two thirds of the 23 million people infected with the HIV virus live in sub-Saharan Africa. In twelve countries, over 10% of women are infected, and vertical transmission rates are high, up to 50% of children born to HIV positive mothers will also be affected. Ainsworth *et al* suggest three reasons why AIDS leads inevitably to higher fertility. First, breast-feeding will stop earlier if a child dies. Second, parents may try to have a replacement child. Third, parents may have more children as insurance against anticipated child mortality (Ainsworth *et al*, 1998, pp. 138, 142).

[78] Srinivason argues that reducing the rates of death and widowhood during reproductive age; reducing post-partum abstinence and lactation and increasing coital frequency will increase fertility (Srinivason, 1986, p. 176).

[79] In the Yaruba tribe in West Nigeria, the average duration of sexual abstention after birth is 30 months, and the average period of lactation is 24 months. More educated couples in Nigeria resume sexual relations and cease breastfeeding on average 10 months after the birth of a child. (See further Leridan and Ferry, 1985). Agnes Riedmann suggests that Western influence upon family planning schemes in developing countries inevitably devalues indigenous knowledge and is based upon the premise that locals cannot solve their own problems (quoted in Pearce, 1996, p. 201).

[80] In Zimbabwe, for example, Kokole argues that "family planning (was) perceived as part of the white racists' grand design to prolong minority rule and deny blacks their birthright" (Kokole, 1994, p. 83). Ojo argues that the introduction of Western birth control programmes was "regarded as a genocidal act perpetrated by the Western World" (Ojo, 1995, p. 53). Mazrui has even suggested that fundamentalist Muslims think that procreation in the name of Allah "can itself be counted as a form of jihad (militant religious struggle)" (Mazrui, 1994, p. 125).

[81] Chamie, 1994, p. 42.

[82] For example GM Shah, the Muslim Chief Minister of the Jammu and Kashmir state in India has contended that "we should reject the Government's family planning programme. This is aimed at further reducing the Muslim population in Kashmir. Every Kashmiri Muslim should have four wives to produce at least one dozen children" (Pai Panandiker and Umashanker, 1994, p. 95). In an article in the New York Times in 1935, CE Silcox commented on the "extraordinary fecundity of the French Canadian", and expressed "the suspicion that the French are deliberately trying to outbreed the English" (quoted in McLaren and McLaren, 1997, p. 130).

adopted quasi-coercive birth control programmes.[83] Curbing population growth in developing countries has also tended to take priority over contraceptive safety and acceptability.[84] So aid programmes have emphasised the benefits of long-acting injections and subdermal implants rather than safer but less effective contraceptives such as condoms, and have paid little attention to the cultural unacceptability of certain side-effects, such as irregular menstruation.[85] In addition, reports of substandard or dangerous contraceptives being "dumped" on developing countries are commonplace,[86] and there has been intense criticism of pharmaceutical companies' decisions to locate trials of new contraceptives in developing countries.[87]

It is important that aid programmes should be concerned *only* to facilitate informed reproductive decision-making in poorer countries, and not to circumscribe individuals' freedom of choice. Access to information about birth control, and to safe and effective contraceptives may help women to exercise control over their fertility, but the decision about whether to use contraception must remain with the woman herself. High mortality rates among children, coupled with non-existent extra-familial support in old age means that having fewer babies might simply be economically irrational. The "quick fix" of supplying contraceptives to women in developing countries, without acknowledging that large families may have considerable material advantages rests upon the patronising assumption that such women are incapable of making informed choices about reproduction.

The existence of a population "problem" in developing countries is itself contentious. Frank Furedi, for example, has argued that the coincidence of high

---

[83] Until 1988 the US Agency for International Development funded an incentive scheme in Bangladesh which paid each man or woman who agreed to be sterilised 175 taka (several weeks' wages) and gave doctors and clinic staff special bonuses for each sterilisation that they performed (see further Hartmann, 1995, pp. 221–241). In the early 1990s Indonesia birth control quotas were enforced by denying women work unless they had a contraceptive registration card (Todd, 1991).

[84] For example, the emphasis on contraceptive drugs and surgery in Nigeria is in sharp contrast with the fact that 40% of women are illiterate, and only 56% of family planning clinics have adequate water supplies (Pearce, 1996, p. 196–7).

[85] For example, Snow *et al* found that the possibility of contraceptive secrecy was of paramount importance to women in North India, this led to intolerance of side-effects such as irregular bleeding which would be noticed by husbands and other family members (Snow *et al*, 1996, p. 25). Ruth Macklin has pointed out that some religious groups prohibit sexual intercourse during menstruation, so that contraceptives which cause irregular bleeding may be unacceptable (Macklin, 1996, p. 174).

[86] The US Agency for International Development shipped 2 million Dalkon Shield IUDs to 79 countries. They were shipped unsterilised with one inserter for every 10 shields, and 1 set of instructions for every 1000. (Grant, 1992, p. 51), Although by 1976 there were 600 lawsuits pending against AH Robins for injuries caused by the Dalkon Shield, in 1979 the devices were still being inserted in Pakistan, India and Kenya (Grant, 1992, p. 65). Although a monthly injectable (dihydrroxyprogesterone acetoplenide) was withdrawn from use in Europe in the 1960s because of safety fears, it was marketed in Brazil in the 1980s (Hardy, 1996, p. 212). And in 1998 Quinacrine was still being used for female sterilisation in 19 countries despite World Health Authority advice against its use (Reproductive Health Matters, 1998, p. 167).

[87] Clinical trials of Norplant in Brazil were eventually stopped after pressure from feminist organisations (see further Finkle and McIntosh, 1994, p. 25).

rates of population growth and widespread poverty does not necessarily establish a causal link.[88] Nevertheless, despite equivocal evidence, high birth rates in the poorest countries have been blamed for poverty, famine, environmental destruction and political instability. Of course poverty may be "caused" by the interaction of many factors, such as corruption, war or inadequate farming practices. A disproportionate emphasis upon population growth inevitably leads to a rather individualistic approach to development. Aid programmes designed to change individuals' attitudes towards their fertility, especially if they can be legitimised by their association with reproductive health and women's rights, may simply be cheaper and more politically expedient than attempts to address the real reasons why some countries are poorer than others.

3. DEFECTIVE BIRTH CONTROL

(a) Defective Sterilisation

(i) What is "Wrongful Birth"?

When a sterilisation operation fails, or when the patient is negligently told that the sterilisation has achieved permanent sterility, the 'harm' that may result is a pregnancy.[89] While it is sexual intercourse, rather than the failed sterilisation that actually *causes* a pregnancy, having unprotected sex will not amount to a *novus actus interveniens*, that is an act which breaks the chain of causation, unless the patient knows that the sterilisation has failed.[90] If a woman believes that either she or her partner is sterile, pregnancy may not be detected until it is too late for her to have an abortion. But even if the pregnancy is discovered in time, the woman may have religious or other objections to abortion, and the law will not impose a duty to mitigate one's loss by terminating an unexpected pregnancy.[91]

[88] Furedi, 1997, p. 34.

[89] For example, in *Crouchman* v. *Burke* [1998] 40 BMLR 163, a sterilisation operation was carried out when, unknown to her, C was several weeks pregnant. Langley J found that the consultant gynaecologist was negligent in failing to warn C of the risk of pregnancy and that the procedure would not necessarily terminate any pregnancy.

[90] In *Sabri-Tabrizi* v. *Lothian Health Board* [1998] BMLR 190, S knew that her sterilisation operation had failed and the Scottish court found that her decision to expose herself to the risk of pregnancy was not reasonable, and constituted a *novus actus interveniens* which broke the chain of causation.

[91] In Park J's first instance decision in *Emeh* v. *Kensington, Chelsea and Fulham Area Heath Authority* [1983] *The Times* 3 January, he suggested that the plaintiff's failure to terminate the pregnancy consituted a *novus actus interveniens*: "Her own unacceptable reasons for not seeking an abortion have convinced me that, in truth, she elected to allow the pregnancy to continue because she wanted to bear another child, and from that time onwards her pregnancy was not unwanted." But this was rejected on appeal, Slade LJ stating that "save in the most exceptional circumstances, I cannot think it right that the court should ever declare it unreasonable for a woman to decline to have an abortion". [1984] 3 ALL ER 1044, at 1053. In *McFarlane* v. *Tayside Health Board* [1999] 3 WLR 1301, Lord Slynn said (at 1311): "It is not contended that the birth was due to her decision not

Where a woman becomes pregnant following a failed sterilisation operation, or negligent advice about her or her partner's sterility, there are three possible outcomes. First, she may miscarry or the baby may be stillborn, in which case an action for her pain and suffering would be uncontroversial, although the sum would be relatively modest. Second, she may decide to terminate the pregnancy. Again, a claim for the costs of an abortion, and any associated discomfort, stress or loss of income would be straightforward, and the award would similarly be fairly small. The third possibility is that the woman carries the pregnancy to term and gives birth to a live baby. In this situation the "damage" caused by the doctor's negligence is a baby. So where a patient can prove that their sterilisation operation was negligently performed, or that they were given negligent pre- or post-operative advice, their claim is for damages to compensate them for the "wrongful birth" of a child that they did not want.

Claims for wrongful conception, pregnancy or birth have raised some complex legal and ethical issues. It is, for example, well established that a child cannot have an action for their "wrongful life"[92] since the courts are not prepared to balance existence with non-existence or to treat life itself as a compensatable injury.[93] A child can, as we see in chapter four, have an action for injuries sustained *in utero*,[94] so if a woman who does not know that she is pregnant undergoes a sterilisation operation that damages her developing fetus, her disabled child may be able to recover damages for their negligently caused injuries. A child cannot, however, bring an action on the grounds that their conception should have been prevented by a sterilisation operation that failed to achieve sterility. Similarly, a child cannot argue that their mother was deprived of the opportunity to terminate the pregnancy. So if, following negligent advice about sterility, or a negligently performed sterilisation, a healthy and normal child is born, the only plausible action lies with his or her parents, although as we see below, the parents' action may also now be disqualified on similar public policy grounds.[95]

---

to have an abortion which broke the chain of causation or made the damage too remote or was a *novus actus interveniens*. If it were suggested I would reject the contention". And Lord Steyn agreed, saying (at 1317): "I cannot conceive of any circumstances in which the autonomous decision of the parents not to resort to even a lawful abortion could be questioned".

[92] In the context of a doctor's failure to identify fetal abnormality, it is clear that a child cannot receive damages for her "wrongful life". In *McKay* v. *Essex Area Health Authority* [1982] QB 1166 a child's complaint that a doctor should have given her mother the opportunity to terminate her pregnancy was dismissed as being contrary to public policy and impossible to assess.

[93] See further Kennedy and Grubb, 2000, pp. 1530–52 for a lucid critique of *McKay* v. *Essex AHA*.

[94] *Burton* v. *Islington HA* [1992] 3 All ER 833; Congenital Disabilities (Civil Liability) Act 1976, s.1.

[95] For example, Trindade and Cane have observed that "it might seem inconsistent to allow a claim by the parents while that of the child, whether healthy or disabled, is rejected. Surely the parents' claim is equally repugnant to ideas of the sanctity and value of human life and rests, like that of the child, on a comparison between a situation where a human being exists and one where it does not" (Trindade and Cane, 1999, p. 434).

(ii) The Failure to Warn

Although a doctor will not be held to have provided a *guarantee* of sterility,[96] it may be negligent to fail to inform the patient that there continues to be a small risk that the operation will not achieve sterility. A claim for wrongful birth based upon a doctor's failure to warn of the risk of pregnancy may arise in one of three situations. First, the doctor may fail to warn his or her patient that there is a small chance that the sterilisation procedure will reverse itself. Second, the patient may not be told that they should continue to use contraception until post-operative tests are completed. Third, a doctor may wrongly inform the patient that sterility has in fact been achieved. In all three circumstances, the patient's action against the doctor would be based upon her negligent misstatement.[97]

The doctor will only owe a patient a duty to warn of the risk of sterilisation failure if no responsible body of medical opinion would have failed to give a warning, or if the court decides that the risk is a substantial one.[98] In relation to

---

[96] *Thake* v. *Maurice* [1986] QB 644.

[97] In *Hedley Byrne* v. *Heller* [1964] AC 465, the House of Lords held that, in relation to negligent misstatements, a duty of care arises where the person making the statement has voluntarily assumed responsibility towards the person receiving the information, who then reasonably relies upon the statement.

[98] In *Sidaway* v. *Board of Governors of Bethlem Royal Hospital and Maudsley Hospital* [1985] AC 871 all of the five Law Lords agreed that doctors had a duty to warn patients about risks associated with treatment as part of their ordinary duty of care. But beyond that the judgements differ markedly. The most extreme judgments were those of Lords Diplock and Scarman, with the other three falling somewhere in between. Lord Diplock thought that a doctor fulfilled his duty to warn if he did as other doctors would do: "To decide what risks the existence of which a patient should be voluntarily warned and the terms in which such warning, if any, should be given, having regard to the effect that the warning may have, is as much an exercise of professional skill and judgment as any other part of the doctor's comprehensive duty of care to the individual patient, and expert medical evidence on this matter should be treated in just the same way. The *Bolam* test should be applied." (at 895).
Lord Bridge, with whom Lord Keith agreed, applied a slightly different test from Diplock's straight application of *Bolam*. He said that "I am of opinion that the judge might in certain circumstances come to the conclusion that disclosure of a particular risk was so obviously necessary to an informed choice on the part of the patient that no reasonably prudent medical man would fail to make it. The kind of case I have in mind would be an operation involving a substantial risk of grave adverse consequences" (at 900). Lord Templeman's judgment was in some respects similar. He said that "There is no doubt that a doctor ought to draw the attention of a patient to a danger which may be special in kind or magnitude or special to the patient." (at 903).
Lord Scarman's judgment was the most radical: "I think that English law must recognise a duty of the doctor to warn his patient of risk inherent in the treatment which he is proposing: and especially so, if the treatment be surgery. The critical limitation is that the duty is confined to material risk. The test of materiality is whether in the circumstances of the particular case the court is satisfied that a reasonable person in the patient's position would be likely to attach significance to the risk" (at 889).
Although Lord Diplock's judgment was followed in *Gold* v. *Haringey* [1988] 1 QB 481, it could be argued that Lords Keith, Bridge and Templeman's slightly modified *Bolam* test in fact represented the majority opinion. Indeed in *Pearce* v. *United Bristol Healthcare NHS Trust* [1999] PIQR P53, Lord Woolf considered that Lord Bridge's judgement most clearly expressed the views of the majority. Lords Keith, Bridge and Templeman all considered that while the *Bolam* test will *normally* determine whether or not a failure to warn amounted to negligence, where the risk is obviously a material one, or is special in kind or magnitude, then the court will find that the failure to warn was negligent even if it is supported by a responsible body of medical opinion.

male sterilisation, there was a clear shift in clinical practice during the 1980s. Before 1984, it was recognised that there was a small risk of recanalisation of the vas following a vasectomy, but this was only thought to be possible shortly after the operation. It was, therefore, assumed that the risk of unwanted conception could be eliminated if two negative sperm samples were taken before a couple abandoned other methods of birth control. Then in 1984 research was published in the *British Journal of Urology* based upon analysis of over 16,797 vasectomies.[99] The study proved that there was a one in two thousand chance of the operation reversing itself several years later, even when initial sperm samples had shown that the patient's sterilisation had been effective. As a result, in *Newell* v. *Goldenberg*[100] the court held that from the mid-1980s no competent body of medical opinion would have omitted to inform a patient of this small risk of reversal,[101] and the failure to give an appropriate warning was therefore negligent.[102]

In the 1990s an action was brought against the Department of Health for failure to take steps to disseminate the information in the 1984 study to the one point five million people estimated to be relying upon pre-1984 vasectomies as their only method of birth control. Mr and Mrs Danns claimed that the Department of Health should have taken space in the national press to publicise the new findings about spontaneous vasectomy reversal.[103] The Court of Appeal found that the Department of Health did not owe Mr and Mrs Danns a duty of care because there was no relationship of proximity between them. The Department did not, according to the Court of Appeal, owe every sterilised man a duty of care to alert him to a newly discovered risk of pregnancy.

A similar change in practice probably exists with respect to the most common method of female sterilisation. In *Gold* v. *Haringey HA*[104] the Court of Appeal found that, in 1979, there was still a responsible body of medical opinion that would not have warned women that there was a small chance that the operation would not be successful. The pregnancy rate after tubal occlusion is now acknowledged to be one in two hundred,[105] and guidelines issued by both

---

   [99] Philp *et al*, 1984.

   [100] [1995] 6 Med LR.

   [101] For example, although Haldar *et al*'s study confirmed that vasectomy is an extremely reliable form of contraception, the risk of recanalisation is such that "all patients should be warned that there is no guarantee that it will not fail at some point in the future" (Haldar, *et al* 2000).

   [102] Mantell J found that in 1985, even if the defendant established that there were other doctors who would fail to give warnings, such doctors would not be considered to be acting reasonably. Damages were, however, reduced on the basis that even if a warning had been given, the plaintiff would probably have proceeded with the operation.

   [103] *Danns* v. *Department of Health* [1998] PIQR P226. Mrs Danns had become pregnant 7 years after Mr Danns was sterilised as a result of late recanalisation of the vas. Initially Mr Danns suspected his wife of infidelity. The Danns sought compensation for the birth of their son Jordan. The Court of Appeal found that although the Department undoubtedly had a power to disseminate medical research, this did not amount to a duty, and the Department could not be held liable to pay compensation to people who claim to have suffered loss because the power was not exercised.

   [104] [1987] 3 WLR 649.

   [105] RCOG, 1999.

the Department of Health and the Royal College of Obstetricians and Gynaecologists recommend full and frank disclosure of this risk of failure.[106] Similarly then, although this has not been tested in the courts, it would now almost certainly be negligent not to warn patients that their operation might fail to achieve sterility.

Changes in medical practice in relation to warning patients about the risk of sterilisation failure mean that it is most unlikely that any new cases in which a patient was not told that the procedure may reverse itself will reach the courts. Because a doctor who had failed to warn their patient would almost certainly be found to have acted negligently, any claims that did arise would tend to be settled by the health authority. For similar reasons, it is unlikely that any future court cases would be based upon a failure to explain to a vasectomy patient that birth control should continue to be used until two negative sperm samples had been taken. So the only remaining scenario in which a statement about sterility might lead to litigation is where the parents were given inaccurate test results,[107] either as a result of negligent testing, or negligent interpretation of the results.

(iii) Differences in the parents' claims

The nature of a claim for wrongful birth may differ slightly depending upon which sexual partner underwent the sterilisation operation, and which intends to bring the action in negligence. In both circumstances, the consequence of a failed sterilisation, or negligent advice about sterility, is that the *woman* becomes pregnant. If it was her sterilisation that failed, her claim for pain and discomfort associated with childbirth is relatively easy to characterise as a personal injury caused by the defendant doctor. Indeed for the purposes of the Limitation Act 1980, it has been held that unwanted conception is a species of "personal injury".[108] Her claims for loss of earnings, and the expenses incurred as a result of the pregnancy can then be reasonably described as economic loss *consequential* upon physical injury, thus raising few difficulties in tort law.

Where a woman's sexual partner's vasectomy was unsuccessful, it would have to be established that her partner's doctor owed *her* a duty of care to prevent her physical injury and her associated economic losses. While this might

---

[106] RCOG, 1999.

[107] This was the case in *McFarlane* v. *Tayside Health Board* [1999] 3 WLR 130, discussed below.

[108] In *Walkin* v. *South Manchester Health Authority* [1995] 1 WLR 1543. Auld LJ said (at 1550) "the failure of the attempt to sterilise the patient was not itself a personal injury. It did her no harm; it left her as before. . . . However, it seems to me that the unwanted conception, whether as a result of negligent advice or negligent surgery, was a personal injury in the sense of an "impairment". . . . The resultant physical change in her body resulting from conception was an unwanted condition which she had sought to avoid by undergoing the sterilisation operation. That conclusion appears to be accepted by both parties". Because this point had been conceded, Roch LJ agreed, but he did express his disquiet at this conclusion. He said (at 1553) "I have some difficulty in perceiving a normal conception, pregnancy and the birth of a healthy child as 'any disease or any impairment of a person's physical or mental condition' in cases where the only reasons for the pregnancy and subsequent birth being unwanted are financial".

be relatively straightforward if she has been in a stable relationship for many years, and her existence is known to her partner's doctor,[109] it may be less easy to establish that a doctor owes a duty of care to *any* woman whom his patient might subsequently impregnate. Although her pregnancy is undoubtedly foreseeable, there might not be a relationship of sufficient proximity between her and the defendant doctor because she would not be identifiable in advance as someone likely to suffer loss should the patient's sterilisation fail. Thus, in 1996, a claim for the costs associated with her pregnancy from a woman whose sexual relationship began three years after her partner's vasectomy was struck out as "vexatious".[110]

A man's loss in the case of his or his partner's unsuccessful sterilisation cannot sensibly be described as personal injury. Instead his claim will be for the economic costs associated with a child's upkeep. Again, if it is his partner whose operation failed, he would have to establish that *her doctor* should reasonably have had him in his contemplation as likely to be affected by any negligence in carrying out the operation. Where it is his own vasectomy that failed, it may be easier for a man to establish a special relationship of proximity between himself and his doctor, although as we shall see, it may not be so easy to establish that it would be fair, just and reasonable for liability to be imposed upon the doctor.

(iv)   Can there be recovery for "wrongful birth"?

There are several possible ways in which the law could resolve the question of the appropriate level of damages in these "wrongful birth" cases. First it could decide that there should be no recovery at all. Second, there could be recovery for the pregnancy and its associated costs and discomfort, but no recovery for the costs of raising the child. Third, the law could give full recovery for both the pregnancy and the costs of the child's upbringing. Fourth, parents could recover in full subject to the costs of the child's maintenance being offset against the benefits gained from the child's life.

The last approach has been rejected because attempting to quantify the benefits that accrue to parents from a child's life is believed to be both infeasible and invidious.[111] The first approach has also been categorically rejected by the

---

[109] In *Thake* v. *Maurice* [1986] QB 644, the advice about sterility was given to both husband and wife, and finding that the surgeon owed the wife a duty of care was unproblematic.

[110] In *Goodwill* v. *British Pregnancy Advisory Service* [1996] 1 WLR 1397, the vasectomy had spontaneously reversed itself and Ms Goodwill became pregnant. The Court of Appeal held that at the time when Mr MacKinlay was told that he need not use contraception, the plaintiff "was merely, like any other woman in the world, a potential future sexual partner of his, that is to say a member of an indeterminately large class of females who might have sexual relations with Mr MacKinlay during his lifetime" (per Peter Gibson LJ at 1405). Her claim was struck out as an abuse of the process of the court.

[111] In *McFarlane* v. *Tayside Health Board* [1999] 3 WLR 130 although those members of the House of Lords who discussed this "benefits rule" agreed that it should be rejected, their reasons

English courts on the grounds that pregnancy and childbirth are precisely what a person undergoing sterilisation is intending to avoid.[112] It is uncontroversial that there are expenses associated with pregnancy, and that pregnant women are subject to some danger, disruption and discomfort. So it is not difficult to characterise an unwanted pregnancy and delivery as an injury that should be compensated in damages. It has therefore proved relatively easy to recover damages for pregnancy-related expenses, and for the pain and suffering caused by pregnancy and childbirth.[113] And these damages for pain and suffering have not been offset by the joy and relief of giving birth.[114]

---

differed. Both Lords Slynn and Hope considered that it would be impossible to quantify with any accuracy the benefit of the child's life. Lord Slynn, for example, said (at 1311–2): "To reduce the costs by anything resembling a realistic or reliable figure for the benefit to the parents is well nigh impossible . . . . Of course there should be joy at the birth of a healthy child, at the baby's smile and the teenager's enthusiasms but how can these be put in money terms and trimmed to allow for sleepless nights and teenage disobedience? If the valuation is made early how can it be known whether the baby will grow up strong or weak, clever or stupid, successful or a failure both personally and careerwise, honest or a crook? It is not impossible to make a stab at finding a figure for the benefits to reduce the costs of rearing a child but the difficulties of finding a reliable figure are sufficient to discourage the acceptance of this approach". Lord Hope's primary concern was that parents might be overcompensated if they could recoup the costs of the child's life without any reduction for the emotional advantages of parenthood, which he believed "in fairness must be set against them" (at 1332). Lord Clyde was less concerned with the problem of quantification, and argued that the emotional benefits of parenthood were in fact entirely different in kind from the financial costs, and therefore could not be offset against each other. He drew an analogy with a parent's claim for the death of a child which could not be offset by the saving in maintenance costs which the parent will enjoy (at 1337). Lord Clyde was also concerned that adopting the "benefits rule" would effectively limit recovery to parents who could establish that their child is "more trouble than he or she is worth" (at 1337). Lord Millett suggested that working out the relative costs and benefits of a child's life "must either be superfluous or produce the very result which is said to be morally repugnant" (at 1345). For if the value of the child exceeds the costs of maintaining her, then this simply confirms that, as a matter of principle, the benefits of parenthood must be assumed to outweigh the financial burden. But if the child's value is assessed to be less than her maintenance costs, the court will have accepted the "unedifying proposition that the child is not worth the cost of looking after him" (at 1345).

[112] According to Kenneth Norrie, "once family planning is accepted as a good, its failure can logically be regarded as a bad" (Norrie, 1991, p. 142).

[113] In *Thake* v. *Maurice* [1986] QB 644, Mr Thake's vasectomy reversed itself and Mrs Thake became pregnant. The Thakes brought actions in both contract [they had paid a small sum for the operation] and in negligence. The contract claim failed, since it could not be said that the consultant had provided a warranty of complete sterility. The negligence claim succeeded since, the Court of Appeal held, it had been negligent not to warn the Thakes that there was a small risk that the operation would reverse itself. It was reasonably foreseeable that Mrs Thake would not recognise the early stages of pregnancy until it was too late to have a termination, and her claim for prenatal pain and suffering succeeded.

In *McFarlane* v. *Tayside Health Board* [1999] 3 WLR 1301, discussed below, the House of Lords held that it was foreseeable that if the operation was unsuccessful and the husband was negligently told that contraceptive measures were unnecessary the wife might become pregnant. The majority of the House of Lords therefore found that she was entitled to general damages for the pain, suffering and inconvenience of pregnancy and childbirth.

[114] *Allan* v. *Greater Glasgow Health Board* [1993] 17 BMLR 135 per Lord Cameron. A reduction was made in *Allen* v. *Bloomsbury* [1993] 1 All ER 651, in order to reflect "the benefit of avoiding the pain and suffering and associated financial loss which would have resulted from the termination of her pregnancy" (per Brooke J at 657).

Whether it should be possible for parents to recover the costs of rearing a normal, healthy child has, however, proved to be extremely controversial.[115] It is not perhaps unusual for a child to know that their conception was unplanned, and perhaps even unwanted,[116] but it is nevertheless often suggested that a child who finds out that they were was the subject of a "wrongful birth" action might feel troubled that their birth led to litigation, rather than happiness.[117] Of course, it could plausibly be argued that unless litigation would be likely to put the child at risk of significant harm,[118] parents should generally be considered to be the best judges of the impact their proposed legal action might have upon their child.[119]

The issue was first considered in *Udale* v. *Bloombsury AHA*,[120] and Jupp J found that the maintenance costs of a healthy child were not recoverable on grounds of public policy. This was overruled by the Court of Appeal in *Emeh* v. *Kensington and Chelsea AHA*,[121] where it was held that public policy did not justify a blanket prohibition on the recovery of the costs of bringing up a healthy child. *Emeh* involved the birth of a handicapped child, but the Court of Appeal judgement did not confine recovery to cases involving disabled children.[122] It should, however, be noted that the judgement in *Emeh* was not so much a robust rejection of the "all children are a blessing" argument, but reflected instead the Court's concern that if damages were unavailable, people might be encouraged to have late abortions. Waller LJ, for example, was minded to award damages since they might "be an encouragement and help to bring up an unplanned child".[123] Nevertheless, since the judgement in *Emeh*, the judiciary had appeared to accept, albeit reluctantly,[124] that recovering damages for the costs

[115] Arras and Blustein have argued that "a child who is doomed to spend his life in a persistent vegetative state, or in severe and intractable pain, would seem to have been wronged by being born. But beyond this, consensus unravels" (Arras and Blustein, 1996, p. 113).

[116] In the House of Lords judgement in *McFarlane* v. *Tayside Health Board*, Lord Slynn said (at 1312): "An unplanned conception is hardly a rare event and it does not follow that if the conception is unwanted the baby when it is born or the baby as it integrates into the family will not be wanted".

[117] In the Scottish inner court decision in *McFarlane* v. *Tayside Health Board* [1997] SLT 211, Lord Gill said that "most people would find it unseemly that a child might later learn not only that his birth was the consequence of negligence, but that his parents had raised an action that implied that they would have preferred that he had not been born".

[118] Children Act 1989 s. 31(2).

[119] This point was made by the Court in the US case *Burke* v. *Rivo* 551 NE 2d 1, 5 (Mass, 1990): "it is for the parents, not the courts, to decide whether a lawsuit would adversely affect the child and should not be maintained".

[120] [1983] 2 All ER 522.

[121] [1985] 2 WLR 233.

[122] Slade LJ said "I can, for my part, see no reason why under public policy, she should not recover such financial damage as she can prove she has sustained by the surgeon's negligent failure to perform the operation properly, *whether or not the child is healthy*" (at 244) (my emphasis).

[123] Ibid at 240.

[124] See for example, the comments of Ognall J in *Jones* v. *Berkshire AHA* (unreported) (2 July 1986): "speaking purely personally, it remains a matter of surprise to me that the law acknowledges an entitlement in a mother to claim damages for the blessing of a healthy child. Certain it is that those who are afflicted with a handicapped child or who long desperately to have a child at all and are denied that good fortune would regard an award for this sort of contingency with a measure of astonishment. But there it is, that is the law". In *Gold* v. *Haringey* [1988] 1 QB 481, Lloyd LJ quoted Ognall J and commented "many would no doubt agree with that observation". See also

of a healthy child's upbringing is not contrary to public policy, and could in principle be a legitimate head of damages.[125] Then in 1999 the House of Lords considered the issue for the first time, and decided that previous authority had been wrong.[126]

Mr McFarlane had undergone a vasectomy in October 1989. In March 1990, the surgeon negligently informed him that his sperm counts were negative and that he no longer need take contraceptive precautions. In September 1991 Mrs McFarlane became pregnant and subsequently gave birth to their fifth child, Catherine. The House of Lords held that it was foreseeable that if the operation was unsuccessful and the husband was negligently told that contraceptive measures were unnecessary, his wife might become pregnant. While the majority of the House of Lords therefore found that she was entitled to general damages for the pain, suffering and inconvenience of pregnancy and childbirth, the Lords were unanimous that the McFarlanes were not entitled to be compensated for the costs associated with Catherine's upbringing.

The House of Lords reviewed the case law in Scotland, England, the United States, Europe and the Commonwealth and found a confusing line of authorities. So in addition to there being no previous decision of the House of Lords to take into account, the Law Lords were similarly unconstrained by any persuasive international consensus. Instead their starting point was the ordinary principles of tort law. With the exception of Lord Millett who argued that drawing a distinction between pure and consequential economic loss in these circumstances would be "technical and artificial, if not actually suspect",[127] the House of Lords considered that the costs of raising a healthy child should be classified as pure economic loss. Applying the principles established in cases such as *Caparo* v. *Dickman*,[128] a three-stage test should then determine whether a duty of care of the scope contended for is owed. First, the loss should be foreseeable. Second there must be a relationship of sufficient proximity between the doctor and the claimant. Third, it should be fair, just and reasonable to impose a duty of care in these circumstances.

Clearly, the birth of a child is a foreseeable consequence of negligently advising a patient that sterility has been achieved. It is also axiomatic that there is a relationship of sufficient proximity between doctors and their patients. The House of Lords' grounds for rejecting the McFarlane's claim was, therefore, that imposing liability on the health authority for the costs of a healthy child's upbringing would not be fair, just and reasonable.

Brooke J in *Allen* v. *Bloomsbury HA* [1993] 1 All ER 651. In *Thake* v. *Maurice* [1986] QB 644, Kerr LJ said (at 682) "The joy of having Samantha should in my view be set off against the time, trouble and care which is inevitably involved in her upbringing. The plaintiffs have rightly made no claim for this".

[125] *Allan* v. *Greater Glasgow Health Board* [1998] S.L.T. 588. *Benarr* v. *Kettering HA* (1988) 138 NLJ 179.

[126] *McFarlane* v. *Tayside Health Board* [1999] 3 WLR 1301.

[127] *Ibid.* at 1343.

[128] [1990] 2 AC 605.

Three different kinds of argument lie behind the Lords' unanimous conclusion that the McFarlanes were not entitled to recover the costs associated with Catherine McFarlane's upbringing. First, several of the Lords were concerned that the size of the claim in damages for a child's upbringing would be disproportionate to the degree of negligence. Lord Clyde, for example, considered that the reasonableness of a claim must include "a consideration of the proportionality between the wrongdoing and the loss suffered thereby".[129] Similarly Lord Hope agreed that full recovery for the costs of a child's upbringing would, in some circumstances, expose the health authority to liability on a scale quite disproportionate to the extent of the doctor's negligence.[130] These arguments based upon proportionality sit rather uneasily with the fundamental principle of tort law that damages should correspond to the loss *actually suffered*, rather than to the degree of fault. Awards of damages in tort are commonly and routinely disproportionate to the extent of the defendant's blameworthiness.

One reason why the Lords were particularly exercised about the potential size of awards was that they anticipated that the costs of private education for the whole of a child's life might have to be recoverable.[131] Not only would this lead to some extremely high awards, but it would also mean that wealthy parents would receive more money for their unexpected child than poor parents. This may seem distasteful, but the principle that damages in tort should put the claimant in the position they would have been prior to the negligent act has always led to invidious differences in the size of awards. For instance, a widow recovering damages for the loss of her husband will receive a large sum if he was a high wage earner, and rather less if he was unemployed. Nor is it clear that this concern justifies a complete prohibition upon recovery for wrongful birth. It might, for example, be possible for the courts to limit the size of an award to costs *reasonably* incurred as a result of the child's life.[132]

The second sort of reason the Lords put forward for dismissing the McFarlane's claim was the familiar[133] argument that it would be unseemly and

---

[129] [1990] 2 AC 605 at 1340.

[130] *Ibid.* at 1327. Lord Millett, on the other hand, was not persuaded by the proportionality argument, and instead was concerned that recovery for the costs of raising the child would have to be contingent upon proving that the parents had had a sterilisation operation in order to avoid the financial burden of another child. He said (at 1344) that there would be "great difficulties both evidential and conceptual in this approach. The parents' motives may have been mixed and the primary motives hard to discern. . . . Moreover, they are unlikely to have been communicated to those responsible for performing the operation. . . . It is difficult to justify a rule which would make their liability depend on facts which were unknown to them and which are, to put it crudely, none of their business".

[131] As happened in *Benarr* v. *Kettering HA* (1988) 138 NLJ 179.

[132] See for example the judgement of Olivier JA in the South African case *of Mukheiber* v. *Raath* (2000) 52 BMLR 49. He argued that a successful wrongful birth action did not necessarily expose the gynaecologist to unlimited liability.

[133] In *Udale* v. *Bloomsbury*, [1983] 2 All ER 522, Jupp J dismissed a claim for the costs of raising a normal healthy child. He said "It is highly undesirable that any child should learn that a court has publicly declared his life or birth to be a mistake—a disaster even—and that he or she is unwanted or rejected. Such pronouncements would disrupt families and weaken the structure of society. . . It has been the assumption of our culture from time immemorial that a child coming into the world,

contrary to public morality to compensate parents for the birth of a healthy child.[134] Lord Steyn, for example, admitted that his was a moral judgement based upon principles of distributive, as opposed to corrective, justice. He specifically appealed to public opinion, saying that:

"it may become relevant to ask of the commuters on the Underground the following question: 'Should the parents of an unwanted but healthy child be able to sue the doctor or hospital for compensation equivalent to the cost of bringing up the child for the years of his or her minority, i.e. until about 18 years?'. . . . I am firmly of the view that an overwhelming number of ordinary men and women would answer the question with an emphatic 'No'. And the reason for such a response would be an inarticulate premise as to what is morally acceptable and what is not".[135]

The "inarticulate premise" underlying the House of Lords' moral judgement in *McFarlane* is that the birth of a healthy baby is always a blessing and an occasion for joy. So even when people have expressly attempted to permanently end their capacity to reproduce by undergoing invasive surgery, the House of Lords considered that the joy and pleasure that any child brings to his or her parents will automatically outweigh the disadvantages of unwanted parenthood. As Lord Millett explained:

"if the law regards an event as beneficial, plaintiffs cannot make it a matter for compensation merely by saying that it is an event they did not want to happen. In this branch of the law at least, plaintiffs are not normally allowed, by a process of subjective devaluation, to make a detriment out of a benefit".[136]

But this must surely be wrong. Where a patient has decided to have an operation in order to irrevocably remove the possibility of conception, it seems perverse to argue that they should regard the failure of this surgery as a

even if, as some say, 'the world is a vale of tears', is a blessing and an occasion for rejoicing . . . (there) should be rejoicing, not dismay, that the surgeon's mistake bestowed the gift of life on the child".

And in *Danns* v. *Department of Health* [1998] PIQR P226 Leggattt LJ concluded his dismissal of Mr and Mrs Danns' appeal by suggesting that "at least they can take consolation from the joy that Jordan must have brought them in the long run".

Similarly in the US case of *Public Health Trust* v. *Brown* (1980) 388 So.2d 1048, the Supreme Court of Florida found that "a parent cannot be said to have been damaged by the birth and rearing of a normal healthy child . . . it is a matter of universally-shared emotion and sentiment that the intangible but all important, incalculable but invaluable 'benefits' of parenthood far outweigh any of the mere monetary burdens involved" (at 1085).

[134] Lord Millett said that "the law must take the birth of a normal, healthy baby to be a blessing, not a detriment . . . it is morally offensive to regard a normal, healthy baby as more trouble and expense than it is worth" (at 1347).

[135] In particular, Lord Steyn was concerned that couples who cannot have children, or who are caring for a disabled child might find it strange that the birth of a healthy child should be compensated with damages. And he also thought it unseemly that, since children born to the wealthy would cost more than children born to poorer parents, such damages would "discriminate between rich and poor".

[136] At 1346.

blessing.[137] If the birth of a child would be a source of unbounded joy to an individual, it is unclear why he or she would want to be sterilised in the first place. In the context of contract law, provided that the event which is contracted for is lawful, whether or not it is "beneficial" does not determine the availability of a remedy for breach of contract. So if a solicitor negligently fails to obtain a divorce for a client, the fact that being married is generally considered beneficial does not mean that the still-married couple should regard the solicitor's oversight as a "blessing".

A third underlying reason for the Lords' rejection of the McFarlane's claim was, I would suggest, less explicitly articulated. Underlying their unease about the possible consequences of recovery may have been the concern that scarce NHS resources should not be diverted to the parents of healthy children.[138] In recent years there has been increasing judicial recognition that the NHS is financially over-stretched.[139] Given that rationing of acute medical treatment is now inevitable the House of Lords may have been alarmed at the prospect that the NHS might have to pay large sums of money towards the maintenance of a healthy child. Although not expressed in these terms by the House of Lords, this underlying concern may reflect a plausible critique of the way in which damages are assessed in tort law. Patrick Atiyah, for example, has already drawn attention to the inequity of a system that gives a few victims of medical negligence

---

[137] And there have been some rare examples of judicial recognition of this. In his first instance decision in *Thake* v. *Maurice* [1986] QB 644, Peter Pain J observed that social policy which permits abortion and sterilisation rests upon the recognition that the birth of a healthy child is not always a blessing. In his dissenting judgment in the US case, *Public Health Trust* v. *Brown* (1980) 388 So.2d 1084, Pearson J said (at 1087) that "there is bitter irony in the rule of law announced by the majority. A person who has decided that the economic or other realities of life far outweigh the benefits of parenthood is told by the majority that the opposite is true". And in the Canadian case of *Caraford* v. *Moreau* (1978) 114 DLR (3d) 585 the court found that it was not justified in concluding "that the undesired birth of a healthy child, especially in a poor family constituting 10 living children, constitutes such a happy and normal event that it would be offensive to the public order to (give) pecuniary compensation in an appropriate case" (at 595).

[138] Tony Weir makes this point forcibly when he says that without the decision in *McFarlane* "English law might have continued blindly, despite occasional plaintive bleats from judges unable to do anything but follow their leader, to transfer to reluctant parents for the upbringing of healthy brats the resources needed by hospitals to cure the sick" (Weir, 2000b, p. 131).

[139] For example, Lord Donaldson's judgement in *Re J (a minor)* [1992] 3 WLR 507 acknowledged that "the court when considering what course to adopt in relation to a particular child has no knowledge of competing claims to a health authority's resources and is in no position to express any view as to how it should elect to deploy them" (at 517). Similarly, in *R* v. *Cambridge DHA ex p. B* [1995] 1 WLR 898 Sir Thomas Bingham said "I have no doubt that in a perfect world any treatment which a patient, or a patient's family, sought would be provided if doctors were willing to give it, no matter how much it cost, particularly when a life was potentially at stake. It would however, in my view, be shutting one's eyes to the real world if the court were to proceed on the basis that we do live in such a world. It is common knowledge that health authorities of all kinds are constantly pressed to make ends meet. They cannot pay their nurses as much as they would like; they cannot provide all the treatments they would like; they cannot purchase all the extremely expensive medical equipment they would like; they cannot carry out all the research they would like; they cannot build all the hospitals and specialist units they would like. Difficult and agonising judgments have to be made as to how a limited budget is best allocated to the maximum advantage of the maximum number of patients. That is not a judgment which the court can make" (at 906).

generous compensatory awards which simultaneously drain scarce health service resources and reduce the quality of care available to the vast majority of
patients.[140] It is almost certainly true that Tayside Health Board has more pressing demands upon its resources than Catherine McFarlane's maintenance. But
the fact that rejecting a claimant's action might enable the defendant to achieve
greater benefits for other people does not normally represent adequate grounds
for its dismissal. In relation to medical negligence, rejecting claims for compensation because the NHS could deploy its resources more efficiently in other ways
would vitiate most, if not all malpractice actions.

So the judgement in *McFarlane* appears to rest upon somewhat shaky foundations.[141] The proportionality argument seems inconsistent with the rules of
tort law. The quasi-theological "all children are a blessing" explanation fails to
treat an individual's preference for sterility with appropriate seriousness or
respect. And the hidden fears about NHS funding, while understandable, do not
justify effectively granting Tayside Health Board immunity from liability for
their negligent after-care of sterilisation patients. Instead, the inadequacies of
the judgement in *McFarlane* may illustrate the compelling need for reform of the
tort system. The number of medical negligence actions against health authori
ties increases each year, inevitably leading to greater expenditure on damages
and litigation costs. It is abundantly clear that the tort system, with its protracted delays, lengthy trials, and duplication of evidence from expert witnesses
is not the most efficient or effective way to deal with injured or disgruntled
patients. If the House of Lords finds itself relying upon the "inarticulate
premises" of passengers on the underground in order to deliver a judgement
which appears to be profoundly inconsistent with the ordinary principles of tort
law, it is perhaps time to look closely at the sustainability of personal injury
litigation.

(v) Disabled Children

In the light of the judgement in *McFarlane* v. *Tayside Health Board*, it would
obviously be extremely difficult to claim the costs of caring for a healthy and
normal child, but the House of Lords specifically declined to consider whether
their judgement would have been the same if the child had been born disabled.
So although the judgement in *Emeh* v. *Kensington and Chelsea and
Westminster AHA*[142] has been overturned insofar as it has been considered
authority for recovery of the costs of bringing up a normal child, it may have
some continued application if the child happens to be born disabled. There is
no requirement that the disability be *caused by* the negligent surgery, if it were
then the child herself would have an action under the Congenital Disabilities

[140] Atiyah, 1997.
[141] An otherwise vocal supporter of the Lords' conclusions admits that "the reasoning is uneasy"
(Weir, 2000a, p. 241).
[142] [1985] 2 WLR 233.

Act 1976, discussed more fully in chapter four. Thus, in *Emeh* the child's disability was not the result of the negligent sterilisation, but simply one of the vicissitudes of life. Waller LJ estimated the chance that any child would be born suffering from congenital abnormalities to be between point two five to point five per cent, which he judged to be plainly foreseeable, and thus not too remote a possibility to be recoverable in negligence.[143]

In a first instance judgement, delivered at the same time as *McFarlane*, a court held that the economic loss which results from the maintenance of a child born with congenital abnormalities following negligent medical advice should be fully compensated according to normal compensatory principles.[144] This means that the parents are entitled to be restored to the position that they would have been in had the negligent advice not been given. Of course, where a disabled child has been born, it is obviously impossible to put the parents in the position they would have been in if the child had not been born. Rather, in applying normal compensatory principles, Morison J found that *all* the costs associated with the birth of the disabled child are potentially recoverable, and that these extend to the costs of caring for the disabled child into adulthood.[145] Similarly in *Taylor* v. *Shropshire HA (No.2)*[146] following a negligently performed sterilisation, a mother recovered the reasonable cost of bringing up and caring for her disabled child for the rest of their joint lives.

Although the disability lobby might be alarmed at the ease with which it seems to be accepted that the birth of a disabled child is *not* a blessing and an occasion for joy, it has been suggested that the public morality cited in *McFarlane* by Lord Steyn might be more sympathetic to recovery where the child is born disabled.[147] But while the costs incurred in caring for a disabled child may be much greater and more debilitating than they would have been if the child had been born free from disability, it is not absolutely clear why these costs should be fully recoverable if the costs of "normal" maintenance are not. If, for example, a child suffers from a minor disability which leads to only slightly increased costs, should the parents still be able to recover the costs of the child's upbringing *in full*? If full recovery is contingent upon the particular abnormality being judged "serious", obvious problems arise in determining whether a particular condition meets the threshold level of seriousness.

Wrongful birth actions are not confined to people who have undergone sterilisation operations. Failure to detect fetal abnormality, or giving a pregnant

[143] Waller LJ said "in my judgment, having regard to the fact that in a proportion of all births—between one in 200 and one in 400 were the figures given at the trial—congenital abnormalities might arise, makes the risk clearly one that is foreseeable, as the law of negligence understands it" (at 239).

[144] *Nunnerley* v. *Warrington Health Authority* [2000] PIQR Q69.

[145] *Nunnerley* v. *Warrington Health Authority* [2000] PIQR Q69.

[146] [2000] Lloyd's Rep Med 96.

[147] According to Tony Weir "it can be hazarded that Lord Steyn's fellow travelers on the Underground would not feel upset if the reluctant parents of a handicapped child were to receive damages denied to the parents of an infant in perfect health (Weir, 2000b, p. 132).

woman incorrect information about the results of a prenatal test may similarly lead to an action in negligence.[148] Similarly, wrongful birth actions might arise following assisted conception if a disabled child is born as a result of inadequate screening of donor gametes, or negligence in preimplantation genetic diagnosis. The courts' decisions in other sorts of wrongful birth claims have, unsurprisingly, tended to be informed by similar concerns to those expressed in the failed sterilisation cases.[149]

(b) Defective Contraception

Over the past forty years, the oral contraceptive pill has been taken by more than two hundred million women throughout the world.[150] Despite the pill's excellent safety record, there is considerable interest in research investigating possible links between the contraceptive pill and, for example, breast cancer or thrombosis.[151] Media reports of any increased risks tend, however, to be both alarmist and misleading.[152] One major problem is the confusion of relative and absolute risk. If a risk is extremely small, then it can double and still be very unlikely to materialise. While informed decision-making may be enhanced by clear and intelligible information about the risks associated with a contraceptive's use, fears about the pill are based upon risks that are in fact minimal when

[148] *Rand* v. *East Dorset HA* [2000] Lloyd's Rep Med 181. Although the courts have been concerned about the risk of fraudulent claims in which, with the benefit of hindsight, parents will claim that they would have aborted the child. In *Gregory* v. *Pembrokeshire Health Authority* [1989] 1 Med LR 81 the court was not convinced that the mother would have had an abortion if she had been told of the risk of Down's syndrome. Rougier J suggested that "the objectivity of an honest witness can fail in circumstances of stress" and this meant that he could "not regard Mrs Gregory's evidence as paramount" (at 86).

[149] In *R* v. *Croydon Health Authority* (unreported) (25 November 1997) damages for the costs of bringing up a healthy child were sought by a woman who had not been told that she suffered from an untreatable condition which was likely to be exacerbated by pregnancy, and could even lead to her death. Mrs R claimed that if she had known about her reduced life expectancy and the difficulties she would have in bringing up her child, she would have taken steps to avoid pregnancy. Her action failed on the grounds that the loss of the opportunity to properly evaluate the risks in becoming pregnant could not amount to a significant head of damages when in the event she had given birth to "a healthy and much-loved child" (per Kennedy LJ).

[150] Baird and Glasier, 1999, p. 969.

[151] See, for example Grabrick *et al*, 2000.

[152] In October 1995 the Committee on Safety of Medicines suggested that "third generation" oral contraceptive pills (these are pills containing desogestrel orgestodene which were introduced in the early 1990s following evidence that they offered superior cardiovascular safety) were associated with twice the risk of venous thromboembolism as older pills. Reports failed to point out that researched had revealed an increase in *relative* risk, the actual risk of thrombosis in young women remained extremely small. The warning led to anxious pill users immediately stopping taking their pills, and in 1996 the abortion rate increased by 9% (Mayor, 1999, p. 1026; Skegg, 2000). The research upon which the CSM announcement was based has subsequently been questioned. Since October 1995, the proportion of women taking the oral contraceptive pill who are taking third generation pills has fallen from 53% to 14%. If third generation pills double the risk of venous thrombolembolism, then some reduction in its incidence should be expected. Farmer *et al* found that rates had, on the contrary, remained consistent (Farmer *et al,* 2000).

compared with the risks of pregnancy and childbirth.[153] A woman is twenty times more likely to die following complications in pregnancy than as a result of using any modern contraceptive.[154] And since the increased risks of the contraceptive pill are almost completely confined to women who exhibit other risk factors, such as smoking or hypertension, for most women the contraceptive pill is extremely safe.[155]

If a woman does suffer injury as a result of using contraception, she may be able to claim damages from the producer of the product if she can establish that it was defective. Or a woman may be able to sue the prescribing doctor if, for example, she presented contra-indications for the prescription of a particular method of birth control. The former type of action is covered by the statutory regime of the Consumer Protection Act 1987, while the latter would lie in the common law tort of negligence.

The oral contraceptive pill has not been the object of litigation under the Consumer Protection Act 1987. The first potential compensation claim involving a defective contraceptive was brought by two hundred and seventy-five women over the alleged side effects of the implant Norplant. Their claim collapsed after the Legal Aid Board withdrew funding for the one hundred and eighty women who were legally aided on the grounds that the chance of success did not justify the high costs of a trial, especially in the light of the small size of the individual claims.[156] Following the Legal Aid Board's decision, the remaining ninety-five women also withdrew their claims.

A case brought under the Consumer Protection Act against a condom manufacturer did get as far as a court hearing, although the claim was ultimately rejected by the court. A woman sued the London Rubber Company following the birth of a child who was conceived after a condom had split during sexual intercourse.[157] Kennedy J found that the fractured condom was not "defective" within the terms of the 1987 Consumer Protection Act. Under section 3 of the statute, a product can only be considered defective if it fails to provide the safety which "persons generally are entitled to expect". According to Kennedy J, consumers are not entitled to expect that any method of contraception will be one hundred per cent effective. But even if the condom were defective within the terms of the statute, Kennedy J suggested that there were two further grounds for rejecting the woman's claim. First, she had known of the existence of the

---

[153] For example, although an increased risk of venous thromboembolic disease (VTE) associated with the use of oral contraceptives is well established, the risk is extremely low. The spontaneous incidence of VTE in healthy non-pregnant women not taking any oral contraceptive is about 5 cases per 100,000 women per year. The incidence in users of oral contraceptive pills is between 15–25 cases per 100,000 women. But the risk of VTE associated with pregnancy has been estimated at 60 cases per 100,000 pregnancies (Department of Health, 1999). The death rate from VTE is lower still, and the annual death rate from VTE among women using oral contraceptives has been estimated to be 1 in 100,000 (Skegg, 2000).

[154] Black, 1999, p. 933.

[155] Pollard, 1994, p. 287.

[156] Dyer, 1999, p. 485.

[157] *Richardson* v. *LRC Products* [2000] Lloyds Rep Med 280.

morning after pill, which she could have taken to avoid her unwanted pregnancy. Second, Kennedy J considered that the judgement of the House of Lords in *McFarlane* v. *Tayside Health Board*[158] had firmly excluded the possibility of recovering damages for the upkeep of a healthy child.

The success of an action in tort against the prescribing doctor will depend upon whether the woman can prove that prescribing her this particular type of contraceptive was negligent. In order to establish negligence, the woman must prove first that the doctor breached his duty of care, and second that this breach caused her injury. Neither of these requirements is straightforward. First, in order to establish a breach of the doctor's duty of care, the woman must demonstrate either that no responsible body of medical opinion would have prescribed her this contraceptive,[159] or the court must be satisfied that, despite expert evidence supporting the doctor's opinion, the decision to prescribe was not logically supportable.[160] Second, she must prove, on the balance of probabilities, that it was the prescription of this contraceptive, rather than any preexisting condition, that caused her injuries.[161] Since most women who should not be prescribed hormonal contraception have some underlying condition, such as diabetes or hypertension, which makes the particular product unsuitable, it will often be extremely difficult to prove that it was *more likely than not* that the injury was caused by the contraceptive pill, rather than by the preexisting illness.

The lack of litigation involving contraceptives in the United Kingdom is in sharp contrast with the United States,[162] where fear of liability has reduced the range of contraceptive options available to women.[163] The burdens faced by contraceptive manufacturers in the US are exacerbated by the fact that women commonly use the same method for many years, and a continuing duty of care may mean that all existing users must be notified as soon as a new risk becomes apparent.[164]

---

[158] [1999] 3 WLR 1301.

[159] *Bolam* v. *Friern Hospital Management Committee* [1957] 1 WLR 582. Under the conventional *Bolam* test, an action against a doctor will fail if he or she can establish that a responsible body of medical opinion would have prescribed this contraceptive in these circumstances.

[160] *Bolitho* v. *City and Hackney HA* [1998] AC 232.

[161] In *Vadera* v. *Shaw* (unreported) (22 July 1998), the plaintiff failed to prove that her stroke had been caused by taking the contraceptive pill. Henry LJ found that since a high proportion of strokes in young people have no identifiable cause, and that infection could be a precipitating cause, it was therefore not possible to conclude that the stroke had been caused by the contraceptive pill.

[162] By 1986, 306,931 compensation claims were filed by women who claimed to have been injured by the Dalkon Shield. This represented 8% of all women who had used the device (Grant, 1992, p. 68).

[163] For example, the Copper-T is an effective intrauterine device, but it was taken off the market as a result of the weight of litigation faced by its manufacturer. Although they had successfully defended numerous lawsuits, their legal bills were still prohibitive (Roberts, 1996).
In the Canadian case of *Buchan* v. *Ortho Pharmaceutical (Canada) Ltd* (1984) 8 DLR (4th) 373 aff. (1986) 54 DLR (4th) 92, a 23 year old woman suffered a stroke shortly after starting to use Depo-Provera. She successfully sued the manufacturers for failure to warn her of the risk of stroke.

[164] For example in *Tresemer* v. *Barke* 86 Cal. App. 3d 656 12 ALR 4th 27 (1978) the court found that the manufacturers had a duty to warn existing Dalkon Shield users as soon as they discovered its risk.

4. INVOLUNTARY BIRTH CONTROL

Could it ever be legitimate to impose birth control measures upon an individual without their freely given consent? In the remainder of this chapter, I intend to argue that the imposition of involuntary fertility control will almost always be inconsistent with respect for an individual's bodily integrity. Although it is undoubtedly possible to envisage situations in which removing someone's reproductive capacity is an inevitable side-effect of an attempt to save their life, undertaken while they are incapable of consenting to medical treatment, such circumstances are likely to be extremely rare. Involuntary birth control more usually involves the judgement that it would be better, either for society or for this individual, that he or she does not reproduce. My argument will be that regardless of whether the justification is utilitarian or paternalistic, taking away an individual's reproductive freedom profoundly violates their interest in making intimate and personal choices for themselves.

In the following sections, we consider three different situations in which birth control has been imposed without consent.[165] First, during the first half of the twentieth century the practice of eugenic sterilisation was widespread and uncontroversial. Second, coercion has undoubtedly been employed within population control programmes. Third, where an individual is mentally handicapped, sterilisation has been authorised where a court has found that it would be in a mentally handicapped woman's best interests. While sterilisation on the grounds of racial inferiority is more obviously sinister than sterilisation which is said to promote an individual's welfare, I intend to argue that apparent concern for their wellbeing cannot justify removing an individual's reproductive capacity without their consent.

(a) A Brief History of Eugenic Sterilisation

At the end of the nineteenth century, increasing knowledge about genetic inheritance was employed to suggest that the "unfit" should be prevented from reproducing.[166] The new science of genetics was used to "prove" that the "feeblemindedness" of the poor was the result of their inherent genetic weak-

---

[165] Trombley (1988) suggests that coercive sterilisation involves one of more of the following:

 (i)   deception (e.g. carrying it out during another operation);
 (ii) undue pressure (e.g. making it a condition of parole);
 (iii) threats (e.g. withdrawal of benefits);
 (iv) if the individual is unable to give consent;
 (v)   lying about the procedure (e.g. telling the individual that its reversible);
 (vi) failing to explain it fully or comprehensibly;
 (vii) pressing it upon someone who has not voluntarily sought it.

[166] In England, Francis Galton founded the Eugenics Education Society in 1907, stating that "the first object of eugenics is to check the birth rate of the unfit".

ness, rather than their appalling living conditions.[167] By prolonging the survival of individuals suffering from genetic disease, modern medicine was also believed to be subverting the natural elimination of those who were "unfit to breed".[168] The discovery of heredity led to two eugenic goals: first that the human race should be improved by selective mating, and second that social ills such as disease, crime and poverty could be eradicated by discouraging "defective" individuals from reproducing.[169] While enhancing the human race may have been an important ideal, negative eugenics was generally considered to be a more pressing disease prevention strategy.[170]

After the Nazi compulsory sterilisation programme it may seem hard to believe that the "science" of eugenics was, at the beginning of the twentieth century, considered politically neutral.[171] In the first half of the twentieth century there was, however, a broad consensus that sterilising the weak or the unfit was in the interests of society as a whole.[172] Mark Haller explains that:

"during the first three decades of the present century, eugenics was a sort of secular religion for many who dreamed of a society in which each child might be born endowed with vigorous health and an able mind".[173]

[167] Dorothy Roberts argues that eugenics "depoliticized social conflict by providing a biological explanation for poverty and crime" and that such "governmental control of reproduction in the name of science masked racist and class-based judgements about who deserves to reproduce" (Roberts, 1993, p. 1964).

[168] For example, in *The Descent of Man* Charles Darwin argued that modern medicine was checking the natural processes by which the weak are eliminated.

[169] In 1877, R Dugdale published a study "proving" that "crime, pauperism and disease" were hereditary conditions (Dugdale, 1877).

[170] Galton, 1908. HG Wells also argued that "it is in the sterilisation of failures, and not in the selection of successes for breeding, that the possibility of an improvement of the human stock lies" (quoted in Trombley, 1988, p. 32). See also Lombardo, 1996.

[171] Atina Grossman has referred to the "remarkable durability over time . . . of an underlying consensus about the paramount importance of motherhood and eugenics for a healthy family and state" (Grossman, 1995, p. 21).

[172] In 1903 Dr Robert Rentoul wrote a book entitled *The Proposed Sterilisation of Certain Mental and Physical Degenerates: An Appeal to Asylum Managers and Others*. In it he listed the conditions he regarded as indications for compulsory sterilisation: "those suffering from leprosy, cancer, epilepsy, idiots, imbeciles, cretins, weak-minded, under restraint lunatics, persons with advanced organic disease of the heart, lungs, kidneys, or any disease likely to be passed from parent to offspring, should, if they wish to marry, be sterilised". In 1906, Dr Rentoul *wrote Race Culture or Race Suicide: A Plea for the Unborn*. In this later book he suggested that "neurotics, erotics, inebriates, drug habitues, kleptomaniacs, drunkards, failures in life, or those who are deaf, dumb or blind" should be sterilised. He thought 25% of the world's population would qualify.(Quoted in Trombley, 1988, p. 18) In 1914 Harry Laughlin argued that "dysgenic groups" should be discouraged from reproducing. Included within his definition of "dysgenic" individuals were "orphans, ne'er do wells, tramps, the homeless and paupers" (Laughlin, 1914). In 1908 the British Government set up a Royal Commission on the Care and Control of the Feebleminded. It estimated that there were over 270,000 persons in England who would qualify for segregation or sterilisation on the ground of mental weakness. James Kerr, the London County Council Medical Officer suggested that parents who wanted their defective children to live at home should have them sterilised before age 13 (see further Trombley, 1988). Paul Lombardo has pointed out that "every president (of the US) from Theodore Roosevelt to Herbert Hoover was a member of a eugenics organisation, publicly endorsed eugenic laws or signed eugenic legislation" (Lombardo, 1996, p. 1).

[173] Haller, 1963, p. 3.

The Fabians, for example, believed that the irresponsible procreation of the unfit would inevitably result in national deterioration unless checked by "surgical solutions".[174] Thus, in response to the economic crises of the 1920s, sterilisation was promoted as a way to ensure that fewer but more productive citizens were born.

Both Marie Stopes and Margaret Sanger, whose pioneering work in promoting access to birth control has been widely praised, also advocated compulsory sterilisation of the "unfit".[175] Marie Stopes, for example, formed the Society for Constructive Birth Control and Racial Progress and argued that:

> "many women and men should be prevented from procreating at all because of their individual ill-health, or the diseased and degenerate nature of the offspring they may be expected to produce".[176]

In the notorious US Supreme Court case of *Buck* v. *Bell*,[177] Justice Oliver Wendell Holmes invoked utilitarian public health imagery to justify the sterilisation of Carrie Buck:

> "It is better for all the world if instead of waiting to execute degenerate offspring for crime, or to let them starve for their imbecility, society can prevent those who are manifestly unfit from continuing their kind".[178]

Eugenic sterilisation laws originated in the United States[179] and were common throughout Europe.[180] Eugenic sterilisation undoubtedly happened in the UK, although it was never directly authorised by statute. In 1934, the Brock Report of the Departmental Committee on Sterilisation had recommended statutory reform that would enable the "voluntary" sterilisation of individuals who were

---

[174] Trombley, 1988, p. 37.

[175] Marie Stopes said that "contraception is obviously indicated rather than the saddling of the community with children of a very doubtful racial origin". She also advocated the compulsory sterilisation of the insane and feeble minded; revolutionaries; "half castes" and the deaf, dumb and blind (*The Control of Parenthood*, 1920) (quoted in McLaren, 1992, p.93). Margaret Sanger suggested the "the most urgent problem today is how to limit and discourage the over-fertility of the mentally and physically defective." Moreover she argued "when we realize that each feeble-minded person is a potential source of an endless progeny of defect, we prefer the policy of immediate sterilization". (*The Pivot of Civilization*, 1923) (quoted in McLaren, 1992, p. 93).

[176] Quoted in Soloway, 1997, p. 61.

[177] 274 U.S. 200 (1927).

[178] *Ibid.* at 207.

[179] In 1896 a Connecticut law prohibited marriage to or sexual relations with the unfit. In Indiana in 1907 the compulsory sterilistion of idiots, imbeciles and rapists was ordered. Iowa passed a law requiring the sterilisation of prostitutes in 1913. In 1913 California authorised the sterilisation of the feeble minded and the insane, in 1917 it extended this to anyone suffering from perversion or a marked departure from normal mentality. And between 1900 and 1970, 100 eugenic statutes were adopted by state legislatures (Lombardo, 1996, p. 1). It is estimated that 60,000 people were sterilised under these provisions (CCNE, 1996, p. 11).

[180] In 1929 in Denmark a law was passed to authorise the sterilisation of those "whose sexual desires are abnormal" or "psychically abnormal persons". In Switzerland, mental patients were sterilised prior to release. In Sweden, laws were passed in 1935 and 1941 authorising the sterilisation of the genetically ill, the feeble-minded, and those deemed "unsuitable parents" (Equinox, 1999).

mentally defective or believed to be likely to transmit mental disorder,[181] but their recommendations never became law.

While the Law for the Prevention of Hereditarily Diseased Offspring passed by the Nazis in 1933 may have been particularly brutal and wide-ranging, resulting in the sterilisation of up to 3.5 million individuals,[182] the principle that individuals who have been classified as unfit to procreate should be compulsorily sterilised was certainly not confined to Nazi ideology,[183] nor did it stop with the end of the Second World War. The Church of England, for example, had repeatedly expressed its support for compulsory sterilisation, and as late as 1949 the Bishop of Birmingham argued that the "sterilisation of the unfit . . . might well be the complement of the welfare state".[184] A course in Eugenics continued to be taught at University College, London until 1951, and the journal *The Annals of Eugenics* was not renamed until 1954.[185] Most of the eugenic sterilisations in the United States actually took place *after* 1945.[186] And the Swedes may even have sterilised proportionately more of their citizens than the Nazis.[187] 63,000 Swedish people were sterilised between 1935 and 1976, on the grounds of undesirable racial characteristics, poor eyesight, mental retardation and sexual deviancy,[188] approximately 32,000 of these sterilisations were involuntary.[189] Apart from the Communist party's dissension, the Swedish policy had had cross-party support and been implemented "in an atmosphere of unanimity".[190] In Japan the Eugenic Protection Law of 1948 allowed involuntary sterilisation for 30 different conditions, and in Canada, the Alberta Eugenics Board was not shut down until 1972[191]. And in China, the sterilisation of anyone with a serious

---

[181] Thom and Jennings, 1996, p. 220.

[182] Lombardo, 1996, p. 12.

[183] In an article in the *American Sociological Review* in 1936 commenting upon the German Hereditary Health Court Marie Kopp argued that "The German legislation.. is a great step ahead as a constructive public health measure, as a method of preventive medicine, and as a contribution to social welfare". (Kopp, 1936, p. 770). Although his decision in *Loving* v. *Virginia* 388 US 1(1967) was eventually overturned, in 1958 the trial judge stated that "the fact that (God) separated the races shows that he did not intend for the races to mix".

[184] Quoted in Trombley, 1988, p. 163.

[185] Thom and Jennings, 1996, p. 223.

[186] Reilly, 1986, p. 161 For example, in Mississippi in 1958 "An Act to Discourage Immorality of Unmarried Females by Providing for Sterilisation of the Unwed Mother" was introduced. Its author explained its purpose: "the negro woman, because of child welfare assistance (is) making it a business in some cases of giving birth to illegitimate children" (Henley, 1993, p. 718).

[187] Equinox, 1999.

[188] Armstrong, 1997.

[189] The Swedish Government set up a commission to investigate enforced sterilisation. The commission's report was published in March 2000 following a three year inquiry. It found that 6000 sterilisations were coerced, a further 15,000 were done in "quasi-coercive" circumstances, for example where having the operation was the condition for discharge from an institution. In a further 6000 cases, there were "signs of . . . exertion of pressure" (Ramsay, 2000).

[190] Tännsjö, 1998, p. 237.

[191] A Canadian Court in 1996 awarded $740,280 (approximately £370,000) to a woman who was sterilised in 1959 after she scored 64 in an IQ test at the age of 14 and was classified as a moron (Dyer, 1996).

genetic disorder continues to be promoted with the explicit purpose of improving the quality of newborn babies.[192]

(b) Compulsory Birth Control

As we saw earlier, the impact that a country's birth rate is assumed to have upon its economic wellbeing has led to governments throughout the world attempting to influence their citizens' contraceptive behaviour. While, as we saw earlier, the state may be able to facilitate access to birth control, through licensing various contraceptive techniques, and regulating their prescription, it is less clear that the state should be trying to shape individuals' decisions about whether to use contraception. In particular, as we see in the following sections, it may be difficult to distinguish between strategies intended to encourage people to use birth control, and policies which reduce individuals' freedom of choice.[193] The line between persuasion and coercion may even be inescapably blurred once governmental power is directed towards enjoining certain groups of people to control their fertility.

(i) Compulsory Sterilisation

In the UK, as we see below, involuntary sterilisation has tended to be justified by the clinical judgement that it would serve a mentally handicapped woman's best interests. In some other countries, compulsory sterilisation has taken place for openly utilitarian reasons. According to India's 1971 census, the population was growing at a rate of 2.25 per cent, and in 1975, India's health minister Karan Singh argued that the population

> "problem is now so serious that there seems to be no alternative to thinking in terms of the introduction of some elements of compulsion in the larger national interest".[194]

By 1976 a variety of policies were adopted to penalise those having three or more children and to make sterilisation a precondition for various benefits.[195] In the year following the Government's decision in June 1976 to assign the task of meeting sterilisation targets to the police, there were 8.1 million sterilisations. A backlash against the brutality of the police's campaign resulted in a change of Government and the number of sterilisations in 1977–8 dropped to 1 million.[196]

---

[192] CCNE, 1996, p. 11.
[193] Anita Hardon and Elly Engelkes argue that "an incentive for a particular contraceptive user often implies a sanction against a non-user", and that "sanctions and incentives are often interrelated" (Hardon and Engelkes, 1997, p. 41).
[194] Pai Panandiker and Umashanker, 1994, p. 89.
[195] In 1976 the Bihar governemnt withdrew ration cards from third and subsequent children. The Pune Hospital Board withdrew hospital care to women bearing a fourth or a subsequent child. In Andrha Pradesh in 1976 sterilisation became a precondition for the allocation of house sites.
[196] Pai Panandiker and Umashanker, 1994, p. 91.

In China since the adoption of the one-child family policy in 1979, sterilisation quotas have been rigorously enforced and over half of all women of childbearing age have been sterilised, many of them involuntarily.[197] Forced sterilisation is not officially authorised by the Government, but it undoubtedly happens,[198] and in the United States and Canada fear of compulsory sterilisation has formed the basis for successful asylum applications.[199] In Peru, hundreds of thousands of women were sterilised after a campaign of bribes and misinformation.[200] In Bangladesh women have been offered saris and food if they agree to be sterilised.[201] Vietnamese women are penalised after the birth of a third child by a fine equivalent to 3 or 4 months wages, and by being given low priority in the allocation of land.[202] In Brazil, politicians have offered women with inadequate access to alternative methods of birth control sterilisations in return for votes, and as a result there are some villages in which every woman of childbearing age has been sterilised.[203] High take-up rates of sterilisation in Brazil have additionally been attributed to women not understanding that it is irreversible.[204]

In the United States attempts to persuade poor women with large families to be sterilised by making continued receipt of state benefits contingent upon their

[197] Bernman, 1999.

[198] Officials are held accountable for the numbers of births in their regions, so local Birth Planning Associations organise sterilisation campaigns each November and December (Greenhalgh *et al*, 1994). Sterilisation is a condition of employment in some workplaces, and generous bonuses are often given to women who "volunteer" to be sterilised (Sills *et al*, 1998).

[199] In *Guo Chun Di v. Carroll* 842 F Supp 858 (E.D. Va 1994) Judge Ellis said that forced sterilisation is "an egregious infringement of the fundamental right to procreate". Section 208 of the US Immigration and Nationality Act 1996 grants asylum protection to victims of forced sterilisation, forced abortion and other forms of compulsory population control, and to opponents of such controls.

In *Cheung v. Minister of Employment and Immigration* [1997] INLR 80, the Canadian Federal Court of Appeal found that women in China who had more than one child and who were consequently faced with forced sterilisation formed "a particular social group" within the meaning of the United Nations Convention relating to the status of Refugees Art. 1A(2); and that the threat of forced sterilisation could ground a fear of persecution within the meaning of the Convention. The Court further held that the forced sterilisation of women was a fundamental violation of basic human rights and violated the United Nations Universal Declaration of Human Rights 1948 Art. 3 and Art. 5.

Although in *A v. Minister for Immigration and Ethnic Affairs* [1998] INLR the Australian High Court suggested that the existence of a "particular social group" depended upon external peceptions and that couples wanting a second child were not identifiable as a social unit, and so could not qualify as a particular social group for convention purposes.

[200] A sterilisation campaign was launched by the Peruvian President Alberto Fujimori in an attempt to reduce poverty. Women were told sterilisation would be good for their health, or that otherwise they would not be given food aid. Some were told that sterilisation was a temporary contraception, and there is evidence that some women were sterilised during caesarean sections. The programme has been described as an "appalling abuse of human rights" (Giulia Tamayo quoted in Lamb, 1999).

[201] Hardon, 1997, p. 11.

[202] Johansson *et al*, 1998, p. 69.

[203] Lamb, 1998.

[204] Hardy, 1996, p. 211.

consent to sterilisation were struck down in *Relf* v. *Weinberger*,[205] where it was held that threatening to withhold welfare unless an individual consents to sterilisation amounted to improper coercion.[206] The US Department of Health, Education and Welfare Regulations of 1979 instituted various safeguards to ensure that consent to sterilisation was freely given, so, for example, consent given while in labour, or before or after abortion would be invalid.[207] The regulations also prohibited the implicit or explicit threat of loss of welfare or medicaid in order to induce consent to sterilisation. But by 1987 the Health Research Group had found extensive violations of the regulations,[208] and Dorothy Roberts has suggested that "sterilization abuse" continues in the US:

> "accomplished through policies that penalise women on welfare for having babies, while making sterilization the only publicly funded birth control method readily available to them".[209]

And, as we see in the following section, the availability of new, long-acting contraceptives has led to a series of analogous misuses of state power over individuals' fertility.

(ii) Compulsory Contraception

Critics of non-consensual sterilisation invariably stress its permanency. For example, Rosalind Petchesky argues that:

> "the virtually irreversible nature of surgical sterilisation makes the choice a more drastic one that it might be otherwise".[210]

And, as we see later, the irreversibility of sterilisation is one of the reasons commonly cited for court involvement in the authorisation of a mentally incompetent woman's sterilisation.[211] New contraceptive techniques which facilitate the *temporary* suspension of a woman's fertility may appear to raise less trenchant ethical dilemmas. If sterilisation could be easily reversed, might objections to its involuntary use be more muted?[212]

---

[205]   372 F Supp 1196 (D.D.C. 1974) 403F Supp (DDC 1975).

[206]   *Ibid.* at 1199: "there is uncontroverted evidence . . . that an indefinite number of poor people have been improperly coerced into accepting a sterilisation operation under the threat that various federally supported welfare benefits would be withdrawn unless they submitted to irreversible sterilization".

[207]   In Brazil it is estimated that 64% of sterilisation operations are performed at the same time as caesarean sections (Hardy, 1996, p. 212).

[208]   Blank, 1991, p. 65.

[209]   Roberts, 1993, p. 1971.

[210]   Petchesky, 1979, p. 29.

[211]   According to Lord Brandon in *Re F* [1989] 2 WLR 1025 court involvement is necessary because "first, the operation will in most cases be irreversible. . .". (at 1068).

[212]   Blank, 1991, 72. George Brown has argued that "provider dependent long-acting contraceptives are more susceptible to ethical abuse than those that are user controlled" (Brown, 1996, p. 45).

In *CDM* v. *State* 627 P. 2d. 607 612 (Alaska 1981) the court found that the duty to "jealously guard an incompetent's rights" derived from the fact that a tubal ligation would "irreversibly curtail procreation". If procreation could be temporarily curtailed, would there be less need to jealously guard the rights of the disabled?

Using most contraceptives requires some direct action, and it is therefore difficult to protect someone against pregnancy without their active participation. The IUD (intra-uterine device) was the first contraceptive that did not presuppose the continued involvement of the user, and new techniques such as contraceptive injections and implants are expanding the range of contraceptive options that are not dependent upon the woman's willingness to act positively to control her fertility. While eliminating the possibility of user-failure is one of the chief advantages of long-acting contraceptives, removing women's control over their use or non-use of contraception may simultaneously represent their principal disadvantage.[213]

Paradoxically then, *improvements* in contraceptive technology may lead to an increased tendency to employ long-acting contraceptives in order to control the fertility of certain groups of women without their freely given consent. As Robert Blank explains:

> "the availability of reversible fertility control techniques makes it easier for many persons to rationalise its use on welfare women and therefore accentuates its potential abuse, ironically, because it is perceived as less extreme an intrusion".[214]

When a woman is fitted with an implant that cannot be removed without medical assistance,[215] or given an irreversible injection, she temporarily loses control over her fertility.[216] It is even possible that a physician who has been taught to insert a long-acting contraceptive implant may not have acquired the skill necessary to remove it.[217] In the US where there is a charge for removal of Norplant, though not for its insertion, some women may find that they cannot afford to regain their fertility.[218] High rates of continued use in some developing countries have been attributed to women not knowing that it is possible to have the implants removed within five years.[219] It is also unclear whether every country in which Norplant has been licensed has a monitoring system in place that is sufficiently sophisticated to ensure that no woman will fail to have it removed after five years.

[213] In Tamil Nadu, IUDs have been routinely inserted following childbirth or abortion. Out of 16,000 women fitted with IUDs, 52% said that they had not been given any option. (van Hollen, 1998, p. 103).

[214] Blank, 1991, p. 88.

[215] Macklin, 1996, p. 176.

[216] Ruth Macklin suggests that unless immediate removal is available at the woman's request, her consent to implantation is invalid (Macklin, 1996, p. 176). In Brazil, the majority of Norplant users have to wait to have it removed (Hardy, 1996, p. 213).

[217] Macklin, 1996, p. 176.

[218] Sally Jacobs has drawn attention to the plight of a Filipino woman in Boston who took up an offer of free Norplant. She suffered intolerable side effects, including heavy bleeding and hair loss, but could not afford the removal fee (Jacobs, 1992). Rosalind Petchesky suggests that African-American women living in rural areas in the South have been told that side-effects such as excess bleeding, weight loss and palpitations are inconveniences rather than medical problems, and hence removal is not covered by Medicaid. Women suffering from these side-effects therefore have to find the $300 removal fee (Petchesky, 1998, p. 315).

[219] In some parts of Indonesia 66% of Norplant users did not know that early removal was feasible (Widyantoro, 1994). One year continuation rates in Scandinavia were 76%, in Sri Lanka they were 99% (Blank, 1991, p. 36).

Given that these long-acting contraceptive techniques largely eliminate the possibility of user-failure, it is obvious why they hold appeal for those anxious to secure the use of contraception in women whose fertility is perceived to be a social problem, and/or who are judged to be incapable of using contraception effectively.[220] While some women will welcome the temporary suspension of their fertility, there is the incipient danger that state encouragement to use long-acting contraception slides inevitably into illegitimate pressure. This slippage has been plainly evident in the United States, where the population *as a whole* is not increasing particularly fast. Rather incentive programmes tend to be targeted at specific groups of women whose unrestrained reproduction is considered to be socially or economically problematic.[221]

There are those who believe that incentives to contraceptive use constitute a legitimate means of implementing policy.[222] John Robertson, for example, argues that:

[220] In 1968 the American Food and Drugs Agency reported that "the underprivileged woman is more effectively served when the need for recurrent motivation, required in most other forms of contraception, is removed" (FDA Advisory Committee on Obstetrics and Gynaecology, 1968, p. 1).

In an American study it was found that Norplant was nineteen times more likely than the pill to prevent pregnancy among teenage girls. Of 98 inner-city teenage mothers, 48 were fitted with Norplant and 50 prescribed the pill. One and a half years later, only 1 of the girls initially fitted with Norplant had become pregnant, compared with 19 of the girls using the pill (Polaneczky *et al* 1994). As a result, John Guillebaud has suggested that long-term contraceptive implants should be provided to all girls considered to be "at risk" of early pregnancy. He says a contraceptive implant "could be fitted into girls once they have had their periods but before they have had sex, for instance at the time when they were having their rubella jabs" (Hall, 1999). Similarly, Robert Blank argues that "evidence suggests that limiting the procreative choice of teenagers, especially those under 17, might benefit both the mother and her potential children" (Blank, 1991, p. 94). It would, of course, be extremely difficult to argue that the implantation of a hormonal implant is in the best interests of an eleven year old girl, especially since its impact upon girls during puberty is not yet fully understood.

Jean Anderson suggests that Norplant's reversibility makes it "ideal" for HIV infected women, because it would be possible for their fertility to be reinstated if a vaccine protecting against perinatal transmission became available (Anderson, 1996, p. 33).

Tannya Lovell Banks suggests that women with HIV/AIDS are regarded as "irresponsible people whose voluntary conduct is responsible for their condition and who are inappropriate parents because of their drug use or association with drug users. Therefore there is less societal resistance to government initiated policies aimed at discouraging these women from bearing children" (Lovell Banks, 1996, p. 144). Beverley Horsburgh has argued that the reasons given for the involuntary sterilisation of the mentally ill could also apply to mothers on welfare. They are thought likely to get pregnant; regarded as unable to care adequately for their children and as unable to use other contraceptive methods effectively (Horsburgh. 1996, p. 535).

[221] Ruth Macklin argues that policies aimed at increasing the use of long-term contraceptives are "designed to save middle-class and wealthy taxpayers money by targeting welfare recipients". The political concern is "the unwillingness of the taxpayers to pay for poor people's babies" (Macklin, 1996, p. 185). Rosalind Petchesky has pointed out that the greatest barrier to services has been poorer women's demeaning and inhumane treatment by health professionals (Petchesky, 1998, p. 314). In the US there are obvious race implications of targeting long-acting contraceptives at underprivileged or welfare dependent women. A controversial scheme in which Norplant was fitted in predominantly black Baltimore schools was labelled genocide by Melvin Tuggle, a black minister (Steinbock, 1996, p.73).

[222] In 1971 Clive Wood argued that "a government financial scheme in which it was in the woman's economic interest to have a device inserted and keep it there . . . might make a great deal of difference to the discontinuation rate in many parts of the world" (Wood, 1971, p. 125). Despite Moskowitz *et al*'s recognition that "the power differences that often exist between health care

"In general incentive programs are designed to preserve autonomy, even though they attempt to influence how the autonomy is exercised".[223]

Arras and Blustein advocate a principle of "reproductive responsibility" and suggest that:

"While coercion may be an extreme response . . ., society may be able to foster adherence to its norms of reproductive responsibility in other non-punitive, non-invasive ways, . . . such as small but meaningful incentives".[224]

In contrast, there are others who consider that financial or other incentives for the poorest sections of the community are inevitably coercive. Katherine Acutt, for example, suggests that:

"Drug using women, particularly pregnant and postpartum women, get strong messages not to reproduce (again) from the negative attitudes of health professionals, drug treatment counsellors and the courts. These messages probably infrequently are coercive in a strict definition of that term, but given the restricted choices of many poor, drug using women, they can come very close".[225]

Two days after Norplant was licensed in the United States, *The Philadelphia Inquirer* printed a now infamous editorial suggesting that contraceptive implants could be used to reduce welfare dependency.[226] Despite widespread condemnation of the editorial's inflammatory language, in the US Norplant has undoubtedly been targeted at certain groups of marginalised women. There have, for example, been attempts to create economic incentives for women on welfare to use Norplant,[227] and consent to its implantation has been used as a

---

providers and patients heighten the risk of wrongful influence", they suggest that, in some circumstances, "it can be appropriate and responsible to use different techniques to influence women to consider long-term contraceptive use, even if she is not immediately inclined to do so" (Moskowitz *et al*, 1996, pp. 16, 7).

[223] Roberston, 1994, p. 79.

[224] Arras and Blustein, 1996, p.130.

[225] Acutt, 1996, p.230. Acutt cites one Baltimore clinic for pregnant drug users in which 95% are sterilised or have Norplant fitted before they leave the programme.

Lovell Banks suggests that low income women are particularly unlikely to question advice given by health care providers, and that such advice "can have a powerful and perhaps coercive effect on some women's reproductive decision making" (Lovell Banks, 1996, p. 159). Indeed the American College of Obstetricians and Gynecologists issued a statement in 1987 suggesting that "women infected with HIV should be strongly encouraged not to become pregnant" (Rothenberg, 1996, p. 186).

[226] In an editorial entitled "Poverty and Norplant: Can Contraception Reduce the Underclass", it was suggested that Norplant could address the social problem that "the people having the most children are the ones least capable of supporting them" (*Philadelphia Inquirer*, 1990, at A18).

[227] Bills have been introduced in Kansas, Louisiana, Mississippi, Tennessee and Ohio offering incentives for women on welfare to use Norplant. A bill introduced in Louisiana would pay $100 per year to women agreeing to the insertion of Norplant (see further Vance, 1994). A Kansas bill would pay $500 to volunteers (Robertson, 1994, p. 87). Bills in Kansas, Ohio, South Carolina and Washington would also permit the involuntary implantation of Norplant in women who have given birth to drug addicted children. A Bill in Ohio would provide a new welfare mother with $1000 and increase her cash assistance by 150% if she agreed to be sterilised by tubal ligation. If she agreed to Norplant instead, she would get $500 and her assistance would increase by 10% every six months until it reached 150% (Steinbock, 1996, pp. 53, 66).

probation condition for women convicted of drug use or child abuse.[228] Because there is no compulsion to accept a financial reward,[229] and probation is a privilege rather than a right, such policies do not overbear an individual's will in the same way as, for example, physical threats. It may not, therefore, be strictly accurate to label them coercive.[230] But I would argue that criticism of state involvement in individuals' reproductive choices should not be confined to examples of narrowly defined and direct coercion. Rather, policies that exert *any* pressure upon disadvantaged women to consent to the semi-permanent removal of their reproductive capacity must, I argue, be *prima facie* illegitimate.

Using long-acting contraception as a sentencing option or a condition of welfare benefits has, unsurprisingly, been subject to considerable criticism, not least from the developer of Norplant himself who said that it had been "developed to enhance reproductive freedom", and that "using Norplant . . . to toss aside rights and trample human dignity would be an intolerable perversion".[231] A woman may have religious objections to birth control which are obviously compromised by limiting her access to probation or to discretionary welfare payments.[232] Additionally, judges and welfare officers are ill equipped to thoroughly assess its clinical suitability for a particular woman. Norplant, for example, should not be used by women who smoke, or who suffer from liver or heart disease; high blood pressure; diabetes; breast cancer or depression.[233] Judges and welfare officers are obviously not qualified to make these sort of informed prescription decisions. A woman should also not be expected to consent to implantation without a full

---

[228] In *People* v. *Johnson* No FO 15316 (Cal.Ct. App) 1992 Darlene Johnson pleaded guilty to inflicting corporal injury on a child. She faced 7 years in prison, but accepted probationary conditions which included a stipulation that she should be implanted with Norplant. An appeal on the ground that such a condition was not rehabilitative was rejected. Although Judge Broadman accepted the existence of a constitutionally protected right to procreate, he said that "it is not absolute and can be limited in a proper case". This was such a case because "it is in the defendant's best interest and certainly in any unconceived child's interest that she not have any more children until she is mentally and emotionally prepared to do so".

The use of Norplant as a probation condition has been heavily criticised on the basis that:

(i)	it only applies to women and thus violates the equal protection amendment;
(ii)	it constitutes cruel and unusual punishment;
(iii)	it violates the right to privacy;
(iv)	there are less restrictive alternatives, such as parenting classes, monitoring etc.;
(v)	minority women are more likely to be affected.

(See further Ballard, 1992).

[229] John Robertson has argued that payments of $100 or $500 are not high enough to make a charge of coercion credible (Robertson, 1994, p. 88).

[230] Rebecca Dresser suggests, for example, that "banning contraceptives from the realm of punishment would leave convicted women to face prison terms and other traditionally accepted forms of punishment, which could be more burdensome and less effective in reducing the possibility of future criminality". Instead she advocates that long-acting contraceptives should be offered only when there is an alternative noncustodial sentence (Dresser, 1996, p. 146).

[231] *Washington Post* 29 December 1990 at A18.

[232] In *People* v. *Garza* No 29794 (Cal Super Ct Tulare County) 1991, the defendant refused a Norplant probation condition because of her religious beliefs. She was sentenced to four years in prison.

[233] See further Stich, 1993, 1021.

description of Norplant's considerable negative side effects. So even if it were argued that it is not actually *coercive* to offer Norplant as a condition of probation or receipt of additional welfare payments, it could plausibly be argued that prescription during sentencing or within the welfare system violates the doctor/patient relationship, and would make fully informed consent a logical impossibility.[234]

It is significant that attempts in the United States to persuade women to use long-acting contraceptive methods have been targeted at the poor and the disadvantaged.[235] Why does the state consider that it has a legitimate interest in shaping such women's reproductive choices? The most obvious answer is that through welfare payments and other subsidies, the state will indirectly be responsible for some of the costs associated with a future child's upbringing. Where birth control is a condition of probation for a woman who has previously been found guilty of child abuse, the state interest is said to lie in protecting the welfare of as yet unborn children. It is not clear that either of these reasons actually represents adequate grounds for state interference with an individual's reproductive freedom. In other contexts, concern about public expenditure, or about future criminal activity would not justify violating an individual's bodily integrity. It would not, for example, be possible to stop someone suffering from a genetic disorder from reproducing on the grounds that their offspring might be a financial burden to the state. Their bodily integrity undoubtedly "trumps" the state's interest in reducing public expenditure. An attempt to prevent the commission of future criminal offences by, for example, the chemical castration of sex offenders would almost certainly amount to "inhuman and degrading"[236] or "cruel and unusual" punishment.[237]

Thus the ostensible public-interest reasons for state concern about certain women's reproductive capacity may in fact obscure more ominous anxiety about the unrestrained fertility of weaker members of society. While not explicitly eugenic, US policies which aim to reduce reproduction among welfare-dependent women reveal the durability of the assumptions that were used in the first half of the twentieth century to justify "surgical solutions" to poverty and criminality. As we see in the next section, in the UK too we can see evidence of a lack of respect for the bodily integrity of some of the weakest members of society, but here the derogation of certain individual's reproductive freedom is even more subtly justified as being in their own best interests.

---

[234] In *People* v. *Gauntlett* 352 NW 2d 310 (Mich Ct App. 1984) a rapist's probation had been conditional upon his use of Depo-Provera, which destroys men's libido. The Michigan appellate court struck down the condition on the grounds that he could not give free and voluntary consent given the coerciveness of probation.

[235] The racial significance of Norplant targeting is discussed by Catherine Albiston, who points out that some clinics in Oakland, California only provide brochures on Norplant in Spanish (see further Albiston, 1994, p. 18).

[236] Human Rights Act 1998 Schedule 1 Article 3.

[237] For example, in the US case *Mickle* v. *Henrichs* 262 GF. 687 D Nev. 1918, the mandatory sterilisation of a rapist was found to be degrading and humiliating and thus to represent cruel and unusual punishment.

(c) Sterilisation in cases of incapacity

There are some members of society who are, as a result of mental incapacity, unable to give consent to medical treatment. Although a patient's consent is necessary in order to prevent any medical intervention from constituting a battery, it is uncontroversial that there are circumstances in which incapable patients can be lawfully treated without their consent. Of course these circumstances should always be defined restrictively: the majority of mentally ill people are undoubtedly capable of making their own health care decisions.[238] Where a proposed treatment would have long-term or permanent effects, it might also be important to recognise that an individual's degree of mental handicap may fluctuate over time.

Where a patient is incapable of giving consent, medical treatment is lawful if it is in the best interests of the patient. Surgical sterilisation is undoubtedly a form of medical treatment, so it therefore follows that mentally incompetent women can be sterilised without their consent if it is considered necessary to preserve their life, health or well-being. And there will be a few instances when sterilisation is necessary to save a mentally incapable woman's life: for example, an operation to remove a malignant tumour may unavoidably result in infertility.[239] But in the vast majority of cases, the sterilisation operation is not sought to treat an illness, but rather to eliminate the possibility that the mentally incapacitated woman will conceive. In the past many mentally ill people spent their lives in single sex hospital wards, thus minimising, although undoubtedly not removing, the opportunity for sexual contact. Today most mentally handicapped people live in mixed environments, either in the community or in residential care, leading inevitably to increased interest in their potential fertility.

It would be a mistake to assume that doctors' support for the sterilisation of their mentally incapacitated patients is always ill-intentioned. On the contrary, while there have been a few instances in which plainly irrelevant factors have prompted applications to the courts,[240] many doctors genuinely believe that

---

[238] *Re C* [1994] 1 WLR 290. According to one study approximately 75% of mentally handicapped individuals are competent to make major health care decisions (Cooney, 1989, p. 58). In *In Re Romero* 790 P 2d 819 (Colo. 1990) 990 the Colorado Supreme Court overturned an order authorising the sterilisation of a woman suffering from brain damage on the grounds that retardation does not necessitate a conclusion of incompetence (at 822–3).

[239] According to Lord Donaldson in the Court of Appeal judgment in *Re F (Mental Patient: Sterilisation)* [1989] 2 WLR 1025 at 1041 "there is a real distinction between medical treatment undertaken with a view to securing abortion or sterilisation and that undertaken for a different purpose, for example the excision of a malignant tumour, which has this incidental result. It is only the former type of treatment which the law regards as being in a special category, probably because of its irreversible and emotive character in the light of the history of our times".

[240] *Re D (A Minor) (Wardship: Sterilisation)* [1976] Fam 185. In this case a mother sought sterilisation of her 11 year old daughter. The girl suffered from Sotos syndrome and "had a dull normal intelligence". Her behavioural problems had improved and were likely to continue to do so. D had "shown no interest in the opposite sex", and Heilbron J considered that her "opportunies for promiscuity, if she ever became so minded, were virtually non-existent, as her mother never leaves her side and she is never allowed out alone" (at 194). Nevertheless D's consultant paediatrician recommended sterilisation: he believed that it was likely that D would have a disabled child, and that

freedom from unwanted pregnancy may, in some circumstances, promote the welfare of a mentally incapacitated woman. My argument is, however, that honourable intentions will invariably fail to offer adequate justification for the non-consensual and permanent removal of an individual's reproductive capacity. That the sterilisation of mentally incapacitated women without their consent is not generally perceived to be an egregious and violatory act reflects, I argue, a web of negative assumptions about the sexuality and possible future maternity of women with mental disabilities.

(i) Court Involvement

In the UK, unlike many other countries, the involuntary sterilisation of mentally incompetent people has never been authorised by statute. Prior to the instigation of court involvement in the 1970s, doctors, parents and institutions made private, unscrutinised decisions to sterilise mentally handicapped women, and there is evidence to suggest that these procedures were in fact fairly common.[241] Ordinarily a doctor is entitled to treat a mentally incapable individual without a court order provided that he or she believes that treatment is in the patient's best interests. So where, for example, a therapeutic operation to treat a medical condition will have the incidental effect of sterilisation, court authorisation is unnecessary.[242]

her epilepsy could cause her to harm her baby. A consultant gynaecologist agreed to perform the operation. On the application of an educational psychologist D was made a ward of court and Heilbron J found that the operation should not take place since it was neither medically indicated nor necessary and would not be in D's best interests. In particular Heilbron J said that she could "not believe that a decision to carry out an operation of this nature performed for non-therapeutic reasons on a minor, can be held within the doctor's sole clinical judgment" (at 196).

Similarly, in the Canadian case of *Re Eve* [1986] 31 DLR (4th) 1 the intended purpose of the proposed sterilisation was to protect Eve's mother from the burden and anxiety of her daughter's pregnancy. As a result, La Forest J held (at 32) that "the grave intrusion on a person's rights and the certain physical damage that ensues from non therapeutic sterilisation without consent when compared to the highly questionable advantages that can result from it, have persuaded me that it can never safely be determined that the procedure is for the benefit of that person".

[241] Peterson, 1996, p. 59.

[242] In *Re GF (Medical Treatment)* [1992] 1 FLR 293 a 29 year old severely mentally handicapped woman suffered from severe menorrhagia and was unable to cope with her condition. Sir Stephen Brown held that provided the hysterectomy was necessary for therapeutic purposes, there was no need for a declaration of the court. He said (at 294) "in a case where the operation is necessary in order to treat the condition in question, it may be lawfully carried out even though it may have the incidental effect of sterilisation. . . . I take the view that no application for leave to carry out such an operation need be made in cases where two medical practitioners are satisfied that the operation is (1) necessary for therapeutic purposes, (2) in the best interests of the patient, and (3) that there is no practicable, less intrusive means of treating the condition" In *Re E (A Minor) (Medical Treatment)* [1991] 2 FLR a 17 year old girl suffered from serious menorrhagia for which the recommended form of treatment was a hysterectomy. In such circumstances, Sir Stephen Brown held that the consent of the court was not required and that the parents of a minor child could give valid consent. In the Australian case of *Re Marion (No. 2)* (1993) 17 Fam LR 337, a hysterectomy and ovariectomy of a 14 year old girl were ordered to minimise her seizures and reduce further brain damage, Nicholson J said "this case probably falls into the category where the court's consent is unnecessary since . . . the procedure was required for medical and therapeutic reasons." (at 355). The use of the word "probably" implies that it may be difficult for doctors to assume that court authorisation is unnecessary.

Sterilisation as a means of fertility control has, however, been recognised to be a special case.²⁴³ In relation to both children and adults, court orders are sought in order to confirm or "declare" the legality of the operation.²⁴⁴ In relation to minors, Lord Templeman has suggested that sterilisation of a girl under eighteen should only be carried out with the leave of a High Court Judge.²⁴⁵ And where the proposed sterilisation is to be carried out on an adult, it has been held that:

> "although involvement of the court is not strictly necessary as a matter of law, it is nevertheless highly desirable as a matter of good practice".²⁴⁶

In *Re F*,²⁴⁷ Lord Brandon listed the special features of sterilisation which he considered necessitated court approval:

> "first, the operation will in most cases be irreversible; secondly, by reason of the general irreversibility of the operation, the almost certain result of it will be to deprive the woman concerned of what is widely, and as I think rightly, regarded as one of the fundamental rights of a woman, namely, the right to bear children; thirdly, the deprivation of that right gives rise to moral and emotional considerations to which many people attach great importance; fourthly, if the question whether the operation is in the best interests of the woman is left to be decided without the involvement of the court, there may be a greater risk of it being decided wrongly, or at least of it being thought to have been decided wrongly; fifthly, if there is no involvement of the court, there is a risk of the operation being carried out for improper reasons or with improper motives; and, sixthly, involvement of the court in the decision to operate, if that is the decision reached, should serve to protect the doctor or doctors who perform the operation, and any others who may be concerned in it, from subsequent adverse criticisms or claims".²⁴⁸

Lord Brandon appears here to suggest that sterilisation might interfere with a fundamental "right" to reproduce. And in *Re D*,²⁴⁹ Heilbron J also attributed overriding importance to a woman's right to reproduce:

²⁴³ The Parliamentary Assembly of the Council of Europe in a recommendation on mental health and human rights adopted on 23 March 1994 requested that "no irreversible injury should be inflicted upon individuals' reproductive capacity" (CCNE, 1996, p. 11).
  In *SL* v. *SL* [2000] 2 F.C.R. 452 Butler-Sloss LJ said that "the patient has the right, if she cannot herself choose, not to have drastic surgery imposed upon her unless or until it has been demonstrated that it is in her best interests".
²⁴⁴ In the Australian case of *Re Jane* (1989) FLC 92–007, 77, 257 it was held that the consent of the court was necessary both because sterilisation involves interference with a basic human right and because its major purpose is non-therapeutic.
²⁴⁵ *Re B (A minor) (Wardship: sterilisation)* [1987] 2 WLR 1213 at 1218.
²⁴⁶ per Lord Brandon at 1068. Similarly Lord Griffiths said (at 1080) "I cannot agree that it is satisfactory to leave this grave decision with all its social implications in the hands of those having the care of the patient with only the expectation that they will have the wisdom to obtain a declaration of lawfulness before the operation is performed". And Lord Goff said (at 1089) "the operation of sterilisation should not be performed on an adult person who lacks the capacity to consent to it without first obtaining the opinion of the court that the operation is, in the circumstances, in the best interests of the person concerned, by seeking a declaration that the operation is lawful".
²⁴⁷ [1989] 2 WLR 1025.
²⁴⁸ *Ibid.* at 1068.
²⁴⁹ [1976] Fam 185.

"The type of operation proposed is one which involves the deprivation of a basic human right, namely, the right of a woman to reproduce, and, therefore, it would be, if performed on a woman for non-therapeutic reasons and without her consent, a violation of her right".[250]

In sharp contrast, in *Re B*, Lord Hailsham appeared to doubt whether mentally incapable women could be said to have any right to reproduce:

"To talk of the 'basic right' to reproduce of an individual who is not capable of knowing the causal connection between intercourse and childbirth, the nature of pregnancy, what is involved in delivery, unable to form maternal instincts or to care for a child appears to me wholly to part company with reality".[251]

Since Article 12 of the European Convention on Human Rights protects "the right to marry and found a family", the question of whether involuntary sterilisation violates mentally incapacitated individuals' right to reproduce may become the subject of litigation under the Human Rights Act 1998. Actions under the Human Rights Act could also plausibly be framed in terms of Article 8's protection of privacy, or Article 3's prohibition upon "inhuman or degrading treatment". There is, as yet, no relevant jurisprudence from the ECHR, although it should be remembered that reproduction has tended to be treated as a subject in which individual member states' margin of appreciation should be especially wide.

(ii) Procedure

Slightly different rules apply depending upon whether or not the woman has reached the age of majority. This is because both the courts' wardship jurisdiction, which gives them extremely wide powers to make decisions about the upbringing of a ward of court, and their powers under the Children Act 1989, cease when the child reaches the age of eighteen. In practice, however, ordinary common law principles have been interpreted to give the courts equally broad powers to authorise the sterilisation of adult women. Similarities in the treatment of mentally incapacitated women and girls are perhaps reinforced by the tendency to infantilise incompetent adult women. Among the judiciary, incompetent adults are commonly described as having the "mental age" of a child, despite modern psychiatry's rejection of this sort of simplistic analogy between normal child development and mental handicap. Clearly, however, describing a woman as having the "mental age" of a four year old may both facilitate treating her as if she were a child,[252] and exacerbate the perception that her status is incompatible with motherhood.

---

[250] *Ibid.* at 193.
[251] [1987] 2 WLR 1213 at 1216.
[252] In *Re X (Adult sterilisaiton)* [1998] 2 FLR 1124, X was 31 years old and described as having a mental age of between 4 and 6. *In the matter of F (adult patient)* (unreported) (26 June 2000), in her opening description of the mentally incapacitated 18 year old, Butler Sloss LJ said that "she is said to have an intellectual age of 5 to 8 years old".

A Sterilisation of mentally incapacitated minors

There are two procedures which might be used to authorise the sterilisation of a mentally incapacitated child. First the child can be made a ward of court, which means that every important decision about the child's upbringing must be made by the court until the child ceases to be a ward, either as the result of a further court order, or because the child has reached the age of eighteen. The wardship jurisdiction was employed in *Re B (A minor) (Wardship Sterilisation)*[253] in order to authorise the sterilisation of Jeanette, a seventeen year old girl suffering from "moderate" mental handicap. The House of Lords found that pregnancy would be a "disaster", and that no other contraceptives were practicable. The House of Lords' judgment in *Re B* was handed down three weeks before Jeanette ceased to be a minor. The advantage in hearing the case before she reached the age of majority was that the Court could use its broad powers under the wardship jurisdiction in order to consent to her sterilisation.[254]

The second possible way in which sterilisation might be authorised is through the making of a specific issue order under the Children Act 1989.[255] The court's powers under the wardship jurisdiction will usually be wider than those available under the Children Act, so the only circumstance in which such an order might have advantages over wardship is that it is possible for the child herself, through her next friend, to make an application to be sterilised using a specific issue order. The mentally incapacitated child's "application" here is obviously a fictional device since the decision to apply for the court authorisation of her sterilisation will not, in any real sense, be an expression of the child's wishes. If the child were mature enough to take this sort of decision for herself, her non-consensual sterilisation would clearly be illegitimate. The practical advantage in "allowing" the child to apply is that she may be more likely to qualify for legal aid than her parents.[256] It might be worth noting that in the only case in which an application was made by the child herself, through her father as next friend, she was nearing her eighteenth birthday.[257] As in *Re B*, the application may then have been prompted by the desire to take advantage of the perceived procedural convenience of making the application during her minority.

---

[253] [1987] 2 WLR 1213.

[254] Norrie, 1989, p. 391.

[255] S. 8. A child can only apply for a s. 8 order after being given leave of the court under s. 10(8).

[256] This was the case in *Re HG (Specific Issue: Sterilisation)* [1993] 1 FLR 587 where the parents were unable to bring proceedings to raise the issue of sterilisation because they were ineligible for legal aid, but could not afford to pay for the action themselves. HG was severely epileptic and mentally handicapped. Pregnancy would be "disastrous" and the contraceptive pill was unsuitable because of her epilepsy. The child's father applied under s. 10(8), as the child's next friend, for leave to apply for a specific issue order under s. 8. Peter Singer QC found that, although this was not the preferred option, a child with a disability could make an application through her next friend.

[257] In *Re HG (Specific Issue: Sterilisation)* [1993] 1 FLR 587.

Where an application is made under the wardship jurisdiction, the Court must only make an order if it is in the best interests of the ward to be sterilised, and Lord Oliver has emphasised that

> "the jurisdiction in wardship proceedings to authorise such an operation is one which should be exercised only in the last resort".[258]

So, for example, in deciding whether sterilisation is in the best interests of a ward, considerations such as the convenience or wishes of carers are plainly irrelevant.[259] Similarly, when making a specific issue order, the child's welfare must be the court's paramount consideration.[260] As we see below, a similar and even perhaps identical test governs decisions regarding the sterilisation of adult women.

B Sterilisation of Mentally Incapacitated Adults

Once a mentally incapacitated woman reaches adulthood, the court loses its ability to consent to her medical treatment through the wardship jurisdiction, or by making an order under the Children Act 1989. And the Mental Health Legislation does not confer any alternative route to authorise the medical treatment of mentally incapacitated individuals, unless they are being treated for their mental disorder.[261] Instead a doctor can lawfully treat an adult patient who is incapable of giving consent if the treatment is in the best interests of the patient.[262]

Given that we have established that the sterilisation of adults and minors is governed by either a best interests test or the welfare principle, it becomes essential to determine precisely when sterilisation will be considered to be in a patient's best interests or to promote her welfare.[263]

(iii) When will the Courts Authorise Sterilisation?

A Best Interests or Medical Necessity?

It is important to remember that deciding that sterilisation is in a woman's best interests is not the same as saying that it is medically necessary. In *Re F (Mental Patient: sterilisation)*[264] the House of Lords considered a test of medical necessity, but rejected it as too "rigid" because it might deprive mentally incapacitated individuals of care which is in their interests but is not necessarily life-saving. While their reasoning is undoubtedly correct with respect to

---

[258] *Re B (A Minor) (Wardship Sterilisation)* [1987] 2 WLR 1213, at 1222.
[259] *Re D (A Minor) (Wardship: Sterilisation)* [1976] Fam 185.
[260] Children Act 1989 s.1(1).
[261] Mental Health Act 1983, s. 63.
[262] *Re F* [1989] 2 WLR 1025, per Lord Brandon at 1068.
[263] In the Australian case of *Secretary, Department of Health and Community Services* v. *JWB and SMB* (1992) FLC 92–293, the High Court of Australia said that "it is not possible to formulate a rule which will identify cases where sterilisation is in his or her best interests".
[264] [1989] 2 WLR 1025.

non-essential medical treatment which nevertheless makes mentally handicapped individuals' lives more comfortable, it is not clear that it should apply
to the permanent removal of a woman's reproductive capacity. In *T* v. *T*,[265]
Wood J offered another criticism of a test based upon medical necessity, which
he said would not be:

> "sufficiently precise as a test of what the courts would consider to be a justification for
> the operative procedures anticipated in the present case".[266]

The judges' preferred test, that a doctor must consider treatment to be in the
best interests of his or her patient, is of course equally imprecise, and in other
contexts has been described as "intellectually flabby";[267] "amorphous and
unpredictable"[268] and as "inevitably reflect(ing) the values and attitudes of individual judges".[269]

B   The (Ir)relevance of the Bolam test?

The relevance of the *Bolam*[270] test to a determination of whether sterilisation is
in the best interests of the patient has been the subject of considerable judicial
disagreement. If *Bolam* were to apply, then a doctor would be entitled to sterilise a mentally handicapped woman if his decision could be accepted as proper
by a responsible body of medical opinion. In *Re F* the Court of Appeal rejected
the first instance judge's view that the *Bolam* test should determine the legality
of sterilisation, and in commenting upon Scott Baker J's reliance upon *Bolam*,
Neill LJ said:

> "with respect, I do not consider that this test is sufficiently stringent. . . ..to say that it
> is not negligent to carry out a particular form of treatment does not mean that that
> treatment is necessary. I would define necessary as that which the general body of
> medical opinion in the particular speciality would consider in the best interests of the
> patient in order to maintain the health and service the well-being of the patient".[271]

The House of Lords then rejected the Court of Appeal's "*Bolam*-plus"[272]
approach and reasserted the primacy of *Bolam*. According to Lord Griffiths:

> "The doctor . . . must give the treatment that he considers to be in the best interests of
> his patient, and the standard of care required of the doctor will be that laid down in
> *Bolam* v. *Friern Hospital Management Committee*".[273]

In recent years, the Court of Appeal has once again, and I argue rightly, challenged
the relevance of the *Bolam* test to the determination of whether sterilisation is in

---

[265] [1988] 2 WLR 189.
[266] *Ibid.* at 199. Instead Wood J advocated that a "medical adviser must..consider what decisions
should be reached in the best interests of his patient's health. What does medical practice demand?"
[267] Kennedy, 1998, p. 100.
[268] Norrie, 1991, p. 120.
[269] Peterson, 1996, p. 64.
[270] *Bolam* v. *Friern Hospital Management Committee* [1957] 1 WLR 582.
[271] *Re F* [1989] 2 WLR 1025, at 1053.
[272] Brazier and Miola, 2000, p. 92.
[273] *Re F* [1989] 2 WLR 1025, at 1080.

the best interests of the patient. The *Bolam* test was developed in order to determine whether a doctor should be liable for medical treatment *that had already
been given, and that had already gone wrong.* Ascribing responsibility in medical
negligence, and determining prospectively what treatment a particular patient
should be given are obviously entirely different exercises.[274] It may be right that a
doctor should not be held liable for a patient's injury unless negligence can be
proved. But where there is an application for the sterilisation of a mentally incompetent individual, the doctor should perhaps have to establish that sterilisation
would be the *best possible option,* not simply that it is a treatment which reaches
some *minimum level of acceptability.* It could even be argued that applying the
Bolam test to an assessment of a patient's best interests effectively emasculates
the court's protective function. A doctor seeking court approval for a proposed
operation in circumstances where *no competent or responsible body of medical
opinion would countenance sterilisation* is extremely unlikely to get as far as a
court hearing.[275]

Butler-Sloss LJ has therefore argued that the *Bolam* test and the "best interests" requirement are better described as two separate duties. First the Court
must establish that the proposed operation would be within the range of reasonable decisions made by a responsible body of medical opinion, and second the
Court should be satisfied that sterilisation is actually in the best interests of this
particular patient.[276] In *SL* v. *SL,* Butler-Sloss LJ explains that:

> "The duty to act in accordance with responsible and competent professional opinion
> may give the doctor more than one option since there may well be more than one
> acceptable medical opinion. When the doctor moves on to consider the best interests
> of the patient he/she has to choose the best option, often from a range of options . . .
> the best interests test ought, logically, to give only one answer".

So a proposed sterilisation could be within the range of acceptable decisions that
might be made by competent and responsible medical practitioners, but it might
not be the *best* option for this particular patient. So if expert opinion is divided
over whether sterilisation or a long-acting method of contraception would be
the most appropriate treatment, the judge must only choose sterilisation if he
considers that permanent deprivation of fertility is the best out of the range of
options that would be judged acceptable according to the *Bolam* test. Where

---

[274] Thorpe LJ in *SL* v. *SL* [2000] 2 FCR 452 says that "at first blush (the *Bolam* test) would seem
an unlikely import in determining the best interests of an adult too disabled to decide for him or herself".

[275] Thorpe LJ in *SL* v. *SL* [2000] 2 FCR 452 confessed to finding "it hard to imagine in practice a
disputed trial before a judge . . . in which a responsible party proposed for an incompetent patient
a treatment that did not satisfy the *Bolam* test".

[276] In *Re A (medical treatment: male sterilisation)* [2000] 1 FCR 193, Butler-Sloss LJ said (at 200)
"Doctors . . . would . . . have to act at all times in accordance with a responsible and competent body
of relevant professional opinion. . . . The doctor, acting to that required standard, has, in my view,
a second duty, that is to say, he must act in the best interests of a mentally incapacitated patient. I
do not consider that the two duties have been conflated into one requirement".

medical opinion is divided, because there should always be a preference for the least invasive option, the judge should have to find extremely compelling reasons to favour sterilisation.

Recent judgements of the Court of Appeal have equated the "best interests" test with the kind of welfare appraisal commonly made in relation to children.[277] This is a far more exacting requirement than the imprecise and forgiving *Bolam* test. But while the need to establish that sterilisation would promote the welfare of a particular individual might hold doctors to a higher standard of proof than simply finding another doctor who would have acted in the same way, the welfare principle might itself be indeterminate and manipulable. In many of these cases the convenience of permanent deprivation of fertility and cessation of menstruation must be balanced against the protection of the mentally incompetent woman's bodily integrity. Without clear rules as to the relative weight to be given to these competing considerations, there is obviously room for widely differing interpretations of where a particular woman's best interests lie. For example, in *Re ZM and OS*[278] although expert witnesses gave conflicting opinions about the relative wisdom of sterilisation and the fitting of an IUD, Bennett J considered that it was in Z's best interests to have a permanent cessation of her periods and complete protection from pregnancy.[279] In the alternative, it could equally plausibly have been argued that an IUD would be in Z's best interests because it would reduce Z's menstrual problems and offer semi-permanent birth control, without resort to major surgery and the permanent removal of Z's fertility.

C *When is sterilisation in a patient's best interests?*

It would seem obvious that certain findings of fact must precede the conclusion that sterilisation is in the best interests of a mentally incapacitated woman, It should, for example, be necessary to establish that the woman actually is incompetent and likely to remain so. There should also be some real likelihood of pregnancy. This involves finding both that the woman is actually fertile, and that she is, or is very likely to become, sexually active. It also needs to be proved that pregnancy poses an unacceptable risk to her physical or mental health, and that it would be impossible for her to use a less invasive contraceptive method.

---

[277] Thorpe LJ in *Re A (medical treatment: male sterilisation)* [2000] 1 FCR 193; and in *SL v SL* [2000] 2 F.C.R. 452, Thorpe LJ said that "in deciding what is best for the disabled patient the judge must have regard to the patient's welfare as the paramount consideration". In *In the matter of F (Adult patient)* (unreported) (26 June 2000), Butler-Sloss LJ referred to these decisions and says that they establish that the court's jurisdiction is "to declare the best interests of the patient on the application of a welfare test analogous to that applied in wardship."

[278] [2000] 1 FLR 523.

[279] Z was 19 years old and had Down's syndrome. Her periods were heavy, irregular and painful. She also experienced personal hygiene difficulties during menstruation, and these were unpleasant and embarrassing for her. Z was going to be moving to a residential unit, and she had a boyfriend. It was accepted that a sexual relationship was probable.

Thus, there are effectively five separate conditions that must be satisfied before a proposed sterilisation should be authorised:[280]

(1) The patient must be incompetent;
(2) The patient must be fertile;
(3) There must be a real likelihood of sexual contact;
(4) Pregnancy must pose an unacceptable risk to the patient's well-being;
(5) It must be impossible for the patient to use a less invasive contraceptive method.

While all of these factors have been considered in the English courts, their application in the cases has not been particularly rigorous. Rather, as we shall see, many of the judgements have appeared to assume that these are simply factors to be taken into account, rather than essential preconditions to the lawful performance of a nonconsensual sterilisation.

First, despite the fact that it has been estimated that only 5 per cent of retarded people do not have the capacity to comprehend reproduction,[281] the English judgements have tended to pay little attention to the question of whether a mentally handicapped woman is in fact incompetent.[282] Deference to medical opinion and a reluctance to meddle with findings of fact result in appellate courts assuming incompetence whenever an application to sterilise a mentally handicapped woman is before them, even where she has expressed a desire to have a child.[283] While it is difficult for an appellate court to overturn a finding of fact made in a lower court, there are obvious dangers in the unqualified acceptance of allegations of incompetence.[284]

The English courts have also tended to ignore the fluidity of incompetence, which is especially important given the irreversibility of sterilisation. Mental incapacity may depend in part upon the quality of social, familial, educational and medical support that is available to the particular woman. Someone who seems to be unable to make her own decisions might, if better care were provided,

---

[280] See further the Official Solicitor's *Practice Note* [1996] 2 FLR 111, which specifies the necessity of proof of incapacity; risk of pregnancy; potential psychological damage from pregnancy and that no reversible method of contraception is appropriate. The Practice Note has no legal force, but may offer some guidance as to the factors that the Official Solicitor may take into account when deciding whether to support an application for a court order authorising sterilisation.

[281] Blank, 1991, p. 79. In France the National Ethics Committee acknowledge that "some minor or mild retardation in young women is entirely compatible with pregnancy, delivery and motherhood" (CCNE, 1996, p. 6).

[282] In contrast in *In Re Romero* the Colorado Supreme Court said that provided a person had some understanding of the link between sex and reproduction and the consequences of sterilisation, then a person who is otherwise incompetent must be able to make their own decision *however unreasonable* (at 823).

[283] Re X [1998] 2 FLR 1124.

[284] In the US case of *In Re Johnson* 263 SE 2d 805 (NC Ct App) (1980) a mildly retarded 23 year old was sterilised because she "had exhibited emotional immaturity, the absence of a sense of responsibility, a lack of patience with children and continuous nightly adventures with boyfriends" (at 809). Such characteristics are not necessarily confined to the mentally ill and could equally apply to a considerable number of "normal" young women.

be capable of autonomous decision-making. In addition, because mental handicap can fluctuate over time, the courts should perhaps insist upon evidence that there is no reasonable prospect of improvement in the individual's condition.

Second, most of the English cases have also tended to take for granted the fertility of the mentally handicapped women whose proposed sterilisations they have considered. In *Re B (A Minor) (Sterilisation)*, for example, the House of Lords assumed, without any supporting evidence, that Jeanette was in fact capable of becoming pregnant. Since the courts have not generally made a fertility assessment an essential precondition to sterilisation, it is undoubtedly possible that some infertile women may have had wholly unnecessary invasive surgery.

Third, although two recent judgements have stated unequivocally that there must be a real risk of pregnancy,[285] there have been many others where sterilisations have been authorised despite no evidence that the mentally handicapped woman either is, or is soon likely to become, sexually active. In *Re W (Mental Patient: Sterilisation)*,[286] for example, there was little chance of the woman becoming pregnant because she was under the constant supervision of her mother. Despite describing the risk of pregnancy as "small", Hollis J considered that the existence of a responsible body of medical opinion that considered the operation to be in her best interests effectively compelled him to declare her sterilisation lawful . Again, in both *Re P(A Minor) (Wardship: Sterilisation)*[287] and *Re HG*,[288] sexual intercourse was unlikely but sterilisation was still held to be in the woman's best interests. Similarly, in the Scottish case of *L* v. *L*,[289] Lord MacLean approved the appointment of a tutor dative who would have power to consent to L's sterilisation even though he found that L "had probably never had sexual intercourse".[290]

At times a mentally handicapped woman's "attractiveness" has been assumed to be synonymous with a real likelihood of sexual activity.[291] Even if it were true

---

[285] In *Re S (Medical Treatment: Adult Sterilisation)* [1998] 1 FLR 944 Johnson J held that sterilisation could only be justified in the event of an identifiable, rather than a speculative risk of pregnancy. And in *Re LC (Medical Treatment: Sterilisation)* [1997] 2 FLR 258 Thorpe J rejected an application for leave to sterilise a patient who currently was at no risk of pregnancy.

[286] [1993] 1 FLR 381.

[287] [1989] 1 FLR 182.

[288] [1993] 1 FLR 588.

[289] [1997] S.L.T. 167.

[290] He nevertheless thought that she was "suggestible", and that a partial hysterectomy would be the best way to deal with the dual problems of menstruation and pregnancy.

[291] In *Re P (A Minor) (Wardship: Sterilisation)* [1989] 1 FLR 182, Eastham J determined that P was at risk of becoming pregnant because, he said, "the evidence is that she is attractive". In *Re LC (Medical Treatment: Sterilisation)* [1997] 2 FLR 258, the application for the sterilisation of LC, who had been indecently assaulted when she was 18 years old, was based upon the local authority's claim that she was "attractive and demonstrative" and therefore vulnerable to sexual abuse. LC was now in a home with an exceptionally high standard of care and Thorpe LJ found that the risk of abuse was now minimal, and sterilisation was not necessary.

Although again, the application for sterilisation was ultimately rejected, within the first page of her judgement in *SL* v. *SL* [2000] 2 FCR 452 Butler Sloss LJ twice referred to S as an "extremely attractive girl".

that a mentally handicapped woman's vulnerability to unwanted sexual attention is increased by her physical attractiveness, sterilisation is obviously not the optimum solution for women at risk of sexual assault. If a severely mentally impaired woman is likely to be sexually assaulted, then removing the threat of abuse by making her living conditions safer would obviously be a better preventative strategy than sterilisation.[292]

Fourth, it also often seems to be taken for granted that pregnancy would be disastrous. For example, it is frequently suggested that a mentally incompetent woman lacks the capacity to care for a child, and so should be sterilised in order to eliminate the need to take her child away from her.[293] But IQ is not the best or the only indicator of parenting inability, and the English courts would not authorise the involuntary sterilisation of mentally competent individuals who are otherwise poorly equipped to care for their children. A competent woman whose children had been taken into care would not be sterilised in order to prevent history repeating itself because her bodily integrity must "trump" concern for the welfare of any future children. Indeed, in such circumstances nonconsensual sterilisation would be an assault.

Alternatively it has been contended that avoiding pregnancy might be in the best interests of mentally handicapped women because it frees them from the constraints of their fertility, and allows them to express their sexuality.[294] Of course it may be possible to achieve freedom from pregnancy using a less invasive contraceptive method, so this argument is only plausible in the rare circumstance in which every other type of contraception both is, and is likely to remain unusable.

---

[292] John Robertson suggests that compulsory contraception might offer one answer to the vulnerability of institutionalised women to rape or sexual sterilisation (Robertson, 1994, p.90). In the American case of *Anonymous* v. *Anonymous* 469 So 2d 588,590 (Ala. 1985) the parents of a 14 year old daughter attending a special school sought her sterilisation. They testified that she was physically attractive and as a result they were concerned that someone might take advantage of her sexuality. Commenting on this case, Beverley Horsbrugh argues that the possibility of sexual harassment and rape appears to render mentally handicapped women vulnerable to the further intrusion of involuntary sterilisation. In the Australian case of *Re L & M* [1993] 17 Fam LR 357, Warnick J said that the problem of abuse was not removed by sterilisation and that any risk of abuse should be tackled directly.

[293] This was one of the arguments put forward in *Re D (A Minor) (Wardship: Sterilisation)* [1976] Fam 185. In *Re M (A Minor) (wardship: sterilisation)* [1988] 2 FLR 997 one reason given for authorising the sterilisation of a 17 year old girl with Fragile X syndrome was that she would never be able to look after a baby and it would have be taken away from her.

Similarly in *Re P (A Minor)(wardship: sterilisation)* [1989] 1 FLR 997 Eastham J approved the sterilisation because it would have been distastrous for the 17 year old girl to become pregnant because the baby would have to be taken away from her and this would "violate" her maternal feelings.

[294] Macklin and Gaylin, 1981. In the American case of *In Re Valerie* N 707 P. 2d. 760 (Cal. 1985) the California Supreme Court found that a mentally handicapped woman had a right to have the decision to be sterilised made for her. In *In Re Moe* 432 NE 2d 712 (Mass. 1982) it was held that sterilisation would facilitate a mentally handicapped woman's exercise of her right to privacy. In *Re Grady* 85 NJ 235 426 A 2d 467 (1981) the New Jersey court found that a 19 year old woman with Down's syndrome had a right to sterilisation in order that she could lead a richer and more active life.

There are sound practical reasons for always favouring the least invasive contraceptive option. First, there will always be the possibility that a more acceptable new birth control method may become available which could prevent conception without permanently removing the woman's reproductive capacity. Sterilisation thus prevents a woman from taking advantage of future developments which might better suit her needs. Second, the woman's degree of mental handicap may alter over time, either as a result of physiological changes or following improvements in the treatments and services that are available to her. Again sterilisation prevents reassessment of a woman's reproductive needs in the light of shifts in her mental capacity.

But this final requirement that the courts should always prefer the least invasive contraceptive option has also been interpreted rather loosely by the English courts.[295] In *Re P (a minor) (wardship: sterilisation)*,[296] for example, Eastham J was impressed by evidence given by Robert Winston suggesting that reversal surgery might have a 95 per cent chance of success. Given improved reversibility, Eastham J questioned whether sterilisation should actually continue to be regarded as a step of last resort.[297] But although reversal might be a technical possibility, it is doubtful whether a woman who is not competent to give consent to a sterilisation operation would be able to consent to its reversal. It also seems unlikely that mentally handicapped women would routinely be offered reversal surgery.[298]

(iv) Practice in other countries

Since the "best interests" of a mentally incapacitated patient are not always immediately apparent, some other countries have specified criteria for determining whether sterilisation is justified.[299] For example, the German Civil Code was amended in 1992 by the *Betreuungsgesetz* or Carership Law, and now offers guidelines which incorporate three precise principles. First, a mentally incapacitated person may nevertheless possess a "natural will" and be able to manifest their opposition to sterilisation, in which case the operation would be unlawful.[300] Second, non-consensual sterilisation must be medically indicated by both

---

[295] In his first instance decision in *SL* v. *SL*, which was subsequently overturned by the Court of Appeal, Wall J decided that in spite of unanimous medical opinion that the immediate preferred option was the Mirena coil, the more invasive procedure was *probably* preferable, but that the decision should be delegated to S's mother in consultation with S's doctors.

[296] [1989] 1 FLR 182.

[297] Brazier points out that "*Re P* illustrates that, in practice, hypothetical reversibility of sterilisation has convinced some responsible gynaecologists that it is now appropriate for a much broader category of women. Sterilisation need no longer be the last resort, merely perhaps the most 'convenient' means of contraception" (Brazier, 1992, p. 392).

[298] Brazier, 1992, p. 390–1.

[299] In Australia, the best interests principle is "confined by the notion of the step of last resort" (Peterson, 1996, p. 73).

[300] This concept of natural will has no parallel in English law. Its function, as George Bradbury Little explains, is that "no matter how beneficial a sterilisation would be to the ward or how benign the intentions of the carers are, this rule protects the kicking, protesting, terrified" or simply obstinate mentally handicapped individual from the indignity of a compulsory sterilisation (Little, 1997, p. 286).

an *immediate* and *serious* risk of pregnancy and an assessment that pregnancy would *endanger the woman's health*. Third, sterilisation *must* be the option of last resort.[301]

The French National Consultative Ethics Committee for Health and Life Sciences (CCNE) has recommended that the following conditions should be satisfied before sterilisation could be performed upon a mentally incapacitated individual:

(1) Incapacity must be established "by thorough and multidisciplinary evaluation";
(2) There must be no prospect of improvement;
(3) The individual must be potentially fertile, sexually active and at least 20 years old;
(4) An effort to consult him or her must be made;
(5) There must be proof that "no other form of contraception can, in practical terms, be used by the individual".[302]

I would argue that British law would be much improved if it ceased to treat the various considerations that inform their judgements about the legitimacy of nonconsensual sterilisation as if they were vague and optionally relevant factors, and instead incorporated a similar set of unambiguous and restrictive conditions.

(v) Sterilising Mentally Incapacitated Men

So far no court has ordered the sterilisation of a mentally incompetent man. A vasectomy is generally a much simpler procedure than female sterilisation, but because a man's *physical* health is not endangered by being capable of impregnating a woman, it would be difficult to establish that a vasectomy was in a patient's medical interest.[303] Yet the female sterilisation cases have indubitably not confined their consideration of the woman's best interests to her *clinical*

---

[301] Paragraph 1905 of the German Civil Code states that:

(1) Where the medical intervention consists of a sterilisation of the ward in which the ward is unable to consent, the carer may only consent if:
    (a) the sterilisation does not contradict the will of the ward
    (b) the ward will remain permanently incapable of giving consent
    (c) it is to be expected that without a sterilisation a pregnancy will occur
    (d) as a result of the pregnancy, a risk of danger to the life, or a risk of serious harm to the physical or mental health of the pregnant woman is to be expected, which cannot be reasonably prevented by any other means and
    (e) the pregnancy cannot be prevented by any other means
(2) ... The preferred method of sterilisation is always that which allows for refertilisation.

[302] CCNE, 1996, p. 2.

[303] In *AL v. GRH* 325 NE 2d 501, 74 ALR 3d 1220 (1975) the Indiana Court of Appeal refused to authorise the sterilisation of a 15 year old mentally handicapped boy who had shown signs of sexual awareness on the grounds that the operation would benefit his sexual partners rather than himself.

needs, but have taken into account a range of *social* reasons why pregnancy might not promote her wellbeing. In other medical contexts, there is also evidence that a patient's best interests are not necessarily confined to their immediate health needs. A bone marrow donation has, for example, been authorised by the Court on the grounds that saving her sister's life would improve a mentally handicapped woman's emotional relationships with her mother and sister.[304] Being a bone marrow donor was held to be in the woman's "best interests" even though it plainly did not promote the woman's *physical* health.

And in *Re A (medical treatment: male sterilisation)*,[305] Butler-Sloss LJ suggested that similar reasoning could be applied to the sterilisation of a mentally incompetent man:

> "In my judgment best interests encompasses medical, emotional and all other welfare issues".[306]

So, although in *Re A*, it was not in this particular man's immediate best interests to be sterilised, the Court of Appeal explicitly left open the possibility that his carers could return to the court for an order authorising a vasectomy if in future his freedom was being restricted for fear of him causing a woman to become pregnant.[307]

5. CONCLUSION

Promoting reproductive autonomy involves respecting choices that individuals make about fertility control. Law may have an important role in facilitating access to birth control, by, for example, ensuring that it is provided free of charge, or by enabling women to purchase the morning-after pill from pharmacists without prescription. But it is of fundamental importance that promoting the availability of contraception does not slide into a series of quasi-coercive measures designed to create more effective contraceptive use by undermining individuals' control over their own fertility. As we have seen in this chapter, the impact of these population policies tends to be uneven, with vulnerable groups

---

[304] *Re Y(Adult Patient)(Transplant: Bone Marrow)* [1997] Fam 110.

[305] [2000] 1 FCR 193.

[306] *Ibid.* at 200.

[307] A was a 28 year old man with Down's syndrome. He was cared for by his mother who was concerned that in the future she would for health reasons be unable to continue to supervise him. She feared that if A moved into local authority care, he might have a sexual relationship and be unable to understand the possibility of pregnancy. The Court of Appeal found that although the fact of a birth, or disapproval of a mentally incapacitated man's conduct were only likely to have a significant impact upon him in exceptional circumstances, it might be possible to argue that restricting his freedom in order to avoid the risk of pregnancy could represent a sufficient justification for a vasectomy. Although the Court of Appeal also pointed out that where a sexual relationship with another resident became probable, the potential female sexual partner would be more likely than A to be subject to extra supervision.

at particular risk from the blurring of the boundary between persuasion and coercion.

Respect for individuals' choices about their fertility means giving priority to an individual's own assessment of whether or not they want to have a child. As a result, wrongful birth actions should not be dismissed on the preposterous grounds that people with an extremely strong desire to have no more children will in fact be delighted when their invasive surgery fails and the "blessing" of another child arrives. There may, of course, be legitimate public interest arguments against using the tort system to deal with medical negligence and these apply equally to the wrongful birth cases as to any other type of claim against a health authority. But the way to deal with disquiet about the implications of "the damages lottery"[308] is not to reject particular claims on spurious moral grounds, but rather to instigate a comprehensive review of personal injury litigation in general, and medical malpractice actions in particular.

Finally, we should acknowledge that fears about overfertility among certain social groups have a long and discreditable history.[309] Explicit support for eugenic policies is undoubtedly now rare, but it may be important to recognise that anxieties about population growth are often unrelated to real demographic trends and may instead reflect some subliminal uneasiness about the long-term social consequences of profligate reproduction among the weakest and most dependent members of society. It has, for example, proved too easy to establish that the best interests of a mentally incapacitated woman require her sterilisation. As we see in the last two chapters of this book, unwanted sterility is extremely distressing, and this is undoubtedly also true for mentally incapacitated individuals. We know, for example, that mentally handicapped women have felt undermined and violated by their involuntary sterilisation.[310] In the next chapter we consider abortion law and policy, and it is perhaps significant that protecting the interests of fetuses has attracted more intensive and vocal interest than safeguarding the bodily autonomy and sexual privacy of mentally incapacitated women and girls.

---

[308] Atiyah, 1997.
[309] In 1909 Whetham and Whetham wrote that "the feeble-minded and weak bodied stock . . . reproduce themselves faster than do the better stocks" (Whetham and Whetham, 1909).
[310] In one survey of 50 mentally handicapped women, 68% disapproved of their sterilisation and felt stigmatised and degraded by their sterility (Cepko, 1993, p. 145).

3

Abortion

1. INTRODUCTION

THE FIRST HALF of this chapter examines the unique place abortion occupies in the practice of both law and medicine. For such a simple and commonplace operation it is, for example, extraordinary that performing an abortion is still, *prima facie*, a criminal offence. I begin by fleshing out some of the reasons for abortion's wholly distinctive regulatory regime, and I describe the conditions of abortion's legality in the UK. The implications of the remarkable authority abortion law vests in medical practitioners are then explored. In the remainder of this chapter, we concentrate upon a few issues that are currently provoking especially intense disagreement. We consider, for example, whether new technologies might be subverting the legal and moral distinctions that are commonly drawn between abortion and contraception. In addition, the prevailing tendency to characterise certain sorts of abortion as "morally worse" than others is interrogated. For instance, diagnostic techniques that facilitate sex-selective abortion have generated considerable anxiety; and disquiet about abortion on the grounds of fetal abnormality has been exacerbated by the proliferation of new genetic tests.

Throughout this chapter, I argue that the decision to have an abortion can only properly be made by the pregnant woman herself. Although an individual doctor may have a conscientious objection to abortion, it is difficult to imagine circumstances in which a doctor's *clinical* judgement could properly offer an adequate justification for refusing a woman's request for abortion. Moreover, given imperfect contraception, and human beings' inability to exercise complete control over their reproductive capacity, unwanted pregnancies are an inevitable side-effect of sexual freedom, and the safety-net of legal abortion is an essential adjunct of effective birth control. Without liberal access to abortion, women's freedom to enter into non-reproductive sexual relationships might be jeopardised by the threat of unwanted procreation. Choosing to carry a pregnancy to term and give birth to a child is undoubtedly one of the most significant decisions a woman will ever take, and it is not, in my opinion, one that anyone else should be able to either veto, or force upon her. Returning to some of the themes of the previous two chapters, I employ a variation upon the liberal ideal of self-government or autonomy in order to argue for a woman's right to determine the outcome of her pregnancy. In the next chapter, I adopt a similarly robust commitment to pregnant women's bodily autonomy in order to defend a woman's right to make decisions about her conduct and medical treatment during a *wanted* pregnancy. In this chapter, my conclusion will be that abortion law should no longer consist in a set of defences to the crime of abortion, but rather should, like the rest of British medical law, be informed by the guiding principle of patient self-determination.

Unwanted pregnancies and attempts to terminate them have always existed.[1] When safe, legal abortion is unavailable, women have unsafe, illegal abortions[2] or they travel to places with more liberal abortion laws.[3] Approximately a quarter of the world's population live in countries where abortion is either illegal or only permitted if the pregnant woman's life is in danger.[4] In these countries, around twenty million women have illegal abortions each year resulting in nearly 80,000 deaths.[5] It is impossible to calculate exactly how many women travel abroad to terminate their unwanted pregnancies. Each year, for example, 2,000 women at English abortion clinics give addresses in Northern Ireland[6] and nearly 6,000 women give addresses in the Republic of Ireland.[7] Undoubtedly the real figures are much higher.[8]

Abortion is a simple, routine and frequently performed operation. It is the most common surgical operation for women of reproductive age,[9] and it has been estimated that between 35 to 40 per cent of all women will have at least one abortion during their lives.[10] The vast majority of abortions take place within the first twelve weeks of pregnancy when it is an extremely simple procedure.[11] Yet despite being a straightforward operation, as we have seen, abortion is subject to a distinctive and extraordinary legal framework. Its

[1] Petchesky, 1984. There is evidence of the use of abortifacients in China in 3000 BC, and abortion was widely practised in Roman times (Hadley, 1997, p. 41).

[2] For example, abortion is absolutely prohibited in Chile, but it is estimated that between 160,000 and 300,000 women have abortions each year (Casas-Becerra, 1997). And in Nepal, abortion is simply classified as infanticide, with no exceptions for life-threatening pregnancies, rape or incest. Two thirds of women in Nepalese prisons are there for *garbaphat* or infanticide. It is estimated that six women die each day in Nepal after illegal abortions, and that 50% of maternal deaths are the result of unsafe abortions (IPPF, 1999). When abortion and contraception was banned in Romania in 1966 in order to encourage population growth, the abortion mortality rate increased to six times its previous level (Kurczycki, 1999, p. 15).

[3] For example, abortion is exported in Germany where restrictive rules have led better off women with unwanted pregnancies to travel to the Netherlands (Hadley, 1997, p. 58).

[4] Kulczycki, 1999, p. 13.

[5] Alan Guttmacher Institute, 1998.

[6] Simpson, 1998, p. 103. The Abortion Act 1967 does not apply to Northern Ireland, where opposition to abortion is one of the only matters upon which unionists and republicans have a history of consensus. In June 2000, for example, politicians from the unionist and the nationalist parties in Northern Ireland joined forces to block any extension of the Abortion Act 1967 to Northern Ireland (Birchard, 2000).

[7] Payne, 1999, p. 593.

[8] Hadley, 1997, p. 22.

[9] Law, 1994, p. 281; Lattimer, 1998, p. 59.

[10] Furedi, 1998a, p. 161.

[11] Of the 183,250 abortions in England and Wales in 1999, 154,682 (84%) were carried out during the first 12 weeks of pregnancy. Only 2,467 were carried out after 20 weeks (Abortion Statistics, Department of Health, HMSO 2000).

legalisation in 1967, for example, simply created a series of defences to the criminal offences contained in the Offences Against the Person Act 1861 and the Infant Life Preservation Act 1929.

Abortion is also a particularly controversial and embattled ethical issue. In the United States disagreements over abortion have determined nominations to the Supreme Court and decided election results.[12] In several countries abortion providers have been subjected to violence, arson and murder.[13] Negotiations over abortion legislation were said to create more difficulties than any other single issue in the reunification of Germany.[14] Although abortion may not inspire quite such fierce controversy in Britain, it remains a highly sensitive and emotionally charged subject. Since 1967 there have been over twenty Parliamentary attempts to restrict access to abortion, and there have been several, albeit ultimately unsuccessful , applications to the courts for injunctions to prohibit terminations.[15]

There are two principal reasons for abortion's enduring contentiousness. First, some people think that abortion is incompatible with respect for the moral value of the fetus.[16] This view is held with varying degrees of intensity. There are those who believe that a fetus is a person from the moment of conception, and that abortion is therefore *always* equivalent to murder, while others consider that fetal life should be protected unless a compelling justification for abortion exists. Very few people hold the former point of view. There would, for example, be little public support for charging a teenage rape victim, who had terminated the resulting pregnancy, with murder. The belief that abortion law should offer the fetus *some* protection, while falling short of endowing it with full legal personhood, is held far more widely, and, as we see below, forms the basis of the Abortion Act 1967.

We return to the moral and legal status of the fetus in the following chapter when we discuss the pregnant woman's decision-making authority during a pregnancy that she intends to carry to term. In relation to both wanted and unwanted pregnancies, protecting the fetus against choices made by the pregnant woman is only possible if her right to take decisions about her body is suspended or abridged. If a conflict exists between respect for fetal life and respect for the bodily integrity and autonomy of the pregnant woman, resolving that conflict in favour of the fetus represents, as I explain in more detail

---

[12] Hadley, 1997, p. 19. In his campaign for the Republican nomination in 2000, in order to defeat his rival John McCain in conservative states like South Carolina, George W Bush declared his support for a complete ban on abortion, without any exceptions, even where the woman is pregnant as a result of rape or incest, or the pregnancy is endangering her life (Greenberg, 2000).

[13] Ellison, 1998, p. 4; Spurgeon, 2000.

[14] Mason and McCall Smith, 1994, p. 106.

[15] *Paton* v. *Trustees of the British Pregnancy Advisory Service* [1978] 2 All ER 987; *C* v. *S* [1987] 1 All ER 1230; *R.* v. *Queen Charlotte's Hospital Ex p. Society for the Protection of the Unborn Child* (Unreported, 1996) discussed in Sheldon, 1997b; *Kelly* v. *Kelly* 1997 SLT 896.

[16] In the Constitution on the Church in the World of Today it is argued that "life must from its very conception be guarded with the greatest care. Abortion (is an) abominable crime" (*Gaudium et Spes*, 1966, p. 54).

in the following chapter, an extraordinary exception to the established principle that no individual can be compelled to use their body in order to save another's life.[17] Given that the fetus has not achieved legal personhood, compelling the pregnant woman to sacrifice her bodily autonomy in order to protect its life seems especially bizarre. Yet the logical corollary of an abortion law that sets limits upon women's access to abortion is that, in certain circumstances, a woman can be obliged to carry her unwanted pregnancy to term. That this is not generally perceived to be an important derogation from the pregnant woman's right to self-determination may derive in part from the second explanation for the antagonism that surrounds the abortion debate, namely that abortion undermines certain dominant cultural assumptions about women's maternal instincts.[18]

A pregnant woman who wants to have an abortion will generally be putting her interests before those of the fetus she is carrying. To choose to terminate a pregnancy may then seem incompatible with the supposed biologically-driven urge towards maternal self-abnegation. In the past, pro-choice campaigners attempted to deflect this second sort of criticism in two ways. First they argued that a woman who wants an abortion is not necessarily rejecting motherhood, she simply cannot continue with *this particular* pregnancy.[19] Indeed many advocates of liberal access to abortion contend that it is precisely because a woman is a good mother that she may need to terminate an unexpected pregnancy in order to continue to nurture and care for her existing children.[20] Alternatively, if the woman seeking an abortion is childless, she can be presented as a woman who is *currently* unable to be a good mother, and who has responsibly decided to delay childbearing until she can give her children a stable and secure upbringing. Presenting abortion as the sensible choice of women with good nurturing instincts was undoubtedly an important campaigning strategy in 1967. However, the argument that abortion's legitimacy derives from the pregnant woman's sense of maternal obligation to present or future children risks inadvertently reinforcing the belief that simply not wanting to be pregnant is not an adequate justification for abortion.[21]

The second way in which pro-choice campaigners have defended women who have abortions from the charge that their decision epitomises a cavalier attitude

---

[17] See further Thomson, 1971.

[18] Kristin Luker has argued that abortion is really a symbolic battleground for the definition of appropriate female roles (Luker, 1984).

[19] Sheldon, 1997a, p.40.

[20] Elizabeth Karlin says that she "know(s) that women have abortions because they have a sense of what it is to be a good mother" (Karlin, 1998, p.273).

[21] A *Daily Mail* editorial referred to "figure conscious women who put work before children" (31.8.93). Jill Knight MP suggested in Parliament that women who want abortions treat babies "like bad teeth to be jerked out just because they cause suffering" Knight, HC Deb Vol. 732 Col. 1100 (22 July, 1966). Clare Murphy has argued that the information given during the mandatory German pre-abortion counselling sessions is intended to draw a bright line between responsible choices made in severely straightened circumstances, and "egotistical choices", based only upon the woman's wishes (Murphy, 1997, p. 56).

towards motherhood is through stressing that the decision to terminate a pregnancy is agonising and traumatic. Sally Sheldon argues that this image of women "at the end of their tether" was a central strategy of abortion reformers in 1967, and the Parliamentary speeches of MPs arguing in favour of legalisation were certainly dominated by descriptions of distraught and unstable constituents for whom abortion might be the only way to preserve their health and sanity.[22] If either unwanted childbearing or unsafe abortion mean that a family's primary caretaker is unable to provide emotional and practical support to her husband and children, it becomes possible to present legal abortion as a necessary way to protect the wellbeing of the family. Portraying women seeking abortions as desperate and disturbed may have been politically astute, but as we see later, the legislation that resulted from these Parliamentary debates converted this argument in favour of legalisation into a *condition of legality*. Accordingly, a woman is not entitled to terminate her pregnancy *unless* she can establish that her mental or physical health would be jeopardised by carrying her unwanted pregnancy to term.

The trauma and regret that are commonly associated with abortion contrast sharply with dominant assumptions about the joy and fulfilment of motherhood. It has, for example, been suggested that the health risks of childbirth tend to be underreported,[23] while conversely, the psychological risks of abortion are commonly overstated.[24] Deciding to terminate a pregnancy is generally understood to be painful and emotionally disturbing, while choosing to have a baby is assumed to be a straightforward and easy decision. Pre and post-abortion counselling is widely available, and in some countries it is compulsory.[25] Women who intend to carry their fetuses to term, on the other hand, are not routinely offered counselling, even though parenthood undoubtedly involves assuming a set of exceptionally challenging and enduring obligations.[26]

[22] Sheldon, 1997a, pp. 38–41.

[23] At least one fifth of all women suffer serious psychological distress in the year after the birth of a child (Boyle 1997, p. 30).

[24] Boyle, 1997, p. 28; Ellie Lee and Anne Gilchrist have argued that "post-abortion syndrome" (PAS) is a myth. Studies have shown that a small percentage of women are diagnosed with psychiatric conditions following abortion. But most of these women in fact exhibited those conditions before the termination. Moreover for the vast majority of women the most stressful time is prior to the abortion, afterwards the most common response is relief. Lee and Gilchrist conclude that "women who have had previous psychological problems are a vulnerable sub-group whether they seek an abortion or continue an unplanned pregnancy" (Lee and Gilchrist, 1997, p. 46).

[25] Under the German Penal Code s. 218, para. 1 abortion is a criminal offence. An exception is created by s.218a para. 1 which permits abortion in the first 12 weeks of pregnancy on condition that a woman obtains counselling three days before the operation. The explicit purpose of the counselling is to protect the "unborn child". The counsellor must encourage the woman to continue with her pregnancy; make her aware of the "unborn child's" right to life and make it clear to her that abortion is only permissible if her circumstances are exceptional.

In the UK, the then Department of Health and Social Security issued a guideline in 1977 recommending that all women requesting abortion should be provided with counselling. More recently the RCOG (2000a) has advised that pre-abortion counselling should be optional.

[26] Boyle, 1997, p. 30.

Underlying this assumption that abortion is uniquely traumatic would seem to be the belief that women have a natural maternal instinct which *always* makes motherhood a much simpler choice than abortion.[27] It appears, therefore, that prevailing attitudes towards abortion may be inseparable from conventional understandings about motherhood. For example, according to John Robertson:

> "the alacrity with which pro-life groups assume that women have a moral duty to lend their bodies to serve fetal needs—far beyond any other duties to rescue recognised in law—betrays an underlying attitude that a woman's role is to sacrifice her own interests and reproduce".[28]

If people generally believe that women's reproductive capacity compels them to be endlessly self-sacrificing, it is unsurprising that the desire for abortion appears to be culturally unacceptable unless accompanied by an acknowledgement of maternal instinct and psychological distress. In the following section, we see how abortion law reinforces some of these assumptions about the relative trauma of abortion.

2. THE LAW

In the United Kingdom, as we have seen, abortion is still a crime. Under sections 58 and 59 of the Offences Against the Person Act 1861 intentionally procuring a miscarriage in oneself or another is a criminal offence, with a maximum sentence of life imprisonment for procuring one's own miscarriage and five years for procuring a miscarriage in another person.[29] Under the Infant Life Preservation Act 1929 section 1, it is an offence to destroy the life of a child capable of being born alive,[30] unless it is done in good faith for the purpose only of preserving the life of the mother. Taken together these statutes could be used to justify therapeutic abortion,[31] and by 1966 "legal" abortions were readily available to

---

[27] In *Udale* v. *Bloomsbury Area Health Authority* [1983] 2 All ER 522, one of the reasons given for rejecting a claim for damages for wrongful life was that such damages would "reward an unnatural rejection of motherhood"(at p.527).

[28] Robertson, 1994.

[29] S. 58 makes it an offence where a "woman, being with child, who, with intent to procure her own miscarriage, shall unlawfully administer to herself any poison or other noxious thing, or shall unlawfully use any instrument or other means whatsoever with the like intent, and whosoever, with intent to procure her miscarriage, whether she be or be not with child, shall unlawfully administer to her or cause to be taken by her any poison or other noxious thing, or shall unlawfully use any instrument or other means whatsoever with the like intent". Under s. 59 it is an offence to unlawfully supply or procure any "poison or other noxious thing knowing it is intended to be unlawfully used with intent to procure a miscarriage".

[30] The Act contains a rebuttable presumption that a child is capable of being born alive at 28 weeks.

[31] In *R* v. *Bourne* [1938] 3 All ER 615, Mr Bourne had performed an abortion on a 14 year old girl who was pregnant as a result of being gang raped by a group of soldiers. He presented himself to the authorities in order to challenge the scope of the law, his contention being that the inclusion of the word "unlawfully" in s. 58 presupposed that abortion could, in some circumstances be "lawful". He

women who could afford them.[32] Safe abortion services did then exist prior to the Abortion Act 1967, but they were inaccessible to the majority of women, and illegal abortions were both common and dangerous.[33] High maternal mortality rates among the poor were undoubtedly a key factor behind the reform of the law governing abortion in 1967. Abortion had become a public health issue and there was broad support for bringing it within the safety of medical control.[34] The births of thousands of children with disabilities caused by thalidomide in the early 1960s may also have furthered the emergence of a climate of public opinion sympathetic to abortion in cases of serious fetal abnormality.[35]

The Abortion Act 1967 did not invalidate the Offences Against the Person Act 1861 or the Infant Life (Preservation) Act 1929, it simply created statutory defences to the crimes of procuring a miscarriage, and destroying a viable fetus. So since 1968, abortion has been lawful in Scotland, England and Wales if two doctors believe in good faith that one of the four grounds in section 1(1) of the Abortion Act 1967 are satisfied.[36] Unlike the abortion laws of many other countries, the grounds for abortion are rather vague. The Act does not, for example, specify that abortion is legal where the pregnancy has resulted from an act of rape or incest.[37] This ambiguity was undoubtedly deliberate. David Steel's

was charged with unlawfully procuring a miscarriage contrary to s. 58 of the Offences Against the Person Act 1861. Macnaughten J described Mr Bourne as "(a) man of the highest skill" who " in one of our great hospitals, , performs the operation as an act of charity, without fee or reward". He then argued that "if the doctor is of the opinion, on reasonable grounds and with adequate knowledge, that the probable consequence of the continuance of the pregnancy will be to make the woman a physical or mental wreck, the jury are quite entitled to take the view that (he) . . . is operating for the purpose of preserving the life of the woman". The jury acquitted Mr Bourne.

[32] Sheldon, 1997, p. 19.

[33] It has been estimated that there were 80,000–110,000 illegal abortions per year in the 1960s (Paintin, 1998, p. 13).

[34] An NOP poll in 1965 showed that two thirds of the population thought that abortion should be legal (Cossey, 1998, p. 24).

[35] Furedi, 1998a, p. 165. Between 1956 and 1961 there were 12,000 children born in 46 countries with severe limb defects. One third of these "thalidomide" babies died within a month (BBC Horizon, 1998b). In the United States, public sympathy was evoked by the plight of a woman whose fetus was affected by thalidomide and who had to travel to Sweden to have an abortion.

[36] s.1(1) Subject to the provisions of this section a person shall not be guilty of an offence under the law relating to abortion when a pregnancy is terminated by a registered medical practitioner if two registered medical practitioners are of the opinion, formed in good faith:

(a) that the pregnancy has not exceeded its twenty fourth week and that the continuation of the pregnancy would involve risk, greater than if the pregnancy were terminated, of injury to the physical or mental health of the pregnant woman or any existing children of her family; or
(b) that the termination is necessary to prevent grave permanent injury to the physical or mental health of the pregnant woman; or
(c) that the continuance of the pregnancy would involve risk to the life of the pregnant woman, greater than if the pregnancy were terminated; or
(d) that there is a substantial risk that if the child were born it would suffer from physical or mental abnormalities as to be seriously handicapped.

[37] More specific indications for abortion are common in other countries, for example under the Choice on Termination of Pregnancy Act 1996 in South Africa abortion is available on request in the first twelve weeks; in the first twenty weeks for rape, incest, socio-economic reasons or to protect physical or mental health; and after 20 weeks, if the woman's life is in danger or the fetus is serious malformed.

Abortion Bill initially contained clauses specifically allowing abortion where the pregnant woman was under sixteen or was pregnant as a result of rape, but these were opposed by both the British Medical Association and the Royal College of Obstetricians and Gynaecologists. Their fear was that a definitive list of situations in which abortion would be lawful might erode medical discretion, and give women the impression that in certain circumstances abortion would be an entitlement.[38] Even where the statutory grounds are made out, doctors' participation in the provision of non-emergency abortion services remains voluntary. The Abortion Act 1967 provides medical personnel with a right of conscientious objection to participation in the provision of abortion services, unless the abortion is necessary to save the woman's life.[39]

While the legalisation of abortion is sometimes assumed to be part of the pattern of liberal law reforms that took place during the 1960s,[40] Sally Sheldon has disputed the characterisation of the 1967 Act as a permissive piece of social legislation.[41] She argues that the principal purpose and effect of the Act was not to promote women's reproductive autonomy, but rather to institute a more rigorous and subtle system of medical control over women's fertility.[42] The 1967 Act does not, for example, entitle a woman to decide to terminate an unwanted pregnancy, even if her circumstances plainly satisfy the section 1(1) criteria. Instead the statute enshrines deference to medical opinion, and legitimises the *doctors'* decision that an abortion would be lawful. In addition, the statute does not even specify that the section 1(1) conditions have to actually *be satisfied*. The legality of an abortion is conditional upon whether the doctor has formed the *opinion* that that woman's case fits within the statutory grounds, not upon whether those grounds in fact *exist*. Thus, an abortion would be legal even if the woman's circumstances did not satisfy the statutory grounds provided that the doctors who authorised her termination had acted in good faith. Insofar as section 1(1) contains a defence to the *prima facie* criminal offence of procuring a miscarriage in another person, it is perhaps interesting that the defendant doctor's *opinion* defines the scope of his own statutory defence.[43] Similarly, judicial review of a decision taken by two NHS

[38]   Keown, 1988, p. 90.

[39]   S. 4(2) excludes the right of conscientious objection if the abortion is "necessary to save the life or to prevent grave permanent injury to the physical or mental health of a pregnant woman".

[40]   For example in 1967, the Sexual Offences Act legalised some homosexual acts, and the National Heath Services Act provided public funding for contraception.

[41]   Sheldon, 1997a, p. 30.

[42]   For example, close monitoring of the incidence of abortion is facilitated by s. 2 of the Act which requires the medical practitioner who performs the termination to complete the relevant form and notify the Chief Medical Officer within seven days of the abortion (Abortion Law Reform Association, 1997, p. 4).

[43]   In *R* v. *Smith* [1974] 1 All ER 376, the only reported case involving prosecution under the Abortion Act 1967, the evidence indicated that the doctor had failed to carry out an internal examination and had made no inquiries into the pregnant woman's personal situation. There was a conflict of evidence on whether the doctor who gave the second opinion had examined the patient. The doctor was convicted on the basis that he had not attempted to balance the risks of pregnancy and termination.

doctors would have to establish irrationality or that no reasonable doctor could have come to the same conclusion. Given the breadth of the discretion granted to doctors by the Abortion Act, it would be extremely difficult to establish that they had exceeded their powers.

In 1999 over 98 per cent of all abortions were authorised under what has become known as the "social" ground,[44] that is:

> "that the pregnancy has not exceeded its twenty fourth week and that the continuation of the pregnancy would involve risk, greater than if the pregnancy were terminated, of injury to the physical or mental health of the pregnant woman or any existing children of her family".[45]

The imposition of a time limit means that it is important to know the moment at which a pregnancy begins. When calculating the length of a pregnancy that is being carried to term, the convention is to treat the first day of the pregnant woman's previous period as the relevant start date, even though conception would usually have occurred approximately two weeks later. The reason for this is that, absent the use of reproductive technologies, the moment at which either fertilisation or implantation takes place is inherently uncertain and unknowable, so the date of the previous period allows doctors to calculate the length of gestation with greater precision. For the purposes of the Abortion Act, however, this convenient though fictional "start date" will not suffice. Insofar as the interpretation of section 1(1)(a) defines the scope of a defence to a criminal offence, any ambiguity must be construed in favour of the defendants, that is the pregnant woman and her doctors. It would obviously be unfair to deny a woman an abortion when she was, as a matter of fact, 22 weeks pregnant, but the date of her previous period fell outside of the 24 week limit. Rather the better interpretation is that the time starts to run when, according to medical judgement, implantation is judged to have taken place. Although this undoubtedly leaves a small margin of uncertainty, basic principles of statutory interpretation again suggest that, if a borderline case were to arise, the ambiguity should be constructed in favour of the pregnant woman and her doctors.

The Royal College of Obstetricians and Gynaecologists contest the description of section 1(1)(a) as the "social" ground, and instead suggest that its reference to health is normally assumed to refer to the World Health Organisation's definition of "health" as "a state of physical and mental well-being, not merely an absence of disease or infirmity".[46] This means that the abortion only needs to be necessary in order to promote the woman's mental wellbeing, rather than to prevent her from suffering psychiatric harm. The mental wellbeing of a woman who does not want to be pregnant is, almost by definition, advanced by termination. In addition, given that pregnancy and childbirth are invariably

[44] OCPS, Abortion Statistics 1998 (London: HMSO, 2000).
[45] Abortion Act 1967 s. (1)(1)(a).
[46] RCOG, 2000a, ch. 2.

more dangerous than abortion, termination will also tend to promote the woman's *physical* wellbeing.[47]

Under section 1(2) the doctor is further directed to take account of the woman's actual or reasonably foreseeable environment, which means that her *social* circumstances are clearly relevant to the assessment of her *medical* need. Given an elastic definition of health, and the relevance of a woman's environment, it could be argued that the "social" ground operates in practice to render every pregnancy lawfully terminable within the first 24 weeks, and as a result is largely redundant as a qualifying condition. Yet despite the apparent ease with which this ground can be satisfied, it would not be true to say that abortion is effectively available upon demand. There *is* an important obstacle to women's access to abortion in section 1(1)(a) of the Abortion Act but it does not consist in the stipulation that pregnancy must be more injurious to health than termination. Rather, the principal statutory barrier to abortion is the need to convince two doctors that abortion is indicated. So, for example, while abortion is in theory relatively freely available until 24 weeks, a growing number of doctors are using their discretion to refuse to authorise abortions after about 16 weeks.[48]

Similarly, the legality of the tiny percentage of abortions carried out under section 1(1)(d), which permits abortion where there is a substantial risk that the resulting child would be seriously handicapped, depends upon two doctors agreeing that a particular handicap is "serious", and that the risk of it materialising is "substantial". With no statutory checklist of qualifying conditions, or guidance as to what criteria should be taken into account, the decision again depends entirely upon the doctors' discretion. As we see below, novel questions of interpretation are emerging as a result of genetic tests' capacity to predict *future* susceptibility to disease. Is a fetus with a predisposition to an adult onset condition at *substantial risk* of suffering from abnormalities that amount to *serious handicap*? If the child must be seriously handicapped from birth, then clearly many genetic diagnoses will not satisfy section 1(1)(d) and abortion would instead have to be justified with reference to the impact that carrying the pregnancy to term would have upon the pregnant woman's mental health. Again it would lie within the discretion of two doctors to decide whether the knowledge that the child might suffer a particular debilitating condition in later life would threaten its mother's mental well being.

It is not self-evident that doctors are well qualified to determine whether or not a pregnancy should be terminated. It would clearly be unacceptable, for example, if doctors exercised their medical discretion and authorised an abortion whenever they encountered a pregnant woman whose mental or physical health they believed would be best served by termination, or whose fetus they judged to be suffering from a serious handicap. Rather, we assume that a

---

[47] On the form authorising an abortion, some doctors have simply given "pregnancy" as the reason for abortion, on the grounds that pregnancy does pose a risk, greater than termination, of injury to the physical or mental health of the pregnant woman (Furedi, 2000).

[48] Furedi, 2000.

doctor will only decide that abortion is medically indicated after a request from a woman who has made the social decision that she does not wish to continue with her pregnancy. While a legal requirement that only qualified medical professionals should carry out surgical abortions makes sense, it is less obvious that their medical training equips doctors to decide *whether* a woman should terminate her pregnancy.

In 1967 the medicalisation of abortion may have appeared to be a pragmatically sensible way of neutralising opposition to the legalisation of abortion. Those in favour of reform argued that women with unwanted pregnancies were facing an invidious choice between giving birth to a child for whom they would be unable to provide adequate care, or risking an illegal abortion. The recognition that the health of women and children was endangered by doctors' inability to provide safe, legal abortion made it possible to justify permissive law reform on public health grounds. Since the reformers had presented abortion as a medical treatment which ought to be available to the caring medical practitioner faced with a "desperate" pregnant woman, it is probably unsurprising that the legislation represents the abortion decision as one to be taken by doctors in the best interests of their patients.

It could, of course, be argued that the Abortion Act simply contains a harmless legal fiction because in practice doctors usually just give their *approval* for decisions that have already been taken. But the requirement that a woman must first satisfy two doctors that she has compelling reasons to terminate her pregnancy is significant for three reasons. First, as I explain below, it is impossible to tell how many women have been given misleading advice about their eligibility for abortion. Second, a woman who wants an abortion must present her circumstances in the worst possible light in order to persuade two medical practitioners that continuing the pregnancy would be injurious to her mental or physical wellbeing. Eligibility for abortion in the United Kingdom is thus contingent upon women describing their circumstances as difficult or desperate. Insofar as the Abortion Act 1967 requires women who want to terminate their unwanted pregnancies to first wrestle with the supposed trauma of abortion, it may offer a particularly clear illustration of Drucilla Cornell's argument that:

> "access to abortion, however liberal, will remain inadequate while women can only experience it through this sort of 'stereotype-like grid' of what having an abortion should mean".[49]

Third, as we see later in this chapter, there are circumstances in which a woman may need medical advice in order to determine whether or not to terminate her pregnancy. Following a complex prenatal diagnosis, I argue that a medical professional's dual role as impartial counsellor and as the ultimate authority over abortion decision-making may undermine the doctor/patient relationship.

---

[49] Cornell, 1995, p. 68. She has also argued that "(i)f a woman's personhood is truly to be respected by the law, then she must also be the ultimate source of both the decision to abort and the meaning given to that decision" (Cornell, 1995, p. 35).

The medicalisation of abortion is further entrenched by section 1(1) which specifies that the statutory defences only exist when a pregnancy is terminated "*by* a registered medical practitioner". While nurses can assist them,[50] doctors must therefore take the decision to terminate a pregnancy, choose the method to be used and be present throughout the procedure. Given that it is now possible to induce abortion chemically using antiprogestin pills,[51] there is no *clinical* reason for requiring a doctor to be present during the taking of the pill. Rather this requirement represents a somewhat artificial legal restriction upon the provision of abortion services.

In its original form, the 1967 Act did not explicitly differentiate between abortions at different stages of pregnancy. Instead it was to be read in the light of the Infant Life (Preservation) Act 1929 which prohibits causing the death of a fetus capable of being born alive. The 1929 Act further provided that a fetus could be presumed capable of being born alive at 28 weeks. Of course, the age at which a fetus achieves viability has been progressively reduced since 1929, and prior to the Act's amendment in 1990, it had become standard practice to assume viability at around twenty-four weeks, and to treat this as the cut-off point for lawful abortions.[52]

Section 37 of the Human Fertilisation and Embryology Act 1990 amended the Abortion Act by breaking the connection with the Infant Life (Preservation) Act 1929, and inserting a fixed time limit of 24 weeks for abortions carried out in order to prevent risk to the health of the pregnant woman or her children. The 1990 amendment also ensured that abortion is lawful until birth if it is necessary to prevent the pregnant woman's grave permanent injury or death, or if the child would be born seriously handicapped. Since very few abortions take place after 24 weeks, and a fetus was already assumed to be viable at twenty-four weeks, this amendment has had minimal impact upon access to abortion. But despite the practical insignificance of the 1990 reform, Sally Sheldon has argued that the Parliamentary debates represent yet another example of the comprehensive medicalisation of abortion law.[53] Despite the existence of intransigent moral disagreement between supporters and opponents of legal abortion, in 1990 a consensus seemed to have emerged that medical knowledge should have a special authority in shaping the substance of abortion law. Members of Parliament

[50] *RCN* v. *DHSS* [1981] 1 All ER 545.
[51] Discussed further below, p. 88.
[52] In *C* v. *S* [1987] 1 All ER 1230 a putative father sought to restrain his girlfriend, who was between eighteen and 21 weeks pregnant, from having an abortion. His argument was that this fetus was capable of being born alive, so abortion could only be lawful if it were necessary to save the life of the pregnant woman. He failed in the Court of Appeal on the basis that this fetus was not capable of being born alive. In *Rance and another* v. *Mid-Downs Health Authority and Another* [1991] 1 All ER 801, a couple brought an action in negligence after Mrs Rance gave birth to a boy with spina bifida. They argued that they should have been given the opportunity of terminating the pregnancy. Their case was dismissed since the diagnosis was only possible at twenty six weeks, at which point the fetus would be capable of being born alive, and an abortion would have been unlawful.
[53] Sheldon, 1997a, ch. 6.

with diametrically opposed views on abortion invoked medical opinion and deployed scientific "facts" about pregnancy to justify their positions.[54]

In addition to being responsible for the relative depoliticalisation of abortion in the UK, the comprehensive delegation of control over abortion to the medical profession may also have helped to deflect men's attempts[55] to use the law to prevent their sexual partners from terminating their pregnancies.[56] The abortion decision is one that must be made by the pregnant woman's *doctor* and not by a third party. It now seems to be settled law in the UK that the pregnant woman's sexual partner has no rights in relation to the fetus,[57] and the European Commission for Human Rights has described a British man's application to prevent his wife's abortion as "manifestly ill-founded".[58] While in practice, of course, a woman's decision to terminate a pregnancy is frequently made in consultation with her sexual partner,[59] respect for the pregnant woman's bodily integrity is obviously incompatible with a third party being able to make a decision about her medical treatment.

So, in addition to the role it played in legalisation in 1967, the medicalisation of abortion may then have helped to emasculate both the anti-abortion lobby and litigious putative fathers. But strategic reliance upon the neutralising impact

[54] David Alton, who believes abortion is immoral, said that ". . . sixty one years ago . . . there was no ultrasound scanning . . ., no electro-cardiograms for a fetus, and no appreciation of the complete sensory development of the unborn child" HC Deb Vol 171 Col 223 (24 April, 1990). David Steel, whose Private Member's Bill became the Abortion Act 1967, cited a study which showed that 75% of gynaecologists supported a 24 week limit: "We are not entitled to case aside all these opinions as though they did not matter, or to pluck out of the air a figure that we think might be better" HC Deb Vol 171 Col 204 (24 April, 1990).

[55] Since 1991, 24 men have approached the courts in order to attempt to prevent abortions taking place. And anti-abortion pressures groups such as Life and SPUC have recently formed alliances with organisations such as Families Need Fathers (Nolan, 1998, pp. 219, 221).

[56] Marie Fox has argued that the exclusion of paternal rights in these cases rests upon the medicalisation of abortion in which third parties are not be allowed to interfere with the privacy of the doctor/patient relationship (Fox, 1998, p. 208).

[57] See for example, *C* v. *S* [1987] 1 All ER 1230. In *Paton* v. *Trustees of the British Pregnancy Advisory Service* [1978] 2 All ER 987, a husband sought an injunction to restrain the defendants from carrying out a termination requested by his wife. Sir George Baker P rejected his application, finding that a husband has no legal right to prevent an abortion. Mr Paton then took his case to the European Commission of Human Rights (*Paton* v. *United Kingdom* [1980] 3 EHRR 408) where his contention that he had standing to protect his unborn child's right to life was rejected. The European Commission further rejected his claim that his right to respect for his private and family life, guaranteed by Article 8 of the European Convention on Human Rights, had been violated. The Commission found that the pregnant woman's right to respect for her private life should prevail, and so the potential father has no right to be consulted nor any right to make applications about a proposed abortion.

In 1997 a Scottish putative father initially won an interdict to prevent his wife from having an abortion. After a protracted series of hearings in which this was struck down and then reinstated (*Kelly* v. *Kelly* [1997] SLT 896), and just before it was to be decided whether the case should go to the House of Lords, the husband decided to drop his case and the woman had the abortion in England.

[58] *Paton* v. *United Kingdom* [1980] 3 EHRR 408.

[59] In one study, 23% of women having terminations reported that one of their reasons was that their partner wanted them to terminate the pregnancy (Torres and Forest, 1988). In a survey of men's attitudes to abortion, 84% regarded the decision to have a termination as a "joint resolution of the matter" (Nolan, 1998, p. 220).

of medical knowledge could have some unanticipated consequences for the regulation of abortion. For example, fetal viability may seem to offer a natural and politically neutral limit for legal abortion, but progress in neonatal medicine is steadily reducing the age at which a premature baby can survive.[60] The 1990 amendment rested upon the assumption that viability was achieved at 24 weeks, but this has already been superseded and it is now possible for a baby to survive at 23, or possibly even 22 weeks.[61] While there may be an age below which independent survival will remain technically impossible, it has not yet been reached.[62]

The rules governing infertility treatment, embryo research and storage that we will consider in detail in chapter five may also have some incidental impact upon attitudes towards abortion. For example, under section 3(4) of the Human Fertilisation and Embryology Act 1990, research on embryos is forbidden after 14 days. A two-week absolute limit upon embryo research may sit uneasily with a law that permits abortion until birth in certain circumstances. And if a fetus can lawfully be destroyed during the first 24 weeks of pregnancy for "social" reasons, the absolute prohibition of potentially invaluable experiments upon 15 day-old embryos may seem illogical. Furthermore, when a frozen embryo is stored *in vitro*, the contributor of the male gametes has a right of veto over its future use and disposal. Of course, treating men differently depending upon whether their interest is in an embryo *in vitro* or a fetus *in utero* is readily explicable given that a man's wishes concerning a cryopreserved embryo may be taken into account without invading his partner's bodily integrity. Nevertheless, insofar as the man's wishes are relevant because an embryo contains his genetic material, pregnant women's sexual partners may feel aggrieved that their interest in the transmission of their genes is not treated with equivalent respect.

Thus, as we have seen, abortion law in the UK has been shaped by a tradition of deference towards medical opinion. Its legalisation in 1967 was almost certainly dependent upon the reformers astute presentation of legal abortion as a measure designed to promote public health, rather than an issue of women's rights. Perhaps unsurprisingly, the statute that emerged from their success therefore entrusts primary responsibility for abortion decision making to medical practitioners and not to pregnant women themselves. In the following section, we consider in more detail the practical significance of the medical profession's pre-eminent authority over abortion.

[60] Dr John Wyatt of University College Hospital has suggested that some medical units should be dedicated to "push(ing) the limits to see what is technically possible, to help babies to survive who were previously incapable of survival" (BBC Horizon, 1998a).

[61] BBC Horizon, 1998a.

[62] Although it should perhaps be noted that improving survival rates of extremely premature neonates may be different in kind from promoting their health. The majority of doctors working in neonatal units, for example, would not want their own twenty-three week old baby resuscitated (BBC Horizon, 1998a).

3. ACCESS TO ABORTION

In England, Scotland and Wales, almost all women under the age of fifty have been able to take abortion's legality for granted throughout their sexually active lives. Yet it is important to remember that the Abortion Act 1967 has never offered women guaranteed access to abortion services, and in practice, pregnant women seeking terminations face multiple practical obstacles. In sharp contrast with the National Health Service's duty to provide comprehensive and free contraceptive services, access to NHS funded abortions is somewhat patchy. There has been some significant recent improvement,[63] but the availability of NHS terminations continues to be subject to wide regional variation.[64] Abortion continues to be the most common privately funded medical procedure,[65] and there seems to be some evidence that better-off women seeking terminations are actively steered towards private clinics by their general practitioners.[66]

One of the reasons for the erratic provision of NHS abortion services is that it is not clear whether a doctor who is unsympathetic to a woman's request for an abortion is under a duty to refer her to a colleague with different views. Certainly, doctors are not obliged to publicise their objections, so women have no way of knowing in advance whether or not their GP is a conscientious objector. As we have seen, the conscience clause in the 1967 act permits doctors to refuse to "participate" in abortion services, and the House of Lords has specifically declined to express an opinion upon whether referring a patient for abortion services constitutes "participation" to which a conscientious objection could be raised.[67] More recently, the Royal College of Obstetrician and Gynaecologist's Guidelines have indicated that doctors should not normally refuse to refer a patient to another colleague:

---

[63] In 1986 only 50% of all terminations performed on resident women in England and Wales were funded by the NHS, by 1999 74% were NHS funded (OCPS, Abortion Statistics 1999, London: HMSO, 2000).

[64] In Teesside 97% of abortions in 1996 were NHS funded, compared with only 34% in Waltham Forest (Office for National Statistics, 1997).

[65] As we see in chap. five, infertility treatment is the other medical procedure that is commonly undergone privately.

[66] Abortion Law Reform Association, 1997.

[67] In *Janaway* v. *Salford Heath Authority* [1989] AC 537 the House of Lords rejected a medical receptionist's claim that she had been wrongfully dismissed for refusing to type a letter of referral for an abortion, but left open the question of whether a GP's right of conscientious objection could extend to refusing to sign the "green" form. While Lord Keith held (at 570d) that participation "in its ordinary and natural meaning referred to actually taking part in treatment administered in a hospital or other approved place", he also said (at 572b) "it does not appear whether or not there are any circumstances under which a doctor might be under any legal duty to sign a green form, so as to place in difficulties one who had a conscientious objection to doing so. The fact that during the 20 years that the Act of 1967 has been in force no problem seems to have surfaced in this connection may indicate that in practice none exists. So I do not think it appropriate to express any opinion on the matter".

> "Practitioners cannot claim exemption from giving advice or performing the preparatory steps to arrange an abortion where the request meets the legal requirements. Such steps include referral to another doctor, as appropriate".[68]

And in a recent case,[69] Alliott J has said that:

> "once a termination of pregnancy is recognised as an option the doctor invoking the conscientious objection clause should refer the patient to a colleague at once".

Nevertheless, some women undoubtedly mistake their doctor's lack of co-operation as an indication of their ineligibility for termination,[70] rather than an expression of his moral convictions. Additionally, women from ethnic minority groups or women who are poorly educated may not have the knowledge or the confidence to seek a second opinion if their general practitioner seems obstructive, and women from rural areas faced with an unsympathetic doctor may not easily be able to find an alternative medical practitioner. Even if a woman does seek another opinion, her encounter with a hostile doctor will invariably delay her abortion. Of course if a woman is able to find and afford a specialist abortion clinic, she will not encounter any doctors with conscientious objections to abortion and will therefore have access to a prompt and supportive service. Inevitably, therefore, the Abortion Act's entrenched deference to medical opinion has disproportionate practical impact upon the choices of poorer women.

Of course it might be argued that a patient never has a positive right to a particular medical procedure, and that pregnant women are not entitled to treat NHS doctors as mere technicians who will perform surgery upon request. Yet aside from his conscientious objection, it is not clear upon what grounds a doctor would be entitled to refuse to perform a termination. Within the NHS, there can clearly be no right to expensive medical treatment because scarce resources have made rationing decisions inevitable. However abortion will invariably cost the NHS much less than a woman's pregnancy and delivery,[71] so a doctor's refusal could not be justified on grounds of cost. Alternatively, a doctor might argue that abortion is not in a woman's *clinical* interest. Again, pregnancy and childbirth is invariably riskier than abortion, so it is not clear how a refusal to carry out a termination would advance the woman's physical health. If the woman has decided that she does not want to carry the pregnancy to term, her mental wellbeing is also unlikely to be furthered by being compelled to carry her unwanted pregnancy to term. Unless he is invoking his right to conscientious objection, I would argue that a doctor's refusal to co-operate with a woman's request for abortion is always unjustifiably paternalistic.

---

[68] RCOG, 2000a, para. 2.3.

[69] *Barr* v. *Matthews* (2000) 52 BMLR 217.

[70] Law, 1994, p. 302. For example, in *Saxby* v. *Morgan* [1997] 8 Med LR 293, a woman who wanted to terminate her pregnancy was told by her doctor that her pregnancy was too far advanced. In fact she was only 18–19 weeks pregnant, and so clearly within the time limits in the Abortion Act. Her action in negligence failed because it was out of time.

[71] The average abortion costs less than £300 (BPAS, 1999), and the health care provided during an average pregnancy costs nearly £2000 (Audit Commission, 1997).

Access to abortion is a classic example of the relative ineffectiveness of negative liberties.[72] Within certain limits, the Abortion Act 1967 provides that abortion is a legitimate medical procedure, but it offers no affirmative right to accessible services. In England, Scotland and Wales women are dependent upon the discretion of the medical profession and the vagaries of NHS funding. Inevitably this means that richer and better educated women will have immediate access to a straightforward and sympathetic service. In the United States the gulf between legality and access is even wider: abortion is both a constitutionally protected right, and widely unavailable.[73]

4. SPECIAL PROBLEMS

(a) Distinguishing between Contraception and Abortion

Many people believe that there is a fundamental moral difference between preventing conception and ending an unwanted pregnancy,[74] and as we have seen, UK law subjects contraception and abortion to entirely different regulatory regimes. But this bright line boundary between contraception and abortion may be unsustainable as new techniques make it increasingly difficult to tell whether a pregnancy is being prevented or terminated. Postcoital contraception, such as the "morning-after" pill, works by preventing the implantation of a fertilised egg. Is a woman pregnant as soon as fertilisation occurs, or is pregnancy only achieved several days later once the fertilised egg has successfully implanted in her uterus? As we saw earlier, the Offences Against the Person Act 1861 defines abortion as "procuring a miscarriage", so our definition of "miscarriage" might

---

[72] Taylor, 1979.

[73] In the United States, since the Supreme Court's decision in *Roe* v. *Wade* 410 U.S, 113 (1973), abortion has been a constitutionally protected right during the first twelve weeks of pregnancy. Access to abortion is, however, restricted. Abortions are not, for example, publicly funded. The Hyde Amendment to the Medicaid Act withdrew Medicaid funding unless the abortion is deemed medically necessary (Congress Pub L No 99–439, §209, 90 Stat 1418, 1434, 1976). An abortion is "medically necessary" following rape or incest, or if it is needed to save the life of the mother (Berenknopf, 1997). In several states minors must have parental consent to their termination (Kolbert and Miller, 1998, p.110) . Some states mandate directive counselling and waiting periods (Kolbert and Miller, 1998, p. 100). Fear of harassment, violence and even death has made abortion practice an unattractive option for doctors (Wilder, 1998, p. 84). From 1990–1998, abortion clinics and their medical staff were subjected to 19 bombings, 100 arson attacks, 7 murders and 621 death threats (Ellison, 1998, p.4). Despite being the most common operation among women of fertile age, it is interesting that student obstetricians and gynaecologists in the United States do not generally learn how to perform abortions (Law, 1994, p. 299). In 84% of all counties in the United States there is no abortion provider (Solinger, 1998, p.xiv). Among non-metropolitan counties, 94% have no abortion provider (Kulczycki, 1999, p. 15). The average age of doctors who perform abortions is now 58 (Ellison, 1998, p. 5).

[74] For example, Mason and McCall Smith have said that they "view the introduction of contragestion therapy with some concern" since they argue that it could "blur the distinction (*a distinction which we regard as essential*) between contraception and abortion" (Mason and McCall Smith, 1994, p. 112) (my emphasis).

be relevant in determining whether an abortion has taken place. In its ordinary linguistic sense, miscarriage must be the antonym of "carriage", a word that seems to imply that the fertilised egg must have attached itself to the pregnant woman's body. The legislation itself is silent on the meaning of miscarriage, leading Glanville Williams to suggest that "there is, therefore, nothing to prevent the courts interpreting the word 'miscarriage' in a way that takes account of customary and approved birth control practices".[75] In a written answer to Parliament in 1983, the Attorney General explained that the words in the 1861 statute should be given the meaning that they had when the statute was passed, and that they should be presumed to have been used "in their popular, ordinary or natural sense".[76] His conclusion that postcoital contraception did not contravene the Offences Against the Person Act was the logical consequence of his judgement that

> "it is clear that, used in its ordinary sense, the word 'miscarriage' is not apt to describe a failure to implant. . .Likewise, the phrase 'procure a miscarriage' cannot be construed to include the prevention of implantation".[77]

Additional, although not in itself determinative support for classifying postcoital birth control as contraception comes, unexpectedly, from the regulation of infertility treatment. During an *in vitro* fertilisation (IVF) cycle, live embryos will be transferred to the woman's uterus. If pregnancy were achieved at fertilisation rather than implantation, then the woman undergoing IVF treatment would be "pregnant" at the moment of embryo transfer. The Human Fertilisation and Embryology Act 1990 thus addresses the definition of pregnancy directly, and states that *"for the purposes of this Act*, a woman is not to be treated as carrying a child until the embryo has become implanted" (my emphasis).

Even if it is settled law in the UK[78] that postcoital birth control is contraception rather than abortion, there are other techniques that further blur the distinction between preventing and terminating a pregnancy. The "abortion pill", mifepristone, commonly known as RU486, operates by inhibiting or interrupting the implantation of a fertilised egg.[79] RU486 can work as a straightforward abortifacient by dislodging an implanted fertilised egg from the lining of the uterus. But if RU486 is used before implantation, there is not

---

[75] Williams, 1983, p. 294.
[76] Sir Michael Havers QC, 42 Parl Deb HC col. 238.
[77] *Ibid*.
[78] The Irish Medicines Board has recently advised the manufacturer of a drug marketed as an emergency contraceptive that it considers it to be an abortifacient. As a result the manufacturers of Levonelle-2 withdrew their application for a licence, Levonelle-2 is licensed as a contraceptive in 13 EU states (O'Morain, 2000).
[79] RU486 is an antiprogesterone agent which occupies the progesterone receptor sites in the cells of the endometrium, preventing an embryo from implanting in the wall of the uterus. If implantation has already occurred the lack of progesterone will cause it to dislodge and be discharged. It is usually used in conjunction with a prostaglandin pessary taken between 36 and 48 hours later which induces uterine contractions. It has a success rate of between 94–97%.

a pregnancy to terminate,[80] and it would effectively act in the same way as postcoital birth control.[81]

More complex issues still are raised by the suggestion that RU486 could be used as a regular "contraceptive" which women would take for three days at the end of each cycle.[82] This would have two practical advantages over the ordinary oral contraceptive pill. First, there would be fewer side effects, and second, there would be less opportunity for women to forget to take the pills. Yet, despite its apparent practical convenience, this sort of birth control would be legally problematic because women would not know whether or not they were pregnant when they took the pills. Most of the time there would be no pregnancy and RU486 would have no effect, whereas in certain cycles an embryo might have implanted and the pills would imperceptibly terminate the pregnancy. A "contraceptive" that were to involve women occasionally and unknowingly having a very early abortion would significantly blur the line between contraception and abortion. If this sort of birth control were subjected to the same regime as abortion, two doctors would have to give their approval, a doctor would have to be present each month while the woman took her pills and the procedure would have to be reported to the Department of Health. Paradoxically, the law would convert it into an extraordinarily inconvenient method of contraception. And given that there would seldom have actually been an abortion, the application of abortion law would usually be illegitimate. On the other hand, if occasional early abortion were to be treated in the same way as contraception, then some abortions would be taking place outside the terms of the statutory defences contained in the Abortion Act, and might therefore amount to criminal offences under the Offences Against the Person Act 1861.

New developments in pregnancy testing also facilitate very early abortions. It is already possible to discover whether a woman is pregnant approximately two weeks after fertilisation when implantation has only just been completed. An abortion procedure carried out shortly after implantation is extremely simple, and as one medical practitioner has pointed out:

> "with these very early abortions, we're talking about a whole gestational sac that's the size of a matchstick head. Its nobody's picture of a little baby sucking its thumb".[83]

It has been argued that if the majority of terminations were to take place shortly after implantation, abortion might become less controversial.[84] But techniques such as RU486 have not had this effect perhaps precisely because their potential to transform abortion from a surgical procedure into something as prosaic as

---

[80] In *R v. Dhingra* (1991) *Daily Telegraph* 25 January p. 5 a doctor fitted an IUD 11 days after intercourse. The judge held that implantation at this stage was "highly unlikely", and that it was "only at the completion of implantation (that the woman can) be regarded as pregnant".

[81] It might be more effective because it requires only one dose, and does not cause nausea (see further Glasier, 1992, p. 1041).

[82] See further Prothro, 1997.

[83] Dr Michael Burnhill quoted in Lewin, 1997, p. 1.

[84] Robertson, 1994, p. 65.

taking a pill seems to make terminating a pregnancy "too easy". The technical simplicity of chemical abortion and the possibility of self-administration might also undermine doctors' tight control over the provision of abortion services.[85]

In the UK, RU486 has been licensed for use during the first seven[86] weeks of pregnancy since 1991,[87] but in 1999, it was used in less than 10 per cent of all abortions performed upon resident women in England and Wales. In part this is due to delays in referral for NHS funded abortions. But low take-up of chemical abortion methods may also result from the regulations governing the prescription of RU486 which, ironically, mandate *more* contact time between doctors and pregnant women than is necessary for surgical abortion.[88] Regardless of the practical similarities between RU486 and postcoital contraception, the law exposes all abortions, including those induced by antiprogestin pills, to a separate and extraordinary regime. Similarly when RU 486 was finally approved for use in the United States on 30 September 2000, it was subjected to restrictive rules quite unlike those governing most prescription drugs.[89]

(b) Are some abortions morally "worse" than others?

It is extremely unlikely that abortion would ever be completely recriminalised, and it is clear that many anti-abortion lobbyists have implicitly accepted that a blanket prohibition upon abortion is not a realistic or achievable goal. During the Parliamentary debates preceding the 1990 amendment, for example, MPs with moral objections to abortion at *all* stages of gestation argued instead for the lowering of the time limit within which abortion is legal. If one believes that the fetus is a person from the moment of conception, abortion must be murder at all stages of pregnancy, and so lobbying for the upper time limit for abortion to be reduced to eighteen weeks obviously reflects a degree of strategic pragmatism, rather than a belief that something miraculous happens at eighteen weeks.

In recent years anti-abortion lobbyists have instead tended to focus their attention upon certain sorts of abortion which are perceived to be more morally problematic than normal. For example, their criticism of fetal reduction, or the

---

[85] Sally Sheldon has argued that "antiprogestins seem to bring the possibility of self-induced abortion much closer to reality (and they) . . . seem to embody the potential to render doctors redundant and their monopoly untenable" (Sheldon, 1997a, p. 131).

[86] Or nine weeks if the first day of the woman's last period is taken as the starting point.

[87] Brand name *Mifegyne*, Product Licence No.: PL 0109/0232.

[88] Women must make at least three visits to the clinic after the decision to abort has been taken by two doctors. First it must be established that RU486 is appropriate and then the pill is taken. Between 36 and 48 hours later the woman must return to receive the prostaglandins which complete the abortion, this must be done under close medical supervision and extended observation; finally she must return within twelve days for an examination to ensure that the abortion is complete.

[89] For example, regulations provide that RU486 can only be prescribed by gynaecologists who have been trained to perform surgical terminations, or within easy reach of a abortion clinic. Since there are comparatively few doctors who perform surgical terminations, RU486 is unlikely to transform the accessibility of abortion (see further, Mishra, 2000).

selective termination of one or more foetuses during a multiple pregnancy, is one reason why anti-abortion campaigners have been vociferous critics of reproductive technologies. In chapter five we consider the high rates of multiple pregnancy that have been an inevitable side-effect of techniques such as IVF, and insofar as some of these multiple pregnancies will be selectively reduced, anti-abortion groups have been able to argue that infertility treatment, para-doxically, causes abortion.

In the light of the international links that exist between anti-abortion cam-paigners, it is worth noting the partial success of US campaigns to ban the proce-dures used in abortions that are carried out at a relatively advanced stage of gestation. Anti-abortion lobbyists have focussed upon late abortions in part because a comparatively well developed fetus cannot be aborted by the simple suction procedures used earlier in pregnancy. If a termination can be described as a "partial birth" abortion, the emotive language of baby-killing is invoked. A fur-ther reason for anti-abortion campaigners' interest in late-term abortions is that they will generally be sought following the detection of a fetal abnormality. Most women who do not want to be pregnant *at all* will seek to terminate their unwanted pregnancy as soon as possible. Women who have late abortions are often carrying pregnancies that were wanted prior to the detection of a serious fetal abnormality. Anti-abortion campaigners have therefore been able to form fruitful alliances with the disability lobby, which is, as we see below, concerned about the social implications of increasingly routine prenatal testing. Similarly, in relation to abortion on the grounds of fetal sex, anti-abortion campaigners have sought to marshal feminist arguments against sex-selective abortion.

This section begins with a brief overview of the special issues raised by selec-tive reduction, and a summary of the "partial birth" abortion debates that have taken place in the US. We then review a variety of fears that have crystallised around the issue of abortion for fetal abnormality. In particular, a disparate range of theoreticians and interest groups have been engaging in intense specu-lation about the long-term implications of increased recourse to prenatal genetic testing. Finally, we consider sex selective abortion, and the somewhat odd coali-tion that has emerged between feminists and the anti-abortion lobby.

(i) Selective reduction

Fetal reduction, or the selective termination of one or more fetuses, is a much more complex procedure than complete termination, and it has only become possible in the last twenty years as a result of advances in ultrasonography.[90] It was initially used to selectively terminate a severely abnormal twin, and was first used to reduce a higher order multiple pregnancy in 1986.[91]

---

[90] The life of one or more fetuses is brought to an end, either using suction or a lethal injection, both of which require considerable technical expertise (see further Ibérico *et al*, 2000).

[91] In 1986 a quintuplet pregnancy in Holland was reduced to a twin pregnancy, which continued to term and resulted in the birth of two healthy babies (Price, 1989, p. 44).

Although assisted conception techniques with their associated risks of multiple pregnancy may have increased demand, in practice selective reduction of multiple pregnancies is rare. In 1999, only 45 selective terminations took place, most of them in triplet or higher order pregnancies.[92] At their inception, none of the statutes governing abortion anticipated selective reduction of a multiple pregnancy, and therefore the conventional rules sit rather uneasily with a scenario in which one or more fetuses is destroyed, but the pregnancy is not terminated. According to the Offences Against the Person Act 1861, for example, the offence lies in "procuring a miscarriage". Yet when selective reduction is carried out at a relatively early stage of gestation, the fetus that is destroyed is not necessarily actually expelled, but may be absorbed by the uterus. Whether or not this amounts to a "miscarriage" is unclear. The defences contained in the Abortion Act 1967 apply to the *termination* of pregnancy. If the woman is still pregnant following selective reduction, is the pregnancy terminated within the terms of the Abortion Act? The intersection of these two provisions is critical. If there is no miscarriage for the purposes of the Offences Against the Person Act, then the inapplicability of the Abortion Act would be irrelevant. If there is no *prima facie* criminal offence, the statutory defences in the 1967 Act would obviously be redundant. If, on the other hand, we consider that miscarriage occurs whenever a fetus dies *in utero*, then the deliberate ending of a fetus's life during selective reduction is *prima facie* a criminal offence. If we were also to decide that the Abortion Act 1967 only applies if the pregnancy is *ended*, then no defence under the statute would exist, and selective reduction would always be a criminal offence under the Offences Against the Person Act 1861.

This confusion has been addressed by a further amendment to the Abortion Act effected by the Human Fertilisation and Embryology Act 1990. Section 5(2) of the Abortion Act 1967 now reads that anything done with intent to procure a woman's miscarriage including "(in the case of a woman carrying more than one foetus, her miscarriage of any foetus) is unlawfully done unless authorised by section 1" of the Abortion Act. Thus the 1990 amendment appears to take for granted that selective reduction *does* involve the miscarriage of a fetus, and is therefore covered by the Offences Against the Person Act. Since section 5(2) specifies that the ordinary Abortion Act grounds apply equally to selective reduction, one or more fetuses can be destroyed if, for example, there is a risk to the woman's mental or physical health, or if there is a substantial risk that a child would be born seriously handicapped.

The application of section 1(1)(a), the so-called "social" ground, to selective reduction is unproblematic given the considerable difficulties commonly encountered in caring for twins, triplets and higher order multiple births. But another indication for selective reduction, namely improving the chances of survival of the remaining fetuses, is not covered by a literal interpretation of section 1 of the Abortion Act. Such abortions would only be lawful if a slightly more

---

[92] Abortion Statistics (HMSO: 2000).

elastic interpretation were accepted, and improving the chances that one or more babies will survive were taken to be necessary to avert a risk to their mother's mental well being, or alternatively to reducing the risk that the child, if born, would be at substantial risk of suffering from a serious handicap.

In addition to its practical and legal complexity, selective fetal reduction is also widely believed to raise especially problematic ethical issues.[93] There has, for example, been anxiety about the psychological well being of children who find out that they were gestated in a pregnancy that was selectively reduced,[94] although in the absence of any evidence, such claims remain speculative.

(ii) Late-Abortion in the US

Anti-abortion campaigners in the United States have concentrated on banning late-term or what they erroneously refer to as "partial birth" abortions.[95] They have had some notable successes, and thirty states have passed laws banning the procedures used in abortions carried out at relatively advanced stages of gestation. Several challenges to the constitutionality of these laws have been mounted in the courts, and by a narrow (five to four) majority, in 2000 the US Supreme Court struck down Nebraska's "partial birth" abortion law on two grounds. First, the Nebraska legislature had failed to include an exception where this type of abortion was necessary to preserve the woman's health. While the statute did contain an exclusion clause if the procedure was necessary to save the woman's life, the majority of the Supreme Court found that this was too narrow to satisfy the constitutional requirement that no state may proscribe abortion where it is necessary to preserve health. As a result the Nebraska statute placed women "at an unnecessary risk of tragic health consequences".[96] Second, the majority found that the wording of the statute was insufficiently precise, and that insofar as its ambiguity might lead doctors to fear prosecution or imprisonment, the statute placed an "undue burden upon a woman's right to make an abortion decision".

The decision in *Stenberg* might initially appear to be a robust defence of a woman's right to choose to terminate her pregnancy in its second or third trimester, but there are several reasons why it is unlikely to lead to the disappearance of statutes designed to prohibit late abortions. First, the narrowness of the majority judgement is itself an indication that one new judicial appointment might be enough to alter the Supreme Court's opinion. Second, it is fairly easy to see how the Nebraska statute could be amended in order to satisfy the Supreme Court's concerns. With tighter legislative drafting and the inclusion of a health exception, a redrawn "partial birth" abortion statute might be upheld.

---

[93] Price, 1992, pp. 110–1.

[94] Price, 1992, pp. 110–1.

[95] The term has no medical meaning, see further Bonavoglia, 1997. It is usually assumed to refer to a procedure called "intact dilation and extraction", but some US courts have found that term is sufficiently ambiguous that it could apply to abortion methods used throughout pregnancy, see for example *Causeway Medical Suite* v. *Foster* US Dist. LEXIS 2756 (ED La Mar 4 1999).

[96] *Stenberg* v. *Carhart* US 120 S. Ct. 2597, 147 L Ed 2d 743 (2000). See further Charatan, 2000.

The broader relevance of the US "partial birth" abortion debates lies in their focus upon a particular sort of abortion for which there may be little public enthusiasm. Throughout the world, research into a fetus's capacity to experience pain is leading to increased anxiety about the ethical probity of late abortions. In the UK as well as the US, it seems clear that the anti-abortion lobby have much greater purchase upon public opinion where their concern is with the unsightly procedures that are used in order to abort fetuses which look like babies. It is also important to remember that women do not have late abortions because they would prefer unpleasant surgery to a quick and painless early termination. Instead women usually have these late abortions following the discovery of a fetal abnormality. So, as we see in the following section, these campaigns against late abortion can also benefit from the range of anxieties that have emerged in relation to abortion in cases of fetal abnormality.

(iii) Fetal Abnormality

A Anxieties

In recent years the acknowledgement that discrimination against disabled people is as illegitimate as discrimination on grounds of sex or race appears to have been accompanied by increased anxiety about the routine abortion of abnormal fetuses.[97] A parallel is commonly drawn between abortion on the grounds of abnormality and the discreditable history of eugenics that we considered in the previous chapter. Evoking the chilling barbarism of Nazism in order to criticise prenatal testing is an extremely powerful rhetorical device, for, as Jonathan Glover has pointed out, "if a policy can be described as eugenic, that is enough for most people to rule it out at once".[98] Unlike the twentieth century's *public* eugenic sterilisation programmes, prenatal screening is criticised for normalising *private* eugenic decision-making. Ulrich Beck, for example, has said that "the eugenics that threatens has shed all the distinguishing marks of a sinister conspiracy, and donned the robes of health, productivity and profit".[99]

One particular focus of concern has been the expansion in testing that is anticipated following the completion of the human genome project. Since isolation of the genetic mutation associated with a particular disease will almost

---

[97] A recent Birth Control Trust/MORI poll found a sharp decline in support for abortion where there was a risk of handicap. In 1980 84% approved of abortion where it is likely that the child would be born mentally handicapped or mentally disabled, by 1997, this figure had fallen to 67%. In 1980 81% approved of abortion where it is likely that the child would be born physically handicapped or physically disabled, by 1997 this figure had fallen to 66%. Disapproval of abortion for fetal abnormality was particularly marked in the young. Only 47% of 15–24 year olds approve of abortion for physical handicap, compared with 81% of those aged between 55–64 (Furedi, 1998a, p. 166). In a follow-up study, Ellie Lee and Jenny Davey found that only 11.4 % of young people thought that Down's syndrome was an acceptable reason for termination (Lee and Davey, 1998, p. 21). This forms an interesting contrast with a survey of geneticists in the US, 85% of whom supported abortion for Down's syndrome (Wertz, 1997, p. 335).

[98] Glover, 1999, p. 102.

[99] Beck, 1995, p. 33.

always precede the development of effective treatment, it is perhaps unsurprising that few adults have opted to find out about their genetic susceptibility to
future ill-health. Prenatal testing, on the other hand, does enable "something"
to be done with a positive diagnosis: the birth of the affected child can be
avoided by abortion. As a result prenatal genetic testing has become one of the
more common uses of new genetic information.

In this section we consider three different types of concern about the implications of increasingly routine prenatal genetic testing and abortion. First,
popular culture and the media have focussed upon the possibility that prenatal
tests will be devised in order to detect and eliminate fetuses with particular
behavioural traits or physical features. Scare stories about screening out fetuses
with a predisposition to, for example, criminality, homosexuality or obesity
are commonplace,[100] despite the improbability that single gene markers exist
for complex behavioural patterns. It would be easy to dismiss this sort of ill-
informed speculation. But fear of these new genetic tests is not limited to the
tabloid's obsession with *Frankenstein* scientists and "designer babies". Second,
there are those who believe that the increasingly routine abortion of abnormal
fetuses will have deleterious consequences for disabled people. The disability
lobby has, for example, argued that disproportionate energy and resources are
currently devoted to preventing the birth of disabled individuals, and that these
would be better spent on improving the quality of their lives. Third, certain
influential sociologists such as Ulrich Beck and Anthony Giddens have
expressed concern about the risks and regulatory vacuums that are opening
up as a result of globalisation and new technological developments.
Biotechnology and expanding genetic knowledge have been a particular focus
of these theories of "reflexive modernisation".[101] And since prenatal testing is
one of the principal uses of genetic information,[102] their arguments have
particular resonance in relation to routine genetic screening and abortion.
Ulrich Beck has, for example, argued that "medically, genetics has so
far achieved almost nothing apart from providing more justifications for

---

[100] On the 12 May, 1992, the *Daily Mail* published an article titled "Your baby is going to be
homosexual so we'll abort him: scientists' nightmare vision of DNA revolution" (quoted in Thom
and Jennings, 1996, p. 243).

[101] Beck, 1992b.

[102] Each human being has 46 chromosomes arranged in 23 pairs. The egg contains one chromosome
from each of these pairs, as does the sperm. When the sperm and the egg (sometimes called the gametes)
unite, the resulting zygote will have its 23 pairs of chromosomes: one chromosome from each pair
comes from the "mother" and one from the "father". Sometimes this process of transmitting chromosomes to the egg or the sperm goes awry and extra chromosomes are created. If fertilisation then
occurs, spontaneous miscarriage is likely, often so early that the pregnancy remains undetected. Not all
extra chromosomes are fatal, for example Down's syndrome occurs when there is an extra chromosome 21. Other abnormalities can occur in the distribution of genetic material. We each have around
30,000 genes. Every individual carries a number of defective genes, but few are ever noticed. There are
two copies of most genes and so a normal gene will usually compensate for a defective one. Genetic
mutations will only cause disease if the disorder is chromosomal (Down's syndrome); if the gene is
dominant (Huntington's disease); if copies of the recessive defective gene have been inherited from both
parents (cystic fibrosis); or, in men, if the mutation only occurs on the X chromosome (haemophilia).

abortion".[103] In the following sections I argue that the fears voiced by the media, the disability lobby and analysts of reflexive modernity all have a tendency to exaggerate prenatal genetic testing's potential for misuse.

I "Designer Babies"?

There is intense speculation in the media about the implications of geneticists' capacity to identify the functions of a growing number of genes. If, so the argument goes, it becomes possible to detect genes associated with certain physical features or behavioural patterns, abortion could be used for reasons that some people may consider to be trivial or grounded in prejudice.[104] The fear is that prenatal screening and abortion might be employed not only to prevent disease and disability but also by prospective parents anxious to maximise their offspring's brains, beauty and conformity to conventional behavioural norms. So, despite broad consensus among scientists that there is no single gene responsible for intelligence, attractiveness or sexual orientation, anxiety about prenatal testing's potential for misuse remains strong. Why?

One factor may be the tendency to use cartographic metaphors in order to describe the achievements being made by scientists working on the human genome project. If told that the human genome has been "mapped", or that we now know the "blueprint" for life, the lay person may understandably fail to appreciate that the functions of each gene will not be identified within the foreseeable future.[105] In addition, the mixture or fascination and fear generated by the familiar image of the mad scientist creating humans to order clearly exercises considerable hold over the popular imagination. We encounter the significance of *Frankenstein* mythology for the public understanding of science again in chapter five when we consider techniques such as preimplantation genetic diagnosis and human reproductive cloning. One recurring theme is the distinction commonly drawn between using new technologies to avoid illness and employing the same techniques for non-therapeutic reasons. Public opinion tends to differentiate sharply between doctors, who are generally assumed to be concerned only to prevent avoidable suffering, and scientists, whose amoral curiosity might propel them to attempt to "play God". Accordingly, in relation to prenatal testing, sympathy for pregnant women who are at risk of passing on a debilitating genetic disease is contrasted with virulent condemnation of anyone who might choose to abort a fetus for a trivial or non-therapeutic reason. As we see below, this distinction is clearly evident in relation to prenatal sex diagnosis, which can be used to prevent the birth of a child with a serious sex-linked disorder, such as Duchenne Muscular Dystrophy, but might also be employed by

---

[103] Beck, 1999, p. 106.

[104] Modell and Modell suggest that "the ability to predict a wide range of genetic characteristics will lead to terminations of pregnancy for minor or even frivolous reasons" (Modell and Modell, 1992, p. 189). Roger Gosden has referred to the "fear that features that were once regarded as trivial blemishes could now be grounds for couples to choose abortion and try again" (Gosden, 1999, p. xiv).

[105] Wertz, 1997, p. 299.

prospective parents who would prefer not to give birth to female offspring. Thus at the same time as science is lauded for reducing the incidence of pain and suffering, an identical technique is denounced for its potential to subvert the natural randomness of human reproduction. The assumption that greater human control over procreation will inevitably lead to its misapplication underpins much of the criticism levelled at prenatal genetic testing and other new reproductive technologies. As we see below, it is an assumption that remains peculiarly resistant to evidence showing the implausibility, or even the impossibility of the particular feared misuse.

II Disability Lobby

There are several interrelated reasons why prenatal testing has attracted the attention of individuals who are concerned to promote the equal treatment of disabled people. First, one recurrent objection to abortion on the grounds of fetal abnormality is that it presupposes a crisp separation between normal and abnormal human development.[106] Normality is not, on this view, an objectively determinable fact, but may instead embody a mutable set of cultural preferences. This sort of argument suggests that if there is no universal and objective definition of abnormality, the decision to have an abortion following a positive prenatal diagnosis must reflect dominant and thus challengeable social or medical assumptions about a particular disability. These critics of prenatal testing are therefore arguing that the decision to abort an abnormal fetus is socially constructed in the same way as it is where the fetus is the "wrong" sex.[107] So an individual who is shorter than normal[108] may argue that it is not being short that makes their life more difficult than that of a person of normal height. Rather their problems are caused both by society's attitudes to physical disability, and by its failure to provide adequate services to accommodate their special needs.[109]

Related to this is the claim that offering prenatal testing when there is no plausible treatment for the particular condition creates a presumption in favour of termination.[110] Pregnant women aged thirty-five and over are, for example, routinely offered either amniocentesis or chorionic villus sampling, both of which carry a risk of miscarriage that would not be worth taking unless termination would be contemplated in the event of a positive diagnosis.[111] Critics of

[106] Sarah Cunningham-Burley has argued that "there is no simple distinction between medical conditions that are serious or not serious, that impact or don't impact on the quality of someone's life; indeed there is no easy distinction between medical conditions and behavioural traits" (Cunningham-Burley, 1998, p. 11).

[107] Gericke, 1990, p. 932.

[108] Achondroplasia is a genetic condition which results in restricted growth.

[109] Tom Shakespeare, for example, has claimed that "people are disabled not by their bodies but by society" (Shakespeare, 1995, p. 24).

[110] Michael Malinowski quotes one genetic counsellor: "its generally accepted that termination is the primary option for most genetic diseases found prenatally" (Malinowski, 1994, p. 1468).

[111] The risk of miscarriage from chronic villus sampling (CVS) is slightly greater than that of amniocentesis. Its advantage is that it can be carried out at nine weeks when abortion is relatively straightforward. Amniocentesis is usually carried out during the second trimester, when abortion is possible but may involve a more complicated procedure (Adler *et al*, 1991).

prenatal tests have therefore argued that their incorporation into standard medical practice creates powerful norms in favour of termination.[112] It is, of course, true that a woman's decision to abort a fetus after a particular prenatal diagnosis is not taken in a vacuum, and may be shaped by both society's attitudes to disability, and by medical advice. It is not, however, obvious that the existence of external influences necessarily undermines the legitimacy of a particular choice. If this were the case, very few of our decisions would withstand scrutiny. As I explained in chapter one, our preferences are always inevitably shaped by the social context in which they are formed but they are the only preferences we have and, provided that their satisfaction does not cause harm to others, they should be treated with appropriate respect.

Of course, some members of the disability lobby would argue that prenatal testing and abortion does cause "harm to others" through its negative consequences for disabled individuals.[113] Just as certain feminists have suggested that sex-selective abortion devalues all women, this second type of argument suggests that the routine abortion of fetuses found to have a particular disability sends a message to people living with that condition that they should "not have been born".[114] While clearly a powerful rhetorical device, this inference presupposes the moral equivalence of a fetus and a person. Disability should not be a legitimate reason for choosing between *people*, but a fetus does not have legal personality and so rules that prohibit discrimination cannot be said to apply *in utero*.[115] It is perfectly plausible to think that a disability makes a life less satisfying without believing that a person with that disability is less valuable. Analogously, if a 48 year old woman decides to terminate an unexpected pregnancy, she is not presumed to be sending a message to all children with older mothers that they should not have been born. Rather she has taken a decision about the course of her life that only she is equipped to make. We should, I argue, allow a woman to assess for herself whether or not she wants to carry this particular pregnancy to term. The responsibilities of parenthood should be

---

[112] Suzanne Tomlinson has even argued that routine prenatal testing "may actually reduce parental choice by subtly conveying that it is unacceptable for someone to bear a child with an imperfection that could have been prevented, albeit by preventing the birth itself" (Tomlinson, 1998, p. 551). For example only about 50% of females with the genetic mutation responsible for Fragile X syndrome will actually be affected by it, and those that are affected are likely to have a borderline normal IQ of 70–85. Nevertheless 64% of female fetuses with the genetic mutation are aborted.

[113] Martha Field vigorously contests the description of abortions for abnormality as "therapeutic". For example, under the Iowa 1991 Acts 267 § 103 an abortion is "medically necessary" if the fetus is certified to be "physically deformed, mentally deficient or afflicted with congenital illness." Field asks "how can an abortion ever be therapeutic to the very fetus it eliminates?" (Field, 1993a, p.112).

[114] Field, 1993a, p. 115. Less stridently Jonathan Glover has suggested that "it cannot do much for someone's self-esteem to have the thought that many parents are choosing abortion rather than have a child with the same condition they have." (Glover, 1999, p. 109).

[115] As John Harris argues, "to believe it right to abort a fetus is not to be necessarily committed to the view that the world would be better off without that individual, nor that the individual would eventually wish she had never been born, nor that that individual will be unhappy, nor that that individual will suffer" (Harris, 1998a, p. 215).

assumed voluntarily, and ought not to be imposed upon an unwilling pregnant woman.

In a similar vein, some critics have expressed misgivings about the practical implications of increased resort to prenatal screening. In the absence of effective fetal therapy, prenatal tests can only promote infant health by enabling the abortion of abnormal fetuses, thus disease is prevented by *selection*, rather than by research into treatment and cures.[116] As a result, it has been predicted that if there were fewer people living with disabilities, interest in devising new treatments and services for them would be correspondingly reduced.[117] It has even been suggested that the state might have a compelling economic interest in the active promotion of prenatal testing[118] because aborting an abnormal fetus will be cheaper than funding the treatment and support needed by disabled people.[119]

However, it is not clear that restricting women's access to prenatal diagnosis or abortion would in fact improve the lives of disabled people. Attempting to reduce the incidence of a particular disease is not necessarily incompatible with trying to improve the lives of people living with that condition. Currently many prospective parents who undergo prenatal or preconception genetic tests have family members or existing children living with a debilitating genetic disease. Their desire to avoid giving birth to another child with the same condition does not mean that they consider their ill relations' lives to be without value, or not worth living. Nor does their willingness to have an abortion in the event of a positive diagnosis reflect their lack of interest in new treatments that might improve the lives of the affected members of their family.

A third and related criticism of prenatal tests is that their routine use might create new standards of perfection, or make physical or mental incapacity appear to be effectively optional.[120] These concerns have considerable resonance with disability activists' objections to the growth of a perceived "tyranny of perfection".[121] Bill Hughes, for example, argues that prenatal genetic testing

---

[116] This has been already been done with some success in some Mediterranean countries with high incidence of B-Thalassemia. In Sardinia 1 in 8 adults was a carrier, and the incidence of B-Thalessemia was 1 in 250 live births. After an intensive screening campaign, 99% of couples who were counselled accepted prenatal diagnosis. 99.7% of the fetuses which tested positive were then aborted. The incidence of B-Thalassemia is now 1 in 1000 live births (Cao, 1991).

[117] Karen Rothenberg says that there is a danger we will develop "genetic myopia" whereby our attraction to genetic explanations of human condiditons such as breast cancer will undermine attempts to find other less dramatic preventative techniques (Rothenberg, 1997, p. 103).

[118] "disguised as responsible planning and . . . resource allocation (this) could lead to the most dangerous and subtle form of eugenics: economic eugenics" (Knoppers and Laberge, 1991, p. 48).

[119] The US National Institutes of Health estimated that the lifetime "cost" of each person with cystic fibrosis ranged from $250,000 to $1,250,000 (NIH 1997, p. 15).

[120] Daniel Callahan has argued that "behind the human horror at genetic defectiveness lurks, one must suppose, an image of the perfect human being. The very language of 'defect', 'abnormality', 'disease' and 'risk' presupposes such an image, a kind of prototype of perfection" (quoted in Miringoff, 1991, p. 53).

[121] Glassner, 1992. Bill Hughes has argued that "not only does contemporary culture exaggerate the extent to which we are able to choose our bodies, but it also conflates the ethical subject with an aesthetic ideal of embodiment" (Hughes, 2000, p. 561).

presupposes both the existence of a "genetic hierarchy" and the categorisation of disabled individuals as "sub-standard human beings".[122] Since wealthier women tend to have more prenatal tests, even where there is no charge for screening,[123] it has also been argued that certain diseases will increasingly correlate with socio-economic status, leading to the creation of a "biological underclass".[124]

As I explain more fully below, the chief defect of all of these arguments is that they massively overstate the social changes that could be wrought by advances in prenatal testing and abortion. New prenatal tests are highly unlikely to transform attitudes to disability because most diseases and disabilities are *not* caused by genetic abnormalities detectable *in utero*, but instead result from poverty, accidents, war, exposure to environmental toxins,[125] or from a complex interaction between an individual's genotype and their environment.

III Reflexive Modernity and Genetic Testing

Until recently, the only way in which the birth of a child suffering from a particular abnormality could be prevented was through prenatal diagnosis of an *existing* fetal handicap. After a positive conventional prenatal test result, the decision may be emotionally fraught, but it is comparatively simple to understand: if this pregnancy were to be carried to term, the resulting child would have the identified disability. If the prenatal test reveals an abnormal gene, on the other hand, this does not necessarily mean that the child will develop a particular condition. Some genetic tests can predict with certainty that a child's life would be both short and excruciatingly painful, and may, for practical purposes, be largely indistinguishable from a conventional diagnosis of abnormality. Others, however, may identify a *predisposition* to an adult-onset disease, or may indicate there would be some statistical *risk* that the resulting child would suffer from a particular abnormality.

Gene penetrance, for example, varies. BRCA1, which is associated with breast cancer, has a penetrance of 85 per cent, meaning that in 15 per cent of women this particular gene will not lead to breast cancer. Some genes may increase an individual's susceptibility to a particular environmental toxin, thus only leading to future ill-health should certain environmental factors obtain. In addition, tests are often unable to predict both the severity of the disability, and the age of onset. So although it is possible to identify the genetic mutation associated with cystic fibrosis, we do not yet know how to tell whether or not the individual will be gravely affected.[126]

It is, therefore, true both that a prenatal genetic diagnosis will often be much more uncertain than results obtained through conventional diagnostic techniques,

---

[122] Hughes, 2000, p. 563.

[123] Lippman, 1991.

[124] Nelkin and Tancredi, 1994, p. 176; Kitcher, 1997, p. 125.

[125] Wertz , 1997, p. 339. In Poland's largest industrial area Katawices, one in two children is born with abnormalities caused by prenatal exposure to pollution (Hellum, 1993, p. 127).

[126] Some men with the gene are infertile, but otherwise healthy; some women develop only mild sinus problems.

and that this uncertainty makes it particularly difficult to digest the results of pre-natal genetic tests. It is especially difficult for an individual to interpret a diagnosis expressed in terms of risk because probability may only make sense at a macro level.[127] The significance of a statistical risk to one's health is almost impossible to grasp, because as far as each individual is concerned the material risk is actually either 100 per cent or 0 per cent: they will or will not develop the particular condition. Since a variety of external factors inevitably feed into our perception of a particular risk, the concept itself may even be essentially meaningless without its subjective and contextual interpretation. For example, the idea that traits "run in the family" is not new, and so popular understandings about the heritability of certain talents, weaknesses or characteristics will shape people's understanding of genetic risk. Similarly individuals faced with a positive prenatal genetic diagnosis may understand it in terms of some resolutely pre-modern concepts such as fate or destiny.

Probabilistic information about a fetus's susceptibility to future ill-health thus converts prenatal diagnosis from a description of current handicap into something much more uncertain. While a completely objective definition of illness or disability has never been possible, and there has always been room for disagreement about precisely what good health consists in, new genetic information unquestionably creates radical new instability in our definitions of health and illness. Genetic risk is not like conventional health hazards because it may simply alert us to uncertainties about whether the future should be considered safe or dangerous.[128] Test results that tell us about *possible* futures thus blur the boundary between illness and health and undermine the clear-cut opposition between good and bad outcomes, which instead may co-exist in a diagnosis that shows no current infirmity, but some increased susceptibility to a late-onset condition.

The analysis of risk has become a central theme in some strands of socio-logical theory. Risk has ceased to be a simple description of the expected frequency of a particular outcome, and has instead become a symbol for the subjective uncertainties created by rapid modernisation. Ulrich Beck, for example, defines risk as:

> "a systematic way of dealing with hazards and insecurities induced and introduced by modernization itself. Risks as opposed to older dangers are consequences which relate to the threatening force of modernization and its globalization of doubt".[129]

The study of risk thus generally involves the analysis of techniques for managing uncertainty. Since risks tend to seem especially threatening if the feared adverse outcome is unfamiliar, uncontrollable or unpredictable, it is probably unsurprising that the uncertainties that emerge from biotechnology, and in particular from genetic knowledge, have appeared to offer a rich source of examples

[127] Warnock, 1998.
[128] Beck, 1999, p. 140.
[129] Beck, 1992a, p. 21.

for sociologists interested in the implications of newly emerging risks. For instance, Beck has suggested that "reproductive medicine and genetic research throw open the door to a new quality of politics",[130] and according to Giddens, the choices offered to pregnant women by modern science and technology are opening up "new ethical spaces".[131] Our unprecedented capacity to control reproductive outcomes is therefore accompanied by the fear that this new technology may itself be uncontrollable.

The modernist assumption that scientific progress is a source of unmitigated health benefits, though still prevalent among scientists, has thus been challenged by sociologists concerned about technology's potential to create unforeseeable hazards. Paradoxically, this heightened risk consciousness actually co-exists with increased life expectancy and our unprecedented capacity to diagnose and treat diseases. Nevertheless, the social implications of knowing much more than ever before about our susceptibility to ill health are commonly perceived to be fundamentally unknowable, and, as a result, our capacity to set up effective regulatory mechanisms to accommodate these novel issues is doubted.[132]

While it is undeniable that genetic test results introduce new ambiguities into the diagnosis of disease, it is less clear that they present potentially uncontrollable hazards. Nor is it obvious that the regulation of prenatal genetic testing needs to be informed by the "precautionary principle" as is commonly advocated in relation to other uses of biotechnology, such as genetically modified food or nuclear power. Prenatal genetic test results may present *individual* pregnant women with information that is more ambiguous than a conventional diagnosis, but it does not necessarily follow that prenatal genetic testing has dangerously uncertain implications for society as a whole.

B Unjustified Fear?

Currently, as I explain below, there are some practical reasons why routine prenatal genetic testing is impracticable, but it is of course possible that new developments will increase the feasibility of comprehensive, population-wide screening. A further and less transient reason to question the various fears that have crystallised around the issue of prenatal genetic testing is that they rely upon a distorted understanding of genetics. In the following sections, I argue that an exaggeration of the dangers posed by genetic screening is thrown into particularly sharp relief by the relative indifference we display towards certain other health risks.

I Practical Difficulties

There are two practical reasons why comprehensive and routine prenatal genetic testing is currently impossible. First, the principal ways to obtain samples of fetal tissue are invasive and carry a comparatively high risk of

---

[130] Beck, 1997, p. 154.
[131] Giddens, 1994, p. 190.
[132] Morgan, 1996a, p. 206.

miscarriage.[133] As a result, prenatal genetic testing is used only where the fetus is judged to be at increased risk of a particular condition as a result of a specific indication, such as a relevant family history. Research into the possibility of isolating fetal cells from a pregnant woman's blood sample is ongoing, and if successful would undoubtedly facilitate some universal testing.

The second practical problem is that there are so many genetic abnormalities that it would simply be impossible to screen for all of them, and the tests that are currently available presuppose that a clinical team knows which condition they are trying to detect. Existing knowledge about a particular fetus's increased susceptibility to a specific abnormality is then a precondition for prenatal genetic testing. Although there are far too many genetic disorders for a single test to ever be able to screen for all of them, in the near future new diagnostic techniques will allow universal screening for some of the most common conditions, such as cystic fibrosis.[134] But while the practical obstacles that have so far prevented routine prenatal genetic testing will eventually be removed, at least in part, there are other more permanent reasons to question the empirical base of the various anxieties associated with prenatal genetic testing.

II Genetic Determinism
There are a few diseases, such as Huntington's chorea, for which prenatal identification of an abnormal gene provides a decisive diagnosis.[135] Because Huntington's disease is monogenic,[136] that is it is caused *only* by this abnormal gene, its elimination is conceivable. If all fetuses with the genetic mutation that

---

[133] Amniocentesis is usually carried out at around 16 weeks gestation, and is the most common prenatal genetic test (ACGT, 2000). It involves the insertion of a needle, guided by ultrasound, through the pregnant woman's abdominal wall and into the amniotic sac around the fetus. A sample of the amniotic fluid is then collected, and tested. There is a risk of miscarriage of around 0.1–0.5%. Chorionic Villus Sampling (CVS) can be performed at around 10 weeks gestation. Under ultrasound guidance, a needle is passed either through the abdominal wall, or through the cervix, and sample of placental tissue is removed. The procedure has a miscarriage rate of 1–3%. It is also possible to obtain umbilical blood samples, again using an ultrasound guided needle. Miscarriage rates are 1–3%.

[134] Kerr and Cunningham-Burley, 2000, p. 287.

[135] Another example might be PKU. Children are now routinely tested at birth for phenylketonuria (PKU) which results, without treatment, in severe mental retardation (it is caused by a recessive allele which means that the enzyme needed to metabolise phenylalanine is not produced, so on a normal diet chemical imbalances in the brain will produce impaired cognitive development). Fortunately, treatment exists (a special diet low in phenylalanine will ensure almost normal development) and so PKU testing is often regarded as a success story. The danger lies in the assumption that identification of the particular gene automatically ensures that a child will not develop PKU. The PKU diet is expensive, unpleasant and extremely difficult to follow. In the United States, only four states require health insurance to cover the PKU diet (Lippman, 1991, p. 35). Moreover, false positives or negatives can cause irreversible damage.

[136] On the tip of chromosome 4 is a trinucleotide repeat in a dominant gene. Unaffected people have between 11 and 34 repeats, Huntington's disease occurs in people who have over 42 repeats. The age of onset is associated with the length of the repeat, so someone who has 100 repeats will develop Huntington's disease earlier than someone with 44 (see further Kitcher, 1997). It is an autosomal dominant disease, which means that possessing a single defective gene is fatal. If someone with Huntington's disease reproduces, their offspring will have a 50% risk of inheriting the gene and developing the disease.

causes Huntington's disease were to be aborted and no babies were born with the relevant gene, it could not be passed on to the next generation and would disappear. Huntington's disease is therefore commonly cited as an example of the revolutionary possibilities being opened up by prenatal genetic screening.[137]

Single gene disorders like Huntington's are, however, extremely rare, and they are the only ones for which a simple genetic "solution" is feasible.[138] Most diseases can be the result of the interaction between several genes, and/or the interaction between an individual's genotype and their environment; or they may be triggered solely by environmental factors.[139] So although genetic markers for certain cancers have been identified, 95 per cent of people who develop colon or breast cancer do not have the particular genetic mutation associated with an increased risk.[140] Conversely, as we saw earlier, those who have the relevant genetic marker do not necessarily develop cancer as a result. Prenatal screening for a genetic predisposition to certain cancers would thus have limited impact upon their population-wide incidence. Similarly, an individual's learning difficulties may be the result of a genetic disease;[141] or environmental factors such as inadequate nutrition, care or education, or it may be caused by a combination of genetic susceptibility and environment. Inordinate interest in the genetic origins of mental disorder might therefore deflect attention from less intriguing but perhaps more statistically significant causes like poverty and childhood deprivation.[142]

It is undeniable that reducing poverty levels would radically alter the physical and mental health of the population to an extent unimaginable through prenatal genetic testing and abortion. Indeed a prenatal test that was capable of predicting future poverty would also represent a fairly accurate predictor of future ill-health. Yet it is perhaps interesting that this sort of knowledge is not perceived to be especially disturbing or threatening. Why are we so fearful about our capacity to single out certain individuals who present a genetic risk, and untroubled by our parallel ability to make predictions about the ill health likely to

[137] However, since Huntington's disease is a late-onset disease in which the symptoms usually begin between the ages of thirty and fifty, prospective parents may not know that they are affected and at risk of passing on the relevant genetic mutation or allele.

[138] It would take several hundred generations to alter the prevalence of most recessive genetic conditions (Cook-Deegan, 1991).

[139] For example, cancer occurs when cell division becomes uncontrolled. An inability to regulate cell division only happens after many changes in a person's DNA. These changes may be the result of a genetic susceptibility to cell copying errors; or they can be stimulated by environmental agents such as radiation, or by an interaction between a person's genetic make-up and their environment.

[140] See further Kitcher, 1997, p. 62; Skene, 1998, p. 2.

[141] Such as Fragile X syndrome which is the result of an abnormal repetition on the X chromosome.

[142] Children from households with lower gross weekly incomes are more likely to suffer from mental disorder. In 1999 16% of children aged 5–15 living in households with a gross weekly income of under £100 displayed a mental disorder compared with 5% of children living in homes where the gross weekly household income was between £600–£770 (Office for National Statistics, 2001, pp. 131). With reference to mental disorders, the chair of the Nuffield Council on Bioethics has referred to the "temptation to rely on 'geneticisation' as the ultimate answer to diagnosis and prevention" (quoted in Brooks, 1998, p. 903).

be suffered by children born into poverty? Like fear of crime, public perceptions of risk in relation to genetics appear to bear little relationship to the actual probability of certain adverse events occurring.[143] Of course, to acknowledge the practical limitations of prenatal genetic screening is not to understate its value and importance for individuals who are at risk of passing on a debilitating genetic disorder. Moreover, misplaced fears about eugenic selection and designer babies should not be allowed to deflect attention from some of the important policy issues that may be raised by prenatal genetic diagnoses.

C New Dilemmas

I Confidentiality

Most women who choose to accept a risk of miscarriage in order to find out whether their fetus is suffering from a particular abnormality will terminate the pregnancy following a positive result. For obvious reasons, a woman who would carry the pregnancy to term in the event of a positive diagnosis will not generally want to go through an invasive and risky procedure. However, as diagnostic techniques improve, a growing number of women will give birth to children with prenatally-detected genetic abnormalities, in which case knowledge about the child's genotype will precede his or her birth. Existing data protection rules governing the disclosure of genetic information to third parties, and to the child herself may need to be adapted to accommodate the acquisition of information about an individual before they have achieved legal personhood.

II Counselling

As we have seen, genetic tests that give a simple yes/no answer are the exception, and it is particularly difficult to interpret diagnoses that consist in a prediction of future risk. In order to digest and evaluate inherently probabilistic and uncertain genetic test results, pregnant women may therefore need professional help, and in practice expert advice is commonly sought in order to translate ambiguous information into intelligible advice. After a positive prenatal genetic diagnosis, a doctor or counsellor's explanation of the risk and description of the various options will often determine whether a woman seeks to terminate her pregnancy. Thus, genetic counselling, whether given by an obstetrician or a specialist counsellor, seldom consists in the neutral provision of information.[144] This is because first, complete value neutrality is probably impossible, and second, pregnant women will generally want help in coming to a decision. So, while information derived from prenatal tests may assist informed decision-making by pregnant women, where that information is predictive of future risk,

---

[143] Williams *et al*, 1995, p. 121.

[144] Robert Wachbroit and David Wassermen have argued that, "in the context of genetic counselling, value neutrality is impossible" (Wachbroit and Wassermen, 1995, p. 103). Indeed it has been suggested that health professionals are not currently following a policy of non-directiveness in genetic counselling, and furthermore that those being counselled may actually prefer to receive some directive advice (Michie *et al*, 1997).

a productive dialogue between doctors and their patients might be of particular importance.

Collaborative decision-making is not, however, fostered by the extraordinary authority vested in doctors by the Abortion Act 1967. As we saw earlier, an abortion's legality depends upon two doctors confirming that, in their opinion, the pregnant woman's reasons for seeking to terminate her pregnancy satisfy the terms of the statute. According to the Abortion Act, a woman who wants to terminate a pregnancy following the identification of a genetic abnormality must either satisfy two doctors that there is a substantial risk that, if born, the child would be seriously handicapped, or she must establish that giving birth to a child with this particular genetic susceptibility would pose a risk to her own mental well-being. Neither is straightforward. First, as we have seen, some genetic test results predict an increased risk of future ill-health, in which case the child might not be born suffering from a serious handicap. Second, a woman will only be able to fit her termination within the so-called "social" ground if the diagnosis and counselling has been completed within the first 24 weeks of pregnancy.

More importantly, given that both grounds leave open the possibility that the doctors will judge the woman's reasons to be inadequate, the statute gives doctors a right to veto any decision made during genetic counselling. If a woman decides during specialist genetic counselling sessions that she does not want to carry the pregnancy to term, that decision cannot stand unless it is subsequently approved by two doctors. Where a pregnant woman has been advised by her obstetrician, he may be responsible for both helping a woman to come to a decision *and then judging its adequacy*. That the facilitator of a decision should also exercise a right of veto over that decision is, perhaps, undesirable. In the light of their twin roles as advisers on the implications of a complex diagnosis and as gatekeepers to abortion services, it is probably unsurprising that there is evidence that genetic counselling given by obstetricians tends to be more prescriptive, albeit covertly, than that given by specialist counsellors.[145]

It could, I suggest, plausibly be argued that the extraordinary control doctors exercise over the decision to terminate an unwanted pregnancy may either disrupt their capacity to offer sensitive and productive advice about the results of genetic tests, or may undermine the finality of specialist genetic counselling. It is at least arguable that an abortion law which gives medical professionals the right to overrule a woman's decision could undermine the efficacy of non-directive genetic counselling.

(iv) Sex selection

The durability of a parental preference for sons is demonstrated by evidence suggesting that a variety of strategies have always been adopted in order to increase the probability that one's progeny will be male. Some advice, such as

---

[145] Marteau *et al*, 1993.

tying off the left testicle prior to sexual intercourse;[146] drinking lion's blood; copulating vigorously or biting the woman's ear during intercourse, was obviously completely ineffective.[147] However, these folk remedies tended to be accompanied by other practices that guaranteed that parents would have more sons than daughters, and continue to do so today. In parts of South East Asia, for example, female infanticide is still practised,[148] and significant gender differences in the allocation of food and medical care exist, especially during the first few years of life.[149] Unsurprisingly, therefore, the mortality rate for Indian girls between one and four years of age is three times that for boys.[150]

As we see in chapter five, it is now possible to identify the sex of an embryo *in vitro* in order to transfer only embryos of the desired sex to the woman's uterus. Preimplantation genetic sex diagnosis is, however, only lawful in the UK if one of the prospective parents is a carrier for a gender-specific genetic disease. Furthermore, removing one cell from a newly fertilised egg is an extraordinarily difficult and highly specialised procedure. It is much easier to identify a fetus's sex *in utero* and terminate the pregnancy if the fetus proves to be the unwanted sex.[151] As a result of improvements in diagnostic techniques, it is becoming possible to find out whether a fetus is male or female increasingly early in pregnancy, and if sex is identifiable at 12 weeks,[152] sex-selective abortion is a relatively simple, and thus potentially routine procedure.

Son preference is not confined to South East Asian countries,[153] but it is especially prevalent in countries such as China, Vietnam and parts of India and Pakistan.[154] Sons are perceived to be more valuable than daughters for a variety

---

[146] This was advocated by Anaxagoras, a Greek philosopher alive in 500BC. Aristotle advised women to lie on their right side after intercourse in the belief that males develop in the right side of the uterus (Danis, 1995, pp. 220, 224).

[147] Jones, 1993, p. 193.

[148] Judith Banister estimates that 50% of the annual shortfall of girls is the result of abortion: "we see a rising number of girls missing as a result of abortion, but it doesn't stop the other categories including infanticide, abandonment and selective neglect" (Weiss, 1996).

[149] A study carried out in Delhi indicated that women who had given birth to girls had significantly fewer visits from family and friends following the birth, and were 75% less likely to seek postnatal care than women who had given birth to boys (Weiss, 1996).

[150] Bhlakrishnan, 1994, p. 274. In Pakistan, mortality among children under four years' old is 66% higher in girls than boys (Wallerstein, 1998, p. 1546).

[151] In a study carried out in Punjab in 1994, it was estimated that fetal sex determination had been carried out in 13.6% of all pregnancies (Booth *et al*, 1994).

[152] John Stephens, an American ultrasonographer claims to be able to detect genitalia at 12 weeks (measured from the date of the mother's last menstrual period). See further Gosden, 1999.

[153] In one survey carried out in the United States, people were asked if they would have a sex preference if they were to only have one child: for every 100 who said that they would prefer an only child to be female, 160 would prefer an only child to be male (Danis, 1995, p. 235). When asked which gender they would prefer for their first child, 60% expressed a preference for a son, only 5% said that they would prefer their first child to be a girl (Cherry, 1995, p. 171). A recent study in Philadelphia showed that sons tended to be breastfed for longer than daughters (Gosden, 1999, p. 71).

[154] Judith Banister of the US Census Bureau has estimated that 1.5 million female fetuses were selectively aborted in China between the mid 1980s and 1990. Monica Das Gupta and Mari Bhat's study in India suggested that 1 million girls were selectively aborted in India between 1981 and 1991 (Weiss, 1996).

of reasons: for example, certain religious ceremonies specifically exclude women, and a family may need a son in order to fully participate in Confucian ancestor worship.[155] In India married women leave their family home in order to live with their husband's family and, despite its illegality, they must often bring some kind of dowry.[156] Since men can earn more, inherit property, have access to their wife's dowry and are expected to support their parents through old age, sons may represent a net gain to a family and daughters a net loss.[157] In addition, a wife's purpose is to provide sons and a woman who repeatedly gives birth to daughters may be judged a failure.[158] In China, population control policies that are intended to limit the number of children in each family have intensified the desire for male children. Couples with a daughter are now permitted to have one more child, but if the second child is also female, the couple are not allowed to try again. As a result there is a strong demand for sex-selective abortion services, especially during second pregnancies.[159]

It has been contended that any gender imbalance that might result from routine sex-selective abortion would be inevitably "self-correcting".[160] While it seems logical that a shortage of one gender would lead subsequent generations to seek to redress the balance, the cultural preference for sons is too deeply ingrained to be mitigated by any practical difficulties that may be caused by a population's gender asymmetry. In India in the nineteenth century, for example, it was reported that the Ranas caste had had no adult daughters for more than 100 years.[161] It has been estimated that one hundred million women are "missing" in Asia as a result of the combined impact of infanticide, relative neglect

---

[155] In traditional Vietnamese society only sons can carry on the family line of descent and are responsible for the care of the elderly and the ancestral altar. After marriage girls become members of the husband's family and are expected to work for their parents-in-law rather than for their own parents. There is a popular Vietnamese folk song which translates as: "Your daughter is a child of the other; only a daughter-in-law is your daughter since you have paid for her" (Hoa *et al*, 1996).

[156] Madhu Kishwar says that dowry payments to the groom's family are "a token of gratitutde for accepting the girl into their family, and for allowing her natal family to get rid of her" (quoted in Rajan, 1996, p. 12).

[157] Monica Das Gupta argues that "son preference is in the interest of the lineage, whose continuity depends on sons alone. It is also in the interest of the household, for whom daughters are transitory members" (Das Gupta, 1987, p. 94).

[158] Flavia Agnes explains that "in (Indian) society, to be a woman is bad enough; to be a mother of girls is a worse humiliation" (Agnes, 1995, p. 177). Monica das Gupta has suggested that "indeed a woman's position in her husband's home is not consolidated unless she produces at least one son" (Das Gupta, 1987, p. 94).

[159] According to the 1990 Chinese Census, sex ratios at birth were only slightly skewed for the first child, whereas second order births revealed a dramatic imbalance in favour of males (Rigdon, 1996, p. 55).

[160] John Robertson has argued that as a consequence of sex selection "women . . . may in fact become more valuable as a result of their shortage" (Robertson, 1996, p. 459). Similarly, John Harris has argued that "(t)he next generation would put a premium on producing children of the gender required to remove the imbalance (Harris, 1998, p. 192).

[161] And in a study carried out in Jiangsu Province in the 1930s, Fei Xiaotung found that for every 100 female births reported, there were 135 male births, a gap which he attributed to infanticide (Gosden, 1999, p. 149).

and sex-selective abortion.[162] Despite a continuing "shortage" of women in parts of China and Northern India,[163] the preference for sons remains strong.

Systemic sex discrimination is undoubtedly responsible for the prodigious demand that exists within certain cultures for prenatal sex screening and abortion. While it is unsurprising that many commentators have expressed concern about the recurrent termination of female fetuses,[164] it is not necessarily obvious that this anxiety is legitimately translated into restrictions upon women's access to prenatal sex screening or abortion. Nevertheless, the 1994 United Nations Cairo Conference on Population and Development advocated the proscription of prenatal sex selection,[165] and despite its relatively infrequency in the United States, a few states do specifically prohibit sex-selective abortion.[166] The legality of sex-selective abortion in the UK has not been tested in the courts. If giving birth to a girl would, as a result of her family's extreme disapprobation, pose a risk to a woman's mental and physical health it is at least arguable that the abortion might be lawful under section 1(1)(a). It is more probable that a woman who has found out that her fetus is female would tell her doctors that she had other reasons for wanting to terminate the pregnancy. As a result, there is anecdotal evidence that some doctors are reluctant to tell women from certain ethnic groups the sex of their fetus during routine ultrasound examinations.[167]

In India, legislation has been directed towards restricting access to diagnostic techniques,[168] and since 1994 it has been illegal to advertise or perform sex determination tests.[169] However, test results are invariably given orally, and without written evidence it has proved impossible for enforcement agencies to bring actions under the statute.[170] With no convictions during its first five years, the Indian statute has been singularly ineffectual,[171] and prohibition has simply

[162] Benegiano and Bianchi, 1999; Sen, 1990.

[163] In China the sex ratio is 100 females to 108–9 males (CRLP, 1995) In the northern Indian states of Bihar and Rajasthan, it has been estimated that there may be only 600 females for every 1000 males. (Mudur, 1999, p. 401). It has been estimated that India is 40 million women short of the numbers that a normal sex ratio would ensure (Gosden, 1999, p. 147).

[164] Holmes, 1995; Warren, 1999. It has been suggested that in sex-selective abortion "women are . . . being required to participate in their own pre-victimization" (Cherry, 1995, p. 166).

[165] Danis, 1995, p. 259.

[166] A Pennsylvania statute states that "no abortion . . . sought solely because of the sex of the unborn child shall be deemed a necessary abortion" 18 PA Cons Stat Ann §3204(a)1983. And a statute in Illinois prohibits abortions performed "with knowledge that the pregnant woman is seeking the abortion solely on account of the sex of the fetus" Ill Ann State Ch 720 para 510/8 (Smith-Hurd 1993).

[167] Modell and Modell argue that "in the UK, it is unacceptable within the NHS to provide fetal sexing with a view to terminating a pregnancy purely on grounds of sex". (Modell and Modell, 1992, p. 187).

[168] In the Indian state of Maharashta, the Regulation of Pre-Natal Diagnostic Techniques Act 1988 prohibited the carrying out of prenatal diagnosis except in registered genetic clinics. It specifically prohibited testing for the purpose of indicating the sex of the fetus (Agnes, 1995, p.183).

[169] In 1994 the Indian Government passed the Pre-Natal Diagnostic Techniques (Regulation and Prevention of Misuse) Act. The doctor; relatives who encourage the test, and the woman herself are punishable with fines of up to 50,000 rupees (£1000) and jail terms of up to 5 years (Rajan, 1996, p. 8).

[170] Mudur, 1999, p. 401.

[171] *Ibid.*

resulted in a flourishing black market in testing and abortion.[172] This is, of course, unsurprising given that the preference for sons is determined not by the availability of prenatal tests, but by the payment of dowry, inheritance rules and wage differentials. Restricting access to information which is so economically and socially valuable has, in practice, simply made the tests more expensive and the resulting abortions less safe.[173] It may then make little sense to tackle the "problem" of sex-selective abortion in isolation from the other social, economic and legal practices that devalue women's lives.[174]

The desire to abort a fetus because it is female may only be comprehensible in the light of a deeply embedded cultural and economic preference for sons. But, as I argued earlier in relation to abortion on the grounds of abnormality, recognising that a decision may be socially constructed does not necessarily mean that it should be ignored. Of course it is possible that a pregnant woman's consent to a sex-selective abortion will have been obtained by duress or undue influence, and thus could not be said to be her own decision.[175] Given the precarious economic and social circumstances of many of the women seeking sex-selective abortions, it may sometimes be difficult to separate real from coerced decisions. But where a competent, adult woman has made her own decision that she wishes to terminate a particular pregnancy, it is not clear that disapproval of her reasons offers a sufficient reason to compel her to carry her unwanted pregnancy to term.[176]

5. CONCLUSION

The regulation of abortion in the UK reflects the social and political context in which it was legalised. The Abortion Act's delegation of decision-making authority to the medical profession may have been a crucial determinant of Parliamentary support for legalisation in 1967. Several decades later, attitudes towards abortion have changed and the law now seems somewhat outdated. The Royal College of Obstetricians and Gynaecologists, for example, consider that women should be entitled to prompt access to abortion services, and that

---

[172] The Indian Medical Association admits that medical practitioners without adequate qualifications in ultrasonography have invested in diagnostic equipment in order to offer sex determination tests to parents (Mudur, 1999, p. 401).

Conspicuous advertisements have urged people that taking the test could save the costs of future dowry (see further Menon, 1993 and Rajan, 1996, p. 8).

[173] See further Bhlakrishnan, 1994, p. 279. Since becoming illegal, charges for sex-determination tests have increased from 700 rupees to 7000 rupees (Rajan, 1996 p. 10).

[174] As Radhika Bhlakrishnan points out "gender preference is articulated at numerous stages in a female life, and . . . it does not start or stop before birth" (Bhlakrishnan, 1994, p.276).

[175] Whether a woman's will has been overborne by relatives would be a question of fact, see further *Re T (adult:refusal of medical treatment)* [1992] 4 All ER 649 in which Lord Donaldson said "the doctors have to consider whether the decision is really that of the patient. . . (P)ersuasion . . . (must) not overbear the independence of the patient's decision."

[176] Jackson, 2000.

abortion should be treated as a routine and non-controversial aspect of medical care.[177] Yet, as we have seen, women have no right to terminate an unwanted pregnancy, and must instead depend upon the beneficent exercise of medical discretion. While this would be comparatively unimportant if the statute was generally working satisfactorily, it is clear that the practical impact of abortion's continued medicalisation is to restrict the reproductive choices of disadvantaged women.

Moreover, we should perhaps consider whether the law's extraordinary treatment of abortion sits uneasily with the rest of British medical law. In particular, the Act's insistence upon two doctors deciding whether a woman should be able to terminate an unwanted pregnancy may be out of step with the increasing priority given to patients' right to make their own decisions about their medical treatment. The logical corollary of the provisions of the Abortion Act is that if two doctors do not consider that the grounds in section 1(1) are satisfied, abortion would be unlawful, and the woman must carry her unwanted pregnancy to term. In the next chapter, we see that pregnant women are entitled to make choices about their medical treatment even if the inevitable consequence is the death of their fetus. It may then be significant that forcing a woman to carry an unwanted pregnancy to term has not been perceived to be an important derogation from her overriding right to make her own decisions about her medical treatment.[178] Pregnancy, especially in its later stages, is an extraordinarily invasive and often painful experience, and unless the baby is immediately given up for adoption, giving birth leads to the onerous and enduring responsibilities of parenthood. Insofar as a non-consensual operation is illegitimate because it would interfere with a person's right to make important decisions about their life according to their own conception of the good, requiring a pregnant woman to carry an unwanted pregnancy to term might be similarly disruptive.

In the light of the increasing availability of prenatal tests, it may also be particularly important that the doctor/patient relationship is not skewed by the Abortion Act's uneven distribution of decision-making authority. Increasingly women may need help in order to digest complex information about genetic risk. This sort of assistance is not necessarily best provided within a framework for abortion decision-making that makes the doctor the ultimate arbiter of whether the woman has a good reason for termination. So in addition to improving abortion law's congruence with the principle of patient autonomy, giving women greater freedom to make their own decision about termination might be an important adjunct of a shift towards a model of medical decision-making based upon partnership rather than power.

[177] In their Guideline *The Care of Women Requesting Induced Abortion*, the RCOG recommend, *inter alia*, that "Services should . . . offer arrangements (e.g. a telephone referral system and direct access from referral sources other than general practitioners) which minimise delay", and that "service arrangements should be such that: ideally, all women requesting abortion are offered an assessment appointment within five days of referral", and " ideally, all women can undergo the abortion within seven days of the decision to proceed being agreed" (RCOG, 2000a, chapter 3).

[178] See further Jackson, 2000.

4

Pregnancy and Childbirth

1. INTRODUCTION

IT IS INDISPUTABLE that an individual's health may be affected by things that happened during their mother's pregnancy. Our constantly expanding knowledge about fetal development means that it is becoming possible to identify an increasingly wide range of prenatal factors associated with future ill health.[1] Although there may be many different social, economic and environmental causes of fetal injury, the behaviour of the pregnant woman has received particular attention. To optimise fetal progress, pregnant women are advised to stop smoking, to stop drinking or reduce alcohol consumption, to eat well,[2] while avoiding certain foods such as soft cheeses, raw eggs, seafood and sometimes nuts, to exercise in moderation and to avoid toxic environments and certain prescription drugs.

Providing information to pregnant women so that they are able to make informed decisions about their pregnancies is clearly both necessary and desirable. Pregnant women are undoubtedly entitled to know about research that shows a correlation between poor health outcomes and prenatal exposure to a particular toxin. But while accurate information is unquestionably one prerequisite for the exercise of free choice, another is the capacity to make a decision that others might consider foolish or reckless. Drawing upon a line of argument developed more fully in chapter one, I argue that proper respect for an individual's autonomy should involve granting them the maximum possible scope for directing the course of their life according to their own values and beliefs. Freedom of choice would be essentially meaningless if only rational and sensible decisions had to be respected. The danger that I explore in this chapter is that a series of assumptions about the proper management of pregnancy may in fact restrict pregnant women's freedom to make unorthodox choices about their lifestyle and medical care.

---

[1] For example, Barker has suggested that a susceptibility to coronary heart disease may be acquired *in utero* (Barker, 1995). Hultman *et al* have found that prenatal malnutrition, smoking, stress or depression and non-compliance with antenatal care routines may influence the development of schizophrenia (Hultman *et al*, 1999, p. 425). Godrey *et al* have suggested that a high carbohydrate intake in early pregnancy suppresses placental growth, especially if combined with a low dairy protein intake in late pregnancy, and that this significantly affects the offspring's risk of cardiovascular disease (Godfrey *et al*, 1996). North and Golding contend that there may be negative consequences from pregnant women following a vegetarian diet (North and Golding, 2000).

[2] Modell and Modell have questioned some of the dietary advice given to pregnant women, they suggest that it is only severe malnutrition which adversely affects fetal development (Modell and Modell, 1992, p. 297).

There are two related situations in which what is sometimes misleadingly referred to as "maternal/fetal conflict"[3] has become an issue for the law: the first is where a pregnant woman is behaving in a way that might harm the developing fetus, and the second is where the pregnant woman refuses to consent to medical treatment that may be necessary to preserve fetal life. In some countries there have been attempts to use the law both to prevent pregnant women from harming the developing fetus, and to punish women who have caused fetal injury. In the United Kingdom, coercive legal intervention in pregnancy is unusual, although not unprecedented.

There are multiple problems in regulating the relationship between a pregnant woman and her fetus, principally because their connection is quite unlike any other recognised by the law. The fetus is not simply a part of the woman's body, in the same way as her arm or her kidney, but nor it is it entirely separate from her. As Ronald Dworkin explains:

> "her fetus is not merely 'in her' as an inanimate object might be, or something alive but alien that has been transplanted into her body. It is 'of her and is hers more than anyone's' because it is, more than anyone else's, her creation and her responsibility; it is alive because she has made it come alive".[4]

Given the uniqueness of the fetus's position inside, but not a part of the pregnant woman, it is probably unsurprising that the regulation of pregnancy appears to be riddled with contradictions and inconsistencies.

The law's difficulty in conceptualising the relationship between the pregnant woman and the fetus may, however, point more to the conventional biases of legal thought than to anything particularly unusual about their connection.[5] In statistical terms at least, the relationship between a pregnant woman and her fetus is, if anything, exceptionally ordinary. Given the rather more transitory physical connection between a man and his offspring, the bond between pregnant woman and fetus is the only corporeal relationship shared, without exception, by every human being. As Cunningham J explained in the American case of *Stallman* v. *Youngquist*, "no one lives but that he or she was at one time a fetus in the womb of its mother".[6] Nevertheless, despite pregnancy's ordinariness, it is undoubtedly true that the relationship between a pregnant woman and her fetus is not easily classified according to conventional legal norms.

This chapter considers the regulation of various aspects of pregnancy and childbirth. First, we investigate the management of prenatal and obstetric care. Echoing themes developed in the previous chapter, we explore the increasing dominance of medical knowledge about pregnancy, and the emergence of the

---

[3] The term is misleading for two reasons. First, because a mother is a woman who has given birth to, or adopted a child, rather than a woman who is pregnant. Second, any legal dispute is not between the pregnant woman and her fetus, rather it is usually between the pregnant woman and those responsible for her health care.

[4] Dworkin, 1993, p. 55.

[5] I am grateful to Ngaire Naffine for this point.

[6] 531 NE 2d 355 (Ill 1988), at 360.

fetus as a patient in its own right. Second, having identified ways in which fetal patienthood may obscure the pregnant woman's right, as a patient, to refuse unwanted interventions during pregnancy and childbirth, we consider the circumstances in which the law permits the treatment of pregnant women without their consent. Third, liability for injuries sustained *in utero* is examined, and we observe the difference between the relatively straightforward ascription of responsibility for fetal harm to third parties, and the infinitely more complex issues raised when it is the pregnant woman's conduct which poses a risk to fetal wellbeing. Finally, we consider health promotion programmes' capacity to exercise subtle and pervasive control over pregnant women's behaviour.

In this chapter, I am principally concerned with the scope of the pregnant woman's autonomy. Unlike the previous chapter, which was devoted to a single decision that might be taken by a pregnant woman, here we are concerned with a broad range of choices about, for example, diet, lifestyle, employment or medical treatment, that may be made during the course of a pregnancy. My argument will be that each individual's freedom to behave in an unconventional or irrational way should not be truncated for pregnant women. Every pregnant woman should, I argue, be allowed to decide for herself the nature and the scope of the obligations she chooses to assume towards her developing fetus.

Of course, as we saw in chapter one, the liberal assumption that each person is an autonomous actor capable of exercising unconstrained free choice has been subjected to an effective and thoroughgoing critique. It is undeniable that we develop preferences within a context that moulds and may even determine what those preferences consist in, but I do not believe that this insight weakens our duty to respect a pregnant woman's decisions about her lifestyle and medical treatment. Rather, I think that it should sharpen society's responsibility to ensure that each pregnant woman has both a range of valuable options from which to choose, and the capacity to articulate her preferences. It might be helpful to bear in mind Jennifer Nedelsky's insight, discussed more fully in chapter one, that for autonomy to flourish, individuals may need a network of supportive relationships.[7] A thin concept of autonomy which is limited to giving effect to a pregnant woman's clearly expressed preferences will obviously not enable all women to exercise effective control over the management of their pregnancies and deliveries. Thus, recognising that a woman's social and economic context may affect her capacity for meaningful, reproductive choice might also help us to challenge the prevailing assumption that a commitment to autonomy is inseparable from an individualistic approach to apportioning responsibility for harm. I argue that we should foster an environment in which a woman is able to make choices about her pregnancy, while recognising that her behaviour is only one of a wide range of factors that may influence fetal health and wellbeing, most of which will be beyond her control. Currently there is, I would suggest, a regrettable and perhaps paradoxical tendency to limit women's capacity to

[7] Nedelsky, 1989.

exercise autonomous choice while simultaneously over-emphasising their individual responsibility for fetal development.

2. REGULATION OF PRENATAL CARE AND OBSTETRIC SERVICES

(a) Access and Accountability

Pregnant women are exempt from prescription charges for the duration of their pregnancy and for 12 months following delivery, and under the National Health Service Act 1977, every health authority is under a duty to ensure universal access to obstetric care. In theory, every pregnant woman is entitled to adequate obstetric care regardless of whether she is cared for in a specialist maternity unit, or is being treated in a prison hospital.[8] In practice, however, there is substantial regional variation in both the nature and the quality of available services.

Although research has shown that the desire to control what happens during the birth may be a predominantly middle-class concern,[9] women's involvement in decision-making during pregnancy and labour is now widely considered to be good medical practice.[10] But while women's involvement in decision-making may have increased, it is noteworthy that this has not led to a rise in the number of home births. On the contrary, fewer than 1 per cent of all births now take place at home. In part this may be because there are seldom sufficient qualified midwives to offer all women the option of home delivery, but as we see below, it also seems clear that both doctors and their pregnant patients increasingly take for granted the need for extensive medical equipment and expertise to be on hand during every delivery.

Even where there is little evidence to support the use of high-tech obstetric interventions, both patients and doctors seem to have confidence in the advantages of technology.[11] Pregnant women are, for example, increasingly demanding access to new technologies, and to elective caesarean sections,[12] and private

---

[8] In *Brooks* v. *Home Office* [1999] 2 FLR 33, a remand prisoner's twin pregnancy was classified as high risk. The prison doctor was insufficiently experienced in obstetrics and waited five days before seeking advice following a scan that provided evidence of abnormal development. Garland J held that a pregnant woman in prison was entitled to receive the same careful standard of obstetric medical care as a woman at liberty.

[9] Fox and Worts, 1999. Margaret Nelson's study found that working class women's principal concern was control over pain (Nelson, 1983).

[10] Cumberledge, 1993.

[11] Marjorie Tew's research indicated that home births appear to have better perinatal outcomes for low, medium and even high risk pregnancies (Tew, 1990). Margaret Donohoe argues that there is a cultural assumption that more machines means better care, and that this is very hard to displace. For example, electronic fetal monitoring continues to be routinely used despite its inaccuracy (Donohoe, 1996). Berkman suggests that the belief shared by both patients and physicians that the use of technology leads to healthier babies is in part responsible for the high caesarean rate in the US (Berkman, 1991 p. 629).

[12] In a survey of London obstetricians' preferences for themselves or their partners, 17% chose elective caesarean section in the absence of any clinical indication (Al-Mufti *et al*, 1997). In the two

patients have the highest rates of both surgical delivery and other types of intervention in labour.[13] Within the NHS, the emphasis on women's active participation in the management of pregnancy does not generally extend to giving women the "right" to choose an elective caesarean section,[14] although patient preference is undoubtedly taken into account.[15] A caesarean birth costs significantly more than a vaginal delivery, and given the inevitability of rationing scarce resources in the NHS, it would be difficult to argue that women have a right to a comparatively expensive procedure requested against medical advice.[16]

Even where the woman's preference for surgical delivery is based upon her perception that the pregnancy may be at risk, a doctor who refuses a woman's request for a caesarean section is extremely unlikely to be found to have acted unreasonably.[17] It is, as we see throughout this book, notoriously difficult to prove that a doctor has been negligent. A court will only find that a refusal to perform a caesarean section was negligent if either responsible medical opinion unanimously agrees that a caesarean should have been performed, or if the court considers that there was a manifest or an obvious risk in vaginal delivery.[18] In

most expensive private maternity hospitals in London, the caesarean section rates are 44% and 38% respectively (Phillimore, 2000, p. 14).

[13] Roberts *et al*, 2000; Belizan *et al*, 1999 . This is partly due to patient preference, and partly the result of their doctors' perception that private patients would be more likely to sue should something go wrong (Meyer, 1997, p. 169).

[14] Paterson-Brown, 1998. Although there are those who would argue that women should have the right to choose caesarean delivery, for example Amu *et al* have argued that "if caesarean section is the preferred mode of delivery by the mother, her choice, however foolish or irrational, must be respected" (Amu *et al*, 1998, p. 464).

[15] In an audit at the Chelsea and Westminster Hospital in London, 14% of elective caesarean sections took place solely because of "maternal" request. Because women who had previously had a caesarean section or breech presentation were given the option of vaginal delivery, "maternal" request also played a part in the numbers of caesarean sections carried out for those indications. Eftekhar and Steer therefore estimate that 72% of elective caesarean sections were wholly or in part the result of "maternal" request (Eftekhar and Steer, 2000).

[16] Drife, 1997, p. 844. A 1% increase in caesarean rates costs the NHS over £5 million per year.

[17] In *Pearce* v. *United Bristol Healthcare NHS Trust* [1999] PIQR 53, Tina Pearce had "begged" for a caesarean section or induction when she was 14 days beyond term. Her consultant advised a natural birth, and seven days later the baby was induced stillborn. Mrs Pearce argued that the consultant had failed to inform her of the risk of stillbirth, and that if he had she would have "insisted" on a caesarean section. The Court of Appeal refused to interfere with the consultant's clinical decision not to inform Mrs Pearce of the minor risk of non-intervention. Moreover, they suggested that even if she had been warned of the risk of non-intervention, she would have followed medical advice and proceeded to a natural birth.

In *Nash* v. *Kingston and Richmond HA* [1997] 36 BMLR 123, N brought an action alleging that there had been an unreasonable delay in performing a caesarean section and that the second attempt at a forceps delivery which caused N's cerebral palsy should not have been attempted. Sir Michael Davies held that there was "ample room" for opposing views to be taken by competent medical opinion, and that the delay was not "unreasonable".

[18] For example in *Dowdie* v. *Camberwell HA* [1997] 8 Med LR 368, Maurice Kay J found that the fact that two distinguished medical experts testified that the persistence towards vaginal delivery was within a range of acceptable practice did not oblige the court to accept their evidence. Here D suffered a serious shoulder injury after a delivery which involved excessive traction, and Maurice Kay J found that a decision that this was unreasonable was within the competence of the court.

addition to overcoming the considerable hurdle of establishing that the doctor breached their duty of care, a woman claiming to have been injured by negligent obstetric care must also prove that it was the actions of the doctor that, on the balance of probabilities, caused their injury.[19] So even where a court finds that a doctor's failure to perform a caesarean section was clearly negligent, it will still be necessary to prove that it was the failure to move more quickly to a surgical delivery that caused the particular injury. Given that a caesarean will only become necessary if there is considerable concern for the health of the fetus, establishing that it was the failure to operate, rather than the pre-existing fetal distress, that caused the injury will be extremely difficult.[20]

Despite the rhetoric of patient involvement in the management of pregnancy and birth, one of the principal mechanisms of accountability for the quality of care operates to vest considerable decision-making authority in individual doctors. The doctor's duty of care towards his pregnant patient means that, unless he has behaved in a way that is not logically supportable, he is absolved of liability provided that other doctors would have treated her in the same way. Moreover, the doctor's duty of care is generally perceived to be to act in the best *clinical* interests of his patients, rather than to enhance their sense of control over the treatment they receive. Nothwithstanding the problems in proving that a failure to respond to a patient's request was a breach of a doctor's duty of care, it would also be difficult to establish that having one's preference ignored, in the absence of any physical injury, counts as "harm" for the purposes of recovery in negligence. This, coupled with the inevitability of rationing within the NHS, means that the emphasis upon patient involvement might be better described as a *service aspiration*, rather than a fundamental component of the obstetrician's duty of care.

Similarly, each health authority's duty to provide adequate obstetric services to women living in its area does not extend to offering every woman the option of a home delivery. And despite indisputable patient preference, health authorities do not have to provide each woman with a named midwife who will be involved in her care throughout her pregnancy and delivery. Rather the health authority will only have breached their primary duty of care to provide adequate treatment if their services pose an unacceptable *health* risk to patients. Its failure to enhance decision-making autonomy among pregnant women will not trigger a health authority's liability in tort.

In the following sections, we first consider other practices that vest the medical profession with considerable authority over the management of pregnancy and childbirth. I then attempt to explain women's apparent enthusiasm for medical involvement throughout their pregnancies.

---

[19] In *Diplul Hoque* v. *Sheffield HA* 19 July 2000 (unreported) Rafferty J dismissed the claimant's action because the obstetric senior registrar's decision to discharge the pregnant woman was supported by expert witnesses. Rafferty J also pointed out that it was not possible to prove that a caesarean section would have averted the claimant's brain damage.

[20] In *Robertson* v. *Nottingham HA* [1997] 7 Med LR 42 Otton J found that although it was negligent not to move to delivery by caesarean section after a series of abnormal cardiograms, it had not been proved that events in the 12 hours before her birth caused the child's cerebral injury.

(b) The Medicalisation of Pregnancy and Childbirth

(i) The Dominance of Obstetrics

It would be a mistake to overstate the novelty of medical involvement in child-birth: the first surgical text to describe a caesarean section, for example, appeared in 1305.[21] From the fifteenth century onwards, there is evidence that women were increasingly excluded from surgical deliveries,[22] and midwives were consistently denigrated by both witch-hunters and the medical establishment.[23] The first professor of obstetrics, Giovanni Antonio Valli, was appointed in Bologna in the middle of the 18th century.[24] Since then the obstetric profession has steadily enlarged its scope,[25] while simultaneously the midwife's role in non-emergency deliveries has declined in importance.[26]

It is at least arguable that falling perinatal and maternal mortality rates owe more to general improvements in women's standard of living than to increased technological intervention in pregnancy.[27] Nevertheless, the assumption that there is a simple causal relationship between new technologies and better health outcomes has dominated attitudes to pregnancy care for hundreds of years, and in the last sixty years there has been a marked trend towards the *routine* clinical management of pregnancy.

Aided by increasingly sophisticated monitoring techniques, the obstetrician has become involved not only in salvaging problem births, but also in *anticipating* and

[21] Bernard of Gordon's *Lilium* (Blumenfeld-Kosinski, 1990, p. 61).

[22] Until 1400 representations of caesarean births showed midwives performing the operation, while after 1400 male surgeons took over responsibility for caesarean sections, with women appearing only as attendants. For an account of medieval and renaissance representations of Caesarean births, see Renate Blumenfeld-Kosinski, 1990.

[23] "The special skills of midwives and female healers as they related to sexuality and procreation not only were assets used in the service of women's health but also threatened some of the most important values of medieval society: the family and male control over women" (Blumenfeld-Kosinski, 1990, p. 110).

[24] See further Karen Newman's history of obstetrics. She argues that "as obstetrics became increasingly technologized with the invention and manufacture of forceps and ever more elaborate pelvimeters and specula, and as an accompanying increasingly positivistic view of anatomy produced the body as a series of parts to be manipulated, obstetrics became professionalized and, ultimately, the province of men" (Newman, 1996, p. 51).

[25] In the 1960s, one of the key textbooks changed its name from *Midwifery by Ten Teachers* to *Obstetrics by Ten Teachers*.

[26] The etymological roots of the word midwife are the Latin "mid" meaning "together with" and "wif" meaning "a woman". Thus a midwife's role is to *assist* the woman in labour, whereas an obstetrician brings his or her clinical judgement to bear upon the diagnosis and treatment of abnormalities in childbirth. Shuman and Marteau studied relative perceptions of the risks of childbirth, and found that obstetricians considered childbirth to be more risky than did pregnant women. Midwives considered childbirth to be less risky than pregnant women (Shuman and Marteau, 1993).

[27] See further Marjorie Tew, 1990. Jo Murphy-Lawless has argued that "the 'dire peril' of maternal death has gradually diminished, for reasons only some of which are attributable to obstetrics" (Murphy-Lawless, 1998, p. 197).

preventing abnormalities during pregnancy.[28] The theory is that if normal physiology is subjected to rigorous control, pathological deviations from the norm can be minimised.[29] Obstetricians' increasing dominance reflects the prevailing assumption that all pregnancies must now be treated as if complications might be imminent. Paradoxically then, despite falling birth rates and falling mortality rates, the number of pregnancies regarded as "abnormal" continues to rise,[30] a trend undoubtedly exacerbated by the increased likelihood of malpractice suits against doctors for failing to intervene in pregnancy.[31]

There are two principal difficulties in defining "normal" childbirth. First, despite its apparent roots in objective medical knowledge, normality may be a context-specific value-judgement rather than a neutral and scientifically verifiable description. For example, in amendments over several recent editions, medical textbooks have steadily reduced the length of a normal labour, thus allowing a delivery to be classified as abnormal, and thus in need of intervention, at an earlier stage.[32] Second, if every pregnancy and its delivery is potentially pathological, it is only possible to define a pregnancy as normal *after* the baby has been safely delivered. Because the normal, pathology-free pregnancy exists only with the benefit of hindsight, all pregnant women tend to be treated as if things *might* go wrong.[33] Obstetric practice is therefore concerned with the management of risk in *all* pregnancies, rather than with interventions

[28] Ann Oakley has said that "when antenatal care began, (its purpose) was to screen a population of basically normal pregnant women in order to pick up the few who were at risk of disease or death. Today the situation is reversed, and the object of antenatal care is to screen a population suffering from the pathology of pregnancy for the few women who are normal enough to give birth with the minimum of midwifery attention" (Oakley, 1984, p. 213). Belinda Pratten has pointed out that "there is a major difference between treating complications which may arise during pregnancy and defining the entire process in terms of pathology" (Pratten, 1990, p. 13).

[29] And one obstetrician has suggested "the active management of labour necessitates that obstetricians take over, not just a single aspect of delivery but responsibility for the whole process of parturition. Our control of the situation must be complete" (Beazley, 1975, p. 161).

[30] It is, for example, ironic that the percentage of deliveries coded as "normal deliveries with no antenatal or postnatal complications" fell from 30.8% in 1989–90 to 18.5% in 1994/5 (Department of Health, 1997). Geoffrey Chamberlain and Philip Steer estimate that one third of all pregnancies are "abnormal" requiring increased surveillance and possibly action to prevent fetal problems (Chamberlain & Steer, 1999, p.1124). And in their survey of obstetric intervention in Australia, Roberts *et al* found that a minority of pregnant women (48%) were categorised as "low-risk" (Roberts *et al*, 2000, p. 137).

[31] Obstetricians and gynaecologists are among the most sued physicians in the United States. 73% of obstetrcians and gynaecologists report that they have been sued at least once (Seymour, 2000, p. 348). The US also has the highest caesarean rate in the world: over 21% of all births are by caesarean section (Gottlieb, 1999). Cheryl Meyer observes that there are higher caesarean rates for those women who are more likely to file a lawsuit if something should go wrong (Meyer, 1997, p. 169).

[32] Donohoe, 1996, p. 227. And in relation to the duration of pregnancy "normal" has been synonymous with "average", thus enabling a pregnancy to be defined as abnormally late when it has exceeded the average length of 280 days, even though only 5% of babies actually arrive on their predicted date of delivery (Murphy-Lawless, 1998, p. 203).

[33] The medical model of childbirth rests upon the assumption "that the body is always ready to fail" (Lane, 1995, p. 56). Jo Murphy-Lawless suggests that according to current obstetric practice "every birth must be managed as having pathological potential until it is over, at which point it can safely be judged normal" (Murphy-Lawless, 1998, p. 198).

in exceptional cases. As we see below, this preoccupation with pregnancy's immanent pathology has been intensified by the development of increasingly sophisticated prenatal tests, and by the emergence of the fetus as a patient in its own right.

(ii) Prenatal Testing

One of the most significant technological developments in the management of pregnancy has been the development of precise, detailed and accurate prenatal diagnostic techniques.[34] Some prenatal testing, most notably ultrasonography and the alpha-foetoprotein test,[35] is already a normal aspect of prenatal care in the UK. Fewer than 1 per cent of British pregnant women receive no prenatal tests,[36] and research has indicated that many women do not realise that routine prenatal screening is optional.[37] Ultrasound, for example, is seldom treated as a diagnostic tool that may have certain unintended side-effects,[38] but rather is perceived to be a simple visualisation technique, and welcomed as the first opportunity to see the "baby".[39] It has even been suggested that ultrasound could be used instrumentally to persuade pregnant women to act more responsibly towards their fetus[40] or to induce paternal sentiments in reluctant fathers.[41]

[34] Until the 1960s, prenatal genetic counselling was limited to advising couples who had already had a child suffering from an abnormality of the statistical chance that another child would be affected (Kolker and Burke, 1994, p. 2).

[35] The AFP test is carried out on a blood sample taken from the pregnant woman. Elevated or reduced levels of a particular protein have been found to correlate with neural tube disorders such as spina bifida and Down's syndrome.

[36] Graham *et al*, 2000, p. 157.

[37] Kolker and Burke, 1994, p. 5.

[38] Studies that have shown an association between exposure to ultrasound and left-handedness indicate that ultrasonic waves may have an impact upon fetal development (Naumberg *et al* 2000 p. 282).

[39] Janelle Taylor describes the marketing tactics of companies which manufacture ultrasound equipment. She quotes one marketing director who says that these machines are marketed differently from cardiology or radiology equipment: "the difference is that in obstetrical ultrasound we're really marketing just as much to the patient as to the physician" (Taylor, 1998, p. 35). Taylor suggests that "women themselves, as avid consumers of prenatal care, are . . . agents in the routinization of ultrasound" (Taylor, 1998, p. 31).

[40] The Royal College of Obstetricians and Gynaecologists' Guidelines at 4.2.2 state that "this new, constantly improving view of the developing fetus brings an earlier recognition of the depth of responsibility towards the fetus as it progresses towards 'personhood'." It has been suggested that if ultrasound were provided in the first trimester of a pregnancy, it would facilitate 'maternal' bonding, and women would be less likely to opt for abortion (Fletcher and Evans, 1983). The concept of maternal "bonding" is relatively new and has its origins in studies that demonstrated the long-term importance of allowing new-born babies to spend time with their mothers immediately after birth. It first emerged in an article by Klaus *et al* in the *New England Journal of Medicine* in 1972. They found that children who had an extra 16 hours contact with their mothers immediately after birth did better in developmental tests (Klaus *et al*, 1972). But the idea was rapidly extended to pregnancy, and it is now widely believed to be valuable for pregnant women to "bond" effectively with their fetus. In Alice Kolker and Meredith Burke's study of women undergoing prenatal testing, one woman said of ultrasound: "I believe it facilitated some bonding." Another said "it made abortion—the thought of it—impossible" (Kolker and Burke, 1994, p. 77). A more extreme example comes from Paul Hill, who said before his trial for several murders committed

As both diagnostic techniques and treatment options become more sophist-icated, a growing number of tests are, like ultrasound, likely to be carried out "routinely", even though they are overwhelmingly likely to give a "normal" result.[42] There are those who would argue that the accumulation of techniques to monitor fetal progress creates needless anxiety,[43] wastes time and resources, does little to improve the proportion of healthy babies[44] and rein-forces the perception that every pregnancy must be subject to as much techno-logical intervention as possible. Yet while the public health benefits of routine prenatal screening may be comparatively small, there is no doubt that many individual pregnant women gain considerable reassurance from undergoing prenatal tests.

A more pressing danger that arises from the incorporation of an increasing number of prenatal tests into standard medical practice is the possibility that women will undergo tests without having given fully informed consent. Since some prenatal tests, such as HIV screening or certain genetic diagnoses, reveal information about the pregnant woman's own genotype or HIV status, it is important that she understands that her "right not to know"[45] is not sus-pended for the duration of her pregnancy. It is also vital that *most* women's willingness to undergo non-invasive prenatal tests should not lead doctors to presuppose the *universal* existence of consent. In the following sections, we consider the implications of routinisation in relation to both HIV screening and genetic testing.

A HIV Testing

Antiretroviral therapy during pregnancy, delivery by caesarean section and refraining from breast feeding can all substantially decrease the chance that an HIV positive mother will transmit the virus to her child. Where no precautions are taken, studies have indicated that the risk of vertical transmission is between

outside abortion clinics in the United States, that if the judge were to view an ultrasound, he would understand his motivation (Taylor, 1998, p. 15). Faye Ginsburg notes that "the idea that know-ledge of fetal life, and especially confrontation with the visual image of the fetus will 'convert' a woman to the pro-life position has been a central theme in . . . right-to-life activism" (Ginsburg, 1988, p. 102).

[41] Janelle Taylor has observed that "ultrasound offers to expectant fathers and mothers alike an equivalent experience of the fetus." (Taylor, 1998, p. 32). As a result, if the primary impulse towards prenatal bonding is the spectatorship of ultrasound, it might cease to be the prerogative of the preg-nant woman, and be equally available to the "father" and other family members (Taylor, 1998, p. 43).

[42] Kolker and Burke point out that 98% of pregnant women will receive "normal" results (Kolker and Burke, 1994, p. 7).

[43] Janet Gallagher has suggested that "the availability of new tests and procedures to detect anomalies before birth, along with new devices to monitor 'distress' or potential problems during labour, freighted prospective parenthood with ever greater apprehension and made the development and wellbeing of the fetus an obsessive preoccupation" (Gallagher, 1995, p. 349).

[44] Ewigman *et al*, 1993.

[45] See further Laurie, 1999.

17 per cent and 25 per cent.[46] With antiretroviral therapy caesarean delivery and avoidance of breastfeeding the risk can be as low as 1 per cent.[47] It is, of course, only possible to take these precautions if the pregnant woman knows that she is HIV positive. It has been estimated that up to 87 per cent of HIV positive pregnant women are not aware of their HIV status, and are therefore unable to benefit from recent advances in preventing perinatal transmission.[48] Unsurprisingly,

[46] Gallagher-Mackay, 1997, p. 353. The Deputy Chief Medical Officer and the Chief Nursing Officer have stated that "Without any treatment one baby in six born to an HIV infected mother is likely to become infected. The rate of mother to child transmission in non-breast feeding populations without therapy in UK and Europe is 15–20% (Peckham and Gibb, 1995). In a large study co-ordinated by Laurent Mandelbort of Cochin-Port Royal Hosptial in Paris of 2834 children born to HIV infected mothers, treatment with zidovudine and elective caesarean reduced transmission rates to less than 1%. Treatment with zidovudine and vaginal delivery led to transmission rates of 7%. Transmission rates for women not treated with zidovudine were 17%, and method of delivery made little difference (Gottlieb, 1998).

[47] Gibb *et al*, 1998, p. 259.

In developing countries it would be impossible to provide a complete course of combination therapy (otherwise known as zidovudine or AZT) for every pregnant HIV positive woman. For example the wholesale cost of a course of zidovudine has been estimated to be over $800 per pregnancy. The per capita annual health care expenditure of Uganda is $10; in Tanzania and Ethiopia its $5, and in Kenya its £13. Moreover, given a lack both of clean water and of adequate sterilisation techniques, routine elective caesarean delivery and the use of formula milk may pose a greater threat to infant health than the risk of HIV infection. The WHO recommends that HIV positive women in developing countries continue to breastfeed, because although up to 18% will infect their babies with the HIV virus as a direct result of breastfeeding, using formula milk without access to clean water poses a more statistically significant risk to infant health (see further Annas and Grodin, 1999, p. 378).

There has been considerable controversy over the ethical acceptability of testing short, and more affordable courses of AZT in developing countries. On the one hand, although it may not represent the optimum therapy, it might be better than nothing, and anything which reduces otherwise high rates of vertical transmission should, perhaps, be welcomed. On the other hand, such research may contravene the 1964 Helsinki Declaration of the World Medical Association, revised most recently in South Africa in 1996, which has been accepted as an authoritative statement of the principles which must be adhered to in all research trials carried out upon human subjects (see further Medical Research Council, 1995). According to the Helsinki Declaration, where the research trial is therapeutic, that is it is carried out on people who are suffering from the relevant condition: "in any medical study, every patient—including those in the control group, if any—should be assured of the best proven diagnostic and therapeutic method" (Section II-3). This section means that if a proven treatment exists, participants in a therapeutic research trial cannot be given treatment that is known to be less effective. Since we know that antiretroviral therapy throughout pregnancy is, combined with other precautions, the best proven therapeutic technique, it would be *prima facie* unethical to give research subjects in developing countries shorter courses of combined therapy. If the Helsinki Declaration were to be reworded, so that patients instead had to be assured of the best *available* therapy, which in many developing countries is nothing, then it would be ethical to conduct research in order to find out whether more affordable short courses of zidovudine could prevent vertical transmission. Of course, amending the Helsinki Declaration in order to offer less protection to people in the poorest countries of the world would appear to set an alarming precedent. It has further been argued that even short courses of AZT, costing around $50, might remain inaccessible to women in the very poorest countries in the world where the annual per capita health expenditure may be as little as $5. In addition, providing supplies of clean water would enable breast feeding to be safely avoided, which might be an equally effective and more appropriate treatment option than relatively high cost drug regimes (see further Annas and Grodin, 1999).

[48] Duffy *et al*, 1998 p. 270. We know a great deal about the prevalence of HIV infection among pregnant women because universal anonymous testing for HIV antibodies has been carried out for many years in the United Kingdom for epidemiological reasons.

despite relatively low rates of infection among both pregnant women and their babies,[49] there have been suggestions that HIV testing in pregnancy should become routine,[50] or even mandatory.[51]

Compulsory testing would undoubtedly violate the pregnant woman's right to refuse an unwanted medical procedure, and as a result it is highly unlikely that prenatal HIV testing would ever become mandatory in the UK. Routine testing might not offend first principles of medical ethics in the same way as a compulsory screening programme, but in practice it may be extremely difficult for many pregnant women to exercise their right to refuse to be tested. Blood tests early in pregnancy are generally perceived to be a normal feature of ante-natal care, and women will not always be told precisely which tests will be carried out on their blood sample.[52] An opt-out system in which women will be tested routinely unless they express an objection is voluntary only in the loosest possible sense.

It is undoubtedly true that improved treatment options have increased the practical value of knowledge about one's HIV status, and that this is the case in relation to a woman's own health as well as that of her children. There is, how-ever, still considerable social stigma attached to being HIV positive, and people who have had a positive test result continue to experience difficulties in obtain-ing insurance. That most people now consider that the health benefits of AZT to outweigh the social and economic disadvantages of a positive HIV test is not a justification for compulsory or quasi-compulsory testing. Rather it should lead health care professionals to offer clear information about the consequences of a positive result, and to explain that not being tested is a choice that will be respected.

[49] In 1997, there were 265 births in Britain to women who were HIV positive, resulting in 71 HIV positive babies (Fitzpatrick, 2001, p. 27).

[50] For example an intercollegiate working party recommended that "testing for HIV should, as far as possible, be 'normalised' that is it should generally cease to be dealt with separately from other conditions discussed within antenatal care" (Intercollegiate Working Party, 1998). Michael Greene, chair of the American College of Obstetricians and Gynecologist's Committee on Obstetric Practice has said "our aim is to make HIV testing as commonplace as urinalysis during the first prenatal office visit. The HIV test would not be mandatory—any woman would have the right to refuse testing. But we'd like to see HIV testing in pregnancy become routine and unexceptional". (ACOG, 2000). In the United States the Public Heath Service has also recommended routine, voluntary prenatal HIV testing, and the rates of perinatal HIV infection have declined drastically (Lindegren *et al*, 1999).

[51] In 1996 the American Medical Association recommended mandatory testing of pregnant women. Theodore Stein suggests that "the vast majority of physicians favour mandatory screening of pregnant women and a number of physicians favour forced intervention to protect the fetus". (Stein, 1998, p. 109). In 1997 the New York Public Health Law §2500-f (McKinney Supp. 1997) intro-duced mandatory HIV testing of newborns. Previously voluntary testing and counselling had iden-tified only 40% of HIV positive babies, since its introduction 98.9% of HIV positive infants are identified and given treatment (Mayersohn, 1997).

[52] For example, dramatic reductions in perinatal transmission of Hepatitis B infection have become possible using immunisation from birth. The discovery that transmission can be prevented in 95% of cases has led the Department of Health to implement a policy of routine universal screening during pregnancy (Department of Health, 1998a). Many women are either unaware that they have been screened for Hepatitis B, or may not fully appreciate that they are entitled to refuse to be tested.

B Genetic Testing

As we saw in the previous chapter, genetic testing is currently confined to women who are known to be at risk of having a child with a particular genetic condition as a result, for example, of a relevant family history. In part this is because it is not yet possible to carry out screening for a wide variety of genetic abnormalities simultaneously, so doctors have to know which genetic abnormality they are attempting to detect. In the future, new testing techniques that enable doctors to diagnose multiple conditions with a single test will undoubtedly promote universal prenatal screening for some of the more common genetic disorders.[53] In addition, samples of fetal DNA are currently only obtainable using relatively invasive and hazardous procedures, such as amniocentesis or chorionic villus sampling. If ongoing research into the feasibility of identifying fetal cells within maternal blood samples is successful, it will be possible to carry out genetic tests without subjecting the pregnant woman to an elevated risk of miscarriage.

There are obvious advantages to less hazardous diagnostic techniques. Their only danger lies in the possibility that the pregnant woman might not appreciate precisely which tests doctors propose to carry out on her blood sample. While it would never be possible for doctors to screen for every rare genetic condition, routine testing for the more common genetic disorders, such as cystic fibrosis, will soon be possible. In relation to genetic testing, properly informed consent is especially important given the genetic connections that exist between the fetus and its progenitors. Thus if a fetus is revealed to have cystic fibrosis, both "parents" have simultaneously been identified as carriers. In some circumstances it will therefore be impossible to inform the pregnant woman about the results of a genetic test without also divulging information about her or her sexual partner's genotype. Genetic information's inherent transmissibility requires intelligible pre-test advice to be available to pregnant women, which might be difficult to provide within a universal screening programme.[54]

As the number of available prenatal tests increases, and as they become safer and cheaper, their routinisation is likely. There is no doubt that many women will find the prospect of more thorough and far-reaching prenatal testing reassuring, although it could plausibly be argued that their net contribution to infant health will be comparatively small. There might then be sound *economic* reasons for the NHS to restrict access to certain prenatal tests to women who present an increased risk of particular conditions. Yet the political enthusiasm for screening programmes and preventative healthcare may mean that considerable resources are diverted to the routine provision of extensive and arguably redundant prenatal tests.[55]

[53] Kolker and Burke 1994, p. 72.
[54] Harper, 1993, p. 397.
[55] See further Fitzpatrick, 2001.

In addition to the possibility that routine testing might be an unwarranted drain on NHS resources, the necessity for informed consent to each test carried out on a woman's blood sample should not be compromised by routinisation. And this is especially true when the test reveals information about the pregnant woman's own future health as well as that of her fetus. It is easy to lose sight of the fact that a fetus cannot undergo any prenatal tests unless the pregnant woman gives her consent, consent that she has the right to withhold. In the following section we explore some of the reasons for the incipient marginalisation of the pregnant woman's status as a patient.

(iii) The Fetus as Patient

At the beginning of the twentieth century anatomists engaged in the new science of embryology assiduously gathered specimen fetuses for research purposes, most of which were derived from miscarriages.[56] Very early embryos could be examined only if women undergoing hysterectomies happened to have conceived just before their operation. While this would normally be a rather haphazard way to obtain embryos, there is evidence that some doctors deliberately timed elective hysterectomies to take place during the two weeks following ovulation, and ensured that patients informed them if they had had unprotected sexual intercourse at the relevant time.[57] But although knowledge about the stages of fetal development has been gleaned from experiments upon expelled or aborted fetuses for many years,[58] until relatively recently the living fetus *in utero* was completely inaccessible and most information about its progress came from the pregnant woman's account of changes within her body.[59]

From the first uses of stethoscopes and X-rays in the late nineteenth century,[60] there has been an accelerating growth in technologies that facilitate external monitoring of the developing fetus. Ultrasound enables both medical staff and

---

[56] Morgan, 1999, p. 50.

[57] A team of Boston physicians, led by John Rock and Arthur Tremain Hertig examined 211 uteri removed during elective hysterectomies between 1938 and 1954. They performed the operations during the two weeks following ovulation, and instructed the women to keep a record of unprotected intercourse. During these experiments they found 34 fertilised ova (Hertig *et al*, 1956). Lynn Morgan suggests that it is interesting that their work was not regarded as ethically problematic, since today there would almost certainly be enormous criticism if scientists "encouraged" women to have hysterectomies when they were most likely to have conceived (Morgan, 1999, pp. 51–2).

[58] Early representations of the fetus, based upon a belief in preformation, depicted a small person, or homunculus (see further Barron, 1995 pp. 2–3). It was, of course, possible for a fetus to be examined following miscarriage, but despite knowledge about fetal appearance, most anatomical illustrations continued to portray a tiny child, rather than the distorted fetal form. In the University of Bologna's Obstetrics Museum set up in the 18th century, the dominant image of the fetus *in utero* is a plump, cherubic baby reminiscent of the omnipresent baby Jesus (Newman, 1996, p. 62).

[59] For example, Barbara Duden has argued that in the past a woman who suspected that she might be pregnant would have this suspicion confirmed by "quickening", or the moment when she first becomes aware of fetal movement. Now, "a scientific technological test rather than a kick urges the woman to change her self-image" (Duden, 1993, p. 80).

[60] Barron, 1995, p. 3.

prospective parents to see the fetus,[61] and foetoscopy can now provide clear moving pictures, and allow doctors to take blood and tissue samples.[62] Embyroscopy techniques, that currently enable doctors to view a four-week old embryo, are progressively lowering the age at which the new human life becomes visible.[63] In almost every wanted pregnancy in the developed world, the fetus makes its first "public" appearance long before it is capable of independent life. Popular culture has embraced this sonographic image of the free-floating fetus, precipitating its characterisation as a tiny, helpless baby.[64] As we have seen, sophisticated prenatal testing is permitting increasingly accurate diagnosis of an expanding range of illnesses, disabilities and even genetic susceptibilities to future ill health. Some fetal abnormalities are now treatable *in utero:* blood transfusions, for example, may be given through the umbilical blood vessels,[65] and fetal surgery has been used to treat a number of conditions, including hydrocephaly and urinary tract obstructions.[66]

Thus, given the increasing range of technological innovations that allow the fetus to be seen, monitored, diagnosed and treated while still *in utero*, it is probably unsurprising that some doctors consider birth to be an arbitrary point at which to recognise the fetus as a patient in its own right. Birth is no longer the point at which the new human life becomes visible and accessible to the doctors involved in its care, and as a result, a significant number of doctors consider fetal medicine to be a discrete medical discipline.[67] Even if it is established law that the fetus is not a person,[68] there is no doubt that the fetus is now widely understood to be a patient.

---

[61] Ultrasound was first applied to the fetus in 1958 in order to measure the dimension of the fetal head (Barron, 1995, p. 5).

[62] Condit, 1995, p. 27.

[63] Reece, 1999.

[64] Feminist critics of reproductive technologies have claimed that ultrasound erases the fetus's connection to, and dependence upon the pregnant woman. Robin Rowland, for example, has argued that the "treatment of the fetus as both person and patient . . . is accompanied by the alienation of women, who now become merely the 'capsule' for the fetus, a container or spaceship to which the fetus is attached by its 'maternal supply line' " (Rowland, 1992, p. 121).

[65] Wyatt, 2000, p. 2.

[66] For example, a fetus can be removed from the woman's body by cutting through the uterus. Surgeons may then repair certain abnormalities. The fetus is then returned to the uterus, and is born a few weeks later (Morris, 1997, p. 61).

[67] In 1985, the first annual symposium of "The Fetus as a Patient" took place (James, 1998, p. 1580) Chervenak and McCullough, for example, contend that the "fetus as a patient" is an essential ethical concept for maternal-fetal medicine, and that the viable fetus must be treated as a patient in its own right (Chervernak and McCullough, 1996). In arguing for the law to impose limits upon a pregnant woman's right of self-determination, John Grace QC says "I pray in aid here what every obstetrician knows namely that he has two patients, and it is time, it seems to me, that the law recognises that" (Grace, 1999, p. 61). Stephen Walkinshaw suggests that in choosing which diagnostic tests to employ,"there may be times when the choice of test will set unreasonable risks for potentially normal fetuses . . . and physicians have in part a duty to protect their 'other' patient" (Walkinshaw, 1995, p. 77). Joseph G Schenker has said that "in modern obstetrics the fetus has rightfully achieved the status of a second patient to be cared for by obstetricians." Moreover Schenker suggests that the fetus is the more vulnerable "patient": "the fetus as a patient usually faces much greater risk of serious morbidity and mortality than the mother" (Schenker, 1991, p. 42).

[68] *Paton* v. *Trustees of BPAS* [1978] 2 All ER 987 at 990 where Baker P said "there can be no doubt, in my view, that in England and Wales, the fetus has no right of action, no right at all, until birth".

The primary focus of obstetric care used to be protecting the life and health of the pregnant woman.[69] But mortality in women as a result of pregnancy and childbirth is now so rare that "maternal" mortality rates may have little value as an indicator of obstetric success or failure.[70] Increasingly the key index for contemporary obstetric practice is fetal health and wellbeing. So, for example, over the course of the last few decades, obstetrics textbooks have devoted progressively more of their pages to treating the fetus, and fewer to the care of the pregnant woman.[71]

Advances in the survival rates of neonates[72] further contribute to the perception that the fetus is a separate patient. If a 23 week-old neonate can be successfully treated after delivery, some doctors may believe that a fetus of identical gestational age deserves equivalent care. In addition, through facilitating detailed study of premature babies, neonatology expands our understanding about the later stages of fetal development.[73] For example, increasing knowledge about fetal physiology has made it possible to identify a fetus's responses to noise, movement and pain.[74] In addition to its obvious significance for the abortion debate, evidence that a fetus can experience pain may reinforce its conceptualisation as an independent patient.[75]

Conferring "patient" status upon a fetus has some important symbolic and practical implications. It invokes, for example, a doctor's primary duty to treat her patients with reasonable care, and to do her best to preserve their lives. If the fetus is their patient, obstetricians must strive to avert fetal death or injury. The possibility that they may be liable for injuries sustained *in utero* or during childbirth undoubtedly further encourages doctors to do all that they can to promote fetal health.[76]

The concept of fetal medicine may present no practical problem when the woman is a willing participant in the proposed treatment, and given that

[69] See further Shorter, 1983.

[70] Lewis and Chamberlain, 1990, p. 340.

[71] Kolker and Burke, 1994, p. 26.

[72] In 1967, it was very rare for a baby born before 32 weeks to survive, and 28 weeks seemed to be an absolute barrier to survival. Survival at 22 weeks is now possible, though rare (Wyatt, 2000, p. 3). Approximately 36% of babies born at 24 weeks now survive, this rises to 38% at 25 weeks, 61% at 26 weeks and 76% at 27 weeks (Paige, 2000, p. 2).

[73] Electroencephalogram (EEG) readings of the brain waves of neonates have revealed that complex brain activity takes place at 24 weeks' gestation.

[74] The first fetal movements can be seen at 7 weeks gestation. By 16 weeks, over 20 different movement patterns are identifiable, including hand-face contact, startle, sucking and swallowing movements. The fetus first responds to sound at 20 weeks (Wyatt, 2000, p. 1).

[75] "Complex cardiovascular and hormonal stress responses to invasive procedures have been detected from before 20 weeks gestation. . . . If facial grimacing and aversive responses to noxious stimuli can be seen in premature babies from before 26 weeks gestation, there is *prima facie* evidence of some form of awareness of pain in the fetus from this gestational age and possibly earlier." (Wyatt, 2000, p. 1). Vivette Glover has suggested that at around 18 weeks a fetus might begin to feel pain "or something like it" (Meek and Barton, 2000).

[76] Janet Gallagher has commented on the fetus's role as both patient and potential plaintiff: "the fetus's emergence as patient, plaintiff and even quasi-religious icon serves as a vehicle for efforts to reinforce . . . traditional maternal norms and gender roles" (Gallagher, 1995, p. 345).

pregnancy is often both a planned and an infrequent experience,[77] many women will actively seek any intervention, however intrusive and debilitating, that might protect the life and health of their fetus.[78] And despite the feminist scepticism we consider in the following section, most women who consent to participate in prenatal intervention have not been duped into sublimating their own interests to those of their fetuses. Nevertheless, as we see later in this chapter, fetal patienthood creates the potential for conflict should a woman seek to exercise her right to refuse unwanted treatment.[79]

Because doctors cannot act to protect the fetus without some impact upon the bodily integrity of the pregnant woman,[80] to suggest that they might be under a duty to preserve fetal life cannot sensibly be described as an uncontroversial aspect of their clinical responsibilities. Acting to save fetal life involves acting upon the body of the pregnant woman, and without the pregnant woman's consent, the practice of fetal medicine will therefore involve a battery or an assault. The term "fetal medicine" may sound like a morally neutral description of a separate field of clinical expertise, but in practice it may deflect attention away from the rights that the pregnant woman has *as a patient* to refuse any unwanted medical treatment. Fetal surgery, for example, is only possible if the pregnant woman has given her consent to surgical intervention, consent that she is entitled to withhold. If the fetus lacks legal personality, it is perhaps illogical to endow it with the status of a patient which could confer upon it extraordinarily powerful rights over the bodily autonomy of the pregnant woman.[81] In its tendency to

---

[77] Janet Gallagher has suggested that women's anxiety about the progression of their pregnancies may be a result of the fact that it may be a "chosen and cherished" experience (Gallagher, 1995, p. 349). Dorothy and Richard Wertz have said that "in the age of choice, the wanted fetus as potentially perfect child and as object of affection has a higher value than in earlier times" (Wertz and Wertz, 1977, p. 241).

[78] Dorothy and Richard Wertz suggest that "when it comes to the health of their children, most (women) are not risk-takers" (Wertz and Wertz, 1977, p. 244). Stephen Walkinshaw points out that "women are increasingly requesting CVS on the basis of age-perceived risk" (Walkinshaw, 1995, p. 74). And Kolker and Burke's study of genetic counsellors revealed that in addition to a family risk, and the woman's age, the pregnant woman's "anxiety about abnormality" was widely believed to be an appropriate indication for CVS (Kolker and Burke, 1994, p. 3).

[79] In *Re Jamaica Hospital* 491 NYS 2d 898 (NY Super Ct, 1985), a pregnant woman was refusing a blood transfusion on religious grounds. The judge appointed the doctor as a "special guardian" to the fetus with "discretion to do all that in his medical judgement was necessary to save its life, including the transfusion of blood into the mother."

[80] Open fetal surgery has been performed over the last decade for a few conditions such as lower urinary tract infections. Two caesarean sections must be performed, and as a result of intraoperative risk and prematurity, there are high perinatal and maternal morbidity rates (James, 1998, p. 1582).

[81] Sheila McLean observes that a mother could not be ordered to donate bone marrow to her living child, and goes on to argue that "showing respect for the embryo or fetus at the expense of the woman's rights is a monumental misunderstanding of the concept of respect and a perverse interpretation of the value of human rights" (McLean, 1999, p. 69). In contrast Joel Jay Fisher mounts a bizarre and illogical argument in suggesting that the law could impose a positive duty to rescue upon a pregnant woman because "she is responsible for placing the being's life in jeopardy by conceiving it" (Finer, 1991, p. 259). It is surely obvious that life cannot be placed in jeopardy by conception. And if the fetus lacks legal personality, then it is illogical to suggest that a woman could owe a duty to "rescue" a fetus, when she owes no such duty to her living children.

eclipse the pregnant woman's status as a patient, fetal medicine may tend to reinforce the prevailing assumption that women *ought* to exercise unremitting self-sacrifice in order to promote fetal health and well being.

(iv) The Feminist critique

Unsurprisingly, feminists from a variety of disciplines have subjected the medicalisation of pregnancy and childbirth to a thoroughgoing critique.[82] Yet, as we have seen, evidence appears to suggest that most women welcome medical intervention during their pregnancies and prefer to give birth in hospital.[83] While this apparent paradox can be crudely explained by the social construction of individual preferences, it would be a mistake to entirely disregard women's agency. As I explained in chapter one, recognising that an individual's preferences may be shaped by dominant cultural norms does not obviate the requirement that we treat them with respect. There is, however, a regrettable tendency implicit within some critiques of medicalised childbirth that women *ought* to be assuming control over their deliveries.[84] Ironically then, this sort of analysis risks suggesting that the pregnant woman herself bears responsibility for the quality of her birth experience.[85]

An alternative explanation for women's enthusiasm for the medical management of childbirth has been suggested by research indicating that women may have two principal reasons for seeking and accepting medical interventions during labour.[86] In addition to their interest in their fetus's safe delivery, women may also be anxious to ensure that they will be capable of assuming the arduous responsibilities of caring for a new baby.[87] Thus where women will have access to extensive social support following the birth, they may be able to afford the "luxury" of rest and recuperation should their natural delivery prove to be both long and painful. Where, on the other hand, the new mother will have comparatively little assistance immediately following the birth, she may quite rationally insist upon any interventions that will speed up labour and/or reduce her pain. Here, we have another example of the relationships that may be necessary preconditions for autonomy to thrive.[88] Without a network of post-birth support, women's capacity to exercise control over their labour may be seriously attenuated.

---

[82] See, for example, Tew, 1990; Katz Rothman, 1982; Kitzinger, 1972; Eakins, 1986; Kay, 1982 and Oakley, 1980.

[83] Lazarus, 1994; Sargent and Stark, 1989.

[84] For example, Janet Gallagher thinks that "pregnant . . . women are altogether too compliant in their dealings with the medical profession and in their willingness to accept invasive procedures." (Gallagher, 1987, p. 13).

[85] Fox and Worts, 1999, p. 330.

[86] *Ibid.*

[87] *Ibid.*

[88] Nedelsky, 1989, p. 12.

(v) The Implications of Medicalisation

In the past, the fetus's position inside the body of the pregnant woman prevented its treatment as a separate patient. New technologies that enable doctors
to monitor fetal progress, diagnose abnormalities and prescribe therapeutic
treatment before birth have steadily reduced the *practical* significance of the
fetus's unique location. Many of these technologies are directed towards
improving health outcomes, and are thus welcomed by pregnant women for
whom having a healthy baby is frequently an overriding priority, and for some
women, medical intervention during their pregnancy and birth has undoubtedly
had tangible health benefits. However, whether the *universal* use of screening
programmes, hospital-based deliveries and certain monitoring techniques is
both clinically and cost-effective has been disputed, and it is probably true that
the widespread preference among patients and doctors for the clinical management of pregnancy and childbirth owes more to certain cultural and political
assumptions about preventative health care, than to any incontrovertible evidence base.[89]

I am not, however, advocating a thorough de-medicalisation of pregnancy
and childbirth, since this would plainly ignore the multiple health benefits that
derive from advances in obstetric care. Rather my point is that we should not
forget that the fetus cannot take advantage of medical treatment unless the
pregnant woman gives her consent to the particular intervention. That most
women are prepared to endure considerable pain and discomfort in order to
benefit their fetus should not lead us to assume that the pregnant woman's consent is a formality. Women are entitled to refuse to consent to prenatal tests or
fetal therapy, and this right should be respected by health care professionals.
Moreover, since properly informed consent undoubtedly involves understanding that you are being given a choice, it might even be important for doctors to
draw pregnant women's attention to their right to refuse any suggested test or
intervention. As we see in the following section, the case law on non-consensual
caesarean sections shows a lamentable tendency on the part of the judiciary to
downplay the pre-eminence of the pregnant woman's right to refuse unwanted
surgical delivery.

3. FORCED CAESAREAN SECTIONS

Medical treatment carried out without the consent of a competent adult
patient amounts to an unlawful touching or battery. Unless a patient is temporarily or permanently incapacitated, they have a right to refuse medical
intervention, even if it would save their life. In the last few years this right
to self-determination has emerged as a guiding principle within medical

---

[89] See further Fitzpatrick, 2001.

law,[90] but in the early 1990s, there were two judicial statements which appeared to suggest that a patient's right to make their own decisions about their medical treatment might be diminished for pregnant women, especially in the later stages of pregnancy. First, in *Re T (Adult: Refusal of Treatment)*,[91] despite Lord Donaldson's conclusion that:

> "the patient's right of choice exists whether the reasons for making that choice are rational, irrational, unknown or even non-existent",[92]

he suggested that there might be one *hypothetical* exception to the principle of patient autonomy:

> "The only possible qualification is a case in which the choice may lead to the death of a viable fetus . . . and, if and when it arises, the court will be faced with a novel problem of considerable legal and ethical complexity".[93]

Second, in *Re S (Adult) (Refusal of Medical Treatment)*,[94] Sir Stephen Brown relied upon Lord Donaldson's caveat in *Re T*, and the American case of *Re AC*,[95] and granted a declaration that a caesarean section could be lawfully performed without the consent of the pregnant woman. In the United States there had indeed been some well publicised cases, most involving women from ethnic minorities,[96] in which caesarean sections had been performed without the pregnant woman's consent.[97] However, Sir Stephen Brown's reliance on the case of

[90] Andrew Grubb, for example, has said that "the golden thread of medical law has become the need to respect a patient's right of self-determination or autonomy" (Grubb, 1999, p. 59). For example, in *Sidaway* v. *Bethlem Royal Hospital* [1985] 1 All ER 643, Lord Scarman said that "the existence of the patient's right to make his own decision, which may be seen as a basic human right, (is) protected by the common law" (at 649). In *Airedale N.H.S. Trust* v. *Bland* [1993] AC 789 there are several references to the primacy of patient self-determination. Lord Mustill said that "If the patient is capable of making a decision on whether to permit treatment, . . . his choice must be obeyed even if on any objective view it is contrary to his best interests" (at 891). Lord Goff similarly found that "it is established that the principle of self-determination requires that respect must be given to the wishes of the patient" (at 891).

[91] [1993] Fam 95.

[92] *Ibid.* at 113.

[93] *Ibid.* at 102.

[94] [1993] Fam 123.

[95] [1990] 573 A 2d 1235.

[96] Gallagher, 1987. While this difference can be partly explained by racial discrimination, it also reflects differences between women's economic circumstances. All the patients subject to non-consensual interventions were being treated in public hospitals. It goes without saying that doctors would be less likely to seek court authorisation for treatment against the wishes of a fee-paying client.

[97] In *Jefferson* v. *Griffin Spalding County Hospital Authority* 247 Ga 86; 274 SE 2d 457 (Ga, 1981), a woman who had been advised that there was a 99% chance of stillbirth unless she consented to a caesarean section refused consent because of her religious beliefs. The court in Georgia granted temporary custody of a 39 week old fetus to the county department giving it authority to make decisions "including consent to the surgical delivery." The court stated that "the intrusion involved into the life of Jessie May Jefferson . . . is outweighed by the duty of the State to protect a living unborn human being from meeting his or her death before being given the opportunity to live" (at 460). In fact the woman did successfully give birth on her own and so the court declaration was never tested.

In *Re Madyun* 114 Daily Wash L Rptr 2233 (1986) (DC Super Ct.) a Muslim woman wanted to walk around during her labour, but her doctors believed that a caesarean was necessary. The court ordered that the caesarean should take place on the basis that "neither parent is a trained

Re AC was bizarre because the judgement of the District of Columbia Court of Appeals had in fact been that a patient's refusal of consent must be inviolable in virtually all cases. In *Re AC*, which incidentally had involved a white, middle class woman, the court decided that the caesarean section should not have been performed on Angela Carder, and that, unless there were "truly extraordinary or compelling reasons", the pregnant woman's wishes should always be determinative.[98]

In addition to its misreading of an American case, the decision in *Re S* also represented an extraordinary exception to the ordinary principles of English medical law. Given that it is not possible to force an individual to act against their wishes to save the life of another person, it would seem anomalous for someone to be forced to submit to unwanted medical intervention in order to preserve a fetus before it achieves legal personhood.[99] Paradoxically, according to the decision in *Re S*, a pregnant woman's responsibilities to her fetus would far exceed those owed by a mother to her children. Even more bizarre, restrictions on the use of organs from cadavers would mean that, on a literal interpretation of *Re S*, a person would have a greater right of veto over unwanted surgical intrusion after their death than would a woman in labour.[100] It seems incredible that the bodily integrity of a corpse should have more legal protection than that of a pregnant woman, nevertheless it is clear that even if an organ transplant would save the life of an identifiable and suffering individual, respect for the dead person's wishes must trump the doctor's duty to act to preserve life.[101]

physician". Janet Gallagher discusses an unreported case in which a court gave the hospital temporary custody of the triplets being carried by a Nigerian woman in Chicago. She refused to consent to a caesarean section in part because she and her husband intended to return to an area of Africa in which caesarean delivery might not be possible for any future pregnancies. Neither she nor her husband had been told of the court order until she went into labour. When they both resisted, her husband was removed from the hospital, and she was placed in leather wrist and ankle cuffs attached to the 4 corners of a bed. Continuing to resist, she bit through her intravenous tubing. (Gallagher, 1995, p. 346; Ikemoto, 1992, p. 1243).

There have also been cases authorising other sorts of medical treatment to be carried out against the wishes of the pregnant woman, for example in *Raleigh-Fitkin Paul Memorial Hospital* v. *Anderson* [1964] 201 A 2d 537 (NJ), a compulsory blood transfusion was authorised upon a pregnant woman who had refused such treatment on religious grounds.

[98] It is unlikely that S's situation could have been distinguished from Angela Carder's as "truly extraordinary or compelling" since Angela Carder's position was desperately serious. She was in the late stages of cancer and died 2 days after the caesarean section, the child died within two hours of the operation. Her death certificate listed the caesarean section as a factor which contributed to her death. In the George Washington University Medical Center's settlement with Angela Carder's parents, the hospital administrator Christin St Andre stated that "we strongly believe that difficult medical decisions should be made within the doctor/patient relationship and not by the courts" (quoted in Gallagher, 1995, p. 360). Angela Carder's case was subsequently dramatised on *LA Law*, but in the TV version the baby survived (Pollitt, 1995, p. 170).

[99] Thomson, 1971.

[100] The Human Tissue Act 1961 s.1(1).

[101] It is clear, for example, that if a mother were to die suddenly having previously expressed an objection to her organs being used for transplantation, then even if removal of an organ would save the life of her dying child, such an operation would be unlawful. If respect for corpses can trump the doctor's impulse to act to save a child's life, it seems absurd for the interests of an entity lacking legal personality to take priority over the bodily integrity of a pregnant woman.

Unsurprisingly,[102] Sir Stephen Brown's decision in *Re S* has been widely criticised,[103] and the case is now assumed to have been wrongly decided. So, for example, guidelines issued by the Royal College of Obstetricians and Gynaecologists the following year instructed medical staff that:

> "to the extent the declaration in *Re S* purports to be in the mother's vital interest, this must surely be wrong. . . It is inappropriate, and unlikely to be helpful or necessary, to invoke judicial intervention to overrule an informed and competent woman's refusal of a proposed medical treatment, even though her refusal might place her life and that of her fetus at risk".[104]

There has also been judicial criticism of *Re S*. In *Re MB (An Adult: Medical Treatment)*,[105] an injection necessary to carry out a caesarean section was authorised by the Court of Appeal on the grounds of MB's temporary incapacity. Nevertheless, Butler-Sloss LJ described the judgement in *Re S* as "a decision the correctness of which we must now call in doubt",[106] and stated unequivocally that:

> "a competent woman, who has the capacity to decide, may, for religious reasons, other reasons, for rational or irrational reasons or for no reason at all, choose not to have medical intervention, even though the consequence may be the death or serious handicap of the child she bears or her own death".[107]

A year later, in *St. George's Healthcare NHS Trust* v. *S*[108] the Court of Appeal again expressed a clear and unambiguous commitment to a pregnant woman's right of self-determination, holding that a caesarean section should not be performed on a competent adult patient without her consent. Judge LJ was adamant that:

---

[102] Such criticism was apparently anticipated by Lord Donaldson who wrote to Sir Stephen Brown after the judgement saying "there will be all sorts of academic problems, but I agree with you" (Brown, 1994).

[103] Jane Mair refers to Sir Stephen Brown's "incredible lack or reasoned and considered opinion. She suggests that Sir Stephen Brown "was caught up in the emergency atmosphere of the operating theatre", and that he "is almost as dismissive of the law as he is of the pregnant woman" (Mair, 1996, p. 84). Katherine de Gama reflects that "the only comfort in this case is that its reasoning is so fatally flawed, it could not survive the scrutiny of the House of Lords" (de Gama, 1993, p. 122).

[104] RCOG, 1994, paras 3.8.7 and 5.12. And in the 1996 supplement, at para. 4.3 "if a patient has an advance directive which specifies refusal of treatment during pregnancy, this should be honoured even at the expense of the fetus" (RCOG, 1996).

[105] [1997] 2 FLR 426.

[106] *Ibid.* at 440.

[107] *Ibid.* at 436.

[108] [1998] 3 WLR 936. A caesarean section had been performed upon a woman in her 36th week of pregnancy without her consent, leading to birth of a healthy baby. She was diagnosed with pre-eclampsia and advised that her life and that of her fetus required urgent medical intervention. She refused to go to hospital. In addition to believing pregnancy to be a natural process, she was also depressed, and her doctors thought that she might be suffering from a mental disorder. A social worker applied for the woman to be sectioned so that she could be assessed at a mental hospital. From Springfield mental hospital, she was transferred to St. George's at which point the hospital applied to the High Court for an order authorising a caesarean section to be performed without consent. The Court of Appeal subsequently decided that the caesarean section had been unlawful and amounted to trespass (at 967).

"pregnancy . . . does not diminish (a woman's) entitlement to decide whether or not to undergo medical treatment. . . Her right is not reduced or diminished merely because her decision to exercise it may appear morally repugnant".[109]

Following the decision in *St. George's* it would be extremely difficult to justify forcing a competent adult woman to undergo a caesarean section without her consent.[110] And a recent Health Service Circular confirms that:

"If a patient is competent and refuses consent to the treatment, an application to the High Court for a declaration would be pointless".[111]

The Health Service Circular is notable for the rigorousness of its defence of a pregnant woman's right to make a decision that will lead to the death or serious handicap of her fetus, even if her choice:

"is so outrageous in its defiance of logic or of accepted moral standards that no sensible person who had applied his mind to the question to be decided could have arrived at it".[112]

Yet despite this broad consensus that a pregnant woman retains the right to refuse unwanted medical treatment, the practical impact of the Court of Appeal's decisions in *Re MD* and *St George's*, and the RCOG and Department of Health guidelines may be undermined in three ways. First, there may be some women who do not understand that they are entitled to refuse to consent to an emergency caesarean.[113] Simply respecting patients' clearly articulated preferences does not ensure informed decision-making, particularly among vulnerable patient groups. Second, deference to medical opinion and reverence for the benefits of technology in practice make it difficult for women to refuse surgical intervention during labour. As I explain in more detail below, advice about optimum behaviour during pregnancy may exert a subtle but powerful influence over a pregnant woman's choices.[114] The prevailing assumption tends to be that every right-minded pregnant woman will eagerly comply with her doctor's requests for cooperation. So, for example, the House of Lords has described a woman who refused an examination and X-ray during pregnancy as a "difficult, nervous and

---

[109] *Supra* at 957.
[110] Among health care professionals there now appears to be a consensus that, as a British Medical Authority spokesman has explained, "the fact that a woman has moral obligations to her fetus does not mean the health professionals or the courts can compel her to fulfil them" (quoted in Dyer, 1998, p. 1477).
[111] Department of Health 1999a, p. 8.
[112] Department of Health 1999a, p. 6.
[113] Donohoe, 1996, p. 230.
[114] Alexander McCall Smith has argued that "even if it is agreed that there is no justification for the use of coercion or compulsion to ensure compliance with medical objectives, there may still be strong pressures on a woman to submit to procedures which are directed towards the benefit of the fetus. These pressures may be coercive in all but name; the creation of a strong social expectation that a particular course of action be followed may be subtly coercive. For this reason it may prove difficult for women to resist intrusive procedures if these are presented as being beneficial for the fetus" (McCall Smith, 1995, p. 170).

at times aggressive patient",[115] with an "obdurate attitude".[116] Third, it remains possible for surgery to be carried out without consent if the woman is temporarily or permanently incapable of making decisions about her medical treatment. If somebody lacks capacity, then the doctor has a duty to act in the patient's best interests. It is obvious that if the result of a finding of incapacity can be that treatment is carried out against their wishes, it becomes crucial to have clear, prospective guidance in order to determine (a) when a patient will be judged incapable of making her own decision,[117] and (b) the circumstances in which a caesarean section will be deemed to be in her best interests.

A caesarean section that would save an incompetent pregnant woman's life could undoubtedly be treatment that is in her best interests. Where it is *fetal* life that may be at risk if a caesarean is not performed, it should be much harder to classify the operation as one that is in the best interests of the pregnant patient. But, as we saw in chapter two when we considered court-ordered sterilisation, in recent years there has been a marked trend towards a rather expansive interpretation of a patient's best interests, which are undoubtedly not now confined to their clinical needs.[118] As we see below, a similarly elastic interpretation of the "best interests" test has been invoked in order to justify nonconsensual caesarean sections.

In addition, the common law presumption of competence[119] appears at times to slide into a presumption of incompetence during labour.[120] This is a particular danger given that the application for a court order to authorise a non-consensual caesarean is usually prompted by a "life and death" emergency situation. As a result the hearings are often *ex parte*, which means that the only evidence before

---

[115] *Whitehouse* v. *Jordan* [1981] 1 WLR 246, per Lord Wilberforce at 250.

[116] *Ibid.* per Lord Edmund-Davies at 275.

[117] For example, minor children who are "Gillick" competent can consent to medical treatment. And minor children of 16 and 17 are able to give effective consent as a result of section 8 of the Family Law Reform Act 1969. It is not, however, clear whether a child is able to refuse a caesarean section. In *Wolverhampton MBC* v. *DB (A Minor)* [1997] 1 FLR 767, B was 17 years old, pregnant and suffered from a cocaine/crack addiction. She also had a phobia about needles, doctors and medical treatment. An *ex parte* order authorising such treatment as was necessary in the opinion of her doctor, with the use of reasonable force if needed, was confirmed by Cazalet J at the full *inter partes* hearing. B's daughter had been born by caesarean section after B accepted treatment. Cazalet J said that although B had a right to refuse treatment because she was over 16 years, that right could be overridden by the court or a person with parental responsibility for her. Cazalet J also suggested that B could not comprehend and retain information about her treatment, or believe it, or make a reasoned choice. It is not clear whether his judgement that B's refusal could be overridden, with force if necessary, was based upon B's incompetence or her minority.

[118] See for example *Re Y* [1996] 4 Med LR 204 in which the court decided that donating bone marrow tissue to her sister would promote the best interests of a profoundly mentally handicapped woman because it was likely to improve her relationships with her mother and sister.

[119] *Re C (Refusal of Treatment)* [1994] 1 FLR 31; Re MB *supra*. If enacted the Government's proposals in *Making Decisions* (Lord Chancellor's Department, 1999) would create a statutory presumption of competence.

[120] Alexander McCall Smith suggests that "the withholding of consent may be portrayed as unreasonable conduct and if this is so the reality of the woman's consent may be questionable. The principle of autonomy may therefore continue to be protected by the law but may be considerably undermined in practice" (McCall Smith, 1995, p. 170).

the judges is from the doctors whose eagerness to carry out the operation has brought them before the court, and a judgement must usually be reached within hours if not minutes.[121] George Annas has therefore suggested that:

> "without time to analyze the issues, without representation for the pregnant woman, without briefing or thoughtful reflection on the situation, in almost total ignorance of the relevant law, and in an unfamiliar setting faced by a relatively calm physician and a woman who can easily be labeled 'hysterical', the judge will almost always order whatever the physician advises".[122]

Given that a protracted and painful labour will often precede the application, the pregnant woman's competence can easily be called into question, and in a number of cases the stress of childbirth has been invoked in order to throw doubt upon the pregnant woman's decision-making capacity. In *Re MB*, for example, it was suggested that temporary factors "including panic brought on by fear" could completely erode a previously competent woman's decision-making capacity. In *Norfolk and Norwich NHS Trust v. W*,[123] although W did not suffer from a mental disorder, it was held that the pain and emotional stress of labour prevented her from weighing the information in the balance and arriving at a choice.[124] This hearing was interrupted so that Johnson J could hear a similar application in respect of another patient[125] in which, after a two-minute *ex parte* hearing, despite having no psychiatric evidence as to her capacity, Johnson J overruled her obstetrician's finding of competence.[126] So in *Rochdale NHS*

---

[121] In *Re MB* , for example, the Court of Appeal heard the case and made its judgement between eleven o'clock at night and one o'clock in the morning (Grace, 1999, p. 60). In *Re S*, court officials were alerted to the matter at 1.30pm, the hearing began at 2pm and the declaration was made at 2.18pm. In *St George's Healthcare NHS Trust v. S* the application was made without informing the pregnant woman and her solicitor.

Although unless the situation is an emergency, there should be a full *inter partes* hearing, with the woman represented by a guardian *ad litem* or by counsel or solicitor, before the court will authorise a caesarean section to be performed on an incapable woman (HSC 1999/031). The guidelines suggest that a declaration granted *ex parte* is not binding upon the patient and so is of no assistance to the doctors. However, the guidelines also suggest that "where delay may itself cause serious damage to the patient's health or put her life at risk then formulaic compliance with these guidelines would be inappropriate."

[122] Annas, 1987, p. 1213. The procedural shortcomings of cases involving non-consensual caesarean sections were also criticised by Butler Sloss LJ in *Re MB*.

[123] [1996] 2 FLR 613.

[124] W was not suffering from any mental disorder, although she did have a history of psychiatric treatment and was denying that she was pregnant. Mr Justice Johnson stated that "although she was not suffering from a mental disorder within the meaning of the statute, she lacked the mental competence to make a decision about the treatment that was proposed because she was incapable of weighing up the considerations that were involved. She was called upon to make that decision at a time of acute emotional stress and physical pain in the ordinary course of labour made even more difficult for her because of her own particular mental history." A caesarean section was ordered.

[125] *Rochdale Healthcare NHS Trust v. C* [1997] 1 FCR 274.

[126] C had said that she "would rather die" than repeat her previous experience of a caesarean section performed under epidural anaesthetic. C's obstetrician had informed the court that C's mental capacity was not in question, and that she appeared to him to be fully competent. Nonetheless, Johnson J found that she was incompetent because she "was in the throes of labour with all that is involved in terms of pain and emotional stress". As a result, he argued, her apparent acceptance of the inevitability of her own death indicated that she was not capable of giving full consideration to the options available: "a patient who could, in those circumstances, speak in terms which seemed

Trust v. *C,* although the only health care professional who had been consulted said that C's competence was not in question and that she was in fact fully competent, Johnson J again held that the pain and emotional stress of labour meant that she was not capable of weighing up the information she had been given.

As well as the common law power to treat incapacitated patients without consent if the treatment is in their best interests, under the Mental Health Act 1983 doctors do not need a patient's consent in order to give *routine* treatment for her mental disorder.[127] In *Tameside & Glossop Acute Services Unit* v. *CH,*[128] CH's gynaecologist feared that placental deficiency might necessitate a caesarean delivery, and that CH's mental instability might lead her to withdraw her consent. The Official Solicitor believed that CH was "clearly aware of the problems suffered by the foetus", and the possible need for intervention.[129] Nevertheless, despite a caesarean section not being immediately necessary and CH's apparent willingness to undergo surgical delivery, a caesarean section was authorised *just in case* it become necessary *and* CH subsequently withdrew her consent.

Wall J considered that, at common law, CH's incapacity entitled the doctor's to treat her in her best interests, and he also found that giving birth to a live baby would promote CH's welfare. He was, however, less certain that the common law entitled him authorise the use of force to ensure treatment.[130] Since the Mental Health Act's Code of Practice permits the use of restraint in order to secure compliance with medical treatment, Wall J characterised the caesarean section, somewhat spuriously, as routine[131] treatment for CH's paranoid schizophrenia,[132] and used section 63 of the Mental Health Act to authorise the performance of a caesarean section, with force if necessary.

to accept the inevitability of her own death, was not a patient who was able properly to weigh up the considerations that arose so as to make any valid decision, about anything of even the most trivial kind, surely still less one which involved her own life".

[127] S. 63 of the Mental Health Act 1983. According to the transcripts of the Parliamentary debates in Hansard, this was intended to cover "routine . . . treatment . . . and general nursing and other care" Hansard (22.3.82) vol 82 column 693. Lord Elton said that it applied to "perfectly routine, sensible treatment" (Hansard (22.3.82) vol. 82 column 1064–5.

[128] [1996] 1 FLR 762.

[129] See further Thomson, 1998, p. 213.

[130] Although in *Rochdale Healthcare NHS Trust* v. *C* [1997] 1 FCR 274, Johnson J had said that he believed that the court has the power at common law to authorise the use of reasonable force in order to carry out a caesarean section.

[131] Under the Mental Health Act 1983, certain "borderline" or "experimental" treatments for mental disorders are subject to rigorous safeguards under ss. 57 and 58, so a second medical opinion and the patient's consent may be necessary. Ceri Widdett and Michael Thomson question the characterisation of a caesarean section as "routine" treatment for a mental disorder, and instead suggest that it raises sufficiently complex ethical issues that the protection of ss. 57 and 58 may be appropriate (Widdett and Thomson, 1997, p. 82).

[132] It was agreed that the death of the baby *in utero* would not cause any physical harm to the mother, but the psychiatrist believed that it would have a "profound deleterious effect" on her mental condition. His argument was that she would blame medical staff for the child's death and that this would undermine her trust in her care workers, thus complicating her treatment for schizophrenia. CH's obstetrician did not go so far as to suggest that a stillbirth would be detrimental to CHs mental health he did say that it would not "benefit her schizophrenia". It could, of course, be argued that carrying out invasive surgery without her consent might have a similar impact upon her ability to trust health care workers.

There are three related assumptions underlying these decisions. First, it tends to be assumed that women have a natural or biological impulse towards maternal self-sacrifice. During labour a "normal" woman is expected to be prepared to do anything to ensure that she gives birth to a live baby. If a woman refuses an intervention that may be necessary to save her fetus's life, her "unnaturally selfish" decision appears to raise the inference that she is not in fact normal, but rather may, perhaps because of the pain and stress of childbirth, be suffering from some temporary incapacity. Even in his apparently robust judgement in *St. George's Healthcare NHS Trust* v. *S*,[133] Judge LJ said of S's persistent failure to follow medical advice, "no normal mother-to-be could think like that".[134]

Second, judges tend to accept the doctors' assessment of incapacity as an uncontestable question of fact and assume that doctors are also best placed to determine where the patient's best interests lie. The tendency to defer to medical expertise is especially pronounced when an application is prompted by an emergency, leading John Grace to suggest that currently there is an:

"entirely artificial situation . . . of judges having to decide in an emergency situation, with very little evidence on which to go, whether or not the woman is competent . . . the issue of competence used to be and still may be, in an emergency, decided on the basis of whether or not the obstetrician thought the woman was competent".[135]

It is clear that the practical impact of doctors' control over the determination of both incapacity and the patient's best interests is to strengthen the medical profession's already considerable power over the management of childbirth. When we take into account the widespread tendency to regard the fetus as a separate patient in its own right, it is clear that there will be some doctors who will seek to exercise this power in order to save fetal life.[136] Third, given the longevity of the association between women's madness or hysteria and the malfunctioning of their reproductive organs,[137] the suggestion that giving birth to a live baby may itself be treatment for a mental disorder clearly has considerable symbolic and cultural resonance.[138]

Thus far, our discussion has focused upon medical treatment during pregnancy and birth. As we have seen, the tendency to defer to medical authority is

[133] [1998] 3 WLR 936.

[134] *Ibid.* at 957.

[135] Grace, 1999, p. 62.

[136] For example, the report of the US National Instiute of Child Health and Human Development Conference on Caesarean childbirth suggested that "in the case of cesarean (*sic*) delivery there are almost always two patients involved, only one of which (the mother) may be able to speak for herself. . . . Usually, but not necessarily, the mother will be assumed (to have) the fetus' best interest at heart." In commenting upon the fact that "the pregnant woman may refuse a blood transfusion or a caesarean section even if she is placing the unborn child at risk", Alec Samuels suggests that "this is not a civilised situation" (Samuels, 1999, p. 17).

[137] Widdett and Thomson, 1997, p. 87; Usher, 1991.

[138] According to Plato "the womb is an animal which longs to generate children. When it remains barren too long after puberty, it is distressed and sorely disturbed, and straying about in the body and cutting off the passages of the breath, it impedes respiration and brings the sufferer into the extremist anguish and provokes all manner of diseases besides" (*Timaeus*, quoted in McLean, 1999, p. 27).

prevalent among both patients and the judiciary. Of course, fetal health can be affected by factors other than the provision of prenatal medical care and obstetric intervention, and the remainder of this chapter concentrates upon the regulation of some of these other sources of fetal harm. In the following section, we consider the law's role in ascribing responsibility for fetal injury.

4. CONTROLLING PREGNANCY

(a) Third parties

It is difficult to use the law to prevent prenatal injury because until it is born, a fetus is not a legal person.[139] Although it is unquestionably foreseeable that a child's health can be affected by injuries inflicted before birth, an action in tort is only possible if a duty of care was owed to the injured *person* at the time when the damage was sustained. So, for example, the thalidomide victims were advised to accept a settlement rather than pursue Distillers through the courts because their counsel doubted their ability to establish that they had been owed a duty of care when their injuries were caused.

There is an obvious opportunity for injustice if a child is born severely disabled as a result of negligently caused harm sustained before he or she achieved legal personhood. As Lamont J remarked in *Montreal Tramways* v. *Leveille*:[140]

"If a child after birth has no right of action for prenatal injuries, we have a wrong inflicted for which there is no remedy. . . . If a right of action be denied to the child it will be compelled, without any fault on its part, to go through life carrying the seal of another's fault and bearing a very heavy burden of infirmity and inconvenience without any compensation therefor".[141]

The common law solution has been to find that there is a *potential* relationship between the wrongdoer and the fetus that "crystallises" at birth, at which point the defendant becomes liable to the child for injuries sustained *in utero*.[142] In

---

[139] Peter Glazebrook has said "it is astonishing what a difference being born makes in English law" (Glazebrook, 1993, p. 20). Although it is surely not at all surprising that the law requires some definite and clear moment at which one achieves legal personhood. In the same way as a legal definition of death (which is usually a process rather than a moment) is necessary in order to determine when someone ceases to be a legal person, similarly it would be difficult if attaining legal personality consisted in a gradual accretion of personhood. Being born represents a definite and clear time at which the child has an existence separate from its mother, and thus it seems logical for birth also to mark the point at which it has a separate legal existence.

[140] [1933] 4 DLR 337.

[141] *Ibid.* at 345.

[142] In *Burton* v. *Islington H.A. De Martell* v. *Merton & Sutton HA* [1993] QB 204 Phillips J said that "in law and in logic, no damage can have been caused to the plaintiff before the plaintiff existed. The damage was suffered by the plaintiff at the moment that, in law, the plaintiff achieved personality and inherited the damaged body for which the defendants were responsible" (at 214). In *Hamilton* v. *Fife Health Board* [1993] 4 Med LR 201, it was suggested that this "potential relationship" was not a fiction, but an application of the *Donoghue* v. *Stevenson* neighbour principle. The

addition, public sympathy for the thalidomide victims led to the creation of a statutory remedy for children born after the 22 July 1976. The Congenital Disabilities (Civil Liability) Act 1976 provides that a child has a cause of action if he is born alive with a disease or abnormality caused by a negligent act that would be actionable by his mother or father.[143] By making the child's action contingent upon a duty owed to their parent, the statute makes the defendant's knowledge, or lack of knowledge of the pregnancy irrelevant. But it also means that there can be no liability to a disabled child unless the defendant owed their parent an independent duty of care. Thus conduct that is *only* likely to have an adverse effect upon the fetus, such as the misreading of fetal monitoring equipment, will not give rise to a duty under the statute. In addition, if her parent had voluntarily assumed the risk of injury, the child will receive no damages;[144] and if her parent was contributorily negligent, the child's damages may be reduced in proportion to the extent of her parent's responsibility.[145]

It is also possible for criminal liability to attach to a third party whose conduct during a pregnancy subsequently causes the resulting child's injury or death. Since homicide is the killing of another human being, a fetus cannot be a

---

child born with injuries sustained *in utero* is in the class of people that a reasonable man would foresee as being closely and directly affected by his actions that he should have had within his contemplation.

In the Australian case of *Watt* v. *Rama* [1972] VR 353, the Supreme Court of Victoria said that "unless a person is injured, there is no tort of negligence. But if a person is injured then the ultimate inquiry to be made is whether or not the injury was a reasonable and probable consequence of the act of carelessness" (at 373). In a case in which a child was born injured as a result of a road traffic accident, it was clearly "reasonably foreseeable that such act or omission might cause injury to a pregnant woman in the car with which his car collided and might cause the child to be born in an injured condition" (at 359). There was then "a potential relationship capable of imposing a duty on the defendant in relation to the child if and when born" (at 360). In *Duval* v. *Sequin* (1972) 26 DLR (3d) 418, a case in which a child was born injured after her mother had been involved in a road accident, Fraser J in the High Court of Ontario said that "procreation is normal and necessary for the preservation of the race. If a driver drives on a highway without due care for other users it is foreseeable that some of the other users of the highway will be pregnant women and a child *en ventre sa mère* may be injured. Such a child therefore falls well within the area of potential danger which the driver is required to foresee and take reasonable care to avoid" (at 433).

143 "s. 1(1) If a child is born disabled as a result of such an occurrence before its birth as is mentioned in subsection (2) below, and a person (other than the child's own mother) is under this section answerable to the child in respect of the occurrence, the child's disabilities are to be regarded as damage resulting from the wrongful act of that person and actionable accordingly at the suit of the child.

(2) An occurrence to which this section applies is one which—
(a) affected either parent of the child in his or her ability to have a normal, healthy child; or
(b) affected the mother during her pregnancy, or affected her or the child in the course of its birth, so that the child is born with disabilities which would not otherwise have been present

(3) . . . a person . . . is answerable to the child if he was liable in tort to the parent or would, if sued in due time have been so."

144 Congenital Disabilities (Civil Liability) Act 1976 s 1(6).
145 *Ibid.* s.1(7).

victim of homicide while still *in utero*.[146] Similarly, threatening to kill a fetus is not equivalent to a threat to kill a person.[147] Nevertheless, should the fetus be born alive and subsequently die as a result of injuries sustained *in utero*, a charge of unlawful homicide may be possible. In *Attorney General's Reference (No. 3 of 1994)*[148] the House of Lords declined to "overstrain the idea of transferred malice" in order to find the requisite intention for murder where the injuries from which the victim died were caused before she acquired legal personality.[149] Somewhat arbitrarily,[150] however, the Lords then resurrected the legal fiction of transferred malice in order to uphold an alternative charge of manslaughter.

Various other legal provisions go some way towards protecting the future interests of the fetus. For example, where a will contains a gift to a class of children alive at a particular date, a fetus will be treated as though it had been living at that date in order to benefit from the gift.[151] Where a man dies before his child is born, the child will be treated as a dependant for the purposes of the Fatal Accidents Act 1976.[152] Prenatal behaviour might also be relevant in care proceedings: in deciding whether a child is at risk of significant harm, a parent's conduct during the pregnancy may be taken into account.[153]

(b) "Maternal" Immunity?

The law recognises that there is a difference between the pragmatic manipulation of legal concepts such as the tortious duty of care in order to attach liability to a third party whose unreasonable conduct has caused foreseeable injuries to a child, and turning the same reasoning upon the behaviour of pregnant women. There are three principal reasons why the law treats pregnant women

---

[146] In contrast in California, the definition of murder specifically includes the unlawful killing of a fetus. Subsequent case law has interpreted this to mean the killing of a *viable* fetus. In Minnesota, specific offences of murder or manslaughter of an "unborn child" have been created, and "unborn child" has been defined as any offspring that has been "conceived but not yet born". In *State* v. *Merrill* 450 NW 2d 318 (Minn, 1990), the statute was held to cover an embryo estimated to be 27 or 28 days old (see further, Seymour, 2000, pp. 141–2).

[147] *R.* v. *Tait* [1990] 1 QB 290.

[148] [1998] AC 245. Lord Mustill quoted Sir Edward Coke's definition of murder: the killing of "a reasonable creature, in rerum natura." And in the context of prenatal injury Coke said "if a woman be quick with childe, and by a potion or otherwise killeth it in her wombe; or if a man beat her, whereby the childe dieth in her body, and she is delivered of a dead childe; this is a great misprision and no murder." Lord Mustill found that "its correctness as a general principle . . . has never been controverted" (at 254).

[149] *Ibid.* per Lord Mustill at 262.

[150] Lacey and Wells, 1998, p. 547.

[151] *Re Wilmer's Trusts* [1903] 2 Ch 41.

[152] *The George and Richard* (1871) LR 3 A and E 466.

[153] For example in *Re D (A Minor)* [1987] AC 317, the mother and father were both drug addicts, and the mother continued to take drugs during her pregnancy. The child was born suffering from withdrawal symptoms, and the Local Authority started child protection proceedings. In determining whether the child's health was at risk, Lord Goff said "I can see no reason why the magistrates should not be entitled to have regard to events which occurred before the child was born" (at 350).

who may injure a fetus differently from third parties. First, the special practical implications of "maternal" liability are taken into account. While the fetus is inside the woman's body, protecting it from harm caused by the pregnant woman would be possible only if the woman's freedom to make decisions about her body were suspended for the duration of her pregnancy. In addition, because almost everything the pregnant woman chooses to do or not do *might* have an impact upon her fetus, in order to minimise fetal harm pregnant women would have to be under almost continual surveillance. Thus, any gains to fetal health would be acquired at the expense of the pregnant woman's autonomy and bodily integrity. As a result, the English courts have acknowledged that:

> "to create conflict between the existing legal interests of the mother (*sic*) and those of the unborn child (*sic*) . . . is most undesirable. . . .There would be insuperable difficulties if one sought to enforce any order in respect of an unborn child against its mother, if that mother failed to comply with the order. I cannot contemplate the court ordering that this should be done by force, nor indeed is it possible to consider with any equanimity that the court should seek to enforce an order by committal".[154]

After birth, there continue to be compelling practical reasons for exempting mothers from liability for prenatal injury. Not only is a woman's capacity to provide effective care for her disabled baby unlikely to be enhanced by an obligation to pay compensation to her, but also the mother would, in effect, be compensating *herself* for the costs of supporting her child. Thus, statute has specifically excluded the possibility of a child bringing an action against their mother for injuries sustained *in utero*, unless those injuries were caused by their mother's negligent driving, when the presence of compulsory insurance means that liability will benefit both the mother and her disabled child.[155]

Second, a further practical difficulty might lie in determining what standard of care the law would require of a pregnant woman. In applying, somewhat ironically, the "reasonable man" test to the behaviour of the pregnant woman, the judiciary would have a flexible tool with which to construct their own subjective evaluation of what acceptable prenatal behaviour consists in. The reasonable

---

[154] *In Re F (in utero)* [1988] Fam 122, per May LJ at 138. *In Re F* involved a pregnant woman who was mentally disturbed and led a nomadic existence. The local authority were concerned that she was unlikely to take care of herself or seek medical attention, and they sought leave to apply to make the fetus a ward of court. The Court of Appeal said that a fetus has no existence independent of its mother (*sic*) and the wardship jurisdiction could not be used to control the actions of the pregnant woman.

Similar decisions have been reached in other countries. For example in the Canadian case of *Re A (in utero)* (1990) 72 DLR (4th) 722, the judge reluctantly concluded that he could not force a pregnant woman who was living in filthy conditions with a very violent man and suffering from severe toxaemia to accept antenatal care. He said "here the child is actually inside of the mother. It is, therefore, impossible in this case to take steps to protect the child without ultimately forcing the mother, under restraint if necessary, to undergo medical treatment and other processes, against her will" (at 731).

[155] Congenital Disabilities (Civil Liability) Act 1976, s. 2: "A woman driving a motor vehicle when she knows (or ought reasonably to know) herself to be pregnant is to be regarded as being under the same duty to take care for the safety of her unborn child as the law imposes on her with respect to the safety of other people".

man is a fictional character which is used to lend apparent objectivity and credibility to a value judgement that is in fact made by the judge. Insofar as the reasonable man is sometimes "an odious and insufferable creature who never makes a mistake",[156] its use in determining the standard of care the law is entitled to expect from the reasonable (pregnant wo)man would present the judiciary with an opportunity to exercise far-reaching control over women's lives.

Third, this distinction between the pregnant woman and third parties has been said to turn upon the unique biological relationship between a pregnant woman and her fetus.[157] Despite, as I explained earlier, this relationship actually being rather commonplace, it is undoubtedly difficult to conceptualise within existing legal classifications. While a woman is pregnant, the law does not identify the fetus as a separate individual, but nor does it treat the fetus as simply a part of the woman's body in the same way as her appendix or her liver. In *Attorney-General's Reference (No. 3 of 1994)*,[158] for example, Lord Mustill:

"reject(ed) the reasoning that since (in the eyes of English law) the foetus does not have all the attributes which make it a 'person' it must be an adjunct of the mother. Eschewing all religious and political debate I would say that the foetus is neither. It is a unique organism".[159]

Their relationship, he said:

"is one of bond not identity. The mother and the foetus were two distinct organisms living symbiotically, not a single organism with two aspects. The mother's leg was part of the mother; the foetus was not".[160]

Yet the insight that the fetus is a unique entity that is not a person, but is also "not nothing" does not help us to determine its moral or legal status.[161] Insofar as the relationship between a pregnant woman and the fetus she carries is quite unlike any other, it is not easily accommodated by a legal system that relies upon the doctrine of precedent and takes for granted the possibility of reasoning by analogy. Hence, although comparisons between the fetus and any other entity are probably futile,[162] they are simultaneously the primary judicial method of

[156] PS Atiyah, quoted in Conaghan and Mansell, 1999, p. 52.
[157] The Royal College of Obstetricians and Gynaecologists' Guidelines state, at para. 4.1.1 that "The maternal-fetal relationship is unique." And at 4.1.2. "The fetus is totally reliant on the mother so long as it remains *in utero*. The protection of the fetus stands on her performance of her moral obligations, not on any legal right of its own."
[158] [1998] AC 245.
[159] *Ibid.* at 256.
[160] *Ibid.* at 255.
[161] Sheila McLean has argued that the question of what status should be given to the fetus is "incapable of resolution by consensus. People's individual or collective morality will relentlessly point them in different directions from each other" (McLean, 1999, p. 49).
[162] Although in her seminal article "A Defence of Abortion", Judith Jarvis Thomson employs a variety of analogies in order to establish that the decision to have an abortion should belong to the pregnant woman. For example, she said that the pregnant woman and fetus are not simply like "two tenants in a small house which has, by unfortunate mistake, been rented to both, The mother *owns* the house" (Thomson, 1971, p. 53).

deductive reasoning. For example, although maternal immunity for negligently caused prenatal harm may initially seem irreconcilable with third parties' obligations to compensate a child for injuries sustained *in utero*, the pregnant woman's position could never be analogous to that of the third party, and will always be distinguishable on the facts. Similarly, as we see later, the uniqueness of pregnancy has posed particular difficulties in sex discrimination cases which depend upon the existence of a relevant male comparator.

Thus, it should be evident that the concept of legal personality has, in the UK, been applied flexibly and instrumentally to cases involving fetal harm. Recognition of the fetus in order to give effect to the presumed desire of a man who dies before his child is born to nevertheless provide for that child does not necessarily depend upon ascribing a particular *moral* value to fetal life. Similarly allowing a child to recover damages for harm sustained as a result of injuries inflicted upon their mother during pregnancy may be consistent with protecting the interests of the pregnant woman herself. The "road traffic" exception to maternal immunity is a particularly striking example of the law's consequentialist approach.[163]

In deciding the legal priority to be given to fetal interests, both biological "facts" about fetal development and moral judgements about the status of the fetus seem to be much less important than normative decisions about the practical consequences of recognising different sorts of obligations. There are clear parallels with the rules governing embryo research that we consider in the following chapter. Rather than engage in an inevitably futile quest to finally resolve the question of an embryo's moral status, the law has declined to make any moral judgement other than the inherently vague maxim that the embryo is "not nothing".

Similarly, in relation to the fetus *in utero*, English law seems to be driven by practical expediency rather than moral absolutes. In *Burton* v. *Islington Health Authority*,[164] for example, Dillon LJ specifically endorsed the context-specific maxim "that an unborn child (*sic*) shall be deemed to be born whenever its interests require it".[165] So where the interests of both the pregnant woman and the fetus would be served by recognising a particular obligation, the courts seem willing to admit the existence of the relevant duty.[166] Similarly, the law's reluctance to recognise maternal liability for prenatal injuries derives in part from the recognition that fear of legal sanctions might deter women from seeking prenatal care, and would therefore be unlikely to improve health outcomes. This

---

[163] See further the Canadian case of *Dobson* v. *Dobson* [1999] 2 SCR 753, in which the Supreme Court of Canada recognised the possible advantages in allowing a child to sue its mother for injuries caused when driving but considered that the common law could not achieve this end without opening up the possibility that a child might have an action against its mother in other circumstances, a consequence that the court was not prepared to countenance.

[164] [1993] QB 204.

[165] *Ibid*. at 226.

[166] Similarly Art. 65 of the United Nations Covenant on Civil and Political Rights prohibits the execution of pregnant women, even where the sentence of death is lawful.

sort of flexible, result-oriented reasoning reveals a softening of conventional tort law principles according to which cases should be decided following the application of abstract rules. In recent years, the judiciary have shown an increased willingness to acknowledge that it is undesirable, and perhaps even impossible, to determine liability without considering its broader implications. In deciding whether a defendant owes the claimant a duty of care, a court will often consider whether it would be just and reasonable for this defendant to bear responsibility for this damage in these circumstances.[167] Central to this determination of the justice or reasonableness of recognising a particular duty of care is a consideration of the likely practical repercussions of liability. Thus, throughout the tort of negligence, the consequences of recognising a duty of care in a given situation are increasingly relevant to judicial determination of whether a duty exists.[168] It may simply be a logical extension of this trend towards "backwards" reasoning for the consequences of liability to also determine whether *a person to whom a duty can be owed* exists at the relevant time.

Despite its inherent pragmatism, English law's position on maternal liability for prenatal harm seems comparatively clear: with the exception of road traffic accidents, it is impossible under English law for women to be liable for injuries to their child which were inflicted *in utero*. But given our ability to detect prenatal injury and its causes with ever greater accuracy, it has been suggested that the common law's refusal to recognise that a mother owes a duty of care to her children before they are born might be anachronistic.[169] In the following section, using the United States as our example, we explore how the ascription of legal responsibility for fetal harm to pregnant women has worked in practice.

In the United States the focus in the case law has not tended to be on the consequences of liability in the instant case, but rather on the innate nature and characteristics of the fetus.[170] John Seymour has described attempts in the US to categorise the fetus in order to divine what, if any, legal rights it possesses as a "definitional" approach. In contrast in the UK, and also in Australia and Canada, what Seymour refers to as a "relational" approach has tended to prevail. By adopting a relational approach the law is able to take into account not only the fetus's characteristics, but also the relationships between the pregnant woman, the fetus and any other relevant actor, thus enabling a distinction to be drawn between maternal liability and the obligations of third parties. As we see in the following section, as a result of the US's concern with the status of the

---

[167] See, for example, *Marc Rich* v. *Bishop Rock Marine* [1996] AC 211.

[168] See further *Smith* v. *Eric Bush* [1990] 1 AC 831; *Caparo* v. *Dickman* [1990] 2 AC 605; *Marc Rich* v. *Bishop Rock Marine* [1996] AC 211; *Stovin* v. *Wise* [1996] 3 WLR 388.

[169] In the dissenting judgments in *Winnipeg Child and Family Services (Northwest Area)* v. *G (DF)* [1997] 3 SCR 1210, Major and Sopinka JJ suggested that the rule that no action could accrue before a live birth was an anarchonism based upon the evidential difficulty of discovering whether there had been fetal injury, and that advances in obstetrics which made such evidence clear and accessible removed the justification for pregnant women's immunity. Major J quoted from an 1826 Midwifery textbook in which it was said that "it is nearly impossible to determine the existence of a pregnancy before the end of the sixth month, let alone whether the baby is alive or dead".

[170] Seymour, 2000, pp. 159–64.

fetus, the pragmatic but comparatively certain maternal immunity that has characterised English law is absent and there is instead a confusing line of authorities in which women have *sometimes* been liable for prenatal harm.

(c) "Maternal" Liability?

An 1884 case in the US, *Dietrich* v. *City of Northampton*,[171] established that the fetus is not a separate entity, but rather "was a part of the mother at the time of the injury"[172] and therefore could not be owed a duty of care *in utero*. Sixty years later, this rule was modified to allow recovery for prenatal injuries provided that the fetus was viable when the injury occurred, and was subsequently born alive.[173] At viability, it was held, the fetus could not be said to be a "part" of its mother. In later cases, the viability requirement waned, in part because it was inherently uncertain,[174] and the chief condition of recovery was, as in England, that the child should be born alive. In 1960, in a much-quoted judgement from the New Jersey Supreme Court, this rule was restated as a child's "legal right to begin life with a sound mind and body".[175]

The focus upon the status of the fetus, rather than the consequences of liability, has led to some inconsistency on the question of maternal liability. Some decisions have explicitly endorsed the reasoning found so compelling in English, Canadian[176] and Australian[177] courts, that giving a child a right of action against their mother would represent an unwarranted intrusion into her freedom of action.[178] For example, in *Stallman* v. *Youngquist*,[179] which involved injuries caused by the mother's negligent driving, the Illinois Supreme Court rejected a child's claim against his mother:

> "Holding a third person liable for prenatal injuries furthers the interest of both the mother and subsequently born child and does not interfere with the defendant's right to control his or her life. Holding a mother liable for the unintentional infliction of prenatal injuries subjects to state scrutiny all the decisions a woman must make in

---

[171] 52 Am Rep 242 (1884).
[172] *Ibid.* at 245.
[173] *Bonbrest* v. *Kotz* (1946) 65 F Supp 138 (DDC).
[174] *Smith* v. *Brennan* (1960) 157 A 2d 497.
[175] *Ibid.* per Proctor J at 503.
[176] For example, the majority in *Winnipeg Child and family Services (Northwest Area)* v. *G (DF)* [1997] 3 SCR 1210 decided that allowing a child to have an action for prenatal injury against their mother would represent an unwarranted intrusion into a "woman's right to make choices concerning herself". See also *Re A (in utero)* (1990) 72 DLR (4th) 722.
[177] See further Seymour, 2000.
[178] In *Thornburgh* v. *American College of Obstetricians and Gynaecologists* 476 US 747 (1986), the US Supreme Court invalidated a Pennsylvania Statute which would require post-viability abortions to be carried out in a way that would maximise the chance that the child could be born alive. The Court found that it was impermissible to require a pregnant woman to bear an increased medical risk to save a viable fetus.
[179] 531 NE 2d 355 (Ill 1988).

attempting to carry a pregnancy to term, and infringes her right to privacy and bodily autonomy. Logic does not demand that a pregnant woman be treated in a court of law as a stranger to her developing fetus".[180]

Other cases have found this objection unpersuasive. For example, in deciding that a mother could be liable for damage to her child's teeth caused by her use of a particular antibiotic during pregnancy, the Michigan Court of Appeals found that the mother "would bear the same liability for injurious, negligent conduct as would a third person".[181] Similarly, a mother has been successfully sued by her child for prenatal injuries sustained as a result of her failure to use reasonable care in crossing a road.[182]

In the United States, the use of proscribed drugs during pregnancy has been the trigger for both criminal prosecution,[183] and the court-ordered removal of the baby immediately after birth.[184] It is undoubtedly true that drugs will sometimes harm a developing fetus, although in practice it is difficult to separate the harmful effects of prenatal drug use from the parallel impact of poor nutrition, inadequate prenatal care, sexually transmitted diseases and a chaotic lifestyle.[185] It is also true that a woman's freedom to take illegal drugs during

---

[180]   531 NE 2d 355 (Ill 1988), at 360.

[181]   *Grodin* v. *Grodin* (1980) 301 NW 2d 869, at 870 *per* Cavanagh PJ.

[182]   *Bonte* v. *Bonte* (1992) 16 A 2d 464 (NH).

[183]   Pamela Rae Stewart was the first woman to be charged with criminal liability for actions during pregnancy. She had used illegal drugs, had sexual intercourse against the advice of her doctors, and she had failed to seek medical attention promptly when she suffered from bleeding. Her son was born with severe brain damage and died six weeks later, she was arrested and prosecuted for causing his death. The precise charge was failure to provide medical treatment to a minor. The case against her failed because the court held that the relevant statute did not apply to a fetus. Subsequently a Bill was introduced to extend the child endangerment statute to fetuses. Jacqueline Berrien points out that there was no attempt to censor Pamela Rae Stewart's sexual partner, even though presumably he was equally responsible for the damaging sexual intercourse (Berrien 1990, p. 246). In addition to taking part in the drug-taking and sexual intercourse for which Stewart was charged, her husband had assaulted her but did not face any charges (Pollitt, 1995, p. 182).

In *State ex rel Angela MW* v. *Kruzicki* 541 N.W. 2d 482 (Wis Ct App 1995) a woman who was five months pregnant tested positive for drugs. She had refused voluntary inpatient treatment and the court construed Wisconsin' s child welfare statute to include "fetus" within the statutory definition of "child". A protective custody order was granted which allowed the court to detain the woman without her consent even though the statute did not formally provide for jurisdiction over the mother.

See also *Whitner* v. *State of South Carolina* App. 141 Cal Rptr 912 (1977) in which the charge of endangering a "child's" life through drug-taking during pregnancy was upheld. More commonly, these prosecutions have failed on the grounds that the fetus is not a child, and therefore not covered by child abuse statutes. See for example *State of Ohio* v. *Grey* 584 NE 2d 710 (Ohio, 1992). Some states in the US, including New Jersey [NJ Stat § 30:4C-11(1999)] and Minnesota [Minn Stat § 626.5561 (1998)], now specifically categorise maternal drug use as child abuse or neglect, thereby imposing an obligation upon doctors to report incidents to the state authorities (Seymour, 2000, p. 9; Gallagher, 1995, p. 354).

[184]   Child removal following a positive drug test at birth is increasing, despite the severe shortage of foster homes.

[185]   In the US it is estimated that 8–18% of pregnant women use cocaine and 10–16% of pregnant women use cannabis. 11% of newborns have positive toxicology screens in the United States, meaning that approximately 375,000 American babies are born suffering from prenatal exposure to drugs. Of those babies between 20–45% are born prematurely; 25% suffer from growth retardation and 50% will need special educational services (Appel, 1992).

pregnancy is not a fundamental liberty deserving rigorous legal protection.[186] Nevertheless, using the law to protect fetuses against the women carrying them has, for several reasons, proved to be both illogical and counter-productive.

First, it is generally supposed that the state's interest in protecting fetal health becomes more weighty the closer the fetus is to term, yet ironically the pregnant woman's behaviour is least likely to have a negative impact upon fetal health during the last weeks of pregnancy.[187] If criminal sanctions are only able toprotect the fetus when it least needs protection, they are plainly a manifestly ineffectual tool. Second, attaching liability to pregnant women serves as a powerful deterrent to antenatal attendance. Women, such as drug users, who particularly need medical assistance during their pregnancies thus tend to avoid seeking help for fear of being penalised,[188] or having their children taken away.[189] Third, the detention of pregnant women is extremely unlikely to benefit the developing fetus. It is, for example, notoriously easy to obtain drugs in prisons.[190] Even if women are successfully removed from drug supplies, sudden withdrawal can cause spontaneous abortion.[191] Antenatal care services in prison are rarely adequate, especially given the complications that are common in the pregnancies of drug addicts, and there tend to be higher than average rates of infant death, late miscarriage and still births.[192]

Third, imposing extra penalties upon pregnant women who use illegal drugs is unlikely to deter other women from taking drugs while pregnant. A deterrence theory of punishment assumes that people are able to engage in some sort of cost-benefit calculation before choosing to do something illegal. A pregnant

[186] For example, Bonnie Steinbock has said that "laws that make it a crime for pregnant women to use illegal drugs and hold them criminally responsible for the effects of such drug use on their offspring . . . do not discriminate against pregnant women since no-one is allowed to use these drugs. If no-one has a right to use cocaine, then a statute that imposes additional penalties on pregnant women who use cocaine is not invasive of their privacy" (Steinbock, 1991, p. 55).

[187] Seymour, 2000, p. 235.

[188] For example, Jennifer Johnson, an American woman who was initially convicted for delivering drugs to her minor children through the umbilical cord during and shortly after birth was prosecuted only because she had tried to get treatment. (*Johnson* v. *State* 578 So.2d 419 Ct App FL 5th Dist. (1991), discussed by Steinbock, 1991, p. 56). The Royal College of Obstetricians and Gynaecologists' Guidelines suggest, at 4.5.5 that "the creation of an 'intentional crime of prenatal injury' . . . is unlikely to be of benefit in the management of the pregnancy."

[189] Cynthia Daniels discusses a study which shows that the threat of losing their children was the least effective way in which to motivate drug-using women to seek help, and it was also the most effective way to drive women away from treatment services (Daniels, 1999, p. 95).

[190] In the light of this it is interesting to note *United States* v. *Vaughn* 117 Daily Washington Law Reporter 441 DC Sup Ct (1988). Brenda Vaughn was found guilty of forging cheques. She was seven months pregnant and had tested positive for crack cocaine. Although her offence would normally have attracted a non-custodial penalty, the judge sentenced her to jail until her child was born. On sentencing Vaughn Peter Wolf J said "I'm going to keep her locked up until the baby is born. . . I'll be darned if I'm going to have a baby born that way."

[191] Appel, 1992, p. 133.

[192] This problem is particularly acute in the United States, which is ironic given the repeated efforts to sentence pregnant women who abuse drugs or alcohol to custodial sentences. For example in Santa Rita County Jail, the miscarriage rate was fifty times the national average, and only 21% of pregnancies ended in a live birth. In the California Institution for Women, there were 2292 female prisoners, and no obstetrician or gynaecologist (Barry, 1989, p. 195).

drug addict may possess the agency that is a precondition of effective deterrence only in an extremely weak sense. If neither existing criminal sanctions against possession of illegal drugs, nor the possibility that her baby may be born suffering from the ill-effects of her drug use deters a woman from using drugs while pregnant, it is improbable that the existence of additional penalties for causing prenatal injury will transform her behaviour. Finally, it is clear that reducing poverty levels and improving access to prenatal care would promote infant health much more effectively and cheaply than the prosecution and incarceration of pregnant drug addicts.[193]

Thus it is clear that the principal purpose of penalising pregnant drug addicts is not the promotion of infant health, but rather the *punishment* of women whose behaviour transgresses certain widely shared moral norms. The particular rage directed at the pregnant drug user may derive from certain cultural assumptions about maternal self-sacrifice and women's natural nurturing instincts. As Iris Marion Young has observed, "the mother who harms her child is not merely a criminal; she is a monster".[194] This may also explain why there has not been equivalent interest in bringing actions against American men for behaviour such as drug use or violence against their pregnant partners,[195] even though it undoubtedly has a similarly negative impact upon the future health of their children.[196]

---

[193] Chavkin *et al* suggest that focussing upon the harm caused by irresponsible pregnant women deflects attention away from the lack of resources available for high quality prenatal care. In New York mandatory drug testing was introduced at the same time as Rudolph Giuliani closed fifteen treatment programmes for drug using mothers. Chavkin *et al* argue that "the symbolic function of depicting the mother in need as a vector of harm to her children is to obscure the dwindling resources available to her" (Chavkin *et al*, 1997, p. 755). Again in the American context, Laura Purdy contends that "until we as a society act to make good, inexpensive, convenient, and respectful care a priority, punishing women for lack of prenatal care reeks of hypocrisy. . . A woman may be denied life saving treatment, yet later be subjected to life-threatening risks to attempt to save her fetus. This state of affairs is all the more angering because it is cheaper to furnish good prenatal care than caesareans, jail, neonatal intensive care or lifetime care for damaged babies" (Purdy, 1996, p.100).

Although subsequently overturned by a court, the Governor of California, Pete Wilson, issued regulations prohibiting state employees from providing pregnancy related care to undocumented immigrants (Finkelstein, 2000). It is significant that in the US fetal protection policies which tend to disproportionately penalise the conduct of poor and marginal pregnant women coexist with policies which deny them prenatal care.

Janet Gallagher has stated that "giving fetuses rights and lawyers, while failing to provide accessible prenatal care and drug treatment on demand for the pregnant women who carry them, is mere posturing—a paradigm of societal bad faith" (Gallgher, 1995, p. 361). And Katha Pollitt says that "the focus on maternal behaviour allows the government to appear to be concerned about babies without having to spend any money, change any priorities or challenge any vested interests" (Pollitt, 1995, p. 173).

[194] Young, 1997, p. 77.

[195] Pollitt cites evidence suggesting that one in twelve women is assaulted by her partner during pregnancy (Pollitt, 1995, p. 182).

[196] Paternal smoking leads to an increase risk of cleft lip, cleft palate, hydrocephalus and low birth weight. It has also been implicated in spina bifida. Similarly alcohol use in men has been linked to low birth weight. (Daniels, 1999, p. 87) The children of men who smoke or take illegal drugs have an increased risk of SIDS (cot death) (Blair *et al*, 1996).

Many feminist writers have advocated a less punitive and more therapeutic approach to the "problem" of prenatal drug use.[197] Yet insofar as the tight network of rules and surveillance which characterises addiction therapy is also directed principally towards controlling pregnant women's behaviour, these apparently benign strategies may also subtly reinforce the individualisation of prenatal harm.[198] Drug treatment programmes usually invite addicts to find the reason for their addiction within themselves or their families. Thus the social, emotional and economic impoverishment that often triggers drug dependency remains unresolved.

Again we have a compelling example of the importance of reconfiguring autonomy so that we acknowledge that a person's capacity to exercise meaningful choice over the course of their life may be dependent upon the existence of a network of relationships and opportunities. Just as punishing the pregnant addict will do little to improve infant health, enrolling her in a drug treatment programme may reduce the impact that her drug dependency has on her developing fetus but unless the circumstances which prompted her addiction are ameliorated, the benefit to her child's health is likely to be both temporary and minimal.

Reducing poverty levels would actually have a much more dramatic positive impact upon fetal development than policies designed to control behaviour during pregnancy. In concentrating upon the harm caused by individual women both punitive and therapeutic strategies may obscure society's responsibility for the health and wellbeing of the next generation.[199] In the next section we explore in more detail the quasi-coercive impact of a variety of health promotion strategies. As we see below, preventative health programmes' tendency to overstate individual pregnant women's responsibility for fetal wellbeing has far-reaching implications.

5. HEALTH PROMOTION

British law may be clear in its non-recognition of maternal liability for fetal harm, but this does not mean that pregnant women in the UK are entirely free to adopt a lifestyle that may damage their developing fetus. Over the past twenty years, one notable trend in sociological and philosophical theory has been "to view with suspicion precisely those liberal, humanist, service-providing practices that seem to be an alternative to overly dominative practices".[200] According to

---

[197] See for example Chavkin, 1991.

[198] See further Young, 1997.

[199] For example, drug addicts are often poor, undernourished, homeless, victims of violence and abuse etc.. It is absurd to isolate the pregnant woman's drug use as the sole factor adversely affecting fetal health. Joan Bertin has suggested that "only by sentimentalizing women and by oversimplifying their lives and choices is it possible to relieve society of its responsibility to protect the next generation from the hazards created by the current one, be they toxic work environments or drug addiction. The incentive to maintain the fiction that this is women's work is powerful" (Bertin, 1995, p. 393).

[200] Young, 1997, p. 89.

this line of analysis, "contemporary structures of domination and oppression appear as often in the bureaucracy of the welfare state as in the prison, although not in the same form".[201] In the following sections, we see how various non-coercive provisions designed to promote infant health may operate subtly and effectively to control pregnant women's behaviour. We first consider the impact of health promotion policies in the workplace, and second we examine the proliferation of prenatal health advice.

(a) Employment

The treatment of pregnancy in the workplace has tended to consist in a mixture of protection, discrimination and paternalism. For example, while women's entitlement to maternity leave is undoubtedly a positive benefit, compulsory leave requirements reveal that there may be a fine line between protection and paternalism.[202] Even if few women would want to return to work soon after giving birth, it is not clear why an early return to the workplace should be *prohibited*.

Initially there were considerable difficulties in applying the Sex Discrimination Act 1975 to pregnancy, principally because its definition of discrimination is dependent upon the existence of a similarly positioned male comparator who has been treated more favourably than the woman who claims to have been discriminated against.[203] Obviously a woman who has been dismissed because she is pregnant will be unable to point to a pregnant man who kept his job in similar circumstances. The Employment Appeal Tribunal found a way around this apparent obstacle by comparing pregnant women with men who are temporarily incapacitated through illness.[204] Of course, pregnancy is not an illness, and

[201] Young, 1997, p. 89.
[202] According to Article 8 of Council Directive 92/85/EEC women must be entitled to a period of at least 14 weeks maternity leave, of which 2 weeks must be compulsory, and in the United Kingdom, a 2 week period after the birth is compulsory. Infringement proceedings are pending against Finland and Sweden for failing to provide for any compulsory period of leave. In other EC countries, compulsory leave is common. For example, in Austria, Luxembourg and Greece there is an absolute ban on working for 8 weeks before and 8 weeks after birth. In Luxembourg the compulsory post natal period is extended to 12 weeks if the woman is breastfeeding. Similarly in Belgium women are not allowed to work for one week before the birth and 8 weeks afterwards. In Denmark there is compulsory leave of 2 weeks after birth. In France the woman is not allowed to work for 8 weeks, of which at least 6 weeks must be after the birth. In Germany work is prohibited for 6 weeks before the birth, although exceptions are possible, and work is absolutely prohibited for 8 weeks after birth. In Ireland, 4 weeks leave before the birth and 4 weeks leave after the birth are compulsory. In the Netherlands women are not allowed to work for 4 weeks before the birth and for 8 weeks following the birth. In Spain women must not work for 6 weeks following the birth. (European Commission, 1999, p. 7).
[203] In *Turley* v. *Allders Department Store* (1980) IRLR 4, the Employment Appeal Tribunal (EAT) drew attention to the difficulties pregnancy poses for conventional legal norms: "when she is pregnant a woman is no longer 'just a woman'. She is a woman . . . with child, and there is no masculine equivalent" (at p. 5).
[204] In *Hayes* v. *Malleable Working Men's Club* (EAT 188/84), the EAT overruled *Turley* and said "we have not found any difficulty in visualising cases—for example, that of a sick male employee and a pregnant woman employee, where the circumstances, although they could never in strictness be called the same, could nevertheless be properly regarded as lacking any material differences" (at p. 8).

resort to this sort of comparison in the employment context illustrates the difficulties in classifying pregnancy according to conventional legal norms.

Differential treatment by employers on the grounds of pregnancy is now *prima facie* automatically discriminatory and thus unlawful, although there is an exception if the pregnant woman would otherwise be exposed to a risk specific to pregnancy or maternity.[205] In the past there were attempts to exclude every woman of child-bearing age from certain sorts of hazardous work, regardless of whether she was in fact likely to become pregnant,[206] and there continue

[205] Under the Management of Health and Safety at Work Regulations 1992, regs 13A–C., derived from the Pregnant Workers Directive 92/85/EEC art 3–6., employers must assess the risks to pregnant employees and new mothers arising from work conditions or physical, biological or chemical agents. If it is not reasonable to alter the working conditions to avoid the risk, then the worker must be given leave. It is unfair to dismiss her because of these requirements (see s.99(1)(d) Employment Rights Act 1996). Under ss. 64 and 66 Employment Rights Act 1996 and the Suspension from Work (on Maternity Grounds) Order SI 1994/2930 a woman is entitled to be paid during this period of leave unless she unreasonably refuses to take alternative employment.

Some areas of work are subject to special regulation, for example in the Merchant Shipping Notice M 1331, the Department of Transport has prescribed certain medical standards for seafarers on United Kingdom ships. The M Notice specifies that in the case of a pregnant employee, she shall not be employed on such ships after the 28th week of pregnancy and at least six weeks after delivery. In *P & O v. Iverson* Appeal No. EAT/322/98 the Employment Appeal Tribunal upheld a woman's right to pay during pregnancy related suspension.

[206] See further *Page v. Freight Hire (Tank Haulage) Ltd* [1981] ICR 299 (EAT) in which a woman HGV driver was removed from her job because the chemical she would have normally carried was reported to be dangerous to women of child-bearing age. She said that she did not want children; did not anticipate becoming pregnant; was aware of the dangers and was prepared to risk them. In his discussion of the employment appeal tribunal's decision to uphold the employer's right to remove Ms Page from her job, Richard Townsend-Smith suggests that "no legislation can avoid a Tribunal's having to balance what may be a rather small risk to a fetus against a woman's expectation of being able to continue in employment. Most tribunals can be expected to play safe and uphold a decision to exclude women" (Townsend-Smith, 1989, p. 133).

Ms Page believed that the tribunal was prejudiced against her because her desire not to have children made her appear monstrous to them. The solicitor for Freight Hire had argued that the decision to have children should be a decision for her future husband, and he apparently said of Ms Page that "she formed the view, as women's libbers and pro-abortionists do that she had the right to decide the future of her own body and her own unborn" (quoted in Kenney, 1986, p. 405).

In 1977 in a notorious US case, American Cynamid introduced a fetal protection policy requiring all women aged 15–55 to produce proof of surgical sterilisation before being permitted to work in the relatively well paid jobs in their Virginia plant. Five women were sterilised as a result (Kenney, 1986, p. 396). Fourteen years later in *International Union UAW* v. *Johnson Controls* SC 113 L. ed (1991) 158, the U.S. Supreme Court found that a policy which excluded "women who are pregnant or who are capable of bearing children" from jobs involving lead exposure was unlawful. Prior to the decision of the Supreme Court, one of the plaintiffs had been sterilised in order to avoid losing her job, while a male colleague who was planning to start a family had had his request for a leave of absence in order to minimise his exposure to lead denied (Meyer, 1997, p. 109). But while the Supreme Court's decision may protect fertile women from discrimination, the Court also suggested that a consequence of an employer's inability to exclude fertile women from hazardous work must be that he/she will not be liable for unintentional prenatal harm. Blackmun J said "without negligence, it would be difficult for a court to find liability on the part of the employer. If, under general tort principles Title VII bans sex-specific fetal protection policies, the employer fully informs the woman of the risk and the employer has not acted negligently, the basis for holding an employer liable seems remote at best" (at 179–80).

Prior to the decision in *Johnson Controls*, fetal protection policies were common in the U.S., and indeed it has been suggested that the decision has not removed fetal protection policies from American industry (Thomson, 1998, p. 123). In *Bourlesan v. Arabian American Oil Company* 111 S

to be some restrictions upon the levels of all fertile women's exposure to certain prescribed toxic hazards.[207]

It is perhaps significant that interest in minimising the impact of toxic environments upon the developing fetus has tended to focus upon reducing *women's* participation in *particular types* of employment. In the past, this disparity could be explained by evidential deficiencies. Analysing chemicals in order to identify their capacity to cause reproductive harm used to mean investigating their effects solely upon the *female* reproductive system.[208] We now know, however, that there are very few occupational hazards that only affect women's reproductive capacity.[209] In fact, exposure to toxic chemicals may be more likely to cause damage to sperm cells that are constantly being regenerated, than it is to fully developed egg cells.[210] But evidence that an individual's future health may be adversely affected by hazardous environments that damage sperm quality,[211] or by exposure *in utero* to affected seminal fluid[212] does not result in restrictions upon the workforce participation of men. A man who is planning to have children cannot be prevented from taking a job that may impair his ability to father a healthy child, although should his reproductive capacity be impaired, he may attempt to sue his employer.[213] So while men have sought compensation for occupational exposure to toxic conditions,[214] similarly positioned women face restrictions upon the range of employment options open to them.[215]

CT 1227, the Supreme Court held that the Johnson decision did not apply to American companies operating outside the US.

[207] For example under Control of Lead at Work Regulations fertile women can be exposed to a maximum of 40μg/100ml compared with the male maximum exposure of 80 μg/100ml. See also the Factories Act 1961 and the Ionising Radiation Regulations 1985.

[208] Kenney, 1986.

[209] Draper, 1991.

[210] This is particularly true where the hazard is a mutagen which is more likely to cause damage to developing cells than to those whose development is fixed. The damage is also likely to be more serious in that it alters the genetic structure of the male reproductive cells, thus passing on the mutation to future generations (Thomsom, 1998, p. 127).

[211] There are over 30 studies showing correlations between male occupations and fetal health. For example childhood brain tumours are apparently more common if the father works in agriculture, the construction industry or in metal-related jobs. Similarly there is a correlation between anencephaly and paternal employment as a painter (Daniels, 1999, p. 86). Davis *et al* suggest that male reproductive exposure can cause miscarriage, low birth weight, congenital abnormalities, cancer and neurological problems (Davis *et al*, 1992). Men's preconception exposure to toxic environments has been associated with childhood cancers, low birth weights and other adverse pregnancy outcomes (Bertin, 1995, p. 392). "Paternal" exposure to lead results in more spontaneous abortions, stillbirths and fetal abnormalities (Narayan, 1995a, p. 399). It has also been linked with certain cancers and mutagenic dysfunction (Thomson, 1998, p. 127). Ionising radiation, benzene, vinyl chloride etc. all pose a serious threat to male reproduction (Thomson, 1998, p. 128).

[212] Some toxins, such as lead, can be transmitted to a fetus during intercourse after conception has occurred (Narayan, 1995a, p. 399).

[213] Purdy, 1996, p. 101.

[214] See for example the campaigns organised on behalf of Vietnam war veterans for the twofold increase in congenital birth defects caused by their toxic exposure to dioxin (TCDD) or Agent Orange (Daniels, 1999, p. 86). There has also been considerable interest in reports that Gulf War veteran's reproductive health has been adversely affected (Daniels, 1999, p. 85).

[215] Joan Bertin suggests that some women were surgically sterilised in order to qualify for lucrative industrial employment (Bertin, 1995, p. 385).

In addition to their focus on *female* workers, fetal protection policies have also tended to concentrate upon the hazards posed by women's participation in *traditionally male* working environments. There has been much less interest in the toxicity of typically female occupations, such as nursing or cleaning,[216] even when they involve exposure to identical toxigens.[217] This discrepancy is particularly striking as a result of the correlation between parental affluence and fetal wellbeing: exclusion from well paid employment may cause fetal harm just as serious as an environmental toxin.

Enabling women *and men* to avoid working in toxic environments that may impair their reproductive capacity might be a proper purpose of employment law. The failure to extend adequate protection to male employees could even be characterised as less favourable treatment on the grounds of sex, and hence actionable under the Sex Discrimination Act 1975.[218] Setting a *single* low standard of exposure to toxic agents might therefore be preferable to sex-specific policies that both fail to acknowledge men's vulnerability to reproductive hazards, and result in women being denied potentially lucrative employment.

(b) Health Promotion Programmes

In recent years, significant public resources have been allocated to health education campaigns, of which pregnant women have been a particular target. Preventative health promotion programmes undoubtedly help some individuals to improve their quality of life and reduce their risk of future infirmity, but at the same time they tend to overemphasise individuals' responsibility for their own ill-health.[219] By alerting the whole population to ways in which they can prevent disease and disability, illness is subtly transformed from an unavoidable misfortune into the inevitable consequence of an individual's lax habits.[220] With quasi-theological zeal, modern therapeutic practices urge the individual to be informed about her own health; to acknowledge her faults and admit her temptations as essential precursors for the adoption of a healthy way of life.[221] If health can be *chosen*, rather than simply enjoyed or missed, it

[216] Narayan, 1995a, p. 401. Cheryl Meyer argues that "when the population exposed to potential reproductive hazards is almost exclusively female, the danger is minimized or not investigated" (Meyer, 1997, p. 110).

[217] Draper, 1991, p. 73.

[218] Kenney, 1996, p. 411.

[219] As Emily Martin explains "medical culture has a powerful system of socialization which exacts conformity as the price of participation" (Martin, 1987, p. 13).

[220] Denise Gastaldo has suggested that "health education is an experience of being governed from the outside and a request for self-discipline. From inside, health education is a constructive exercise of power that improves the medical gaze; the promotion of health it circulates everywhere in spheres that are new to biomedicine" (Gastaldo 1997, p. 118). R. Crawford has observed that being healthy has become "the mark of distinction that separates those who deserve to succeed from those who will fail" (Crawford, 1994, p. 1354).

[221] Young, 1997, p. 87.

becomes "a visible sign of initiative, adaptability, balance and strength of will".[222] Conversely, a person's poor health provides indelible evidence of their inability to conform with dominant behavioural norms.

Thus, the failure to adopt a healthy lifestyle is increasingly perceived to be not only foolish, but also morally reprehensible,[223] and taking responsibility for one's health has become a key obligation of productive or virtuous citizenship.[224] It would be easy to cynically attribute successive governments' enthusiasm for the "victim-blaming" ideology of health promotion to the economic and political convenience of deflecting attention away from both the major social causes of disease[225] and endemic underfunding of the NHS.

By focusing upon *lifestyle* risk factors, health promotion programmes emphasise individual agency and accountability, and where their target is the pregnant woman, she is exhorted to assume personal responsibility for the health of her fetus. The wellbeing of future generations depends, according to these preventative health strategies, upon the pregnant woman's capacity to modify her lifestyle appropriately.[226] This individualistic approach to prenatal harm leads to the pathologising of certain behaviours, and their attribution to moral failure and personal inadequacy. Underlying this analysis is the assumption that all pregnant women are equally willing or able to adopt some optimum prenatal lifestyle, whereas in fact, health promotion initiatives tend to be taken up most enthusiastically by the more affluent members of the community. This focus upon pregnant women's personal responsibility for fetal wellbeing also tends to obscure the close correlation between socio-economic class and high-risk conduct, such as smoking or the use of illegal drugs.[227]

A healthy prenatal lifestyle is frequently presented as a norm from which deviant behaviours are both distinguished and judged.[228] If certain prenatal conduct is assumed to reflect a pregnant woman's lack of self-control, a women who does not conform to dominant health norms may become the object of pity, scorn or intolerance. Her freedom to choose to behave in an unorthodox way may be subtly restricted by the prevailing assumption that no sensible pregnant woman would fail to follow medical advice. Unsurprisingly pregnant women

---

[222] Greco, 1993, p. 369.

[223] Salstanhall, 1993; Lupton, 1996.

[224] Petersen and Lupton, 1996, p. 68. See also Backett, 1992; Crawford, 1977; Lupton, 1993. A Government White Paper published in 1977 asserted that "much ill-heath in Britain today arises from over-indulgence and unwise behaviour. The individual can do much to heal himself, his family and the community by accepting more direct responsibility for his own health and well-being" (DHSS, 1977, p. 39).

[225] Crawford, 1977.

[226] As Petersen and Lupton have explained "the woman as 'healthy' citizen. . .is understood as a resource for the reproduction and maintenance of other 'healthy' citizens" (Petersen and Lupton, 1996, p. 73).

[227] 14% of women in professional employment smoke, compared with 33% of unskilled women. The use of the most harmful illegal drugs, such as heroin and crack, also correlates with relative deprivation (Office for National Statistics, 2001, pp. 135–6).

[228] Michael Fitzpatrick highlights our collective willingness to condemn people who fail to conform with "the new moral code of healthy living" (Fitzpatrick, 2001, p. 70).

absorb this persistent interest in their responsibility for fetal health, so a woman may, for example, only feel confident that her baby's ill health is a tragic accident, rather than her fault, if she behaved in an exemplary way throughout her pregnancy. Submitting to the medical management of pregnancy, and following every health promotion edict, have become necessary strategies in order to avoid feelings of guilt and responsibility should the pregnancy prove to be abnormal.[229]

The provision of information to pregnant women about the best ways to maximise fetal health reflects health education's dual function as a provider of information to assist informed decision-making, and as a refined and pervasive system of control.[230] The accumulation and dissemination of vast and detailed expertise about how to optimise fetal development may enable pregnant women to make choices about their lifestyle, but it simultaneously represents a powerful stimulus towards self-discipline.[231] The identification both of risk factors, and of appropriate tactics for risk-avoidance is in a constant state of flux with new research published each week. Pregnant women are, therefore, not only supposed to follow medical advice, but also to be alert to the possibility of new guidance, and endlessly receptive to it.[232] The proliferation of advice about the best ways to promote fetal health thus constitutes pregnant women as self-policing subjects.[233]

[229] Monica Greco has said that "disease will be treated as if it were an accident so long as the authority of the physician is not put into question and is effectively complied with" (Greco, 1993, p. 366).

[230] Abby Lippman has argued that "it is generally assumed that (the pregnant woman) must do all that is recommended or available to foster her child's health. At its extreme, this represents the pregnant woman as obligated to produce a healthy child" (Lippman, 1991).

[231] For example, there was intensive media coverage of a study carried out by Jennifer Little testing the response time of 25 week old fetuses to a noise made by a buzzer. Her results showed slower activity where the pregnant woman had drunk alcohol moderately and within the government's recommended limit of 4 glasses of wine a week. Dr Little said that "It's worrying because current recommendations generally say that some alcohol during pregnancy is OK. However, the results would suggest that women shouldn't drink any alcohol during pregnancy. Even low amounts may have an effect on their fetus" (quoted in Boseley, 2000a). There is a clear dual effect here since such a study both gives information which pregnant women may find useful, and it attempts to exercise normative control or influence over pregnant women's behaviour. It was interesting that the results were presented as "facts" even though they are disputed by the Department of Health and other scientists.

[232] This omnipresent need for reflexive adaptability to newly identified risks has resonance with the concept of "risk society" (Beck, 1992a).

[233] Michel Foucault's analysis of bio-power has had considerable resonance for the analysis of health promotion programmes. Foucault considered that medicine was a key site for the exercise of disciplinary power: "For the first time in history, no doubt, biological existence was reflected in political existence; the fact of living was no longer an inaccessible substrate that only emerged from time to time, amid the randomness of death and its fatality; part of it passed into knowledge's field of control and power's sphere of intervention" (Michel Foucault, 1981, p. 142). But he did not suggest a simple and explicit domination of patients by doctors, rather power is located in techniques of surveillance and in the production of knowledge: "a power whose task is to take charge of life needs continuous regulatory and corrective mechanisms. . .Such a power has to qualify, measure, appraise and heirarchize" (Foucault, 1981, p. 144). The individual is not, therefore, repressed by biopower, but rather is constituted as an agent able to exercise control over his or her own health and wellbeing. Power which consists in the subtle, ubiquitous and continuous promotion of a productive population may be both effective and invisible.

Its grounding in the apparently objective findings of scientists lends particular weight to health promotion advice. Yet this assumption of neutrality may be misplaced. For example, there tends to be much more interest in studies that find a *negative* correlation between a pregnant woman's behaviour and fetal development, than in those indicating that prenatal exposure to a particular toxin has no discernible impact upon fetal wellbeing.[234] Any bias in medical journals will inevitably be amplified by the media's relative indifference to research with no headline-grabbing potential.

In addition to news coverage of scientific research that identifies ways in which the pregnant woman can influence fetal development, there is a burgeoning "self-help" literature directed towards pregnant women. These magazines and books offer women who are, or who intend to become pregnant advice about their diet and behaviour. Deciding to become pregnant, or to carry an unexpected pregnancy to term is frequently accompanied by the desire to acquire expert knowledge about pregnancy. There seems to be a tendency, particularly among affluent pregnant women, to see themselves as "researchers", reading voraciously about pregnancy and childbirth in order to promote optimum fetal development and enhance their capacity to control the management of their pregnancy.[235] The concept of "preconceptive health" even encourages women to modify their lifestyle *before* they conceive because, as one manual explains:

> "there is so much less to worry about or brood over when you know you've provided a pristine environment for your unborn baby from day one".[236]

By focussing almost exclusively upon the individual woman's capacity to influence the outcome of her pregnancy, these self-help manuals reinforce the idea that women's self-discipline is the primary determinant of fetal progress. While it is undoubtedly true that fetal development is affected by the conduct of the pregnant woman, women's responsibility for the health and wellbeing of the next generation may be overstated,[237] in comparison with a widespread underestimation of the impact of "paternal" behaviour.[238] In addition to direct impact through men's sperm, for example, male violence towards their pregnant partners is often triggered by their drug and alcohol use.

---

[234] Joan Bertin suggests that there is a significant difference between publication rates of studies showing negative effects of pregnant women's behaviour as compared with those that show no adverse effects. Her example is that 11% of studies which concluded cocaine use has no adverse effect were accepted for publication, whereas 57% of studies showing that prenatal cocaine use had an adverse impact were accepted (Bertin, 1995, p. 388).

[235] Bailey, 1999, p. 343.

[236] Graham, 1991, p. 4.

[237] The link between IQ at age 4 and maternal and paternal education is more statistically significant than the connection between alcohol use and IQ (Bertin, 1995, p. 389).

[238] Cynthia Daniels says that "it is clear that responsibility for fetal harm is so deeply shared with men, with public institutions, and with social structures, that it makes little sense to try to tease out individual from collective responsibility for fetal harm. How are we to separate poor nutrition from drug use from lead paint from poverty from genetics from chronic violence and abuse as causes of fetal harm?" (Daniels, 1999, pp. 83–4).

It could even be argued that the most dangerous behaviour of both men and women is eclipsed by the risks to which fetuses are exposed as a result of environmental hazards and socio-economic inequalities.[239] By individualising the problem of prenatal harm, and concentrating almost exclusively upon steps that a pregnant woman can take to ensure a healthy baby, preventative health programmes tend to deflect attention away from collective responsibility for toxic environments[240] and inadequate social care. The persistent focus upon individual responsibility for disease inevitably tends to obscure its social causes. In part this may be because we seem to have little control over external risk factors such as poverty, so stressing individual agency may seem to have more immediate potential to transform infant health than utopian ideas about distributive justice.

We should, however, remember that their mother's poverty represents a more statistically significant risk to future wellbeing than her failure to adhere to health promotion advice. The development of fetal alcohol syndrome (FAS), for example, is closely associated with the socio-economic class of the pregnant woman, and it is actually relatively uncommon among the children of wealthy women who drink heavily during pregnancy but who have other material advantages such as good nutrition and prenatal care.[241] So while advising women not to drink excessively during pregnancy may help to prevent FAS, improving the living standards of poorer women would actually be a more effective strategy.

6. CONCLUSION

In this chapter, we have considered how women's capacity to make free and informed choices about the management of their pregnancy and childbirth may be constrained by dominant assumptions about both medical authority and maternal self-sacrifice. We have seen how the significance of the fetus's lack of legal personhood may be substantially undermined in practice by the fetus's status as an independent patient. If doctors consider the fetus to be a separate patient, their perceived "duty" to preserve fetal life may be in tension with their common law duty to respect the pregnant woman's right to refuse unwanted intervention. While pregnant women are undoubtedly uniquely placed to influence the health and wellbeing of future generations, this should not eclipse their right to self-determination.

---

[239] Daniels, 1999, p. 97.

[240] For example, women living near landfill sites have a statistically significant increased risk of giving birth to a baby with congenital malformations. This increased risk is not confined to women living near hazardous waste sites, but extends to women living in proximity to household waste landfill sites (Fielder *et al*, 2000).

[241] Neurin Bingol *et al* studied pregnant women drinking more than 3 units of alcohol a day. Among upper middle class women, the prevalence of FAS in their offspring was 4.5%. For poor women drinking identical amounts, 70.9% of their children developed FAS (Bingol *et al*, 1987).

I do not, however, intend to suggest that the choices of all pregnant women have been predetermined, and that autonomous decision-making has become impossible. Rather, my point is that we should enhance a woman's capacity to exercise free and informed choice over the management of her pregnancies. Undeniably this involves providing clear and intelligible advice and information to pregnant women, but crucially it is also contingent upon respect for their unconventional decisions. It is also important to remember that while the pregnant woman and the fetus are connected by a bond of unparalled intimacy, fetal development may be affected by multiple external factors. So in addition to obscuring the pregnant woman's right to make unorthodox decisions about her body, the dominant focus on the mother's behaviour may also overshadow collective responsibility for environmental toxins, inadequate prenatal care or endemic poverty.

5

Reproductive Technologies

1. INTRODUCTION

IT IS AT least arguable that assisted conception techniques represent one of the most important and spectacular scientific developments of the last 25 years. In addition to transforming some people's reproductive lives,[1] infertility treatment has also wrought a profound change in the relationship between law and reproduction. Until recently parenthood was only regulated *after* children had been born. With the exception of the instances of sterilisation abuse discussed in chapter two, the decision to procreate was not susceptible to legal control. Assisted conception, on the other hand, is intensely regulated, and the announcement of any new technique is invariably followed by demands for further regulation. There are very few people who would advocate the completely unregulated provision of reproductive technologies: a system in which there were no prior licensing requirements for the setting-up of an infertility clinic would obviously be open to abuse. The disagreement that exists is rather between those who believe that regulation should be broadly facilitative, and those who would restrict or even remove access to assisted conception techniques.

My first task in this chapter is to explain what infertility treatment involves, and define some of the different techniques. We then consider the various arguments commonly put forward by critics of assisted conception. Having explained why I believe that regulation should facilitate, rather than restrict access to infertility treatment, this chapter then covers six key areas of regulation, drawing particular attention to the social, ethical and legal implications of some of the more controversial technologies and practices. First, we consider the role of the Human Fertilisation and Embryology Authority (HFEA) in controlling the provision of assisted conception services. Second, the restrictions upon access to treatment are examined. Third, we investigate the rules governing the status, use and donation of gametes.[2] Fourth, we explore the moral status of the embryo and the regulatory framework within which it can be used, stored, researched upon and destroyed. Fifth, the rules determining the parentage of children born through assisted conception are explained. Finally, we consider the regulation of innovative developments in biotechnology and reproductive genetics.

The British regulatory scheme undoubtedly has many merits, not the least of which is that it offers some prospective guidance to doctors, scientists and

---

[1] One child in 80 in the UK is now born following assisted conception (Boseley, 2000b).
[2] Sperm and ova.

patients. My principal criticism of the current regime will be that it does not always provide people who cannot have children without medical assistance with an adequate range of reproductive options from which to choose. As I explained in chapter one, I believe that respect for reproductive autonomy should involve more than the absence of state constraints upon the decisions of fertile heterosexual couples, and might sometimes require the active provision of resources to enable biologically unlucky people to exercise meaningful reproductive choice.

2. WHAT IS INFERTILITY?

The standard medical definition of infertility is the failure to conceive after twelve months of regular, unprotected sexual intercourse, or the occurrence of three or more consecutive miscarriages or stillbirths.[3] An objective definition of infertility is, however, probably impossible.[4] The World Health Organisation, for example, classifies infertility as the failure to conceive after two years, and some demographers would favour a five year cut-off point. Approximately half of all couples who qualify as infertile on the 12 month definition will conceive naturally during the following year,[5] so it would certainly be a mistake to equate the failure to conceive during 12 months with a diagnosis of sterility.[6]

In addition, since a diagnosis of clinical infertility can only be made once an individual has articulated an unfulfilled desire for a child within a heterosexual relationship,[7] the actual incidence of fertility problems is unknowable. But despite the inevitable imprecision of definitions, it is now assumed that approximately one in six heterosexual couples in developed countries will experience infertility at some point while of reproductive age. For some their infertility will be temporary and/or unexplained, while for others sterility is permanent and procreation without medical intervention will remain impossible. While not usually counted as "infertile", homosexual couples and individuals with no sexual partner are also, of course, unable to reproduce without some external assistance.

Infertility is sometimes mistakenly assumed to be a modern social problem. Historical accounts of women's lives which concentrate upon the domestic drudgery that resulted from women's uncontrollable fecundity often convey the impression that there were hardly any women who wanted children but could

---

[3] Macpherson, 1995, p. 252.

[4] Douglas, 1991, p. 105.

[5] Te Velde *et al*, 2000.

[6] It has even been suggested that there may be people associated with the provision of assisted conception services who have a vested interest in progressively shortening the period of time that must elapse before infertility can be diagnosed and treatment started. Susan Faludi, for example, contends that "the twelve month rule is a recent development, partly inspired by 'infertility specialists' marketing experimental and expensive new reproductive technologies" (Faludi, 1992, p. 47).

[7] Farquhar, 1996, p. 83.

not have them.[8] The concern about overpopulation among the poorer sections of society, considered in more detail in chapter two, also tended to deflect attention away from the problems faced by infertile men and women. It was not until the 1930s, when the declining birthrate became a matter of political interest, that involuntary childlessness also came to public attention.[9] In the 1940s, the Family Planning Association became actively involved in the provision of clinics to investigate and treat sterility, although in the majority of cases there was little that could be done. Most "treatment' was confined to helping women to work out the optimum time to conceive.

It is undoubtedly true that unwanted childlessness is extremely distressing,[10] and that the existence of infertility treatment offers hope to people who would otherwise be unable to have children. It must be remembered, however, that reproductive technologies do not always offer a solution to involuntary childlessness. As we see later, many people are unable to afford assisted conception services, and low success rates ensure that a significant proportion of people who do undergo infertility treatment will remain childless.[11] The fact that most infertility treatment fails is obscured by media coverage that tends to focus upon the "miracle" babies born through assisted conception, rather than the high rates of continued childlessness.[12] Similarly, academic interest in reproductive technologies is inevitably weighted towards discussion of issues that simply do not arise if treatment fails, such as the welfare of children and the attribution of legal parenthood. For example, an examination of the academic literature could give the impression that donor anonymity is the most compelling issue raised by donor insemination (DI), whereas the chief concern for people undergoing DI might actually be the 90.1per cent chance that their treatment will fail. Thus, bearing in mind that reproductive technologies have not eliminated involuntary childlessness, let us now turn to a brief description of some of the various techniques.

3. WHAT ARE REPRODUCTIVE TECHNOLOGIES?

(a) Cryopreservation

The cryopreservation of both sperm and embryos is a well-established practice: sperm was first frozen in 1949,[13] and it has been possible to freeze embryos since

---

[8] For a lucid account of the invisibility of infertility in the past, and the tendency of contemporary oral historians to concentrate upon women as mothers, see Pfeffer, 1993.

[9] Pfeffer, 1993, p. 99.

[10] In addition to the fact of childlessness, infertility can threaten people's self-esteem and their sense of control over their lives. Where a couple have assumed that they would have children, a diagnosis of infertility disrupts their assumptions about the trajectory of their shared future.

[11] In the year to March 1999, 21.9% of IVF treatment cycles resulted in a clinical pregnancy, and 18.2% resulted in a live birth (HFEA, 2000c, p. 11). Success rates for DI are even lower, in 1998/9 12.1% of DI cycles resulted in a clinical pregnancy, and 9.9% in a live birth (HFEA, 2000c, p. 12).

[12] Mulkay, 1997, p. 76.

[13] Corea, 1990, p. 57.

1983.[14] In addition to the obvious practical advantage in being able to store donated sperm until it is needed, cryopreservation also enables all donors to be tested for HIV six months later, thus ensuring that the donor was not infected at the time of donation. Embryos may be frozen so that they can be transferred to the woman's uterus at the optimum time in her cycle, and cryopreservation also enables any spare embryos to be stored and used in subsequent treatment cycles, or donated to other patients, or to research. Until recently, cryopreservation of eggs was not thought to be safe, and so no clinic was licensed to use frozen eggs in treatment. Some women had, nevertheless, had some of their eggs frozen prior to elective hysterectomy or chemotherapy treatment in the hope that the use of their frozen eggs would be licensed as safe during their reproductive lifetime. In January 2000, the HFEA decided to allow one clinic to use frozen eggs in fertility treatment, on condition both that it should be subject to close monitoring, and that women should be warned that it is a new technique with a low success rate.[15]

(b) Assisted insemination by husband/partner (AIH/AIP)

In the past laboratory manipulation of sperm was employed in order to increase the chance of fertilisation in women whose partners had an abnormally low sperm count. The development of ICSI, discussed below, means that AIH/AIP is no longer the optimum treatment for men with poor quality sperm. AIH/AIP continues to be used when a man has stored some of his sperm prior to undergoing medical treatment, such as chemotherapy, that will render him infertile. Assisted insemination with the sperm of a living[16] husband or partner is specifically excluded from the list of treatments requiring a licence from the HFEA.[17] As we see later, this means that it does not have to be performed in a licensed clinic, and is subject neither to the "welfare principle" in section 13(5) of the Human Fertilisation and Embryology Act 1990,[18] nor to the consent provisions in Schedule 3.[19] It is perhaps significant that artificial insemination within a heterosexual family unit is subject to minimal regulatory control in comparison with identical treatment that uses the gametes of an anonymous donor, or that involves the treatment of a single or lesbian woman.

---

[14] Channel 4, 1999.

[15] HFEA, 2000a.

[16] If insemination takes place after the husband or partner's death, the treatment must then be regulated by the HFEA. As we shall see below, for posthumous insemination a man must have given specific consent to the posthumous use of sperm in accordance with Schedule 3, and the clinic must take into account the welfare of any child who may be born before deciding to treat the woman.

[17] As a result of section 4(1)(b) "No person shall . . . in the course of providing treatment services for any woman, use the sperm of any man unless the services are being provided for the woman and the man together . . . except in pursuance of a licence".

[18] See page 192.

[19] See page 206.

(c) Donor Insemination (DI)

The first recorded birth through donor insemination occurred towards the end of the nineteenth century,[20] but it was not perceived to be an acceptable way to conceive until much more recently. In addition to disapproval of its reliance upon masturbation, it used to be thought that a woman's insemination with the sperm of a third party was tantamount to adultery,[21] and that any child conceived following DI would be illegitimate.[22] It was not until the 1970s that a panel appointed by the BMA concluded that there were grounds for making DI available within the NHS,[23] provided that its use was confined to married women.[24]

DI is commonly sought because a woman's partner is infertile, either as a result of a biological incapacity or a previous vasectomy, but it might also be used where the male partner is a carrier for a genetic disease or suffers from sexual dysfunction. As we see below, a new treatment called ICSI, which enables the child to be genetically related to both parents, is steadily reducing the numbers of heterosexual couples opting for donor insemination.[25] DI is still, of course, the only option where the male partner produces no sperm at all, or where a woman seeking treatment does not have a male partner. A DI treatment cycle may involve hormonal stimulation of the woman's ovaries, and insemination will often be through direct injection into her uterus (intra-uterine insemination (IUI)). Success rates are low: only 9.9 per cent of cycles performed in 1998/9 led to the birth of a child.[26]

(d) Oocyte (egg) Donation

There are some important differences between egg and sperm donation. First, each woman has a finite, if large, number of eggs whereas sperm is a renewable

---

[20] The first successful case of donor insemination took place in 1884, and an account of this was first published in 1909 (Haimes and Daniels, 1998, pp. 1–2). It may be interesting that donor insemination has never attracted the same levels of attention as IVF, perhaps because it is a less miraculous, and less glamorous technological achievement. Yet some of this issues raised by DI are clearly of similar complexity.

[21] As a result the BMA considered donor insemination to be an "offence against society" (Corea, 1990, p. 61). Daniel Wikler has argued that the medicalisation of donor insemination "cloak(s) the act of insemination with the aura of the clinic . . . transforming what might in other circumstances be regarded as a sin . . . into therapy" (Wikler, 1995, p. 50). The 1960 Feversham Committee Report into Artificial Insemination thought that donor insemination might lead to indifference towards the marriage vows, and thus weaken the institution of marriage (Feversham Committee, 1960).

[22] For example the Archbishop of Canterbury's Commission in 1948 considered that the practice of donor insemination amounted to official endorsement of adultery and illegitimacy, and that therefore it should be criminalised (Haimes, 1998, p. 56).

[23] Panel on Human Artificial Insemination, 1973.

[24] Pfeffer, 1993, p. 158.

[25] Lasker, 1998, p. 7. The number of DI cycles dropped by 57% between 1992/3 and 1998/9 (from 25,623 a year to 11,035) (HFEA, 2000c, p. 12).

[26] HFEA, 2000b.

resource. Second, egg donation is much more uncomfortable and invasive than masturbation. Third, donor insemination was first employed over a hundred years ago, while donated eggs were first used in IVF treatment in 1984.[27] Fourth, it has been possible to freeze sperm since the middle of the twentieth century, whereas cryopreservation of oocytes is, as we have seen, in its infancy. Fifth, there seems to be some evidence that the donation of eggs may be less widely accepted than sperm donation, with some countries that allow sperm donation also specifically prohibiting egg donation.[28] In this country, it could be predicted that a husband's attempt use to his deceased wife's eggs in treatment with another woman would attract greater opprobrium than has the posthumous use of a deceased husband's sperm.

Donated eggs might be used by women who have suffered ovarian failure or who have a serious genetic abnormality that they would prefer not to pass on to their offspring. Women who have had multiple failed IVF cycles using their own eggs might also attempt treatment with donated eggs. The oocyte donor has hormone treatment and her eggs are surgically retrieved in the same way as a woman having IVF treatment. The eggs are fertilised *in vitro*, usually with the infertile woman's partner's sperm, and the embryos are then transferred to her uterus. Oocyte donation has an obvious advantage over DI because although she will not be genetically related to her baby, the infertile woman will become pregnant and give birth to her partner's child. Thus following oocyte donation, the infertile partner has a biological, albeit not genetic connection with her child.[29] Additionally, since the woman who gives birth is, as we see later, *always* treated as the legal mother of a child,[30] no special problems arise in relation to legal parentage.

(e) *In Vitro* Fertilisation (IVF)

Because a woman's ovaries normally produce only one mature egg in each monthly cycle, in an *in vitro* fertilisation cycle, women commonly have hormonal treatment in order to stimulate the over-production of eggs. The eggs are then removed from the ovarian follicles through laparoscopy[31] or transvaginal aspiration[32] and placed in a culture that allows them to mature further. The mature eggs are put into a petri dish with sperm, usually from the woman's partner, and if fertilisation occurs the resulting zygote(s)[33] may be placed in the woman's uterus, or frozen to be used at a later date.

[27] Bonnicksen, 1996, p. 156.
[28] Several countries in Europe have legislation prohibiting oocyte donation, e.g. Germany, Norway, Austria (Schenker, 1997, p. 178).
[29] Schenker, 1997, p. 178.
[30] Human Fertilisation and Embryology Act 1990, section 27(1).
[31] This involves the insertion of a hollow needle into the woman's abdomen.
[32] This involves the threading of a probe, guided by ultrasound, through the woman's vagina and uterus.
[33] A zygote is a very early embryo.

Research into the possibility of *in vitro* fertilisation had begun in the 1930s, and it was first successfully performed on mouse ova in 1958.[34] Its use with human gametes was pioneered by Robert Edwards and Patrick Steptoe during the 1960s and 1970s, culminating in the birth of the first IVF baby, Louise Brown, on the 25 July 1978. Initially there was considerable hostility to IVF, and scepticism about its safety and efficacy.[35] For example, James Watson, who along with Francis Crick discovered the structure of human DNA, had warned that IVF might produce children suffering from severe abnormalities, and predicted that its use in humans could become another "Thalidomide" tragedy.[36] Fortunately for the scientists, and unfortunately for their critics,[37] Louise Brown was completely normal. IVF is now the most common treatment for infertility, with over 35,000 cycles taking place in the UK each year.[38] On average, 18.2 per cent of IVF treatment cycles in the UK result in a live birth, but significant disparities exist between different clinics' success rates. There are, for example, clinics with live birth rates as low as 5.6 per cent per IVF cycle, while rates of 31.2 per cent are achieved elsewhere.[39]

(f) Gamete Intra-Fallopian Transfer (GIFT)

This involves egg retrieval in the same way as IVF, but instead of being placed in a petri dish with the sperm, the eggs and the sperm are injected into the woman's fallopian tube so that fertilisation can occur *in vivo*. GIFT is commonly used where there is no abnormality in a woman's fallopian tubes and the couple's infertility is "unexplained". GIFT is not regulated by the Human Fertilisation and Embryology Act because no embryo is ever created or kept outside the woman's body.[40] However, given that the eggs and the sperm may be in contact with each other before being transferred to the woman's fallopian tube, it is *possible* that fertilisation could have occurred before injection. Virtually all GIFT treatments do in fact take place in licensed assisted conception clinics, so as we see later, the chief practical impact of its exclusion from the HFEA's regulatory scheme is that more than three eggs can be transferred during each cycle of treatment.

---

[34] Mulkay, 1997, p. 8.

[35] The Medical Research Council, for example, had rejected a request for funding on the grounds that IVF was too dangerous (Channel 4, 1999).

[36] Channel 4, 1999.

[37] Phyllis Bowman for example, has said "I think it's a real tragedy that it was successful" (Channel 4, 1999).

[38] From April 1998 to March 1999, there were 35,363 cycles of IVF treatment (HFEA, 2000c, p. 10).

[39] HFEA, 2000b.

[40] Human Fertilisation and Embryology Act s.1(3) "This Act, so far as it governs the keeping or use of an embryo, applies only to keeping or using an embryo outside the human body."

(g) Micromanipulation: Intra-Cytoplasmic Sperm Injection (ICSI) and Sub-Zonal Insemination (SUZI)

ICSI was first performed successfully in 1992. It involves the injection of a single sperm into an egg with a very fine glass needle. If fertilisation occurs, the resulting zygote(s) will be transferred to the woman's uterus in the same way as in conventional IVF treatment. ICSI may be used when sperm cannot penetrate an egg naturally, this might be because a man's sperm count is extremely low or his sperm may have poor motility. If the male partner's semen contains no sperm as a result of an abnormality in his reproductive organs, sperm might be surgically removed from his testes and used in ICSI. Of course, where a man's infertility is caused by a genetic abnormality, the use of ICSI raises the possibility that any male children born as a result will also be infertile.[41] SUZI similarly involves the microinjection of a small number of sperm into the egg, and again it might be used if normal fertilisation has failed to occur. The number of treatment cycles involving micromanipulation has increased significantly from 244 in 1992/3 to 10,630 in 1998/9.[42] Success rates have also improved dramatically, only 5.7 per cent of treatment cycles using micromanipulation led to a live birth in 1992/3, compared with 21.8 per cent seven years later.[43]

(h) Cloning

Since the announcement of the birth of the first sheep cloned from an adult cell in February 1997, there has been intense speculation about the possibility of human cloning. Nuclear substitution, the technique involved in the creation of Dolly, has not yet been tried on humans, and reproductive cloning is likely to remain unlawful. Cell mass division, on the other hand, which involves splitting an embryo at the 2–8 cell stage into single embryo cells, was first performed in 1993.[44] In theory, this could be used to increase the numbers of embryos created in an IVF cycle, or to create a duplicate embryo that could be tested for genetic abnormalities and discarded, while its intact "twin" could subsequently be implanted. Its use in infertility treatment has, however, been prohibited.[45]

Before we move on to discuss the regulatory framework within which these various reproductive technologies are provided in the UK, I shall summarise some of the criticisms commonly levelled at infertility treatment and explain why I find none of them convincing. It is undoubtedly true that regulating assisted

---

[41] Gordts *et al*, 1998.
[42] HFEA, 2000c, p. 12.
[43] *Ibid*.
[44] Harris, 1999b [1997] p. 143.
[45] The HFEA Code of Practice para. 7.22 states: "Centres must **not** attempt to produce embryos in vitro by embryo splitting for treatment purposes" (emphasis in original) (HFEA, 1998).

conception services is a novel and complex task for the law, and that some exceptionally difficult moral and ethical dilemmas are raised by our unprecedented capacity to intervene in the once invisible and mysterious process of conception. I intend to argue that regulation should strive, as far as possible, to enhance rather than inhibit reproductive freedom, but first I need to address the arguments of those who would prefer a much more restrictive regulatory scheme.

4. CRITICS OF REPRODUCTIVE TECHNOLOGIES

People with a wide variety of disparate concerns have expressed reservations about both infertility treatment and embryo research. For the sake of clarity, I will identify three different types of argument commonly deployed by reproductive technologies' critics: first that the techniques are unnatural; second that they do not promote children's welfare and third that they reinforce damaging gender stereotypes. Of course, these concerns often overlap, so someone who believes that reproductive technologies are an attempt to "play God" may also consider that natural procreation is "better" for children.

It is important to remember that anyone who has moral objections to assisted conception is obviously entitled to live their own life according to their own values and beliefs. Thus, if they discover that they or their partner is infertile, they are absolutely entitled to resign themselves to their childlessness, or find other ways to forge meaningful relationships with children. But their point is seldom simply to explain why they personally would refuse to use assisted conception services should they find themselves unable to conceive. Few critics of reproductive technologies believe that their use is simply a matter of individual freedom. Rather, the preferred outcome for most of infertility treatment's detractors would be either the contraction or the eradication of assisted conception services. In order to restrict other people's reproductive freedom, these critics must do more than establish personal distaste for artificial means of reproduction. The onus must be on them to find public policy arguments against assisted conception techniques that are sufficiently compelling to justify restricting other individuals' reproductive options. In the following sections I argue that none of the various objections to reproductive technologies have satisfied this burden of proof.

(a) Unnaturalness

Repeated references to Aldous Huxley's novel *Brave New World*[46] or to Mary Shelley's *Frankenstein* convey the fear that the development of artificial means of reproduction will inexorably lead to their uncontrollable abuse. Futuristic

---

[46] For example, Lee and Morgan, 1989, p. 1; Farquhar, 1996, p. 27; HGAC and HFEA, 1998, para. 5.1; Putnam, 1999, p. 8.

images and narratives drawn from popular culture tend to activate collective suspicion of scientists[47] and have even been said to constitute "an extremely effective antirationalist critique of science".[48] The word *Frankenstein*, for example, has a strikingly specific cultural meaning:[49] it communicates both wonder at the extraordinary power of science, and fear of the horrifying reper-cussions if scientists are allowed to give their amoral curiosity free reign.[50] In the context of reproductive technologies, we can trace this ambivalence in popular representations both of "miracle" babies bringing unprecedented joy to the infertile, and of the dangers to society if "designer" babies are produced to order.

This kind of slippery slope or "don't-trust-human-beings objection"[51] has been a common response to the development of all new reproductive techno-logies.[52] Yet it is not clear that the possibility that a technique might be abused offers, on its own, sufficient reason to prohibit its use, especially given the enor-mous potential benefits that might flow from helping involuntarily childless people to reproduce. Must we deny infertile people access to technology that might enable them to overcome their biological bad luck because there can be no guarantee that the techniques will never fall into the hands of unscrupulous scientists? I would argue that a more logical response to these sorts of concerns would be to construct an effective and comprehensive regulatory structure that might be better able to police undesirable practices than an unworkable blanket ban. However, it is not only the possibility of reproductive technologies' misuse that concerns some critics. Others are dubious about the moral propriety of any human interference in the process of conception. Of course, human beings have *always* tried to control the reproductive process, through, for example, rules governing sexual relations and the capacity to marry. Thus, while technical intervention in the process of *conception* may be new, "however primitive the means may have been: the attempt to exercise control over human reproduction

---

[47] Eric Hirsch's research into public attitudes confirmed the prevalence of this dual image of reproductive cloning. As one of his interviewees' commented: "if you can give a couple, who want children, the ability to have children by artificial insemination by fertilising the egg inside, outside the body whatever, then reimplanting, fine, you're giving Nature a helping hand. But if you're try-ing to create the master race, by fiddling around with genetics, that's wrong" (quoted in Hirsch, 1999, p. 102).

[48] Toumey, 1992, p. 434. Robert Edwards has argued that "whatever today's embryologists may do, Frankenstein or Faust or Jekyll will have foreshadowed, looming over every biological debate" (Edwards, 1989, p. 70).

[49] Turney, 1998, p. 6. Willard Gaylin, co-founder of the US ethics institute the Hastings Center, has said that the *Frankenstein* myth "has a viability that transcends its original intentions and a rel-evance beyond its original time (quoted in Kolata, 1997, p. 73).

[50] See further Tudor, 1989.

[51] Fletcher, 1998 [1974], p. 120.

[52] According to Michael Mulkay "in the Parliamentary debates of the 1980s, the dominant metaphor was that of the 'slippery slope' " (Mulkay, 1997, p. 148). James Watson, for example, explicitly used this sort of "thin end of the wedge" argument to justify his scepticism about the devel-opment of *in vitro* fertilisation. If embryo manipulation becomes possible, he argued, "the situation would then be ripe for extensive efforts, either legal or illegal, for human cloning" (quoted in Kolata, 1997, p. 70).

is as old as the human race itself".[53] Nevertheless, it is axiomatic that infertility treatment is not the natural way to reproduce, and for some its unnaturalness is sufficient reason to discourage or prohibit its use.[54]

The equation of that which is "natural" with that which is "good" has a long history. John Stuart Mill, for example, described the word "unnatural" as "one of the most vituperative epithets in the language".[55] Yet it is perhaps interesting that human intervention in the process of procreation provokes much greater repugnance and outrage than similarly unnatural attempts to reduce pain, or cure disease. Moreover, this uneasiness tends to be confined to interventions only in the very earliest stages of human reproduction: technical interference in pregnancy and childbirth through, for example, fetal monitoring, prenatal testing or surgical delivery, is seldom condemned on the grounds of its *unnaturalness*.

Nor is it clear that there is a crisp boundary between natural and unnatural reproduction, rather the reality may be that "unnatural" interventions in the procreative process exist on a continuum, from simple ovulation-predictor kits to high-tech procedures such as ICSI.[56] The line between natural and unnatural reproduction is further blurred by some of the processes involved in assisted conception. If a woman conceives following intra-uterine insemination (IUI), for example, the fertilisation of her egg and its implantation in her uterus takes place in the "natural" way.[57] IUI is only unnatural because the sperm does not enter the woman's body though ejaculation during sexual intercourse. Similarly, when eggs and sperm are mixed in a petri dish, fertilisation takes place naturally, albeit in an unnatural environment.[58] A woman who conceives following donor insemination or IVF may otherwise experience a completely "normal" pregnancy, and a woman who conceives as a result of heterosexual sexual intercourse may go on to have multiple technological interventions during her pregnancy and childbirth. Pregnancies are not then self-evidently either natural or unnatural, rather these allegations of unnaturalness consist in the judgement that a particular method of *conception* is morally defective.

---

[53] Bayertz, 1994, p. 21. Plato advocated control over sexual partnerships in order to promote optimum reproductive outcomes. And the Dominican monk, Tommaso Campanella, writing in 1602 believed that "matters of reproduction should be tended to above all else", and that sexual intercourse between appropriate individuals should be supervised (see further Bayertz, 1994, pp. 23–7).

[54] According to Leon Kass "what has been violated, even if only slightly, is the distinction between the natural and the artificial, and, at its very root, the nature of man himself. For man is the watershed which divides the world into those things that belong to nature and those that are made by men. To lay one's hands on human generation is to take a major step toward making man himself simply another of the manmade things (Kass, 1972, p. 54).

[55] Mill, 1874 [1969], p. 377.

[56] See further Michie and Cahn, 1997, p. 129.

[57] Indeed some providers of infertility services stress that they are facilitating natural processes. Barad and Cohen, for example argue that they "bring the components needed for reproduction into contact with each other (so that) nature will take its course" (Barad and Cohen, 1996, p. 27).

[58] Sarah Franklin has remarked upon patient leaflets' tendency to represent IVF as a simple, natural procedure through the use of phrases such as "giving Nature a helping hand" (Franklin, 1997, p. 103).

So this revulsion at the artificiality of infertility treatment does not consist in a general criticism of all that is unnatural, but instead embodies a much more specific belief in the impropriety of separating sex from conception.[59] According to this critique, the unity of sexuality and reproduction is not simply a biological fact, like the existence of disease, that humans can legitimately attempt to manipulate, rather it is a fundamental moral principle.[60] The mystery and invisibility of conventional conception is thus imbued with a moral significance quite unlike other previously immutable biological processes such as infection, or the spread of contagious diseases.[61]

There are those who believe that human life is inevitably degraded if conception takes place in a laboratory following masturbation and surgical egg retrieval, rather than inside a woman's body after sexual intercourse.[62] Family bonds that result from the randomness of love can more easily be attributed to divine providence than kinship relations created by scientists.[63] The Catholic Church, for example, believes that children should "be brought about as the fruit of the conjugal act specific to the love between spouses".[64] Yet even if we accept that the existence of a loving relationship between a child's parents promotes her emotional wellbeing, there is manifestly no guarantee of a loving relationship between two people who have engaged in unprotected sexual intercourse. Neither does their sexual encounter ensure that a couple will prove to be stable and caring parents. It could even plausibly be argued that the commitment necessary to endure repeated cycles of infertility treatment offers better evidence of the resilience of the parents' love for each other than the simple fact of intercourse.

It is, however, undeniable that the discontinuity between conception and sexual contact may complicate the narrative of our origins, and reconfigure

---

[59] This was especially notable in the "virgin-birth" hysteria that accompanied the announcement in 1991 that women who had never had sexual intercourse were being given infertility treatment (Strathern, 1999a, p. 10; Faludi, 1992, p. 461).

[60] For example, Nicholas Tonti-Filippini says that "the Church gives sexual expression a very high status, it is the altar on which a family is founded" (Tonti-Filippini, 1999 [1994] p. 94).

[61] Joseph Fletcher explains how "the respect-for-life objection is often tied psychologically to the feeling that mastery of life will kill its mystery and that the mystery of life is essential to respect for it. This attitude in turn reinforces the 'stop meddling' attitude which favors blissful ignorance. If it were to dominate it would stifle or at least hobble not only biology but the chemistry on which biology is built" (Fletcher, 1998 [1974] p. 119).

[62] An example of this comes from Leon Kass who says that "with *in vitro* fertilisation, the human embryo emerges for the first time from the natural darkness and privacy of its own mother's womb, where it is hidden away in mystery, into the bright light and utter publicity of the scientist's laboratory, where it will be treated with unswerving rationality, before the clever and shameless eye of the mind and beneath the obedient and equally clever touch of the hand" (Kass, 1998 [1979] p. 113).

[63] For example, Thomas Murray argues that "certain values at the core of new reproductive technologies are at odds with the values most central to creating and sustaining the relationships that are at the heart of family life. The new reproductive technologies emphasise values such as control, choice and contract" (Murray, 1996, p. 60).

[64] Congregation for the Doctrine of the Faith, 1990, p. 28.

some conventional understandings about the foundations of kinship.[65] Procreation which requires neither a heterosexual sexual relationship nor biological fertility opens up the possibility of parenthood, with all its social and cultural significance, for people whose age or way of life would previously have been incompatible with reproduction. The fact that biological connections, or the "facts of life" have traditionally been the foundation of kinship relations[66] convinces some people that genetic relatedness must be the normatively desirable basis for family life.[67] Marriage, which is a voluntarily assumed relationship between people without any "blood" ties becomes, on this view, a valid kinship relationship because its purpose is the mixing of the couple's genes through procreation.[68] But the heterogeneity of family life in the twenty-first century means that increasing numbers of children grow up within step-families and form complex sets of non-blood relationships. Reproductive technologies are not then a unique threat to the conventional bonds of kinship.

Moreover, despite their radical transformative potential, almost all assisted conception techniques are in fact directed towards creating families based upon biological connections between parents and their children. The vast majority of children born following infertility treatment are genetically related to one or both of their parents. Most children conceived through IVF or ICSI are their parents' genetic offspring, while children born as a result of gamete donation are usually genetically related to one of their parents. So unless infertility is perceived to represent divine judgement that an individual would be an inadequate parent, those who believe in the moral priority of "blood relationships" should, perhaps, celebrate reproductive technologies' capacity to enable infertile people to have genetically related offspring.

(b) Child Welfare Arguments

We return to the "child welfare" arguments against assisted conception several times in this and the following chapter. Critics of infertility treatment, and of surrogacy, often cite the possibility of a negative impact upon children's welfare

---

[65] According to Marilyn Strathern, reproductive technologies "have the potential to make us think again about what we take for granted, what we look for in family life, how we regard the relationship between parents and children" (Strathern, 1999b, p. 180). Jeanette Edwards explains that the anthropologist's interest in reproductive technology stems from the premise that "human reproduction not only creates new human beings but also kin relations" (Edwards, 1999, p. 61).

[66] Although it must be remembered that the significance accorded to conception is culturally specific. Other cultures have, for example, placed more emphasis upon nurture and feeding as the foundation of kinship relations (Strathern, 1999a, p. 24).

[67] Cynthia Cohen says that "part of what gives meaning and cohesiveness to our lives and helps us to feel recognised as individuals is our biological connectedness to others in our families" (Cohen, 1996, p. 98).

[68] According to Lisa Cahill "when we consider our responsibility to a family member, the fact that he or she is related to us by blood or genes counts. Biological relationship is cross-culturally the foundation of the social meaning of family. Even marriage, which is itself not a blood relation, is consummated biologically through sexual union and the procreation of offspring who are the genetic combination of both parents" (Cahill, 1996, p. 74).

as though this in itself provides sufficient reason to restrict or prohibit alternative methods of conception. My argument in both chapters will be that unless we are concerned to prevent reproduction in anyone who may offer a suboptimal environment for their children's upbringing, then restricting the reproductive options of infertile people on the basis of some vague appeal to child welfare may be both disingenuous and discriminatory.

Unsurprisingly, there is considerable interest in the emotional development of children born following assisted conception. Because the first IVF birth took place in 1978, there is little empirical evidence of its long-term impact upon children. But such studies as have been completed, and the evidence from children born following donor insemination,[69] appears to show that children conceived in non-traditional ways do not suffer particular psychological trauma as a result.[70] Because the children are wanted, valued and loved, it is probably unsurprising that the great majority of families created using DI or IVF seem to be functioning well.[71]

A different sort of child welfare objection to infertility treatment is the contention that it might be immoral to create new babies when there are already so many abandoned or ill-treated children who would benefit from being adopted.[72] But since procreation among the fertile population is not similarly dismissed as selfish and immoral, even if a conception was deliberately achieved for ill-considered or self-regarding reasons, it is unclear why moral responsibility for the world's neglected children should be assigned to infertile men and women.[73]

(c) The Feminist Critique

Some of the most vocal critics of reproductive technologies have been feminists. In 1984 Gena Corea, Renate Klein, Janice Raymond and Robyn Rowland were instrumental in setting up the Feminist International Network on the New Reproductive Technologies (FINNRET), later FINRRAGE (Feminist International Network of Resistance to Reproductive and Genetic Engineering), with the purpose of publicising their hostility to reproductive technologies. Despite FINRRAGE's coherent manifesto, it would be a mistake to imagine that there has been a single feminist response to infertility treatment. Rather, feminists have

---

[69] Snowden and Snowden, 1998.

[70] Golombok *et al*,1995; Golombok *et al*, 1996; Brewaeys *et al*, 1997.

[71] Snowden and Snowden, 1998, p. 36.

[72] Patricia Smith, for example says "the world does not need babies any more, at least not very many of them" (Smith, 1995, p. 113). The Wellcome Trust's survey of public attitudes found "some suggestion that adoption was a socially preferable solution for infertility" (Wellcome, 1998, p. 27).

[73] According to Derek Morgan the argument that adoption of marginalised children is the solution to infertility is in fact "a cheap and convenient way to alleviate guilt . . . helping us to overcome two difficult and very different social problems by the quick fix of alloying the selfishness of the infertile with the plight of the helpless, the abandoned, rejected or destitute" (Morgan, 1988, p. 235).

raised a variety of disparate concerns, unified only by their conviction that reproductive technologies' may have some negative impact upon women's physical or mental wellbeing.

The diversity between different feminist analyses of reproductive technologies derives, in part, from the existence of profound ambivalence about whether motherhood should be considered empowering or oppressive or both.[74] There are, for example, feminists who argue that reproductive technologies reinforce the cultural assumption that a woman's primary purpose is to become a mother. In contrast, other feminists argue that assisted conception degrades women by corrupting the positive experience of natural maternity and supplanting women's biological monopoly over certain aspects of procreation. The medicalisation of conception is thought by some feminists to raise similar issues of control and power as the medicalisation of pregnancy and childbirth, discussed in chapter four. Additionally, there has been concern that women may be undergoing infertility treatment without having adequately appreciated the strain and risks involved, while some feminists have doubted whether fully informed consent to infertility treatment is even possible.

There are, of course, interesting parallels between feminist opposition to infertility treatment, and the feminist criticism of paid surrogacy that I consider in detail in the following chapter. In both chapters, I argue that not only do these various objections to alternative procreative strategies rely on ultimately unconvincing arguments, they also betray a regrettable tendency to disregard or trivialise the experiences and preferences of people who are unable to reproduce without external assistance.

(i) Motherhood

Some feminists have suggested that reproductive technologies degrade women by reinvigorating the patriarchal premise that a woman's principal function is to become a mother.[75] The availability of infertility treatment, according to these critics, reinforces the pro-natalist bias within society and exerts pressure upon women to consent to potentially risky and unpleasant procedures.[76] By assuaging the (socially constructed) desires of infertile women, assisted conception is accused of harming *all* women by amplifying the message that childbearing is

---

[74] Dion Farquhar describes how, on the one hand maternity keeps women dependent, but on the other it is a site of positive ethical experience. So motherhood is associated with both self-sacrifice, and with personal enrichment (Farquhar, 1996, pp. 101, 3).

[75] For example Joan Callahan and Dorothy Roberts argue that "reproduction-assisting technologies . . . contribute to the subordination of women by continuing to tie the value of women to reproduction" (Callahan and Roberts 1996, p. 1211).

[76] Rosemarie Tong, for example, believes that infertility treatment imposes a pressure upon infertile couples to keep trying: "not wanting to let any stone go unturned, such couples often find it extremely difficult to say 'no' to this one last chance. Very likely they will think, or be caused to think, that were they to forsake this final opportunity, they might never forgive themselves" (Tong, 1996, p. 138).

their natural destiny.[77] Yet without equivalent criticism of the desire for motherhood in fertile, heterosexual women, this sort of criticism embodies a curious disdain for the preferences of infertile women. It is undoubtedly true that a woman's decision to have children is shaped by a complex network of social expectations and cultural norms, but this is true for everyone, not only for those whose decision is subsequently thwarted by their or their partner's biological incapacity. Few feminists object to motherhood in principle, rather their concern is with dominant gendered assumptions about familial roles. In the absence of oppressive maternal stereotypes, this derivative objection to infertility treatment would surely disappear. In fact it could be argued that far from reinforcing prevailing familial norms, reproductive technologies' separation of heterosexual sex and procreation might help to subvert them by, for example, facilitating motherhood in single or lesbian women.[78]

That most of the invasive processes involved in assisted conception are performed upon the female body, even where it is the male rather than the female partner who is infertile, is cited by some feminist critics as yet another example of women unilaterally assuming all of the physical burdens of reproduction.[79] But while it is undoubtedly true that fertile women undergo invasive procedures because of their partner's infertility, this does not necessarily reveal fundamental gender bias in the provision of assisted conception services. Infertility is not like other diseases because the capacity to conceive is necessarily collaborative. A fertile woman with an infertile partner is, unless she has sexual intercourse with another man, unable to have children. ICSI, which allows a woman to conceive using her partner's sperm, may be more intrusive than donor insemination but this does not necessarily reflect men's obsession with genetic lineage taking priority over women's comfort and safety.[80] Women who claim to prefer to conceive using their partner's sperm rather than that of an anonymous stranger, despite the additional risks and inconvenience involved in ICSI, are not necessarily sublimating their own needs to those of their partner. If the desire to have one's partner's child is socially constructed, this must be equally true for women who have the good fortune to have fertile partners. Insofar as most women take

---

[77] For example April Cherry has suggested that "there must be a point at which the rights of individual women impinge so strongly on women as a social group that social or legal regulation is required" (Cherry, 1997, p. 439). Deborah Steinberg has criticised analyses which take infertile women as their starting point, which, she says, "may suggest. . .that the experiences of infertile women are more important than other women, and indeed, in the context of IVF, that theirs are the only experiences that must be considered" (Steinberg, 1997, p. 7).

[78] Lublin, 1998, p. 137.

[79] See further Arditti et al, 1984. Barbara Katz Rothman explains that "(i)f a man has a high sperm count the infertility problem is treated entirely as the woman's, whereas if the man has a low sperm count, the problem is *still* treated largely as the woman's" (emphasis in original) (Rothman, 1989, p. 149). According to Deborah Steinberg "it would seem an unprecedented move in medical circles to subject a person to such an invasive and risky treatment regimen for the purpose of treating someone else's condition when that condition is non-fatal (and that person is himself not undergoing treatment)" (Steinberg, 1997, p. 46).

[80] Callahan and Roberts argue that liberalism's tendency to privilege genetic procreation is socially constructed (Callahan and Roberts, 1996, p. 1214).

the satisfaction of their preference for bearing their partner's child for granted, it is not clear why the validity and authenticity of an equivalent preference among women with infertile partners should be impugned.

(ii) Usurping Women's Natural Power

Women's innate biological monopoly over certain aspects of the reproductive process is celebrated by certain other feminists as a particularly potent source of power for women, which is threatened by the encroachment of (male) medical expertise into the process of conception.[81] The medicalisation of conception is sometimes treated as a logical progression from the medicalisation of childbirth and pregnancy that we considered in chapter four.[82] Infertility treatment's dependence upon techniques of visualisation that open up the female body to intense scrutiny and minute analysis leads to the charge that its primary purpose is to discipline and manipulate the female reproductive body.[83] Since control over reproductive technologies lies with health care professionals, rather than with women, (male) doctors are accused of wielding unprecedented power over women's reproductive lives.[84] According to this view, by appropriating and manipulating women's bodies for their own nefarious scientific purposes, (male)[85] fertility specialists are usurping natural female power.[86]

There are several reasons why this feminist critique of unnatural reproduction is unconvincing. Contraception and safe abortion are, for example, similarly unnatural medical interventions in the reproductive process, however few feminists would deny fertile women access to artificial methods of birth

[81] For example Mary O'Brien argues that even though women's reproductive capacity has been a source of oppression for women, it has simultaneously been a source of power over life itself: so women have both an individual power to determine whether a partcular child will be born, and the collective power to determine whether the human species will continue (O'Brien, 1981). Similarly Robyn Rowland says that "for the history of 'mankind' women have been seen in terms of their value as childbearers. We have to ask, if that last power is taken and controlled by men, what role is envisaged for women in the new world?" (quoted in Tong, 1996, p. 185).

[82] See further Ehrenreich and English, 1978.

[83] Baruch, 1988.

[84] Sherwin, 1992, p. 120. Commenting on the process of ovarian stimulation, Gena Corea says "through these powerful hormones, men controlled the ovulation of women . . . here are men taking over one function of a woman's brain" (Corea, 1985, p.110).

[85] According to Rosi Braidotti, "the test-tube babies of today mark the long-term triumph of the alchemists' dream of dominating nature through their self inseminating, masturbatory practices. What is happening with the new reproductive technologies today is the final chapter in a long history of fantasy of self generation by and for men themselves—men of science, but men of the male kind, capable of producing new monsters and fascinated by their power" (Braidotti, 1994, p. 88).

[86] For example Sara Ruddick argues that "maternal thinking" has been an important part of the peace movement. She believes that because motherhood involves protection and nurturing, women are naturally non-violent (Ruddick, 1989). Susan Griffin advocates "the rejection of technology and the modern world in order to realign themselves with their true and essential source of strength: a pre-patriarchal affinity with nature" (quoted in Lublin, 1998, p. 47).

control.[87] There is an obvious inconsistency here: feminists have tended to embrace technological developments that enable fertile women to avoid the course of their lives being governed by their reproductive capacity. Yet an infertile woman's equivalent desire to use technology to prevent her future being determined by her reproductive *incapacity* is simultaneously challenged or even condemned.[88]

This celebration of natural maternity coupled with the denigration of artificial conception is puzzling because it implies that only fertile women in heterosexual relationships should become mothers. Given feminisms' concern with the structural limits that ingrained sexism has imposed upon women's freedom and opportunities, it seems odd that the biological restrictions of infertility are treated by some feminists as simply "the way things are".[89] This argument risks reinforcing the conservative message that the course of a woman's life should be determined by her natural procreative capacity *or incapacity*, and that families constituted through conventional heterosexual intercourse are preferable to those formed in non-traditional ways. It is, perhaps, strange for feminists to be troubled by an artificiality which consists in the absence of a penetrative heterosexual encounter.[90] Yet some feminists' suspicion of reproductive technologies undoubtedly leads them, rather paradoxically, to characterise the male/female sexual partnership as the only legitimate place to conceive children.

(iii) The Strain of Treatment

Research into the motivations of women who go through the emotionally, physically and financially demanding processes involved in infertility treatment has revealed that they tend to have two primary aims. First and most straightforward is the desire for a baby. But a second, less obvious goal is to exhaust every possibility before being able to come to terms with their childlessness.[91] However, it has been suggested that the peace of mind which women assume will come from knowing that they have tried everything tends, in practice, to be elusive.[92] The procedures are so complex that there is no obvious point of closure when patients can

[87] Although there are certainly some anti-technology feminists who are suspicious of any reproductive intervention: Feminists for Life, for example, describe abortion as "surgical rape" (for a thorough description of "ecofeminism" and its critique of reproductive technology, see further Lublin, 1998, p. 51).

[88] Rosalind Petchesky has attempted to circumvent this apparent contradiction by maintaining that abortion allows women to assert their independence from dominant cultural expectations, while infertility treatment reinforces the assumption that maternity is women's destiny (Petchesky, 1984, p. 388). But as I explained above, reproductive technologies can be used to subvert certain maternal stereotypes by enabling single, lesbian or older women to conceive.

[89] For example, Caroline Whitbeck appears to condemn reproductive technologies on the grounds that they "require that we make explicit decisions where formerly we made none" (Whitbeck, 1991, p. 58). It seems curious, to say the least, for feminists to celebrate women's lack of control over their fertility.

[90] Holmes *et al*, 1981, p. 255. It could even been argued that in separating reproduction from coitus, reproductive technologies render conception "less phallocentric" (Farquhar, 1996, p. 32).

[91] Sandelowski, 1993.

[92] Franklin, 1997, p. 11.

be satisfied that a successful outcome has become impossible.[93] During the course of infertility treatment, many women will come closer than they have ever been before to being pregnant by, for example, having live embryos transferred to their uterus.[94] As a result, the pressures of infertility treatment have been accused of intensifying the very desire for children that it is supposed to relieve.[95] The physical demands of ovulation induction and egg retrieval, coupled with the multiple points at which the process can fail mean that IVF is often experienced as an obstacle course. Repeated visits to the clinic for injections and scans, as well as for egg retrieval and the embryo transfer add to the perception among patients that infertility treatment "takes over their lives".[96] A woman's fertility declines with age, and so the disappointment of a failed treatment cycle is exacerbated by patients' perception that they do not have much time left.[97]

Research that highlights the inevitable strain of infertility treatment is undoubtedly valuable. By focusing doctors' attention upon the difficulties encountered by their patients, this sort of research might enable clinics to provide more accurate information prior to treatment and thus gain more fully informed consent. But while it may be true that infertility treatment is emotionally and physically taxing, this cannot be a sufficient reason to restrict women's access to treatment. Given that there are now various techniques which can alleviate involuntary childlessness, preventing women from using them on the grounds that they might suffer stress, discomfort and exhaustion would be unjustifiably paternalistic. We do not prevent someone from consenting to any other medical treatment because we think that they might find it tiring or upsetting. Provided that a women's consent is real, informed and voluntary, she must be allowed to decide for herself whether she wants to embark upon treatment for her or her partner's infertility.

(iv) Consent

Some feminists have, however, doubted whether informed consent to infertility treatment is even possible.[98] Women, it has been argued, only submit to the

---

[93] Charis Cussins explains that "the structuring of treatment is open-ended in the sense that there is always another combination of hormones, another cycle of artificial insemination, another go at IVF that can be embarked upon" (Cussins, 1998, p. 76). Similarly, Gena Corea argues that "there is no easy way off of the medical treadmill" (Corea, 1985, p. 6).

[94] It has, for example, been suggested that IVF patients may become emotionally attached to their frozen embryos, which can seem to represent hope and future parenthood, and if their IVF treatment is ultimately unsuccessful, their cryopreserved embryos may have been the closest an infertile couple ever came to becoming parents (Overall, 1995, p. 189).

[95] Franklin, 1997.

[96] In Sarah Franklin's study of women undergoing IVF treatment, 70% had either already left full time employment or were planning to do so for reasons directly related to their treatment (Franklin, 1997, p. 124).

[97] A clinician interviewed in Frances Price's study remarked that infertile women were "some of the most impatient patients in the world" (Price, 1999, p. 31).

[98] Renate Klein has argued that informed consent to IVF is a "farce" (Klein, 1989, p. 246). Similarly Gena Corea suggests that "the appearance of voluntarism is deceptive, for the control over women begins long before they can voice a 'free choice' " (Corea, 1985, p. 169). Joan Callahan and Dorothy Roberts say that "pronatalist social attitudes do exert a troubling often insidious influence on women's choices to reproduce in general, and to seek potentially painful, risky and expensive

gruelling procedures involved in infertility treatment as a result of overwhelming pressure either from their male partner, or from society. A woman's reluctance to accept her unwanted childlessness is thus assumed to be both inauthentic and socially-constructed.[99] Aside from the rather patronising assumption that women who use assisted conception services are "acting out of mindless socialization",[100] it is odd that an infertile woman's desire for the nearest possible approximation of a natural pregnancy and birth is seldom treated with equivalent respect to a fertile woman's preference for a natural delivery.

Given the high failure rates[101] and possible side-effects[102] of treatment, some feminists have claimed that IVF should be classified as an experimental treatment.[103] The significance of this would be that the voluntariness of women's consent would be subjected to more rigorous scrutiny. It would, for example, have to be established that women had given fully informed consent to taking part *in a research trial*, and had been told that they were free to withdraw their consent at any time. Yet it is doubtful whether these extra safeguards would actually make much difference to women's willingness to consent to IVF. Certainly in the early days of their research into the possibility of *in vitro* fertilisation, Robert Edwards and Patrick Steptoe "soon discovered that patients needed to be restrained from volunteering too much".[104] In the UK doctors are now under a duty to inform prospective patients about a treatment's success rate, both nationally and in the particular clinic.[105] The Royal College of

reproduction in particular" (Callahan and Roberts, 1996, p. 1227). Sheila McLean has argued that "the decision to embark on sometimes painful, often unsuccessful and frequently costly treatment is one which is only arguably representative of a free choice" (McLean, 1999, p. 40).

[99] Gena Corea has said that "(t)he propaganda . . . that women are nothing unless they bear children, that if they are infertile, they lose their most basic identity as women . . . has a coercive power. It conditions a woman's choices as well as her motivations to choose. Her most heartfelt desire, the pregnancy for which she so desperately yearns, has been—to varying degrees—conditioned" (Corea, 1985, p. 170). Sharyn L. Roach Anleu has said that "women are more concerned with infertility because the social consequences of childlessness, that is the absence of children . . . are greater for them than for men because of the pervasive norms surrounding motherhood as central to an adult, heterosexual, married woman's identity" (Roach Anleu, 1997, p. 109).

[100] Berg, 1995, p. 85.

[101] Elizabeth Heitman has argued that the proportion of infertile couples who can actually be helped by infertility treatment has been exaggerated (Heitman, 1995). According to Callahan and Roberts "if enrolling women do not understand the failure rates of these programs, their participation in them is not acceptably voluntary" (Callahan and Roberts, 1996, p. 1229).

[102] There have been suggestions that superovulatory drugs create an increased risk of certain sorts of cancer, although the evidence seems inconclusive (Venn *et al*, 1999). The HFEA's Working Group on New Developments in Reproductive Technology reviewed the literature in 1998 and concluded that there was no convincing evidence for such an association (HFEA, 1999, p. 31).

[103] Rowland, 1999, p. 96. Gena Corea has suggested that IVF was not sufficiently thoroughly tested on animals before it was used on humans. According to Corea, scientists' desire for self-aggrandisement through achieving the first IVF birth took precedence over the minimisation of risk (Corea, 1985, pp. 99–186). Sheila McLean describes how women "have been used more frequently, and more damagingly, than others as a vehicle for inadequately tested or researched procedures, techniques and technologies", and asks "why should we believe that these new technologies will be any different?" (McLean, 1999, p. 37).

[104] Edwards and Steptoe, 1981, p. 93.

[105] HFEA Code of Practice 1998, para. 4.4a.

Obstetricians and Gynaecologists' Guidelines stress that couples should be clearly advised of the probability of achieving a live birth,[106] and in her study of women participating in IVF treatment, Sarah Franklin found that "95 per cent of the women interviewed were well aware of the low success rate of IVF before they decided to attempt it".[107]

(v) Ignoring Infertile Women

Within feminist criticism of reproductive technologies, the perspective of women who have chosen to undergo infertility treatment is often conspicuously absent.[108] This is particularly curious given feminists' recognition in other contexts of the illegitimacy of presuming to understand the experiences of differently situated women. The anti-essentialist critique, developed in the 1980s, undoubtedly had a profound impact upon feminist theory, much of which is now self-consciously attentive to the multiple differences that exist between women.[109] Yet no equivalent reticence is evident within feminist criticism of the women who choose to undergo infertility treatment. To judge and make assumptions about the experience of infertility without knowing what it is like to be a woman who wants to have children but whose only chance of becoming pregnant is with medical assistance, is, I would argue, as illegitimate as any other exclusionary tendency.

In sum, all of the various criticisms made of infertility treatment and associated embryo research fail, in my opinion, to treat the life plans of infertile men and women with appropriate respect. For most human beings, having children is of profound importance and this is no less true for people for whom unassisted conception has proved to be impossible. Of course it is unnatural for conception to take place outside of a woman's body, but almost all of modern medicine is directed towards improving people's quality of life by interfering with nature. Once we have established that a technique that can alleviate involuntary childlessness is safe, it seems to me that we should be concerned to facilitate its use by individuals whose lives may have been blighted by their biological misfortune. The child welfare objection to infertility treatment lacks any empirical basis, and it is simply implausible to suggest that a child conceived in a certain way will inevitably have parents who are incapable of meeting her needs throughout her childhood. Being fertile is not necessarily synonymous with being a good parent, and *vice versa*. The quality of a child's upbringing is principally determined by

---

[106] RCOG, 2000.

[107] Franklin, 1997, p. 83.

[108] Barbara Berg says that "fertile individuals demonstrate an amazing lack of concern for the perspective of those who experience difficulty having children" (Berg, 1995, p. 94). Naomi Pfeffer has commented upon the fact that "the one voice that is never heard is that of the most directly implicated: the voice of infertile women. Because of their absence, this debate appears, from the perspective of an infertile woman, to be curiously ill-informed about what it is like to be infertile, socially, medically and emotionally" (quoted in Lublin, 1998, p. 68). Sarah Franklin's perceptive and sympathetic account of women undergoing IVF treatment is a useful antidote to this tendency, see further Franklin, 1997.

[109] For a lucid account of this process, see further Conaghan, 2000.

the ways in which she is treated by her parents, rather than by the manner in which her mother's egg was fertilised. The various feminist objections to reproductive technologies again reveal differential treatment of fertile and infertile women. Women have infertility treatment because they want to be mothers. That this desire emerges from a cultural context in which women expect, and are expected to become mothers is undeniable, but this is equally true for fertile heterosexual couples whose desire for children is seldom similarly dismissed on grounds of inauthenticity. Recognising that a woman's preferences are shaped by her environment is not, in itself, a cogent reason to question the existence of technologies that may enable her to meet a valued life goal.

We return to some of these criticisms of reproductive technologies when we consider the regulation of specific techniques or procedures. In the following sections, we consider the framework within which assisted conception services are provided in the UK, with a particular focus upon some of the more contentious ethical dilemmas raised by reproductive technologies.

5. REGULATION IN THE UK

The birth of Louise Brown in 1978 was followed, throughout the world, by the setting up of national commissions to make recommendations about the regulation of infertility treatment.[110] In the United Kingdom, scepticism about the wisdom and moral acceptability of embryo research and assisted conception led to several attempts to foreclose embryo disposal, and thereby effectively prohibit treatment. Since embryo research is an essential precursor of infertility treatment, unsurprisingly the anti-abortion movement has objected vociferously to reproductive technologies' reliance upon embryo destruction.[111] Anti-abortion lobbying groups such as SPUC (Society for the Protection of the Unborn Child) and LIFE were instrumental in the organisation and briefing of MPs and peers opposed to the relatively liberal proposals for regulation of embryo research and infertility treatment laid out in the Warnock Report.[112]

[110] In 1982 Norman Tebbit commissioned the Committee of Inquiry into Human Fertilisation and Embryology, chaired by Mary Warnock. The Committee published its Report in 1984. The Report was debated in the House of Lords in 1984, although the Human Fertilisation and Embryology Bill, based upon Warnock's principal recommendations, was not introduced to Parliament until 1989. In 1989, the Canadian Government set up the Royal Commission on New Reproductive Technologies which consulted with 40,000 Canadians in the preparation of its report into the regulation of assisted conception. In the same year Canada also created the National Council on Bioethics, which issues guidelines on different areas of biomedicine. In France, the National Consultative Ethics Committee on Life and Medical Sciences (CCNE) was set up in 1983 to advise the government on bioethical issues (Bonnicksen, 1996, p. 167).

[111] LIFE, 1984. See further Yoxen, 1990 pp.184–8.

[112] Mulkay, 1997, p. 22. Leo Abse observed that in the debate in the House of Lords following publication of the Warnock Report "the overwhelming majority of Peers who spoke (against the Report) were supporters of SPUC" (Abse, 1986, p. 210). Given its religious roots, unsurprisingly the anti-abortion movement was also critical of the Warnock Report's failure to insist that infertility treatment should be available only to married people (Mulkay, 1997, p. 17).

Initially those opposed to embryo research were much better organised and appeared to have both public and parliamentary opinion on their side.[113] In 1985, their efforts were very nearly successful, and but for some effective delaying tactics in Parliament, embryo research and almost all IVF treatment would have become unlawful.[114] Between 1985 and 1990 the scientific and medical community campaigned to sway public and Parliamentary opinion, largely by stressing the potential health benefits of embryo research.[115] The passing of a relatively liberal statute in 1990 has been attributed, in part, to the fortuitous announcement that doctors and scientists working at Hammersmith Hospital had successfully performed preimplantation sex diagnosis in order to prevent the birth of a child suffering from a sex-linked genetic disorder.[116] Five days before the House of Commons voted on the Human Fertilisation and Embryology Bill, newspapers published a picture of Professor Robert Winston with the pregnant women who would be the first to benefit from this new technique when their healthy children were born in a few months time.[117] That IVF could be used to prevent serious disease and acute suffering significantly advanced the case for facilitative regulation. It should, however, be noted that while the arguments advanced by those who object on principle to embryo research and assisted conception were defeated in 1990, their right to live their lives according to their own moral convictions has been respected. In a clear parallel with abortion law,[118] health care professionals who have a moral objection to involvement in any activities licensed under the statute have a right to conscientious objection.[119]

In the following sections we consider the various functions fulfilled by the Human Fertilisation and Embryology Act 1990 and by the licensing authority set up by the statute. The regulation of reproductive technologies has two principal

[113] Michael Mulkay points out that the conservative lobby opposed to any embryo research, and therefore to treatment "was well organised, virtually unopposed and in control of a large section of parliamentary opinion" (Mulkay, 1997, p. 19).

[114] Enoch Powell's Bill would have permitted the creation of embryos only if they were going to be implanted into an identifiable woman, which would have stopped most IVF treatment, and all research. It passed its first reading on the 14 February 1985 by an overwhelming majority (238 MPs voted in favour of Powell's Bill, only 66 MPs voted against it). It only failed to become law because an alliance of scientists and Members of Parliament succeeded in talking it out of time. In 1986 Ken Hargreaves reintroduced the Unborn Children (Protection) Bill, and again it was initially approved by the House of Commons, this time by 229 votes to 129, although lack of Parliamentary time meant that it had no chance of becoming law. See further Mulkay, 1997, pp. 24–9.

[115] An organisation called the Progress Educational Trust was set up in November 1985 to work for increased public understanding of embryo research and the benefits of infertility treatment. Prior to the Parliamentary debates on the Human Fertilisation and Embryology Bill, Progress arranged for members of the House of Lords to be visited by families affected by genetic disease (Mulkay, 1997, pp. 28, 38). Arrangements were also made for MPs and members of the House of Lords to visit clinics and talk to patients and clinicians (Franklin, 1999, p. 157).

[116] Handyside *et al*, 1990.

[117] Mulkay, 1997, p. 41.

[118] Abortion Act 1967 s. 4.

[119] Human Fertilisation and Embryology Act 1990 s. 38 (1). It is, however, unlikely that this section would give a doctor working in an assisted conception clinic the right to refuse to treat a lesbian patient because he disapproved of her lifestyle because his objection would not then be to an *activity* governed by the Act, but to the treatment of a particular patient.

purposes: first to ensure that the techniques are safe and second that their use is ethical. As we see below, while setting minimum levels of safety might be relatively straightforward, policing the ethical acceptability of reproductive technologies has proved to be a far more divisive and difficult task.

(a) Controlling the Provision of Treatment

We begin our consideration of the control of assisted conception services with an overview of the licensing procedure and a summary of the licensing authority's role in the provision of treatment. In the second part of this section, we focus upon control of one particular practice, namely the use of techniques that inevitably increase the risk of multiple pregnancy.

(i) Licensing and Accountability

The pace of scientific progress in the field of assisted conception means that primary legislation has an inevitable in-built obsolescence. As a result, the Human Fertilisation and Embryology Act 1990 set up the Human Fertilisation and Embryology Authority (HFEA)[120] which operates as a licensing body,[121] allowing the integration of new technical developments without the need to return to Parliament for amendment to the primary legislation.[122]

One of the HFEA's most important purposes is to control the activities of licensed clinics and research centres. Sections three and four of the Human Fertilisation and Embryology Act 1990 provide that the creation and storage of an embryo, and the storage and use of gametes,[123] can only be carried out under licences granted by the Human Fertilisation and Embryology Authority. Failure to obtain a licence before carrying out any of these activities is a criminal offence.[124]

There are, however, some types of assisted conception which are not regulated by the HFEA. Self-insemination with fresh sperm can be accomplished without any professional assistance, and is not subject to any regulatory control. As a result there is no compulsory HIV screening, and the HFEA's strict rules relating to the donor's consent[125] and the need to consider the welfare of

[120] The Authority was established in August 1991. The Authority's twenty members are appointed by the UK Health Ministers, and at least half of them must not be scientists or doctors.
[121] The HFEA took over from the Voluntary (and then Interim) Licensing Authority which was established by the Royal College of Obstetricians and Gynaecologists and the Medical Research Council in 1985 following the publication of the Warnock Report (Price, 1989, p. 38). By 1989 it had approved 38 *in vitro* fertilisation centres (Morgan and Lee, 1989, p. xv).
[122] One of the duties of the Authority is to keep under review information about human embryos and assisted conception services. Although, as Christine Gosden from the Human Fertilisation and Embryology Authority has argued, any amendments to the regulation of embryo research "has to be at a pace that the public can support" (BBC2 Newsnight, 1998).
[123] Other than the gametes of the live husband/partner (section 4(1)(b)).
[124] Human Fertilisation and Embryology Act 1990 s. 41.
[125] Human Fertilisation and Embryology Act 1990 Schedule 3.

the child[126] do not apply. In addition, with no reporting requirements, we have little information about the incidence of informal gamete donation. So although we know that gay individuals or couples seeking reproductive partners regularly advertise in the gay press,[127] our understanding of the frequency or outcomes of these arrangements is extremely limited. GIFT's exclusion from the HFEA's regulatory framework[128] means that there are no restrictions upon the number of eggs that may be transferred, thus creating the risk of a multiple pregnancy. Similarly, super-ovulatory drugs can be prescribed by a general practitioner, again increasing the chance of a multiple pregnancy.[129]

It is not clear that these excluded treatments are necessarily less risky than those which are monitored and controlled by the HFEA.[130] Rather this regulatory lacuna derives from the preoccupation with embryology evident in both the Warnock Report and the Parliamentary debates on the Human Fertilisation and Embryology Bill.[131] In practice, of course, it would be difficult to maintain rigorous control over the practice of self-insemination with fresh sperm. Nevertheless, the HFEA's ability to comprehensively ensure the safe and ethical provision of infertility treatment in the UK is undoubtedly undermined by the existence of a few largely unregulated techniques.

There are currently 116 clinics licensed to carry out activities under the Act.[132] Licenses are granted for three-year periods, and a full inspection must precede license renewal. Interim or "focussed" inspections may be carried out more frequently depending upon the nature and licensing history of the clinics.[133] The conditions under which licenses will be granted and renewed are laid out in the Code of Practice that the HFEA was required to establish by the Act.[134] The HFEA Code of Practice is now in its fourth edition with a fifth edition due in 2001. In order to secure the safe use of gametes and embryos, the Code contains rules designed to ensure that clinics employ suitably qualified and experienced staff, and that proper procedures are followed.[135]

[126] Human Fertilisation and Embryology Act 1990 s.13(5).

[127] Hogben and Coupland, 2000.

[128] Although interestingly, the HFEA Code of Practice purports to subject GIFT to the "welfare of the child" condition (para. 3.13). However, because a license is not needed to carry out GIFT, it is not clear how there could be any sanction for failing to follow HFEA advice.

[129] In a highly publicised case Mandy Allwood conceived octuplets following her use of super-ovulatory drugs without adequate monitoring by specialist clinicians (Sheldon, 1997b). In 1987 septuplets were born to a woman in Liverpool who had used ovulation inducing drugs, the longest surviving child lived for only 16 days (Price, 1992, p. 97).

[130] Margaret Brazier has argued that "the composition of the regulated group is not dictated by the level of risk they pose to the woman being 'treated', the child or any donor" (Brazier, 1999a, p. 171).

[131] Mulkay, 1997.

[132] HFEA, 2000c, p.6.

[133] HFEA, 2000c, p.6.

[134] Human Fertilisation and Embryology Act 1990 s. 25.

[135] HFEA 1998, paras. 1.4–2.19; part 7. For example, sperm should only be produced outside of a licensed centre in exceptional circumstances, and all reasonable steps must be taken to ensure that the sperm was produced by the particular donor (HFEA Code of Practice 1998, para. 7.3).

The Code of Practice also lays out certain information that clinics are obliged to provide to potential patients. The clinic must, for example, inform the client of its own live birth rate per treatment cycle, and the national live birth rate for the particular treatment.[136] The side effects of ovarian stimulation, the risks of multiple pregnancy and the "possible disruption of the client's domestic life which treatment will cause" must be discussed.[137] The clinic is also under a duty to explain the rules governing the child's legal parentage.[138] Unlike consent to other medical procedures, consent to any treatment licensed under the Act must be in writing,[139] and adequate time for reflection must be permitted following the discussion of treatment with donated gametes.[140]

The provision of counselling to couples undergoing infertility treatment is widely assumed to be good clinical practice,[141] and the Human Fertilisation and Embryology Authority insists that all couples must be offered "implications"[142] counselling before consent is given to treatment.[143] Similarly, potential donors of gametes must be given the opportunity to have counselling. Yet confining the mandatory counselling requirement to an *offer* of services is unlikely to ensure its use. As we see later, infertility treatment is extremely expensive and most people have to pay for it themselves. As a result, very few patients will want to incur the additional expense of counselling, and unless counselling is provided free of charge, the uptake is likely to be low.

In addition to controlling the activities of licensed clinics, the HFEA collects and maintains a formal register of information about research projects, donors,

[136] HFEA Code of Practice 1998, para. 4.4a.
[137] HFEA Code of Practice 1998, paras. 4.4b, 4.4e.
[138] HFEA Code of Practice 1998, para. 4.4l.
[139] HFEA Code of Practice 1998, para. 5.2.
[140] HFEA Code of Practice 1998, para. 5.3.
[141] RCOG, 2000b.
[142] According to the HFEA Code of Practice (1998) para. 6.10, implications counselling involves inviting potential clients or providers of gametes and embryo to consider the following issues:

a. the social responsibilities which centres and providers of genetic material bear to ensure the best possible outcome for all concerned, including the child;
b. the implications of the procedure for themselves, their family and social circle, and for any resulting children;
c. their feelings about the use and possible disposal of any embryos derived from their gametes;
d. the possibility that these implications and feelings may change over time, as personal circumstances change;
e. the advantages and disadvantages of openness about the procedures envisaged, and how they might be explained to relatives and friends.

According to para. 6.11 counsellors should invite clients to consider in particular:

a. the client's attitude to their own, or partner's infertility;
b. the possibility that treatment will fail.

And para. 6.12 provides that where treatment using donated gametes or embryos is contemplated, clients should also be invited to consider:

a. their feelings about not being the genetic parents of the child;
b. their perceptions of the needs of the child throughout their childhood and adolescence.

[143] HFEA Code of Practice 1998, para. 6.1.

treatments and children born as a result of treatment. Information about the progress of research projects, and about the incidence and outcomes of infertility treatment must be published by the HFEA in its Annual Report, and its detailed records about licensed activities in the UK forms the largest database of its kind in the world.[144]

The HFEA seldom becomes involved in decisions about the treatment of individual patients. Only where a prospective patient's treatment involves a novel or especially complex ethical issue might the HFEA be called upon to express an opinion about the merits or otherwise of the proposed procedure. Thus, when a woman sought permission to export sperm taken from her deceased husband without his written consent, the HFEA was consulted.[145] Similarly, a couple who wanted to use preimplantation sex selection following the death of their only daughter had their case considered by the authority. In most cases, however, decision-making is delegated to the clinic with the threat of licence withdrawal for any failure to comply with the HFEA's Code of Practice. *Doctors*

Of course the HFEA is not the only mechanism through which clinics are accountable for their treatment of patients. Doctors in assisted conception clinics obviously owe their patients a duty of care just like any other medical practitioner.[146] An action in negligence would therefore be possible if the standard of care at a licensed clinic fell below that of "a responsible body of medical men skilled in that particular art",[147] and the patient could establish that they had suffered injury or loss as a result of the clinic or doctor's negligence.[148] This would generally only be possible where a patient has suffered physical injury as a result of negligent treatment. It is unlikely that the failure to achieve a pregnancy or a live birth could found a successful claim in damages. Even if continued unwanted childlessness were to be considered compensatable "damage", a couple would have to prove on the balance of probabilities that, but for the clinic's negligence, a pregnancy or live birth would have been achieved. Because the processes involved in fertilisation and implantation continue to be fundamentally unpredictable, establishing causation would be impossible.

Where a clinic's negligence, such as their failure to screen donated gametes, leads to the birth of a disabled child, the child will have an action against the clinic under section 1A of the Congenital Disabilities (Civil Liability) Act

---

[144] HFEA, 2000c, p. 10.

[145] See below, p. 208.

[146] In many states in America, malpractice litigation is the primary means for the regulation of infertility treatment (National Bioethics Advisory Commission, 1997, p. 89). Although guidelines exist in the US, compliance with them is voluntary, which means that malpractice litigation operates as the only legal sanction against poor practices (Klotzko, 1997, p. 434).

[147] McNair J in *Bolam* v. *Friern Hospital Management Committee* [1957] 1 WLR 582.

[148] For example in the American case of *Del Zio* v. *Columbia Presbyterian Hospital* (unreported) 74 Civ 3855 (US Dist Ct, SDNY November 9, 1978), a couple were awarded damages of $50,000 for their emotional distress after a physician, who believed that IVF was immoral, deliberately destroyed their stored embryos.

1976.[149] It is unclear whether gametes or an embryo could be treated as a "product" for the purposes of the Consumer Protection Act 1987. If this were possible, then an action could be brought if it could be established, as a result perhaps of HIV infection, that the gametes or embryos were not as safe as persons generally are entitled to expect.[150]

Because most treatment is carried out privately, there will often also be a contract between the clinic and the patient(s). Thus a private patient could have an action for breach of contract if a clinic failed to meet its contractual obligations. In November 2000, a couple succeeded in an action for breach of contract following the transfer of more embryos than originally agreed.[151] The consent form had specified that a maximum of two embryos were to be transferred, although the clinic claimed the patient had later agreed verbally to the transfer of three embryos. Following the birth of triplets, Hooper J held that Sheffield Fertility Centre had broken a term of their contract with the Thompsons. At the time of writing, the quantum of damages has yet to be assessed, but the public policy considerations found so compelling by the House of Lords in the *McFarlane*[152] case discussed in chapter two are likely to mean that the Thompsons will receive a relatively small, or possibly even nominal award for the costs of bringing up their unexpected child.

(ii) Multiple pregnancies

It has become standard practice in IVF treatment to transfer more than one embryo in order to increase the chance of achieving a pregnancy.[153] For the same reason, prior to donor insemination, women usually take super-ovulatory drugs.[154] Unsurprisingly, these techniques have also increased the likelihood of multiple pregnancy, with its associated risks of miscarriage, abnormality, perinatal mortality[155] and prematurity, and 47 per cent of babies born following *in vitro* fertilisation now come from a multiple pregnancy.[156]

[149] Inserted by s. 44 of the Human Fertilisation and Embryology Act 1990.

s.1A(1) In any case where—

(a) a child carried by a woman as the result of the placing in her of an embryo or of sperm and eggs or her artificial insemination is born disabled,

(b) the disability results from an act or omission in the course of the selection, or the keeping or use outside the body, of the embryo carried by her or of the gametes used to being about the creation of the embryo, and.

(c) a person is under this section answerable to the child in respect of the act or omissions,

the child's disabilities are to be regarded as damage resulting from the wrongful act of that person and actionable accordingly at the suit of the child.

[150] S. 3.

[151] Dyer, 2000b.

[152] *McFarlane* v. *Tayside Health Board* [1999] 3 WLR 1301.

[153] In the early years of IVF practice up to six embryos would be implanted at any one time (Price, 1989, p. 42).

[154] Bhattacharya and Templeton, 2000.

[155] The stillbirth and neonatal death rate for a triplet pregnancy is 6%, compared with 1% for singleton pregnancies (HFEA, 2000c, p. 11).

[156] HFEA, 2000c, p. 11.

AREA OF
NEGLIGENCE

In addition to the health problems common in multiple pregnancies and the additional strain upon parents,[157] provision of extra maternity and neonatal services[158] leads to increased costs to the National Health Service.[159] The chief priority of predominantly private infertility clinics is to maximise the "take home baby" rate per cycle of treatment, rather than to minimise NHS expenditure on associated maternity and neonatal services.[160] In addition to the pressure to achieve high live birth rates in order to retain their HFEA license and attract new clients, clinics may find that individual patients are eager to have as many embryos transferred as possible. The prospect of a multiple pregnancy holds understandable appeal for patients who are simply unable to imagine having *too many* babies.[161]

As we saw in chapter three, one way to avoid some of the problems associated with carrying a multiple pregnancy to term is for the pregnant woman to undergo fetal reduction, or the selective termination of one or more fetuses.[162] In practice, however, selective terminations are rare,[163] and are beset by legal and ethical complexity. A more effective solution to concerns about the dramatic increase in multiple births, especially higher order multiple births such as triplets and quadruplets,[164] has been the placing of an upper limit upon the number of embryos that may be transferred in any one cycle of IVF treatment.[165]

---

[157] Rates of postnatal depression are significantly higher following a multiple birth (Price, 1992; CCNE, 1991). Unlike some other European countries, such as Belgium where mothers of triplets are entitled to a full-time nanny and a part-time domestic help for three years, the UK has no organised system of public assistance to families with higher order births (Denton, 2000). Frances Price quotes a local authority social services department manager who said that cases of triplets and above "do not easily 'fit' in terms of local authority provision—i.e. not elderly, not handicapped, no real question of reception into care" (Price, 1992, p. 107).

[158] According to one study, 28% of triplets, and 62% of quadruplets spend a month or more in neonatal intensive care units (Price, 1999, p. 41), and another study found that 50% of triplet pregnancies and 75% of quadruplet pregnancies required extended periods of prenatal hospitalisation (Iberico *et al*, 2000, p. 2232).

[159] Naomi Pfeffer suggests that the extra demands upon neonatal care means that "National Health Service staff resent the pressure on their resources, especially where they have no control over the circumstances which generate that demand" (Pfeffer, 1993, p. 170).

[160] Most women who have private infertility treatment transfer to NHS care if they become pregnant. So, as Frances Price explains "private clinicians thereby relinquish responsibility for these (multiple) pregnancies to the public sector" (Price, 1999, p. 39).

[161] France Price refers to a French study in which only 7% of people attending an IVF programme expressed reservations about the possibility of multiple pregnancy. In a survey of patients at a London clinic 62% thought that twins would be the ideal result of their treatment, only 29% said that they would prefer a singleton pregnancy (Price, 1999, p. 41).

[162] The survival rate of the remaining fetuses in a quintuplet pregnancy following fetal reduction is 75.2%, compared to a 40% survival rate if the pregnancy is not reduced (Fasouliotis and Schenker, 1999, p. 32).

[163] 45 took place in 1999 (Abortion Statistics HMSO: 2000).

[164] The number of twin births has doubled and that of triplets has trebled since the development of IVF (Fisk and Trew, 1999, p. 1572). In 1997/8, there were 3 quad pregnancies, 283 triplet pregnancies, 1647 twin pregnancies and 4746 singleton pregnancies as a result of IVF treatment (HFEA, 1999, p. 16).

[165] It became evident that the percentage of women becoming pregnant did not increase dramatically with the transfer of more than three embryos, although the risk of multiple pregnancy was significantly higher. So in 1987, the Voluntary Licensing Authority introduced an upper limit of three

Currently the HFEA Code of Practice specifies that no more than three embryos can be transferred,[166] but the continued risk of triplet pregnancies has led to suggestions that a maximum transfer of two embryos would be preferable.[167] This would largely avoid triplet pregnancies, but would inevitably have some impact upon pregnancy rates, particularly among older women.[168] Abdalla *et al* suggest that for women aged 35–39, transferring two embryos rather than three would avoid nine triplet pregnancies per 1000 treatment cycles, at the expense of nineteen patients who would fail to achieve a live birth.[169] Similarly Craft *et al* argue that a blanket upper limit upon the number of embryos that may be transferred is "too crude and imprecise an approach", and they advocate instead that the number of embryos should be determined by an individual assessment of a particular woman's reproductive potential and risk of multiple pregnancy.[170]

Thus, as we have seen, through its guidance to clinics, and its role in monitoring the activities of licensed centres, the HFEA is the principal mechanism through which assisted conception services are controlled. As we see in the following section, control over who should have access to treatment consists in a mixture of statutory rules, health authority funding priorities and delegated clinical authority.

(b) Regulating Access

In the UK there are two types of restrictions upon who may have access to infertility treatment. First, the statute itself lays down provisions designed to ensure that treatment is most readily accessible to heterosexual couples. Second, in

embryos unless there were exceptional clinical reasons for transferring four embryos (Price, 1989, p. 43). Nevertheless in 1989 the then Interim Licensing Authority's Sixth Report found that 9.9% of all IVF embryo transfers were of four or more embryos, and that 59% of all GIFT transfers were of four or more eggs (Price, 1999, p. 39).

[166] HFEA Code of Practice 1998, para. 7.9.

[167] Templeton and Morris (1998) argue that the transfer of two embryos rather than three would not reduce the pregnancy rate. Although it should be noted that the studies that have been carried out have tended not to adjust for variations in embryo quality.

The Royal College of Obstetricians and Gynaecologists have suggested that a national move to transfer no more than two embryos would have the biggest impact on the current "unacceptably high" rate of multiple births (RCOG, 2000b). According to the HFEA, there has been a steady decrease in the number of transfers where the maximum of three embryos were replaced [68.6% in 1995/6 to 50.5% in 1998/9], and corresponding increase in the number of transfers where only two embryos were replaced [30.9% to 48.6% in the same period] (HFEA, 2000c, p. 11).

[168] Abdalla *et al* say that a transfer of two embryos is appropriate for women under 38 years where the embryo quality is high, or for women who would not consider fetal reduction in the event of a triplet pregnancy. But where women are older, or embryo quality is poor or variable, or where a woman has had repeated failed cycles in the past, Abdalla *et al* argue that transferring three embryos will have better results (Abdalla *et al*, 2000). The Royal College of Obstetricians and Gynaecologists have recommended that a maximum of two embryos should be transferred in women under forty (RCOG, 2000).

[169] Abdalla *et al*, 2000.

[170] Craft *et al*, 2000.

many parts of the country restrictions upon NHS funding largely confine access to people with considerable financial resources. Taken together, as Derek Morgan and Robert Lee have noted, these restrictions mean that "assisted conception is to be, for the most part, for the married, mortgaged middle-classes".[171]

Within the European Union, there is considerable variation between different countries' regulation of access to treatment. There are some countries where there are few restrictions upon access for single, lesbian or older women.[172] And there are other countries, such as France, where provided strict eligibility criteria are met, couples are entitled to publicly funded infertility treatment.[173] This variation of course raises the possibility that people unable to gain access to assisted conception services in their home country might seek treatment abroad. Because Article 59[174] of the European Treaty only applies to services which are "normally provided for remuneration", there could be no right to publicly funded treatment in another member state.[175] Consequently, it is only where a citizen is able to pay for infertility treatment in another country that the possibility of "reproductive tourism" arises. So, if they can afford it, postmenopausal women who have been denied treatment in the UK may travel to Italy for treatment, and single women who are unable to obtain treatment in France might travel to Spain.[176] In addition, then, to their privileged access to infertility treatment in the UK, wealthy infertile people may also be able to take advantage of less restrictive regulatory regimes within the European Union.[177]

In the following sections, we first consider the statutory framework within which clinics' decisions must be taken. We then examine the practical significance of constraints upon NHS funding for assisted conception services. Finally, we look at one particularly controversial group of potential patients, namely post-menopausal women, and I challenge the prevailing assumption that they are unsuitable or undeserving recipients of assisted conception services.

[171] Morgan and Lee, 1991, p. 146.

[172] For example Greece and Italy have virtually no regulatory measures, and in Spain any competent and healthy adult woman can make use of assisted conception techniques (Hervey, 1998, pp. 226–7).

[173] See further Latham, 1998.

[174] Article 59 of the E.C. Treaty specifies that restrictions on European nationals' access to services in other member states should be progressively abolished.

[175] Hervey, 1998, p. 215.

[176] Similarly, Swedish couples wanting to use anonymously donated sperm could seek treatment in other countries, such as the UK, where donor anonymity is guaranteed.

[177] Tamara Hervey says that this means that the "ability to rely on European rights is limited to those whose financial position permits them to pay for services sought in another member state", and she asks "whether it is equitable that some people can in effect 'buy their way out' of ethical or moral choices given legislative force in their own Member State" (Hervey, 1998, pp. 228–9).

(i) Statutory restrictions on access

There are some countries where access to infertility treatment is confined either to married[178] or to cohabiting heterosexual couples,[179] but an attempt in 1990 to amend the Human Fertilisation and Embryology Bill to similar effect was defeated, albeit narrowly.[180] In the United Kingdom, therefore, there is no absolute prohibition upon the treatment of single or lesbian women.[181] Instead the Warnock Report's conclusion that:

> "we believe that as a general rule it is better for children to be born into a two-parent family, with both father and mother"[182]

is given statutory effect by section 13(5) of the Human Fertilisation and Embryology Act 1990 which imposes a duty upon clinics to take account of:

> "the welfare of any child who may be born as a result of the treatment, (*including the need of that child for a father*)" (my emphasis).

If interpreted literally, this section is rather puzzling insofar as it exhorts a clinician to base his decision as to whether to attempt to bring a child into the world upon a consideration of that child's welfare. Given that, as we saw in chapter two in the context of wrongful life actions, the law generally presupposes that existence is better than non-existence, it is difficult to see how a clinician could decide that a child would be benefited by not being born.[183] Thus section 13(5) cannot in fact be directed towards assessing whether being conceived would promote the child's welfare, because if the alternative is not being conceived, it obviously would. Instead section 13(5) requires clinics to take into account the prospective patient's aptitude for parenthood.

Importantly, section 13(5) has to be read in the light of the provisions governing paternity that, as we see below, contemplate the birth of children who will have no legal father. Thus because children born to single or lesbian women treated in licensed clinics with anonymously donated sperm will be legally

---

[178] For example, Iran, Saudi Arabia and Jordan (Fasouliotis and Schenker, 1999, p. 27).

[179] For example, in Western Australia s. 23(c) of the Human Reproductive Technology Act 1991 specifies that IVF may only be carried out if the persons seeking to be treated are married to each other, or have been cohabiting in a heterosexual relationship as husband and wife for periods aggregating at least 5 years during the immediately preceding 6 years (Roach Anleu, 1997, p. 116). Similarly in Israel only married or long-term cohabiting couples can use infertility services. In Sweden only married or cohabiting couples can have access to assisted conception and in Denmark priority is given to married or cohabiting couples (Blank, 1998, pp. 143–4). Joseph Schenker points out that within Europe, most countries that have regulations restrict access to assisted conception to heterosexual couples, either married or in stable relationships, and even those countries without regulations in practice tend to confine access to heterosexual couples (Schenker, 1997, p. 175).

[180] An amendment which would have limited fertility treatment to married couples lost by one vote in the House of Lords (Brazier, 1998, p. 69).

[181] Single or homosexual men could only become parents by using surrogacy, discussed in the next chapter.

[182] Warnock, 1984, para. 2.11.

[183] *McKay* v. *Essex AHA* [1982] AB 1166, in which the Court of Appeal was not prepared to weigh existence against non-existence.

father*less*, clinics' duty to consider their child's *need for a father* translates into a statutory obligation to take into account the undesirability of single or lesbian motherhood.

Of course, the existence of a potential father-figure when assisted conception services are sought offers no guarantee of his continued presence.[184] Nevertheless, the purpose of this part of the Act is clear: it incorporates the political and moral belief that the heterosexual, two-parent family is the optimum, or even the only legitimate place to bring up children. Given that so many children conceived naturally do not grow up in two parent families, it is perhaps interesting that access to assisted conception should be dependent upon conformity with some notional ideal model of the family, rather than with the heterogeneous empirical reality of family life. Perhaps it is precisely because reproductive technologies have the *potential* to radically transform family relationships by facilitating procreation among single or lesbian women that the Act reasserts the desirability of the two-parent heterosexual family unit. It may also be worth noting that section 13(5) was drafted, debated and passed at a time when there was intense political interest in the "problem" of single parent families.[185] In 1990, infertility treatment's acceptability was therefore widely believed to be contingent upon it being used to support rather than to undermine the conventional nuclear family.[186]

Despite politicians' claims, this equation of children's best interests with the presence of a father-figure at the moment of conception lacks any sound evidential basis. There is no empirical evidence to support the view that lesbian parents impair their children's social and emotional development.[187] And while there have been many studies that purport to demonstrate a link between single parenthood and impaired future life chances, they may have little relevance for children born to single women following assisted conception. The chief causes of problems experienced by children who grow up with a single mother are poverty, isolation, residential mobility and the family discord associated with parental separation.[188] Women who choose to have fertility treatment on their own will be neither poor nor young, and they will not have had single motherhood thrust upon them as a result of either an unplanned pregnancy or a relationship breakdown.

The translation of unease about single and lesbian women's access to treatment into the structured exercise of medical discretion has clear parallels with abortion law.[189] And in the debates in Parliament in 1990, similar arguments to those used in 1967 were employed by MPs who advocated delegating the gatekeeping role to the medical profession. Rather than a blanket ban upon

---

[184] McLean, 1999, p. 41.

[185] Culminating in the passage of the Child Support Act 1991. For more on the "family values" debates of the early 1990s, see Jackson, 1997.

[186] Dewar, 1989, p. 123.

[187] See further Reece, 1996a.

[188] McLanahan and Sandefur, 1994.

[189] Thomson, 1998, p. 182.

treatment for single or lesbian women, which might simply encourage them to organise their own self-insemination in a regulatory vacuum, the medicalisation of access to treatment was promoted as the optimum way to persuade such women against autonomous motherhood. According to the then Lord Chancellor, Lord Mackay:

> "through counselling and discussion with those responsible for licensed treatment, (single women) may be discouraged from having children once they have fully considered the implications of the environment into which their children would be born or its future welfare".[190]

Just as it was thought that women seeking abortions might be persuaded to carry their pregnancy to term by discussions with a calm, rational medical practitioner, so it was argued that a single or lesbian woman would, through her encounter with an authoritative infertility specialist, come to recognise that her status might be incompatible with proficient motherhood. Yet as we saw in chapter three, the decision about whether or not to have a child is not one requiring clinical expertise, but is instead a social judgement made in the context of a woman's psychological, cultural and economic circumstances. Just as deciding *not* to become a mother is a decision that a woman may be best equipped to take for herself, so positively deciding to become a mother might also be a choice that a woman should be able to make without professional scrutiny.

A further parallel with abortion law is the relative invisibility of control once it has been delegated to doctors. This has two principal consequences. First, because decisions regarding eligibility are made on a case by case basis, there is considerable variation in practice. Just as women's access to abortion may depend upon the attitudes of both her general practitioner and her health authority, so there is little uniformity in the application of the statutory eligibility criteria for infertility treatment. Second, clinical judgement is, as we have seen at several points during this book, extraordinarily resilient to legal scrutiny. Clear statutory prohibition upon infertility treatment outside of the heterosexual nuclear family might seem obviously and unacceptably discriminatory. It is much more difficult to challenge discrimination when it is obscured by the interjection of the supposed neutrality and beneficence of the infertility doctor's discretion. For example, in a case[191] decided prior to the implementation of the Human Fertilisation and Embryology Act 1990, Schiemann J rejected an application for judicial review of a consultant's decision to remove a woman from the waiting list for IVF treatment on the grounds of her perceived unsuitability for parenthood,[192] arguing that:

[190] Lord Mackay HL Deb Vol 516 col. 1098, 1990 (6 March).
[191] R v. *Ethical Committee of St Mary's Hospital (Manchester) ex parte Harriott* [1988] 1 FLR 512.
[192] The clinic had discovered that she had been turned down for adoption on the grounds of her previous convictions for prostitution. Schiemann J said that "if the committee had advised, for instance that the IVF unit should in principle refuse all such treatment to anyone who was a jew or coloured (*sic*), then I think the courts might well grant a declaration that such a policy was illegal."

"it is not, and could not be, suggested that no reasonable consultant could have come to the decision to refuse treatment to the applicant".[193]

The BMA has suggested that when health professionals positively assist people to become parents, they have a special responsibility to protect the welfare of children born as a result of treatment, and of course, a clinician's concern for the wellbeing of children created with his assistance is readily understandable.[194] It is, for example, easy to imagine circumstances in which a doctor might be extremely reluctant to offer infertility treatment to a particular couple or individual. Yet the fact that an individual's infertility gives the opportunity for professional scrutiny of their fitness to parent does not necessarily mean that such scrutiny is either justified or desirable. Since respect for the civil liberties of the fertile population limits our capacity to determine whether or not they should be permitted to reproduce, it seems rather invidious and discriminatory to subject only the infertile population's fitness for parenthood to rigorous scrutiny.[195] People who seek infertility treatment will invariably have given considerable thought to the responsibilities of parenthood. On average, therefore, their aptitude for parenthood may even be greater than that of people who conceive haphazardly through unprotected sexual intercourse And if we respect the procreative choices of alcoholics, and people with a record of violence and abuse, even when we *know* that their children are likely to be disadvantaged, is it disingenuous to require infertile people to satisfy a conceptually incoherent version of the welfare principle prior to reproducing?[196]

It could be countered that we do restrict and regulate parenthood in the fertile population through provisions that allow a child to be taken into care[197] and even adopted[198] without their parents' consent.[199] But family law's protective function only applies to a child who already exists, and has no bearing upon a couple's choices prior to conception. Family law does not prohibit reproduction among the fertile population because values such as the protection of autonomy

---

[193] *Ibid.* at 519.

[194] For example, Guido de Wert argues, that "a doctor assisting in reproduction shares the responsibility for creating a new human being . . . judging the suitability for parenthood of infertile prospective patients is part of the professional responsibility of the physician" (De Wert, 1998, p. 231). And according to Rosemarie Tong "physicians argue that . . . they are partially responsible for the well-being of a child who would not have existed were it not for the interventions of medicine" (Tong, 1996, p. 152).

[195] John Harris has argued that procreative liberty is important "even though it may result in suboptimal outcomes for children" (Harris, 1999c, p. 128). And Heather Draper and Ruth Chadwick suggest that "parents can make mistakes without losing. . .the right to parent. We have, therefore to accept that parents can make misguided judgements" (Draper and Chadwick, 1999, p. 117).

[196] John Harris explains that "if we are serious that people demonstrate their adequacy as parents in advance of being permitted to procreate, then we should license all parents. Since we are evidently not serious about this, we should not discriminate against those who need assistance with procreation" (Harris, 1998b, p. 7).

[197] Children Act 1989, s. 31(2).

[198] Adoption Act 1976 s. 16(2).

[199] Deech, 1999, p. 97.

take priority over future children's welfare. Section 13(5), on the other hand, attempts to regulate certain people's capacity to conceive. So we reach the conclusion that the law is not in fact concerned to restrict childbearing among unsuitable parents, or to ensure that all children live with a parent of each sex. Rather, the law purports to restrict access to infertility treatment *because it can*. I would argue that the ease with which certain people's freedom can be restricted does not, without more, justify such restrictions.

It must also be admitted that doctors are manifestly not well positioned to make complex judgements about whether a couple will prove to be competent parents.[200] Doctors are not trained to be proficient judges of future parenting ability, and unless we give infertility clinics access to more detailed information about potential patients' backgrounds, personalities, previous relationships etc., then we are expecting them to make complex assessments with wholly inadequate knowledge. Either we do require serious and thorough consideration of a person's aptitude for parenthood, involving full investigation of their circumstances, or we do not. Although the HFEA's Code of Practice gives guidance on the interpretation and implementation of section 13(5),[201] given the

[200] For example, Robert Blank suggests that "expertise in a technical area does not ensure, and in some cases might even obscure, attentiveness to the social implications of technology" (Blank, 1998, p. 138). The Glover Report admitted that "it is hard to know who will be a good or bad parent" (Glover, 1989, p. 48).

[201] According to the Human Fertilisation and Embryology Authority Code of Practice (4th ed.) July 1998, para. 3.17:

"Where people seek licensed treatment, centres should bear in mind the following factors:

a. their commitment to having and bringing up a child or children;
b. their ability to provide a stable and supportive environment for any child produced as a result of treatment;
c. their medical histories and the medical histories of their families;
d. their health and consequent future ability to look after or provide for a child's needs;
e. their ages and likely future ability to look after or provide for a child's needs;
f. their ability to meet the needs of any child or children who may be born as a result of treatment, including the implications of any possible multiple births;
g. any risk of harm to the child or children who may be born, including the risk of inherited disorders or transmissible diseases, problems during pregnancy and of neglect or abuse; and.
h. the effect of a new baby or babies upon any existing child of the family."

and para. 3.18 states:

"Where people seek treatment using donated gametes, centres should also take the following factors into account:

a. a child's potential need to know about their origins and whether or not the prospective parents are prepared for the questions which may arise while the child is growing up;
b. the possible attitudes of other members of the family towards the child, and towards their status in the family;
c. the implications for the welfare of the child if the donor is personally known within the child's family and social circle and
d. any possibility known to the centre of a dispute about the legal fatherhood of the child"

and according to para. 3.19a:

"where the child will have no legal father centres are required to have regard to the child's need for a father and should pay particular attention to the prospective mother's ability to meet the child's needs throughout their childhood. Where appropriate, centres should consider particularly whether

inevitable superficiality of the information with which clinics are expected to determine prospective patients' fitness for parenthood, their assessments are likely to be perfunctory and at times ill-judged. Perhaps, therefore, section 13(5) is not actually motivated by profound concern for the welfare of children born following assisted conception, which would indubitably require a far more intensive and exacting scrutiny of prospective patients. Rather it may in fact be an essentially cosmetic provision designed to appease Members of Parliament whose fragile support for the Human Fertilisation and Embryology Bill was dependent upon infertility treatment being confined to "deserving" infertile heterosexual couples, and denied to "undeserving" single or lesbian women.

Not for welfare but so it got passed

(ii) Financial Restrictions on Access

Infertility treatment is expensive,[202] and it is seldom available within the National Health Service.[203] Even when treatment takes place in an NHS Hospital, it will often be within a quasi-private clinic.[204] According to the Royal College of Obstetricians and Gynaecologists, there is evidence of both inadequacy and inequity in the provision of infertility services in the UK.[205] Some health authorities do not pay for any infertility treatment, while others will fund up to three cycles of treatment per couple.

Where NHS treatment is available it is invariably subject to strict eligibility criteria and long waiting lists. Since success rates decline with a woman's age, health authorities invariably set an upper age limit for publicly funded treatment.[206] When coupled with a waiting list of two to three years, the common

there is anyone else within the prospective mother's family and social circle willing and able to share the responsibility for meeting those needs, and for bringing up, maintaining and caring for the child."

The Code of Practice also stresses that although centres must take account of both the wishes and needs of the people seeking treatment and the needs of any children "neither consideration is paramount over the other, and the subject should be approached with great care and sensitivity. Centres should avoid adopting any policy or criteria which may appear arbitrary or discriminatory" (para. 3.3.). Michael Thomson has argued that the use of the word "appear" here is revealing, suggesting, perhaps, that the HFEA is principally concerned to avoid the *appearance* of discrimination (Thomson, 1998, p. 184).

[202] One cycle of IVF treatment costs between £900 (in a not-for-profit facility) and £2200 (Bourn Hall clinic price list). While this may not seem too high a price for a much-wanted baby, given the 82% failure rate, this is a great deal of money to pay for nothing.

Throughout the world the accessibility of assisted conception services tends to correlate with a country's wealth. For example, countries in the former Soviet Union have one clinic for every 10–30 million people, whereas Scandinavian countries have two to three clinics per million (Schenker, 1997, p. 174).

[203] It may be worth noting that the other area of medical practice where private treatment is the norm is abortion.

[204] Naomi Pfeffer has argued that "the very existence of these quasi-private clinics within NHS hospitals serves an important ideological purpose: they are . . . an emblem of the new political economy of health care" (Pfeffer, 1992, p. 67).

[205] RCOG, 2000b.

[206] Tizzard, 1998, p. 3.

upper age limit of 35 requires a woman to be diagnosed as in need of assisted conception services by the age of 32 or 33. But since failure to conceive is only recognised as an indication for treatment after a year of unprotected sex, to be eligible for public funding, a woman must start trying to become pregnant at least 12 months earlier. So women who decide to abandon contraception in their early thirties, even if they are fortunate enough to live in an area where infertility treatment is available within the NHS, may nevertheless discover that, by the time their problem has been diagnosed and they have climbed their health authority's waiting list, they are too old for publicly funded treatment.

In rejecting an application for judicial review of Sheffield Area Health Authority's decision to refuse to fund treatment for women over 35 years old, Auld J held that health authorities were entitled to make decisions on the basis of the financial resources available, and given that infertility treatment is generally less effective in women aged over 35 years, it proved impossible to establish that the health authority's policy was illegal or irrational.[207]

Other common criteria for NHS treatment are evidence of the stability of a nonmarital relationship,[208] and that a couple has no existing children, either natural or adopted.[209] Some NHS clinics will only treat women who are close to their ideal body weight,[210] and most will fund no more than three cycles of treatment. Although these eligibility guidelines may seem overly restrictive, it must of course be remembered that funding *any* infertility treatment is more generous than the norm.

There are unknown numbers of infertile people who will never use assisted conception techniques.[211] Even people who do manage to pay for one or more cycles of treatment may not be able to afford the repeated attempts that are often necessary before a pregnancy is achieved. Since patients in assisted conception

---

[207] *R* v. *Sheffield AHA ex p. Seale* [1994] 25 BMLR 1.

[208] 49% of Health Authorities have criteria related to the length of a couple's relationship. One region in Scotland sets a minimum of five years (Caroline Spelman MP, Hansard 6 May 1998, col. 658). St Mary's Hospital (Manchester) requires couples to have been living together for at least three years. (McHale and Fox, 1997, p. 671).

[209] Tizzard, 1998, p. 3; Caroline Spelman MP, Hansard 6 May 1998, col. 658; Brazier, 1999a, p. 176.

[210] Being either overweight or underweight is associated with reduced fertility (Wang et al., 2000, p. 1320) St Mary's Hospital (Manchester) IVF guidelines state: "if you are overweight, it is difficult to see the ovaries on a scan and dangerous to undertake a laparoscopy or have a general anaesthetic. We treat women who are close to their ideal body weight for the height" (McHale and Fox, 1997, p. 671).

[211] In discussing egg donation and IVF, David Barad and Brian Cohen from the Montefiore Medical Center in the US say that "it has been our experience that only people with considerable disposable income have sufficient funds to undertake this procedure (Barad and Cohen, 1996, p. 22). In Canada the Royal Commission on New Reproductive Technologies found that 80% of IVF users had incomes over three times the national average (Royal Commission on New Reproductive Technologies, 1993, p. 554).

Joan Callahan and Dorothy Roberts point out that in the United States "specialised infertility services are twice as likely to be obtained by non-Hispanic white women than by Hispanic or Black women" (Callahan and Roberts, 1996, p. 1199). And this is despite the fact that the prevalence of infertility among black women is approximately 1.5 times greater than the rate among white women (Heitman and Schlachtenhaufen, 1996, p. 195).

clinics are the primary source of epidemiological data about infertility, our understanding of infertility and its treatment may itself be skewed by the under-representation of poorer sections of society in treatment services.[212]

Hostility to public funding for assisted conception services derives in part from the common perception that infertility treatment is a "luxury" that should not be paid for with scarce NHS funds.[213] According to these critics, infertility is best understood not as a disease but as an incapacity, in which case infertile individuals are not ill and needing treatment to restore their health, but instead are simply unable to perform a socially desirable function. It might plausibly be argued that it is particularly easy for people who know that they will never need infertility treatment, either because they have had children or do not intend to have them, to object to its provision within the NHS. Unlike treatment for cancer or heart bypass surgery, for many people there could be no possible future self-interest in broad and unconditional access.[214]

The description of assisted conception services as medical treatment is commonly challenged on the grounds that reproductive technologies do not treat the underlying cause of the infertility.[215] It is therefore argued that if some infertility is caused by pelvic inflammatory disease following IUD use, or by inadequately treated infections, medical resources should be diverted towards reducing the incidence of infertility, rather than providing children for the infertile.[216] Because producing "miracle" babies for infertile people is more glamorous than primary prevention strategies,[217] it has been suggested that disproportionate resources tend to be allocated to investigating new assisted conception techniques.[218] Of course, research into the causes of infertility is

---

[212] See further Heitman and Schlachtenhaufen, 1996. The Warnock Report acknowledged this difficulty: "we recognise the difficulty of providing reliable statistics on infertility because of the number of infertile couples who do not seek treatment or are voluntarily childless" (Warnock, 1984, para. 2.14).

[213] For example, Margaret Brazier suggests that a right to infertility treatment would mean that "one woman's right to reproduce would have to be weighed against her mother's right to preventive care to ensure breast cancer is detected early enough, against her grandmother's need for a hip-replacement, against perhaps her great grandmother's life itself" (Brazier, 1998, p. 74). Leon Kass says that "much as I sympthasize with the plight of infertile couples, I do not believe that they are entitled to the provision of a child at public expense" (Kass, 1998 [1979] p. 113).

[214] Brock, 1996.

[215] Patricia Spallone says "IVF does not cure infertility. IVF does not heal women's blocked tubes or the subfertility in men . . . IVF is a 'technical fix' in that it bypasses the causes of fertility problems" (Spallone, 1989, p. 70). Similarly, Deborah Steinberg suggests that the term infertility treatment "misleadingly implies that IVF treats or cures the causes or source of 'infertility'. This is not the case. IVF only bypasses 'infertility' " (Steinberg, 1997, p. 47).

[216] Leon Kass, for example, says that infertility treatment "represents yet another instance of our thoughtless preference for expensive, high-technology, therapy-oriented approaches to disease and dysfunctions. What about spending the money on discovering the causes of infertility? (Kass, 1998 [1979] p. 110).

[217] Sheila McLean, for example, says that "developing sophisticated techniques and technologies is more glamorous than arguing for changes in society, in the environment and in sexual practices, all of which may affect fertility" (McLean, 1999, p. 26).

[218] This was alluded to by the Warnock Report: "we would not want to see IVF with its present relatively low success rate, cream off all the resources available for the treatment of infertility just because it has the glamour of novelty" (Warnock, 1984, para. 5.11).

undeniably important, but for women and men who find themselves unable to have children, primary prevention is almost certainly too late, and assisted conception may represent the best available treatment.[219] Moreover, many conventional medical therapies, such as prosthetic limbs, hearing aids or drugs to control certain mental illnesses, enable people to live a more normal life without curing their underlying disability. In other circumstances we do not base funding decisions upon whether a treatment corrects or circumvents the particular disability. According to the Royal College of Obstetricians and Gynaecologists, infertility should be classified as a disease that significantly impairs normal functioning.[220] While it is true that infertility is not life-threatening, nor are many other conditions that are routinely treated within the NHS. Alternatively, it could be argued that the psychological pain of infertility might give rise to more conventional stress-related illnesses for which assisted conception services may be the optimum solution. Yet both these justifications for wider public funding of assisted conception services have their limitations. First, if we were to limit NHS provision of infertility treatment to those whose infertility fits within the definition of disease, then we would only allow state funded treatment for those whose inability to have children is the result of impaired biological function.[221] Post-menopausal or single women, and homosexual couples would therefore be excluded. Second, to argue that assisted conception services are in fact treatment for the stress of infertility would make access to NHS treatment dependent upon proof of psychological problems.

A different sort of solution would be to argue that state funding for assisted conception services is necessary according to basic principles of redistributive justice.[222] The desire for genetically related offspring is not an unreasonable preference, indeed having one's own children is widely regarded as a necessary constitutive element of a fulfilling and meaningful life.[223] The relative importance of childbearing within the life plans of most people might then lead us to conclude that alleviating involuntary childlessness should be a high priority for

[219] Dion Farquhar even suggests that "the imposition of a strict, politically pure double standard on infertile people who wish to use such technologies is like blaming cancer patients for 'choosing' individualist therapies like chemotherapy or radiation rather than campaigning for the reduction of pesticides or pollutants" (Farquhar, 1995, p. 7).

[220] RCOG, 2000b. This is also the position adopted by the American College of Obstetricians and Gynecologists (Brock, 1996, p. 224). The definition of disease is that it is a physical or mental condition that results in deviations from normal functioning. Even if we were to add the gloss that the deviation from normal function must be bad for the individuals suffering from it, infertility would still undoubtedly qualify.

[221] In commenting upon the provision of infertility treatment to single or lesbian women, Daniel Wikler says that the "lack of a male reproductive partner may be a misfortune, or a preference, but it is not a disease state" (Wikler, 1995, p. 51).

[222] Justine Burley offers a persuasive application of Ronald Dworkin's theory of the just distribution of resources to state funding for assisted conception (Burley, 1998).

[223] John Robertson says that "depriving persons of the ability or opportunity to reproduce is a major burden and should not occur without their consent" (Robertson, 1998, p. 1389). In a similar vein Dan Brock argues that "for many people, the opportunity to become a parent and raise a child is one of, if not the most important and valuable parts of their lives" (Brock, 1996, p. 222).

state-funded healthcare.[224] If people's capacity to follow their own conception of the good life is restricted by the unequal distribution of natural resources, public funding for treatment to reverse this biological bad luck may be demanded by principles of fairness and justice.

An equality-based argument for publicly funded infertility treatment was made in a Canadian case in 1999.[225] The Nova Scotia Court of Appeal found that the infertile are unequally treated because they are denied a medically recommended treatment that is appropriate for them. Yet despite the Court's conclusion that this unequal treatment is discriminatory, scarce health care resources meant that ultimately this discrimination could be justified. Similarly, although some American cases have indicated that interfering with access to infertility treatment might be unconstitutional,[226] it has simultaneously been accepted that scarce resources and other legitimate public concerns[227] might justify placing limitations upon individuals' freedom.[228]

Assuming that a case for public funding of assisted conception services could be made out, infertility treatment would clearly not be immune from the rationing decisions that are now inevitable in every field of clinical practice. The NHS is subject to infinite demands upon its finite resources, and there will always be treatments that have to be excluded from NHS coverage on grounds of cost. Infertility treatment is no exception, and should be rationed according to the same principles as other non-emergency medical treatments.[229] My argument is not, therefore, that infertility treatment should be provided on demand to every citizen, but rather that rationing decisions should be taken for *relevant* and *fair* reasons. Thus an assessment of a procedure's clinical and cost-effectiveness ought to determine what services are available within the NHS, rather than arbitrary health authority exclusions or disingenuous claims to have evaluated future parenting ability. So, for example, the chance of achieving a pregnancy might be a relevant consideration, and a maximum number of treatment cycles per patient would almost certainly be necessary in order to ensure fair and equitable access to treatment.

Fairness based arguments for publicly funded infertility treatment rest upon the assumption that involuntary childlessness is a serious misfortune that

[224] Brock, 1996, p. 223.

[225] *Cameron* v. *Nova Scotia (Attorney General)* [1999] NSJ No 297 (CA) (unreported).

[226] The federal district court in *Lifchez* v. *Hartigan* 908 F. 2d 1395 (8th Cir 1990) found that "it takes no great leap of logic to see that within the cluster of constitutionally protected choices that includes the right to have access to contraceptives, there must be included within that cluster the right to submit to a medical procedure that may bring about, rather than prevent, pregnancy".

[227] For example, the "right" of prisoners to participate in infertility treatment has been restricted for security reasons.

[228] *Lifchez* v. *Hartigan* 908 F. 2d 1395 (8th Cir. 1990); *Percy* v. *New Jersey* 651 A.2d 1044 (NJ Super Ct App Div 1994); *Anderson* v. *Vasquez* 827 F Supp 617 (ND Cal 1992).

[229] In addition to their consideration of social reasons for restricting access to treatment, the Warnock Report also considered that sometimes a clinical judgement, taking into account considerations such as the patient's age, the duration of infertility and the likelihood that treatment will be successful may be necessary (Warnock, 1984, para. 2.12).

202   *Reproductive Technologies*

should, if possible, be alleviated with state assistance. But of course not everyone would accept that infertility is the result of brute bad luck, in the same way
as, for example, facial disfigurement. The belief that infertile individuals,
particularly perhaps women, must be in some way to blame for their failure to
reproduce has its roots in the belief that barrenness is a sign of God's disfavour,
or evidence of involvement in witchcraft.[230] In the nineteenth century, both
male and female sterility was assumed to the price to be paid for "slack moral
habits",[231] such as excessive sexual activity or masturbation.[232] While few
people still believe that infertile people are being punished for their sins, the
assumption that they may be in some way responsible for their inability to conceive continues to have considerable resonance.[233] The stigma of infertility is
reinforced by popular myths about the role of abortion or sexually transmitted
diseases in causing fertility problems.[234] References to a wholly fictitious[235]
"infertility epidemic" exacerbate the misperception that infertility is a modern
problem caused by (and perhaps, punishment for) women's promiscuity and/or
deferral of childbearing.[236]

(iii) Post-Menopausal Women's Access to Infertility Treatment

The average woman goes through the menopause in her early fifties, although
some women can experience premature menopause much earlier. Women's fertility declines from their mid-twenties onwards, and the rate of this decline
accelerates rapidly from a woman's mid-forties, with births over the age of 45
relatively uncommon, and natural conceptions over the age of 50 extremely
rare, although not unprecedented.[237] IVF using donated eggs can now allow
women to give birth after their menopause. This is relatively uncontroversial

[230] See further Vaux, 1989, p. 121; Sandelowski, 1990.
[231] Pfeffer, 1993, p. 33.
[232] Although Victorian doctors were apparently reluctant to investigate the possibility of male
infertility, perhaps because doctors were reluctant to ask men to produce a semen sample "in case
its production corrupted them" (Pfeffer, 1993, p. 39).
[233] Today it is widely assumed that women are infertile as a result of their own choices, for example, by choosing to delay childbearing, by having had an abortion, through contracting sexually
transmitted infections, or by over-use of particular contraceptives. So a woman's inability to
conceive is commonly thought to be the consequence of her deviation from conventional gender
roles, through an over-zealous pursuit of her career or through sexual promiscuity. She is then
responsible for her infertility, which is "nature's" punishment for her unnatural behaviour (see
further Michie and Cahn, 1997, p. 145).
[234] Margaret Tighe, for example, says that abortion and IUDs are the "major cause" of infertility, and that "sexually transmitted diseases notoriously can cause infertility" (Tighe, 1999 [1994]
p. 93). Dion Farquhar considers that the "invisibility" of infertility among black people may in part
derive from the belief that any problems they may have conceiving are the "price" of their "previous
sexual excesses" (Farquhar, 1996, p. 91).
[235] Berg, 1995, p. 97.
[236] See further Michie and Cahn, 1997, pp. 150–2; and Faludi, 1992 pp. 46–54. In fact, female fertility may actually be increasing because despite some evidence of declining sperm counts a recent
study has concluded that there has been "a clear rise in couple fertility in recent decades" (Joffe,
2000, p. 1963).
[237] Fisher and Somerville, 1998, p. 206.

where women have suffered premature menopause, but has proved extremely contentious where the patient is in her fifties. In the United Kingdom, there is no fixed upper age limit for infertility treatment. Instead, each clinic must take into account potential patients' "ages and likely future ability to look after or provide for a child's needs".[238] In practice, most clinics refuse to treat women over the age of about 50.[239]

There are several different reasons commonly given for denying infertility treatment to post-menopausal women. It could, for example, be argued that the infertility of a woman who has gone through the menopause is not pathological, but entirely normal. Infertility treatment is not then necessary to restore normal functioning in the same way as it is for women who have blocked fallopian tubes or ovarian dysfunction. Underlying this sort of argument may be the assumption that a post-menopausal woman's childlessness is in fact her own fault, resulting from her decision to postpone having children until it is too late. Just as single or lesbian women are thought to be responsible for their inability to conceive without assistance, a post-menopausal woman's reproductive incapacity is sometimes considered to be the just dessert for the choices she made earlier in her life.[240] However, as we saw earlier in this chapter, the demonisation of unnatural childbearing sits rather uneasily with our unqualified acceptance of other unnatural aspects of modern medicine. Hence, although it is unnatural for a woman to have a child after the menopause, it may be similarly unnatural for a young woman who has suffered from ovarian cancer to subsequently bear children, and it is probably unnatural for her to be alive. Instead of relying on the facile equation of unnatural childbearing with undesirable childbearing, its critics should find substantive reasons why fertility treatment should not be provided to post-menopausal women.

It could, for example, be argued that the chances that treatment will be successful are much lower, although the use of donated oocytes undoubtedly avoids some of the problems with low fertilisation rates among older patients.[241] Alternatively, it might be argued that the physical risks of pregnancy are significantly higher for older women. Because of the tiny numbers of women who become pregnant over the age of fifty, there is little evidence to support, or discount claims that post-menopausal women might suffer

---

[238] HFEA Code of Practice, 1998, para. 3.17e.

[239] In other countries practice varies considerably. For example, in Canada, the Royal Commission on New Reproductive Technologies recommended that "women who have experienced menopause at the usual age should not be candidates to receive donated eggs (Royal Commission, 1993, i. 590) whereas many American clinics routinely offer egg donation to older women (Sauer and Paulson, 1992). France limits infertilty treatment to couples of reproductive age (Nau, 1994, p. 48), whereas in Italy the absence of regulations have made its clinics attractive to older British women who have been rejected by clinics in the UK.

[240] The presumption is that such women have chosen not to have children in order to pursue a successful career.

[241] The success rates of IVF drop by one third for women aged 35–40, and by two-thirds for women over 40 (de Wert, 1998, p. 221).

increased risks in pregnancy.[242] Nevertheless, extrapolating from research which indicates that the chances of stillbirth, miscarriage and ectopic pregnancy increase with age,[243] it seems probable that pregnancy in post-menopausal women might be associated with some increased health risks. Screening potential patients for known risk factors such as cardio-vascular dysfunction and diabetes might help minimise some of these dangers. Hence, these practical clinical arguments against treatment of post-menopausal women do not justify a *blanket* prohibition, but simply indicate a need for careful medical assessment of the chance of achieving a pregnancy and its associated risks.

It is also sometimes argued that even if a post-menopausal woman may be able to cope with the rigours of pregnancy, she is not a suitable candidate for motherhood because women who give birth in their fifties are likely to be in their sixties and seventies when their children are teenagers.[244] Of course this is also true of men who may even be able to father children when they are in their eighties and nineties.[245] In any event, improving standards of health mean that people's sixties and seventies are no longer necessarily a time of chronic ill-health and dependency. On the contrary, it is now commonplace for people in their sixties and seventies to take responsibility for the care of their very elderly parents, which may be much more physically demanding and psychologically dispiriting than looking after young children.[246]

Nevertheless, it is indisputable that children born to post-menopausal women are more likely to experience the death of their mother at an early age than children born to younger women. It is also undeniable that the death of a mother during childhood is a particularly traumatic experience, although not perhaps such that it would be better if the child had never been born. Of course, children born to women who suffer from, or have a genetic predisposition to a serious illness may also be statistically more likely to experience bereavement during childhood. Thus a requirement that potential parents should have certain characteristics such as longevity, energy and agility would necessarily debar many ill or disabled people from procreation.

Women's increased life expectancy (currently 80 years)[247] means that women now giving birth in their fifties may have a greater chance of seeing their children reach adulthood than women who gave birth in their twenties 100 years

---

[242] On the inconclusive evidence of increased health risks of post-menopausal pregnancy, see further Fisher and Sommerville, 1998, p. 215.

[243] Stein and Susser, 2000.

[244] For example, Guido de Wert quotes the French Health Minister, Philippe Douste-Blazy who said "it is absolutely shocking to think that when a baby is eighteen years old, his mother will be 80" (de Wert, 1998, p. 221).

[245] Guido de Wert points out that such men will have much younger partners, thus reducing the psychosocial risks to the child (de Wert, 1998, p. 236). It is of course possible that postmenopausal women might also have younger partners, although de Wert says that "partners of women of advanced age also tend to be older" (*ibid.*).

[246] Harris, 1998b, p. 20.

[247] Office for National Statistics, 2001, p. 127.

ago when life expectancy for women was 49.6 years.[248] But even if we were to accept that having elderly parents is not ideal, few parents are able to offer their children a perfect upbringing, and the disadvantages of their advanced age might be balanced by the advantages of having more stable, experienced and economically secure parents.[249]

It may also be worth noting that in the context of reproductive hazards in the workplace, women of reproductive capacity are typically defined as women between the ages of 15–55.[250] In one American case, a fetal protection policy even purported to exclude all women up to the age of 63.[251] If a woman of 55, or 63 is considered to be a *natural* potential mother for the purposes of excluding her from certain types of employment, it is interesting that her potential maternity is commonly perceived to be an *unnatural* aberration when she seeks infertility treatment.

(c) Regulating the Status and Use of Gametes

(i) Status

The cryopreservation of gametes raises new questions about their status. We might, for example, assume that a person should have the right to decide what happens to their gametes, but is this control over the disposition of frozen sperm or ova equivalent to ownership?[252] Bonnie Steinbock suggests that the question of whether sperm is property can only be resolved by determining what we think may permissibly be done with it. If we believe that it should be possible, for example, to bequeath frozen sperm in a will, then, she says, it must be considered property for that purpose.[253]

While the regulatory scheme set up by the Human Fertilisation and Embryology Act 1990 undoubtedly gives people considerable power to decide what should be done with their stored gametes, the question of whether this amounts to a property right has not yet been tested. The question of ownership was not, for example, raised in Mrs Blood's high profile dispute with the HFEA, discussed below, over whether she should be allowed access to her dead husband's sperm. Cases in other countries have tended to agree that an individual does have some special dispositional authority over their stored gametes, but there is little consensus over whether that authority derives from a quasi-proprietorial interest in one's gametes.

---

[248] *Ibid.* p. 128.
[249] Stein and Susser, p. 1682.
[250] Kenney, 1986, p. 409.
[251] *Wright* v. *Olin* 697 F.2d 1172 (1982).
[252] Stephen Munzer suggests that property rights in one's body parts exist when one can transfer those rights to another. He distinguishes between weak property rights in which only gratuitous transfer is permitted (such as donating a kidney) and strong property rights when transfer for value is possible (such as in countries where the sale of semen is permitted) (Munzer, 1990).
[253] Steinbock, 1998.

In a French case[254] in 1984 a deceased man's widow and parents tried to argue that, as heirs to his estate, they had become the owners of his frozen sperm. The Court rejected an argument based upon Corinne Parpalaix's *ownership* of her deceased husband's sperm. Rather the Court held that the question of what should happen to Alain Parpalaix's sperm had to be determined by his *intention*, which was, according to the Court, that his wife should have access to his sperm after his death. In contrast, in an American case,[255] a Court found that "the decedent had an interest in his sperm which falls within the broad definition of property"[256] and was "in the nature of ownership".[257] Despite clear differences in reasoning, in practice the question of whether the interest is proprietorial or not made little difference since in both cases the deceased's partner was able to decide what should happen to his frozen sperm.

(ii) The Use of Gametes

A Consent

Consent to the storage and use of one's gametes must be voluntary and fully informed.[258] For egg donors this also involves giving informed consent to the physical risks involved in egg retrieval.[259] Consent must specify the maximum period of storage, if this is to be less than the statutory storage period of five years, and must state what is to be done with the gametes in the event of the donor's death.[260] Unlike other much more invasive medical procedures,[261] consent to the creation of an embryo, or to the use of one's gametes in the treatment of others *must* be in writing.[262] Prior to donation certain information must be

---

[254] *Parpalaix* v. *CECOS* (unreported) discussed in Atherton, 1999.

[255] *Hecht* v. *Superior Court* 20 Cal Rptr 2d 274 (Ct App 1993). Deborah Hecht and William Kane had cohabited for five years. Prior to his suicide, Mr Kane made deposits of his sperm so that Ms Hecht could conceive his child after his death. He left his residual estate, including 15 vials of frozen sperm, to Ms Hecht. Mr Kane's children from a previous marriage contested the will on the ground that to permit posthumous conception would violate the integrity of their family and open Mr Kane's estate to additional claims. The Court of Appeal of California decided that sperm is property capable of bequest in a will. A similar question arose in *Hall* v. *Fertility Institute of New Orleans* 647 So. 2d 1348 (La Ct App 1994). A man had attempted to leave his frozen sperm to his girlfriend, and the Louisiana Court of Appeal rejected the argument that a gift of frozen sperm would be contrary to public policy.

[256] *Hecht* v. *Superior Court* 20 Cal Rptr 2d 274 (Ct App 1993), at 283.

[257] *Ibid*, at 281.

[258] In February 2000 it was reported that the London Gynaecology and Fertility Centre had settled a claim by an Austrian man that his sperm had been used without his consent. He claimed that he provided sperm samples for his ex-partner in order to assess her fertility problems, but subsequently discovered that a daughter had been born following her treatment with his sperm (Dyer, 2000a).

[259] In one American clinic, potential egg donors are shown a video of vaginal aspiration in order to underline the fact that the procedure is sufficiently painful to require administration of a general anaesthetic (Tong, 1996, p. 151).

[260] HFEA Code of Practice 1998, para. 5.9.

[261] Margaret Brazier points out that "English law imposes no legislative rule requiring that I consent in writing to surgical removal of all my reproductive organs. Yet I must consent in writing to the less invasive procedure of egg retrieval if those eggs are destined for another recipient" (Brazier, 1999a, p. 184).

[262] HFEA Code of Practice 1998, para. 5.12.

given to potential donors,[263] and they must be offered counselling, with their partner if relevant, which would address their reasons for wanting to become a donor and their attitudes to the prospective parents and any resulting children.[264]

Why are the rules concerning consent to gamete donation so strict? It could be argued that because gamete donation may involve passing on one's genes to future generations, particular care must be taken to ensure that consent is freely given and fully informed. But the claim that we have a strong right to control the destiny of our genetic material is perhaps undermined by the complete absence of control over the reproductive choices of one's children, which will also involve the transmission of one's gene pool.[265] John Harris has also argued that the overriding priority given to the necessity of explicit, informed and written consent for the use of a man's gametes is "over-precious" and may be inconsistent with men's complete lack of control over procreative outcomes when their gametes are disseminated through sexual intercourse.[266] Without equivalent protection of the right to control the destiny of one's genetic material in other contexts, it might be more accurate to locate the justification for these rigorous consent provisions in the assumption that maintaining an adequate supply of

---

[263] According to the HFEA Code of Practice 1998 para. 4.5 the following information should be given to people consenting to the donation or storage of gametes:

a. the procedures involved in collecting gametes, the degree of pain and discomfort and any risks to that person, e.g., from the use of superovulatory drugs;
b. the screening which will be carried out, and the practical implications of having an HIV antibody test, even if it proves negative;
c. the genetic testing that will be carried out, its scope and limitations and the implications of the result for the donor and their family;
d. the purposes for which their gametes might be used;
e. whether or not they will be regarded under the Act as the parents of any child born as a result;
f. that the Act generally permits donors to preserve their anonymity;
g. the information which centres must collect and register with the HFEA and the extent to which that information may be disclosed to people born as a result of the donation;
h. that they are free to withdraw or vary the terms of their consent at any time, unless the gametes or embryos have already been used;
i. the possibility that a child born disabled as a result of a donor's failure to disclose defects, about which they knew or ought reasonably to have known, may be able to sue the donor for damages;
j. in the case of egg donation, that the woman will not incur any financial or other penalty if she withdraws her consent after preparation for egg recovery has begun;
k. that donated gametes and embryos created from them will not normally be used for treatment once the number of children believed to have been born from them has reached 10, or any lower figure specified by the donor; and.
l. that counselling is available.
[264] HFEA Code of Practice 1998, paras. 6.16–7.
[265] See further Erin, 1998, p. 173; Brazier, 1999a, p. 185.
[266] "Men are notorious for leaving their gametes behind in all sorts of places, some of which may well result in the creation of life. They do so almost always without all these requirements for opportunities for counselling, formal consent and time for reflection, and usually without missing them and without mishap without them. We normally accept that they have no say in the outcome one way or another. They cannot control their partners' use of contraception, not insist on an abortion if they do not want their genes to survive in this way, or be mixed with those of this woman" (Harris, 1998b, p. 18).

donated gametes may be dependent upon our capacity to reassure potential donors that their gametes will be used only according to their wishes.[267]

B Consent and the posthumous use of gametes: the Blood case[268]

Despite the Warnock Report's hostility to the posthumous use of gametes,[269] it is not prohibited by the Human Fertilisation and Embryology Act 1990,[270] and according to one survey, 74 per cent of UK clinics would agree, subject to certain conditions, to the posthumous use of sperm or embryos.[271] Section 28(6)(b) specifically envisaged the use of sperm after the provider's death and determined that any child born as a result should be legally fatherless.[272] Since, as we saw earlier, section 13(5) discourages the creation of fatherless children, the statute enshrines, by implication, a presumption against the posthumous use of sperm. It is of course possible that a child whose father was dead at the moment of conception might find this knowledge troubling,[273] although for obvious reasons, there is no evidence to support or discount speculation about posthumous conception's negative impact upon the child's wellbeing.

The case of *R* v. *Human Fertilisation and Embryology Authority ex parte Blood*[274] involved a widow who wanted to be inseminated with her deceased

---

[267] Brazier, 1999a, p. 186.

[268] Michael Thomson argues that the term "posthumous pregnancy", with its connotations of "a pregnant cadaver, a monstrous act of procreation" is misleading but revealing (Thomson, 1998, p. 187).

[269] "We have grave misgivings about AIH in one type of situation. A man who has placed semen in a semen bank may die and his widow may then seek to be inseminated. . . This may give rise to profound psychological problems for the child and the mother" (Warnock, 1984, para 4.4). "The use by a widow of her dead husband's semen for AIH is a practice which we feel should be actively discouraged" (Warnock, 1984, para. 10.9).

[270] The Government's 1987 White Paper *Human Fertilisation and Embryology: A Framework for Legislation* (Cm 259) acknowledged that "many people are uneasy about this practice", and while not recommending prohibition, the White Paper stated that "obviously it is not a practice which should receive active encouragement"(para. 59).

[271] Cited in McLean, 1997, para. 9.11. In France the position is somewhat different. Assisted conception is limited to married couples both of whom must be alive and must give their consent at the moment of embryo transfer or insemination. Simone Bateman Novaes and Tania Salem describe a case known in the press as the "widow of Toulouse" in which a woman's miscarriage of her twins conceived following six unsuccessful attempts at IVF was immediately followed by her husband's death. She requested the transfer of their two remaining embryos, but her request was refused, and her appeals to the courts were unsuccessful. The final Court order was that the remaining embryos be left to perish (Novaes and Salem, 1998). Posthumous assisted conception is also prohibited in Canada, Germany and Sweden (McLean, 1997, para. 9.32).

[272] "where the sperm of a man, or any embryo the creation of which was brought about with his sperm was used after his death, he is not to be treated as the father of the child". This is similar to the position in the United States where s. 4(b) of the 1988 Uniform Status of Children of Assisted Conception Act (USACA) provides that "an individual who dies before implantation of an embryo, or before a child is conceived other than through sexual intercourse, using the individual's egg or sperm, is not a parent of the resulting child".

[273] Commenting on Mrs Blood's case in *The Guardian*, Martin Kettle said he found the idea of conception with a dead person misguided, undesirable and morbid and that "the whole thing (is) decidedly creepy" (Kettle, 1996, p. 23).

[274] [1996] 3 WLR 1176; [1997] 2 WLR 806 (CA).

husband's sperm. Her case raised a novel problem because although Mrs Blood claimed that they had discussed the posthumous use of his sperm, Mr Blood had not given written consent. While Mr Blood was in a coma after contracting bacterial meningitis, sperm samples were extracted at Mrs Blood's request. Since medical treatment can only be carried out on an unconscious patient if it is both necessary and in their best interests, the sperm retrieval almost certainly amounted to an unlawful touching or battery.[275] It is hard to see how creating posthumous genetic offspring could have been said to have been either necessary, or in Mr Blood's best interests. Given the absence of written consent it was also undoubtedly unlawful for Mr Blood's sperm to be stored by a licensed clinic, and insemination with the stored sperm would have contravened the provisions of the Human Fertilisation and Embryology Act.[276]

Mrs Blood sought judicial review of the HFEA's decision to refuse permission for her to export the sperm to Belgium, where she would have been able to use it in treatment. At first instance, Sir Stephen Brown P dismissed her claim and found that the HFEA had acted within their discretion, although he did go to considerable lengths to express sympathy for her plight,[277] and to describe her

---

[275] Stuart Horner, then chairman of the British Medical Association's ethics committee wrote to the HFEA following the initial decision of the High Court that their decision to deny Mrs Blood access to her husband's sperm was correct. The HFEA had agreed to reconsider the ban following the public outcry. Dr Horner urged them not to change their mind, and said: "we believe that the doctrine of informed consent, which is central to medical ethics, must not be eroded. . . . Law and ethics should not be adjusted to accommodate isolated cases. . . . There will always be a new case to challenge the previously accepted view and to evoke our sympathy. The inevitable consequence will be a steady erosion of ethical standards" (quoted in Dyer *et al*, 1996).

[276] Section 12 sets out what are to be the "conditions" of every licence granted under the Act. One of these is condition (c) which requires compliance with the provisions of Schedule 3 to the Act. Schedule 3 is headed "Consents to use of gametes or embryos." Paragraphs 1 and 2 deal with the form of consent and provide.

"(1) A consent under this Schedule must be given in writing and, in this Schedule 'effective consent' means a consent . . . which has not been withdrawn. . . .

(2) A consent to the storage of any gametes . . . must—(a) specify the maximum period of storage . . . and (b) state what is to be done with the gametes or embryo if the person who gave the consent dies or is unable because of incapacity to vary the terms of the consent or to revoke it . . ."

Paragraph 3 deals with the procedure for giving consent:

"(1) Before a person gives a consent under this Schedule—(a) he must be given suitable opportunity to seek proper counselling about the implications of taking the proposed steps, and (b) he must be provided with such relevant information as is proper."

The use of gametes for the treatment of others is dealt with in paragraph 5:

"(1) A person's gametes must not be used for the purpose of treatment services unless there is an effective consent by that person to their being so used and they are used in accordance with the terms of the consent. (2) A person's gametes must not be received for use for those purposes unless there is effective consent by that person to their being so used. (3) This paragraph does not apply to the use of a person's gametes for the purpose of that person, or that person and another person together, receiving treatment services."

[277] "It cannot assist the applicant for the court to express the view that it might itself have made a different decision if it had had the authority to do so. I have found this to be a most anxious and moving case. My heart goes out to this applicant who wishes to preserve an essential part of her late beloved husband" (at 1191).

aptitude for motherhood.[278] Following a public outcry, the HFEA reconsidered its ban but decided again to refuse Mrs Blood's request.

On appeal Mrs Blood succeeded. The Court of Appeal found that despite the unlawfulness of the sperm retrieval, in exercising their discretion the HFEA had not taken adequate account of Mrs Blood's right under EC law[279] to receive treatment in another member state,[280] and it was this failure to consider EC law, rather than the ban itself that led the Court of Appeal to allow Mrs Blood's appeal.[281] The HFEA was entitled to place restrictions upon the export of sperm, but such restrictions had to be justified on grounds of public policy,[282] and the Court of Appeal was not satisfied that the public interest was served by refusing Mrs Blood permission to export the sperm for treatment elsewhere in Europe.

It could, of course, be argued that the export provisions issued by the HFEA under section 24(4) ought to be subject to the presumption that the gametes must first been obtained and stored in conformity with national law.[283] As Sheila McLean's Report to Health Ministers explained:

"it surely cannot have been intended that the discretion to permit export was intended to cover gametes which were unlawfully obtained and/or unlawfully stored. It would be a most unusual piece of legislation which created regulations only to build into itself the power to defeat them by the exercise of discretion".[284]

---

[278] "The applicant is a widow now aged 30 years. She was married to her husband Stephen in 1991. They had been courting for nine years before that. They lived a happy married life and greatly wished to have a family. They had married according to the rites of the Anglican Church using the traditional service contained in the 1662 Book of Common Prayer. The applicant had her own business. She had set up her own company in advertising and public relations dealing particularly with matters concerning nursery products. They lived a normal sex life. Towards the end of 1994 they began actively trying to start a family" (at 1178).

[279] Article 59 of the EC Treaty reads: "Within the framework of the provisions set out below, restrictions on freedom to provide services within the Community shall be progressively abolished during the transitional period in respect of nationals of member states who are established in a state of the Community other than that of the person for whom the services are intended."

[280] Lord Woolf said "the first reason given by the authority is a correct statement that in this case there has not been compliance with the Act of 1990 in relation to storage or use in the United Kingdom. This is the starting point for the subsequent reasoning which is the essence for the explanation why the authority was not prepared to exercise its undoubted discretion to permit export in Mrs. Blood's favour. It was a permissible and proper starting point: in giving a particular direction, the authority is using delegated powers, which should be used to serve and promote the objects of the legislation, which clearly attach great importance to consent, the quality of that consent, and the certainty of it. The authority must balance that against Mrs. Blood's cross-border rights as a Community citizen."

". . . The reasons given by the authority, while not deeply flawed, confirm that the authority did not take into account two important considerations. The first being the effect of article 59. The second being that there should be, after this judgment has been given, no further cases where sperm is preserved without consent" (at 821).

[281] McLean, 1997, para. 8.21.

[282] Article 56(1), applied to article 59 by article 66, states: "The provisions of this Chapter . . . shall not prejudice the applicability of provisions laid down by law . . . providing for special treatment for foreign nationals on grounds of public policy . . ."

[283] Morgan and Lee, 1997, p. 851. For example, without the written evidence demanded by Schedule 3, it is simply impossible to judge the truth or otherwise of Mrs Blood's assertion that her husband would have consented to the sperm retrieval and to its posthumous use.

[284] McLean, 1997, para. 7.4.

Nevertheless, following the decision of the Court of Appeal, the HFEA reconsidered its position. The HFEA took into account first, that there could be no precedent set because sperm should never again be taken without consent, and second, that they had failed to establish a sufficiently compelling public policy exception to Mrs Blood's cross border rights. Mrs Blood was therefore allowed to export her deceased husband's sperm, and following treatment in Belgium, she gave birth to a son on the 11 December 1998.[285]

Judicial sympathy for Mrs Blood's predicament was echoed in the media,[286] and in Parliament where two Bills were introduced which if passed would have made it possible to waive the requirement for written consent in certain circumstances.[287] Interestingly, public support for Mrs Blood extended beyond compassion for a young widow, to include support for her decision to have a child who will never meet his father. This is obviously in sharp contrast with the widespread disapproval of other single women's desire to use reproductive technologies in order to conceive a fatherless child. It may seem rather macabre that the presence of a dead father-figure should displace the accusations of narcissism and selfishness that frequently accompany single women's requests for infertility treatment.

Following the *Blood* case, and in the light of Sheila McLean's Report to Ministers, the Government has indicated its intention to amend the Human Fertilisation and Embryology Act in order to accommodate some of the difficult issues raised by Mrs Blood's case.[288] As we see below when we consider the rules governing paternity, the posthumously created child will no longer be legally fatherless, and this amendment is likely to have retrospective effect. Their proposed reform would, however, retain the provisions that require a person's written consent prior to the removal of gametes. The Government has insisted that the only circumstance in which gametes might lawfully be removed without a person's consent would be if the retrieval would be in their best interests. For this to be the case, the individual would have to be *temporarily* incapacitated, and likely to suffer from impaired fertility on their recovery. The Government have proposed that in such circumstances, storage of the temporarily incapacitated individual's gametes would be lawful *only until he or she is capable of deciding what should happen to his or her gametes.*[289] The principal beneficiaries of this provision would be children who are about to undergo treatment such as chemotherapy that might affect their future fertility, but who do not yet have sufficient understanding to give a valid consent to gamete retrieval. In such cases, the HFEA would be able to waive the requirement of consent to the storage of the child's gametes until he or she

[handwritten margin note: Ammended after Blood]

---

[285] Thomas, 1998.

[286] See further McLean, 1997, para. 6.24.

[287] Human Fertilisation and Embryology (Amendment) Bill (HL Bill 19, 1996); Human Fertilisation and Embryology (Consents) Bill (Bill 28, 1996).

[288] Department of Health, 2000.

[289] *Ibid.*

achieved capacity. Retrieval of sperm without the man's written consent when he is unlikely to regain consciousness would continue to be unlawful.

C Gamete donation

I Anonymity

Several reasons are commonly given for maintaining donor anonymity. Historically, one of the most compelling reasons for preserving the donor's anonymity was that it enables a couple to keep their infertility secret, and allows them to pretend both to their child and to the outside world that their family was created "naturally". Although there appears to be some evidence of a shift in attitudes in recent years, the use of donated gametes has traditionally been characterised by high levels of secrecy.[290] Secrecy has been of particular importance for couples using donated gametes because of male infertility, for whom the stigma of infertility may be particularly acute.[291] Secrecy has tended to be less important for single or lesbian women who may be happy for others to know that their conception was deliberate and planned, rather than the result of a casual sexual encounter.[292] And in relation to oocyte donation, it is more common for the donor to be a friend or relative of the recipient.[293]

In addition to facilitating secrecy, donor anonymity is also intended to protect the privacy and security of the recipient family, and shield the donor from parental obligations, inheritance claims and unwanted contact with his progeny. It used to be assumed that a donor's willingness to be identified was tantamount to an "unhealthy" desire to interfere in the family life of their genetic offspring, and thus evidence of his unsuitability as a donor. The 1960 Feversham Committee Report on artificial insemination by donor, for example, expressed the concern that non-anonymous sperm donation might appeal to "the abnormal and the unbalanced".[294] Given the prevailing assumption that a normal individual's willingness to donate is dependent upon a guarantee of non-identification, donor anonymity has also been directed towards maintaining adequate stocks of donated gametes.

In most European Countries, sperm donor anonymity is the norm and donations from family members or friends are discouraged, largely in order to preserve family privacy and avoid ambiguous familial relationships.[295] And there does seem to be some evidence that foreclosing any future relationship

[290] For example, Judith Lasker found that while 96% of people who had conceived through IVF intended to tell their children about the circumstances of their conception, only 50% of those who had conceived using DI intended to tell their children (Lasker, 1998, p. 24).
[291] For example David Berger reported that over half of all men who are told that they are infertile became impotent for several months following diagnosis (Berger, 1980). John Dewar suggests that "the silence surrounding the practice of AID may have something to do with men's reluctance to face the consequences of their own infertility, possibly because our culture attaches much significance to the association between fertility and power" (Dewar, 1989, p. 116).
[292] Lasker, 1998, p. 27.
[293] Murray and Golombok, 2000, p. 2134.
[294] O'Donovan, 1989, p. 109.
[295] Schenker, 1997, p. 176; Price 1999 p. 46.

with the gamete donor is the reason why some couples prefer to undergo donor insemination in a licensed clinic, rather than attempting self-insemination with the gametes of a friend or relative.[296] The abolition of donor anonymity in Sweden, for example, was accompanied by a decline in demand for donor insemination services with many couples choosing to travel abroad for treatment with anonymous sperm.[297]

The compromise position reached following the Warnock Committee's commitment to both anonymity and a child's need to know about their genetic and ethnic origins is that non-identifying information about the donor can be made available to the child when he/she reaches the age of 18.[298] But although the HFEA's Code of Practice insists that would-be patients are informed before treatment of "a child's potential need to know about their origins",[299] continued donor anonymity is sending confusing messages to parents about the wisdom of telling children about the circumstances of their birth.[300]

In recent years, some of these justifications for retaining donor anonymity have been challenged. There are, for example, those who would argue that the need to know one's biological parents is of such overriding importance that if infertility treatment using donated gametes is not sustainable without anonymity, it should cease to be an option for childless couples.[301] A flippant response would be that a significant proportion of the population, perhaps as many as 10 per cent,[302] are in fact biologically unrelated to their presumed

[296] Lasker, 1998, p. 12. In her interviews with members of the Warnock Committee, Erica Haimes found that this was a primary concern, she quotes one member saying "if the donor has a name and address and a profession and an image, if they'd met him or her, then it would be much more a real person, a real third person intruding in their marriage. I think that would make it more difficult" (Haimes, 1992, p. 130).

[297] Glover, 1989, p. 36.

[298] The Warnock Report states that "there is a need to maintain the absolute anonymity of the donor" (Warnock, 1984, at para. 4.22), but also that the child born following donor insemination "should have access to basic information about the donor's ethnic origin and genetic health" (Warnock, 1984, at para. 4.21). Human Fertilisation and Embryology Act 1990 s. 31.

[299] HFEA Code of Practice (1998) para. 4.4o.

[300] According to Snowden and Snowden "many couples assert that if they cannot tell the child everything then it is preferable to tell them nothing." (Snowden and Snowden, 1998, p. 49). Susan Golombok claims that since "they will never be able to trace them. Their parents feel that it's better for them not to know" (quoted in Dillner, 1994a, p. 290).

[301] Neil Leighton, for example, argues that "bioengineering appears to have gone ahead without due regard to the creation of alien persons separated from the true beginnings of their personal narrative, having false relationships with the significant persons with whom they have an important connection in the world" (Leighton, 1995, p. 103). In 1948, the Archbishop of Canterbury's Commission found that donor insemination "defrauds the child begotten and deceives both his putative kinsmen and society at large" (quoted in Haimes, 1998, p. 56). The Feversham Committee report found that to be conceived by donor insemination could only be a handicap and that "in the interests of the child alone . . . the practice should be discouraged" (Feversham, 1960, p. 46). In Sweden, the Policy Committee Report in 1983 concluded that "If AID is considered from the viewpoint of the prospective child, there are weighty reasons in favour of a decision—despite the risk that in an initial stage the activity would decrease in hospitals, to demand that only such sperm donors are used who do not oppose that their identity may subsequently be disclosed to the child" (quoted in Haimes, 1998, p. 60).

[302] Reiss, 2000, p. 11.

Need to know - DNA, ORGAN DONATION

fathers. Infidelity may then be a statistically greater threat to accurate knowledge of our biological origins than the relatively small number of DI births.

Many people have also questioned the prevailing assumption that donor identification would have disastrous consequences for the donor and/or the recipient family. The Glover Report to the European Commission, for example, argued that there might be more dignity for the donor in a system in which openness rather than anonymity was the norm.[303] The presumption that anonymity is necessary in order to protect the continued availability of donated gametes has been undermined by several studies which have indicated that a significant proportion of donors would be willing to be identified.[304] In some other countries it is now possible for children to gain access to identifying information about the gamete donor,[305] and this does not appear to have dramatically depleted the supply of donated gametes. In Sweden, for example, the decline in the numbers of donors that initially followed the abolition of donor anonymity was short-lived.[306]

In addition to the belief that children have a psychological need to understand something about their genetic origins,[307] increased understanding about the importance of family history in determining future health means that there may now be important practical health benefits in knowing about inherited genetic susceptibilities. As genetic tests proliferate, it may become increasingly difficult to conceal the lack of a genetic link between a child and his or her social mother or father. And although it is clearly highly improbable that a child conceived using donor sperm will meet and have sexual intercourse with one of their "siblings", the powerful symbolic resonance of incest and in-breeding leads to demands that children should have sufficient information to avoid sexual contact

[303]   Glover, 1989, p. 36.

[304]   For example, Sauer *et al* (1989) found that 36% of donors would like to meet their offspring; Mahlstedt and Probasco (1991) reported that 72% of donors would like to leave a message for their offspring. Ken Daniels describes two studies carried out in the UK, one study involved older donors 53% of whom would not mind if their offspring were able to trace them; the other study involved students, only 18% of whom would continue to provide sperm if their offspring could learn their identity (Daniels, 1998, p. 94). Research into the wishes of oocyte donors has reached similar conclusions, with 80% of donors in one study having no objection to the recipients of their eggs being told their names (see further Cohen, 1996, p. 99).

[305]   For example in Austria, Sweden and France identifying information may be given. In Australia identifying information may be given with the written consent of the gamete donor (Haimes, 1998, p. 61). And in New Zealand, current practice means that it is possible to find out the donor's identity (Daniels, 1998, p. 77). Germany and Switzerland have also abolished sperm donor anonymity (Freeman, 1996, p. 285). In some countries, such as Belgium and the Netherlands, anonymity is optional, and in the Netherlands approximately two thirds of donors opt to remain anonymous, while about a third register their willingness to be identified (Shenfield, 2000).

[306]   Daniels, 1994.

[307]   It has been suggested that children born following anonymous gamete donation may suffer "genealogical bewilderment" (Wikler, 1995, p. 49). And Michael Freeman has argued that "the right to identity is a right not to be deceived about one's true origins" (Freeman, 1996, p. 291). The Glover Report said that "a life where the biological parents are unknown is like a novel with the first chapter missing" (Glover, 1989, p. 37).

with their genetic relatives.[308] It is, however, interesting that the legislation in fact just allows the disclosure of information directed towards the avoidance of *marriage* between two genetic siblings,[309] which obviously fails to capture all of the "feared horrible consequence of their mating".[310]

Over the course of the twentieth century, attitudes towards anonymity in relation to adoption underwent a complete reversal, and although initially also characterised by secrecy and concealment, openness about the fact of adoption is now considered good practice.[311] In 1975, it became possible, once they had reached the age of 18, for adopted children to receive their original birth certificate.[312] Comparatively few adopted children attempt to trace their biological parents, and the experiences of those that do "do not necessarily suggest that such quests should be encouraged".[313] In addition, adopted children tend to be much more interested in tracing their mothers than their fathers, perhaps as a result of the perception that gestation and childbirth creates a bond which is absent in the genetic connection between a father and his child.[314] It is not clear whether this might lead children born through sperm or egg donation to have less interest in tracing the gamete donor.

Nevertheless, evidence from adopted children has suggested that secrecy about a child's biological parentage may not be in the best interests of the child.[315] The existence of family secrets can lead to insecurity and instability,[316] and since most people using donated gametes will have told someone about their treatment, the parents may live in fear of disclosure.[317] A child who learns about the circumstances of their conception accidentally will undoubtedly be shocked and hurt by their parents' deception.[318]

---

[308] Jeanette Edwards' research into public attitudes to infertility treatment found that the possibility that children might meet and want to marry their genetic siblings was a recurrent concern to her interviewees (Edwards, 1999, p. 65). Michael Freeman has suggested that infertility specialists have a vested interest in avoiding inter-marriage and in-breeding since "the cause célèbre that would result could lead to blame being attributed to them" (Freeman, 1996, p. 278).

[309] Human Fertilisation and Embryology Act 1990 ss. 31(4)(b), 31(6). → *only against marriage, not sex*

[310] Freeman, 1996, p. 278.

[311] See further O'Donovan, 1989.

[312] Although it should be remembered that this does not reveal very much about one's genetic origins, and that an adopted person who wants to discover his or her biological parents "will require persistence and tenacity as well as skills of detection" (Freeman, 1996, p. 278).

[313] O'Donovan, 1989, p. 102.

[314] O'Donovan, 1989, p. 105.

[315] For example the British Agency for Adoption and Fostering's Medical Group found that "on the basis of this adoption experience we recommend that serious account should be taken of the possibility that AID (Artificial Insemination by Donor) adults will have a similar desire for true knowledge of their origins and will wish to be reared by parents who do not deceive them on this score" (BAAF, 1984, p. 11).

[316] Haimes and Timms have suggested that "children and adults are likely to suspect something, not just through family interaction but also through basic genetic knowledge" (Haimes and Timms, 1985, p. 97).

[317] In Gottlieb *et al*'s study, 59% of DI couples had told someone else (Gottlieb *et al*, 2000, p. 2054).

[318] According to Katherine O'Donovan "the evidence from life histories of adopted persons is that discovery is more than a shock; it can undermine a lifetime's security" (O'Donovan, 1989, p. 99). Jeanette Edwards says that: "ultimately the secret (which, when it emerges becomes a lie) is

But despite an indisputable connection between anonymity and secrecy, it is important to remember that they are not synonymous.[319] A couple could know the identity of the gamete donor, but still keep the fact of gamete donation to themselves. Or a couple could be open about their use of anonymously donated gametes. So less secrecy about the circumstances of a child's conception does not necessarily mean that the child must have access to identifying information about the gamete donor. A child could, for example, be given a great deal of information about the donor, without being told their name. So even if we acknowledge that secrecy may be damaging, this does not necessarily require the removal of anonymity.

Conversely, any right to information about the gamete donor, whether identifying or non-identifying, does not in itself eliminate secrecy surrounding the circumstances of a child's conception. Unless the use of donated gametes must be recorded on the child's birth certificate, or a duty is imposed upon parents to tell their child that they were conceived using donated gametes, the right to information will not automatically lead to greater openness.[320] The Warnock Report had initially proposed that the words "by donation" should be entered on the child's birth certificate,[321] but this was rejected by Parliament. Even in Sweden where a child can find out the identity of the gamete donor, there is no corresponding duty to disclose the circumstances of the child's conception. The Swedish National Board of Health and Welfare does explicitly encourage parents to tell a child about the use of donor insemination, but it continues to be possible for children to remain ignorant about their parents' use of DI,[322] and in a recent study, 89 per cent of Swedish parents of children created using donated gametes had not yet told their children about the circumstances of their conception.[323]

In 2001 the Department of Health will publish a consultation paper considering various options for reform, the most radical of which would be allowing future gamete donors to register their willingness to have their name passed on to any child born using their gametes. The legislation would not have retrospective effect. In some countries, such as Belgium, there is a two tier system in which gamete donors can choose at the time of donation whether or not they would be prepared to be identified, and recipients can choose between

thought to be more damaging to family relationships than the facts of DI" (Edwards, 1998, p. 157). And in her research into public attitudes to reproductive technology, Edwards found that people believed that "secrets have a nasty habit of being disclosed when least expected" and that "the truth will always out" (Edwards, 1999, p. 76).

[319] Katherine O'Donovan has observed that "secrecy is a darker concept than anonymity" (O'Donovan, 1989, p. 98).

[320] The Warnock Report had initially proposed that the words "by donation" should be entered on the birth certificate (Warnock, 1984, paras. 4.25, 6.8). But an amendment to the 1990 Bill aimed at ensuring that the birth certificate of a child born following infertility treatment had this fact endorsed upon it was defeated in the House of Commons.

[321] Warnock, 1984, paras. 4.25, 6.8.

[322] Blank, 1998, p. 146.

[323] Gottlieb *et al*, 2000, p. 2053.

identifiable and non identifiable donors.[324] Given that parents who would prefer an anonymous donor can, in any event, simply not tell their child that their
conception involved the use of donated gametes, this two-tier system may
acknowledge that, absent endorsed birth certificates, parents inevitably exercise *de facto* control over their child's access to information.

II Payment
Paying people for their gametes undoubtedly involves the commodification of
human body parts,[325] and an analogy could plausibly be drawn with payment
for human organs, such as kidneys, which is a criminal offence.[326] Yet unlike a
person's kidneys, their sperm or eggs are in plentiful supply. In addition, the
health risks to an egg donor are comparatively small, with sperm donation pos-
ing no risk at all.

An alternative analogy could be drawn with payments to surrogate mothers
for their reproductive services. In relation to surrogate motherhood, as we shall
see in the next chapter, a consequentialist analysis might lead us to conclude that
paying women for their gestational services may be preferable to non-payment.
If we think that banning payments might drive potential surrogates and would-
be commissioning couples abroad, or into an unregulated "black market", a ban
will simply reduce the possibility of effective regulatory control, which is
unlikely to be in the best interests of the resulting children. A similar argument
might plausibly be mounted in relation to payments for human gametes; a ban
upon payments might result in fewer donations, thus restricting access to infertility treatment,[327] or it could lead to a flourishing black market in donated
gametes, with fewer protections for donors, recipients and children.

Both the Glover Report to the European Commission[328] and the Human
Fertilisation and Embryology Authority agree that it would be preferable to move
towards a system in which donors were not paid, but for pragmatic reasons both

---

[324] Pennings, 2000.

[325] There is considerable disagreement about the acceptability of commodification of human
body parts. For example, Daniels has asked "is it possible to show respect for a person when we buy
and sell major components of his or her personhood?" (Daniels, 2000, p. 209), while David Resnik
believes that human body parts, including gametes, should be treated as "incomplete commodities"
and that regulatory control of the market in gametes would be sufficient to allay fears about the
potential threat to human dignity (Resnik, 1998).

[326] Human Organ Transplant Act 1989. See further Macklin, 1996.

[327] The British Fertility Society estimate that in order to meet demand, about 500 donors must be
recruited per annum in the UK. As a result of the very strict criteria which are used to select semen
donors, only 5% of those who enquire about sperm donation are accepted, which means that 10,000
potential donors must be found and assessed (British Fertility Society, 1996 para. 1.2). King's
College Hospital attempted to set up an exclusively altruistic Sperm Bank in 1988. It accepted about
5 donors per year, resulting in sufficient semen for only 38.8% of their needs. The British Fertility
Society estimates that this might represent the shortfall in donor recruitment if payments in the UK
were to be stopped (British Fertility Society, 1996, para. 4).

[328] For example, the Glover Report expressed the concern that "as with blood donation, payment
may lead unsuitable people to apply, lying about their medical history (perhaps one of AIDS) in
order to be paid" . . . and that payment "deprives donors of the chance of doing something purely
for others" (Glover, 1989, pp. 83–4).

stopped short of advocating an immediate ban on payments.[329] In addition to the fear that without payment it might prove difficult to recruit sufficient donors in the UK, the HFEA was also "mindful of an emerging international trade in gametes and of the increased use of the internet to advertise donors from abroad".[330] The HFEA therefore decided that the supply of safe, screened sperm through licensed clinics was more important than their ideological preference for altruism.[331]

Of course, one practical danger in paying gamete providers is that it might encourage repeat donations. While frequent donation would pose no risk to a sperm provider's health, the feared social consequences of one donor being the genetic father to hundreds of children have led to an upper limit of 10 pregnancies per donor.[332] For female egg donors the same limit applies, but since oocyte donation is an invasive and possibly risky procedure[333] most clinics also set a maximum number of egg donation cycles per woman.

Sperm

In the United Kingdom sperm donors or providers[334] are paid a small sum, up to £15, which is intended to compensate for their expenses and inconvenience.[335] For low-income men, such as students, £15 undoubtedly represents a

[329] The HFEA has explained that "we became increasingly aware that the issue of payment could not be considered as an issue of principle in isolation from others" (HFEA, 1999, p. 28). Following the announcement of the HFEA decision, Ruth Deech stated "we do not feel that payment of £15 is so wrong that we are prepared to threaten the entire service" (Deech, 1999).

[330] HFEA 1999, p. 28. Although it would probably be unlawful to receive sperm from abroad because the frozen sperm would inevitably have to be stored prior to use, and storage is only lawful in licensed clinics (Low, 1998).

[331] This preference for altruistic donation, coupled with the recognition on the part of those involved that payment may be necessary is also evident in a study conducted by Lyall *et al* into attitudes towards payments to sperm donors: 58% of the general public were against payments, compared with 29% of potential donors, and 43% of potential recipients (Lyall *et al*, 1998 p. 772).

[332] According to the HFEA Code of Practice para. 7.18: "Donated gametes or embryos should not be used for treatment once the number of live children believed to have been born as a result of donations from that donor has reached 10. It is the responsibility of the supplier and of the user to agree an appropriate procedure for ensuring that the limit is not exceeded". The only exception is contained in para. 7.19: "This limit of 10 may be exceeded only in exceptional cases, e.g. where a recipient wishes to have a subsequent child from the same donor. The HFEA should be notified whenever the limit is exceeded. If the donor has specified a limit, this must never be exceeded" (HFEA, 1998).

Other countries set different maximum numbers of children per donor, for example in South Africa one donor can have up to five children, in Spain the upper limit is six. Because of its tiny population and the danger of consanguinity, Iceland imports all of its sperm from Denmark (Blank, 1998, p. 145). In Switzerland, the maximum number of offspring per donor is also ten (Bonnicksen, 1996, p. 165). And in Israel, the upper limit is seven children per donor (Schenker, 1997, p. 178).

[333] It is unclear whether there might be adverse consequences following multiple cycles of ovulation induction (Klein *et al*, 1996, p. 9).

[334] The routine payment of donors has led some to suggest that the term donor is a misnomer and should be replaced by a term such as "provider" (Daniels, 1998, p. 76), or "vendor" (Murray, 1996, p. 63).

[335] Section 12(e) of the Human Fertilisation and Embryology Act states that "no money or other benefit shall be given or received in respect of any supply of gametes or embryos unless authorised by directions".

financial incentive.[336] In addition to helping to recruit new donors from the student population,[337] it could be argued that payment reinforces the finality of the transaction between the donor and the clinic. And given that the majority of donated sperm is used in private clinics, where patients are charged around £150 per straw, it is unclear whether men would be willing to make altruistic donations in the knowledge that their sperm will then be "sold" to its users.[338]

The profile of sperm donors differs between countries according to whether they are paid. In the United Kingdom, 75 per cent of donors are students,[339] whereas in New Zealand where donations must be altruistic, they tend to be older, and in professional employment.[340] In France the Centre d'Études et de Conservation des Oeufs et du Sperme humains (CECOS) sperm banks demand that their donors are married,[341] or in a stable relationship; their wife or partner must have consented to their donation; they must have fathered at least one child and there must be no payment.[342] While France is often offered as an example of how a donor insemination programme can be sustained without payments for donors, the British Fertility Society has argued that the supply of sperm is maintained at the expense of a rigorous screening programme, and that there are in fact extended waiting lists for treatment.[343]

Eggs

In the United Kingdom, like sperm donors, egg donors may be paid up to £15 per donation. But because egg retrieval is a time-consuming and invasive procedure, £15 would not be likely to encourage donation among poorer women. More attractive inducements such as free IVF treatment, or avoiding a long waiting list for sterilisation might, however, amount to indirect payment. Since one IVF cycle typically costs around £2000, it is clear that egg-sharing schemes represent substantial, albeit indirect, payment for egg donation. And given the anguish of involuntary childlessness, the possibility that "donating" eggs could lead to one's own pregnancy may also represent a significant non-financial incentive.[344]

---

[336] Cooke and Golombok studied 144 semen donors from 14 Centres and found that 71% felt that payment was very or moderately important (Cooke and Golombok, 1996).

[337] Murray and Golombok, 2000.

[338] British Fertility Society, 1996, para. 5.2.

[339] Barratt, 1993.

[340] Daniels, 1987.

[341] Donors in Poland must also be married. Interestingly in Israel for religious reasons, donors must be single (Schenker, 1997, p. 176).

[342] Novaes, 1998, p. 118.

[343] According to the British Fertility Society, of 674 donors who applied to CECOS in 1995, 61% were accepted after screening, compared with a 5% acceptance rate in the UK. The BFS also claims that one third of CECOS donors may carry some risk of passing on an inherited disease. There is a significant waiting list for DI in many CECOS centres. According to the BFS, the average time between acceptance for treatment and the start of treatment is 6 to 12 months (BFS, 1996, paras. 3.1.3 and 3.1.4.).

[344] As a result the HFEA Code of Practice (1998) para. 3.55 states that the possibility of donating gametes should not be raised during the potential donor's treatment cycle, or by a member of staff involved in the potential donor's treatment.

Egg sharing schemes carry no extra *clinical* risk, since the donor would be having the egg retrieval in any event, however the HFEA requires participants to contemplate the possibility that the recipients of their eggs may be treated successfully while their own treatment may fail.[345] Since the eggs will, of necessity, be retrieved from a woman who has experienced difficulty in conceiving, there is the possibility that success rates may be lower. Women undergoing surgical sterilisation may also be prepared to donate their eggs, particularly if they are offered immediate sterilisation as an incentive.[346] Again, since such women are likely to be older, fertilisation rates may be correspondingly reduced.

In its consultation on payments to gamete donors, the HFEA decided against banning egg-sharing schemes on the grounds that they "can be beneficial to both sharer and receiver",[347] but it also recommended that they should be closely controlled to minimise the possibility of exploitation. In addition, the HFEA recognised the possibility that prompt access to sterilisation might encourage consent to egg donation, and its information leaflet for potential egg donors specifically states that if a woman chooses to withdraw her consent to egg collection, "sterilisation or other related surgery . . . will still be performed on the terms already agreed".[348]

In the United States, managing egg "donation" is now a lucrative business. Although the American Fertility Society has recommended that there should be no financial compensation for the donation of the egg itself, reimbursement for expenses,[349] time, risk and discomfort may be substantial.[350] Egg donors are typically given approximately $2000 per donation,[351] which is undoubtedly enough to operate as an incentive to donate.[352] Much higher sums[353] have been

[345] Bonnicksen, 1996, p. 157. The HFEA Code of Practice 1998 para. 6.16c suggests that pre-donation counselling should invite potential donors to consider "the possibility of their own childlessness".

[346] Kan *et al*, 1998.

[347] HFEA, 1999, p. v.

[348] HFEA, 1995.

[349] Ruth Macklin points out that if payment represents actual compensation for lost wages, well-paid women will be given more money for donating their eggs than low-income or unemployed women. But if payment is for the service of egg donation, then the principle of equal pay for equal work demands that their compensation should be identical (Macklin, 1996b, p. 114).

[350] Macklin, 1996b, p. 107.

[351] Steinbock, 1998, p. 150.

[352] Ruth Macklin argues that "$2000 is a significant sum for students or for poor or lower-class women; and they are surely being induced to undergo something they would not otherwise be doing" (Macklin, 1996b, p. 111). Similarly Rosemarie Tong suggests that "in an ever shrinking and increasingly lower-paying job market, an unskilled woman, or a woman who needs money fast, might be tempted to sell her oocytes for a $750–$3000 fee even if the process constitutes a threat to her health" (Tong, 1996, p. 143).

[353] Tall, intelligent young women have been offered up to $50,000 to donate their eggs (Mead, 1999).

reported in the flourishing market for the eggs of models and Ivy League graduates, with egg donors frequently recruited on university campuses.[354]

We shall explore the arguments put by those who believe that human reproduction should never be the subject of a commercial transaction more fully in the following chapter when we consider the practice of surrogacy. In relation to oocyte donation, the argument might be made that paying women to "donate" their eggs is exploitative since it may persuade poor women to undergo an invasive and unpleasant procedure. Of course, having one's choices influenced by the prospect of financial reward is not necessarily inherently exploitative. There are many types of employment, such as mining or the armed forces, which involve doing something which may be physically uncomfortable and/or dangerous, in return for financial reward. Any health risks associated with repeated ovulation induction and retrieval could be minimised by imposing a maximum number of donations per woman, as in fact already happens in the UK. But paying women substantial sums of money for donating their eggs is likely to remain unlawful in the UK. Given that egg donation is both uncomfortable and extremely time-consuming, it is unsurprising that clinics find it difficult to recruit altruistic donors.[355] As a result, there will continue to be an acute shortage of eggs, and British women may increasingly try to obtain eggs from countries such as the US where greater compensation to donors means that eggs are more readily available.

III Alternative Sources of Eggs

As a result of the multiple practical and ethical difficulties in recruiting egg donors,[356] there is a huge shortfall in the number of donated eggs available for treatment and it is not uncommon for would-be recipients to wait three years for eggs to become available.[357] Women from certain ethnic groups may have to wait for five years or more for same race eggs.[358] One possible solution would be to lift the ban on the retrieval of eggs from cadavers or aborted fetuses. When a female baby is born, its ovaries contain a lifetime's supply of eggs. These eggs are produced while the fetus is still *in utero*, which means that

---

[354] The University of Washington Medical Center recruits oocyte donors by "the posting of flyers around campus" (Klein *et al*, 1996, p. 7). Given the risks inherent in egg retrieval, one US clinician points to "an inherent moral ambiguity in a practice of medicine that simultaneously places young women at risk of infertility while treating the childlessness of other women (Mark Sauer, quoted in Price, 1999, p. 55).

[355] Unlike the profile of sperm donors in the UK, egg donors tend to be older and have children of their own. In Kan *et al*'s study of anonymous oocyte donors, their mean age was 31.2 years and 89% had their own children (Kan *et al*, 1998).

[356] Kan *et al*, 1998; Murray and Golombok, 2000.

[357] Ian Craft has said "I favour egg donation without financial reward but the demand for eggs far outstrips the supply from women who donate for altruistic reasons. The end results are an inordinate delay . . . and the proliferation of private organisations that put donors and recipients in contact for financial reward" (Craft, 1997, p. 1400).

[358] In Kan *et al*'s study, 96.7% of anonymous oocyte donors were Caucasian (Kan *et al*, 1998, p. 2764).

it might be possible to retrieve eggs from the ovaries of aborted fetuses and mature them *in vitro* prior to their use in infertility treatment. If it were both lawful to extract eggs from aborted fetuses and possible to use them in treatment, the shortage of eggs would disappear. While there would obviously be clear practical benefits in locating a plentiful supply of donated eggs that is not dependent upon women undergoing ovarian stimulation and surgical egg retrieval, public hostility to the use of fetal eggs tends to outweigh sympathy for infertile women.[359]

The Polkinghorne Committee was set up in 1989 to consider the use of fetal material, and they concluded that the donation of gametes is different in kind to the donation of other sorts of tissue[360] because they contain genetic material which will be passed on to future generations. Five years after the publication of the Polkinghorne Report, the HFEA issued a public consultation document and found that there was still a "widespread and fundamental objection" to the use of fetal ovarian tissue.[361] The HFEA therefore decided that although it would be prepared to licence *research* on fetal ovarian tissue, provided that it is not investigating the use of fetal eggs in IVF treatment,[362] no licences would be granted to anyone proposing to use fetal eggs in infertility treatment. In addition to the HFEA's licensing policy, the prohibition upon the use of fetal eggs was also incorporated into the primary legislation by the Criminal Justice and Public Order Act 1994.[363] Although the HFEA had "no objection in principle" to the use of eggs from adult female cadavers, it also decided that it would not currently approve their use in infertility treatment, although again, licences may be granted for *research* on cadaveric ovarian tissue.

The most frequently cited objection to the use of fetal or cadaveric ovarian tissue is uncertainty about the long-term psychological impact upon the recipients and any resulting children.[364] Of course, in both legal and social terms, the child's mother would be the woman who became pregnant and gave birth to the child, rather than the oocyte source. But it is nevertheless argued that to find out that half

[359] The HFEA's consultation on the use of fetal and cadaveric eggs found that 83% of respondents were against the use of fetal eggs in infertility treatment (HFEA, 1994, p. 9).

[360] And other sorts of fetal tissue have been used in the treatment of conditions such as leukaemia, diabetes and Parkinson's disease. In the UK the Medical Research Council's fetal tissue bank was established in 1957 and disperses about 5000 tissues each year (Savulescu, 1999b, p. 92).

[361] HFEA, 1994, p. 5. It is perhaps interesting that a public opinion poll conducted at the same time as the publication of the HFEA's public consultation document showed that 57% of respondents said that it was not right to use eggs from aborted fetuses, while 35% were in favour (Dillner, 1994b, p. 158). So although most respondents were against the use of eggs from aborted fetuses, this is by no means an overwhelming majority.

[362] HFEA, 1994, p. 2.

[363] S. 156 of the Criminal Justice and Public Order Act 1994 inserted section 3A into the Human Fertilisation and Embryology Act 1990: "No person shall, for the purposes of providing fertility services for any woman, use female germlines taken or derived from an embryo of a fetus or use embryos created by using such cells." Similarly, in the US the NIH Human Embryo Research Panel concluded that fetal egg donation was ethically unacceptable (Bonnicksen, 1996, p. 162).

[364] HFEA, 1994, p. 5. As an example of the sort of scenario for which people tend to feel instinctive revulsion, Kathleen Guzman points out that "scientists could soon create an embryo by joining sperm recovered from a decedent and an egg retrieved from a fetus" (Guzman, 1997, p. 203).

of one's genetic material came from an aborted fetus or a corpse would be unbearably disturbing. For obvious reasons, there is no evidence to support or discount this objection, so the claim that it would be better not to be born than to have this sort of knowledge about one's genetic origins is likely to remain speculative.[365]

IV Selection

There are certain limits upon who may donate their gametes. The HFEA imposes an upper age limit of 55 for male donors and 35 for female donors,[366] and a lower age limit of 18 for both sexes.[367] These restrictions are relaxed for the storage of an individual's gametes for their own treatment, so a 16 year old who is about to undergo radiotherapy could legitimately have their gametes stored for their own future use.[368]

It is common practice for infertility clinics to attempt to match the physical characteristics of the donor with those of the infertile partner, so that, as nearly as possible, the lack of a genetic link is not obvious.[369] More controversial are requests for a donor from a *different* racial group,[370] and the HFEA Code of Practice has explicitly proscribed the selection of a donor of different ethnic origins *for social reasons*.[371] It should, of course, be remembered that using a different race donor may not always indicate a positive request for gametes of a different racial origin. There are massive shortages of donated gametes among certain racial groups, and so it may prove impossible for a clinic to locate same-race gametes.

There has also been condemnation of attempts to select a donor with traits that are thought especially desirable.[372] There can of course be no guarantee

---

[365] John Harris argues that "it is surely unlikely to be so disturbing as to make it certain that no compassionate parent nor such a society would or should permit its birth" (Harris, 1998b, p. 15).

[366] HFEA Code of Practice (1998) para. 3.36.

[367] HFEA Code of Practice (1998) para. 3.38.

[368] HFEA Code of Practice (1998) paras. 3.37 and 3.40.

[369] HFEA Code of Practice (1998) para. 3.22: "when selecting donated gametes for treatment, centres should take into account each prospective parent's preferences in relation to the general physical characteristics of the donor."

[370] It was reported in 1993 that an infertile black woman whose husband was white, had chosen a white egg donor "because she believed a white child had a better future than one of mixed race" (Willan and Hawkes, 1993, p. 1). Robyn Rowland suggests that "we have people who are black wanting to carry children from white eggs, thereby attempting to resolve the problems of racism and violence by whitening the population" (Rowland, 1999, p. 98). Heitman and Schlachtenhaufen argue that transracial gamete donation raises similar issues to transracial adoption in that a child could grow up without an appreciation of his or her ethnic origins (Heitman and Schlachtenhaufen, 1996, p. 202). Jonathan Berkowtiz and Jack Snyder insist that "racism in medically assisted conception can be prevented by insisting that . . . children only represent a reasonable phenotypic approximation of their parents" (Berkowitz and Snyder, 1998, p. 35).

[371] HFEA Code of Practice (1998) para. 3.22.

[372] The Warnock Committee said that "as a matter of principle we do not wish to encourage the possibility of prospective parents seeking donors with specific characteristics by the use of whose semen they hope to give birth to a particular type of child" (Warnock, 1984, para. 4.21). The Wellcome Trust's survey of public attitudes found that "there was strong disapproval of the use of sperm selected from a sperm bank on the basis of the donor's characteristics" (Wellcome, 1998, p. 27).

In an American survey of sperm banks and physicians providing DI, 90% would match for height and 82% for body type; while fewer providers would be prepared to screen for characteristics such as educational attainment (66%), IQ (57%) or athletic skill (45%) (Strong, 1996, p. 132). Rosemarie

that the child will inherit the particular trait, and this sort of gamete selection is undoubtedly based upon an over-simplistic understanding of the role of genetics in human achievement. But the fact that it is unlikely to work is not the primary reason for disapproval of attempts to enhance a child's genotype by gamete selection. Because access to assisted conception tends to be confined to relatively wealthy members of society, endeavouring to "improve" a child's genotype by selecting donated gametes from people with particular characteristics would be restricted to couples who already have considerable material advantages, thus, according to these critics, exacerbating existing inequalities.[373] The desire to influence one's child's genetic make-up is also often assumed to spring from discreditable quasi-eugenic sentiments,[374] although John Harris would argue that choosing a *same* race donor or one with *similar* physical characteristics to the infertile partner is no less an exercise of parental preference than choosing a donor from a different racial group or with different attributes.[375] If fertile people's choice of their mating partner is often influenced, or even determined by the characteristics a potential partner might pass on to their child, it is unclear why similar choices made by infertile people are singled out as being especially invidious.

V Screening

All donated sperm must be frozen to enable the HIV status of the donor to be conclusively established by a further HIV test six months after the donation was made. Clinics must also give careful consideration to the suitability of donors, taking into account their personal and family medical history,[376] their potential fertility including whether they have children of their own, and their attitude towards donation.[377] At the moment it would be impossible to test sperm or egg donors for all hereditary conditions, or to independently ascertain the truth or

Tong suggests that "it is one matter to enable an infertile couple to conceive a child that resembles the one they might have conceived 'naturally' and quite another to enable them to conceive a child appreciably 'better' than that one" (Tong, 1996, pp. 150–1).

In America The Repository for Germinal Choice specialises in providing sperm from men who are particularly highly educated and successful, where enhancement is clearly the intention of the purchasing couples.

[373] See further Strong, 1996, p. 134.

[374] For example, the Benda Report in Germany in 1980 rejected the practice of DI in part because of concern about the eugenic selection of semen providers (Edwards, 1998, p. 152).

[375] "It is a truism that bears repeating, that once you have the capacity to choose and the awareness of that capacity, then choice is inevitable. It is not the less an exercise of choice because the choice is exercised in a traditional way, nor because the choice may involve doing nothing at all" (Harris, 1998b, p. 22).

[376] A medical history questionnaire must be taken (HFEA Code of Practice (1998) para. 3.43).

The American Fertility Society Guidelines apply to both sperm and oocyte donation. They recommend excluding donors with any of the following: a major Mendelian disorder; a major multifactorial or polygenic malformation; a familial disease with a major genetic component; a chromosomal rearrangement; carriers of an autosomal recessive gene known to be prevalent in the donor's ethnic background and for which carrier status can be detected; advanced age (females 35 or older; males 40 or older); or a first degree relative (parents or offspring) with any of the above conditions (Strong, 1996, p. 123).

[377] HFEA Code of Practice (1998) para. 3.47.

falsity of would-be donors' answers to questions about their family's medical history.[378] The only test that the HFEA recommends should be routinely carried out on all donated gametes is for cystic fibrosis.[379] Screening for conditions such as Tay-Sachs, thalassaemia and sickle cell anaemia is recommended for population groups with an increased susceptibility.[380]

It is of course possible that a donor's genetic condition might be detected after their gametes have been used in treatment. Where this happens both the donor and the patient must be offered counselling, and the HFEA Code of Practice recommends that particular care should be taken in informing a woman who is pregnant as a result of treatment with the donated gametes.

As the number of identifiable genetic conditions increases, and the costs of screening decrease,[381] there will inevitably be pressure upon clinics to carry out more extensive tests on donated gametes.[382] There is also the inevitable possibility of malpractice litigation for failure to warn recipients of the risk that their child could inherit certain genetic conditions. Parents of a child born suffering from a condition passed on by the gamete donor could argue that failure to inform them of the existence of genetic testing, or failure to screen for the particular disease was a breach of the clinic's duty of care, owed both to them and to any child that might be born. Such actions would be similar to the "wrongful birth" litigation discussed in chapter two, and would derive from the claim that if the parents had been told of the risk of a particular genetic condition, they would have rejected these gametes and the harm, that is the child's disease, would have been avoided. The HFEA Code of Practice insists that clinics should inform potential donors that they may be sued personally by any child born disabled as a result of their failure to disclose information about an inherited disorder,[383] but this has not yet been tested in the courts.

A further problem in relation to routine genetic screening of donated gametes is the possibility that the donor may be affected by the disclosure of any positive test results. Fully informed and specific consent to genetic screening may then be necessary in addition to the consent required for the storage and use of the

---

[378] Although according to the HFEA Code of Practice (1998) para. 3.44, centres should, wherever practicable, ask a potential donor's GP if there is any reason why the potential donor might be unsuitable.

[379] HFEA Code of Practice (1998) para. 3.50 "in relation to cystic fibrosis, centres should normally screen donors especially those from population groups with high frequencies of cystic fibrosis carriers. If a centre uses unscreened donors, the centre should inform the patient and offer screening and counselling".

[380] HFEA Code of Practice (1998) para. 3.51.

[381] At present tests for some genetic markers are expensive, and so it is more efficient to reject all potential donors with a relevant family history, rather than test the individual donor to discover whether he or she carries the genetic mutation. For example, people at risk of developing hereditary nonpolyposis colorectal cancer can be identified by a genetic test which costs £1500; it is currently much cheaper to reject anyone with a family history of colorectal cancer (Strong, 1996, p. 130).

[382] HFEA Code of Practice (1998) paras. 3.58–9.

[383] HFEA, 1998, para. 4.5i: donors must be told about " the possibility that a child born disabled as a result of a donor's failure to disclose defects, about which they knew or ought reasonably to have known, may be able to sue the donor for damages".

gametes. If a potential donor is turned down as a result of the detection of a genetic abnormality, the HFEA Code of Practice insists that the clinic should give him or her all reasonable assistance in obtaining treatment or counselling.[384]

(d) Regulating the Status and Use of the Embryo

(i) Moral Status

The moral status of the human embryo is undoubtedly one of the most complex and divisive questions in medical ethics.[385] Despite our increasingly sophisticated understanding of *how* new human life is created, there may be no objectively determinable scientific answer to the question of *when* morally significant life begins. Thus, for example, biological facts about the processes involved in conception are commonly invoked both by those who want to argue that human life begins at the moment of fertilisation, and by those who believe that individuated human life begins somewhat later.

On the one hand it is argued that at the moment of fertilisation a new and unique genotype is formed which will continue to grow autonomously, and which is continuous with the resulting person.[386] On the other hand, the fertilised egg or zygote is not a unique new person in microcosm, because its cells may subsequently divide and become two new living entities. So while fertilisation results in a genetically distinct biological entity, there is not yet an ontologically distinct individual.[387] Furthermore, some of the zygote's cells will become the placenta and umbilical cord, material that is readily discarded at birth. It is only the cells in the inner cell mass that go on to form the embryo itself, and at fertilisation there is no way to determine which cells will become disposable matter and which will constitute the first stages of the new human embryo.[388] Occasionally, a fertilised egg will even develop into a type of tumour

---

[384] HFEA, 1998, para. 3.57.

[385] The ongoing debates about precisely when human life begins also have an interesting resonance with anthropology's interest in the cultural significance of different societies' "conception accounts". Anthropologists have been preoccupied by the cultural significance of what a society believes about conception for many years. And according to Sarah Franklin, one notable feature of the embryo research debates in Parliament 1999 is "their saturation with conception litanies" (Franklin, 1999, p. 133).

[386] For example, Margaret Tighe says that "from that time when the father's (*sic*) sperm begins to penetrate the mother's (*sic*) ovum, a new life has begun and, unless man or nature intervenes, has commenced the journey of life only requiring time, optimum conditions and natural development to become a full-fledged member of the human family—male or female—with all of the characteristics unique to that person" (Tighe, 1999 [1994] p. 91). Although it should be noted that it is rather misleading to refer to the *moment* of fertilisation since the merging of the sperm and the egg might be better described as a *process* of fusion (Eberl, 2000, p. 143).

[387] Ford, 1988, p. 117.

[388] Ford, 1988, pp. 148–9.

known as a hydatidiform mole rather than a human embryo. So while it may be new human life, the zygote is not then a new human *individual*: it may turn out to be two individuals and some of its cells are destined to become disposable extraembryonic structures.[389] It could therefore be argued that a unique individual entity does not exist "until all the cells that will contribute to the formation of the embryo proper are determined to that end and no other",[390] which would be the case at around 14 days.[391]

Moreover, an embryo will not autonomously become a baby, rather this collection of cells will perish unless subsequently implanted in a woman's uterus and carried for at least five months. These are substantial prerequisites: most fertilised eggs fail either to implant or to complete their development, and the vast majority of this natural wastage remains unnoticed.[392] As a result, the Royal College of Obstetricians and Gynaecologists' Ethics Committee has argued that

"It is morally unconvincing to claim absolute inviolability for an organism with which nature itself is so prodigal".[393]

But even if we accept that the newly fertilised egg is not yet a person, its potential to become one is often offered up as a compelling reason for its protection.[394] There are, however, multiple problems with this "argument from potential". First, it is not clear that X's potential to be Y obliges us to treat X as if it already were Y.[395] Nor does the possibility that X *might* one day become Y tell us very much about precisely how X should be treated. Second, although an embryo obviously has the potential to become a person, this may also be true of gametes, which could, if certain things happen, also become a new human

---

[389] Known as trophoblast.

[390] Eberl, 2000, p. 146.

[391] The primitive streak is the first indication of neural development, and it occurs approximately 14 days after fertilisation. According to Norman Ford, 1988 "the appearance of one primitive streak signals that only one embryo proper and human individual has been formed and begun to exist" (Ford, 1988, p. 172). Ingmar Persson has argued that "it is better to adopt the view that we begin to exist *no earlier* than at the stage of implantation" (Persson, 1999, p. 131) (emphasis in original). And Jeff McMahan suggests that "although it is not unreasonable to believe that an organism begins to exist at fertilisation, it is more plausible to suppose that a human organism does not begin to exist until about fourteen days after fertilisation" (McMahan, 1999, p. 82).

[392] Alto Charo, 1995, p. 16. About half of all fertilised eggs are lost before the woman's period is due (Lockwood, 2000).

[393] Quoted in Alto Charo, 1995, p. 16. Similarly, Jason Eberl argues that religious claims for the personhood of the newly fertilised zygote may be unconvincing since "it seems odd to believe that God . . . would permit the needless death of so many persons. It seems more reasonable to conceive of them as naturally rejected biological material—not persons" (Eberl, 2000).

Ian Kennedy, on the other hand, rejects these arguments on the ground that they rely on the false premise that everything which happens in nature is necessarily good (Kennedy, 1991, p. 126).

[394] The chairman of the HFEA, Ruth Deech, has said that "the embryo is the first step to the creation of a human being and always deserves respect and protection" (HFEA, 1999, p. vi).

[395] HT Engelhardt says that the argument from potentiality "is in itself misleading, for it is often taken to suggest that an X that is potentially a Y in some mysterious fashion already possesses the being and significance of Y" (Engelhardt, 1986, p. 111).

life.[396] If the embryo is special because it has the potential to become a human being, then since the egg and sperm have the potential to become an embryo, logically they must also have the potential to become a human being.[397] Yet gametes' potential does not lead to their protection as if they already were full human beings.[398] The difference perhaps is that the embryo contains a new genetic code, so it is clearly a significant step further on in the process of becoming a person than a spermatazoa or an unfertilised egg.[399] But while it is undoubtedly true that most human gametes have the potential to be a person only in a rather remote sense,[400] Peter Singer has argued that it is not necessarily obvious that a fertilised egg in a petri dish should have an entirely different moral status to the egg and sperm in the petri dish immediately prior to fertilisation.[401] Third, the possibility of human cloning adds a new dimension to the potentiality argument. Nuclear transfer means that, in theory at least, *any cell* could become a new human being if certain conditions were to obtain. Just because a skin cell might have the potential to become a person, we would obviously not be compelled to treat it as though it already were a person.[402]

Christine Overall suggests that some of this confusion can be avoided if we are careful to distinguish between what it means to be human, and what it means to be a person.[403] An embryo is undoubtedly human, in the sense that it belongs to the human species, but this is not the same thing as saying that an

[396] Mary Warnock has said that "human semen is potential human material, if it fertilises an egg and is implanted. Human ova are likewise potential human beings if they are fertilised by semen, and implanted. Yet no-one supposes that sperm and egg are in themselves to be protected, although they are plainly of value, and are not to be thought of just like anything else" (Warnock, 1987, p. 12). Jason Eberl suggests that sperm, ova and the fertilised zygote all have a *passive potentiality* for human personhood, although the zygote may be slightly closer to realising that potentiality (Eberl, 2000, p. 153).

[397] Harris, 1989, p. 91. Taken to its logical extreme, it could even be argued that the parents decision to have sexual intercourse has the potential to produce a baby, and that the argument from potential should question the morality of refusing to have sexual intercourse (Reichlin, 1997, pp. 3–4).

[398] Although some religions do believe that sperm and eggs deserve moral concern and respect, and should not, for example, be wasted or misused (Kennedy, 1991, p. 129).

[399] Leon Kass says that "while the egg and sperm are alive as cells, something new and alive *in a different sense* comes into being with fertilization . . . For after fertilization is complete, there exists a new individual with its unique genetic identity, fully potent for the self-initiated development into a mature human being, if circumstances are cooperative. Though there is some sense in which the lives of egg and sperm are continuous with the life of the new organism-to-be . . . in the decisive sense there is a discontinuity, a new beginning, with fertilization" (Kass, 1998 [1979] p. 97) (emphasis in original). Ian Kennedy agrees that "once united, there is a new entity which, for the first time, at least has the chance to become a human person" (Kennedy, 1991, p. 127).

[400] Reichlin, 1997, p. 4.

[401] "If potentiality is a matter of degree, the embryo is a degree closer to being a person than a collection of egg and sperm in a petri dish before fertilisation has taken place. What I still cannot find is any basis for the view that this difference of degree makes an enormous difference in the moral status of what we have before us" (Singer, 1998 [1985], p. 88).

[402] Julian Savulescu eloquently explains that "if all our cells could be persons, then we cannot appeal to the fact that an embryo could be a person to justify the special treatment we give it. Cloning forces us to abandon the old arguments supporting special treatment of fertilised eggs" (Savulescu, 1999b, p. 91).

[403] Overall, 1995, p. 180.

embryo is a person, which is, according to Overall, a moral judgement rather than a species classification.[404] Overall identifies a similar slippage between the terms "life" and "alive".[405] So an embryo is alive in the sense that it is not dead, but that does not mean that it has the capacity to perform the functions that we associate with possessing life, such as a heart beat or brain activity.

Related to this, it might be argued that the definition of death could prove useful in determining when human life becomes significant. Dying, like conception, is usually a gradual process. The moment of death, nevertheless, has a precise legal definition that consists in determining when certain factors and characteristics which are associated with being a human being, are irrevocably absent. If we say that someone is dead when they have lost the capacity for consciousness or sentience, then it might seem logical to say that the first appearance of the capacity for consciousness or sentience marks the beginning of a valuable human life. This argument has a pleasing symmetry, although there would obviously be those who would argue that the capacity for *future* consciousness is present at fertilisation, thus returning us again to the argument from potential.

In its deliberations, the Warnock Report reached the conclusion that an embryo is not a person, but also that it is not nothing.[406] According to Warnock, the embryo is "special" and should be treated with "respect".[407] Yet, as we see in the following section, there is, a profound ambiguity at the heart of the Warnock Report's recommendation that legislation should both permit research on human embryos and prohibit their "frivolous or unnecessary" use.[408] Perhaps it simply needs to be admitted that the law is not capable of divining any absolute truths about the moral status of the embryo, and the only certainty is probably the continued absence of any consensus.[409] So rather than attempt to justify embryo research and/or destruction through moral reasoning, it might be preferable to acknowledge that the instrumental use of the early human embryo inevitably offends some people's cherished belief in the moral significance of fertilisation,[410] but that that offence has to be put into

[404] In a similar vein, Walter Glannon says that "'person' is a psychological concept, while 'human organism' is a biological concept . . . The zygote, embryo, fetus and person are distinct but biologically related stages in the development of a human organism . . . A person begins to exist when the fetal stage of the organism develops the structure and function of the brain necessary to generate and support consciousness and mental life" (Glannon, 1998, pp. 189–90).

[405] Overall, 1995, p. 181.

[406] According to Leon Kass, "the blastocyst is not nothing; it is at least potential humanity, and as such it elicits, or ought to elicit, our feelings of awe and respect" (Kass, 1998 [1979] p. 98).

[407] Warnock, 1984, para. 11.17.

[408] Warnock, 1985, p. 64. Daniel Callahan believes that it is disingenuous to claim to have respect for human embryos while simultaneously permitting their destruction, he argues that " 'respect' for prenatal life is really just a way to feel less uncomfortable by its destruction", and that it is "an odd form of esteem, at once high minded and altogether lethal" (quoted in Alto Charo, 1995, p. 12).

[409] Arlene Judith Klotzko believes that the "Human Fertilisation and Embryology Act is a legislative tour de force in that it creates a legal framework for embryo research in the absence of moral consensus" (Klotzko, 1997, p. 437).

[410] The Human Genetics Advisory Commission and the Human Fertilisation and Embryology Authority's joint consultation on human cloning found that 23% of their respondents believed that *any* form of embryo research is simply wrong (HGAC and HFEA, 1998, para. 3.3).

the balance with the benefits that may flow from embryo research and infertility treatment. Thus the statutory restrictions upon embryo research that we consider in detail below may not embody a coherent resolution of the question of the embryo's moral status, but might instead be an arbitrary and politically expedient compromise designed to safeguard some scientific research within limits that are intended to convey the intrinsic moral importance of the early human embryo.

(ii) Embryo Research

There have been attempts to draw a moral distinction between creating embryos in order to achieve a pregnancy, and using embryos for research.[411] And initially there might seem to be a plausible moral boundary between fertilising an egg with the intention that it should become a baby, and carrying out an experiment on an embryo and subsequently discarding it.[412] Yet IVF treatment and embryo research are not readily separable because *in vitro* fertilisation techniques would not exist without research on human embryos. Given the imprecision of IVF, it would also be impossible to fertilise only the exact number of eggs that will be transferred to the woman's uterus in any one treatment cycle. IVF treatment therefore necessarily involves the creation of spare embryos that may have to be destroyed. If the disposal of spare embryos is inevitable, it is difficult to see why washing an embryo down the drain would be morally preferable to using it in order to carry out valuable research.

As we have seen, the regulatory scheme embodied in the Human Fertilisation and Embryology Act 1990 represents a compromise between the view that the early embryo's membership of the human species means that it is deserving of special respect, and the acknowledgement that the potential benefits of research on embryos are so great that some research ought to be permitted.[413] The Act therefore permits research on embryos within certain limits. First, an embryo cannot be kept or used after the appearance of the primitive streak,[414] which is taken to be no later than 14 days from the mixing of the gametes.[415] Second, licences authorising embryo research may only be granted for certain purposes, such as promoting advances in the treatment of infertility and increasing knowledge

---

[411] For example Enoch Powell's Unborn Children Protection Bill 1985.

[412] According to the Warnock Committee "some people hold that if an embryo is human and alive, it follows that it should not be deprived of a chance for development, and therefore it should not be used for research. They would give moral approval to IVF if, and only if, each embryo produced were to be transferred to a uterus" (Warnock, 1984, para 11.9).

[413] Michael Mulkay suggests that the legislation embodies an "uneasy balance between endorsement and restriction" (Mulkay, 1997, p. 3).

[414] S. 3(3)(a).

[415] S. 3(4).

about the causes of congenital diseases.[416] Third, there are limits upon what can be done with embryos, so nuclear substitution,[417] or placing an embryo in any animal[418] are both expressly forbidden. Fourth, the HFEA will only consider applications for research licences that have already been approved by a properly constituted research ethics committee. Finally, all applications for research licences are submitted for peer review before being approved by a Licence Committee.[419]

Unlike the laws of most European Countries,[420] and contrary to the European Convention on Human Rights and Biomedicine,[421] the Human Fertilisation and Embryology Act permits the creation of embryos for research purposes. Since the spare embryo created in IVF treatment is essentially the same thing as the embryo created for research, those who would argue against the deliberate creation of research embryos are not concerned with the harm to the embryo itself. Instead, in their focus upon the embryologist's *intention*, their uneasiness is clearly with the symbolic harm of creating human life in order to conduct research upon it.[422] While the Warnock Report avoided this ambiguous moral distinction, it resurrected a similar one by sanctioning the deliberate creation of research embryos[423] while simultaneously condemning the mass production of *in vitro* research embryos on a commercial basis.[424] The committee believed

---

[416] Schedule 2(3)(2) A licence under this paragraph cannot authorise any activity unless it appears to the Authority to be necessary or desirable for the purpose of—

(a) promoting advances in the treatment of infertility;
(b) increasing knowledge about the causes of congenital disease;
(c) increasing knowledge about the causes of miscarriages;
(d) developing more effective techniques of contraception or;
(e) developing methods for detecting the presence of gene or chromosome abnormalities in embryos before implantation.

or for such other purposes as may be specified in regulations. In January 2001, regulations extended this list to cover stem cell research.

[417] S. 3(3)(d).

[418] S. 3(3)(b).

[419] Between 1991 and 2000, the HFEA received 131 applications for research licences, of these 111 were granted, although 12 were subsequently refused a renewed licence (HFEA, 1999, p. 26; HFEA, 2000c, p. 26). At 31 August 2000, there were 32 licensed research projects ongoing, most of which are concerned with the promotion of advances in the treatment of infertility (HFEA, 2000c, p. 26).

[420] For example, the French law of 29 July 1994 proscribes the creation of human embryos unless it is "in the context of a parental project" (CCNE, 1997).

[421] The European Convention on Human Rights and Biomedicine was adopted by the Parliamentary Assembly on 26 September 1996 and first came into force at the end of 1999. Article 18 of the Convention permits embryo research, but prohibits the creation of embryos for research purposes.

[422] For example, Ian Kennedy finds "compelling" "those arguments which suggest that the research is morally wrong because the intention of the researcher is morally repugnant" (Kennedy, 1991, p. 124).

[423] Nine members of the Warnock committee favoured permitting research on deliberately created embryos; four believed research should only take place on spare embryos donated by IVF patients, and three opposed all research on human embryos.

[424] "We feel very strongly that the routine testing of drugs on human embryos is not an acceptable area of research because this would require the manufacture of large numbers of embryos . . . the testing of such substances on a very small scale may be justifiable" (Warnock, 1984, para. 12.5).

that the large-scale manufacture of human embryos for research might occasion greater moral outrage than the creation of a very small number of embryos destined for research. But of course an embryo is the same thing regardless of how many other embryos were created at the same time. Again the concern is with the researcher's profligate or cavalier *attitude* towards the embryo rather than with any harm it might suffer.

Clearly then the restrictions placed upon embryo research are not principally concerned to protect the individual human embryo, since the rules contemplate that this early form of human life can be both experimented upon and destroyed. Rather, the rules are directed towards the mind of the scientist who must have good reasons for carrying out research on early human life, and must do so with appropriate respect. The question of the moral status of the embryo has therefore become less focused upon whether we are prepared to sanction its instrumental use, and instead is concerned principally with ensuring that scientists' behaviour minimises, as far as possible, moral offence. But since it will never be possible to persuade everybody that embryo research is both necessary and desirable, rules that are designed to that end will inevitably be perceived to be too lax by those whose moral qualms are being addressed. Conversely, scientists may argue that the attempt to achieve a political compromise where none is possible has led to an overly restrictive regime.[425] It might, for example, be argued that the 14-day limit is radically out of step with the law on abortion, which permits the destruction of a fetus until birth in certain circumstances, and until 24 weeks gestation under the "social" ground.[426]

(iii) Dispositional Authority

Unless an embryo created *in vitro* is immediately either transferred to a woman's uterus or discarded, it will be frozen and stored.[427] Because it is common for a cycle of IVF treatment to create more than the two or three embryos that will be transferred to the woman's body in any one treatment cycle,[428] tens of thousands of "spare" embyros are currently in storage. If the couple from

[425] Robertson, 1994, p. 201.

[426] John Harris says that he "cannot imagine the moral argument that would support the killing of 150,000 embryos annually to safeguard the 'health' of women, where 'health' is very broadly conceived and where their lives are seldom at risk, which would at the same time suggest that no comparable embryos should be studied, experimented upon or used as a source of transplant or graft material, where such use would very probably save lives and be of substantial benefit to the health of present and future individuals". As a result he concludes that "if the moral reasons which justify abortion are sound then we should permit embryo research and experimentation and the use of embryonic material on the same terms and set a limit to such research *at the same point* as the upper limit for abortion"(Harris, 1989, pp. 89, 94) (emphasis in original).

[427] According to the HFEA Code of Practice, 1998, para. 5.9 consent must be given to the storage of embryos and this should specify a maximum period of storage, if this is to be less than the statutory period of five years, and what should be done with the gametes if the progenitors die.

[428] This is because in order to avoid repeated egg retrieval cycles, doctors harvest as many eggs as possible in one cycle, and since it is more straightforward to freeze embryos than to freeze eggs, it is also common practice to attempt to fertilise all of the retrieved eggs.

whose gametes they were created do not want to use these frozen embryos in future treatment cycles, what should be done with them? The HFEA initially set a maximum storage period of five years, and so in 1996, five years after the first licences for the storage of embryos had been granted, the fate of thousands of frozen embryos had to be decided. The Government decided to introduce regulations extending the permitted storage period for embryos to ten years,[429] provided that the people storing their embryos consented to the five-year extension. It proved impossible to contact all of the "parents", and without their consent for extending the storage period, around four thousand embryos had to be destroyed. Although this initial destruction attracted particular attention from the media, and condemnation from the anti-abortion lobby,[430] the disposal of unwanted or unclaimed embryos has become common practice.[431]

There is also, of course, the possibility that the gamete contributors will subsequently disagree about the disposal or use of their frozen embryos. How should such disputes be resolved? Unlike the embryo or fetus[432] *in utero*, the female progenitor does not necessarily have a special claim to determine the fate of the frozen embryo *in vitro*. As we saw in chapters three and four, respect for the pregnant woman's decision-making autonomy in relation to her own body gives her unique authority to make decisions, such as whether to have an abortion or a caesarean section, that will affect the survival of the fetus *in utero*. Where an embryo has been frozen and is being stored in a clinic's freezer, neither gamete provider has such an obvious claim to have their preference ratified. To some extent then, embryo cryopreservation reduces the asymmetry that normally exists between men and women's interest in their fertilised gametes.[433]

Yet one major difference between the male and the female partner's interest in the frozen embryo remains. It is possible for the female gamete provider to unilaterally decide to have the embryos transferred to her uterus, and to carry the resulting pregnancy to term, while the male gamete provider seeking to create a baby needs the co-operation of a woman. What difference should this biological disparity make? On the one hand, it could be argued that the woman's unique capacity to autonomously give the embryo life should give her the right

---

[429] Statutory Instrument 1991 No. 1540. Subsequent regulations (SI 1996/375) have provided that the ten year upper limit may be exceeded in exceptional cases, where, for example, embryos are frozen because a woman is about to undergo cancer treatment that will destroy her eggs.

[430] The Pope described the impending thawing of these so-called "orphan" embryos as "genocide" (Franklin, 1999, p. 167).

[431] See further J O Oghoetuoma *et al* (2000) who reported that of 1344 embryos cryopreserved between 1988 and 1994 at two centres in Manchester, 67% (904 embryos) had to be destroyed at the end of the first 5-year interval, even if the couples involved remain childless, 74% of these embryos were destroyed after couples failed to respond to letters sent from the clinics and 26% after couples gave instructions to destroy.

[432] The "embryo" becomes a "fetus" at eight weeks gestation.

[433] Novaes and Salem have suggested that this might be the logical progression of the argument we considered in ch. 4, namely that technology which makes the embryo/fetus more visible as a discrete entity inevitably tends to obscure the pregnant woman (Novaes and Bateman, 1998, p. 117).

to determine its fate.[434] On the other hand, if the embryo's storage and use depends upon the ongoing consent of *both* gamete providers, either provider's objection to the embryo's use would have to be decisive.

In the United Kingdom the position is relatively straightforward. The Human Fertilisation and Embryology Act allows for the variation or withdrawal of consent to the use or storage of an embryo.[435] Once either gamete provider has withdrawn their consent to its use or continued storage, the embryo must be destroyed or allowed to perish. Thus, whichever partner does not want the embryos to be used in treatment effectively has a right of veto. In other countries, the position has been rather more complicated.[436] In one American case, the court ultimately preferred to respect the man's right to be free from unwanted reproduction, rather than the woman's right to reproduce with an embryo created using her gametes,[437] while in another case, custody of the frozen embryos was awarded to the wife on the grounds that following *in vitro* fertilisation a man had no more rights over the reproductive process than if conception had occurred through sexual intercourse.[438]

Again it is unclear whether a gamete contributor's right to decide the fate of their frozen embryos derives from some kind of quasi-proprietorial interest.[439] Although the Warnock Report stated that "the concept of ownership of human embryos seems to us to be undesirable",[440] it also suggested that a couple who have stored an embryo should have "rights to the use and disposal of the embryo".[441] It could plausibly be argued that having the right to use and dispose of something looks very like ownership.[442]

---

[434] Christine Overall thinks that the woman's future gestational involvement "gives her the entitlement to decide what happens to the embryos", and that "men are . . . entitled to exercise reproductive choice at the time that sperm leaves their body and is conveyed to another location— whether a woman's vagina or a test tube; there are no grounds for extending male reproductive freedom beyond this point" (Overall, 1995, pp. 191, 182).

[435] Schedule 3 para. 2(4).

[436] In France, the state's interest in confining assisted conception to *living* married couples has taken priority over a woman's request for implantation with an embryo that had been created while her deceased husband was alive (See further Novaes and Salem, 1998).

[437] In an American divorce case *Davis* v. *Davis* 842 SW2d 588 (Tenn 1992), the couple had had an unsuccessful cycle of IVF treatment and had frozen their remaining seven embryos. They had no prior agreement about what should happen to their seven frozen embryos on their divorce. The wife sought "custody" of the embryos for subsequent donation or implantation, while the husband wanted them to be destroyed. The trial judge treated the embryos as children, and awarded custody to the wife on the grounds that this would be in the embryos' best interests since she was the one capable of giving them life. But this was overturned by the Tennessee Supreme Court who awarded joint custody to the couple, and found that the husband's right to procreational autonomy outweighed the state's interest in the potential life of these four to eight cell embryos. The Court also decided that the wishes of the gamete provider who does not want to become a parent should take priority over the other's desire to use the embryos. Following the wife's unsuccessful appeal, the seven embryos were destroyed.

[438] *Kass* v. *Kass* (1995) WL 110368 NY Sup Ct 18.1.95.

[439] Barry Brown, for example, thinks that "proprietary rights can enhance the public policy debate regarding the limits of dispositional authority over pre-embryos", and that we "should not reject property rights out of simple distaste" (Brown, 1995, p. 74).

[440] Warnock, 1984, para. 10.11.

[441] Warnock, 1984, para. 10.11.

[442] Kennedy, 1991, p. 134.

In addition to uncertainties about whether embryos themselves can be owned, disputes have also arisen over whether a frozen embryo could itself have a proprietary claim over the estate of one of its 'parents'. So, bizarrely, a frozen embryo might be treated as if it were property in order that someone should be able to bequeath their interest in it; while simultaneously a frozen embryo could be treated as if it were in the process of becoming a person for the purpose of inheriting from its "parents'" estates.[443] The concept of a frozen embryo with substantial assets, ownership of which crystallises upon their birth, undoubtedly seems rather bizarre,[444] although, of course, rules concerning the inheritance rights of posthumously born children have been in existence for hundreds of years. For example, a child's claim when she was *en ventre sa mère* at the time of her father's death is that she has a contingent interest in his estate which crystallises on birth.[445] Could it be argued that a frozen embryo has a similarly contingent interest?[446]

Until recently there was a clear practical time limit upon the claims of posthumously born children: a man could not be considered the father of a child born more than 300 days after his death. Obvious problems for inheritance law might be raised by the cryopreservation of embryos or gametes, which could result in the birth of a child several years after its "father's" death.[447] The administration of an estate might therefore remain fundamentally uncertain until all of the frozen embryos created using a man's gametes had either been used or allowed to perish.[448] There are two possible solutions to the problem of testamentary uncertainty. First, finality could be achieved by the setting of a limitation period consonant with the need for reasonably prompt and final administration of estates.[449] Second, and this has been the preferred solution in the UK, children who are not yet *in utero* at the time of their "father's" death are disregarded for inheritance purposes because, as we

---

[443] Atherton, 1999, p. 142. Kathleen Guzman suggests that "allowing frozen embryos to be both the subject and the recipient of . . . transfers seems to blur the person/property line and affront traditional categorical sensibilities" (Guzman, 1997, p. 250).

[444] For example, Kathleen Guzman raises the possibility that "prospective social parents could 'shop' for frozen embryos that either had or stood to inherit substantial sums" (Guzman, 1997, p. 234).

[445] e.g. *Re Wilmer's Trusts* [1903] 2 Ch 41.

[446] For example, in the Australian case of *In Re K (deceased)* (1996) 5 TR 365 the court had to consider whether a frozen embryo of a deceased man and his widow was a child of the marriage for inheritance purposes. The court held that "if a child *en ventre sa mère* is not regarded as living . . . but has a contingent interest dependent on birth, then *in loci* the same status should be afforded an embryo. That would be so whether or not 2 cells, 4 cells or a developed fetus was existent" (at 373).

[447] Of course an embryo created using a woman's gametes could be used after her death, but because the woman who gives birth is always the child's legal mother, no inheritance issues would arise.

[448] Such offspring have been described as "extreme posthumous children" (Atherton, 1999, p. 146).

[449] Ronald Chester suggests a period of two years, plus a gestation period of 300 days (quoted in Atherton, 1999, p. 162). Kathleen Guzman argues that "allowing the transfer of property to frozen embryos or subsequent children is desirable. It reinforces responsibility by allowing decedents to provide for entities they played a significant role in creating" (Guzman, 1997, p. 232).

have seen, they will be legally fatherless.[450] The Government has confirmed that, in amending the legislation so that a man who was dead at the time of conception can nevertheless be registered as the child's father, he will not be recognised as the father for the purposes of inheritance.

(e) Parentage

Identifying the connection between a man and his offspring requires knowledge of the biological "facts of life", and some anthropologists have considered interest in paternity to be a defining moment in the transition from primitive to more sophisticated models of social organisation.[451] The law's preoccupation with determining paternity certainly long predates the complex questions raised by fertility treatment. The security of family property, and the smooth running of primogeniture have, for example, always depended upon a clear mechanism for assigning paternity.[452] Maternity, on the other hand, has traditionally been of little concern to the law. The existence of a connection between a mother and her child has, until recently, been assumed to be self-evident.

Reproductive technologies have the potential to separate various aspects of both maternity and paternity, and one of the key functions of the regulations is to provide clear rules to identify a child's legal parents. In the UK the legislation, rather confusingly, both reaffirms and disrupts conventional understandings about kinship. At times the status provisions appear to rest upon the assumption that parenthood is a non-negotiable and immutable "fact of life", despite the new technologies' capacity to subvert traditional reproductive norms. So, for example, rather than recognise that a child born following oocyte donation has two *biological* mothers, the law instead determines which one shall be considered the *only* biological mother. On the other hand, at other times the rules appear to recognise that the natural biological facts of procreation do not accurately reflect the realities of assisted reproduction. Hence, for example, although a child born to a single woman treated with donor sperm undoubtedly has a *biological* father, he or she will be *legally* fatherless.[453]

---

[450] Warnock, 1984, para. 10.9. In the United States the Unified Status of Children of Assisted Conception Act 9B ULA 161 (Supp 1995) excludes posthumously implanted embryos from inheritance unless the bequest contains a specific gift to a posthumously implanted child.

[451] For an account of the importance of understandings of conception to anthropology, see Franklin, 1997, pp. 17–72. Bronislaw Malinowski, for example, described the question of physical paternity as "the most exciting and controversial issue in the comparative science of man" (Malinowski, 1937, p. xxxiii).

[452] The Archbishop of Canterbury's Commission into artificial insemination condemned the practice in part because "it would change the whole basis of society if a man could not safely regard his brother's child as of the proper common stock of his and his brother's parents, and could not feel assured that it was not the product of an anonymous donor" (quoted in Dewar, 1989, p. 121). The 1960 Feversham Committee Report stated that "succession through blood descent is an important element in family life and as such is at the basis of society" (Feversham Committee, 1960, para. 163).

[453] Human Fertilisation and Embryology Act 1990 s. 28.

Definitions of biological parenthood following assisted conception are also susceptible to unprecendented cross-national variation. Different countries have different rules governing parentage following the use of assisted conception, so a woman who would be treated as the legal mother of a child in one jurisdiction would not necessarily be so treated in another. Deciding which of the various candidates should be considered the child's legal parents is now obviously a *choice,* revealing that our definitions of mother and fatherhood may have become culturally variable in the same way as, for example, the nature of kinship networks or conventions of marriage.[454] We now consider the rules governing paternity and maternity in detail.

(i) Maternity

As we see in the next chapter, the most dramatic fragmentation of motherhood occurs in surrogacy arrangements where the woman who gives birth to the child is not the intended mother. In this chapter our concern is with the separation of genetic and gestational motherhood which occurs following egg donation. The law is unambiguous: the woman who gives birth to a child is its mother.[455] The maternity of the woman who gave birth to the child could not subsequently be challenged on the grounds that she has no genetic connection with her child.[456] While, as we see in chapter six, the application of this rule to surrogacy subverts the parties' pre-conception agreement, in relation to egg donation, the law reflects the intentions of both the egg donor and the recipient.

(ii) Paternity

Before the enactment of the Human Fertilisation and Embryology Act, proof of biological paternity trumped the common law presumption of paternity within marriage. So where a woman had been treated with donor sperm it used to be possible for her husband to subsequently deny that he was the child's father, even if he had consented to the treatment.[457] A DNA test which established that

---

[454] For example, John Dewar considers that DI "offers an illustration of the constructed and flexible notion of paternity" (Dewar, 1989, p. 128).

[455] Human Fertilisation and Embryology Act 1990 s. 27 (1) "The woman who is carrying or has carried a child as a result of the placing in her of an embryo or of sperm and eggs, and no other woman, is to be treated as the mother of the child".

In *The Ampthill Peerage Case* [1977] AC 547, Lord Simon said (at 577) "motherhood, although also a legal relationship is based on fact, being proved demonstrably by parturition".

[456] In an American case *McDonald* v. *McDonald* 196 A.D.2d 7; 608 N.Y.S.2d 477(1994), a divorcing husband tried to gain sole custody of twins born following anonymous egg donation. His claim was that his wife was not the children's natural mother and should therefore be denied custody. Unsurprisingly, the court rejected his claim. Custody of the twins was awarded instead to his wife.

[457] In *Re M (Child Support Act: Parentage)* [1997] 2 F.L.R. 90 the issue was whether a husband was a "parent" within the meaning of the Child Support Act 1991 in respect of two children born in 1981 and 1986 by artificial insemination with donor sperm. Bracewell J held that because the children were born before the enactment of the Human Fertilisation and Embryology Act 1990, under the law applicable at the time of their births a male parent meant the biological father. Therefore the husband was not liable to maintain the children under the 1991 Act.

the woman's husband was not the biological father of her child thus enabled him to abandon his parental obligations. The sperm donor would in theory be the legal father of the child, although in practice his anonymity would mean that the child would have no identifiable father.

Since 1991, where a donor's gametes are used in accordance with the consents required in Schedule 3, the donor is not to be treated as the father of the child.[458] Of course, the obverse may also be true: where there has not been compliance with the consent provisions in Schedule 3, the donor will be treated as the child's father, unless the woman is married.[459] As a result, if an unmarried woman inseminates herself at home with fresh sperm from a friend or relative, the sperm donor will be the child's legal father and under a duty to support that child until it reaches the age of majority.[460]

If a child is conceived in a licensed clinic using donated sperm, the mother's husband will be the child's father unless he can prove that he did not consent to her treatment; and if the mother is unmarried, her male[461] partner is the child's father if the couple were provided with the treatment together.[462] On a literal interpretation, the wording of this section is puzzling: if donor sperm is used, it is not clear in what sense the woman's partner is actually being *treated* by the

---

[458] S. 28(6)(a).

[459] S.28(2) applies to *all* cases of artificial insemination (including those not carried out in licensed clinics), whereas s. 28(3) only applies to treatment in a licensed clinic.

[460] Child Support Act 1991 s. 1(1).

[461] In *X, Y and Z* v. *United Kingdom* (1997) 24 EHRR 143, X, a female to male transsexual, lived with a woman, Y, who in 1992 gave birth to Z, who had been conceived through artificial insemination by donor. X was refused permission to be registered as the father of Z. X, Y and Z applied to the ECHR, claiming that the refusal to register X as Z's father was an infringement of their right to respect for family life under the European Convention on Human Rights 1950 Art. 8 and was discriminatory in breach of Art.14. The European Court of Human Rights found that there was little agreement between the contracting states on these issues, so the UK should be afforded a wide margin of appreciation, and although the Court recognised that X,Y, and Z had *de facto* family ties, the UK was not in breach of Art. 8 by failing to formally recognise X as Z's father.

[462] Section 28 of the Human Fertilisation and Embryology Act states:

(1) This section applies in the case of a child who is being or has been carried by a woman as the result of the placing in her of an embryo or of sperm and eggs or her artificial insemination.
(2) If—
 (a)   at the time of the placing in her of the embryo or the sperm and eggs or of her insemination, the woman was a party to a marriage and.
 (b)   the creation of the embryo carried by her was not brought about with the sperm of the other party to the marriage,
then, subject to subsection (5) below, the other party to the marriage shall be treated as the father of the child unless it is shown that he did not consent to the placing in her of the embryo or the sperm and eggs or to her insemination.
(3) If no man is treated by virtue of subsection (2) above, as the father of the child but—
 (a)   the embryo or the sperm and eggs were placed in the woman, or she was artificially inseminated, in the course of treatment services, provided for her and a man together by a person to whom a licence applies, and.
 (b) the creation of the embryo carried by her was not brought about with the sperm of that man,
then, subject to subsection (5) below, that man shall be treated as the father of the child.
Subsection (5) states that (2) and (3) do not apply to any child treated as the child of the parties by any other enactment or by common law.

clinic.[463] Instead the treatment will be said to have been provided for the couple together if the clinic is responding to a request for treatment made jointly by the man and woman, as a couple.[464]

There is an important practical difference between these two provisions. Where a woman is married, the assumption is that her husband is the father of her child and it would be for him to prove otherwise. Conversely if the woman having treatment is unmarried, the onus is on her partner to prove that he was treated together with the child's mother. That it should be more difficult to establish non-genetic paternity outside of marriage is not perhaps surprising.[465] In fact section 28(3) represents an exception to the impossibility in any other area of English law for an unmarried man to acquire non-genetic paternity together with the mother.[466]

Using marriage, rather than biology, as the principal means to identify a child's father is not new:[467] as we have seen, at common law there is a presumption that a mother's husband is the father of her child. Section 28(5) retains this common law presumption of paternity. This means that a husband who is seeking to deny paternity of a child conceived following donor insemination might have to rebut two presumptions of his paternity. First, he could rebut the common law presumption of paternity by having a DNA test that would establish that he is not the biological father of the child. Once the common law presumption is rebutted, the presumption in section 28(2) would come into operation, and his second task would be to prove that, at the time of the insemination, he did not consent to his wife's treatment. Although this may seem a rather tortuous process, husbands and partners are invariably asked to sign consent forms that specify their agreement to being treated as the child's legal

---

[463] *In Re Q (Parental Order)* [1996] 1 FLR 369, Johnson J said "it seems plain to me that the subsection envisages a situation in which the man involves himself received medical treatment, although . . . I am not sure what treatment is envisaged since the subsection refers to a man whose sperm was not used in the procedure" (at 371). In *Re B (Minors) (Parentage)* [1996] 2 FLR 15, insemination using the unmarried partner's sperm was said to be treatment together, although he had not given express consent. Because the unmarried partner was the biological father of the child, finding that he should be treated as the father was less problematic than if donor sperm had been used. Bracewell J found that in the absence of express consent the father would be considered to have given consent if he and the mother were together receiving treatment and he had not subsequently withdrawn such consent.

[464] See the comments of Wilson J in *U v. W (Attorney General Intervening)* [1998] Fam 29.

[465] There are also differences in the consequences of fatherhood depending upon whether the man is married to the mother. Although the obligation to support one's children exists regardless of marital status, unlike married fathers, unmarried fathers do not automatically acquire parental responsibility. Instead under s. 4 of the Children Act 1989 they must apply to the court for a parental responsibility order, or make a formal parental responsibility agreement with the mother which must subsequently be registered with the court. The Government intends to bring forward legislation granting unmarried fathers automatic parental responsibility.

[466] An adoption order can only be made in favour of two people if they are married to each other (Adoption Act 1976, s. 14), and access to a parental order for a child born to a surrogate mother is again confined to married couples (Human Fertilisation and Embryology Act 1990 s. 30(1)).

[467] See Smart, 1987, p. 101.

father prior to the provision of infertility treatment,[468] so in practice disputes about the existence of consent are rare.

Once paternity is established under section 28 it is equivalent in almost every respect to paternity established by DNA tests or through the common law presumption of paternity.[469] As a result, if the relationship between the parents subsequently breaks down, it will not be possible for either the father or the mother to seek to deny his paternity.[470] It should, however, be noted that couples treated abroad may not be covered by these presumptions of paternity. In *U v. W (Attorney General Intervening)*[471] even though the couple were undoubtedly "provided with treatment together" in Rome, the male partner was not considered to be the children's legal father.

Where a woman's husband does not consent to her treatment, or where an unmarried woman is not treated "together" with a man, then the child will have no legal father. Section 28 of the Human Fertilisation and Embryology Act thus creates what Derek Morgan and Robert Lee have referred to as "a new class of child, the (legally)'fatherless child'".[472] As noted earlier, the introduction of this new category of fatherless children must be read in the context of section 13(5)'s presumption that the creation of fatherless children should be avoided. The interaction between these provisions leads, as we have seen, to an indirect presumption against the treatment of single or lesbian women.

If a woman is inseminated with the sperm of her partner after his death, then according to section 28 of the Human Fertilisation and Embryology Act 1990, the child would again be legally fatherless.[473] This latter provision has been the

---

[468] HFEA Code of Practice 1998, para. 5.7 "the centre should take all practicable steps to obtain his written consent", or it he does not consent or the woman does not know "centres should, if she agrees, take all practicable steps to ascertain the position and (if this is the case) obtain written evidence that he does not consent". Where the woman is unmarried, according to para. 5.8 "centres should try to obtain the written acknowledgement of the man both that they are being treated together and that donated sperm is to be used".

[469] Except, under s.29(4) for the succession to dignities or transmission of titles of honour.

[470] In *Re CH (Contact: Parentage)* [1996] 1 FLR 569, the husband had given written consent to his wife's treatment with donor insemination and he was registered as the father of the child. The couple had divorced and the woman sought to deny contact to her former husband on the grounds that he was not the child's biological father, and so the presumption in favour of contact did not apply. Callman J found that severing the legal ties between the father and his child would be contrary to the intentions of Parliament, and to principles of justice.

[471] [1998] Fam 29. In this case the applicant and her partner, who were not married, had fertility treatment in Rome. Although they had expected the treatment to involve the partner's sperm, in the event donor sperm was used. Twin boys were born and the applicant sought a declaration of paternity under s.28(3). Wilson J found that the presumption of paternity could only apply if it could be ensured that the Act's provisions regarding consent, of both the donor and the potential father, had been complied with. Because the acquisition of paternity under s.28(3) has significant consequences, full, informed consent must be given. Records of this consent must be kept in order that disputes about paternity, which might arise long after a child's birth, can be resolved. So although Wilson J did find that s.28(3) restricted the freedom to provide services within Europe under Article 59, he found that the there were good reasons for the requirements of informed consent and record-keeping, and these provided objectively valid and proportionate justification for the restriction.

[472] Morgan and Lee, 1991, p. 154.

[473] S. 28(6)(b).

subject of particular criticism[474] since in these circumstances the child's mother will undoubtedly regard her dead partner as the child's father, and will inevitably communicate this to her child. That the law treats the child as if she did not have an identifiable father reveals an obvious discontinuity between social and legal perceptions of paternity.[475] Following Sheila McLean's Report to Ministers,[476] the Government has indicated its intention to amend the Human Fertilisation and Embryology Act with retrospective effect, so that any child born since the 1990 Act came into force, whose deceased father has not been recorded on their birth certificate, would be able to have their birth re-registered.[477] A new birth certificate would be issued containing the father's details. At the time of writing the statute has not yet been amended.

(f) Regulating New Technologies

The HFEA has a duty not only to supervise the provision of existing techniques, but also to anticipate and assess the safety and ethical implications of innovative procedures. In the light of the rapidity of scientific progress in areas such as human genetics and biotechnology, the HFEA's responsibility for monitoring novel developments undoubtedly represents one of its more complex and difficult tasks. Certainly its inability to single-handedly provide expert analysis of every scientific advance that has some bearing on the provision of assisted conception services has been acknowledged, and the Government has set up a variety of other bodies to consult and advise on future regulation. In relation to preimplantation genetic diagnosis, for example, the Human Genetics Commission has worked with the HFEA in producing a consultation document and proposing options for reform. In this section, we concentrate upon two techniques that are currently provoking particular controversy: preimplantation genetic diagnosis (PGD) and human reproductive cloning. While PGD has

---

[474] Following a complaint from a constituent whose deceased husband had agreed to the posthumous use of his sperm, but who cannot be registered as the father of her child, Debra Shipley MP introduced the Human Fertilisation and Embryology (Amendment) Bill 2000. In introducing the Bill Debra Shipley quoted Sheila McLean's comment that "now, it might be thought that by taking the trouble to make a written statement of intent concerning the use of gametes after death, the man is intending that the child should be regarded as his" (Hansard 7 June 2000 column 291).

Debra Shipley's Bill would have amended section28(6)(b) so that it did not apply "where at the time of the man's death the woman and the man–

(a) were married to each other
(b) were otherwise living as man (*sic*) and wife, or
(c) had been receiving treatment services together from a person to whom a license applies

[475] Rosalind Atherton has argued that "if a child is born to a man's widow which is genetically his child—and he was a willing participant in the process—then it should be considered his child if indeed the child is born alive. Not to reach such a conclusion is historically regressive: placing the children back in the era of bastards, with all their disabilities, if not necessarily the same social stigmas" (Atherton, 1999, p. 161).

[476] McLean, 1997.

[477] Department of Health, 2000.

been practised for over ten years, rapid developments in our understanding of human genetics are thought to raise complex new questions about the extent to which would-be parents should be allowed to select their offspring prior to conception. Reproductive cloning is not currently believed to be sufficiently safe to attempt in humans, but given the pace of scientific innovation and increasing globalisation within the biotechnology industry, we cannot rely upon its continued impossibility.

(i) Preimplantation Genetic Diagnosis (PGD)

All of the cells in a human zygote at the four to ten cell stage are totipotential, which means that it is possible to remove one or two of its cells without interfering with its capacity for normal development. Those cells can then be analysed and certain genetic abnormalities may be detected.[478] PGD thus allows doctors to transfer only unaffected embryos to the woman's uterus. For couples who are at risk of passing on a genetic disorder,[479] PGD enables them to avoid undergoing prenatal diagnosis and (possibly repeated) abortion, and instead start a pregnancy in the knowledge that the resulting child will not have a particular abnormality. The sex of a zygote can also be identified, thus making it possible for a couple to avoid having a child with a sex-linked recessive condition.[480]

Although IVF is a necessary prerequisite of PGD, it is not a type of infertility treatment and is usually provided to couples who could conceive naturally. Some health authorities that have decided not to fund infertility treatment may elect to fund IVF and PGD on the grounds that its principal purpose is the prevention of disease. It would be possible for PGD to be routinely carried out on every IVF embryo, but this would significantly increase the already high costs of IVF treatment. In addition, it is currently only possible to carry out PGD for one disorder at a time. Its use is then dependent upon the clinical team knowing

---

[478] It is currently possible to diagnose chromosomal abnormalities, such as Down's syndrome, and some genetic defects such as cystic fibrosis, Duchenne muscular dystrophy, Tay-Sach's syndrome or Lesch-Nyhan syndrome (Holm, 1998a p. 177). It is also possible to detect polyposis coli (inherited colon cancer) and Marfan's syndrome (HFEA and ACGT, 1999, para. 12) The most common uses of PGD are sexing an embryo to avoid X-linked disorders and testing for age-related aneuploidy (an abnormal number of chromosomes). Cystic fibrosis is the single-gene disorder most frequently tested for using PGD (HFEA and ACGT, 1999, para. 11).

[479] PGD is commonly used when a couple have had one affected child and/or one or more terminations of pregnancy following conventional prenatal diagnosis (Draper and Chadwick, 1999, p. 114).

[480] Because females have two X-chromosomes, they will invariably have a "normal" gene that can correct a defective gene on the other X chromosome. Males, on the other hand, have only one X-chromosome, so if they inherit a defective gene on the X chromosome, they will develop the particular disease. A man with an X-linked disease can only pass the gene to his daughters, because he gives his sons his Y-chromosome. A female carrier of an X-linked gene has a 50% chance of passing it to her sons, who will then have the disease, and a 50% chance of passing it to her daughters, who will then be carriers. So only women are able to pass on the disease to their sons, while both men and women can pass on the carrier gene to their daughters.

what it is they are trying to detect. Without a family history of a particular condition, there would be no reason to test for one abnormality rather than any other. It is possible that in the future PGD might be able to increase the success rates of IVF treatment by screening out embryos that are, for some reason, less likely to implant. But until such tests are devised, or until it becomes possible to screen embryos for multiple abnormalities, screening all IVF embryos would be of little value.

Removing one cell from a four cell embryo, and testing it is an extremely complex and time-consuming process, requiring considerable technical expertise.[481] As yet the number of false negatives,[482] and possibly false positives remains relatively high, and rates of misdiagnosis are exacerbated by problems with contamination[483] and difficulties in ensuring that the cell that is removed is representative of the embryo's genetic characteristics.[484] The non-transfer of affected embryos coupled with the possibility that embryos may be damaged during the biopsy means that it will often be possible to transfer only one embryo,[485] thus reducing pregnancy rates.

Current practice of the HFEA equates preimplantation diagnosis with abortion in cases of serious abnormality.[486] Hence, PGD can lawfully be carried out only to detect conditions where there is "a substantial risk that, if the child were born, it would suffer from such physical or mental abnormalities as to be seriously handicapped".[487] So, although it would technically be possible for PGD to be used by couples who want to choose the sex of their child, sex selection for social reasons has been prohibited by the HFEA.[488] Preimplantation sex identification is lawful only if it is carried out in order to prevent the transfer of male embryos where there is a risk that the parents will pass on an X-linked disease. A couple with four sons whose only daughter had died failed to persuade the HFEA that their circumstances merited preimplantation sex selection. Inevitably, condemnation of pre-implantation sex selection tends to consist in arguments similar to those employed against sex-selective abortion which were considered in detail in chapter three.[489]

---

[481] In the UK, four centres are currently licensed to carry out PGD (HFEA, 1999, p. 29).

[482] Holm, 1998a, p. 177.

[483] Such as sperm left over from the *in vitro* fertilisation procedure (HFEA and ACGT, 1999, p. 5).

[484] This may happen as a result of mosaicism, which means that the genetic code in one cell may not be the same as in the rest of the embryo.

[485] HFEA and ACGT, 1999, para. 16.

[486] "The HFEA and the ACGT (Advisory Committee on Genetic Testing) do not think it would be acceptable to test for any social and psychological characteristics, normal physical variations, or any other conditions which are not associated with disability or a serious medical condition" (HFEA and ACGT, 1999, para. 22).

[487] Abortion Act 1967, s. 1(1)(d).

[488] Following a public consultation in 1993, the HFEA decided not to permit sex selection for social reasons (HFEA, 1993).

[489] For example, Jonathan Berkowitz and Jack Snyder have said that "to choose a boy or girl, parents must have preconceived notions, however vague, about the ramifications of having a certain sexed child: notions which are fundamentally sexist as they are predicated upon anticipated gender based behaviour" (Berkowitz and Snyder, 1998, p. 32).

It would also be possible for PGD to be employed in order to ensure that the resulting child would be a good tissue match for a relative in need of, for example, a bone marrow transplant. This has happened in the United States and in 2000 Adam Nash was born following PGD in which an embryo was selected that was not only free from the genetic disease suffered by an older sibling, but was also a tissue match for her.[490] It is not clear what the HFEA would decide were a similar case to arise in the UK. In part the selection was done in order to prevent the birth of a child affected by Fanconi's anaemia, and this aspect of the screening procedure would have been unproblematic. For a couple to prefer an unaffected embryo that *also* happens to be a good tissue match for their dying child over an unaffected embryo with incompatible tissue seems readily understandable, although a literal interpretation of the HFEA's guidance would make it difficult to justify any selection that is not directed towards avoidance of disease in the child that will be born following PGD.

While the abortion model may initially appear to offer a useful framework for the regulation of PGD, there are plainly some crucial differences. First, it is, as we saw in chapter three, possible for a woman to be denied access to abortion if her circumstances do not fit within the Abortion Act's grounds. If, for example, two doctors consider that a fetus's abnormality is insufficiently serious, the pregnant woman can be compelled to carry the pregnancy to term. In contrast, it is impossible to see how a woman could be under a duty to have a particular embryo transferred to her uterus should her doctors decide that it is not at substantial risk of serious handicap.[491]

Second, because PGD is carried out when the embryo is outside the woman's body, it can be destroyed without invading her bodily integrity. It has therefore been suggested that decisions over the fate of the embryo could become the subject of *greater* professional control than is the case with abortion.[492] This might be especially relevant if a couple wanted to select embryos affected by a particular

---

[490] Dobson, 2000.

[491] John Harris argues that the decision not to have embryos implanted must lie within the unfettered discretion of the woman herself (Harris, 1998b, p. 33). This must be right, there could be no legal duty to implant any particular embryo. For example, if the sex of a couple's embryos are known and the couple have expressed a clear preference for a female baby, then it is hard to imagine what harm would be caused if the doctors replaced only female embryos. Given that it is impossible to see how a woman could be obliged to have a particular embryo transferred into her uterus, it would be difficult to place her doctors under a duty to transfer a male embryo. So rather than prohibiting this sort of selection, the HFEA instead prohibits access to information that would enable this choice to be made.

[492] David King has argued that "preimplantation diagnosis thus represents a new intensification of the medical surveillance of human reproduction, which would institute a far more preventive regime than currently operates for prenatal testing" (King, 1999, p. 180). According to Julian Savulescu, "doctors cannot and should not force couples to have a termination of pregnancy for some serious genetic condition, but they might decide not to assist couples to have a child suffering from such a condition" (Savulescu, 1999a, p.121). And Heather Draper and Ruth Chadwick suggest that "once (women) have parted with their gametes and once the resulting embryos are tested, it is possible for them to lose control over what happens next . . . she cannot compel him to implant embryos against his wishes" (Draper and Chadwick, 1999, p. 119).

condition, such as achondroplasia[493] or congenital deafness. So while a doctor could not force a woman to abort a fetus with a particular abnormality, a refusal to transfer an abnormal embryo would not violate her bodily autonomy. It is unclear whether section 13(5) of the HFEA, which as we have seen incorporates a direction to consider the child's welfare prior to treatment, applies to the decision to transfer particular embryos to the woman's uterus. While usually assumed to be concerned with *access* to infertility treatment, rather than choices made once treatment has begun, it could plausibly be argued that in deciding which embryos to transfer, section 13(5) demands that clinics take account of "the welfare of any child who may be born as a result of the treatment." If this were the case, doctors might be able to use section 13(5) in order to justify their refusal to transfer an embryo affected by, for example, congenital deafness.

It is also, as we noted in chapter three, not necessarily self-evident whether a particular condition amounts to a serious handicap. While conditions such as Lesch-Nyhan[494] or Tay-Sachs[495] syndrome are obviously extremely disabling, others may be less easy to categorise. For example, the severity of a particular disability may depend in part upon the availability of treatments or services that relieve an individual's difficulties, or upon the particular family's socio-economic circumstances. In addition, carrying out PGD for late onset genetic disease, or an increased susceptibility to a particular condition may further complicate our capacity to draw a clear boundary between serious and trivial abnormalities. Where a woman could choose between several embryos, one of which has a gene associated with an increased risk of an adult onset disease, it might seem odd to choose to transfer the affected embryo rather than one without this increased risk.[496] But where the only embryos available for transfer have a particular genetic susceptibility, the decision may be less straightforward. A similar issue arises in relation to embryos that have been identified as carriers of recessive disorders. If a carrier embryo implants and is successfully carried to term, the resulting child will be free from the particular condition, but may face some difficult reproductive choices in the future. Again, where there are a number of unaffected embryos to choose from, choosing non-carrier embryos for transfer would seem logical. But where only carrier embryos are available, their transfer may be preferable to abandoning treatment. The current policy of the HFEA is to leave these decisions to the patients in consultation with their clinical team.[497]

[493] This is an inherited condition which results in restricted growth.
[494] A child with Lesch-Nyhan disease will suffer from limb spasms, and self-mutilation and aggressive behaviour, and will usually die in his teens.
[495] Children with Tay-Sachs appear quite normal at birth, but in their first year of life their nervous systems degenerate and they usually die within three or four years.
[496] John Robertson, for example, argues that "avoiding offspring with genes that make them more susceptible to diseases such as cancer . . . would . . . appear to be an exercise of procreative liberty" (Robertson, 1996, p. 433).
[497] HFEA and ACGT, 1999, para. 36.

Critics of PGD are alarmed by the possibility that potential parents might routinely be in a position to choose between various potential children.[498] As the number of genetic tests multiplies, the number of conditions that can be diagnosed before implantation inevitably increases, as does the associated moral panic. For example, alarmist, and almost certainly impracticable suggestions that sexual orientation might be detectable through PGD have led to proposals that research into a genetic component to sexual orientation should be discouraged or prohibited.[499] We considered a variety of anxieties that have crystallised around prenatal genetic testing in detail in chapter three,[500] and these misguided assumptions about the inevitable misuse of genetic diagnoses are equally evident within the criticisms that are commonly levelled at PGD.

Currently the only way in which genetic knowledge can be used before implantation is by discarding embryos discovered to have some genetic abnormality. Preimplantation gene therapy is not yet possible, but at some point in the future scientists may be able to alter the genetic make-up of an early embryo.[501] If this were to happen before cell differentiation, it would cause a biologically different individual to come into existence.[502] Contrary to media speculation, it is unlikely that it would ever be possible to modify multifactorial characteristics such as height, beauty or intelligence via preimplantation gene therapy. Rather, simple gene insertion, which could be used to treat a very limited number of recessive disorders,[503] is all that is likely to be possible in the foreseeable future. Yet despite the practical limits of what could actually be achieved by single gene manipulation, there will be some people who will condemn any attempts to alter an embryo's genetic make-up.[504]

Generally opinion is likely to follow a similar pattern to the current perception of PGD, namely that therapeutic intervention to prevent the birth of a child

---

[498] David King, for example argues that in preimplantation diagnosis "parents adopt a far more pro-active, directing role, choosing their children in a way which is not so far removed from their experience as consumers, choosing amongst different products . . . selecting the 'best' amongst multiple embryos sets up a new relationship between parents and children" (King, 1999, p. 180).

[499] Stein, 1998, p. 20.

[500] pp. 94–106.

[501] As John Robertson points out "the genome project will almost certainly accelerate a growing tendency of parents to choose or exercise control over offspring characteristics" (Robertson, 1996, p. 422).

[502] Walter Glannon says that this sort of genetic manipulation is incorrectly referred to as therapy, which implies that there is a disease to be treated or cured, "because when the gametes are altered, there are no existing persons who might benefit from this act" (Glannon, 1998, p. 195).

[503] Recessive disorders are ones where a single copy of the normal gene is sufficient to prevent the development of the disease, inserting one copy of a normal gene into an embryo with a double-dose of the abnormal gene will enable them to avoid developing the disease. Dominant disorders develop even when the affected individual only has one abnormal gene, inserting a normal gene into an affected embryo would not stop them developing the condition (Glannon, 1998, p. 196).

[504] Since *in vitro* gene therapy is likely to be expensive, those familiar arguments about the creation of both a biological underclass, and a genetically enhanced "master-race" are commonly invoked. Although Adam Moore points out that banning a medical advancement because initially it is available only to the rich would have prevented "almost every" development in modern medicine (Moore, 2000, p. 117).

who would suffer from a serious and debilitating disease might be acceptable, but that attempts to enhance a normal genotype in order to create a child with particular traits or characteristics should be precluded.[505] Thus gene therapy would be employed to restore normal functioning and not to improve functioning for embryos that are within the range of what is considered normal.[506] Yet is there really a bright line boundary between gene enhancement and the restoration of normality? If we accept that an objective definition of normality is impossible, it becomes difficult to distinguish between "acceptable" and "unacceptable" gene therapy. Similarly, if we were to argue that medicine should be concerned only to prevent disease, rather than to enhance a normal genotype, we would be ruling out gene enhancements such as boosting an embryo's immune system or its resistance to malaria.

In sum, PGD is currently used by people who have family members whose lives have been blighted by a particular genetic abnormality. Their decision to pre-select embryos that are not similarly affected does not, in my opinion, reflect insidious eugenic sentiment, but rather acknowledges that a child's life may be easier and more agreeable if it does not inherit a particular genetic disease. Of course as our understanding of the functions of various genes increase, it will become possible to carry out preimplantation genetic diagnosis for less serious conditions. Given its dependence upon IVF, and the technical complexity of extracting and carrying out tests upon a single human cell, PGD is not, in the foreseeable future, likely to become widely used. Thus it would be a mistake to restrict developments that can indubitably improve the lives of families that are at risk of passing on debilitating genetic diseases in order to prevent the entirely speculative and inherently unlikely spectre of routine PGD for trivial behavioural traits.

(ii) Human Reproductive Cloning

Speculation about the possibility of cloning has a long history,[507] and research with animals started in the 1950s.[508] Before the birth of Dolly, scientists had produced clones from totipotent embryonic stem cells,[509] but had assumed that

[505] For example, John Robertson says that "a couple who seek to alter the genes of an embryo to enhance an otherwise normal child's capabilities is in danger of being more interested in genes than in the child for her own sake" (Robertson, 1998, p. 1455). Kurt Bayertz concludes that "the application of gene technology should be deemed morally permissible, providing it has a therapeutic objective" (Bayertz, 1994, p. 314).

[506] Walter Glannon, for example says that "the aim of any medically and morally defensible form of genetic intervention should not be to enhance people's genotype or phenotypic traits, but only to ensure that the people we do cause to exist have normal or close to normal, cognitive and physical functioning over the balance of their lives" (Glannon, 1998, p. 205).

[507] In 1938 Hans Spemann had considered the possibility of cloning (see further Kolata, 1997, pp. 36–59) see also Muller 1936, pp. 136–7.

[508] For example, Robert Briggs and Thomas King transferred complete genetic material into denucleated frogs' eggs in 1952 (Briggs and King, 1952). And John Gurdon produced tadpole clones in 1962 (Gurdon, 1962; Bayertz, 1994, p. 69).

[509] HGAC and HFEA, 1998, para. 1.3.

cloning a differentiated adult cell would be impossible.[510] The announcement on 23 February 1997[511] that an *adult* sheep had been successfully cloned, albeit from an unusual and perhaps relatively undifferentiated mammary cell,[512] the previous year[513] led to immediate demands for the complete prohibition of human cloning.[514] The House of Commons Select Committee on Science and Technology produced a report on the implications of human cloning within weeks of the Roslin Institute's announcement.[515] The European Commission has prohibited the issue of any patent on work leading to the cloning of human beings,[516] and the Council of Europe issued a protocol forbidding human

---

[510] In order to do this, it would be necessary to "trick" the adult cell's DNA into reverting to its undifferentiated state.

[511] Wilmut *et al*'s paper was published in Nature on 27 February, but the story was broken a few days earlier in *The Observer*.

[512] Dolly, named after Dolly Parton (Miller, 1998, p. 78), was cloned from a cell taken from a pregnant six year old ewe's mammary gland. And Wilmut *et al* said that they "could not exclude the possibility that there is a small proportion of relatively undifferentiated stem cells able to support regeneration of the mammary gland during pregnancy" (Wilmut *et al*, 1997, p. 813). And it has been suggested that "some mammary cells, though technically adult, may remain unusually labile or even 'embryo like', and thus able to proliferate rapidly to produce new breast tissue at an appropriate stage of pregnancy. Consequently, we may only be able to clone from unusual adult cells with effectively embryonic potential, and not from any stray cheek cell, hair follicle, or drop of blood" (Gould, 1998, p. 45).

[513] Wilmut *et al*, 1997.

[514] For example, Daniel Tarschys, the Secretary General of the Council of Europe, insisted that "the cloning of an adult sheep may be an impressive scientific achievement but it also demonstrates the need for firmer rules on bioethics . . . No human cloning whatsoever is acceptable" (quoted in Cox, 1999, p. 35). On March 4 1997, President Clinton issued an executive order banning federal funding for research into human cloning (Klotzko, 1997, p. 432). Dr Hiroshi Nakajima, Director General of the World Health Organisation reported that "WHO considers the use of cloning for the replication of human individuals to be ethically unacceptable". Frederico Mayor of UNESCO said that "human beings must not be cloned under any circumstances". A month after the announcement of Dolly's birth, the European Parliament passed a resolution on cloning, the preamble of which said "the cloning of human beings . . . cannot under any circumstances be justified or tolerated by any society" (Harris, 1999b [1997] p. 144). On its opinion of the 22 April, The French National Consultative Ethics Committee for Health and Life Sciences (CCNE) said reproductive cloning "would be a grave moral regression in the history of civilisation" (CCNE, 1997, p. 21).

Media Reports were frequently ill-informed and alarmist, for example, the *Daily Mail*'s headline on the 24 February, the day after news of Dolly's birth was broken, was "Could We Now Raise the Dead?" (Klotzko, 1997, p. 429).

And in a CNN/*Time Magazine* survey conducted a week after the announcement of Dolly's birth, 93% of the people questioned said that they disapproved of human cloning (Brazaitis, 1997). In the UK a national opinion poll conducted by Harris Research and published in *The Independent* on the 7 March 1997 found that 72% thought human cloning "should never be allowed and all research should be stopped" (Wellcome, 1998, p. 7). The HGAC and the HFEA's consultation on cloning found that 80% of their respondents thought reproductive cloning is an "ethically unacceptable procedure" (HGAC and HFEA, 1998, para. 4.3).

[515] Science and Technology Committee, 1997. In France the National Consultative Ethics Committee for Health and Life Sciences published a special report on cloning on the 22 April 1997 (CCNE, 1997).

[516] European Parliament, 1997.

cloning.[517] Several countries have legislation banning human cloning, either directly,[518] or by implication.[519]

Whether or not cloning by nuclear substitution is covered by the Human Fertilisation and Embryology Act 1990 is a matter of some disagreement.[520] Section 3(3)(d) of the Act prohibits replacing the nucleus of a cell of an *embryo* with a cell taken from another person or embryo, but Dolly was created by replacing the nucleus of an *egg* with a cell taken from an adult sheep. Similarly, although a licence from the HFEA is necessary to bring about the creation of an embryo, an embryo is defined as being "a live human embryo where *fertilisation* is complete".[521] Since fertilisation does not takes place when a cell is cloned, there might not be an embryo for the purposes of the Act. But regardless of whether there is currently a statutory prohibition upon cloning techniques, the HFEA has indicated that it will not issue any licences for research into reproductive cloning.[522]

Because this is a book about law and reproduction, we will concentrate here upon reproductive cloning, as opposed to what it sometimes described as "therapeutic" cloning, or the production of tissue from embryonic stem cells.[523] In the years following the announcement of Dolly's birth, public and political opinion has become more accepting of cloning as a technique to produce replacement tissue for people suffering from degenerative diseases, and in January 2001, Schedule 2(3)(2) of the Human Fertilisation and Embryology Act was amended in order to permit the HFEA to grant licences to carry out stem cell research. Reproductive cloning, on the other hand, will remain illegal, although the prohibition will no longer consist only in the HFEA's licensing policy, instead an anti-cloning statute will probably be passed in order to allay public fears.

There are people for whom cloning might offer the only plausible or appealing reproductive option. There are those, such as couples in which both partners are infertile, who might prefer to avoid using donated gametes.[524] And, of course, duplication of one's genetic material might hold a certain appeal for

[517] Council of Europe, 1997. Article 1 of the Additional Protocol states: "Any intervention seeking to create a human being genetically identical to another human being, whether living or dead, is prohibited."

[518] Germany, Denmark and Spain (Savulescu, 1999b, p. 87).

[519] Norway, Slovakia, Sweden and Switzerland (Savulescu, 1999b, p. 87).

[520] Brazier, 1999a, p. 189.

[521] S. 1(1)(a).

[522] The HGAC and HFEA consultation on cloning concluded that the existing safeguards are "wholly adequate to forbid human reproductive cloning in the UK" (HGAC and HFEA, 1998, para. 9.2).

[523] Schedule 2 of the Human Fertilisation and Embryology Act initially did not cover research into the generation of tissue, or into degenerative diseases. New regulations were necessary before such research could take place.

[524] In addition, a lesbian couple could clone one partner, and each could contribute some genetic material, one the nuclear DNA and the other the egg and mitochondrial DNA.

people with more dubious motives.[525] In the following sections we consider the reasons commonly given for maintaining an absolute prohibition upon human reproductive cloning. I argue that the only convincing, and as yet decisive argument is that reproductive cloning is not yet sufficiently safe.

A Arguments against cloning

I Safety

The most compelling reason not to allow human reproductive cloning is that it would currently present intolerable health risks. Before research can be conducted upon humans, trials in animals must establish that the experiment has a reasonable prospect of success and that any associated risks are not unacceptably high. The burden of proof lies with the researcher, and although an absolute guarantee that a procedure is risk-free would be unworkable, cloning in animals has not reached this threshold level of safety or efficacy. Dolly was the sole survivor following the successful transplantation of nuclei to 277 enucleated ewe's eggs.[526] Cloning experiments on animals have found high rates of spontaneous late abortion and early postnatal death.[527] Given that there seems to be some evidence that "somatic cloning may be the cause of long-lasting deleterious effects"[528] in animals, it would obviously be unethical to conduct research into human reproductive cloning.

When reproduction consists in the mixing of two sets of genetic material, an abnormal gene from one parent may be paired with a normal gene from the other parent, thus diluting the impact of any genetic mutations. Because cloning bypasses this random mixing of genes, there has been speculation that it might thereby lose its associated benefits and lead to an increased risk of cancer or immunological disease.[529] In addition to the risks of multiple miscarriages[530] and serious abnormalities,[531] we do not yet know the extent to which the advanced age of the cloned cell would affect the ageing process in the cloned person.[532] This problem might be avoided if cloning techniques were only employed on early embryonic cells, but this would then only be a reproductive option for people who had *already* produced an embryo *in vitro* and wanted to create a duplicate. There might be advantages in replicating an existing embryo if, for example, the prospective parents are at risk of passing on a genetic disease, and

[525] Commonly cited examples are that "narcissistic tycoons might clone themselves to extend their power", and that "those with . . . commercial appeal could . . . sell their DNA to others" (Robertson, 1998, p. 1384). Media reports of a millionaire who paid scientists $5 million to try to clone his dog add to the perception that cloning will appeal to the rich and unbalanced (Radford and Dodd, 1998).

[526] Wilmut *et al*, 1997.

[527] Kato *et al*, 1998.

[528] Renard *et al*, 1999, p.1489.

[529] Galton and Doyal, 1998.

[530] In the research that led to Dolly's birth, 62% of fetuses were lost, compared with a loss rate of 6% in normal mating (Wilmut *et al*, 1997).

[531] Weiss, 1999.

[532] Colman, 1999, p. 16.

cloning an unaffected embryo could increase the number of embryos available for transfer. Making identical copies of an embryo created *in vitro* might also have some advantages over conventional IVF's dependence upon repeated cycles of ovarian stimulation and surgical egg retrieval.[533]

While concerns about the safety of reproductive cloning currently undoubtedly require a moratorium upon research,[534] for most people, the fact that it is not currently safe is not the principal reason for continuing the blanket prohibition upon human reproductive cloning. Rather there is a widely shared assumption that there is something unacceptably disturbing about the possibility of cloning human beings. Opinion differs as to whether this visceral unease derives from a principled ethical objection to cloning, or whether it amounts to little more than an irrational gut reaction.[535] While it may be true that some people are repelled by the prospect of human reproductive cloning, intuitive feelings of disgust do not necessarily justify restricting other individuals' reproductive options. So assuming that at some point in the future experiments upon animals indicated that cloning could safely be attempted on humans, are there other reasons that would justify maintaining the prohibition upon human reproductive cloning?

II Dignity

There are those who would argue that cloning an existing child to produce another who would be, for example, a perfect match for a bone marrow transplant violates the Kantian imperative that we should never treat a person solely as a means to another's end. Stephen Robertson, for example, has suggested that cloning presents "the greatest opportunity so far in history actually to treat people merely as means and not as ends".[536] But this "Kantian principle, invoked without any qualification or gloss is seldom helpful in medical or

---

[533] Kolata, 1997, p. 206.

[534] Ian Wilmut has said that "at present, with the likelihood of abortions and infant deaths, it is surely obscene to even consider applying these techniques in humans" (Wilmut, 1999, p. 22).

[535] For example, Ezekiel Emanuel, a member of the US presidential ethics commission on human cloning, suggests that any apparent inadequacy in the arguments against human cloning reflects instead deficiencies in our capacity to articulate deeply held beliefs: "the strong public reaction suggests a strong argument" (quoted in Kolata, 1997, p.195). John Harris quotes from Leon Kass who has said that "we are repelled by the prospect of cloning human beings not because of the strangeness or novelty of the undertaking, but because we intuit and feel, immediately and without argument, the violation of things that we rightfully hold dear". John Harris describes this trust in one's capacity to sniff a situation and determine right from wrong as "nasal reasoning", and he argues that "we should be suspicious of accepting the conclusions of those who use nasal reasoning as the basis of their moral convictions" (Harris, 1999a, p. 82).

[536] Robertson, 1998, p. 282; Caroline Spelman MP has said "surely a couple who plan to have a family should not, ethically, be able to plan for that family's genetic characteristics" (Caroline Spelman MP, Hansard 6 May 1998, col. 659). And the French National Consultative Ethics Committee for Health and Life Sciences (CCNE) refers to the prospect of "intolerable lowering of a person to the status of an object". And their report goes on to argue that "the organism of (a cloned) individual would . . . serve as a means of expression of a genome chosen by a third party. Could a project of this nature be judged as being anything but an offence against the human condition?" (CCNE, 1997, pp. 18, 19).

bio-science contexts",[537] otherwise we should have to prohibit blood donation, non-therapeutic research on human subjects and live donor organ transplants. It is also unclear that a child created in such circumstances would be treated *exclusively* as a means to the end of helping their older twin. If the child were abandoned following the donation, then this would undoubtedly be an unacceptable exploitation of a human life. But once a child has been born, parents are under a legal obligation to support her until she reaches the age of majority. Parents can already choose to have another child because there is a good chance that that child may prove to be a compatible bone marrow donor for an older sibling, and it is surely probable that in such circumstances the child will be loved and cherished as an individual in his or her own right.[538] It could even be argued that people frequently decide to reproduce for reasons much less honourable than saving an existing child's life, such as wanting an heir or trying to salvage a failing relationship. We might not approve of their motives, but neither would we feel that application of the Kantian imperative compels us to prevent them from reproducing.

III Identity

Popular science fiction has contributed to the public misperception that human cloning would lead to the manufacture of "photocopied" individuals on an automated artificial production line.[539] The assumption that cloning violates the right to one's own unique identity[540] is, however, founded upon some fundamental misunderstandings about genetics.[541] Monozygotic twins share identical DNA, yet there is no doubt that each twin is a separate person with his or her own identity. The human brain is extraordinarily complex and even genetically identical twins will be born with different neural connections.[542] These differences will increase as their experiences and environment shape their

---

[537] Harris, 1999c, p. 67. Harris goes on to say that Kant's principle "is so vague and so open to selective interpretation and its scope for application is consequently so limited, that its utility as one of the 'fundamental principles' of modern bioethical thought . . . is virtually nil" (Harris, 1999c, p. 68).

[538] For example in a highly publicised American case, Mr and Mrs Ayala chose to have another baby because there was a one in four chance that he or she would be a compatible bone-marrow donor for their elder daughter Anissa, who had leukaemia. Marissa proved to be a good match. Her parents have been adamant that Marissa is loved and valued as an individual in her own right (Robertson, 1998, p. 1420).

[539] Wellcome, 1998, p. 13. Our cultural fascination with identical twins has a long history, and as Wendy Doniger explains "mythology comes down strongly against cloning. The case against cloning is made over and over; even the comedies have a tragic aspect and the tragedies are grim indeed" (Doniger, 1998, p. 135).

[540] Robert Williamson argues that "the single most important feature of autonomy (is) the fact that each of us is genetically unique and individual" (Williamson, 1999, p. 96). Similarly Frederico Mayor has said that "cloning would remove the uniqueness that ensures that no one has chosen and intrumentalized another person's identity" (Mayor, 1998, p.13).

[541] The French National Consultative Ethics Committee for Health and Life Sciences (CCNE) has stated unequivocally "the notion that perfect genetic similarity would in itself lead to perfect psychic similarity is devoid of any scientific foundation" (CCNE, 1997, p. 18).

[542] See further Johnson, 1998.

neural development. Having a unique genotype is not, therefore, an essential prerequisite of individual identity.

Since a clone and its DNA source will not usually share the same mitochondrial DNA,[543] their genotypes may even be subtly differentiated. There are 37 genes in human mitochondrial DNA and their principal role is to control energy metabolism in human cells.[544] The contribution mitochondrial DNA makes to differences between individuals is not fully understood, although mutations in maternal mitochondrial genes undoubtedly increase susceptibility to certain rare but fatal human diseases.[545] Hence, it may not even be strictly accurate to describe a clone as a delayed twin. But even if it were, the existence of this delay will mean that the clone and the DNA source will be less alike than monozygotic twins. Their uterine environments;[546] their childhood experiences and their upbringing will all necessarily be entirely different. Since the way in which genes express themselves is influenced by a person's environment, the clone and the DNA source will not be identical in either appearance or character.[547]

But even if it is accepted that a clone will not be an exact duplicate of the DNA source, and that monozygotic twins do not offend against the principle that we each have a right to our own identity, there will probably be significantly more similarity between a clone and his or her DNA source than happens with the intrinsic genetic randomness of an egg's fertilisation by a spermatazoa. So although parents can already reproduce because they would like offspring that resemble them, or because they want to produce a tissue donor for an older sibling, cloning would considerably increase their chance of success. That reproduction could consist in the duplication of an existing person's DNA, rather than the random lottery of inherited appearance and characteristics to which we are accustomed, is undeniably unsettling.[518] Unlike other forms of assisted conception that continue to rely upon the haphazard mixing of two sets of genetic material, cloning would introduce a new element of human control over the transmission of our genes. It should, however, be remembered that preimplantation gene therapy,

[543] The denucleated egg will contain mitochondrial DNA.

[544] Tanne, 1999.

[545] Gardner, 1999, p. 36.

[546] As we saw in ch. 4, the contribution one's uterine environment makes to susceptibility to disease has only recently been recognised.

[547] As Eisenberg explains "to produce another Mozart, we would need not only Wolfgang's genome but mother Mozart's uterus, father Mozart's music lessons, their friends and his, the state of music in eighteenth century Austria, Haydn's patronage, and on and on, in ever-widening circles . . . we have no right to the . . . assumption that his genome, cultivated in another world at another time, would result in an equally creative musical genius" (Eisenberg, 1976, p. 326).
There is an important difference between someone's genotype, which is their genetic code, and their phenotype, which is their characteristics. An individual's phenotype is controlled both by the expression of the genome during development and by environmental factors.

[548] John Robertson says that "the idea of turning out replicas of persons was deeply unsettling, for it appeared to contradict the very notion of respect for individual persons that undergirds our moral and legal system" (Robertson, 1998, p. 1383). William Ian Miller suggests that "nature gave us just about as much doubling as we can handle without getting too spooked" (Miller, 1998, p. 87). The team of scientists which had produced Dolly anticipated this reaction, and apparently consulted a public relations firm to advise them about how to present their achievement (Harris, 1999a, p. 63).

when it becomes possible, will offer greater opportunities for directing the transmission of genetic material than the simple reproduction of an existing person's genotype.

The argument is further made that even if we acknowledge the differences that will exist between the clone and the DNA source, the *expectation* of similarity will significantly impair a clone's capacity for individuality.[549] For example, the Explanatory Report to the Additional Protocol to the European Convention on Human Rights and Biomedicine which specifically prohibits human cloning argues that "naturally occurring genetic recombination is likely to create more freedom for the human being than a predetermined genetic make-up".[550]

According to this line of argument, every individual should have the right to an open future, and someone who is the clone of their parent will instead be burdened by the anticipation of uncanny resemblance between the lives of the parent and his or her clone.[551] And it may be true that a parent might be particularly fascinated by the development of a child who has been cloned from their DNA. Yet is this actually very different from the interest parents commonly have in their children's inherited characteristics? People who grow up in the shadow of a successful older sibling already often feel constrained by their parents' unreasonable expectations. So if we are really concerned to protect children from oppressive parental pressure and a correspondingly "closed future", we should have to closely examine the parenting practices of many people who reproduce in the ordinary way.

This argument against cloning is further weakened by the fact that this supposedly oppressive expectation of similarity is, as we have seen, based upon a series of mistaken assumptions about genetic determinism. The clone would not be a "carbon copy" of the DNA source, and their personality, appearance and health would all differ markedly. Expectations that are grounded in ignorance are surely not a good justification for restricting reproductive freedom, otherwise we might also have to consider preventing reproduction among people who believe, for example that boys are cleverer than girls.[552]

IV Family Relationships

Because a cloned child would not be produced through the mixture of his or her parents' gametes, but through the replication of one person's DNA, some people have expressed concern about its impact upon family relationships.[553] It has even been suggested that such a fundamental change in the nature of kinship would in turn have a profound effect upon social stability.[554] For

---

[549] Holm, 1998b.

[550] Quoted in Cox, 1999, p. 36.

[551] Hilary Putnam, for example, suggests that cloning might give rise to a novel human right: "the 'right' of each new-born child to be a complete surprise to its parents" (Putnam, 1999, p. 13).

[552] Justine Burley and John Harris have argued that "it is morally problematic to limit human freedom on the basis of false beliefs" (Burley and Harris, 1999, p. 111).

[553] Wellcome, 1998, p. 17.

[554] Hilary Putnam, for example, argues that "our moral image of a good family strongly conditions our moral image of a good society" (Putnam, 1999, p. 11).

example, cloning raises the possibility that a woman could reproduce without using a man's gametes. If lesbian and single women could have children entirely autonomously, there is inevitable speculation about the future redundancy of men.[555] While children conceived using DI also have no genetic connection with one of their parents, a cloned child would have an unprecedented genetic identity with one parent and it is impossible to tell what impact this might have upon the child and her parents.[556] However, speculation about the dangers for intra-family relationships may rest in part upon the misguided assumptions about genetics that we considered earlier. The child will not be a miniature version of their DNA source, rather, just like children born following DI, they will share certain inherited characteristics with only one of their parents.

V Diversity

This argument against cloning rests upon the assumption that procreation which involves the random redistribution of genetic material from two different genotypes leads to a healthy genetic diversity among the population, and that this would necessarily be impaired by permitting reproduction that consists in the replication of an individual's DNA.[557] This sort of anxiety is misplaced for several reasons. First, the clone's genotype will in fact be the result of the mixing of two sets of genes: those of the DNA source's mother and father. Second, the clone will also inherit the mitochondrial DNA from the de-nucleated egg, so its genetic inheritance is not completely identical to that of the nuclear DNA provider. Third, as John Harris points out, the human genome was not threatened two thousand years ago when the world's population, and hence genetic diversity, was perhaps 1 per cent of what it is today.[558]

If cloning becomes possible, the number of clones is likely to be infinitesimal, compared with the number of babies produced "normally" by the world's six billion people. Given the cost and inconvenience of cloning, the number of artificially produced clones is not even likely to be as high as the number of clones

---

[555] For example, William Eskridge and Edward Stein suggest that "one result of the development of these technologies will be to reinvigorate the feminist utopian idea of women reproducing without men" (Eskridge and Stein, 1998, p. 97).

[556] The HGAC and HFEA consultation on human cloning said that "this complete genetic identity between the child and one parent would constitute a novel situation of which there is no previous experience and there must be uncertainites and doubts about the effects this would have on the family and the child" (HGAC and HFEA, 1998, para. 4.7). Ian Wilmut asks "could I have an effective, healthy relationship with someone who is a copy of me? Could my wife? And, importantly, could the child have a good relationship with me?" (Wilmut, 1999, p. 23). In a similar vein Ruth Deech says "would cloning represent the desire of one parent to have a monopoly of control, annihilating any possibility of a second parent and family?" (Deech, 1999, p. 98). And Caroline Spelman MP has said "if I could clone my husband, the clone would be (his) twin, not our child" (Caroline Spelman MP, Hansard 6 May 1998, col. 660).

[557] David Tracy, for example, says that "human cloning certainly sounds like the ultimate contribution to an undesirable monoculture" (Tracy, 1998, p. 193). Hilary Putnam claims that "the unpredictability and diversity of our progeny is an intrinsic value" (Putnam, 1999, p. 12).

[558] Harris, 1999b [1997], p. 147.

that result from natural twinning.[559] As a result, it would be difficult to argue that the health of the human species would be endangered by reproductive cloning.

VI Slippery Slope

Slippery slope or "thin end of the wedge" arguments are commonly cited as good or even sufficient reasons to prohibit any research into human cloning. Three related assumptions underpin slippery slope arguments. First, it is predicted that a new technology could be put to some extremely undesirable uses. Second, there is judged to be a high chance that someone will employ the new technology to these undesirable ends. Third, our capacity to institute effective regulation to prevent this undesirable use of the new technology is doubted.

If, so the argument goes, we permit scientists to conduct research into cloning human embryos in order to grow replacement tissue for people suffering from degenerative diseases, we automatically face an unacceptably high risk that disreputable scientists will offer to clone narcissistic millionaires or mad dictators.[560] According to this sort of argument, if it would be unethical to produce 100,000 clones of one person, then it must also be unethical to produce one clone.[561] But this is simply illogical. We might similarly want to argue that it would be undesirable for one sperm donor to father thousands of children, but this does not mean that we have to prohibit the practice of donor insemination. Rather, this concern instead leads us to impose upper limits on the numbers of children who can be born from one donor's gametes.

And what exactly is this abuse of which we are so afraid? The slippery slope argument against cloning undoubtedly relies upon a disproportionate fear of legions of mad scientists whose curiosity and desire for self-advancement will always impel them to go beyond the limits set for them by the law.[562] As we saw earlier, the stereotype of the crazed scientist pushing back the frontiers of knowledge regardless of the social consequences has developed a strong hold upon the popular imagination.[563] Gradual public acceptance of therapeutic cloning reveals an interesting distinction that tends to be drawn between doctors, who

---

[559]   3.5 births in every 1000 produces natural monozygotic twins (Harris, 1999a, p. 79).

[560]   The Wellcome Trust report on public attitudes to human cloning found that "the public have fearful perceptions of human cloning" (Wellcome, 1998, p. 4).

[561]   Williamson, 1999, p. 96.

[562]   For example, media reports of Korean scientists who were said to have cloned a human embryo in Seoul University Hospital, and then destroyed it at the 4 cell stage fuel this assumption that human cloning experiments are going on anyway (BBC Panorama, 1999). Similarly, the Chicago scientist, Dr Richard Seed announced that he was going to attempt human cloning regardless of public opinion (Berlins, 1998).

[563]   Frances Price suggests that "trust both in science and the regulation of scientists has declined since the late seventies" (Price, 1989, p. 37). And according to the Wellcome Trust report on public attitudes to human cloning "a striking theme found throughout the research was the lack of trust that participants expressed in scientists and those perceived to be in control of scientific research". Researchers found that "there was a belief that regulation would not be able to prevent those determined to attempt human cloning. For many, illegal research seemed inevitable and impossible to prevent" (Wellcome, 1998, pp. 35, 29).

are assumed to act ethically and beneficently in their patient's best interests, and scientists, who are assumed to be prepared to act unethically in their pursuit of knowledge and self-aggrandisement.

Slippery slope arguments therefore rely both on some alarmist ideas about scientific amorality and on the rather defeatist assumption that our ability to control inappropriate applications of cloning technology is inevitably and irreparably undermined by a decision to permit some scientists to carry out research into the cloning of human embryos. The claim that a technique could be abused is not an adequate justification for banning it unless we have also established that it would be impossible or exceptionally difficult to prevent its abuse. So we can only prohibit human cloning on the grounds that it might be abused once we have concluded that there is little or nothing we could do to stop that abuse materialising. Rather than pessimistically presuming that satisfactory regulation is a logical impossibility, it might be more logical to consider how the feared misuse of reproductive cloning techniques could be prevented.

VII Confidentiality

Although it is undoubtedly true that a person's appearance, characteristics and abilities are not determined by their DNA, there are, as we saw in chapter three, a few medical conditions that are caused by genetic abnormalities. If someone with the gene that causes Huntington's Disease were to be cloned, the clone would also have the relevant gene, and would therefore develop the disease. Since the DNA source's knowledge of their genetic make-up translates (aside from mitochondrial differences) into identical knowledge about the clone, significant questions about genetic confidentiality may arise. By the time human reproductive cloning becomes safe enough to attempt in humans, this problem is likely to have been exacerbated by advances in the breadth and accuracy of genetic testing.

Confidentiality issues already arise between family members who undergo genetic tests, and these are obviously especially pronounced for identical twins where the discovery of a genetic abnormality in one twin is tantamount to a positive diagnosis for the other one. The existence of confidentiality problems is not, however, a sufficient reason to prevent cloning. Rather if human reproductive cloning were to become possible, rules which already exist in relation to the cross-referencing of information from different family members would need to accommodate the special implications of a parent and child with a shared genotype.

B Arguments in favour of human reproductive cloning

In the next few years, human reproductive cloning is likely to remain too hazardous to satisfy the threshold safety requirements for research trials on human subjects. The chief argument in favour of allowing reproductive cloning if and when it ever becomes sufficiently safe is that it would add to the reproductive options already available, and enhance procreative choice for people who might not otherwise be able to have children.[564] Despite the extraordinary advances in infertility treatment over the last twenty-five years, there are still people who cannot be helped to reproduce using the existing technologies. The principal argument in favour of reproductive cloning is simply that we should do all that we can to alleviate involuntary childlessness. There are also, of course, compelling practical reasons for bringing every available reproductive technique within the control of the law. If human reproductive cloning becomes safe enough to attempt on humans, it is obviously preferable that it should be carried out within a rigorous regulatory framework than in some shadowy black market.

Full consideration of what a human reproductive cloning statute would look like is beyond the scope of this book. But it is undeniable that the regulation of human reproductive cloning would raise some novel dilemmas. Who, for example, are the parents of a child born following human reproductive cloning? There are even more possibilities than the multiple options created by existing assisted conception techniques. Relatively straightforward is the scenario in which a man's nuclear DNA is inserted into an egg retrieved from his partner, who then gestates the cloned embryo to term. Then we realistically have two biological parents: mother and father. But if the egg and its mitochondrial DNA were to be contributed by a third party, would we have a third biological parent? Similarly, if a lesbian couple were to use one partner's nuclear DNA and the other partner's egg and mitochondrial DNA, does that child have two biological mothers? Where the DNA source is also the gestating woman, does the child have only one biological parent? None of these permutations has a simple solution, and all are further complicated by the fact that the parents of the person contributing their nuclear DNA may also have a plausible claim to be treated as the parents of their child's "delayed twin".

In addition, new consent provisions might also be important to ensure that the DNA source had given free and informed consent to be cloned.[565] And just as restrictions are already put upon the number of children who can have the same gamete source, there might need to be some limit on the number of clones derived from one person's DNA.

6. CONCLUSION

In this chapter we have considered some of the legal, social and ethical questions raised by reproductive technologies. As we have seen, this is a fast-moving area

---

[564] John Robertson, for example, says that "if the safety and efficacy of cloning are established, . . . a persuasive case can be made for its use as a technique to assist infertile or genetically-at-risk couples to have healthy children" (Robertson, 1998, p. 11372).

[565] John Robertson argues that "even if clone sources have no direct legal rights or duties toward their later born twin, the relationship is a novel one with potential psychological complications that persons should be free not to incur" (Robertson, 1998, p. 1432).

of clinical practice and research, and any legislation has an inevitable in-built obsolescence. Nevertheless, the nature of the techniques involved and the special vulnerability of would-be patients mean that clear, prospective regulation is necessary. In the UK, considerable ongoing decision-making authority is vested in the HFEA, and the flexibility this offers is to be welcomed, as is the HFEA's broadly facilitative approach.

As will have been obvious in this chapter, I would advocate even greater facilitation of access to assisted conception services, including public funding for treatment and an abolition of the disingenuous and arguably cosmetic "welfare of the child" condition upon access to treatment. My argument is a simple one. Wanting to have a child is not equivalent to other desires that we might consider undeserving of public subsidy, like an aesthetic preference for a more attractive nose. For most adults, having children is both fulfilling and profoundly important, and involuntary childlessness should, I argue, be recognised as a serious misfortune. Given that it is a misfortune that can now be alleviated, respect for each individual's interest in planning their lives according to their own conception of the good should incline us to facilitate wanted childbearing. Like other medical treatments, clinical and cost-effectiveness must be relevant to the extent of NHS provision, but doctors, legislators and regulators are indubitably ill equipped to make moral judgements about whether an individual deserves to procreate.

6

Surrogacy

1. INTRODUCTION

SURROGACY IS, IN the words of the Warnock Report, "the practice whereby one woman carries a child for another with the intention that the child should be handed over after birth".[1] Agreements may be reached between strangers, usually involving the payment of expenses; or a woman may offer to act as a surrogate for a friend or relative. In this chapter I describe the woman who gives birth as the "surrogate mother" and the individual(s) for whom she agrees to bear the child as the "commissioning couple". I use these terms because they are in common usage, but it should be acknowledged that there is some controversy over the description of the woman who gives birth as a "surrogate" mother.[2] It is also possible, although in practice rare, for a single man or woman to engage a surrogate mother and my references to the commissioning couple should be understood as a convenient shorthand, rather than a normative exclusion.

The two most common sorts of surrogacy arrangement are "full" surrogacy, where an embryo created *in vitro* using the egg and sperm of the commissioning couple is transferred to the surrogate mother's uterus, and "partial" surrogacy where the surrogate mother is inseminated with the commissioning father's sperm.[3] Full IVF surrogacy first took place in 1985 in the United States,[4] whereas partial surrogacy has been practised for hundreds, and possibly thousands of

---

[1] Warnock Report, 1984, para. 8.1.

[2] For example, John Robertson suggests that "the term 'surrogate mother', which means substitute mother, is a misnomer. The natural mother, who contributes egg and uterus, is not so much a substitute mother as a substitute spouse who carries a child for a man whose wife is infertile. Indeed, it is the adoptive mother who is the surrogate mother for the child, since she parents a child borne by another" (Robertson, 1990, p. 157). Rosemarie Tong argues that "to term the child's gestational mother, who may or may not also be the child's genetic mother, the 'surrogate mother', is to imply that she is not the real mother of the child when it is precisely her claim to 'motherhood' that is at stake" (Tong, 1995, p. 57). Derek Morgan, on the other hand, notes that if the word "surrogate" applies to maternity, rather than motherhood, then the conventional terminology is sustainable (Morgan, 1989).

[3] There are, of course, various other possible scenarios, such as insemination with an anonymous donor's sperm; or IVF with a donated embryo, or natural conception with the surrogate's own partner, but these are comparatively rare.

[4] Utian *et al*, 1985. In 1985, despite opposition from the BMA Patrick Steptoe and Robert Edwards first proposed treating a patient with IVF surrogacy in Britain at Bourn Hall Clinic. Following extensive consultation with the clinic's independent ethics committee, the couple were treated and the first British IVF surrogacy baby was born in 1989 (Brinsden *et al*, 2000, p. 924).

years.[5] Because full surrogacy arrangements involve *in vitro* fertilisation they come under the regulatory umbrella of the Human Fertilisation and Embryology Authority, considered in detail in the previous chapter. Conception in partial surrogacy, on the other hand, usually takes place at home, by self-insemination with fresh sperm. The ease with which a woman can inseminate herself undoubtedly undermines effective legislative control, so, for example, the informal surrogacy arrangements entered into by gay or single men tend to be made in a regulatory vacuum.[6] Additionally, in contrast to the comprehensive records kept and published by the HFEA, information about the incidence and outcomes of partial surrogacy arrangements is inevitably incomplete.

Despite the existence of the Surrogacy Arrangements Act 1985, and the passage of further statutory provisions in 1990, the law governing surrogacy remains unclear. In part this is a result of the Warnock Report's ambivalence about the purpose of regulation.[7] The majority of the Warnock Committee concluded that surrogacy was almost always unethical.[8] But despite this antipathy, the Committee "recognise(d) that there will continue to be privately arranged surrogacy agreements", and were "anxious to avoid children being born to mothers subject to the taint of criminality".[9] Their judgement that surrogacy arrangements are flawed but inevitable led to the passage of legislation with two disparate goals: the rules are intended both to offer some protection to the vulnerable parties (believed principally to be the surrogate mother and the child), and to discourage involvement in surrogacy.[10]

---

[5] Examples from the book of Genesis in the Bible are frequently cited (Genesis xvi, 1–15; 17:15–19,21:1–4; Abraham's wife Sara was infertile and enlisted her maid Hagar to bear Abraham's child; similarly Isaac and his infertile wife Rachel used Rachel's servant Bilhah to bear Isaac's child). Since these arrangements involved slaves bearing children for their masters, the comparison is rather flimsy. And although it may be true that it has been quite normal in other cultures for women to bring up other women's children, this is not necessarily evidence of the practice of surrogacy, but may simply reflect cultural differences in the organisation of family life.

Derek Morgan suggests that the Canadian case of *R* v. *Armstrong* [1850] PR 6 may be one of the first litigated surrogacy arrangements. The mother of an illegitimate child had agreed to transfer all rights in respect of the child to its father. Subsequently she wanted to keep the child and sought a *habeus corpus* writ, the court decided in favour of the father on the ground that he had obtained the child by a consensual agreement with the mother and that in the absence of force or fraud the agreement should not be revoked (Morgan, 1988 p. 227).

[6] van den Akker, 1999.

[7] Mary Warnock has explained that "(t)he inquiry then, while unanimously answering the first-order question negatively, holding that surrogacy was wrong, nevertheless held that legislation should not be invoked to prevent it (Warnock, 1985, p. xii).

[8] "Even in compelling medical circumstances the danger of exploitation of one human being by another appears to the majority of us far to outweigh the potential benefits, in almost every case." (para. 8.17).

[9] Para. 8.19. In some other countries, participation in surrogacy arrangements is a criminal offence. In most states in Australia, the contracting parties commit a criminal offence if they enter into a commercial surrogacy arrangement. In Queensland, the criminal prohibition extends to parties entering into non-commercial arrangements (see further Otlowski, 1999).

[10] And in the United States, most state legislation governing surrogacy rests "upon the assumption that the practice presents intolerable risks and should be discouraged" (Andrews, 1995, p. 2349).

By 1997 it had become clear that, for a variety of reasons, the patchwork of provisions regulating surrogacy was unsatisfactory. Of particular concern was the ineffectiveness of the prohibition upon paid surrogacy. So only three years after the relevant parts of the Human Fertilisation and Embryology Act 1990 had come into force,[11] a committee, chaired by Margaret Brazier, was commissioned to make recommendations for further law reform. Their report was published in 1998, and we consider its substance in detail below. At the time of writing the Government have not indicated when or if the proposals contained in the Brazier Report will form the basis of new legislation.

Some regulation of surrogacy is almost certainly necessary. Without a mechanism for the transfer of legal parenthood, for example, informal arrangements might leave children in an undesirable legal limbo in which their primary caretakers would owe them no formal obligations. It might also be important for the law to offer people contemplating entering into a surrogacy agreement some prospective guidance about the legality or otherwise of payments. In this chapter we first consider the current regulatory scheme and highlight its chief defects. Having identified gaps and inconsistencies in the law, we evaluate the options for reform.

In working out how surrogacy should be regulated, the problem is not so much an absence of law, but rather that there are multiple existing bodies of law that could plausibly accommodate surrogacy arrangements. First, surrogacy could be subsumed within the ordinary rules of contract law. Second, the arrangement could be treated as a contract of employment, and subject, for example, to the protections of the Health and Safety at Work Act 1974 and the minimum wage. Third, surrogacy might be covered by the prohibition upon trade in human beings. Fourth, it could be classified as a particular type of adoption and thus governed by family law. Finally, surrogacy could be classified as one of the range of assisted conception services that are provided in licensed clinics and regulated by the Human Fertilisation and Embryology Authority. These are not mutually exclusive options, and an effective regulatory scheme might borrow elements from more than one legal tradition. Currently, as we see below, the rules governing surrogacy consist in an uncomfortable combination of adoption law and the regulations that govern infertility treatment, and the reforms proposed by the Brazier Report would maintain this family/medical law hybrid. Towards the end of this chapter, I argue that the refusal to countenance the incorporation of certain principles from modern contract law into the regulation of surrogacy might be hampering the development of a more imaginative regulatory framework. This is not to say that adoption law or the rules governing the provision of infertility treatment should be irrelevant. Rather my point will be that in rejecting the relevance of contract law *on principle*, an opportunity for some productive cross-fertilisation between different legal disciplines might have been missed.

[11] S. 30 came into force in November 1994.

While there may be some consensus that regulation of surrogacy arrangements is necessary, it is obviously important to decide whether that regulation should be broadly facilitative or restrictive. Having considered some of the arguments commonly put both for and against the practice of surrogacy, I shall argue that the law should not be concerned to restrict individuals' reproductive options, but rather to offer a clear set of rules in order to promote certainty and fairness. Contrary to the prophesies of many of its critics, disputes between surrogate mothers and commissioning couples are in practice rare,[12] nevertheless there is the inevitable possibility that arrangements may go wrong. I argue that this small, inescapable risk does not offer a good reason for discouraging people from entering into surrogacy arrangements,[13] but instead should prompt us to institute comprehensive, prospective regulation.

2. THE LAW

(a) Commercialisation

The Surrogacy Arrangements Act 1985 prohibits the initiation and negotiation of surrogacy arrangements "on a commercial basis",[14] and makes the publication or

---

[12] For example, there is no data to support the fear that imperfect babies will be abandoned by both commissioning parents and surrogate mothers (Gostin, 1990, p. 7). In van den Akker's survey of surrogacy in the UK "no commissioning couple has been known to refuse to adopt a baby following the arrangement" (van den Akker, 1999, p. 264). The Stiver-Mallahoff case in the United States has received a great deal of publicity: the facts were that after a surrogacy arrangement with the Mallahoffs, Mrs Stiver gave birth to a child who was almost certainly mentally retarded. Initially neither the Stivers nor the Malahoffs wanted the child, who was subsequently discovered to be Mr Stiver's baby, rather than Mr Malahoff's. The Stivers agreed to keep the baby (see further Corea, 1985, p. 215). While undoubtedly regrettable, it is undeniable that handicapped children conceived naturally are sometimes rejected by their parents, and so it is unclear that any general lessons can be learnt from the Malahoff case. John Robertson argues that rejection of a severely disabled child "reflects common attitudes toward handicapped newborns as much as alienation in the surrogate agreement" (Robertson, 1990, p. 162).

There is also, as we see later in this chapter, little evidence to suggest that women regret agreeing to be surrogate mothers (Baker, 1994, p. 608). Lori Andrews' research demonstrated that 1% of surrogates changed their minds about giving up the child (Andrews, 1995, p. 2351). Yet, as Michael Shapiro argues, "in surrogacy the small failure rate gets 'writ large'" (Shapiro, 1994, p. 648).

Brazier *et al* cite the small "failure rate", but then suggest that "we need to ask what constitutes 'success' in a surrogacy arrangements. The fact that the child is handed over to the commissioning parents without contest may not be a reliable criterion of success" (Brazier *et al*, 1998, para. 6.2).

[13] For example, Carl Schneider has argued that "the number of things that can go wrong with surrogacy contracts is great enough that there is an argument to be made that, despite their potential advantages to some people, the law should channel people away from the institution of surrogacy" (Schneider, 1990, p. 130).

[14] S. 2 (1) No person shall on a commercial basis do any of the following acts in the United Kingdom, that is—
(a) initiate or take part in any negotiations with a view to the making of a surrogacy arrangement,
(b) offer or agree to negotiate the making of a surrogacy arrangement, or
(c) compile any information with a view to its use in making, or negotiating the making of, surrogacy arrangements

distribution of advertisements indicating a willingness to take part in surrogacy arrangements a criminal offence.[15] But while commercial surrogacy is, in theory, forbidden, the Brazier report was instigated in part as a result of the recognition that "surrogacy is, in effect, increasingly practised on a commercial basis",[16] with typical payments of around £10,000. The reason for this gap between theory and practice is that the courts are entitled to authorise payments made in contravention of the ban on commercial surrogacy. If the court considers that it is in the child's best interests to remain with the commissioning couple, retrospective authorisation of any illegal payments will, as we see later, be relatively straightforward. Although a court will seldom have the opportunity to prevent people from entering into surrogacy arrangements that contemplate the making of an unlawful payment, prospective authorisation of illegality would, of course, be an entirely different matter. In *Briody v. St. Helen's & Knowsley Health Authority,*[17] following a negligently performed hysterectomy, Ms Briody had argued that her compensation should include the costs of entering into a surrogacy arrangement. Her claim was rejected by Ebsworth J, who considered that:

"it is one thing for a court retrospectively to sanction breaches of statute in the paramount interests of an existing child, it is quite another to award damages to enable such an unenforceable and unlawful contract to be entered into".

(2) A person who contravenes subsection (1) above is guilty of an offence; but it is not a contravention of that subsection—
(a) for a woman, with a view to becoming a surrogate herself, to do any act mentioned in that subsection or to cause such any act to be done, or
(b) for any person, with a view to a surrogate mother carrying a child for him, to do such an act or cause such an act to be done
(3) For the purposes of this section, a person does an act on a commercial basis (subject to subsection (4) below) if—
(a) any payment is at any time received by himself or another in respect of it, or
(b) he does it with a view to any payment being received by himself or another in respect of making, or negotiating or facilitating the making of, any surrogacy arrangement
In this section "payment" does not include payment to or for the benefit of a surrogate mother or prospective surrogate mother.

[15] S. 3 (1) This section applies to any advertisement containing an indication (however expressed)—
(a) that any person is or may be willing to enter into a surrogacy arrangement or to negotiate or facilitate the making of a surrogacy arrangement
(b) that any person is looking for a woman willing to become a surrogate mother or for persons wanting a woman to carry a child as a surrogate
(2) where a newspaper or periodical containing an advertisement to which this section applies is published in the United Kingdom, the proprietor, editor or publisher of the newspaper or periodical is guilty of an offence.

[16] Brazier *et al*, 1998, para. 1.13. And at para. 3.20 "Payments for the service provided by the surrogate, in excess of any reasonable level of actual expenses incurred as a result of the pregnancy, are currently being made." Brazier found that payments of over £15,000 had been made, with a number of payments in the range of £10,000–£15,000 (para 5.4).

[17] [2000] 2 FCR 13 Ms Briody would only be able to fund the surrogacy arrangement she had organised in California if the defendants were liable to pay her damages for the costs of surrogacy.

(b) Status

Following a full surrogacy arrangement using a donated embryo, a child could potentially have six adults with an apparent claim to parenthood: their genetic mother and father; the couple who intend to bring them up, and the surrogate mother and her husband or partner. In partial and most full surrogacy arrangements, the number of potential parents will be limited to four (the surrogate, her husband or partner, and the commissioning couple). Nevertheless, with so many plausible candidates, identifying the legal parent(s) following a surrogacy arrangement is obviously both complex and important.

(i) Maternity

There are three possible ways in which a child's mother could be identified. First, the legal mother could be the woman who gestates the pregnancy and gives birth. Second, legal motherhood could be synonymous with genetic motherhood, so that the woman whose egg was fertilised would be the resulting child's mother. Third, legal motherhood could vest in the woman who intends to raise the child, sometimes referred to as the social mother. In full surrogacy where the embryo is created using an egg from the commissioning woman, there are only two possible mothers because the child's intended or social "mother" is also his or her genetic "mother". Similarly in partial surrogacy, there are only two candidates because the child's genetic "mother" is also the woman who gives birth to the child. Only in IVF surrogacy using a donated egg will each of the three definitions identify a different woman.

The legal definition of "mother" in British law is clear and unequivocal: the woman who gives birth to a baby is its mother.[18] British law does not distinguish between different types of surrogacy when determining maternity, rather the same test applies to all births regardless of whether the woman who gives birth is genetically related to the baby. As the legal mother, the woman who gives birth to the child has the absolute right to decide whether to keep the child, or hand it over to the commissioning couple. And protecting the surrogate's right to keep the child to whom she has given birth appears to be a non-negotiable part of the British regulatory scheme. In this *prima facie* allocation of legal motherhood, the presumed interests of the surrogate mother even take priority over the interests of the child.

The principal merit of the British approach is that it unambiguously identifies the child's legal mother. A genetic test would also promote certainty, although

---

[18] Human Fertilisation and Embryology Act 1990 section 27 (1) "The woman who is carrying or has carried a child as a result of the placing in her of an embryo or of sperm and eggs, and no other woman, is to be treated as the mother of the child".

In the *Ampthill Peerage Case* [1977] AC 547, Lord Simon said (at 577) "motherhood, although also a legal relationship is based on fact, being proved demonstrably by parturition".

it would obviously lead to different results depending upon the type of arrange-ment. In partial surrogacy, a genetic test would vest motherhood in the surro-gate, while in a full surrogacy arrangement, the commissioning mother would, unless a donated egg was used, be the child's legal mother from birth.[19] If a donated egg was used in IVF surrogacy, a genetic test would vest motherhood in the egg donor. In this last, and it must be admitted, rather unusual scenario, the child's legal mother would be the woman least likely to want to raise the child.

A further problem with a test based solely upon genetic contribution is that it obscures the gestational mother's physical connection with the child.[20] So, in cases of full surrogacy it might be more accurate to admit that there are two women who have each played a necessary *biological* role in the child's creation. That a child might have two *biological* mothers is, as Michael Shapiro has sug-gested "conceptually explosive".[21] It is, however, unlikely that any legal system would formally recognise the coexistence of two biological mothers. One legal mother will usually be identified,[22] although interestingly the definition of motherhood now varies between different jurisdictions.[23] In the United

[19] For example, in West Virginia, there is no need to adopt following a full surrogacy arrange-ment, instead there is a procedure through which a new birth certificate reflecting the "correct" information about the child's parentage may be created.

[20] For example in the American case of *Johnson* v. *Calvert* 286 Cal Rptr 369,372 (Cal Ct App 1991) Cert. Granted, 822 P. 2d 1317 (Cal, 1992). Mr Calvert was white and his wife Crispina was Phillapino. They provided both the egg and the sperm, and agreed to pay Anna Johnson, who was black, $10,000 to carry their child. Although Anna Johnson had agreed that she would relinquish her parental rights, when she was 7 months pregnant she indicated that she was having doubts and might try to seek custody of the baby. When she was 8 months pregnant, the Calverts sought and gained a declaration of legal parenthood. Using the results of blood tests the California Appellate Court declared that Crispina Calvert was the "biological, natural and legal mother of the child". It is of course questionable whether "natural" accurately describes Crispina Calvert's claim to moth-erhood. While DNA tests may be able to conclusively establish whether or not a man either is the child's father, the division between the genetic and the gestational contribution of motherhood makes identifying the "mother" in a full surrogacy arrangement less clear. There are perhaps two women who have a legitimate claim to be considered the child's mother. In the United Kingdom, Anna Johnson would have been considered this child's legal mother, but the opposite result was reached by the Californian court.

It is perhaps significant that the Court in *Johnson* v. *Calvert* determined legal motherhood in a similar way to the resolution of conventional paternity disputes. In commenting upon this case, Janice Raymond suggests that "women's parenthood is recognised only to the extent that it con-forms to the legal determination of male parenthood and is 'similarly situated' . . . meaning meas-ured by the same criteria" (Raymond, 1993, p. 68).

[21] Shapiro, 1994, p. 649.

[22] Although in Arkansas, it is possible for a child born through a surrogacy arrangement with a single man to have no legal mother, see below footnote 27.

[23] In the American case of *Buzzanca* v. *Buzzanca* Sup Ct No 95D002992, a child was born fol-lowing the implantation of an anonymously donated embryo into a gestational surrogate, so the child was not genetically related to the commissioning couple or to the surrogate mother. The trial judge had held that Jaycee had no legal parents, but this was overturned on appeal. The California Court of Appeal were anxious to avoid the conclusion that a parentless child had been created, and found that although conventionally the parent and child relationship has been established through genetic ties, giving birth or adoption, the means through which parenthood is identified should not be closed, and could therefore be expanded to keep up with new technologies. As a result, the court

Kingdom the gestational mother will always be considered the legal mother unless and until a parental order or an adoption order is made. Whereas in the United States, a distinction has been drawn between the relatively simple allocation of motherhood to the genetic *and* gestational mother in partial surrogacy,[24] and the more complex considerations that obtain in full surrogacy arrangements, in which genetic and gestational motherhood are separated. A US court has, for example, accepted that if a genetic father of a child conceived following a full surrogacy arrangement can be considered the legal father, it might be discriminatory to preclude the genetic mother from mounting a similar claim.[25] In some states, the woman who provided the genetic material[26] and/or the woman who intended to become the mother[27] has been given priority over the gestational mother.

found that a parent/child relationship might also exist following medical procedures which were initiated and consented to by the intended parents, even when there is no genetic relationship between them and the child: "Jaycee would never have been born had not Luanne and John both agreed to have a fertilized egg implanted in a surrogate." Drawing an analogy with the legal fatherhood of a man whose wife is inseminated with donor sperm, the court saw no reason why basing parenthood upon the intention to become a parent should not apply equally to a couple who arrange for a donated embryo to be implanted in a surrgate mother. The Court quoted from the decision in *People* v. *Sorenson* 68 Cal. 2d 280 (1968) 285: "by consenting to a medical procedure which results in the birth of a child . . . by common law estoppel a husband incurs the legal status and responsibility of fatherhood." The Court in *Buzzanca* v. *Buzzanca* found that this definition could be extended to establishing maternity.

[24] In *Marriage of Moschetta* (1994) 25 Cal App 4th 1218; 30 Cal Rptr 2d 893 17,32, 34, the combination of genetic parentage and maternity meant that the surrogate should automatically be considered the child's legal mother. Her legal relationship with the child would thus have to be terminated before the "intended" mother could acquire legal parenthood.

[25] In *Soos* v. *Superior Court of Maricopa* 897 P.2d 1356 (Ariz App Div 1 1994) the Appellate Court found that an Arizona surrogacy statute which provided that the gestational surrogate is the legal mother of the child to be born violated the biological mother's equal protection rights.

[26] In *Belsito* v. *Clark* 644 N.E.2d 760 (Ohio Com Pl 1994) the Ohio Court of Common Pleas determined that the "birth" test should be subordinate to the genetic test, so that if the individuals who have been identified as the genetic parents do not waive their rights to parenthood, they become both the natural and the legal parents: "the natural parents of the child shall be identified by a determination as to which individuals have provided the genetic imprint for that child". Anonymous sperm, egg or embryo donors will not then be treated as a natural and legal parent because they will have relinquished their rights to parenthood.

[27] The California Supreme Court in *Johnson* v. *Calvert* (1993) 5 Cal 4th 84 found that "she who intended to procreate the child . . . is the natural mother under California law . . . intentions that are voluntarily chosen, deliberate, express and bargained-for ought presumptively to determine legal parenthood . . . a rule recognizing the intended parents as the child's legal, natural parents should best promote certainty and stability for the child" (at 93–96). The intention test has also been adopted in New York, see further *McDonald* v. *McDonald* (1994) 196 AD2d 7, 608 NYS2d 477.

In Arkansas, a state not generally noted for its progressive legislation, the Arkansas Code (Annotated Section 9–10–201 et seq.) provides that a child born as the result of artificial insemination pursuant to a surrogacy contract is deemed to be the child of the biological father and his wife, if he is married. If he is not married, then the child is his alone. The child's birth certificate recognises the paternity and maternity as contemplated by the surrogacy contract. Similarly, in Florida, New Hampshire, North Dakota and Virginia the intended rearing parents are viewed as the legal parents (NBAC, 1997, p. 90).

A test based solely upon intention would of course be open to dispute and might result in prolonged uncertainty about a child's parentage.[28] Nevertheless, an intention-based test of maternity might more accurately reflect the reproductive choices being made when individuals negotiate a surrogacy arrangement.[29] Our ability to control our fertility means that procreation increasingly involves both the biological process of reproduction *and the intention to become a parent*. During a "normal" wanted pregnancy, a couple often expend considerable effort in preparing themselves for parenthood. If we understand the mental and practical preparations for the birth of a child to be a part of the reproductive process, it might be important to recognise that procreative intent can be separable from the biological fact of gestation.[30]

Furthermore, if the surrogate mother has no interest in bringing up the child, imposing the obligations of parenthood upon her may not be in the child's best interests. If the child is born disabled and the commissioning couple decide that they do not want to take him or her, a test based upon the pre-conception intentions of the parties would hold the commissioning couple to their agreement.[31] The British approach would, less satisfactorily, put the surrogate mother in the difficult position of having *prima facie* responsibility for a child that she never wanted, and leave the commissioning couple with no legal responsibility towards a child whose creation they brought about.

A further objection to the British definition of mother is its conservatism. The idea that the familial norms derive from the state of nature may be inherently regressive. In recent years there has been a dramatic shift away from thinking about the family as a natural and indissoluble entity. Instead the organisation of family life is now characterised more by diversity and voluntarism than by the rigid ascription of indivisible biological roles. An intention-based test of parenthood has the potential to be much more inclusive of

---

[28] In the United States, the *Baby M* case involved a protracted battle about who should be considered baby M's parents which would have been avoided if the British approach had been adopted. And in *Buzzanca* v. *Buzzanca* Sup. Ct. No. 95D002992, before Jaycee's birth John Buzzanca argued that he had not intended to become her legal father, He alleged that Luanne Buzzanca had promised to assume all responsibility for Jaycee. Despite his denial, the court found that both he and Luanne were the intended parents of Jaycee. Although written evidence would offer helpful proof of intention, the California Supreme Court found that full knowledge of the facts and willing participation was enough.

In *Belsito* v. *Clark* 644 N.E.2d 760 (Ohio Com Pl 1994) the Ohio Court of Common Pleas rejected an intention-based test of parenthood on the grounds that intent is often difficult to prove, disputes can arise, and there may even be a joint intent on the part of the surrogate and the genetic mother to bring up the child, which would make determination of the child's legal mother impossible.

[29] In *Johnson* v. *Calvert,* the California Supreme Court ruled that "a woman who enters into a gestational surrogacy arrangement is not exercising her own right to make procreative choices; she is agreeing to provide a necessary and profoundly important service without (by definition) any intention that she will raise the resulting child as her own" (at 505).

[30] Stumpf, 1986, p. 194.

[31] For example, in Florida (statute 742.14) the Statute specifically addresses this situation: "the couple agrees to accept custody of and assume full parental rights and responsibilities immediately upon the child's birth regardless of any impairment of the child."

alternative family structures than one which vests legal parenthood in the woman giving birth and her husband or partner.[32]

We can therefore see that a family law model, which has traditionally ignored intention, might not be the most helpful way to think about surrogacy arrangements. In family law, obligations have tended to be imposed involuntarily, whereas within other legal disciplines, intention has often determined the scope of an individual's legal duties. Criminal responsibility is, for example, largely inseparable from intention. And multiple rules of contract law are directed towards divining the intentions of the parties.[33] Of more immediate relevance might be the "medical law" model for the allocation of parenthood following the use of assisted conception, which again makes intention determinative. Thus the British status provisions might also be criticised for discriminating between different sorts of infertility. Where a woman's husband or partner is infertile and she conceives as a result of donor insemination, as we saw in the previous chapter, her husband or partner's *intention* determines his paternity. But where a surrogate is employed because a couple's infertility derives from the female partner's inability to carry a child, the intentions of the parties are largely irrelevant to the ascription of parenthood.

In a surrogacy arrangement, the child only exists because the commissioning couple intended its birth. To ignore the centrality of their intention and instead ascribe *prima facie* parenthood to a couple that never intended to keep the child may not promote the child's welfare. Where the surrogate mother is happy to hand over the child at birth, the British approach to parenthood nevertheless demands that the child's life starts with litigation, albeit amicable. If we instead recognised that the initiation of the biological process manifests procreative intent, a presumption in favour of the intended parents might promote the stability and security of the child's first months.[34] Such a presumption could, of course, be rebuttable should the surrogate mother object, and replaced instead with a default rule, such as the conventional British definition of motherhood, or a "best interests" test.

(ii) Paternity

There are four ways in which legal paternity is determined. First, there is the rebuttable common law presumption of paternity within marriage. Applied to a surrogacy arrangement, this would lead to the surrogate's husband being treated as the legal father of the child until legal parentage is transferred to the commissioning couple through adoption or a parental order. Second, there is a

---

[32] Stumpf, 1986, p. 196.

[33] For example, no contract will exist absent the intention to create legal relations, and the imposition of implied terms has conventionally rested upon the courts determining what the parties must have intended at the time when the contract was made.

[34] Andrea Stumpf, for example, has argued that ignoring the importance of procreative intention leads to the "egregious . . . failure . . . to acknowledge the role of the infertile wife" (Stumpf, 1986, p. 196).

rebuttable presumption that the man who is registered as the father on the birth certificate (normally the surrogate's husband or partner) is the child's father.[35] Third, both of these presumptions of paternity are rebutted if DNA tests establish that the mother's husband, or the man registered on the birth certificate, is not in fact the father,[36] which would of course be the case following a surrogacy arrangement. Fourth there is the statutory definition of "father" in section 28 of the Human Fertilisation and Embryology Act 1990. As we saw in the previous chapter, this section has two related purposes. It vests legal paternity in men whose wives or partners have been inseminated using donated sperm, and it excludes the sperm donor from any of the rights or responsibilities of parenthood. Its application to surrogacy arrangements is incidental to its original purpose, and leads to some rather strange results.

A literal interpretation of section 28 would, for example, treat the commissioning father in the same way as an anonymous sperm donor, even though in a surrogacy arrangement, the provider of the sperm is not only identifiable, but also intends to become the child's father. Section 28 treats the surrogate mother's husband as the father of the child provided that he consented to the procedure.[37] If the surrogate has an unmarried partner, he will be treated as the father if the couple were being treated "together", which seems unlikely.[38] If the surrogate is single, or if her husband does not consent, or if she is not being treated "together" with her partner, then the child will have no legal father.[39] It would not be possible for a commissioning father to acquire legal paternity via section 28 by arguing that *he* is being treated "together" with the surrogate because first, this provision only applies when the embryo is created with the sperm of a third party, and second it is generally assumed that the treatment must have been provided for the man and a woman "as a couple".[40]

---

[35] Births and Deaths Registration Act 1953 s.34(2).

[36] Family Law Reform Act 1969 s. 20(1).

[37] Human Fertilisation and Embryology Act 1990 section 28(2) If.

(a) at the time of the placing in her of the embryo or the sperm and eggs or of her insemination, the woman was a party to a marriage and

(b) the creation of the embryo was not brought about with the sperm of the other party to the marriage,

then . . . the other party to the marriage shall be treated as the father of the child unless it is shown that he did not consent to the placing in her of the embryo or the sperm and eggs or to her insemination

[38] Human Fertilisation and Embryology Act 1990 section 28(3) If. . .

(a) the embryo or the sperm and eggs were placed in the woman, or she was artificially inseminated, in the course of treatment provided for her and a man together by a person to whom a licence applies, and

(b) the creation of the embryo carried by her was not brought about with the sperm of that man,

then . . . that man shall be treated as the father of the child

[39] *In Re Q (A Minor)(Parental Order)* [1996] 1 FLR 369 the surrogate mother was unmarried, and the IVF surrogacy involved the implantation of an embryo created using the egg of the commissioning mother and donated sperm. Johnson J found that there was no person with whom the surrogate mother had received treatment services together.

[40] See the comments of Wilson J in *U v. W (Attorney General Intervening)* [1998] Fam 29.

So both the common law presumption of paternity within marriage and the Human Fertilisation and Embryology Act's provisions result in paternity usually being granted to the man least expecting to be treated as the child's father. And the HFEA Code of Practice confirms that the surrogate mother must register the baby to which she has given birth in the normal way, and that "her husband or partner should *normally* be registered as the father"[41] (my emphasis). The HFEA Code of Practice then envisages that there will be *abnormal* situations where the surrogate's partner will not be registered as the father. One obvious example is where the surrogate mother is single. But it is unclear what would happen if the surrogate mother and the commissioning father both attended the Registrar of Births and jointly requested that his name should be recorded on the birth certificate.[42] Since DNA tests will only serve to confirm his paternity, it is unclear what sanction there might be for failing to follow HFEA advice.

In the light of the somewhat awkward application of rules governing the acquisition of paternity to surrogacy, it seems clear that separate status provisions might more easily accommodate the special issues raised by surrogacy arrangements.[43] In addition to allocating the legal obligations of parenthood to a man who will usually want to play no role in the child's life, the paternity rules laid out in the 1990 Act might also be criticised for creating an incentive for anyone contemplating entering a surrogacy arrangement to do so covertly.[44] If, for example, conception occurs following sexual intercourse between the commissioning father and the surrogate mother, his registration as the child's father will be straightforward. If, on the other hand, a couple seek assistance with insemination from a licensed clinic, and thus subject themselves to the scrutiny of the clinic's ethics committee, the surrogate mother's husband will be treated as the child's father, or the child will be legally fatherless. Where a regulatory scheme offers both compelling incentives to avoid its protection, and no sanctions for doing so, we should, perhaps, be alerted to its failings.

(c) Acquiring Legal Parenthood

The definition of mother in English law means that the commissioning mother will never automatically acquire legal responsibility for a child born through surrogacy. And, as we saw above, the commissioning father will not *usually* be

[41] HFEA Code of Practice 4th ed. July 1998 Annex B.

[42] Where the child's mother is unmarried, the father's name can only appear on the birth certificate if one of the criteria in section 10 of the Births and Deaths Registration Act 1953 (as amended) is satisfied. For our purposes, the relevant circumstances would be that the parties jointly request registration either by personal attendance or by providing a statutory declaration of paternity.

[43] For example, in Arkansas where the birth certificate reflects the intended parenthood of the surrogacy arrangement, there is no need for subsequent adoption, and no possibility for subsequent custody battles between the surrogate mother and the couple. The clarity of the Arkansas approach means that there have been no disputes.

[44] I am grateful to Katherine O'Donovan for this point.

considered the legal father of the child. So if commissioning parents want to be treated as their child's legal parents they will either have to adopt her, or be granted a parental order under section 30 of the Human Fertilisation and Embryology Act 1990.

The acquisition of parenthood after a surrogacy arrangement is based upon a family law model. As we see below, even the specific "fast-track" parental order embodies conditions, such as the requirement that the applicants be married, that owe more to adoption law than to the regulation of infertility treatment. Assisted conception services are, as we saw in the previous chapter, routinely available to unmarried couples, and may be accessible to single women or lesbian couples. In sharp contrast, a couple who use surrogacy to overcome their infertility can only jointly acquire legal parenthood if they are married to each other. In addition, when male infertility is tackled using DI, the partner with no genetic connection to "his" offspring becomes the child's legal father simply by signing the clinic's consent form. When a particular sort of female infertility is addressed by entering into a surrogacy arrangement, the intended parents are treated as strangers to the child, and legal parenthood can only be acquired through a series of burdensome and complex legal procedures.

(i) Section 30 Parental Orders

The granting of a section 30 Order by a court will result in the Registrar General re-registering the child's birth. Just as with adoption, it will not be possible for the public to make a link between entries in the Register of Births and the Parental Order Register, but once a child reaches adulthood, she will, after being offered counselling, have access to her original birth certificate.[45] Section 30 was inserted at the Report stage of the Human Fertilisation and Embryology Bill after a proposal by an MP who had received a complaint from a couple in his constituency who had gone through a full surrogacy arrangement resulting in the birth of twins, and then been informed that they would have to apply to adopt their biological children.[46] With little opportunity for parliamentary debate or extra-parliamentary consultation, the proposal was accepted and section 30, which lays out the minimal criteria for eligibility for a parental order[47] came into force in November 1994.

[45] HFEA Code of Practice 4th ed. July 1998 Annex B.
[46] Michael Jopling MP was responding to the case *of Re W (Minors)(Surrogacy)* [1991] 1 FLR 385, see Hansard (1990) vo.l 170, cols. 944–5.
[47] Human Fertilisation and Embryology Act 1990 section 30

(1) The court may make an order providing for a child to be treated in law as the child of the parties to a marriage (referred to as "the husband" and "the wife") if
    (a) the child has been carried by a woman other than the wife as the result of the placing in her of an embryo or sperm and eggs or her artificial insemination
    (b) the gametes of the husband or the wife, or both, were used to bring about the creation of the embryo and
    (c) the conditions in subsections (2) to (7) are satisfied

cont. over/

In 1994, guidance was issued to Local Authorities and Health Authorities explaining how the section 30 regulations should operate.[48] When a Local Authority is aware that a child has been or is about to be born following a surrogacy arrangement, its Social Services Department is required to make enquiries in order to satisfy itself that the child is not at risk of harm as a result of the arrangement. Following the child's birth, if the local authority have reasonable grounds to believe that the child is suffering, or is likely to suffer significant harm, they would be entitled to seek a care order.[49]

Although a report from a guardian *ad litem* is needed before a parental order can be made,[50] a section 30 application effectively short-circuits some of the more cumbersome aspects of the adoption process. As a result, access to this fast-track procedure is limited. The applicants must be married to each other;[51] at least one of the applicants must be genetically related to the child, conception must not have been by natural intercourse, the child must be living with the applicants, the surrogate and the child's legal father (usually her husband) must have given consent and the court must be satisfied that no money or benefit, other than for expenses reasonably incurred, has been paid, unless subsequently authorised by the court.[52] In deciding whether to make a section 30 order, the court is directed to "have regard to all the circumstances, first consideration

(2) The husband and the wife must apply for the order within six months of the birth of the child...
(3) At the time of the application and of the making of the order—
    (a) the child's home must be with the husband and the wife
    (b) the husband or the wife or both of them must be domiciled in the U.K....
(4) At the time of the making of the order both the husband and the wife must have attained the age of 18
(5) The court must be satisfied that both the father of the child (including a person who is the father by virtue of section 28), where he is not the husband, and the woman who carried the child have freely, and with full understanding of what is involved, agreed unconditionally to the making of the order
(6) Subsection (5) does not require the agreement of a person who cannot be found or who is incapable of giving agreement and the agreement of the woman who carried the child is ineffective ... if given by her less than six weeks after the child's birth
(7) The court must be satisfied that no money or other benefit (other than expenses reasonably incurred) has been given or received by the husband or the wife for or in consideration of—
    (a) the making of the order
    (b) any agreement required by subsection (5)
    (c) the handing over of the child to the husband and the wife, or
    (d) the making of any arrangements with a view to the making of the order, unless authorised by the court

[48] s.30(9) authorised the modification of the adoption legislation by subsequent regulations: now the Parental Orders (Human Fertilisation and Embryology) Regulations 1994, Local Authority Circular LAC (94) 25.

[49] Children Act 1989 s. 31(2).

[50] Parental Orders (Human Fertilisation and Embryology) Regulations 1994, Local Authority Circular LAC (94) 25.

[51] John Miller notes that "politicians clearly express a desire to simulate conventional parenting in surrogate arrangements" (Miller, 1994, p. 630).

[52] In *Re Q (A Minor)(Parental Order)* [1996] 1 FLR 369 Johnson J found that the payment of £8280 was reasonable in the circumstances and that the court would use its power to retrospectively authorise it.

being given to the need to safeguard and promote the welfare of the child".[53] Since section 30 applications are classified as "family proceedings",[54] the courts are entitled if they see fit, to make an alternative order, such as a residence order, or an additional order, such as an order that the child should continue to have contact with the surrogate mother.[55]

Given that around 40 per cent of all children are now born to unmarried parents, confining access to parental orders to married couples seems overly restrictive. In addition, there are two practical problems with the operation of section 30.[56] First, eligibility for a parental order is conditional upon the child *already living with* the commissioning couple. Yet prior to the making of the order the commissioning couple will usually have no legal relationship with the child because, as we have seen, it is the woman who gives birth and her husband who will be considered the child's legal parents. Thus section 30 demands that a child should live for a period of time with people who have no legally recognised responsibility for him or her. Given the prevailing emphasis upon the best interests of the child, this requirement is rather puzzling. Second, by leaving the assessment of the reasonableness of any "expenses" to the *post hoc* discretion of the court, judged on a case by case basis, there is no prospective guidance for people contemplating involvement in surrogacy.

An application for a parental order may be made in the Family Proceedings Court. The guardian *ad litem* must first establish that the section 30 criteria are satisfied, and second, must determine whether there is any reason why a parental order would not be in the best interests of the child.[57] So guardians *ad litem* are charged with policing the "genetic link" and "no payment" requirements, *and* with protecting the child's welfare. In carrying out their role, guardians *ad litem* face two major problems. First, their powers are extremely limited, so in ensuring both that the child was created using the gametes of at least one of the applicants, and that there have been no unlawful payments, they only have access to information provided by the surrogate and the commissioning couple. Second, their two duties are not necessarily compatible with each other. Because the child must already be living with the commissioning parents before an application is made, her welfare will seldom be promoted by removing her from a settled home. So even if there has been a blatant contravention of, for example, the "no payment" rule, the child's interests may still be best served by making a parental order, and indeed the Brazier Committee was

---

[53] Parental Orders (Human Fertilisation and Embryology) Regulations 1994, schedule 1(1)(a). This is based upon the welfare principle contained in section 6 of the Adoption Act 1976.

[54] S. 30(8).

[55] Children Act 1989 s. 8.

[56] Jonathan Montgomery has said that "the provisions of section 30 represent the worse features of a legislative system which allows anecdotal evidence to determine the shape of reform" (Montgomery, 1991 p. 230).

[57] The Parental Orders Regulations provide that "first consideration" must be given to the welfare of the child. Although this is consistent with s. 6 of the Adoption Act, it differs from the welfare principle embodied in s. 1(1) of the Children Act 1989 which makes the welfare of the child the court's paramount consideration.

unable to find any case in which an application for a section 30 Order was refused on the grounds that an unacceptably large sum of money had changed hands.[58]

Where the surrogate mother is happy to hand over the child, and the commissioning couple fulfil the other section 30 criteria, an application for a parental order will be the simplest way for the commissioning couple to acquire legal parenthood. If the surrogate mother does not want the child, unless the commissioning couple would obviously be woefully inadequate parents, it would rarely be in the child's best interests for the parental order to be refused and the child to be taken into the care of the local authority. Hence, provided that the section 30 conditions are satisfied, obtaining a parental order will be relatively straightforward.

There are, however, several different reasons why a commissioning couple might not be able to apply for a section 30 order. They might, for example, not be married to each other, or the surrogate mother might have refused to consent to the making of an order. If for any reason the intended parent(s) are ineligible for a section 30 parental order, the only way in which they can acquire legal parenthood is through adoption.

(ii) Adoption

The adoption process is extremely onerous and time-consuming. In order to be eligible to adopt a child, the criteria in the Adoption Act 1976 must be satisfied. So, for example, the parent(s) must give their unconditional consent to the adoption or a court must determine that consent is being unreasonably withheld,[59] the court must consider that adoption is in the child's best interests and in order to adopt jointly, a couple must be married to each other. These statutory criteria are the *minimum* requirements, and in practice local authorities supplement these with additional conditions, such as upper age limits. Potential adopters must also endure rigorous scrutiny by social workers over a prolonged period of time.

In deciding whether to make an adoption order, the child's welfare will be the court's first consideration. If the surrogate mother does not want the child, but

---

[58] Brazier *et al*, 1998, para. 5.3. Brazier *et al* argue that the "courts find themselves in effect 'forced' to authorise expenses which are simply covert payments" (at para. 4.41), and describe the reference to expenses reasonably incurred as "laconic" (at para. 7.11).

[59] This was the case in the Scottish case of *C* v. *S* [1996] SLT 1387. S and C had entered into a surrogacy arrangement. C, who was ineligible for a section 30 order because there had been a payment contrary to s.30(7), applied to adopt X. S, the natural mother of X, refused to consent to the adoption and sought custody. The Court of First Division found that S had withheld her consent unreasonably and made an adoption order in favour of C. The Court argued that if S had placed X's welfare first she would have recognised that X had been living with C since birth and that C had a secure relationship and was able to provide a balanced home environment. In contrast S had demonstrated her irresponsibility by involving a tabloid newspaper, abusing drugs and lying about a previous miscarriage.

for some other reason the couple are ineligible for a section 30 order, adoption will usually be in the best interests of the child. But where the surrogate mother has changed her mind and an adoption application is made, applying a "best interests" test may prove to be much more problematic. Is there a presumption that it is in a child's best interests to be brought up by the woman who gave birth to her?[60] Are the circumstances in which the child was conceived relevant to an assessment of the child's welfare?[61] And if the child has been living with the commissioning couple, are the short term interests in avoiding disruption

[60] Because of the Australian courts' tendency to conclude that the child's long term ability to cope with the circumstances of their conception would be promoted by granting custody to the gestational mother, and that it was entitled to give priority to the child's long-term welfare interests rather than the short-term consequences of disruption to their living arrangements, Otlowski has argued that only in the most exceptional circumstances will the Australian gestational mother fail to be awarded residence of the child (see further Otlowski, 1999, p. 46).

Martha Field has argued that the surrogate mother ought to have the right to custody of the child. She argues that in the United States the non-enforceability of surrogacy contracts is undermined by the subsequent application of a "best interests" test which, she says, favours fathers so often that "birth mothers are discouraged from withdrawing from the surrogacy contract even when they know they have a legal right to back out and would like to exercise it." Indeed Field goes so far as to suggest that "a custody contest to determine 'the best interests of the child' in itself is actually contrary to the child's best interest" (Field, 1993b, pp. 224, 230). In a similar vein, Janice Raymond suggests that "the far greater legal and financial resources of the 'ejaculatory father'—the middle-class home, education, and upbringing that he can provide—measured against the usually financially disadvantaged position of the so-called surrogate mother and her often insecure family situation privileges the sperm source immediately in any court battle" (Raymond, 1993, p. 80). In addition to the material advantages offered by the commissioning couple, any custody battle may be further weighted in favour of the commissioning couple in cases of full surrogacy where the commissioning mother is also the genetic mother of the child. While in the United Kingdom the law remains clear that the birth mother is always a child's legal mother, this is not universally the case, and in *Johnson* v. *Calvert* in the United States (discussed above, footnote 20) the genetic links of both commissioning parents have been found to be decisive. Critics of the decision have said that the commissioning couple in *Johnson* v. *Calvert* benefited from three factors which militated against giving custody to the birth mother: they were more financially secure; they were genetically related and unlike Anna Johnson, they were white. Some feminists have suggested that a black woman's claim to a white child is so unlikely to succeed that the colour difference may have been a factor in the Calvert's selection of Anna Johnson as a surrogate mother. For example, Janice Raymond says "it appears that the Calverts may have selected Johnson precisely because her Black skin would ensure the Calverts' claim to the resultant child" (Raymond, 1993, p. 69). Martha Field agrees that "gestational surrogacy . . . (will) make it more likely that those who hire surrogates will use women of other races to have their children" (Field, 1993b, p. 228).

[61] In the first instance decision in the Australian case of *Re Evelyn* No BR 7321 of 1997 (unreported); (1998) F.L.C. 92–807, Jordan J, whose judgment was approved on appeal said that "it is appropriate that I take account of the intentions and expectations of the four adults who co-operated to bring about her birth. Whilst, of course, such considerations are secondary to an independent determination of what is in Evelyn's best interests, the circumstances surrounding her creation are pertinent to such an assessment" (at p. 29). Perhaps as a result of the altruistic basis of the surrogacy arrangement in *Re Evelyn*, the judge was not especially critical of the parties: Jordan J accepted that the agreement had been based upon the "noblest of motives and that the adults were "genuine and well intentioned." Margaret Otlowski contrasts this with the remarks of Ormrod LJ in *A* v. *C* [1985] FLR 445 describing the surrogacy arrangement as a "sordid commercial bargain which should never have been made" (Otlowski, 1999, p. 45).

"trumped" by the supposed long term psychological benefits in being brought up by one's gestational mother?[62]

Where, as is usually the case following surrogacy, the proposed adopters are non-relatives, only licensed adoption agencies are permitted to make arrangements for the adoption of a child. A privately arranged adoption following a surrogate birth may, therefore, be unlawful.[63] In addition, any payment or reward made in consideration of the adoption of a child is a criminal offence.[64] Yet if a child has settled with adopters following an adoption procedure tainted by illegality, removing the child from his or her home in order to "punish" the wrongfulness of the circumstances in which the child was adopted would not necessarily be in the best interests of that child. As a result, both unlawful private placements, and illegal payments made in consideration of adoption can subsequently be "authorised" by the court.

This pragmatic approach to illegal placements is clearly evident in the case law on adoption applications following surrogate births.[65] In *Re an Adoption Application (Surrogacy)*,[66] Latey J argued that the payments that had been made to the surrogate mother had not been made in consideration for the adoption, but instead to compensate for the inconvenience and expense of pregnancy. Yet he also indicated that even if the payments had contravened the Adoption Act, he would have used his power to authorise them retrospectively. The child was, by the time of the application, nearly two and a half years old, and had spent his entire life with the commissioning couple who were, according to the pre-adoption reports, excellent parents. To remove the child from his

---

[62] In *Re Evelyn* No BR 7321 of 1997 (unreported); (1998) FLC 92–807, Mr and Dr S agreed that Dr S would bear a child for close friends, Mr and Mrs Q. The child was handed over shortly after her birth and "Evelyn" had lived with Mr and Mrs Q for most of her first year. Dr S changed her mind 8 months after Evelyn's birth, and a contested application for residence ensued. Although the court recognised that disturbing the established status quo might have negative short-term implications for Evelyn's welfare, these were outweighed by the longer term advantages in placement with her biological mother, who, it was held, would be better able to help Evelyn cope with psychological problems relating to abandonment and identity.

[63] Under section 29 of the Adoption Act:

(1) A person other than an adoption agency shall not make arrangements for the adoption of a child, or place a child for adoption, unless.
  (a) The proposed adopter is a relative of the child, or
  (b) He is acting in pursuance of an order of the High Court

Gatehouse v. *R* [1986] 1 WLR 18 involved a prosecution under this section. It was not strictly a surrogacy case, in that the arrangement to hand over the child was made when its mother was already heavily pregnant. The Court of Appeal found themselves unable to overturn the first instance decision that there had been no offence under s. 29 of the Adoption Act 1958, although Watkins LJ thought that "it may well be if the justices had asked themselves the right question . . . they would have convicted these two defendants" (at 27).

[64] Adoption Act 1976 s. 57.

[65] A similar approach is adopted in the United States In *Adoption of Matthew B* (1991) 232 Cal App 3d 1239 the Court found that "even if we assume that the parties' conduct was illegal, the state's paramount interest in Matthew's welfare overrides its interest in deterring illegal conduct" (at p. 1257).

[66] [1987] Fam 81.

settled and happy home in order to deter other people from engaging in similar arrangements would have amounted to a wilful disregard of the child's welfare. Similarly in *Re MW (Adoption: Surrogacy)*,[67] despite the applicants' clear breach of the prohibition upon payment, Callman J found that the court's primary duty must be to safeguard and promote the welfare of the child. In the light of the surrogate mother's media publicity campaign, and given that the child had lived with the applicants for two and a half years and that there were "glowing" reports of his progress, the surrogate mother's consent was dispensed with; the payments were retrospectively authorised and an adoption order was made.[68] And in a case[69] in which an English couple made an agreement with a pregnant woman in Germany that her child should be handed over to them in return for £1000, and where the judge admitted that there were "grave concerns" about the prospective adopters' behaviour, their health and the state of their marriage, the welfare of the child still demanded that she should remain with them while progress reports were prepared.[70]

(iii) Informal Transfers

While adoption and section 30 parental orders are the only ways in which the commissioning couple can become the legal parents of the child born following a surrogacy arrangement, this does not mean that every surrogate birth is followed by a formal application for legal parenthood. A child may be handed over by the surrogate mother, and live with the commissioning couple without any legal formalities. And it is, of course, impossible to tell how many unofficial transfers of children take place each year, although the Brazier Report suggests that "a substantial proportion of commissioning couples are failing to apply to the courts to become the legal parents of the child".[71]

The surrogate mother is not supposed to register the commissioning father's name on the birth certificate, although as we noted above, it is not clear what sanction there might be for failing to follow HFEA advice. His paternity would

[67] [1995] 2 FLR 789.

[68] There had been a payment of £7500 on condition that the surrogate mother supported the adoption process. There had also been a breach of section 11 of the Adoption Act since it was a non-agency adoption which should be confined to adoption by family members, here the wife was not a relative of the child.

[69] *Re AW (Adoption Application)* [1993] 1 FLR 62.

[70] Although an order authorising the breaches of the Adoption Act was made, legal authority would only be vested in the applicants for a probationary period of two years while the local authority and the guardian *ad litem* were provided with progress reports.

[71] Brazier *et al*, 1998, para. 5.7. They reached this conclusion because of the discrepancy between the levels of payments recorded by guardians *ad litem*, and those reported by Childlessness Overcome Through Surrogacy (COTS). The maximum payment recorded by a guardian *ad litem* was £12,000. 22% of section 30 applications involved payments of less than £1000; 47% involved payments of between £1000 and £4999; 28% were between £5000 and £9999. Only 3% of section 30 applications were accompanied by payments of more than £10,000. Since COTS report payments of between £10,000 and £15,000 as standard, Brazier *et al* suggest that the commissioning couples who are paying the most may be the ones who are also avoiding the courts (para. 5.7).

be confirmed by DNA tests so the information given to the registrar would not have been false. Because he will not be married to the legal mother, even if he is registered on the birth certificate, or his paternity is established by DNA tests, the commissioning father will not automatically acquire parental responsibility for the child. He might, however, be entitled to register a parental responsibility agreement made with the legal mother, or to apply for parental responsibility either directly under section 4 of the Children Act 1989, or indirectly via an application for a residence order under section 12.[72] These informal transfers have two principal defects. First, the child may have absolutely no legal relationship with her "mother", even if she is the child's genetic mother. Second, the surrogate mother retains parental responsibility, meaning that she would have to be consulted about any important decisions the "parents" wanted to take about their child's upbringing. The potential for acrimonious disputes is obvious.

(d) (Non) Regulation

Full surrogacy arrangements involve *in vitro* fertilisation and are therefore regulated by the Human Fertilisation and Embryology Authority.[73] The HFEA Code of Practice controls the practice of IVF surrogacy by, for example, specifying that in deciding whether to provide IVF surrogacy, the welfare of the surrogate's existing children must be taken into account.[74] Similarly, the sperm used in IVF surrogacy must, just like donor sperm, be subject to a six-month "quarantine" period in order to eliminate the risk that it might be contaminated with the HIV virus. In addition, treatment in an assisted conception clinic will be subject to supervision by the clinic or hospital's independent ethics committee, which may impose its own restrictions upon access to surrogacy.[75] In sharp contrast, aside

[72] In the future, it is anticipated that parental responsibility for unmarried fathers will become automatic. In a British case involving two gay men employing a surrogate mother, the one who provided the sperm was registered as the legal father, and thus eligible for a parental responsibility order or agreement under s. 4 of the Children Act 1989. His partner would, after three years, be entitled to apply for a residence order, which would automatically give him parental responsibility as well. Although not a problem unless there was some conflict or dispute in the future, the surrogate mother would retain her parental responsibility (Barton, 1996).

[73] 29 out of the 115 licensed fertility clinics questioned by Brazier would provide assistance with surrogacy, either through IVF, or less frequently through insemination with the commissioning father's sperm. About 60 couples per year seek IVF surrogacy (Brazier *et al*, 1998, para. 6.9).

[74] Para. 3.19b of the HFEA's Code of Practice states that "where it is the intention that the child will not be brought up by the carrying mother . . . centres should also take into account the effect of the proposed arrangement on any child of the carrying mother's family as well as its effect on any child of the commissioning parent's family" (HFEA Code of Practice 4th ed. July 1998).

[75] For example, the Bourn Hall Clinic's independent ethics committee imposes the following conditions upon access to IVF surrogacy

(i)   surrogacy must only be undertaken "as a last resort";
(ii) social reasons for surrogacy are unacceptable;
(iii) prospective parents with severe health problems should only be considered if the clinicians and the committee are satisfied that the strain of bringing up a child will not damage the mother's health and jeopardise the child's welfare;

from the broad, and to some extent ineffective prohibitions upon commercial surrogacy, partial surrogacy arrangements remain largely unregulated.

This absence of official control is in part a result of the Warnock Report's conclusion that regulation might appear to offer official endorsement of the practice of surrogacy.[76] The majority of the Warnock Committee rejected the instigation of a "limited, non-profit making surrogacy service, subject to licensing and inspection," on the grounds that "the existence of such a service would in itself encourage the growth of surrogacy".[77] The minority of the Warnock Committee reached a somewhat different conclusion, and found that the dangers of "do-it-yourself" surrogacy arrangements outweighed the risk of conferring legitimacy on the practice of surrogacy.[78] They recommended that a non profit-making body, such as a fostering or adoption agency, could be licensed by the HFEA in order to assist couples after referral from a gynae-cologist.

While doctors may assist conception within a surrogacy arrangement, the Surrogacy Arrangements Act 1985 prohibits them from helping commissioning couples to find a surrogate mother.[79] Couples must therefore find a woman will-ing to act as a surrogate themselves. There are currently at least two non profit-making organisations which help to put potential surrogate mothers in touch

---

(iv) every case must be looked at by the ethics committee on its own merit;
(v) the relationship between the genetic couple and the host must be carefully considered in order to avoid creating conflicting family relationships;
(vi) Independent counselling must be available to both genetic couples and host couples;
(vii) HIV, hepatitus B and C antibody tests are required of both genetic and host couples;
(viii) the genetic mother should be no older than 35;
(ix) the host should be less than 40 years old;
(x) the principal motive of the prospective host must be to help an infertile couple;
(xi) the prospective host must already have had at least one child;
(xii) the commissioning couple must be married, and the host should preferably be in a stable rela-tionship;
(xiii) cases must be rejected if there is any doubt that the genetic couple will comply with the requirements for a parental order under section 30 of the Human Fertilisation and Embryology Act 1990;

In the period 1989–98, Bourn Hall Clinic's independent ethics committee rejected 12 couple's appli-cations for the following reasons

(i) genetic mother more than guideline age
(ii) host mother more than guideline age
(iii) perceived psychological unsuitability of genetic or host mother;
(iv) perceived concerns about the welfare of the planned or existing children;
(v) inappropriate indications for surgery (Brinsden *et al*, 2000, pp. 925, 926).

[76] Similarly, in commenting upon greater acceptance of surrogacy within the medical profession, the Brazier Committee suggest that "medical endorsement of surrogacy adds to its respectability" Brazier *et al*, 1998, para. 3.2.
Janice Raymond opposes regulation of surrogacy for similar reasons: "laws that claim to regulate surrogacy end up promoting it" (Raymond, 1993, p. 207).
[77] *Ibid*. para. 8.18.
[78] For a consideration of the minority's viewpoint, see Brazier *et al* 1998, paras. 2.14–2.23.
[79] Surrogacy Arrangments Act 1985 s. 2(1).

with would-be commissioning couples,[80] but these agencies currently operate within a regulatory vacuum.[81] For example, there are no rules governing access to treatment, the use of fresh sperm inevitably raises the possibility of HIV infection and there is no formal data collection about the incidence and outcomes of surrogate births. There are no standard procedures for screening surrogate mothers and commissioning couples, there are no pre-treatment counselling requirements or waiting periods prior to conception,[82] and "the very ease of the process may preclude time for reflection".[83] The ban on commercial involvement in surrogacy means that access to professional expertise is extremely limited.[84] Given the almost complete absence of legal advice, it is perhaps surprising[85] that the proportion of arrangements that go wrong is so small.[86] It might, nevertheless, be important to note that the incidence of disputes both in IVF surrogacy, which is regulated by the HFEA, and in commercial surrogacy in the US, is even lower.[87]

The assumption that formal regulation would lend surrogacy respectability and invite more people to consider taking part in surrogacy arrangements has, paradoxically, resulted in a complete absence of official control over inappropriate involvement in surrogacy. There have been suggestions that this lacuna encourages "procreative tourism"[88] whereby would-be parents from countries with more restrictive regimes attempt to find surrogate mothers in Britain.[89]

---

[80] Childlessness Overcome Through Surrogacy (COTS), set up by Kim Cotton in 1988 is the best known organisation. It has a subsidiary group, called TRIANGLE, which introduces infertile couples to potential surrogate mothers. The Surrogacy Parenting Centre (SPC) was set up in 1993, and its subsidiary group HOPE puts potential surrogates in touch with infertile couples.

[81] In discussing the practices of COTS, Brazier *et al* said that "we have questions about the adequacy and impartiality of the advice and support offered to the various parties" (Brazier *et al*, 1998, para. 6.4).

[82] In a survey of agencies and clinics involved with surrogacy in the UK, van den Akker found that "knowledge of surrogacy by both commissioning couples and surrogates was generally seen as poor by 75% of organisations", and that "criteria for suitability were relatively vague". Van den Akker also discovered that "numbers of rejections were marginal" (van den Akker, 1999, p. 263 and 264). It is interesting to contrast Parkinson *et al*'s study of 95 IVF surrogates in the US. In commenting upon the absence of postpartum depression among surrogates, Parkinson *et al* say "credit should be given to the expert selection of IVF surrogates who undergo meticulous screening as well as intense and careful psychological counselling throughout the surrogacy process" (Parkinson *et al*, 1998, p. 675).

[83] Brazier, 1999a, p. 181.

[84] Margaret Brazier has argued that "in navigating the uncharted waters of surrogacy the principal sources of advice, the voluntary surrogacy agencies, are essentially amateur operations" (Brazier, 1999a, p. 181).

[85] Kim Cotton herself suggests that partial surrogacy arrangements "go surprisingly well despite the huge hazards attached" (Cotton, 2000, p. 929).

[86] Brazier *et al* found that the surrogate refused to hand over the child in 4–5% of surrogacy arrangements (Brazier *et al* 1998, para. 3.38).

[87] Brinsden *et al* report that only one IVF surrogacy arrangement has ended in the courts in a dispute between the genetic and host mothers (Brinsden *et al*, 2000, p. 927). Bill Handel, director of the Centre for Surrogate Parenting and Egg Donation in California reported that of the 500 births arranged by his centre during its 18 year existence, only one mother had ever sought to keep the child (quoted in Watson-Smyth, 1997).

[88] Nielsen, 1996.

[89] Brazier *et al* 1998, para. 3.43.

Within Europe, several countries completely prohibit the use of surrogacy,[90] while others ban any sort of payment to a surrogate mother:[91] the attraction of the relatively unregulated British system is obvious.

Acknowledging this danger, the Brazier Committee agreed with the approach taken by the minority on the Warnock Committee, and concluded that non-regulation is simply not an option.[92] Brazier *et al*'s regulatory model would not, however, be neutral as to surrogacy's acceptability. The Brazier Committee were undoubtedly persuaded by the argument that regulating payments might appear to offer official endorsement of commercial surrogacy, and "imply a normalisation of what we believe to be a difficult personal choice".[93] Their proposed regulatory scheme has instead been described as a "policy of containment".[94] We explore it in more detail below.

(c) Reform

(i) Is reform necessary?

As we have seen, surrogacy is currently regulated by a combination of surrogacy-specific rules and provisions that apply incidentally to the practice of surrogacy. Of the provisions expressly designed to control surrogacy arrangements, the prohibition of commercialisation has plainly failed to prevent the making of considerable payments to some surrogate mothers. Similarly, the restrictions upon access to the surrogacy-specific parental orders are undermined by the limited powers granted to guardians *ad litem*. So aside from my disagreement with the substance of the Surrogacy Arrangements Act 1985 and section 30 of the Human Fertilisation and Embryology Act 1990, there might be reason to doubt their effectiveness.

The Human Fertilisation and Embryology Act's status provisions apply awkwardly and inappropriately to surrogacy arrangements. Where all the parties are happy with the surrogacy arrangement, the status provisions nevertheless require them to go through court proceedings which will, almost inevitably, simply confer legality upon their intentions. Given the supposed primacy of the child's best interests, it is at least arguable that requiring largely redundant judicial hearings at the start of the child's life is at best a waste of court time, and at worst an unwarranted and potentially stigmatising intrusion. By completely ignoring the parties' pre-conception intentions, adoption law's application to surrogacy is also rather clumsy. Even when the commissioning couple are the

---

[90] Including Germany, Austria, Sweden and Norway.

[91] Including Denmark, the Netherlands and France.

[92] Elsewhere Margaret Brazier has suggested that "the current state of the law on surrogacy suggests a scenario in which the most dangerous infertility 'activity' is the least regulated" (Brazier, 1999, p. 181).

[93] Brazier *et al*, 1998, para. 4.25.

[94] Brazier, 1999, p. 183.

child's genetic mother and father, they are treated in the same way as strangers would be if they sought to adopt the child. The complexity of the rules governing the transfer of legal parenthood undoubtedly deters some commissioning parents from acquiring a formal relationship with "their" child, and it is clearly not in a child's best interests for her social parents to have assumed none of the legal obligations associated with parenthood.

Perhaps the most pressing reason for reform is that the combined effect of the various rules governing surrogacy is that arrangements remain largely unregulated, thus encouraging would-be commissioning couples and potential surrogates to make agreements without any formal prospective guidance or professional advice. Given the ease with which self-insemination can be accomplished, the absence of an effective regulatory framework is unlikely to discourage participation in surrogacy arrangements. Effective legal reform might therefore be directed towards offering clear guidance to parties contemplating entering into a surrogacy agreement in order to avoid unfairness, uncertainty and protracted disputes. In the following section, I offer some criticisms of the most recent proposals for reform.

(ii)   The Brazier Report's Recommendations:

The Brazier Report advocated the complete prohibition of any payments to surrogate mothers, other than compensation for certain expenses actually incurred as a result of the pregnancy. The Report suggests several reasons for favouring an outright ban on supplementary payments, none of which, in my opinion, is entirely convincing. The first reason given is that if no money has changed hands, the commissioning parents would not have to explain to a teenage child that they made a payment to his or her gestational mother. This concern is largely speculative given that there is no evidence to suggest that children born following commercial surrogacy suffer particular harm because of the payment to their gestational mother. Second, and again without any supporting evidence, they predict that arrangements founded upon altruism are less likely to break down. It could equally plausibly be argued that disputes might be *more* common if surrogates were unpaid,[95] especially since failure rates in the US, where commercial surrogacy is the norm, are much lower than in the UK. Third, the Brazier Report suggests that in an unpaid surrogacy arrangement, commissioning parents would be less likely to face increased financial demands from the surrogate mother once the pregnancy has been established.[96] Insofar as the possibility of extortion exists, it is not clear that a ban on *all* payments is necessary in order to prevent sharp practices in a minority of cases. In a similar vein, Brazier *et al* predict, again without any evidence, that unless payments are prohibited the sums involved "will increase exponentially", which in turn would

---

[95]   Freeman, 1999, p. 7.
[96]   Brazier *et al*, 1998, para. 5.21.

mean that "the incidence of surrogacy would increase". We should, I suggest, be suspicious of these sort of slippery slope arguments.[97] To argue that we must prohibit *all* payments to surrogates because extortionate payments might be undesirable is to be overly pessimistic about our capacity to regulate the size of awards. Were payments to surrogates to receive legislative endorsement, there is no reason why regulations could not specify a maximum upper limit, or some sort of reasonableness test to be administered by the courts.

In rejecting payments to surrogates greater than expenses actually incurred,[98] the Brazier Report argued that surrogacy should be "a fully informed and free act of giving".[99] The comparison is made with blood, tissue and organ donation, all of which are, in the UK, legitimate only within a "gift relationship".[100] In addition to resting upon the dubious assumption that gifts are always a spontaneous act of altruism,[101] an interesting analogy could be drawn with the HFEA's policy on payments for sperm donation and egg-sharing schemes.[102] The HFEA had advocated removing payments for similar reasons to those given by Brazier, yet as we saw in the previous chapter, their proposal was short-lived. The ease with which human gametes can be obtained from abroad, or via the internet, means that anyone denied treatment in licensed and regulated clinics as a result of a shortage in donated gametes is likely to look elsewhere for their treatment. The HFEA therefore concluded that the dangers in increased resort to unscreened gametes outweighed the undesirability of payments.[103]

Brazier *et al* admit that one consequence of eliminating payments for surrogacy may be that "few women will be willing to undertake such a commitment, except for a relative or close friend",[104] but a drop in the number of surrogacy arrangements is not, according to Brazier, necessarily a bad thing. The Brazier Report rejects the argument found so compelling by the HFEA in the context of donated gametes, that prohibiting payments will inevitably reduce access to surrogacy for British couples and, *as a result,* might propel them into going abroad to find women to bear their children.[105] In a subsequent article, Margaret Brazier has criticised the HFEA's pragmatic toleration of payments for gametes,

---

[97] For an effective exposition of the logical fallacy behind slippery slope arguments, see further Frederick Schauer, 1985.

[98] See below, footnote 133.

[99] Brazier *et al*, 1998, para. 4.37.

[100] See further Titmuss, 1970.

[101] Janice Raymond draws an analogy between the assumption that women will behave altruistically in surrogacy and the prevailing belief that pregnant women and mothers are essentially self-sacrificing" (Raymond, 1993, p. 51).

[102] For more discussion on this, see chapter 5, p. 220.

[103] Similarly Brinsden *et al* who provide IVF surrogacy at Bourn Hall clinic in Cambridge "believe that altruism in surrogacy arrangements is ideal but, to make surrogacy a viable treatment option, a modest and sensible payment to the hosts for their services is a reasonable and practical solution" (Brinsden *et al*, 2000, p. 927).

[104] Brazier *et al*, 1998, para. 4.37.

[105] For example, restrictions upon surrogacy in Australia have simply resulted in growing numbers of Australian couples going to the United States in order to enter into surrogacy arrangements (Otlowski, 1999, p. 57).

advocating instead an absolute commitment to altruism. She argues unequivocally that the "good" of treating infertile couples should not be allowed to trump
the "evil of abandoning altruism".[106] It is clear that prohibiting payments to
surrogates may have the same effect as an outright ban upon surrogacy arrangements.[107] In addition to the dangers inherent in exporting our market for fertility treatment, it is likely that potential British surrogates will be driven away
from lawful, regulated surrogacy arrangements into a "black" market where
fees are likely to become higher and protection against exploitation and abuse
would be non-existent.[108] Although the Brazier Report rejects the total prohibition of surrogacy on the grounds that this might send the practice underground,
it appears unconcerned that a ban upon payments might have the same outcome. The Brazier Report thus seems to assume that reducing the number of
women willing to become surrogate mothers within the terms of the legislation
will simply reduce the incidence of surrogacy.[109]

Various regulatory proposals were considered by the Brazier Committee. The
British Fertility Society, for example, had suggested that all surrogacy arrangements should take place in licensed fertility clinics. Although this would have
the advantage of reducing the risk of transmission of HIV and hepatitis, it was
rejected on the grounds that surrogacy should not be just another option in the
treatment of infertility, but instead "require(s) a consideration of other factors,
much more akin to the dilemmas of adoption than those of infertility".[110]
Brazier *et al* were also fearful that its routine provision in assisted conception
clinics might lead to its use as an alternative to failed IVF much sooner than at
present.[111] This seems unlikely. IVF enables the would-be parents to experience
a normal pregnancy, and if feasible, will undoubtedly be the preferred option.

Elsewhere, Margaret Brazier has suggested that surrogacy should not be
managed within assisted conception clinics because "the professional expertise
required to advise and assist those contemplating surrogacy is not a clinical
expertise".[112] Yet an identical point could be made in relation to clinics'

[106] Brazier, 1999b, p. 353.
[107] In the context of his discussion of the existing restriction on payments other than expenses in s. 30, Eric Blyth argues that while prohibiting payments "is clearly designed to prevent a market in children..(it) may be a surreptitious attempt to deter surrogacy altogether" (Blyth, 1990, p. 255).
[108] Michael Freeman suggests that potential surrogates will be driven "into an invisible and socially uncontrolled world where the regulators will be more like pimps than adoption agencies." (Freeman, 1999, p. 10).
[109] In arguing for the complete prohibition of surrogacy, Janice Raymond acknowledges that one consequence might be that surrogacy is driven underground, but she is confident that "the number of surrogate arrangements would be minuscule compared to the explosive growth of surrogacy that would result from permissive regulation" (Raymond, 1993, p. 206). She cites no evidence to back up this claim, but even if she were right that the numbers of "underground" arrangements might be rel-atively small, the potential for abuse is surely so great that it would be indefensible to relegate some women to a black market in surrogacy just because relatively few women would be ill-treated.
[110] Brazier *et al*, 1998, para. 6.13. The HFEA too consider that "the nature of the regulation required for surrogacy agencies is outside the HFEA's remit and area of expertise" (submission to the Brazier Committee, quoted in Brazier *et al* 1998, para. 6.18).
[111] Brazier *et al*, 1998, para. 6.15.
[112] Brazier, 1999a, p. 182.

control over access to assisted conception services. As we saw in the previous chapter, clinics are already charged with considering the welfare of any child who may be born when determining whether a particular couple should undergo infertility treatment. Judging the suitability of potential parents is clearly not an exercise of clinical judgement. Similarly, Margaret Brazier's argument that clinics' impartial participation in surrogacy would be undermined by the fact that the commissioning couple would be paying for their services[113] could equally apply to infertility treatment. It is standard practice for assisted conception clinics to charge would-be patients for an initial consultation, and this is not thought to jeopardise the clinic's capacity to exercise its discretion to refuse treatment.

A surrogacy licensing authority was also rejected by the Brazier Report on the grounds that the small number of surrogate births do not justify the expense of a new regulatory agency.[114] And given Brazier's proposed prohibition on payments other than actual expenses, the number of surrogacy births is expected to decrease, thus bolstering Brazier's contention that a new licensing authority would be "an excessive reaction to current concerns".[115] Instead the Brazier Committee's preferred option is a new Surrogacy Act which would provide that all agencies involved in surrogacy should be required to be registered by the UK Health Departments, and operate in accordance with a statutory Code of Practice to be drawn up by the UK Health Departments in consultation with other relevant bodies.[116] The Code of Practice would be binding upon registered agencies, but Brazier *et al* also envisage that it should be consulted as a statement of good practice in surrogacy arrangements between friends or family members,[117] and that relevant parts of it could be incorporated into the HFEA Code of Practice and thus be binding upon clinics providing IVF surrogacy and assisted insemination.[118]

In addition, the Brazier Report envisages provision in the Code of Practice for the compiling of statistics and for research into the outcomes of surrogacy arrangements.[119] The Code of Practice would also contain details of the allowable expenses, specify safe insemination procedures; have minimum counselling and information requirements, set criteria for the selection of both commissioning couples and surrogate mothers[120] and draw up a model "memorandum

---

[113] Brazier, 1999a, p. 182.

[114] Brazier *et al* estimate that there are between 100–180 surrogacy arrangements each year, and 50–80 surrogacy births (Brazier *et al* 1998, para. 6.22).

[115] Brazier *et al* 1998, para. 6.22.

[116] Michael Freeman argues that given the small number of surrogacy arrangements, Brazier's proposal for decentralisation makes little sense (Freeman, 1999, p. 11).

[117] Brazier *et al* 1998, para. 7.18.

[118] Brazier *et al* 1998, para. 7.19.

[119] Brazier *et al* 1998, para. 6.26.

[120] Such as the suggestion in the Brazier Report that "the surrogate should have given birth and have living with her at least one child of her own" (Brazier *et al* 1998, para. 8.8).

of understanding"[121] between the parties.[122] The Code of Practice might stipulate a minimum age for surrogate mothers,[123] a minimum interval to elapse between pregnancies,[124] and a maximum number of times that any woman could undergo a surrogate pregnancy.[125] Brazier *et al* would prefer that a woman acts as a surrogate mother on one occasion only, unless providing a sibling for an existing child.[126] The Report also advocates raising the minimum age for commissioning couples to 21,[127] and setting a maximum age limit.[128]

The Brazier Report further recommends that the Code of Practice explicitly states that the welfare of the child must be the "paramount" concern of all parties, and that participation in surrogacy arrangements must be conditional upon establishing that both the surrogate and the commissioning couple have given the requisite consideration to the child's welfare[129] and to the impact the surrogate pregnancy may have upon the surrogate's own children.[130] The use of the word "paramount" in relation to the child's welfare is, however, problematic. The paramountcy principle means that the child's welfare is not just the most important consideration, but that it must determine the course of action to be followed.[131] Given the emphasis in the Brazier report on the parallel need to protect the surrogate mother, its use of the paramountcy principle is puzzling. If

---

[121]   The memorandum should define and clarify the expectations of the parties. Brazier *et al* propose, in para. 8.12, that it "should record the parties' arrangements to secure the future welfare of the child, including agreements about contact between the surrogate and the child and/or what the child is to be told about his or her origins. It should address how pregnancy is to be established and what screening processes pre-conceptually and pre-natally are agreed to safeguard the health of the surrogate and the child". Additionally "issues relating to the conduct of pregnancy should be addressed, such as any undertaking the surrogate may have offered in relation to smoking, alcohol, diet and anti-natal care. Arrangements for the commissioning couple to keep in contact with and provide support for the surrogate in the course of pregnancy must be spelled out. What arrangements will follow the birth for the child to be entrusted to the couple, and how the couple will acquire joint parental responsibility in relation to the child should be agreed. What is to happen in certain contingencies such as the detection of fetal abnormality, miscarriage, stillbirth, the birth of a disabled child, or injury to or the death of the surrogate herself should be agreed. Arrangements for the provision of life and disability cover for the surrogate should be included" (para. 8.13).

[122]   Brazier *et al*, 1998, para. 6.25.

[123]   The Brazier Report advocates a minimum age of 21 (Brazier *et al* 1998, para. 8.8).

[124]   The Brazier Report advocates a minimum period of 2 years (Brazier *et al* 1998, para. 8.8).

[125]   Brazier *et al*, 1998, para. 7.20.

[126]   Brazier *et al*, 1998, para. 8.8.

[127]   Currently no-one under 18 may apply for a parental order, raising this to 21 would bring surrogacy into line with adoption. But Michael Freeman argues "it is inconceivable that people not at least in their twenties would contemplate surrogacy. I have my doubts as to the necessity to specify an age at all" (Freeman, 1999, p. 15).

[128]   Brazier *et al*, 1998, para. 8.4. Though no age is proposed in the report, so there is no consideration of whether surrogacy could be provided to post-menopausal women.

[129]   "The commissioning couple must be able to demonstrate that they are able to care for the child and have adequately considered questions of continuing contact between the surrogate and the child and whether, how and when the child will be informed of the circumstances of his or her birth. . . . Where a couple resort to surrogacy because the intending mother suffers from a medical condition making pregnancy dangerous to her, there must be clear evidence that nonetheless she is able to rear the child" (Brazier *et al* 1998, para. 8.4).

[130]   Brazier *et al* 1998, para. 8.5.

[131]   Children Act 1989 s.1(1). See further Reece, 1996b.

the child's welfare were effectively the only relevant matter, there would be little scope for taking the surrogate mother's interests into account. And at other points in the Brazier Report, the Committee appear to endorse a rather more limited version of the "welfare principle" in which the child's best interests are the "highest priority".[132] This latter formulation in which a child's welfare is the most important, but not the only consideration, would be consistent with the Parental Order regulations and the Adoption Act both of which, in contrast to the Children Act 1989, also make the child's best interests the *first*, but not the paramount consideration.

The new Act would continue the non-enforceability of surrogacy contracts, and the prohibition on advertising and involvement of commercial agencies, and new provisions would specify which of the surrogate mother's expenses could legitimately be reimbursed by the commissioning couple.[133] There would be a revised procedure for granting parental orders to commissioning couples[134] after application to the High Court,[135] including an express provision making access to parental orders conditional upon *full compliance* with the statutory rules.[136] Their ineligibility for a parental order would mean that a couple who had made an illegal payment could no longer argue that the order would nevertheless be in the child's best interests. Guardians *ad litem* would

---

[132] Brazier *et al* 1998, paras. 4.46 and 4.50.

[133] Documentary evidence would be required (para. 5.24), and the allowable expenses would have to fall into one of the following categories (para. 5.25):

  (i)   maternity clothing
  (ii)   healthy food
  (iii) domestic help
  (iv)   counselling fees
  (v)   legal fees
  (vi)   life and disability insurance
  (vii) travel to and from hospital or clinic
  (viii) telephone and postal expenses
  (ix)   overnight accommodation
  (x)   child care to attend hospital/clinic
  (xi)   medical expenses
  (xii) ovulation and pregnancy tests
  (xiii) insemination and IVF costs
  (xiv) medicines and vitamins

Similarly, although the Brazier Report would allow surrogate mothers to be compensated for actual loss of earnings, it envisages that such payments would in practice be minimal since they would be confined to the difference between the surrogate mother's usual earnings and state benefits. Again documentary proof would be required. The loss of potential earnings would not be compensated (para. 5.26).

[134] Both members of the couple must have lived in the United Kingdom for at least 12 months immediately prior to their application (Brazier *et al*, 1998, para. 7.24).

[135] Brazier *et al* found that the "current arrangements whereby magistrates may be confronted at random with one or two applications for parental orders are unsatisfactory." Accordingly, they suggest that approval of a surrogacy arrangement should be given only "by judges of the highest experience." Centralising applications in the High Court would, they argue, "result in the development of the necessary expertise by a small group of judges and would allow similarly for a small panel of Guardians to specialise in surrogacy" (Brazier *et al* 1998, para. 7.24).

[136] Brazier *et al* 1998, para. 7.3.

be given additional powers to investigate whether unlawful payments had been made, and courts would not be able to retrospectively authorise payments on the grounds that the welfare of the child demanded the making of an order.[137] Instead couples who had made payments other than the permitted and fully documented expenses would be required to go through the ordinary adoption process in order to become the legal parents of the child.

In addition to their powers to investigate the making of unlawful payments, the powers of guardians *ad litem* would be further strengthened to enable them to detect arrangements where there is in fact no genetic link with the "commissioning" couple. At present there is a suspicion that some women who are already pregnant are persuaded to agree to give up the child at birth under cover of an apparent surrogacy arrangement, and that even when guardians *ad litem* suspect that there was no preconceptual agreement, they are powerless to prevent parental orders being made.[138] The new Act would give judges the power to order DNA tests, and without a genetic link there could be no eligibility for a parental order. Guardians *ad litem* would also be given powers to check criminal records to ensure that neither of the prospective parents has a previous record of offences against children.

Brazier *et al* rejected a suggestion that couples who had acted unlawfully should also be denied access to adoption. Although they accepted that it might be a more effective deterrent, the Report concluded that it could leave some children, unwanted by the surrogate mother, in an unacceptable legal limbo.[139] It has already been noted that it is possible for a child born following a surrogacy arrangement to be handed over to the commissioning couple without any formal transfer of legal parenthood. The non-availability of adoption would simply encourage more people to avoid acquiring full legal responsibility for "their" child. Similarly, Brazier *et al* rejected the criminalisation of unauthorised payments on the grounds first, that the child might be tainted by the criminality of their conception, and second, that it would provide a further incentive for couples to avoid acquiring any formal relationship with their child.[140]

The Brazier Committee's compromise solution to the problem of payments is, however, rather odd. Currently, in relation to both adoption and section 30 orders, the prohibition upon payments can be circumvented relatively easily by *post hoc* judicial approval. Brazier's proposal would remove one mechanism for the subsequent authorisation of payments, while leaving the other intact. Thus, it is at least arguable that their proposal would not end the *de facto* commercialisation of surrogacy, but rather would divert more couples towards the adoption process. Since applying for an adoption order is more cumbersome

---

[137] Brazier *et al*, 1998, para. 7.11.

[138] Brazier *et al*, 1998, para. 7.24.

[139] Brazier *et al*, 1998, para. 7.13.

[140] And although it would be a criminal offence for any non-registered organisation or individual to assist in the creation of a surrogacy arrangement, if neither the couple nor the surrogate were aware of this requirement, the making of a parental order would not be precluded (Brazier *et al*, 1998, para. 7.23).

and time-consuming than the section 30 procedure, the principal effects of Brazier's compromise position might therefore be longer delays and greater public expense. Given that it is the received wisdom that delays are prejudicial to children's welfare,[141] giving couples an incentive to avoid the streamlined surrogacy-specific procedure might be unwise. Moreover, the assumption underlying Brazier's proposal appears to be that the defects or inconvenience of the adoption process might act as a deterrent to couples contemplating making unlawful payments. There are two problems with this. First, adoption should be a "service for children",[142] and children's interests are unlikely to be best served by a regulatory scheme that relies upon adoption being perceived to be second-best. Second, the imminent reform of adoption law will rightly be directed to eliminating some of the obstacles currently faced by potential adopters.[143] If adoption law reform successfully simplifies the adoption process, it will cease to operate as an incentive to comply with the prohibition upon payments, and there will be little point in retaining the separate section 30 procedure.

Thus far, we have seen that both the current regulatory structure, such as it is, and the latest proposals for reform rest upon the belief that surrogacy should not be encouraged. We need, therefore, to work out why there continues to be so much antipathy towards surrogacy. In the following section, I suggest that the arguments commonly used to justify restrictive regulation are weak. I challenge the assumption that family law offers the most appropriate model for the regulation of surrogacy, and argue instead that contract law's capacity to police the fairness of surrogacy arrangements has been overlooked. In common with my conclusions in the previous chapters, I believe that the regulation of surrogacy should start from the premise that, as far as possible, the law should respect individuals' reproductive decisions.

3. IS SURROGACY ACCEPTABLE?

The Brazier Report rehearsed the arguments for and against surrogacy described in the Warnock Report,[144] and concluded that in 1998 "across a wide

[141] Children Act 1989 s.1(2).
[142] Department of Health, 2000b.
[143] *Ibid.*
[144] In the Warnock Report, the arguments against surrogacy were that

(i) it amounts to third party intrusion into the marital relationship
(ii) the use of a woman's uterus for financial profit is inconsistent with human dignity
(iii) it distorts the relationship between the mother and child and might be psychologically damaging to the child
(iv) no woman should be asked to bear the risks of pregnancy for another person

The arguments in favour of surrogacy were that.

(i) those who regard it as degrading the sanctity of marriage need not take part, but should not restrict the freedoms of others

cont. over/

spectrum of opinion, we judge that the existence of surrogacy is now accepted".[145] However, the Brazier Report also proposes that "surrogacy should remain an option of the last resort available only to couples where the intending mother's condition renders pregnancy impossible or highly dangerous to her".[146] There has been a similar shift in position by the British Medical Association who in 1990 considered doctors' involvement in surrogacy to be "unethical".[147] Now the BMA's position is that surrogacy may be "an acceptable option of last resort"[148] for women suffering from a recognised clinical indication.[149] Similarly the Human Fertilisation and Embryology Authority's Code of Practice permits licensed clinics to become involved in surrogacy only where "it is physically impossible or highly undesirable for medical reasons for the commissioning mother to carry the child".[150] As we have seen both the current regulatory scheme and the Brazier Committee's proposals for reform reflect this official consensus that surrogacy should only ever be used as a last resort in the face of a woman's clinical inability to bear a child.[151] Is this prevailing hostility towards surrogacy is justified? In the following sections, I evaluate a variety of criticisms commonly levelled at the practice of surrogacy.

(ii)   it might not be degrading or commodifying, but instead a supremely altruistic act
(iii) the psychological risks are speculative, and already accepted in relation to adoption
(iv)   women should be entitled to choose to enter surrogacy arrangements

Michael Freeman contends that "the Warnock case against surrogacy is thin, distorted and unconvincing" (Freeman, 1989, p. 172).

[145] Brazier *et al*, 1998 para. 4.5.
[146] Brazier *et al*, 1998, para. 8.9.
[147] British Medical Association, 1990.
[148] British Medical Association, 1996. Although it should be noted that there are still disagreements within the medical profession about the acceptability of surrogacy. In *Briody* v. *St. Helen's & Knowsley Health Authority* [2000] 2 FCR 13, a case involving a woman claiming the costs of surrogacy as compensation for a negligently performed hysterectomy, Ebsworth J summarised the evidence of Lord Winston, who had told the court that "the majority of gynaecologists regard surrogacy as a rather questionable procedure", and that "the pendulum of opinion is swinging further and further away from surrogacy".
[149] The BMA suggests that surrogacy should only be an option where is it "impossible or highly undesirable" for the commissioning mother to carry a child (British Medical Association, 1996).
[150] HFEA Code of Practice 4th ed. July 1998, para. 3.20.
    The Bourn Hall Clinic's independent ethics committee has guidelines which limit its provision of IVF surrogacy to women in the following circumstances:

(i)   Total or partial absence of the uterus either of congenital origin or after surgery
(ii)   Repeated failure of IVF treatment, the clinicians must be satisfied that there is no reasonable prospect of success
(iii) Severe medical conditions incompatible with pregnancy
(iv)   Repeated miscarriage

(Brinsden *et al*, 2000, p. 924).
[151] Similarly, the Warnock committee unanimously agreed that surrogacy for convenience alone was "totally ethically unacceptable" (Warnock, 1984, para. 8.17).

(a) An Option of Last Resort?

If natural reproduction is possible and safe, it is difficult to imagine why anyone might contemplate engaging a surrogate mother. There is certainly no evidence[152] to support the common references to the "nightmare vision" of a world in which an underclass of breeder women produce offspring for the privileged classes.[153] Instead surrogacy is sought by couples and individuals for whom pregnancy and childbirth is infeasible.[154] Usually this is because a woman is physically unable to bear a child.[155] In addition to cases where pregnancy would be impossible as a result, for example, of a woman having no uterus, as we have seen, medical indications for surrogacy have more controversially included

---

[152] Brazier *et al* refer to the concern, raised in the Warnock report that surrogate mothers might be employed "where wealthy career women simply wished to avoid the inconvenience of pregnancy", and conclude "we have seen no evidence of such practices" (Brazier *et al*, 1998, para. 4.7).

[153] Patricia Spallone calls surrogacy "the use of women as breeders" (Spallone, 1989, p. 82). Gena Corea also describes surrogate mothers as "breeders" (Corea, 1985, p. 214), and suggests that full surrogacy facilitates the employment of third world women as fetal incubators (Corea, 1985 p.215). Martha Field argues that "a fully developed surrogacy system would doubtless include shipments of frozen sperm or embryos around the world to be implanted in Third World women at bargain rates" and "career women who want to be mothers (would) have the option of hiring another woman to gestate their child even if they themselves are fertile" (Field, 1993b, pp. 224, 226). Elsewhere Field suggests that "surrogacy-by choice could become such a norm that employers would pressure women to employ a surrogate rather than allow their own pregnancy to inconvenience their employer or impede their career. Employers might, for example, confer health insurance that would cover hiring a surrogate instead of giving women maternity leave" (Field, 1990, pp. 30–1). Janice Raymond invokes the spectre of "an international market in surrogacy where women of color could easily be exploited and hired at a lower rate than the current market price" (Raymond, 1993, p. 69). Katha Pollitt suggests that one consequence of surrogacy might be that "enterprising poor women take up childbearing as a cottage industry and conceive expressly for the purpose of selling the baby to the highest bidder" (Pollitt, 1995, p. 76). The reference is usually made to Margaret Atwood's novel *The Handmaid's Tale* in which fertile women become breeders or "handmaids" for the ruling elite, see for example Thomson, 1998, p. 125; de Gama, 1993, p. 127; Tong, 1995, p. 66.

[154] Brinsden *et al* argue against banning surrogacy because "for the small group of women for whom this is the only available treatment of their infertility, it would be unreasonable and unfair to do so" (Brinsden *et al*, 2000, p. 927).

[155] Full surrogacy could be used where a woman produces eggs but is unable to carry a child. This might be the result of a natural physical incapacity where, for example, she does not have a uterus. Women who undergo hysterectomies while still of reproductive age may have some of their eggs frozen for use in a surrogate pregnancy. Alternatively, pregnancy might be too hazardous due to her history of high blood pressure, kidney disease or because of previous ectopic pregnancies or repeated miscarriages. For example, in the (in)famous American case *In the matter of Baby M* (1988) 537 A 2d 1227, Elizabeth Stern had been warned that pregnancy would aggravate her multiple sclerosis.

Partial surrogacy might be needed by women who do not produce eggs and cannot gestate a pregnancy.

repeated failed IVF cycles.[156] Less frequently,[157] surrogacy might be employed by transsexuals,[158] or gay or single men.[159]

Why do the HFEA, the BMA and the Brazier Report all distinguish between the use of surrogacy by women who are clinically incapable of bearing a child, and its use by people whose childlessness is the result of not being in a heterosexual relationship? Why is surrogacy perceived to be less acceptable in the latter situation? Of course, there are those who believe that procreation is only acceptable within the heterosexual, two-parent family unit,[160] but some people's preference for conventional family norms does not in itself offer a compelling justification to restrict other individuals' reproductive options. Since the proportion of all children who are brought up by both of their biological parents living in a stable marital relationship continues to decrease, the deliberate separation of biological and social parenthood is not confined to surrogacy, but is actually experienced much more frequently by children conceived in the normal way.[161]

(b) Why don't "they" adopt instead?

As we saw in the previous chapter, there is a strain of thought that criticises infertile couples for a narcissistic or egotistical desire to bear a child genetically related to one or both of them. Given that there are thousands of disadvantaged and unwanted children who would benefit immeasurably from being adopted, there are those who believe that it is immoral to devote any energy or resources to producing more babies.[162] According to these critics, adoption is a response

---

[156] Brazier *et al* state that "establishing a pregnancy in a healthy and provenly fertile surrogate might be perceived as preferable to continued attempts at IVF. Whether such cases constitute use of surrogacy as "a last resort" where pregnancy is impossible may be open to question." (Brazier *et al*, 1998, para. 3.24).

[157] Van den Akker 1999, p. 263 According to R Alto Charo less than 1% of people seeking surrogacy arrangements are homosexual (Alto Charo, 1990, p. 89). Of course when surrogacy is used by gay men, there tends to be intense media interest (see further Barton, 1996).

[158] *Noyes* v. *Thrane* No. CF7614 (LA Super Ct 1981) involved a contract between a surrogate mother and a commissioning couple in which the "wife" was subsequently revealed to be a male to female transsexual. During her pregnancy the surrogate had changed her mind, and the couple withdrew from an action for custody on the grounds that revelations about Mrs Noyes' sex change operation would be likely to jeopardise their case.

[159] For examples see Keane and Breo, 1983.

[160] Michael Freeman quotes Peter Bruinvels MP in his contribution to the Parliamentary debates prior to the passing of the Surrogacy Arrangements Act. The Bill would, he argued "preserve family life, stabilise society and do away with this unnatural and unfortunate practice which has sickened so many decent-living and family-loving people" (Freeman, 1989, p. 165).

[161] John Robertson suggests that surrogacy's "threat to the family is trivial compared to the rapid changes in family structure now occurring for social, economic and demographic reasons" (Robertson, 1990, p. 160).

[162] Martha Field, for example, has said that the real social harm of surrogacy is that it involves creating babies "at the expense of babies who already exist and need homes" (Field, 1992, p. 1592). In responding to the argument that surrogacy may be a preferred treatment for infertility, Nadine Taub has suggested that "we must make plain that adoption, foster care, step-parenthood and numerous other less formal arrangements offer equivalent possibilities" (Taub, 1990, 229). In her discussion of the American case *In the matter of Baby M* (1988) 537 A 2d 1227, Katha Pollitt criticises

to the child's less than ideal situation, whereas in surrogacy the "less than ideal" circumstances result from a deliberate and premeditated arrangement. Adoption then can be presented as a way of promoting the best interests of a child who has already been born, whereas surrogacy is perceived to be only in the self-regarding interest of the infertile couple.[163] Yet it is surely overly simplistic to suggest that adopters are always only motivated by altruism, and that commissioning parents are universally selfish and egotistical. Nor, as we saw in the previous chapter, is it clear why infertile individuals should be responsible for the world's neglected children, especially since fertile people's preference for having their own biological children is not similarly condemned.

(c) Harm to Children

The possibility that children may be scarred by the knowledge that their gestational mother gave them away, in return for money, shortly after their birth is commonly cited as another reason to discourage surrogacy arrangements.[164] Being "given away" by one's gestational mother, especially in return for payment is thus assumed to be qualitatively worse than learning that your genetic father was a sperm donor, or that your genetic mother was an egg donor, or that you were conceived outside of your mother's body. It is, perhaps, interesting that speculation about possible psychological harm to children tends to focus on the effect of discovering that one's birth was the result of a *commercial* transaction. The Brazier Report appears to assume that there would be less risk of emotional trauma following surrogacy arrangements between friends or relatives, despite the inevitable possibility of ambiguities in family roles following intra-familial surrogacy.[165]

There is little information about the long-term impact of surrogacy arrangements upon children, so any argument against surrogacy based upon the possibility of psychological harm to children is largely speculative. There is, as we saw in chapter five, a growing body of research into the psychological development of children conceived as a result of assisted conception. The results appear

---

the commissioning couple, the Sterns, because they "did not, in fact, seriously investigate adoption". In an essay in which she mentions her own experience of pregnancy, she is scathing about the Stern's desire to have a child genetically related to one of them (Pollitt, 1995, p.79).

[163] Nelson and Nelson, 1989.

[164] Wertheimer, 1997. In her introduction to the subsequent publication of the Warnock Report as a book, Mary Warnock says that the committee's unanimous disapproval of surrogacy was "largely because of possible consequences for the child" (Warnock, 1985, p. xii). In the Warnock Report, surrogacy was said to be "degrading to the child . . . since, for practical purposes, the child will have been bought for money" (Warnock, 1984, para. 8.11).

[165] For example in the UK in 1996 Edith Jones gave birth to a baby girl after being implanted with an embryo created using the eggs from her daughter and the sperm of her son-in-law. This child's gestational mother was her genetic and social grandmother (Gould, 1996). M Wright argues that adoption following "domestic" surrogacy arrangements may in fact be more problematic because of its potential to confuse family relationships (Wright, 1986).

to show that the children are functioning at least as well as children conceived naturally. Research into the experiences of adopted children appears to show that the younger children are at the time of the adoption, the less likely they are to suffer from psychological difficulties. Since children born through surrogacy are generally handed over at birth, it might be supposed that surrogacy would have comparatively little impact upon children's long term wellbeing. It is impossible to judge whether continued contact between the surrogate mother and the commissioning parents might be confusing for children. Because open adoption is generally confined to older children who already have a good relationship with their birth family, research showing its potential psychological benefits has little relevance for surrogacy.

It is often suggested that the surrogate mother's children sense of security might be undermined by witnessing their mother giving away a child.[166] There is no evidence to support or discount this claim, and unless children are likely to suffer significant harm, the law normally assumes that parents are best able to make decisions about their children's upbringing.[167] Accordingly, without evidence of a risk of harm to her existing children, a surrogate mother must be assumed to be the best judge of a surrogacy arrangement's impact upon their wellbeing. Further, as Lori Andrews points out, feminists should be particularly wary of embracing this criticism of surrogacy too enthusiastically since an identical argument could be mounted against relatively late abortions. If we believe, as I think we must, that a woman is capable of explaining to her children why their expected new sibling is dead, we must also trust surrogate mothers' capacity to help their children through the process of surrogacy. Speculation about the psychological risks of surrogacy is common, evidence to support these allegations is rather thin on the ground. Yet despite the lack of evidence of psychological harm either to children born through surrogacy, or to the surrogate's existing children, the Brazier report judged that "there is a clear potential risk to the welfare of such children".[168] And although Brazier *et al* admitted that they had found no clear proof that children's welfare is endangered by surrogacy, they nonetheless decided that surrogacy should be restricted in part because of the possibility that it *might* cause psychological harm to children.[169] They argue that preventing a particular conception does not cause harm to a child, because there is no child who is capable of suffering through their non-existence. So while denying an infertile couple access to surrogacy may cause them distress, this "harm" is, according to Brazier *et al*, outweighed by the risk of harm to future children.

---

[166]   Wertheimer, 1997.

[167]   Children Act 1989 s. 31(2).

[168]   Brazier *et al*, 1998, para. 4.16.

[169]   "we do not have to show certainty of major harm to potential children before we are justified, either through personal decision or legislative restriction, in avoiding conceptions on grounds of risk to the welfare of the child" (Brazier *et al*, 1998, para. 4.29).

It is not self-evident that a speculative risk to future children is a more import-ant consideration than the distress of involuntary childlessness. And without equivalent concern for the welfare of *all* future children, this argument reveals discriminatory tendencies similar to those embodied in the rules governing access to infertility treatment that we considered in the previous chapter. So, for example, there may be evidence that children born to parents who are alcoholics face an increased risk of emotional and behavioural problems, and if we were to prevent two alcoholics from conceiving there would, in the words of Brazier, be "no person who suffers from not being alive".[170] Yet the reproductive freedom and bodily autonomy of two alcoholics undoubtedly trumps our concern for the wellbeing of their future children. It seems inequitable that the ease with which the state can prevent procreation among people with a pre-existing biological incapacity should be treated as if it were in itself a sufficient reason for inter-fering with their reproductive choices

People who engage in surrogacy arrangements only do so because they have a strong desire to have a child. So unlike many children conceived naturally, these children may have the psychological advantage of knowing that their birth was planned and wanted. But regardless of where the balance of risk lies, the most compelling answer to this criticism of surrogacy is that we do not burden fertile people with the requirement that they demonstrate that they are capable of producing psychologically well-balanced individuals before they conceive. If protecting the civil liberties of the fertile population prohibits us from policing conception among individuals whom we *know* are likely to cause psychological harm to their offspring, it seems illogical that a possibly groundless fear of harm to children born through surrogacy should justify its prohibition.

(d) Risk of Exploitation

There are two different sorts of exploitation of which surrogacy stands accused. The first derives from the philosophical objection to treating another human being as a means to an end. Any departure from this Kantian imperative, includ-ing a case where an individual chooses to use themselves as a means to another's end, is sometimes assumed to be morally objectionable. Hence, there are those who would argue that in surrogacy, the surrogate is being treated as a means to the ends of the infertile couple, and the child is treated as a means to the ends of both the surrogate and the commissioning couple.[171] If it is always wrong to treat oneself or someone else as a means to another's ends, and if surrogacy involves so treating someone, then, so the argument goes, surrogacy must be

---

[170] Brazier *et al*, 1998, para. 4.28.
[171] For example, Herbert Krimmel says that "what is fundamentally unethical about surrogate mother arrangements is that they, of necessity, treat the creation of a person as the means to the grat-ification of the interests of others, rather than respect the child as an end in himself" (Krimmel, 1992, p. 58).

condemned.[172] Of course, as we saw in the previous chapter, an absolute prohibition upon treating one person as a means to the ends of another is, in practice, infeasible,[173] otherwise we should have to forbid the donation of sperm, eggs, embryos, non-vital organs, human tissue and blood, and it would be impossible to justify non-therapeutic research on human subjects. If it is *sometimes* legitimate to use one person's body in order to relieve another person's suffering, then we cannot rely on an unqualified application of the Kantian imperative in order to justify proscribing surrogacy arrangements.

Further, it is not obvious that the commissioning couple would be treating the child as the means to their own selfish ends. In fact, given that many fertile people may have children for self-regarding reasons, such as trying to save a failing relationship, or anticipating some desired change in their social status, it is not clear that we can single out an infertile person's desire to have a child as necessarily more selfish than that of a fertile person.[174] The circumstances of a child's conception do not necessarily determine whether or not parents are capable of respecting their child's right to be treated as an end rather than a means.

Most critics of surrogacy have, however, tended to accuse surrogacy of being exploitative in the second sense: that is they believe that the very nature of a surrogacy contract is such that the risk that there will be actual exploitation, chiefly of the surrogate mother, is too great. According to some commentators, simply offering a woman money to bear a child for someone else creates the possibility of exploitation. Both the existence of a financial incentive and the nature of the transaction are therefore criticised for inducing poor women to become surrogates, and for keeping them to an agreement that they may find insupportably difficult.

The common disparity between the economic circumstances of commissioning parents and surrogate mothers is often cited to support allegations of exploitation.[175] That surrogate motherhood may be chosen by women with

[172] The Warnock Report appeared to adopt this position: "that people should treat others as a means to their own ends, however desirable the consequences must always be liable to moral objection" (Warnock, 1984, para. 8.17).

[173] In the previous chapter I cited John Harris's claim that the Kantian imperative "is so vague and so open to selective interpretation and its scope for application is consequently so limited, that its utility as one of the 'fundamental principles' of modern bioethical thought . . . is virtually nil" (Harris, 1999c, p. 68).

[174] Although there are some who would go this far, Herbert Krimmel, for example says that "surrogate mother arrangements . . . are condemned because they cannot, by their very nature, rise to an ethical treatment of children that is possible for natural parents" (Krimmel, 1992, p. 60). To suggest that fertile people have a monopoly upon the ethical treatment of children seems to me to wholly part company with reality.

[175] See further Farquhar, 1996, p. 152. According to Beverley Horsburgh, less than 35% of surrogate mothers in the United States attended college, and 60% earn less than $30,000 per year (Horsburgh, 1998, p. 37). Katha Politt argues that "women to whom $10,000 is a significant amount of money are the ones who live closest to the edge and have the fewest alternative ways of boosting their income in a crisis" (Pollitt, 1995, p. 71). Janice Raymond says that "most so-called surrogates arrive in court from a background of economic disadvantage or dead-endedness" (Raymond, 1993, p. 81).

The Brazier Report states that "payments may operate as an inducement to enter into surrogacy for women suffering financial hardship. There is evidence that the majority of surrogates are significantly poorer than commissioning couples and have relatively low educational attainments. A

limited alternative opportunities for earning money is seen by some as raising the possibility, or even the inevitability[176] of coercion and/or exploitation. In practice, there is little evidence of exploitation of surrogate mothers by commissioning couples,[177] nevertheless, Brazier *et al* found that payments to surrogates "create a danger that women will give a less than free and fully informed consent to act as a surrogate".[178]

For certain feminists, surrogacy arrangements exist only because there are women sufficiently economically disempowered to find becoming a surrogate an attractive way to earn money.[179] According to this argument, it is gender inequality which "forces" women to resort to supplementing their income through surrogacy, so the removal of inequalities between men and women would effectively end surrogacy as an economic exchange. Yet financial hardship is not confined to women and it is extremely unlikely that greater equality between the sexes would remove all the other factors which lead some people to be worse-off than others, and hence more likely to accept underpaid and perhaps unpleasant employment. It may be true that surrogate mothers might prefer to have an abundant range of convenient, well-paid and fulfilling jobs from which to choose, although there are never going to be many other sources of income that simultaneously enable women to be full-time carers of their own children. Thus, if surrogacy is preferable to the other options available to would-be surrogate mothers, denying them this source of income and satisfaction because the lack of alternative employment opportunities is to be deplored, seems perverse.

There are undoubtedly women who choose to become surrogate mothers in order to earn money, but, as Michael Freeman points out, we are untroubled by the possibility that a fertility specialist may have chosen his or her profession for personal aggrandisement or financial gain.[180] Moreover while money may influence a woman's decision to become a surrogate mother, it is seldom

---

number are unemployed, unsupported by a partner and responsible for children of their own. 'Professional' surrogacy may appear to be an attractive option for women in these circumstances" (Brazier *et al*, 1998 para. 4.19). They go on to say "we . . . have reservations about facilitating a situation whereby some relatively poor and less educated women are having babies for their wealthier and better educated counterparts" (para. 5.17).

[176] Beverley Horsburgh says that "since . . . Black women in our society exercise little if any power in the public sphere, it is difficult to justify enforcing a surrogacy contract on the grounds that the Black surrogate has made a meaningful choice" (Horsburgh, 1998, p. 52).

[177] Appleton, 1993.

[178] Brazier *et al*, 1998, p. i.

[179] Helene Ragone has said that "if American society accorded women equal access to education, employment, and other related opportunities, fewer women would elect to participate in surrogacy as a means by which to attain satisfaction and fulfilment" (Ragone, 1994, p. 3). Janice Raymond has argued that "a legal recognition of male dominance, thus a legal recognition of the ways in which women have been channelled into surrogacy and motherhood at any cost to themselves, is a necessary legal precondition to women's equality" (Raymond, 1993, p. 81).

[180] Freeman, 1999, p. 4.

her only reason.[181] Women often become surrogate mothers after being affected by the plight of infertile friends or family members. In Lori Andrews' interviews with surrogate mothers, 75 per cent found the most rewarding aspect of surrogacy to be helping to create a family.[182] Andrews found that women who had enjoyed parenting themselves "describe tremendous psychic benefits from helping someone meet a joyous life goal".[183] Similarly Phillip Parker's study found that women willing to become surrogate mothers had several motives: in addition to finding the financial rewards appealing, some women enjoyed being pregnant, and others gained satisfaction from giving the "gift of life" to another woman.[184] Fisher and Gillman's follow up interviews with surrogate mothers discovered that the majority of them had found surrogacy to be a positive and fulfilling experience.[185] Even the Brazier Report acknowledges that "many women have found being a surrogate an emotionally rewarding experience, with no obvious ill effects on them or their families".[186] Of course, many feminists would argue that surrogate mothers' claims to have enjoyed the experience are inauthentic and the product of illegitimate social conditioning.[187] Yet to return to a theme from the first chapter of this book, all of our preferences are inevitably shaped by the context in which we form them and this insight does not necessarily make those preferences less real or valuable. It is not clear to me why a surrogate mother's assertion that she gained satisfaction from helping an infertile couple to have a child should be less worthy of respect or treated as less genuine than a university lecturer's claim to enjoy writing a book about reproduction and law.

[181] *In re Adoption Application* [1987] Fam 81, Latey J acknowledged that Mrs B, who became a surrogate mother, "was deeply and genuinely moved about the plight of childless couples". After placing an advertisement in a magazine advertising her willingness to become a surrogate mother, she had responses from other couples, including one who offered a "very large sum of money". She worked full-time and she and her husband were comfortably off, money was not her motivation. The guardian *ad litem*'s report stated "The mother does not appear to have been primarily motivated in entering into the arrangements by financial considerations. She appears to have felt strongly that through a surrogacy arrangement she could offer an important service to a childless couple and to have regarded the money mainly as the equivalent of compensation for loss of earnings while pregnant".

Mrs B said that she wanted to help a childless couple with whom she could be friendly, empathise and have a rapport. She declined the couple offering the very large sum in favour of Mr and Mrs A with whom she agreed a payment of £10,000. Although initial payments of £5000 were made, the mother refused to accept the balance because she had made money from a book she had written under a pseudonym about her experience as a surrogate mother.

[182] Andrews, 1995, p. 2353.

[183] Andrews, 1995, p. 2354. Eric Blyth's study of a small sample of British surrogate mothers found that any distress experienced as a result of parting from the child was accompanied by feelings of satisfaction from having helped the commissioning couple to achieve parenthood (Blyth, 1994).

[184] Parker, 1983.

[185] Fisher and Gillman, 1991.

[186] Brazier *et al*, 1998, para. 4.26.

[187] Janice Raymond suggests that surrogate mothers are recruited by "using the appeal of altruism as a seasoning process—a gentle strategy of procurement casting surrogacy as a supreme act of female giving" (Raymond, 1993, p. 44).

Those who argue that surrogacy is exploitative are not only concerned about inducements to enter into surrogacy arrangements, they also suggest that it is simply not possible for a woman's consent to bear a child for someone else to be fully informed and entirely voluntary.[188] Their anxiety is principally that before conception, a woman cannot know whether she will want or be able to hand over the child to whom she has given birth. Dion Farquhar describes this assumption of women's victimisation and lack of judgement as a "fundamentalist feminist analysis".[189] To argue that a woman may be incapable of agreeing to give up a child before its conception[190] may also reflect both a particular image of the indissoluble bond created during pregnancy, and the presumption that hormonal changes associated with pregnancy inhibit rational choice.[191] It is interesting that a woman is presumed able to give a valid consent both to give up a child for adoption six weeks after its birth,[192] and to destroy a fetus during its gestation. Why should her pre-conception decision to hand over the child at birth automatically be flawed?

Feminists who claim to be suspicious about whether any woman would ever genuinely consent to giving away a child to whom she has given birth risk amplifying the anti-feminist message that pregnancy automatically creates an unconditional bond of love with the developing fetus. The suggestion that women are biologically incapable of deciding in advance to bear a child for someone else implies that women's capacity for careful and reasoned decision-making is inevitably impaired by their maternal instincts.[193] Arguing that the experience of pregnancy and giving birth creates inalienable duties that no woman would relinquish unless coerced embodies a curiously traditional

[188] Katha Pollitt argues that "in areas of profound human feeling, you cannot promise because you cannot know . . . When Mary Beth Whitehead signed her contract, she was promising something it is not in anyone's power to promise: not to fall in love with her baby" (Pollitt, 1995, p. 73–4). In a similar vein Elizabeth Anderson believes that the surrogate mother is required "to repress whatever parental love she feels for the child . . . a form of alienated labor" (Anderson, 1990, p. 81).

[189] Farquhar, 1996, p. 152.

[190] For example, Brazier *et al* say that "in our judgement, surrogacy does carry some unpredictable risks which become fully evident only after an agreement has been entered into, perhaps even some time after the baby has been handed over to the commissioning parents" (Brazier *et al*, 1998, para. 4.25).

[191] Lori Andrews urges that feminists should be wary of hormone-based arguments suggesting women cannot be expected to abide by their contracts because of the hormonal changes of pregnancy (Andrews 1990 p. 173). And Carmel Shalev argues that "the paternalistic refusal to force the surrogate mother to keep her word denies the notion of female reproductive agency and reinforces the traditional perception of women as imprisoned in the subjectivity of their wombs" (Shalev, 1989, p. 121).

[192] Adoption Act 1976 s. 16(4).

[193] Marjorie Shultz suggests that the unenforceability of surrogacy contracts "expresses the idea that the biological experience of motherhood 'trumps' all other considerations . . . it exalts a woman's experience of pregnancy and childbirth over her formation of emotional, intellectual and interpersonal decisions and expectations, as well as over others' reliance on the commitments she has earlier made" (Shultz, 1990, p. 384).

conception of motherhood.[194] The biological essentialism[195] of the argument that motherhood is a universal natural fact, determined only by women's unique relationship with the fetus that they carry is radically at odds with the conventional feminist position that motherhood, as traditionally understood, is socially constructed. Taken to its logical conclusion, this "feminist" suggestion that motherhood is always indivisible, and that a sacred[196] bond of love between mother and child is symbiotically created during gestation would endanger access to abortion[197] and lend support to the regressive belief that childrearing is women's natural destiny.

Similarly, the analogy that Andrea Dworkin draws between surrogacy and prostitution is meant to invoke the powerful negative image of women being forced to sell their sexual or reproductive capacity.[198] Yet it also comes close to the conservative idea that women's sexual and procreative lives should be confined to the private sphere, and driven only by altruism and care for others. For a woman to reject the biological bond of motherhood, and simultaneously to combine economic and altruistic motives may be deeply disturbing to the conservative right, but it is perhaps bizarre that feminists should be equally contemptuous.

Moreover, if informed consent to a surrogacy arrangement must be a logical impossibility until the woman has actually given birth and knows how she feels, consents given to a range of other as yet unexperienced things, such as sterilisation or gender-reassignment surgery, or perhaps even marriage must also be *prima facie* invalid. In practice the proportion of women who regret agreeing to become a surrogate has proved to be less than the proportion of women who subsequently change their mind about sterilisation.[199] Comparatively high rates of regret are not considered a sufficient justification to prohibit people from

---

[194] For example Margaret Brinig says "women are not programmed to have children and then part with them" (Brinig, 1995, p. 2384). Elizabeth Bartholet warns that "parenting is or should be about relationship, about holding on to and nurturing those to whom we are connected rather than letting go" (Bartholet, 1993, p. 227).
As Derek Morgan points out, this argument involves "the uncritical assumption that pregnancy is the only fit state of preparation for the role of caring and nurturing a young child and providing it with a loving and caring environment in which to grow up" (Morgan, 1988, p. 220).

[195] In her criticism of the *Johnson* v. *Calvert* case, a full surrogacy case discussed above in footnote 20, Martha Field appears to argue that women are biologically programmed to assume the primary care-taking role by suggesting that one reason why the birth mother should have priority over the genetic mother is that "she has the capacity to breastfeed the child" (Field, 1993b, p. 228).

[196] Martha Field suggests that "having a baby is . . . (an) almost sacred thing" (Field, 1990, p. 27).

[197] There is a strong similarity between the position of radical feminists and the pro-life lobby. Nuala Scarisbrick from the anti-abortion organisation Life says "women . . . bond with the child in the womb and there is bound to be an adverse affect [*sic*] when the child is given up. Surrogacy devalues motherhood" (quoted in Watson-Smyth, 1997).

[198] Dworkin, 1983. And according to Katha Pollit, "take away the mothers' delusion that they are making babies for other women, and what you have left is what, in cold, hard, fact, we already have: the limited-use purchase of women's bodies by men—reproductive prostitution" (Pollit, 1995, p. 69). Thomas Shannon agrees that "in renting her uterus the surrogate is assuming the role of a reproductive prostitute . . . like the prostitute, the surrogate takes a capacity intimate to herself, objectifies it, prices it, and puts it on the market" (Shannon, 1988, p. 152).

[199] Andrews, 1995, p. 2351.

consenting to sterilisation, rather they draw attention to the need for full and intelligible pre-operation advice.

A further strand to this argument from exploitation is that the risks associated with pregnancy and childbirth are so grave that we should be alerted to the improbability that a woman would freely and voluntarily assume them for someone else's benefit.[200] Maternal morbidity is, however, now extremely rare, and although pregnancy is not completely without risk, it is considerably less hazardous than some other jobs where we do not question the employee's capacity to voluntarily accept the possibility of harm.[201] Nevertheless the possibility that payments might induce some women to enter into repeated surrogacy arrangements against their better judgement is cited as a further reason to restrict the practice of surrogacy.[202] These critics of surrogacy are invoking the rather dubious device of "necessarily impaired consent",[203] which differs markedly from a more appropriate case-by-case consideration of whether, in any particular situation, autonomous decision making has been compromised by the existence of, for example, duress or undue influence.

There is an interesting parallel between this contention that the surrogate's apparent agreement cannot reflect her true will, and feminist scepticism about the authenticity of the commissioning mother's desire for a child.[204] Just as surrogate mothers are presented as suffering from false consciousness in agreeing to take part in an arrangement to which, so the argument goes, no woman with any control over her life would consent, so infertile women who seek to employ surrogate mothers are similarly accused of being deluded in the importance they attach to becoming a mother.[205]

It is significant that concern that the surrogate mother may be pressurised into entering a surrogacy arrangement derives principally from the existence of

---

[200] For example, Katha Pollitt asks: "how can it be acceptable to pay a woman to risk her life, health and fertility so that a man can have his own biological child" (Pollitt, 1995, p. 71).

[201] The Brazier report admits that "even where there is risk in an occupation (e.g. working as a solider, or in the police or fire service) payment does not of itself necessarily constitute exploitation" (Brazier *et al*, 1998, para. 4.24).

[202] Brazier *et al*, 1998, para. 5.17.

[203] There are a few other situations where doubts about the validity of anyone's consent to a particular procedure have resulted in its blanket prohibition. For example, under the Prohibition of Female Circumcision Act 1985 a patient cannot give a valid consent to female circumcision; and the Human Organ Transplants Act 1989 prohibits anyone from consenting to the removal of an organ for payment.

[204] Mia Kellmer-Pringle, for example, denounces the belief that children complete a family by likening a couple's wish for a baby to their desire for a fridge or a television (Kellmer-Pringle, 1977, pp. 69–70). Thomas Shannon argues that surrogacy "denigrates the infertile woman. In essence, she is told that since she simply cannot meet her partner's need to have a child, he has to go out and rent a woman who can do this for him. . . . Although many report that wives freely co-operate with this process, one has to wonder whether or not this is a survival mechanism" (Shannon, 1988, pp. 157–8).

[205] Janice Raymond says that "the assumption is that a woman is only fulfilled through breeding. She enters reality only as a mother, and any woman who rejects that role is unnatural, suspect, and out of place . . . (the) romanticizing of motherhood sentimentalizes women's subordination in the family as well as in society at large". She goes on to argue that "underlying this demand for children is the patriarchal perception of childlessness as a disease and misfortune that elicits sympathy and pity, a perception that fosters the social pressure not to be childless" (Raymond,1993, pp. 73, 153).

financial incentives.[206] Social and emotional pressure to agree to bear a child for a distraught friend or family member is seldom presented as an equivalent obstacle to a potential surrogate's free and autonomous decision-making,[207] although in practice it may be extremely difficult to refuse a request from a close friend or relative.[208] The Brazier Report acknowledges that where a sister, cousin or close friend is unable to bear a child "the pressure on a potential surrogate to assist her may be extreme",[209] but it nevertheless considers these "altruistic" arrangements preferable to those involving payment.

The argument that paying women to become surrogates jeopardises the possibility of free and informed consent is, I argue, unconvincing. The absence of attractive alternative sources of income for poor women does not invalidate their consent to other types of work that may be much more disagreeable.[210] And unlike other badly paid jobs, it is seldom argued that surrogacy would be less exploitative if the surrogate were paid *more* for her services. Ironically, as we have seen, unpaid surrogacy is frequently perceived to be the least exploitative option.[211] Instead anxiety about the possibility of exploitation only makes sense if we think that there is something especially unacceptable about being paid to produce a child. This argument against surrogacy is not then concerned with the possibility that a commissioning couple may take advantage of a woman's economic desperation by offering an inadequate financial reward for her reproductive services, rather it is the existence of a commercial exchange which is condemned.

---

[206] And in the United States, the National Association of Surrogate Mothers recommends that financial security should be a prerequisite for acceptance as a surrogate mother in order to minimise the risk of exploitation, and the risk that she might subsequently claim economic duress (Baker, 1994, p. 610. Andrews, 1995, p. 2365). The Centre for Surrogate Parenting and Egg Donation in California refuses to accept applications from would-be surrogate mothers who are claiming welfare benefits (Watson-Smyth, 1997).

[207] For example in the American case *In the matter of Baby M* (1988) 537 A 2d 1227, the New Jersey Supreme Court found that surrogacy contracts were contrary to the law and the public policy of the state, but found that there were no legal impediments to arrangements "when the surrogate mother volunteers, without any payment, to act as a surrogate" (at 1274). Thomas Murray argues that "a woman who is willing to bear her sister's or best friend's child out of loyalty and affection is acting in harmony with the values we prize in families" (Murray, 1996, p. 67).

[208] Kim Cotton, a surrogate mother and founder of COTS, says that in her experience, "surrogacy within families can be more problematic than with strangers . . . family members can feel pressurised and obliged to help" (Cotton, 2000, p. 928).

Uma Narayan points out that "gift surrogates who have prior friendship or kinship ties with the receiving parents may be as economically or psychologically vulnerable as commercial surrogates. . . . Indeed, the gift surrogate's relationship and emotional ties to the receiving parents—ties the commercial surrogate usually lacks—may make her more vulnerable to emotional pressure and coercion concerning the conditions of pregnancy and childbirth" (Narayan, 1995b, p. 179).

[209] Brazier *et al*, 1998, para. 7.19.

[210] As John Robertson explains, "offering money to do unpleasant tasks is not in itself coercive" (Robertson, 1990, p. 163).

[211] Lori Andrews quotes one surrogate mother's question: "Why am I exploited if I am paid, but not if am not paid?" (Andrews, 1989, p. 259).

(e) Commodification of reproduction

It could be argued that every adult of working age, with the exception of the independently wealthy and the unemployed, takes money for the use of some part of their body.[212] Martha Nussbaum has drawn attention to the cultural specificity of any stigma associated with using certain physical attributes in order to generate income. For example, in the medieval church accepting fees in return for education was condemned as a "base occupation".[213] Similarly, in *The Wealth of Nations*, Adam Smith drew an analogy between prostitution and opera singing, acting or dancing on the grounds that certain "very agreeable and beautiful talents" should never be exploited for financial gain.[214] Nevertheless, censure of commercialised procreation has a long history and considerable symbolic resonance,[215] leading Brazier *et al* to suggest that, in addition to inducing imperfect consent, payments to surrogates:

"risk the commodification of the child to be born . . . (and) contravene the social norms of our society".[216]

Their conclusion, therefore, is that an arrangement which involves remuneration greater than actual expenses "has to be regarded as a form of child purchase".[217]

To put a price on a baby, or on the reproductive capacity of a woman is, to many people, morally insupportable.[218] This criticism of surrogacy suggests that the symbolic and practical harm done by converting procreation into an economic transaction outweighs the benefits in facilitating parenthood for people who could not otherwise reproduce.[219] Margaret Radin, for example, has argued that:

"if a capitalist baby industry were to come into being . . . how could any of us . . . avoid subconsciously measuring the dollar value of our children? How could our children

---

[212] Nussbaum, 1999, p. 276.
[213] *Ibid.* p. 279.
[214] Quoted in Nussbaum, 1999, pp. 276.
[215] In the United States, for example, fecund female slaves were commonly impregnated in order to produce children that could replenish the slave labour force or be sold for profit (see further Sanders, 1992).
[216] Brazier *et al*, 1998, p. i.
[217] Brazier *et al*, 1998, para. 4.35.
[218] For example, Martha Field has argued that "(s)ociety . . . has an interest in keeping certain subjects outside of the market economy. The transfer of children is one of these subjects" (Field, 1992, p. 1591). In commenting upon Islam's approach to surrogate motherhood, Sherifa Zuhur observes that the loudest objection is "to the overt assignation of a stated price of motherhood" (Zuhur, 1992, p. 1733). According to Capron and Radin "during the process of commissioning a pregnancy, the woman becomes a breeder to be bargained over in a market that will place a specific (monetary)value on personal traits that she may pass on to her offspring" (Capron and Radin, 1990 p. 63).
[219] For example, Thomas Shannon says that "by pricing babies . . .we are making an explicit frontal assault on human dignity and the moral worth of an individual. Such pricing of an individual, by its nature reduces the individual to what he or she can be exchanged for on the market" (Shannon, 1988, p. 157).

avoid being preoccupied with measuring their own dollar value?. . . . In the worst case, market rhetoric could create a commodified self-conception in everyone, as the result of commodifying every attribute that differentiates us and that other people value in us, and could destroy personhood as we know it".[220]

This is another slippery-slope argument revealing again, in my opinion, un-warranted pessimism about our capacity to institute effective regulation. Moreover, it is simply not true that the commissioning couple buy the right to treat a child as a commodity, since if they did in fact treat the child as an object, they would clearly fail to meet the basic standard of adequate parenting required by law. There is no doubt that a child who was being treated as a prod-uct would, as a result, be at risk of significant harm, and her compulsory removal from her parents would therefore be justified under section 31(2) of the Children Act 1989.

It is true that it is particularly easy to invoke dramatic and affecting metaphors in relation to surrogacy.[221] Choosing to discuss surrogacy in terms of selling babies and hiring wombs, rather than as a means to alleviate a particular sort of infertility, is emotive and politically charged.[222] It is, perhaps, interesting that payments made in infertility clinics are not looked upon as the "price" of a child, even though the infertile person or couple pays this money precisely in order to acquire a "take home baby". Of course in assisted conception clinics the money must be paid regardless of whether a pregnancy or a live birth is achieved, whereas in a surrogacy arrangement, full payment is generally depen-dent upon the handing over of the baby. It is also clear that buying the services of an assisted conception clinic does not invoke the same stark symbolism as paying for the gestational services of a fertile woman.

In partial surrogacy, some feminists have argued that the commissioning father buys the right to impregnate the surrogate mother with his sperm.[223] Gena Corea considers that this loosens women's claims to maternity while strengthening men's paternity rights.[224] Yet this argument obviously goes into reverse where the infertility treatment is donor insemination,[225] in which only the female partner will have a biological connection with the child. Given that each year approximately ten times as many children are born through DI as

[220] Radin, 1987, p. 1926.

[221] Katha Pollitt has said that "it seems that a woman can rent her womb . . . and get a check upon turning over the product to its father", and she alleges that surrogacy arrangements "bear an uncanny resemblance to the all-sales-final style of a used car lot" (Pollitt, 1995, pp. 63–4).

[222] For example In *Re Baby M* 537 A. 2d 1227 (NJ 1988) in particularly loaded language, the judge (at 1241) said "the evils inherent in baby bartering are loathsome for a number of reasons. . .".
Richard Epstein describes the use of the word "commodification" as a "descriptive rebuke" (Epstein, 1995, p. 2328).

[223] Katha Pollitt has argued that surrogacy is "a way for men to get children, and that "maternity contracts make one woman a machine and the other irrelevant" (Pollitt, 1995, pp. 68–9).

[224] Corea, 1985, p. 244. Similarly, Mary Lyndon Shanley says that "viewed in its social context, contract pregnancy . . . enabl(es) economically secure men to purchase women's procreative labor" (Lyndon Shanley, 1995, pp. 164–5).

[225] Farquhar, 1996, p. 156.

through surrogacy, Corea's criticism seems unfounded. It could even be argued that the separation of social, gestational and biological parenthood immanent in surrogacy arrangements might contribute to the *erosion* of biological determinism in relation to both maternal and paternal roles.[226]

In sum, critics of surrogacy arrangements claim that they harm children, exploit women and commodify reproduction. As yet, there is little research on children born through surrogacy, although we do know that children conceived in other non-traditional ways tend to be wanted, loved and psychologically well-balanced.[227] The arrangements rarely go awry, and interviews with surrogate mothers have found that the concerns raised about the voluntariness of their participation "are rashly speculative and bear no relation to the arrangements as they currently exist".[228] Pessimistic prophesies of the damage wreaked by surrogacy thus seem unfounded. Moreover, given the prevailing recognition that formal disapproval will not stop people from engaging in surrogacy arrangements,[229] insofar as the possibility of unfairness exists, regulation might be preferable to prohibition. If we know that these contracts are going to be made regardless of their non-recognition, and we believe there to be a risk of complications, then the development of expertise to predict, avoid or resolve problems might be a more logical response than the "ostrich like"[230] belief in the dangers of assigning them the legitimacy of regulation.[231]

There are various forms that facilitative regulation could take. As we saw earlier, an intention-based parenthood test would side-step the need for the formal transfer of legal parenthood by recognising the commissioning couple as the child's parents from birth. Any ambiguity in divining the parties' intentions could be resolved either by reference to the pre-conceptual arrangement, or by a default presumption in favour of the gestational mother or a "best interests of the child" test in the event of subsequent disagreement. Another possibility might be to ascribe responsibility for controlling and monitoring all surrogacy arrangements to the Human Fertilisation and Embryology Authority, or a similar body. This would have the advantage of consistency between different solutions to the problem of involuntary childlessness. Primary legislation might contain surrogacy-specific status provisions, and a simplified mechanism for acquiring legal parenthood. A final possibility might be to make surrogacy contracts enforceable, and I argue below that the assumption that surrogacy

[226] Marjorie Shultz believes that surrogacy can "soften and offset gender imbalances that presently permeate the arena of procreation and parenting" (Shultz, 1994, p. 304).
[227] Golombok, 2000.
[228] Andrews, 1995, p. 2350.
[229] Indeed in Australia criminal prosecution of parties entering into surrogacy arrangements has had little impact upon the practice of surrogacy, Margaret Otlowski argues that "the existing legislative policy of prohibition is ineffective and even the threat of criminal penalty does not deter couples from entering into such arrangements" (Otlwoski, 1999, p. 51).
[230] Shultz, 1994, p. 619.
[231] Marjorie Shultz has argued that "exploitation is more likely in a black or grey market" (Shultz, 1994, p. 620).

arrangements must, as a matter of fundamental principle, remain unenforceable may be based upon a series of outdated assumptions about the scope of contract law.

These several options are not necessarily mutually exclusive, and my argument is rather that facilitative regulation might involve an amalgam of regulatory techniques. For example, a *prima facie* intention test for parenthood would avoid the need for cumbersome legal proceedings in cases where all the parties are content to keep to their prior arrangement. Where there is a dispute, a best interests test, interpreted in the light of guidance from a regulatory authority, such as the HFEA, might be necessary. In addition, there are two key features of contract law that might prove helpful in devising new ways to think about the regulation of surrogacy arrangements. First, contract law is now accustomed to shaping the *content* of contractual arrangements in order to facilitate both planning and fairness. Second, insofar as there are those who believe that the surrogate mother's right to resile from her undertaking to hand over the child should be paramount, contract law is also well adapted to resolving contractual disputes without violating individual freedom.

4 LESSONS FROM CONTRACT LAW

Non-enforcement of surrogacy contracts has been a central part of the United Kingdom's strategy to discourage participation in surrogacy arrangements.[232] If, so the argument goes, commissioning couples have no "right" to the child, and the surrogate mother has no "right" to receive the agreed expenses, surrogacy contracts will seem precarious, and people will be unwilling to risk so much upon such a patently insecure arrangement. It is impossible to tell how many people may be dissuaded from engaging in surrogacy contracts as a result of their unenforceability, but the continued practice of surrogacy shows that this is an imperfect deterrent. As I have explained, I do not consider deterring participation in surrogacy arrangements to be a proper purpose of regulation. But the fear that it might encourage the practice of surrogacy is not the only argument against enforceability. It is also suggested that non-enforcement is an essential protection for women who should never be forced to give up a child to whom they have given birth.[233] Yet, as I explain below, it is not clear that this concern requires the complete non-enforceability of surrogacy agreements. My argument here is that contract law might offer a productive framework for *some*

---

[232] Under s. 1A of the Surrogacy Arrangements Act 1985 (as amended by s. 26 of the Human Fertilisation and Embryology Act 1990) "no surrogacy arrangement is enforceable by or against any of the persons making it".

This position is mirrored in other jurisdictions. In Australia, for example, surrogacy contracts are "void and unenforceable" (Otlowski, 1999, p.40).

[233] Larry Gostin argues that "the rights of a gestational mother to make future decisions about her body, lifestyle and an intimate future relationship with her child are so important to her dignity and human happiness that they should be regarded as inalienable" (Gostin, 1990 p. 14).

aspects of the facilitative regulation of surrogacy. In order to test this thesis, I consider how first principles of contract law might apply to surrogacy arrangements.

Like other contractual agreements, a surrogacy arrangement usually consists in a discrete and finite relationship containing a set of specific undertakings, and based upon some sort of exchange or reciprocity. The principle of freedom of contract means that we should, as far as possible, respect individuals' freedom to enter into binding agreements about whatever subject they choose. If surrogacy contracts were subject to the ordinary rules of contract law, we should therefore be slow to interfere with individuals' private ordering arrangements. Yet, contract law has always reserved the right to influence the shape of legally binding agreements, through, for example, implying certain "necessary" terms, and invalidating other unfair terms. Similarly, respect for individual liberty has always restricted the availability of remedies that might restrict one parties' freedom or bodily autonomy. I intend to show, therefore, that contract law is accustomed to limiting the scope and impact of oppressive agreements. Given its capacity to promote reproductive freedom while simultaneously policing onerous or unconscionable bargains, unlike the commonly favoured family law model some aspects of modern contract law might offer a flexible and accommodating framework for the voluntary transfer of parental obligations

It is, however, usually assumed by family lawyers and contract lawyers alike that the ordinary law of contract has no place in the regulation of surrogacy. Contract law's abstention from involvement in family matters has a long history,[234] and it is undoubtedly true that contractual ordering is often assumed to be an inappropriate way to organise domestic relationships.[235] In order to draw a line between the public and the private spheres, contract law has traditionally relied upon the doctrine of consideration, that is the need for the goods or services to be in some sense "paid for", supplemented by a residual refusal to enforce any agreement in which the court retrospectively decides that there was no intention to create legal relations. Yet surrogacy contracts may on their face satisfy both elements: there is often consideration, or some sort of exchange relationship, and there may be a clear intention to create legal relations.

The ordinary law of contract could potentially resort to two other doctrines in order to render surrogacy contracts unenforceable. First, to be valid a contract must have been entered into voluntarily, and, as we have seen, there are those who would argue that the inequality of bargaining power between the

---

[234] See further Collins, 1997, 56–70.

[235] Roberto Unger has said that "the rules of contract law that discourage contract in noncommercial settings . . . express a reluctance to allow contract law to intrude at all upon the world of family and friendship, lest by doing so it destroy their peculiar communal quality. . . . The social realm is rich in precisely the attributes that are thought to be almost wholly absent from the economic sphere. The communal forms in which it abounds, islands of reciprocal loyalty and support, neither need much law nor are capable of tolerating it" (Unger,1983, pp. 61, 3).

surrogate and the commissioning couple may reveal duress, undue influence[236] or an "unconscionable" bargain.[237] But this common assumption that the relative wealth of the commissioning couple inevitably results in a significant disparity in bargaining power may be misguided for two reasons. First, people whose infertility leads them to consider surrogacy are not necessarily wealthy, instead their desperation for a child may lead them to incur significant financial debts. Second, it is at least possible that the surrogate's knowledge that the law will protect her right to be considered the mother of any child to whom she gives birth may give her considerable bargaining leverage.

In addition, the existence of inequality of bargaining power does not invalidate every contract made on an uneven playing field. Rather, a sharp inequality of bargaining power has tended to be a background consideration that might alert a court to the possibility that the stronger party may have taken advantage of their dominant position. Even if we were to accept the *possibility* that a surrogacy contract may contain oppressive or unconscionable terms, this does not necessarily represent an adequate justification for the general unenforceability of *all* surrogacy arrangements. Instead, just as in the regulation of standard form consumer contracts, where there may be a similar risk that the stronger party has inserted unfair terms, should terms be found to be substantively unfair, the offending term could be severed, or, if necessary, the contract invalidated.

Second, a contract may be invalidated on the grounds that it is contrary to public policy if it contemplates conduct that is immoral; or contrary to the public interest; or unduly restrictive of individual liberty. To find a contract to be immoral or contrary to the public interest is to make a value judgement that needs to be defended,[238] rather than to describe an essential characteristic of a particular arrangement. So, for example, it might be argued that there are some things, such as having babies, which should never be the subject of an economic transaction.[239] Yet assisted conception clinics typically charge around £2000 for each IVF cycle, and although the money is consideration for the treatment, rather than the baby, no woman ever has infertility treatment for its own sake. Patients are not, therefore, paying for the various procedures as an end in themselves, but as the means to acquire a take-home baby. If the treatment cycle has to be abandoned because there is no chance that it will lead to a pregnancy, the patient will be reimbursed for treatment that has not yet

---

[236] In order to strike down a contract on the grounds that the stronger party has taken advantage of his or her position, the contract must be disadvantageous to the weaker party such that "it would have been obvious . . . to any independent and reasonable persons who considered the transaction at the time with knowledge of all the relevant facts." Per Slade LJ *Bank of Credit and Commerce International SA* v. *Aboody* [1989] 2 WLR 759, at 780.

[237] For example in *Cresswell* v. *Potter* [1978] 1 WLR 255, relief was given to a wife on the grounds that she was the equivalent of a "poor and ignorant person" who had been taken advantage of by her husband.

[238] And Richard Epstein has said that "a prohibition on voluntary exchange for . . . moral reasons should be narrowly circumscribed" (Epstein, 1995, p. 2308).

[239] For example the revised code of Washington (RCW 26.26.210 et seq.) prohibits surrogacy contracts for compensation over and above medical expenses as contrary to public policy.

been received. Thus, if the salient moral difference between infertility treatment and surrogacy is that *some* money, though not necessarily the full cost of
treatment, has to paid to an assisted conception clinic regardless of whether
the treatment is successful, would a surrogacy contract be legitimate provided
that *some* money had to be paid regardless of whether the baby was in fact
transferred after birth? Do we therefore defeat this public policy argument
against surrogacy by inserting a clause that respects the surrogate mother's
absolute right to resile from her agreement and to retain *some* of the money
that she has received?

Another "public policy" argument is suggested by Martha Field who argues
that surrogacy is analogous to some other sorts of promises which are considered "so deeply personal" that we do not think people should be bound by
them.[240] Her examples include a promise to marry, to have sex, to donate an
organ or to give up one's child for adoption.[241] It is, of course, perfectly lawful
to promise to do all of these things, so Field's argument is rather that there are
some promises where the right to change one's mind ought to be protected.
Again, this does not necessarily mean the contract must be invalid, just that the
surrogate mother must be given the option of changing her mind throughout
the pregnancy. After the baby had been handed over, her right to withdraw from
the agreement might, however, be diminished. If we examine the British case
law on mothers who initially consent to their child's adoption, and subsequently
have a change of heart, we can see that her right to withdraw her consent is seriously attenuated by the courts' concern to protect the welfare of the child by
avoiding disruption.[242] Thus, after placement there is no absolute right to resile
from a promise to give up one's child for adoption, instead the right is qualified
by the "best interests" test.

I am not convinced by these public policy arguments against surrogacy contracts. As will be obvious, I consider the alleviation of unwanted childlessness to
be a worthwhile enterprise, and I do not believe that surrogacy arrangements
are necessarily oppressive or exploitative. If the agreement is entered into voluntarily, and benefits the surrogate, the infertile couple and the resulting child,
I would argue that the public policy objection embodies unwarranted moral

[240] Field, 1993, p. 225.
[241] *Ibid.*
[242] See for example, *Re H (Infants) (Adoption:Parental Consent)* [1977] 1 WLR 471 in which
Ormrod LJ said (at 472) "it ought to be recognised by all concerned with adoption cases that once
the formal consent has been given . . . or perhaps once the child has been placed with the adopters,
time begins to run against the mother and, as time goes on, it gets progressively more and more difficult for her to show that the withdrawal of her consent is reasonable". Similarly, in *Re A
(Adoption: Change of Mind)* [2000] 1 FLR 665, A's mother had started making arrangements for A's
adoption while still pregnant. A was placed with foster parents two days after his birth, and before
he was 3 months old he was placed with the prospective adopters. Three months later the mother
changed her mind. Sumner J ruled that the couple caring for A could adopt him, and that the mother
had been unreasonable in changing her mind. A was almost 1 year old, and Sumner J decided that
to return him to his natural mother, would pose too great a risk of disturbance and lasting damage
to him. See also *Re V (Adoption: Parental Agreement)* [1985] FLR 45 and *Re T* [1986] Fam 160.

paternalism. Yet even if I am wrong, as we have seen, these policy reasons do not necessarily mean that the whole arrangement must be struck down, rather they point towards a requirement that we protect the surrogate mother's right to change her mind. This could be accommodated while also recognising that allowing her to keep *all* of the money paid by the commissioning couple might amount to her being "unjustly enriched" at the expense of the commissioning couple.

A further superficially compelling public policy argument from contract law against the enforceability of surrogacy arrangements is that the contracts are unduly restrictive of individual liberty. The argument might be made that "selling" one's reproductive services is analogous to selling oneself into slavery, and should therefore be prohibited.[243] The parallel with slavery is, however, a weak one since the commissioning parents could not be said to own the surrogate. John Stuart Mill's classic objection to allowing someone to sell themselves into slavery was that it would represent an exercise of autonomy which thereafter precluded the individual's future capacity to exercise any autonomy at all.[244] The surrogate mother's contract is for a finite and relatively short period of time, and, as I explain below, clauses which might be unduly restrictive of her autonomy, such as a term specifying that she should have an abortion in the event of fetal abnormality, would undoubtedly be unenforceable, if not unlawful. Instead, the surrogacy arrangement may be more akin to a contract *for services*, in which an individual agrees to surrender some portion of their liberty in return for something, such as an income, that may be more valuable to them. And just as in a contract for services, if either party were to fail to fulfil their obligations under the agreement, the remedy would lie in damages, rather than specific performance.[245]

Arguments against the enforceability of surrogacy contracts that derive from the premise that an order for specific performance would be insupportable are built upon a misunderstanding of contract law. There are many contracts where specific performance would be oppressive, and this is not generally regarded as a sufficient reason for them to be entirely unbinding. Rather, the ordinary remedy in contract law is damages. An order that a party who fails to fulfil their obligations under a contract should compensate the other party for their disappointment would not have the same potential to wreak havoc with the basic liberties of the surrogate mother. So just as contract law will not force an actor who refuses to go on stage to complete his performance, so a

[243] Mary Lyndon Shanley has argued that "pregnancy contracts might..usefully be compared to contracts for consensual slavery" (Lyndon Shanley, 1995, p. 165).
[244] "By selling himself for a slave, [a person] abdicates his liberty; he forgoes any future use of it beyond that single act. . . It is not freedom, to be allowed to alienate his freedom" (Mill, 1859, [1975] 126).
[245] Specific performance means that the party in breach could be forced to complete the contract. So if a surrogate mother were to decide she wanted to keep the baby, a remedy of specific performance would require her to hand over the baby to the commissioning couple.

surrogate mother would not necessarily be compelled to complete her contractual obligations.[246]

Similarly, if the surrogacy arrangement were to specify that the surrogate should undergo particular prenatal tests or have an abortion if the fetus proved to be abnormal, her decision not be tested, or not to have an abortion should be respected. It is inconceivable that a court would entertain an order for specific performance of obligations in a surrogacy contract that purported to interfere with the bodily integrity of the surrogate mother. And in any event, since to carry out any medical intervention without the consent of the surrogate would be both an assault and a battery, such a term would be unlawful. Just as unfair terms in consumer contracts may be severed, and the contract can continue without the offending term, any term that purported to restrict the surrogate mother's decision-making authority about the management of her pregnancy could be struck out.

Were we to learn some lessons from contract law, we could see how legislation has determined the legitimacy or otherwise of certain contractual terms. Terms guaranteeing the surrogate mother's freedom of conduct during her pregnancy could be implied, and terms restricting her freedom could be invalidated. A compulsory term could give the surrogate the right to retain the baby, and perhaps to keep some of the money she has already received. Similarly, the commonly expressed fear that surrogacy contracts might contain a warranty[247] as to the "quality of the end-product" could also be dealt with by the statutory prohibition of terms relating to the health of the child. Insofar as the risk of an unwanted baby exists, default rules could allocate responsibility for that risk to the individuals responsible for the child's conception, namely the commissioning couple.

The classification of surrogacy as a family law matter entirely outwith the reach of the law of contract excludes the possibility of productive cross fertilisation between legal disciplines.[248] The recent history of contract law suggests that far from facilitating the wild excesses of the free market, it has instead been concerned to remedy some of the problems that arose from the universal application of abstract principle. Not only were the common law rules found to be incapable of differentiating between large commercial contracts, and consumer transactions, they also seemed to rest upon the absurd legal fiction that every contractual term is negotiated anew. Legislation has therefore introduced a

---

[246] Although there are those who argue that specific performance ought to be the ordinary remedy in disputes over surrogacy contracts, for example Marjorie Shultz believes that failing to give effect to the intentions of the parties "is to disregard one of the most distinctive traits that makes us human. . . . To disregard such intention with reference to so intimate and significant an activity as procreation and child-rearing is deeply shocking." As a result she believes that "specific performance of agreements about parenthood in some sense confirms core values about the uniqueness of life" (Shultz, 1990, pp. 377–8, 364).

[247] Brazier, 1999b, p. 348.

[248] On the blindness produced by the legal classification system, see further Collins, 1999, pp. 44–5.

subtly differentiated system of contract law in which context-specific regulations are directed towards efficient dispute avoidance and the elimination of abusive practices. In some types of contract, mandatory rules now largely define the terms upon which the parties are entitled to contract. In relation to surrogacy, there is no reason why a statute could not define and limit the parties' obligations under the contract. I do not intend to suggest the wholesale reclassification of surrogacy as a subset of contract law. Instead my point is simply that modern contractual regulation might offer some productive alternative models for the allocation of responsibilities within a surrogacy arrangement.

The law's failure to enforce surrogacy contracts inevitably contributes to their insecurity. It could even be argued that their complete unenforceability may persuade women to become surrogates even if they are not sure that they would want to give up the child after birth.[249] Giving the surrogate mother complete freedom to withdraw from the contract and keep all of the money that she has been paid might also provide the opportunity for extortion.[250] Once conception has occurred the commissioning couple may be vulnerable to threats from the surrogate mother that she intends to keep the baby, or have an abortion, unless she receives more money.

Unlike other domestic agreements that are outside the scope of contract law, surrogacy arrangements are often based upon an entirely illusory relationship of "trust" or "friendship" between strangers.[251] And unlike ordinary contracts, surrogacy arrangements are seldom entered into as a result of the trust that may obtain from reputation and/or a pre-existing relationship, or because effective sanctions exist should the other party fail to keep their promise. Clearly people only enter into such patently risky arrangements because their desire for the best-case outcome is so overwhelming. Nor should we be surprised that involuntarily childless people are prepared to gamble so much upon the unreliable promise of a baby: each cycle of IVF is equivalent to staking as much as £2000 on a chance roughly equivalent to rolling a six. This special vulnerability does not seem to me to be a good reason to deny individuals any remedy if the arrangement breaks down. Rather the law should be able to offer a remedy that protects the interests of the various parties to the agreement. A remedy in

---

[249] Epstein, 1995, p. 2329. In a much publicised case of a surrogate changing her mind in 1997, the surrogate mother claimed to have had an abortion as a result of her doubts about the commissioning couple's suitability, it later turned out that she had decided to keep the child. Although the parties had been introduced through COTS, Kim Cotton said that neither side had followed the COTS guidelines and had rushed into the pregnancy (Boseley, 1997).

[250] See further Field, 1990, pp. 101–3.

[251] Both COTS and SPC, and some assisted conception clinics encourage commissioning couples to have faith in the surrogate's behaviour during pregnancy and in her willingness to hand over the baby. Similarly the surrogate is encouraged to have faith in the commissioning couple's promise to make the agreed payments and in their desire to adopt the child. Van den Akker argues that "an arrangement based on faith in the unknown may be unacceptable" (Van den Akker, 1999, pp. 264–5).

John Robertson believes that "uncertainty and anxiety about the surrogate's trustworthiness" is inevitable (Robertson, 1990, p. 159).

damages for breach of contract would protect the surrogate mother's "right" to keep the child, while compensating the commissioning couple for at least some of their losses. It is perfectly plausible for a surrogate mother's right to resile from her undertaking to hand over the child to coexist with the commissioning couple's right to compensation for losses resulting from their misplaced reliance upon the agreement.

The commissioning couple's change of heart is slightly more complicated. Insofar as they will not, absent reform of the status provisions, be the child's parents, specific enforcement of their undertaking to take the child would be difficult, and probably undesirable. Neither is payment of damages to the surrogate mother, if she does not want the child, necessarily particularly helpful. Here the *prima facie* intention-based test of parenthood might be a more productive solution, although it would obviously offer no guarantee that the commissioning couple would be prepared to offer the child a loving and secure upbringing. Its merit would simply be that it would fall to the commissioning couple, rather than the surrogate mother, to go through the process of giving *their* child up for adoption.

5. CONCLUSION

In this chapter we have seen that the law governing surrogacy consists in an incomplete patchwork of provisions which mean that, despite the arrangements' practical and moral complexity, surrogacy is comparatively unregulated. The two official reports into the practice of surrogacy have advocated regulation that is supposed to restrict or even prevent people from engaging in surrogacy arrangements. Hostility to facilitative regulation is based upon two principal misconceptions. First, as we have seen, there is little evidence to support the twin assumptions that surrogacy exploits women and harms children. Second, making it difficult to engage lawfully in surrogacy arrangements is unlikely to lead people who cannot have children in any other way to simply resign themselves to their childlessness. Rather restrictive regulation may be the catalyst for them to travel abroad to find a surrogate mother, or to make unlawful contracts in a regulatory vacuum.

There are several ways in which the law relating to surrogacy could be reformed so it more accurately reflected the intentions of the parties. Much depends upon the status provisions because if intention governs the determination of parenthood, then the commissioning couple simply *are* the child's parents, and there is no need for any rules governing the transfer of legal parenthood. Although this solution would have an appealing simplicity, it might also lack clarity and certainty, and would require some default position in the event of a dispute. A second possibility might be to make surrogacy contracts enforceable, provided that they satisfied various conditions. So contracts which had been made in circumstances of undue influence, or which were oppressive or unconscionable would be unenforceable. The surrogate mother would continue to be considered the child's legal mother at the moment of birth, and if she chose not to perform her side of the bargain by carrying the pregnancy to term and handing the child over, she would be in breach of contract. If this is characterised as a contract for services, it would not be specifically enforceable and she would instead be liable in damages. Although there would be the usual objections to the commercialisation of something as sacred as childbearing, it might be important to recognise that the real danger posed by surrogacy is the creation of a legal framework which encourages would-be surrogates and would-be commissioning couples to have children without the safeguards that can exist within an effective regulatory scheme.

---

[252] Golombok, 2000

7

Postscript

JUST AS THE rules governing new technologies such as genetic screening or infertility treatment may have an inevitable built-in obsolescence, so any book attempting to offer a definitive overview of the regulation of this rapidly shifting terrain will almost certainly soon suffer a similar fate. Within the next few years, for example, someone will probably attempt to clone a human being, and their success or failure may transform discussion about the ethics of reproductive cloning. The development of less invasive prenatal testing techniques could lead to routine screening for some of the more common genetic disorders. New post-coital methods of birth control may further blur the line between contraception and abortion, and improvements in semi-permanent contraceptive techniques might alter prevailing judicial attitudes towards controlling the fertility of mentally disabled women and girls.

Not only is technological progress in the field of reproduction unquestionably a moving target, but regulation itself also seems to be in a constant state of flux. A new Surrogacy Act may implement some or all of the proposals in the Brazier Report. The government intends to allow the 'fathers' of posthumously conceived children to have their names recorded on their children's birth certificates[1]. At the time of writing, the National Institute for Clinical Excellence (NICE) is appraising the availability of assisted conception within the NHS. And there is considerable speculation about whether the continued anonymity of sperm donors is either necessary or desirable. In the UK there will be an increasing number of cases brought under the Human Rights Act 1998 to test both the scope of the right to found a family[2], and the extent to which the

---

[1] The Human Fertilisation and Embryology (Deceased Fathers) Bill, if passed, would enable certain men to be registered as the father of a child that was conceived after their death. The Bill would have retrospective effect and would apply to married couples, or to unmarried couples provided that they were being provided with treatment services together before the man's death. The recognition of these deceased fathers' paternity would only be for the purpose of registration on the child's birth certificate. None of the other normal incidents of paternity, such as inheritance rights, would apply, thus avoiding the problem of testamentary uncertainty that might otherwise arise if a child could be conceived many years after her "father's" death. Despite cross-party support for the Bill, it was talked out of time at its third reading on 27 April 2001 by Desmond Swayne MP, a Conservative health spokesman, who claimed to have been speaking in a personal capacity upon an issue of conscience. Although a debate upon the Bill was rescheduled, it had no chance of becoming law before the general election in June 2001. At the time of writing, it is not clear if or when it will form part of the new Government's legislative programme.

[2] Article 12. *R* v. *Secretary of State for the Home Department, ex parte Mellor*, unreported, 4th April 2001 was a case brought under Article 12. Gavin Mellor is serving a life sentence for murder at Nottingham prison. The Home Secretary refused permission for him to visit a clinic in order to provide sperm with which his wife could be artificially inseminated. The policy of the prison

right to privacy[3] can be invoked in order to protect reproductive autonomy. Arguments for liberalising women's access to abortion, for example, could be framed in terms of the right to privacy, and nonconsensual sterilisations or caesarean sections carried out upon women who lack capacity might also have their legitimacy tested under Article 8.

Thus if the purpose of this book had only been to provide a comprehensive and up-to-date description of the regulation of reproduction, its shelf-life would inevitably be limited. Biotechnology and its regulation is subject to rapid and dramatic change, and within the next year or so there will be aspects of this text which will have been superseded by events. Nevertheless, I hope that some of the broader themes that I have pursued here will have ongoing relevance. Whatever happens in the future, reproduction will continue to be intensely regulated by a complex amalgam of statute, common law and the work of regulatory agencies, such as the Human Fertilisation and Embryology Authority. In order to work out the optimum nature and content of this regulatory mix, it might be useful to have reached some prior conclusions about the proper purposes and legitimate scope of the regulation of reproduction.

In this book I have argued that regulation should, as its central guiding principle, strive to carve out maximum possible respect for the reproductive autonomy of individual men and women. Of course, as we have seen, our procreative choices will be shaped by multiple different relationships, experiences and other external influences; they are indubitably not decisions that are inherently individualistic. Yet while collaborative and contextualised reproductive decision-making is undoubtedly the norm, the intimacy and importance of the decisions we take about reproduction should lead to a strong presumption in favour of freedom of choice.

In arguing for respect for individual liberty in questions of reproduction, I do not, however, advocate a kind of Nozickian minimal state[4]. *Unregulated* reproduction would unquestionably not be the best way to enhance reproductive freedom. Not only must the safe provision of medical procedures such as abortion and *in vitro* fertilisation be guaranteed by legislation, it is also important to recognise that reproductive autonomy is not synonymous with an absence of external constraints. Procreative freedom is not something that every individual *already* possesses, rather it may be a goal to be actively pursued. The

service is to refuse all such requests unless there are exceptional circumstances which would mean that refusal would not just delay the prisoner's capacity to found a family, but might eliminate it altogether. This might be the case if either the prisoner or his female partner were about to undergo medical treatment that would render them infertile. There were no such exceptional circumstances in Mr Mellor's case. His reason for seeking this permission was simply that he would first be eligible for parole in 2006 and his concern was that Mrs Mellor's fertility—she was 25 years old at the time of the application—might be impaired by the time of his release. The Court of Appeal decided that the Home Secretary's decision was neither irrational nor unreasonable. Imprisonment necessarily involved the deprivation of liberty, and so the right to found a family could not be said to be an absolute one.

[3] Article 8
[4] Nozick, 1974

uneven natural distribution of fertility means that there are some people whose reproductive options are, absent the provision of resources and services, extremely impoverished. The state therefore has a key role to play in enabling its citizens to maximise the scope of their reproductive autonomy through, for example, public funding of birth control, abortion, obstetric care and assisted conception services. While birth control, abortion and obstetric services also happen to be comparatively cheap, and thus represent efficient uses of public resources, the provision of assisted conception services at taxpayers' expense has proved to be much more controversial.

Fertile, sexually-active heterosexual people of reproductive age may be able to take their capacity to conceive for granted, but for many individuals, pro-creation without external assistance is simply impossible. It is indisputable that their infertility may be natural, but this could only offer a sufficient reason to deny them access to reproductive technologies if we were to embrace a Luddite rejection of all medical interventions that are directed towards enabling people to avoid the incapacitating impact of natural processes. Of course, no state could afford to pay for each of its citizens' unlimited use of the various assisted conception techniques, and rationing decisions are therefore inevitable. My argument in this book has not been that we must divert infinite sums of public money towards the satisfaction of reproductive preferences. Rather, I argue that we should acknowledge that the protection of procreative liberty may involve questions of distributive justice. Given the inevitability of financial constraints in the public sector, once we acknowledge that the positive provision of resources may be necessary for autonomy to flourish, we will obviously need to make some difficult choices about the relative merit of various competing claims upon state funds. Determining precisely how much public money we are pre-pared to devote to the promotion of procreative freedom is, therefore, a *political* decision. There is no easy answer to this question, instead the merit of this approach is its definition of reproductive liberty as a public good, rather than a purely private interest. As a result, decisions about the allocation of state resources to reproductive services should be subject to the same requirements of transparency, non-discrimination and relevance that apply to other public goods, such as education or health care. So, for example, in common with other comparatively expensive medical procedures, funding decisions should be made only for reasons that go to the heart of the clinical and cost effectiveness of the particular treatment, and criteria which purport to distinguish between deserv-ing and undeserving "parents" ought to have no place in the just distribution of NHS resources.

One of the things that I have found especially interesting while writing this book is that some of the conclusions I reach as a result of my commitment to reproductive autonomy are relatively uncontroversial, and would be broadly, although obviously not universally, supported by public opinion. Examples might be free access to birth control or pregnant women's participation in obstetric decision-making. However, some of the other consequences that I believe must also flow from a belief in the importance of procreative self-determination appear to be much more contentious. The enforceability of surrogacy contracts; the availability of abortion upon request; the provision of infertility treatment to postmenopausal women, and my acceptance—should it become sufficiently safe—of human reproductive cloning, would all tend to provoke widespread antipathy. Why is this? Why do some reproductive preferences tend to be treated with less respect than others?

It is, of course, axiomatic that reproductive freedom cannot be an absolute right admitting of no exceptions or qualifications. Consider a man who disapproves of his pregnant partner's decision to have an abortion. He can only have his right to make choices about his reproductive future respected if his partner's right to make decisions about her body is overridden. Thus when resolving a conflict between these two people's procreative choices, one person's preferred outcome will necessarily be ignored. In a similar vein, in the absence of unlimited state resources, some people's interest in publicly funded infertility treatment may have to be balanced with the whole population's need for a functioning National Health Service. Because it would leave no scope for the resolution of these sorts of conflicts, an absolute right to reproductive autonomy would clearly be unworkable.

The important question, therefore, is how we should define the circumstances that might justify interference with reproductive autonomy. Here I believe that John Stuart Mill's "harm principle" continues to offer a useful framework within which competing procreative choices may be weighed against each other:

> "The only purpose for which power can rightfully be exercised over any member of a civilised community against his will is to prevent harm to others. His own good either physical or moral is not a sufficient warrant. He cannot rightfully be compelled to do or forbear because it will be better for him to do so, because it will make him happier, because in the opinions of others, to do so would be wise or even right".[5]

In sum then, the harm principle means that we should respect each person's freedom to act as they wish unless to do so would infringe someone else's capacity to exercise their rights and freedoms. Of course, without some prior hierarchy of interests, the harm principle does not necessarily dictate any particular solution to disputes in which respect for one person's reproductive decision-making may jeopardise someone else's capacity to pursue their own procreative preferences. To return to the abortion example: the man who wants his partner's pregnancy to continue cannot have his choice respected unless her freedom is compromised; and conversely, if the woman is permitted to exercise procreative self-determination, her partner's preference will have been disregarded. This conflict can only be resolved if we judge that one of these two competing interests should trump the other. How then might their relative priority be evaluated?

[5] Mill, 1859

The simple answer is that we must give most protection to people's right to self-determination when their bodily integrity is at stake. So while it is understandable that a male progenitor's opinion about how his partner's pregnancy should proceed may be profoundly important to him, his point of view can be ignored without violating his interest in making decisions about his body. On the other hand, were we to give his preference priority, his partner would effectively be compelled to submit herself, against her will, to the physical strain of pregnancy and childbirth. Thus we can interfere with a man's desire for his pregnant partner to carry her pregnancy to term because to respect it would cause *greater* harm to his partner's freedom to make critical choices about her body and her life. Sometimes, of course, it will prove extremely difficult to weigh incommensurate interests against each other. There is, for example, no right answer to the relative priority infertility treatment should given within a publicly funded health service, as evidenced by the wide variation in policy within the European Union. Again, this question is simply one of the exceptionally tough political choices that are an inevitable consequence of the gap that now exists between the demand for health care services and taxpayers' willingness to pay for them.

There is another sense in which Mills' harm principle has to be fleshed out in order to offer an effective basis for regulation. If we judge the legitimacy of a particular decision according to whether it is likely to cause harm to others, it is obviously necessary to specify what we mean by "harm". If we were to adopt a very broad and expansive definition of harm, then it could incorporate feelings of disgust, upset or offence. This would mean that we could prohibit post-menopausal women from having access to assisted conception services because some members of society disapprove of such women's attempts to overcome their natural infertility. Or, similarly, we could outlaw the third-trimester abortion of abnormal fetuses on the grounds that many people find it repugnant. However, interpreting "harm" to include moral offence must be wrong because it would undermine the whole purpose of the harm principle which is, in essence, to introduce a presumption in favour of individual self-determination. If my liberty could be restricted just because what I choose to do might annoy someone else, my sphere of self-government would be vanishingly small. As H.L.A. Hart has explained

> "Recognition of individual liberty as a value involves, as a minimum, acceptance of the principle that the individual may do what he wants, even if others are distressed when they learn what it is that he does . . . No social order which accords to individual liberty any value could also accord the right to be protected from distress thus occasioned".[6]

"Harm", therefore, must receive a more restricted definition. Mere offence is simply not a good enough reason to limit the reproductive freedom of others.

[6] Hart, 1963, p. 47

Yet much media coverage of reproductive issues, and this applies almost equally to tabloids and broadsheets, appears to assume the opposite. Press coverage of the more controversial applications of reproductive technologies, such as their use by postmenopausal women, invariably encourages readers to feel that their sense that this is "not natural" or "not right" offers a sensible and appropriate basis for regulation. Whereas, on the contrary, I would argue that one person's personal morality should never dictate the extent to which another person is permitted to make reproductive choices according to their own conception of the good. Even where the revulsion at the prospect of, for example, postmenopausal motherhood is widely shared, and could even be said to be the opinion of the majority of the population, this cannot justify the imposition of popular morality upon the reproductive choices of individual citizens. Particularly when a person's choice pertains to something as personal and important as reproduction, I would argue that she has a legitimate interest in having her decision respected, despite widespread, or even near universal disapproval. Again H.L.A. Hart makes the point forcefully when he argues that

> "no one should think (that) even when popular morality is supported by an overwhelming majority or marked by widespread intolerance, indignation and disgust, that loyalty to democratic principles requires him to admit that its imposition on a minority is justified".[7]

Rather, unless a person's preferences would cause *harm* to others, as opposed to offence or disgust, they should always be treated with appropriate seriousness and respect.

Of course, critics of some of my more controversial conclusions in this book would say that their disapproval of, for example postmenopausal motherhood, derives from the "harm" that they believe it would cause to children born to older mothers. In a similar vein, as we saw in chapter three, there are people who object to abortion for fetal abnormality because of the "harm" they think it causes to disabled people. Yet all of the various "harms" that are posited as inevitable consequences of a broad conception of reproductive autonomy seem to be inherently speculative. There is, for example, no evidence that children born to women in their fifties fare worse than other children. Fifty and sixty year old adults are not necessarily inactive or prone to ill-health, and older parents may have the considerable advantages of maturity and stability. Nor is there any proof of a connection between a woman's decision to abort an abnormal fetus and the difficulties faced by disabled people.

So these various attempts to justify interfering with some individuals' reproductive autonomy on the basis of "harm", other than mere offence or disgust, caused to others by their unconventional procreative preferences tend to rely on conjecture or intuition, rather than clear documentary evidence. These broad and unsubstantiated allegations of 'harm' are seldom rigorously interrogated, but

---

[7] Hart, 1963, p. 81

instead are generally assumed to be self-evidently true. Yet because an individual's decisions about reproduction are of such critical importance to her sense of self, unfounded speculation about largely hypothetical risks cannot, without more, offer a sufficient reason for disregarding her preferences.

In the second half of the twentieth century, there was increasing recognition that the sexual predilections of all consenting adults should lie within that "realm of private morality and immorality which is, in brief and crude terms, not the law's business"[8]. At the beginning of the twenty-first century it is clear that while certain individuals' reproductive preferences are similarly protected, other people may find that their procreative choices are constrained and/or condemned. Just as the capacity to exercise and explore one's sexuality with other consenting adults may be a necessary constituent element of a fulfilling existence, so I would argue that having one's reproductive choices taken seriously and treated with respect may be similarly integral to a satisfying and self-authored life. A commitment to liberty and to moral pluralism should lead us to restrict an individual's reproductive autonomy only where the risk of harm to another person outweighs her undeniably compelling interest in deciding for herself whether and how to reproduce.

[8] Wolfendon, 1957, para. 61

Bibliography

Abdalla, Hossam, Gearon, Ceinwen and Wren, Marie (2000) "Swedish in-vitro fertilisation study" *Lancet* vol. 355 pp. 844–1.

Abortion Law Reform Association (1997) *A Report on NHS Abortion Services* (London: ALRA).

Abse, Leo (1986) "The Politics of In Vitro Fertilisation in Britain" in Fishel, S and Symonds EM (eds.) *In Vitro Fertilisation: Past, Present, Future* (Oxford: IRL Press) pp. 207–13.

ACGT [Advisory Committee on Genetic Testing] (2000) *Prenatal Genetic Testing: Report for Consultation* (London: Human Genetics Commission).

Acutt, Katherine (1996) "Perinatal Drug Use: State Interventions and the Implications for HIV Infected Women" in Faden, Ruth and Kass, Nancy (eds.) *HIV, AIDS and Childbearing: Public Policy, Private Lives* (Oxford UP) pp. 214–253.

Adler, Nancy, Keyes, Susan and Robertson, Patricia (1991) "Psychological Issues In New Reproductive Technologies: Pregnancy Inducing Technology and Diagnostic Screening" in Rodin, Judith and Collins, Aila (eds.) *Women and New Reproductive Technologies: Medical, Psychological, Legal and Ethical Dilemmas* (Hillsdale, New Jersey, Lawrence Erlbaum) pp. 111–133.

Agar, N (1995) "Designing Babies: Morally Permissible ways to Modify the Human Genome" *Bioethics* vol. 9 no. 1 pp. 1–15.

Agnes, Flavia (1995) *State, Gender and the Rhetoric of Law Reform* (Bombay: Research Centre for Women's Studies).

Ainsworth, Martha, Filmer, Dean and Semali, Innocent (1998) "The Impact of AIDS Mortality on Individual Fertility: Evidence from Tanzania" in Montgomery, Mark and Cohen, Barney (eds.) *From Death to Birth: Mortality Decline and Reproductive Change* (Washington DC: National Academy Press) pp. 138–180.

Alan Guttmacher Institute (1998) *Into A New World: Young Women's Sexual and Reproductive Lives* (New York: AGI).

—— (1998) *Sharing Responsibility: Women, Society and Abortion Worldwide* (New York: AGI).

Albiston, Catherine (1994) "The Social Meaning of the Norplant Condition: Constitutional Considerations of Race, Class and Gender" *Berkeley Women's Law Journal* vol. 9, pp. 9–57.

Al-Mufti R, McCarthy A, Fisk NM (1997) "Survey of obstetricians' personal preference and discretionary practice" *European Journal of Obstetrics, Gynecology and Reproductive Biology* vol. 73 no. 1 pp. 1–4.

Alto-Charo, R (1990) "Legislative Approaches to Surrogate Motherhood" in Gostin, Larry (ed.) *Surrogate Motherhood: Politics and Privacy* (Bloomington: University of Indiana Press) pp. 88–102.

—— (1995) "The Hunting of the Snark: The Moral Status of Embryos, Right-to-Lifers and Third World Women" *Stanford Law and Policy Review* vol. 6 no. 2 pp. 11–37.

American College Obstetricians and Gynecologists (2000) *HIV Tests Urged for All Pregnant Women* Press Release 23 May 2000 (Washington: ACOG).

Amu, Olubusola, Rajendran, Sasha and Bolaji, Ibrahim (1998) "Maternal Choice Alone Should Not Determine Method of Delivery" *British Medical Journal* vol. 317 pp. 463–5.

Anderson, Elizabeth (1990) "Is Women's Labor a Commodity?" *Philosophy and Public Affairs* vol. 19 pp. 71–92.

Anderson, Jean (1996) "Gynecological and Obstetrical Issues for HIV Infected Women" in Faden, Ruth and Kass, Nancy (eds.) *HIV, AIDS and Childbearing: Public Policy, Private Lives* (Oxford UP) pp. 31–62.

Andrews, Lori (1989) *Between Strangers: Surrogate Mothers, Expectant Fathers and Brave New Babies* (New York: Harper and Row).

—— (1990) "Surrogate Motherhood: The Challenge for Feminists" in Gostin, Larry (ed.) *Surrogate Motherhood: Politics and Privacy* (Bloomington and Indianapolis: Indiana UP) pp 167–182.

—— (1995) "Beyond Doctrinal Boundaries: A Legal Framework for Surrogate Motherhood" *Virginia Law Review* vol. 81 pp. 2343–2375.

Annas, George (1987) "Protecting the Liberty of Pregnant Patients" *New England Journal of Medicine* vol. 316 no.19 pp. 1213–1214.

—— (1990) "Mapping the Human Genome and the Meaning of Monster Mythology" *Emory Law Journal* vol. 39 no. 3 pp. 629–664.

—— and Grodin, Michael (1999) "Human Rights and Maternal-Fetal HIV transmission Prevention Trials" in Mann, Jonathan, Gruskin, Sofia, Grodin, Michael and Annas, George (eds.) *Health and Human Rights* (London: Routledge) pp. 373–379.

Appel, Deborah (1992) "Drug Use During Pregnancy: State Strategies to Reduce the Prevalence of Prenatal Drug Exposure" *University of Florida Journal of Law and Public Policy* vol. 5, pp. 103–148.

Appleton, Susan (1996) "When Welfare Reforms Promote Abortion: 'Personal Responsibility'; 'Family Values' and the Right to Choose" *Georgetown Law Journal*, vol. 85, no. 1 pp. 155–190.

Appleton, TC (1993) "Counselling in IVF surrogacy: An emotional minefield" *Journal of Obstetrics and Gynaecology* vol. 13 pp. 393–8.

Aramburu, Carlos (1994) "Is Population Policy Necessary? Latin America and the Andean Countries" in Finkle, Jason and McIntosh, Alison (eds.) *The New Politics of Population: Conflict and Consensus in Family Planning* (Oxford UP) pp. 159–178.

Arditti, R, Duelli-Klein, R, Minden, S (eds.) (1984) *Test Tube Women* (Boston: Pandora Press).

Armstrong, Claire (1997) "Thousands of Women Sterilised in Sweden without Consent" *British Medical Journal* vol. 315 pp. 563–568.

Arras, John and Blustein, Jeffrey (1996) "Reproductive Responsibility and Long-Term Contraceptives" in Moskowitz, Ellen and Jennings, Bruce *Coerced Contraception? Moral and Policy Challenges of Long-Acting Birth Control* (Washington DC: Georgetown UP) pp. 108–133.

Atherton, Rosalind (1999) "En ventre sa frigidaire: posthumous children in the succession context" *Legal Studies* vol. 19 no. 2 pp. 139–64.

Atiyah, PS (1997) *The Damages Lottery* (Oxford: Hart Publishing).

Audit Commission (1997) *First Class Delivery: Improving Maternity Services in England and Wales* (Abingdon: Audit Commission Publications).

Backett, K. (1992) "Taboos and excesses: lay moralities in middle class families" *Sociology of Health and Illness* vol. 14 pp. 255–74.

Badawi, N, Kurinczuk, JJ, Keogh, JM, Alessandri, LM, O'Sullivan, F, Burton, PR, Pemberton, PJ, and Stanley, FJ (1998) "Antepartum risk factors for newborn encephalopathy: the Western Australian case-control study" *British Medical Journal* vol. 317 pp. 1549–1553.

Bailey, Lucy (1999) "Refracted Selves? A Study of Changes in Self-Identity in the Transition to Motherhood" *Sociology* vol. 33 no. 2 pp. 335–52.

Baird, David T and Glasier, Anna F (1999) "Science Medicine and the Future: Contraception" *British Medical Journal* vol. 319 pp. 969–71.

Baker, Valerie (1994) "Surrogacy: One Physician's View of the Role of Law" *University of San Francisco Law Review* vol. 28 no. 3 pp. 603–612.

Ballard, Megan (1992) "A Practical Analysis of the Constitutional and Legal Infirmities of Norplant as a Condition of Probation" *Wisconsin Women's Law Journal* vol. 7 pp. 85–106.

Barad, David H and Cohen, Brian L (1996) "Oocyte Donation at Monte-Fiore Medical Center, Albert Einstein" in Cohen, Cynthia (ed.) *New Ways of Making Babies: The Case of Egg Donation* (Bloomington and Indianapolis: Indiana UP) pp. 15–28.

Barber, John (1998) "Code of Practice and Guidance on Human Genetic testing Services Supplied Direct to the Public" *Journal of Medical Genetics* vol. 35 no. 6 pp. 443–445.

Barker, DJP (1994) "The Fetal Origins of Adult Disease" *Fetal and Maternal Medicine Review* vol. 6 pp. 71–80.

—— (1995) "Fetal Origins of Coronary Heart Disease" *British Medical Journal* vol. 311 pp. 171–4.

Barratt, CLR (1993) "Donor Recruitment, Selection and Screening" in Barratt, CLR and Cooke, ID (eds.) *Donor Insemination* (Cambridge UP) pp. 3–11.

Barron, SL (1995) "The Galton Lecture for 1992: The Changing Status of the Fetus" in Barron, SL and Roberts, DF (eds.) *Issues in Fetal Medicine: Proceedings of the 29th Annual Symposium of the Galton Institute* (Basingstoke: Macmillan) pp. 1–21.

Barry, Ellen (1989) "Pregnant Prisoners" *Harvard Women's Law Journal* vol. 12 pp. 189–205.

Bartholet, Elizabeth (1993) *Family Bonds: Adoption and the Process of Parenting* (New York: Houghton Mifflin).

Barton, Chris (1996) "Two men and a baby: what of the law" *The Times* Tuesday 1 October 1996 p. B6.

Baruch, EH (1988) "A Womb of his Own" in Baruch, EH, D'Adamo, AF and Seager, J (eds.) *Embryos, Ethics and Women's Rights: Exploring the New Reproductive Technologies* (New York: Haworth) pp. 135–9.

Baucher, Jean (1991) "Tribal Conflict over Abortion" *Georgia Law Review* vol. 25 pp. 595–624.

Bayertz, Kurt (1994) *GenEthics: Technological Intervention in Human Reproduction as a Philosophical Problem* (Cambridge UP).

BBC Horizon (1998a) "The Limits to Birth" 26 March 1998 BBC2.

BBC Horizon (1998b) "Thalidomide: A Necessary Evil?" 29 October 1998 BBC2.

BBC Newsnight (1998) 5 November 1998 BBC2.

BBC Panorama (1999) 8 February 1999 BBC1.

Beazley, J (1975) "The Active Management of Labour" *American Journal of Obstetrics and Gynecology* vol. 122 pp. 161–8.

Beck, Ulrich (1992a) *Risk Society: Towards a New Modernity* (London: Sage).

Beck, Ulrich   (1992b) "The Reinvention of Politics: Towards a Theory of Reflexive Modernization" in Beck, U, Giddens, A and Lash, S (eds.) *Reflexive Modernization: Politics, Tradition and Aesthetics in the Modern Social Order* (Cambridge: Polity) pp. 1–55.

—— (1995) *Ecological Politics in an Age of Risk* (Cambridge: Polity).

—— (1997) *The Reinvention of Politics: Rethinking Modernity in the Global Social Order* (Cambridge: Polity).

—— (1999) *World Risk Society* (Cambridge: Polity).

—— and Gernsheim Beck, Elizabeth (1995) *The Normal Chaos of Love* (Cambridge: Polity).

Belizan, José, Althabe, Fernando, Barros, Fernando C and Alexander, Sophie (1999) "Rates and implications of caesarean sections in Latin America: ecological study" *British Medical Journal* vol. 319 pp. 1397–402.

Benagiano, G and Bianchi, P (1999) "Sex preselection: an aid to couples or a threat to humanity?" *Human Reproduction* vol. 14 pp. 868–70.

Berenknopf, Sandra (1997) "Judicial and Congressional Back-Door Methods that Limit the Effect of *Roe v. Wade*: There is no Choice if there is no Access" *Temple Law Review* vol. 70 pp. 653–698.

Berg, Barbara J (1995) "Listening to the Voices of the Infertile" Callahan, Joan (ed.) *Reproduction, Ethics and the Law: Feminist Responses* (Bloomington and Indianapolis: Indiana UP) pp. 80–108.

Berger, Abi (2000) " 'Kits' for male contraceptive pill" *British Medical Journal* vol. 320 p. 468.

Berger, David (1980) "Couples' Reactions to Male Infertility" *American Journal of Psychiatry* vol. 137 pp. 1047–9.

Berkowitz, Jonathan M and Snyder, Jack W (1998) "Racism and Sexism in Medically Assisted Conception" *Bioethics* vol. 12 no. 1 pp. 26–44.

Berlins, Marcel (1998) "Cloned Alone" *The Guardian* 3 February 1998 G2 p. 17.

Bernman, Jessica (1999) "China Attempts to Soften its One-Child Policy" *Lancet* vol. 353 13 February 1999 www.thelancet.com.

Berrien, Jacqueline (1990) "Pregnancy and Drug Use: The Dangerous and Unequal Use of Punitive Measures" *Yale Journal of Law and Feminism* vol. 2 pp. 239–250.

Bertin, Joan (1995) "Regulating Reproduction" in Callahan, Joan (ed.) *Reproduction, Ethics and the Law: Feminist Responses* (Bloomington and Indianapolis: Indiana UP) pp. 380–97.

Bevir, Mark (1999) "Foucault and Critique: Deploying Agency against Autonomy" *Political Theory* vol. 27 no. 1 pp. 65–84.

Bhattacharya, Siladitya and Templeton, Allan (2000) "In treating infertility, are multiple pregnancies unavoidable?" *New England Journal of Medicine* Vol. 343, No. 1, p. 58.

Bhlakrishnan, Radhika (1994), "The Social Context of Sex-Selection and the Politics of Abortion in India" in Sen, Gita and Snow, Rachel (eds.) *Power and Decision: The Social Control of Reproduction* (Cambridge MA: Harvard UP) pp. 267–286.

Bingol, N, Schuster C, Fuchs M, Iosub S, Turner G, Stone RK and Gromisch DS (1987) "The influence of socio-economic factors on the occurrence of fetal alcohol syndrome" *Advances in Alcohol and Substance Abuse* vol. 6 no. 4 pp. 105–18.

Birchard, Karen (2000) "Northern Ireland resists extending Abortion Act" *Lancet* vol. 356 p. 53.

Black, Tim (1999) "Impediments to effective fertility reduction" *British Medical Journal* vol. 319 pp. 932–3.

Blair, Peter S, Fleming, Peter J, Bensley, David, Smith, Iain, Bacon, Chris, Taylor, Elizabeth, Berry, Jem, Golding, Jean and Tripp, John (1996) "Smoking and the sudden infant death syndrome: results from 1993–5 case-control study for confidential inquiry into stillbirths and deaths in infancy" *British Medical Journal* vol. 313 pp. 195–198.

Blank, Robert (1998) "Regulation of Donor Insemination" in Daniels, Ken and Haimes, Erica (eds.) *Donor Insemination: International Social Science Perspectives* (Cambridge UP) pp. 131–50.

—— (1991) *Fertility Control: New Techniques, New Policy Issues* (New York: Greenwood Press).

Blumenfeld-Kosinski, Renate (1990) *Not of Woman Born* (Ithaca: Cornell UP).

Blyth, Eric (1994) "I wanted to be interesting. I wanted to be able to say 'I've done something with my life': Interviews with surrogate mothers in Britain" *Journal of Reproductive and Infant Psychology* vol. 12 pp. 189–198.

Bonavoglia, Angela (1997) "Late Term Abortion: Separating Fact from Fiction" *Ms Magazine* vol. 7 no. 6 pp. 54–71.

Bonnicksen, Andrea L (1996) "Private and Public Policy Alternatives in Oocyte Donation" in Cohen, Cynthia (ed.) *New Ways of Making Babies: The Case of Egg Donation* (Bloomington and Indianapolis: Indiana UP) pp. 156–74.

Booth, BE, Verma M and Beri, RS (1994) "Fetal sex determination in infants in Punjab, India: correlations and implications" *British Medical Journal* vol. 309 pp. 1259–1261.

Boseley, Sarah (1997) "What Price Parenthood?" *The Guardian* 15 May 1997 G2 p. 6.

—— (1998) "Let Chemists Sell Next-Day Emergency Pill say MPs" *The Guardian*, 12 June 1998 p. 11.

—— (2000a) "Danger to foetus in glass of wine" *The Guardian* 27 January 2000 p. 1.

—— (2000b) "One Birth in 80 from a test-tube" *The Guardian* 28 June 2000.

Botting, R, Rosato, M and Wood R (1998) "Teenage Mothers and the Health of their Children" *Population Trends* Autumn p. 93.

Boyle, Mary (1997) *Re-thinking Abortio: Psychology, Gender, Power and the Law* (London: Routledge).

Brahams, Diana (2000) "Condom maker wins against pregnancy claim" *Lancet* vol. 355 p. 560.

Braidotti, Rosi (1994) *Nomadic Subjects: Embodiment and Sexual Difference in Contemporary Feminist Theory* (New York: Columbia UP).

Brazaitis, Tom (1997) "Amid the Cloning Debate, We'll Repeat Ourselves" *Cleveland Plain Dealer* 9 March 1997 p. 3E.

Brazier, Margaret (1992) *Medicine, Patients and the Law*, (London: Penguin).

—— (1998) "Reproductive Rights: Feminism or Patriarchy" in Harris, John and Holm, Søren (eds.) *The Future of Human Reproduction: Ethics, Choice and Regulation* (Oxford: Clarendon Press) pp. 66–76.

—— (1999a) "Regulating the Reproduction Business?" *Medical Law Review* vol. 7 pp. 166–193.

—— (1999b) "Can you buy children?" *Child and Family Law Quarterly* vol. 11 no. 4 pp. 345–54.

Brazier, Margaret, Campbell, Alastair and Golombok, Susan (1998) *Surrogacy: Review for Health Ministers of Current Arrangements for Payments and Regulation* (London: HMSO) Cm 4068.

Brazier, Margaret and Miola, José (2000) "Bye-Bye Bolam: A Medical Litigation Revolution" *Medical Law Review* vol. 8 pp. 85–114.

Brewaeys, A, Ponjaert, I, Van Hall, EV and Golombok, S (1997) "Donor Insemination: Child development and family functioning in lesbian mother families" *Human Reproduction* vol. 12 no. 6 pp. 1349–59.

Briggs, R and King, TJ (1952) "Transplantation of living nuclei from blastula cells into enucleated frogs' eggs" *Proceedings of the National Academy of Sciences of the USA* 15 May 1952 pp. 455–463.

Brinig, Margaret (1994) "A Maternalistic Approach to Surrogacy: Comment on Richard Epstein's 'Surrogacy: The Case for Full Contractual Enforcement' " *University of San Francisco Law Review* vol. 28 no. 3 pp. 2377–2399.

—— (1995) "A Maternalistic Approach to Surrogacy" *Virginia Law Review* vol. 81 pp. 2377–99.

Brinsden, Peter, Appleton, Time, Murray, Elizabeth, Hussein, Mohammed, Akagbosu, Fidelis and Marcu, Samuel (2000) "Treatment by *in vitro* fertilisation with surrogacy: experience of one British centre" *British Medical Journal* vol. 320 pp. 924–928.

British Agencies for Adoption and Fostering Medical Group (1984) *AID and After* (London: BAAF).

British Fertility Society (1996) *Payment of Semen Donors* (Bristol: BFS).

British Medical Association (1990) Annual Report of Council 1989–90, Appendix V: Surrogacy Report *British Medical Journal* vol. 300 pp. 39–48.

—— (1996) *Changing Conceptions of Motherhood: The Practice of Surrogacy in Britain* (London: BMA).

—— (1998) *Human Genetics: Choice and Responsibility* (London: BMA).

British Pregnancy Advisory Service (1999) *Pricelist of Services* (London: BPAS).

Brock, Dan W (1996) "Funding New Reproductive Technologies: Should they be included in health insurance benefit packages?" in Cohen, Cynthia (ed.) *New Ways of Making Babies: The Case of Egg Donation* (Bloomington and Indianapolis: Indiana UP) pp. 213–30.

Brooks, Alex (1998) "Mentally ill patients need protection from inappropriate genetic testing" *British Medical Journal* vol. 316 p. 903.

Brown, Barry (1995) "Reconciling Property law with Advances in Reproductive Science" *Stanford Law and Policy Review* vol. 6 no. 2 pp. 73–88.

Brown, George (1996) "Long-Acting Contraceptives: Rationale, Current Development and Ethical Implications" in Moskowitz, Ellen and Jennings, Bruce *Coerced Contraception? Moral and Policy Challenges of Long-Acting Birth Control* (Washington D.C.: Georgetown UP) pp. 34–49.

Brown, Stephen (1994) "Matters of life and death: the law and medicine" *Medico-Legal Journal* vol. 62 52.

Bunker, John, Houghton, Joan and Baum, Michael (1998) "Putting the Risk of Breast Cancer into Perspective" *British Medical Journal* vol. 317 pp. 1307–1309.

Burley, Justine (1998) "The Price of Eggs: Who Should Bear the Costs of Fertility Treatments?" in Harris, John and Holm, Søren (eds.) *The Future of Human Reproduction: Ethics, Choice and Regulation* (Oxford: Clarendon Press) pp. 127–149.

Burley, Justine and Harris, John (1999) "Human Cloning and Child Welfare" *Journal of Medical Ethics* vol. 25 pp. 108–113.

Cahill, Lisa Sowle (1996) "Moral Concerns about Institutionalized Gamete Donation" in Cohen, Cynthia (ed.) *New Ways of Making Babies: The Case of Egg Donation* (Bloomington and Indianapolis: Indiana UP) pp. 70–87.

Callahan, Joan C and Roberts, Dorothy, E (1996) "A Feminist Social Justice Approach to Reproduction Assisting Technologies: A Case Study on the Limits of Liberal Theory" *Kentucky Law Journal* vol. 84 no. 4 pp. 1197–1234.

Cao Antonio (1991) "Antenatal Diagnosis of B-Thalassemia in Sardinia" in Bankowski Z and Kapron AM (eds.) *Genetics, Ethics and Human Values: Human Genome Mapping, Genetic Screening and Gene Therapy, Proceedings of the XXIVth CIOMS Round Table Conference* (Geneva: CIOMS) pp. 72–77.

Capron, AM and Radin, MJ (1990) "Choosing Family Law over Contract Law as a Paradigm for Surrogate Motherhood" in Gostin, Larry (ed.) *Surrogate Motherhood: Politics and Privacy* (Bloomington: University of Indiana Press) pp. 59–76.

Casas-Becerra, Lidia (1997) "Women Prosecuted and Imprisoned for Abortion in Chile" *Reproductive Health Matters* vol. 9 pp. 29–36.

CCNE [Comité Consultatif National d'Ethique pour les sciences de la vie et de la santé] (1991) *Opinion on embryonic and foetal reduction* Opinion no. 24 (Paris: CCNE).

—— (1997) *Reply to the President of the French Republic on the subject of reproductive cloning* Opinion no. 54 (Paris: CCNE).

Center for Reproductive Law and Policy (1995) *Women of the World: Laws and Policies Affecting their Reproductive Lives* (New York: CRLP).

—— (1998) *Emergency Contraception: Contraception not Abortion* (New York: CRLP).

Cepko, Roberta (1993) "Involuntary Sterilisation of Mentally Disabled Women" *Berkeley Women's Law Journal* vol. 8 pp. 122–165.

Chamberlain, Geoffrey and Steer, Philip (1999) "ABC of labour care: Labour in special circumstances" *British Medical Journal* vol. 318 pp. 1124–1127.

Chamie, Joseph (1994) "Trends, Variations and Contradictions in National Policies to Influence Fertility" in Finkle, Jason and McIntosh, Alison (eds.) *The New Politics of Population: Conflict and Consensus in Family Planning* (Oxford UP) pp. 37–50.

Channel 4 (1999) *The Baby Makers* 11 May 1999.

Charatan, Fred (2000) "US court refutes Nebraska's antiabortion law" *British Medical Journal* vol. 321 p. 70.

Chavkin, Wendy (1991) "Mandatory Treatment for Drug Use During Pregnancy" *Journal of the American Medical Association* vol. 260 pp. 1556–61.

——, Elman, Deborah and Wise, Paul H (1997) "Mandatory Testing of Pregnant Women and Newborns: HIV, Drug Use and Welfare Policy" *Fordham Urban Law Journal* vol. 14 no. 4 pp. 749–755.

Cherry, April (1995) "A Feminist Understanding of Sex-Selective Abortion: Solely a Matter of Choice?" *Wisconsin Women's Law Journal*, vol. 10, pp. 161–223.

—— (1997) "Choosing Substantive Justice: A Discussion of 'Choice', 'Rights' and the New Reproductive Technologies" *Wisconsin Women's Law Journal vol.* 11 pp. 431–441.

Chervenak, FA and McCullough, LB (1996) "The fetus as a patient: an essential ethical concept for maternal-fetal medicine" *Journal of Maternal and Fetal Medicine* vol. 5 no. 3 pp. 115–19.

Clarke, Linda (1989) "Abortion: A Rights Issue?" in Lee, Robert and Morgan, Derek (eds.) *Birthrights: Law and Ethics at the Beginnings of Life* (London: Routledge) pp. 155–171.

Cleland, John, Philips, James, Amin, Sajeda and Kamel, GM (1994) *The Determinants of Reproductive Change in Bangladesh: Success in a Challenging Environment* (Washington DC: The World Bank).

Cohen, Cynthia (1996) "Parents Anonymous" in Cohen, Cynthia (ed.) *New Ways of Making Babies: The Case of Egg Donation* (Bloomington and Indianapolis: Indiana UP) pp. 88–105.

Cohen, Joel E (1999) "How Many People can the Earth Support?" in Beauchamp, Dan and Steinbock, Bonnie (eds.) *New Ethics for the Public's Health* (Oxford UP) pp. 330–8.

Collins, Hugh (1997) *The Law of Contract* 3rd edition (London: Butterworths).

——(1999) *Regulating Contracts* (Oxford UP).

Colman, Alan (1999) "Why Human Cloning Should not be Attempted" in Burley, Justine (ed.) *The Genetic Revolution and Human Rights* (Oxford UP) pp. 14–18.

Conaghan, Joanne (2000) "Reassessing the Feminist Theoretical Project in Law" *Journal of Law and Society* vol. 27 no. 3 pp. 351–85.

—— and Mansell, Wade (1999) *The Wrongs of Tort* 2nd edn. (London: Pluto).

Condit, Deirdre Moira (1995) "Fetal Personhood: Political Identity Under Construction" in Boling, Patricia (ed.) *Expecting Trouble: Surrogacy, Fetal Abuse and New Reproductive Technologies* (Oxford: Westview) pp. 25–54.

Congregation for the Doctrine of the Faith (1990) "Instruction on Respect for Human Life in its Origin and on the Dignity of Procreation" in Hull, Richard (ed.) *Ethical Issues in the New Reproductive Technologies* (Belmont, Ca: Wadsworth) pp. 21–39.

Cook-Deegan, Robert Mullan (1991) "Public Policy Implications of the Human Genome Project" in Bankowski Z and Kapron AM (eds.) *Genetics, Ethics and Human Values: Human Genome Mapping, Genetic Screening and Gene Therapy, Proceedings of the XXIVth CIOMS Round Table Conference* (Geneva, CIOMS) pp. 56–71.

Cooke R and Golombok S (1996) "A survey of semen donation—phase 2: the view of the donors" *Human Reproduction* vol. 10 pp. 951–959.

Cooney, Tom (1989) "Sterilisation and the Mentally Handicapped" *Dublin University Law Journal* vol. 11 pp. 56–73.

Corea, Gena (1985) *The Mother Machine: Reproductive Technologies from Artifical Insemination to Artificial Wombs* (New York: Harper and Row).

—— (1990) "The Subversive Sperm: 'A False Strain of Blood' " in Hull, Richard (ed.) *Ethical Issues in the New Reproductive Technologies* (Belmont, Ca.: Wadsworth) pp. 56–68.

Cornell, Drucilla (1995) *The Imaginary Domain: Abortion, Pornography and Sexual Harassment* (London, Routledge).

Cossey, Dilys (1998) "Campaigning for Abortion Law Reform" in Lee, Ellie (ed.) *Abortion Law and Politics Today* (London, Macmillan) pp. 20–28.

Cotton, Kim (2000) "Surrogacy should pay" *British Medical Journal* vol. 320 pp. 928–9.

Council of Europe (1997) *Additional Protocol to the Convention for the Protection of Human Rights and the Dignity of the Human Being with Regard to Application of Biology and Medicine on the Prohibition of Cloning Human Beings* (Strasbourg: Council of Europe).

Cox, Neville (1999) "The Failure of 'Rights Talk' in the Field of Bioethics: The European Convention on Human Rights and Biomedicine" in Junker-Kenny, Maureen (ed.) *Designing Life? Genetics, Procreation and Ethics* (Aldershot: Ashgate) pp. 23–53.

Craft, Ian (1997) "Should egg donors be paid?" *British Medical Journal* vol. 314 pp. 1400–1.

——, Gorgy, Amin, Podsiadly, Barbara and Venkat, Geetha (2000) "Limiting Multiple Births" *Lancet* vol. 355 pp. 1103–4.

Cramb, Auslan (1998) "Schoolgirls are left holding the Virtual Baby" *Electronic Telegraph* issue 1084 *www.telegraph.com*.

Crawford, R (1977) "You are dangerous to your health: the ideology and policits of victim-blaming" *International Journal of Health Services* vol. 7 no. 4 pp. 663–80.

—— (1994) "The Boundaries of the self and the unhealthy other: reflections on health culture and AIDS" *Social Science and Medicine* vol. 38 no. 10 1347– 65.

Cumberledge, J (1993) *Changing Childbirth* (London HMSO).

Cunningham-Burley, Sarah (1998) "Understanding Disability" *Progress in Reproduction* vol. 2 pp. 10–11.

Cussins, Charis (1998) "Producing Reproduction: Techniques of Normalization and Naturalization in Infertility Clinics" in Franklin, Sarah and Ragone, Helene *Reproducing Reproduction: Kinship, Power and Technological Innovation* (Pennsylvania UP) pp. 66–101.

Daniels, Cynthia (1999) "Fathers, Mothers and Fetal Harm" in Morgan, Lynn M and Michaels, Meredith W (eds.) *Fetal Subjects: Feminist Positions* (Philadelphia: Pennsylvania UP) pp. 83–98

Daniels, Ken (1987) "Semen Donors in New Zealand: Their Characteristics and Attitudes" *Clinical Reproduction and Fertility* vol. 5 no. 4 pp. 177–90.

—— (1994) "The Swedish Insemination Act and its Impact" *Australian and New Zealand Journal of Obstetrics and Gynaecology* vol. 34 no. 4 pp. 437–9.

—— (1998) "The Semen Providers" in Daniels, Ken and Haimes, Erica (eds.) *Donor Insemination: International Social Science Perspectives* (Cambridge UP) pp. 76–104.

Daniels, KR (2000) "To give or sell human gametes—the interplay between pragmatics, policy and ethics" *Journal of Medical Ethics* vol. 26 pp. 206–11.

Danis, Jodi (1995), "Sexism and 'The Superfluous Female': Arguments for Regulating Pre-Implantation Sex Selection" *Harvard Women's Law Journal* vol. 18 pp. 219–264.

Das Gupta, Monica (1987) "Selective Discrimination Against Female Children in Rural Punjab, India" *Population and Development Review* vol. 13, no. 1, pp. 90–95.

David, Henry and Radenakers, Jani (1996) "Lessons from the Dutch Abortion Experience" *Studies in Family Planning* vol.27 no.6, pp. 341–343.

Davis, DL, Friedler G, Mattison D and Morris R (1992) "Male mediated teratogenesis and other reproductive effects: biological and epidemiologic findings and a plea for clinical research" *Reproductive Toxicology* vol. 6 pp. 289–92.

Dawkins, Richard (1998) "What's Wrong with Cloning?" in Nussbaum, Martha and Sunstein, Cass (eds.) *Clones and Clones: Facts and Fantasies about Human Cloning* (New York: Norton) pp. 54–66.

Deech, Ruth (1999) "Payment to gamete and embryo donors" *Journal of Fertility Counselling* vol. 6 no. 1 pp. 6–7.

De Gama, Katherine (1993) "A Brave New World? Rights Discourse and the Politics of Reproductive Autonomy" in Bottomley, Anne and Conaghan, Joanne (eds.) *Feminist Theory and Legal Strategy* (Oxford: Blackwell) pp. 114–130.

Denton, Jane (2000) "Twins, Triplets and More: Implications for the Families" Paper presented at Comment on Reproductive Ethics' conference *What About Me? The Child of ART* 28 March 2000, Royal Society, London.

Department of Health (1998) *HIV/AIDS strategy report of a conference held on 27 October 1998* (London: HMSO).

—— (1999a) *Consent to Treatment: Summary of Legal Rulings* HSC 1999/031 19 February 1999.

—— (1999b) *Oral Contraceptives: Clearer Information for Women and Health Professionals* 1999/0206 Wednesday 7 April 1999.

—— (2000a) *Government Response to the McLean Review on Consent to Storage and Use of Human Sperm and Eggs* 2000/0486 25 August 2000.

—— (2000b) *Adoption: A New Approach* Cm 5017 (London: HMSO)

Department of Health and Social Security (1977) *Prevention and Health: Everybody's Business* Cmnd 7047 (London: HMSO).

Dewar, John (1989) "Fathers in Law? The Case of AID" in Lee, Robert and Morgan, Derek (eds.) *Birthrights: Law and Ethics at the Beginnings of Life* (London: Routledge) pp. 115–131.

De Wert, Guido (1998) "The Post-menopause: Playground for Reproductive Technology? Some Ethical Reflections" in Harris, John and Holm, Søren (eds.) *The Future of Human Reproduction: Ethics, Choice and Regulation* (Oxford: Clarendon Press) pp. 221–237.

Dillner, L (1994a) "Use of fetal eggs for infertility treatment is banned" *British Medical Journal* vol. 309 pp. 289–290.

—— (1994b) "British public will rule on fertility advances" *British Medical Journal* vol. 308 pp. 153–158.

Dobson, Roger (2000) " 'Designer baby' cures sister" *British Medical Journal* vol. 321 p. 1040.

Doniger, Wendy (1998) "Sex and the Mythological Clone" in Nussbaum, Martha and Sunstein, Cass (eds.) *Clones and Clones: Facts and Fantasies about Human Cloning* (New York: Norton) pp. 114–38.

Donohoe, Margaret M (1996) "Our Epidemic of Unnecessary Cesarean Sections: The Role of the Law in Creating it, the Role of the Law in Stopping it" *Wisconsin Women's Law Journal* vol. 11 pp. 197–241.

Donovan, P. (1998) "Falling Teen Pregnancy Birthrates: What's Behind the Declines?" *The Guttmacher Report on Public Policy* Vol. 1 No. 5 October 1998.

Dorozynski (2000) "France bans morning after pill from schools" *British Medical Journal* vol. 321 p. 70.

Douglas, Gillian (1991) *Law, Fertility and Reproduction* (London: Sweet and Maxwell).

Doyal, Len (1999) "Informed Consent: A response to recent correspondence" *British Medical Journal* vol. 316 pp. 1000–1.

Draper, Elaine (1991) *Risky Business: Genetic Testing and Exclusionary Practices in the Hazardous Workplace* (Cambridge UP).

Draper, Heather and Chadwick, Ruth (1999) "Beware! Preimplantation genetic diagnosis may solve some old problems but it also raises new ones" *Journal of Medical Ethics* vol. 25 pp. 114–20.

Dresser, Rebecca (1996) "Long-Term Contraceptives in the Criminal Justice System" in Moskowitz, Ellen and Jennings, Bruce *Coerced Contraception? Moral and Policy Challenges of Long-Acting Birth Control* (Washington DC: Georgetown UP) pp. 134–50.

Drife, James (1997) "Maternity Services: The Audit Commission Reports" *British Medical Journal* vol. 314 p. 844.

Duden, Barbara (1993) *Disembodying women: perspectives on pregnancy and the unborn* trans. Lee Hoinacki (Cambridge, Mass.: Harvard UP).

—— (1999) "The Fetus on the 'Farther Shore': Toward a History of the Unborn" in *Fetal Subjects: Feminist Positions* Morgan, Lynn M and Michaels, Meredith W (Philadelphia: Pennsylvania UP) pp. 13–25.

Duffy, Teresa A, Wolfe, Charles DA, Varden, Claire, Kennedy, Jane, Chrystie, Ian L and Banatvala, Jangu E (1998) "Antenatal HIV testing: current problems, future solutions, survey of uptake in one London hospital" *British Medical Journal* vol. 31 pp. 270–271.

Dugdale, R (1877) *The Jukes: A Study in Crime, Pauperism, Disease and Heredity* (New York: GP Puttnam & Sons).

Dunstan, GR (1995) " 'Calming or Harming?' The Ethics of Screening for Fetal Defects" in Barron, SL and Roberts, DF (eds.) *Issues in Fetal Medicine: Proceedings of the 29th Annual Symposium of the Galton Institute* (Basingstoke: Macmillan) pp. 134–141.

Dworkin, Andrea (1983) *Right Wing Women* (London: Women's Press).

Dworkin, Gerald (1988) *The Theory and Practice of Autonomy* (Cambridge UP).

Dworkin, Ronald (1993) *Life's Dominion: an argument about abortion and euthanasia* (London: Harper Collins).

Dyer, Clare (1998) "Trusts Face Damages after Forcing Women to Have Caesareans" *British Medical Journal* vol. 316 p. 1477.

—— (1999) "Legal Suit over Norplant collapses" *British Medical Journal* vol. 318 p. 485.

—— (2000a) "Clinic sued for unauthorised use of sperm" *British Medical Journal* vol. 320, p. 464.

—— (2000b) "Triplets' parents win right to damages for extra child" *British Medical Journal* vol. 321 p. 1306.

——, Boseley, Sarah and Radford, Tim (1996) "Fight goes on for new life after death" *The Guardian* 23 November 1996 p. 3.

Dyer, Owen (1996) "Canadian Women Compensated for Sterilisation" *British Medical Journal* vol. 312 pp. 330–331.

Eakins, Pamela (1986) *The American Way of Birth* (Philadelphia: Temple UP).

Eberl, Jason (2000) "The Beginning of Personhood: A Thomistic Biological Analysis" *Bioethics* vol. 14 no. 2 pp. 134–57.

Edwards, Jeanette (1998) "Donor Insemination and 'Public Opinion' " in Daniels, Ken and Haimes, Erica (eds.) *Donor Insemination: International Social Science Perspectives* (Cambridge UP) pp. 151–72.

—— (1999) "Explicit Connections: Ethnographic Enquiry in North West England" in Edwards, Jeanette, Franklin, Sarah, Hirsch, Eric, Price, Frances and Strathern, Marilyn (eds.) *Technologies of Procreation: Kinship in the Age of Assisted Conception* 2nd edn. (London: Routledge) pp. 60–90.

Edwards, Robert (1989) *Life Before Birth: Reflections on the Embryo Debate* (London: Hutchinson).

—— and Steptoe, Patrick (1981) *A Matter of Life: The Sensational Story of the World's First Test-Tube Baby* (London: Sphere).

Eftekhar, Kathy and Steer, Philip (2000) "Women Choose Caesarean Section" *British Medical Journal* vol. 320 p. 1074.

Ehrenreich, B and English, D (1978) *For Her Own Good: 150 Years of the Experts' Advice to Women* (London: Pluto Press).

Eisenberg, L (1976) "The outcome as a cause: predestination and human cloning" *Journal of Medicine and Philosophy* vol. 1 no. 4 pp. 318–31.

Ellison, Michael (1998) "Triumph of Terror" *The Guardian* 29 October 1998, G2 pp. 4–5.

Engelhardt, HT (1986) *The Foundations of Bioethics* (Oxford UP).

Epstein, Richard (1995) "Surrogacy: The Case for Full Contractual Enforcement" *Virginia Law Review* vol. 81 pp. 2305–2341.

Equinox (1999) *Sweden, Sex and the Disappearing Doctors* Channel 4, 26 April 1999.

Erin, Charles (1998) "The Use of Ovarian Tissue" in Harris, John and Holm, Søren (eds.) *The Future of Human Reproduction: Ethics, Choice and Regulation* (Oxford: Clarendon Press) pp. 162–175.

Eskridge, William N and Stein, Edward (1998) "Queer Clones" in Nussbaum, Martha and Sunstein, Cass (eds.) *Clones and Clones: Facts and Fantasies about Human Cloning* (New York: Norton) pp. 95–113.

European Commission (1999) *Report from the Commission on the implementation of council directive 92/85/EEC of 19 October 1992 on the introduction of measures to encourage improvements in the health and safety at work of pregnant workers and workers who have recently given birth or are breastfeeding* (COM/99/0100).

European Parliament (1997) *European Parliament and Council Directive on the Legal Protection of Biotechnologies Inventions* (COM/97/446).

Evans, Heidi (1993), "Womb with a View: Unborn Babies Star in Fetal Film Fests" *Wall Street Journal*, 30 November 1997, at A1.

Everett, Hilary and Turner, Anne (1997) "Aims in Termination Counselling" in Lee, Ellie and Lattimer, Maxine (eds.) *Issues in Pregnancy Counselling: What do Women Need and Want?* (Canterbury, Pro-Choice Forum) pp. 47–53.

Ewigman BG, Crane JP, Frigoletto FD, LeFevre ML, Bain RP and McNellis D (1993) "Effect of Prenatal Ultrasound Screening on Prenatal Outcome" *New England Journal of Medicine* vol. 329 no 12 pp. 821–7.

Faludi, Susan (1992) *Backlash: The Undeclared War Against Women* (London: Chatto and Windus).

Family Planning Association (1993) *Children who have Children* (London: FPA).

Farmer, RDT, Williams, TJ, Simposon, EL and Nightingale, AL (2000) "Effects of 1995 pill scare on rates of venous throboembolism among women taking combined oral contraceptives: analysis of General Practice Research Database" *British Medical Journal* vol. 321 pp. 477–9.

Farquhar, Dion (1995) "Reproductive Technologies are Here to Stay" *Sojourner* vol. 20 no. 5 pp. 6–7.

—— (1996) *The Other Machine: Discourse and Reproductive Technologies* (London: Routledge).

Farrell, S (1997) "Screen Yourself by Mail Order" *The Times* 24 September 1997 p. 6.

Fasouliotis, Sozos, J and Schenker, Joseph G (1999) "Social Aspects in Assisted Reproduction" *Human Reproduction Update* vol. 5 no. 1 pp. 26–39.

Fathalla, Mahmoud (1994) "Fertility Control Technology: A Woman Centred Approach" in Sen, Gita, Chen, Lincoln and Germain, Adrienne (eds.) *Population Policies Reconsidered: Health, Empowerment and Rights* (Cambridge, Mass: Harvard UP) pp. 223–234.

FDA Advisory Committee on Obstetrics and Gynaecology (1968) *Report on Intrauterine Devices Document* No, 290–137 0–68–3.

Feinberg, Joel (1986) *The Moral Limits of the Criminal Law. Vol. 3 Harm to Self* (Oxford, OUP).

Feversham Committee (1960) *Report of the Departmental Committee on Human Artificial Insemination* Cmnd 1105 (London: HMSO).

Field, Martha (1990) *Surrogate Motherhood: The Legal and Human Issues* (Cambridge, Mass: Harvard UP).

—— (1992) "Reproductive Technologies and Surrogacy: Legal Issues" *Creighton Law Review* vol. 25 no. 5 pp. 1589–1598.

—— (1993a), "Killing the Handicapped—Before and After Birth" *Harvard Women's Law Journal* vol. 16, pp. 79–138.

—— (1993b) "Surrogate Motherhood" in Eekelaar, J and Šarčević, P (eds.) *Parenthood in Modern Society: legal and social issues for the twenty-first century* (London: Nijhoff) pp. 223–232.

Fielder, HMP, Poon-King CM, Palmer, SR, Moss, N and Coleman, G (2000) "Assessment of impact on health of residents living near the Nant-y-Gwyddon landfill site: retrospective analysis" *British Medical Journal* vol. 320 pp. 19–22.

Finer, Joel Jay (1991) "Towards Guidelines for Compelling Cesarean Surgery: Of Rights, Responsibility and Decisional Authenticity" *Minnesota Law Review* vol. 76 pp. 239–94.

Finkelstein, Katherine Eban (2000) "Medical Rebels: When Caring for Patients means Breaking the Rules" *The Nation* 21 February 2000.

Finkle, Jason and McIntosh, C Alison (1994) *The New Politics of Population: Conflict and Consensus in Family Planning* (Oxford UP).

Fisher, Fleur and Sommerville, Ann (1998) "To Everything there is a Season? Are There Medical Grounds for Refusing Fertility Treatment to Older Women?" in Harris, John and Holm, Søren (eds.) *The Future of Human Reproduction: Ethics, Choice and Regulation* (Oxford: Clarendon Press) pp. 203–220.

Fisher, S and Gillman, I (1991) "Surrogate motherhood: attachment, attitudes and social support" *Psychiatry* vol. 54 pp. 13–20.

Fisk, Nicholas and Trew, Geoffrey (1999) "Two's company, three's a crowd for embryo transfer" *Lancet* vol. 354 pp. 1572–3.

Fitzpatrick, Michael (2001) *The Tyranny of Health: Doctors and the Regulation of Lifestyle* (London: Routledge).

Fletcher, Joseph (1998) [1974] "Ending Reproductive Roulette Revisited" in Pence, Gregory E (ed.) *Classic Works in Medical Ethics* (Boston Mass.: McGraw Hill) pp. 118–124.

Fletcher, JC and Evans, MI (1983) "Maternal bonding in early fetal ultrasound examinations" *New England Journal of Medicine* vol. 308 no. 7 pp. 392–3.

Ford, Norman (1988) *When Did I Begin?* (Cambridge UP).

Foucault, Michel (1981) *The History of Sexuality Volume One* (London: Penguin).

—— (1982) "Afterword: The Subject and Power" in Dreyfus, H and Rabinow, P (eds.) *Beyond Structuralism and Hermaneutics* (University of Chicago Press).

—— (1984) "Space, Knowledge and Power" in P Rabinow (ed.) *The Foucault Reader* (New York, Pantheon).

Fox, Bonnie and Worts, Diana (1999) "Revisiting the Critique of Medicalized Childbirth: A Contribution to the Sociology of Birth" *Gender & Society* vol. 13 no. 3 pp. 326–46.

Fox, Marie (1998) "Abortion Decision-making—Taking Men's Needs Seriously" in Lee, Ellie (ed.) *Abortion Law and Politics Today* (London, Macmillan) pp. 198–215.

Franklin, Sarah (1997) *Embodied Progress: A Cultural Account of Assisted Conception* (London: Routledge).

—— (1999) "Making Representations: The Parliamentary Debate on the Human Fertilisation and Embryology Act and Orphaned Embryos" in Edwards, Jeanette, Franklin, Sarah, Hirsch, Eric, Price, Frances and Strathern, Marilyn (eds.) *Technologies of Procreation: Kinship in the Age of Assisted Conception* 2nd edn. (London: Routledge) pp. 127–170.

Freeman, Michael (1989) "Is Surrogacy Exploitative?" in McLean, Sheila (ed.) *Legal Issues in Human Reproduction* (London: Gower) pp. 164–84.

—— (1996) "The New Birth Right? Identity and the child of the reproduction revolution" *International Journal of Children's Rights* vol. 4 pp. 273–97.

—— (1999) "Does Surrogacy Have a Future After Brazier?" *Medical Law Review* vol. 7 pp. 1–20.

Friedman, Marilyn (1996) "Autonomy and Social Relationships: Rethinking the Feminist Critique" in Meyers, Diana Tietjens (eds.) *Feminists Rethink the Self* (Boulder: Westview) pp. 40–61.

Furedi, Ann (1998a), "Wrong but the Right Thing to Do: Public Opinion and Abortion" in Ellie Lee (ed.) *Abortion Law and Politics Today* (London: Macmillan), pp. 159–171.

—— (1998b) "Medical Ethics Forum: Ethics and Abortion for Abnormality" in Lee, Ellie and Davey, Jenny *Attitudes to Abortion for Fetal Abnormality* (Canterbury: Pro-Choice Forum) pp. 42–58.

—— (2000) *Abortion: A Provider's Perspective* Paper presented at Strategic Thinking for the Millenium: Women and Law University of Westminster, 23 June 2000.

Furedi, Frank (1997) *Population and Development: A Critical Introduction* (Cambridge: Polity).

Gallagher, Janet (1987) "Prenatal Invasions and Interventions: What's Wrong with Fetal Rights?" *Harvard Women's Law Journal* vol. 10 pp. 9–41.

—— (1995) "Collective Bad Faith: 'Protecting the Fetus' " in Callahan, Joan (ed.) *Reproduction, Ethics and the Law: Feminist Responses* (Bloomington and Indianapolis: Indiana UP) pp.343–79.

Gallagher-Mackay, Kelly (1997) "Routine Offering of HIV Tests to Pregnant Women: Foetal Supremacy, Medical Authority and Invisible Effects on Women" *Canadian Journal of Women and the Law* vol. 9, no. 2, pp. 336–364.

Galloway, Patrick, Hammel, Eugene and Lee, Ronald (1994) "Fertility Decline in Prussia 1875–1910: A Pooled Cross-Section Time-Series Analysis" *Population Studies* vol. 48 no.1 pp. 135–158.

Galton, Francis (1908) *Memoirs of my Life* (London: Methuen).

Galton, RDJ and Doyal, L (1998) "Goodbye Dolly? The ethics of human cloning" *Journal of Medical Ethics* vol. 24 p. 279.

Gaudium et Spes (1966) *Pastoral Constitution on the Church in the World of Today* (London: Catholic Truth Society).

Gardner, RL (1999) "Cloning and Individuality" in Burley, Justine (ed.) *The Genetic Revolution and Human Rights* (Oxford UP) pp. 29–37.

Gastaldo, Denise (1997) "Health Education and the Concept of Biopower" in Peterson, Alan and Bunton, Robin (eds.) *Foucault, Health and Medicine* (London: Routledge) pp. 113–133.

Gelb, Joyce (1996) "Abortion and Reproductive Choice: Policy and Politics in Japan" in Githens, Marianne and McBride Stetson, Dorothy (eds.) *Abortion Politics: Public Policy in Cross-Cultural Perspective* (London: Routledge) pp. 119–137.

Gerber-Fried, M (1997) "Abortion in the United States: Barriers to Access" *Reproductive Health Matters*, vol. 9, pp. 37–45.

Gericke, G (1990) "The Role of Human Genetics in Society: Implications for Legal Involvement" *Medicine and Law* vol. 9 no. 3 pp. 930–938.

Gibb DM, MacDonagh SE, Gupta R, Tookey PA, Peckham CS and Ades AE (1998) "Factors affecting uptake of antenatal HIV testing in London: results of a multicentre study" *British Medical Journal* vol. 316 pp. 259–61.

Giddens, Anthony (1991) *Modernity and Self-Identity: Self and Society in the Late Modern Age* (Cambridge: Polity).

—— (1994) "Living in a Post-Traditional Society" in Beck, U, Giddens, A and Lash, S (eds.) *Reflexive Modernization: Politics, Tradition and Aesthetics in the Modern Social Order* (Cambridge: Polity) pp. 56–109

Gillis, John, Tilly, Louise and Levine, David (1992) *The European Experience of Declining Fertility 1850 1970: The Quiet Revolution* (Oxford: Blackwell).

Gillon, Ranaan (1985) *Philosophical Medical Ethics* (Chichester: John Wiley).

Ginsburg, Faye (1998), "Rescuing the Nation: Operation Rescue and the Rise of Anti-Abortion Militance" in Rickie Solinger (ed.) (1998) *Abortion Wars: A Half Century of Struggle 1950–2000* (Berkeley, University of California Press) pp. 227–50.

Glannon, Walter (1998) "Genes, Embryos and Future People" *Bioethics* vol. 12 no. 3 pp. 187–211.

Glasier, Anna (1992), "Mifepristone (RU486) Compared with High Dose Estrogen and Progeston for Emergency Postcoital Contraception" *New England Journal of Medicine* vol. 327 pp. 1041–1044.

Glassner, B (1992) *Bodies: The Tyranny of Perfection* (Los Angeles, CA: Lowell House).

Glazebrook, Peter (1993) "What care must be taken of an unborn baby?" *Cambridge Law Journal* vol. 52 pp. 20–2.

Glover, Jonathan (1977) *Causing Death and Saving Lives* (London: Penguin).

—— (1989) *Fertility and the Family: The Glover Report on Reproductive Technologies to the European Commission* (London: The 4th Estate).

—— (1999) "Eugenics and Human Rights" in Burley, Justine (ed.) *The Genetic Revolution and Human Rights* (Oxford UP) pp.101–24.

Godfrey K, Robinson S, Barker DJP, Osmond C and Cox V (1996) "Maternal nutrition in early and late pregnancy in relation to placental and fetal growth" *British Medical Journal* vol. 312 pp. 410–4.

Golombok, S, Brewaeys, A, Cook, R, Giavazzi, MT, Guerra, D, Mantovani, A, Van Hall, E, Crosignani, PG and Dexeus, S (1996) "The European Study of Assisted Reproduction Families: Family Functioning and Child Development" *Human Reproduction* vol. 11 no. 10 pp. 2324–31.

——, Cook, R, Bish, A and Murray, C (1995) "Families created by the new reproductive technologies: quality of parenting and social and emotional development of the children" *Child Development* vol. 66 no. 2 pp. 285–98.

Gordts S, Rombauts L, Roziers P, Serneels A, Gaurois B, Vercruyssen M, and Campo R (1998) "Intracytoplasmic sperm injection in the treatment of male subfertility" *European Journal of Obstetrics, Gynecology and Reproductive Biology* vol. 81 no. 2 pp. 207–11

Gosden, Roger (1999) *Designer Babies, The Brave New World of Reproductive Technology* (London: Victor Gollancz).

Gostin, Larry (1990) "A Civil Liberties Analysis of Surrogacy Arrangements" in Gostin, Larry (ed.) *Surrogate Motherhood: Politics and Privacy* (Bloomington and Indianapolis: Indiana UP) pp. 3–23.

Gottlieb, Claes, Lalos, Othon and Lindblak, Frank (2000) "Disclosure of donor insemination to the child: the impact of Swedish legislation on couples' attitudes" *Human Reproduction* vol. 15 no. 9 pp. 2052–6.

Gottlieb, Scott (1998) "Elective caesarean and zidovudine cuts HIV transmission *British Medical Journal* vol. 317, p. 11.

—— (1999) "US effort to cut caesarean section rate may be harmful" *British Medical Journal* vol. 318 p. 147.

—— (2000) "UN says up to half the teenagers in Africa will die of AIDS" *British Medical Journal* vol. 321 p. 67.

Gould, Mike (1996) "First surrogate granny gives birth to girl" *The Observer* 8 December 1996 p. A2.

Gould, Stephen Jay (1998) "Dolly's Fashion and Louis's Passion" in Nussbaum, Martha and Sunstein, Cass (eds.) *Clones and Clones: Facts and Fantasies about Human Cloning* (New York: Norton) pp. 41–53.

Grabrick DM, Hartmann LC, Cerhan JR, Vierkant RA, Therneau TM, Vachov CM, Olson JE, Couch FJ, Anderson KE, Pankratz VS, Sellers TA (2000) "Risk of Breast Cancer with Oral Contraceptive use in Women with a Family History of Breast Cancer" *Journal of the American Medical Association* vol. 283 no. 14 pp. 1791–8.

Grace, John (1999) "Should the Foetus have Rights in Law?" *Medico-Legal Journal* vol. 67 no. 2 pp. 57–67.

Graham, Janice (1991) *Your Pregnancy Companion* (New York: Pocket Books).

Graham, Wendy, Smith, Pat, Kamal, A, Fitzmaurice, A, Smith, N, Hamilton, N and Wyatt, Jeremy (2000) "Randomised controlled trial comparing effectiveness of touch screen system with leaflet for providing women with information on prenatal tests" *British Medical Journal* vol. 320 pp.155–160.

Grant, Nicole (1992) *The Selling of Contraception: The Dalkon Shield Case, Sexuality and Women's Autonomy* (Ohio State UP).

Greco, Monica (1993) "Psychosomatic Subjects and the Duty to be Well: personal agency within medical rationality" *Economy and Society* vol. 22 no. 3 pp. 357–72.

Greenberg, Daniel S (2000) "Abortion returns to haunt US Presidential Campaign" *Lancet* vol. 355 p. 1165.

Greenhalgh, S, Chuzhu, Z and Nan, L (1994) "Restraining Population Growth in Three Chinese Villages 1988–1993" *Population Development Review* vol. 20 pp. 365–95.

Griffiths, M (1990), "Contraceptive Practices and Contraceptive Failures Among Women Requesting Termination of Pregnancy" *British Journal of Family Planning* vol.16, pp. 16–18.

Grossman, Atina (1995) *Reforming Sex: The German Movement for Birth Control and Abortion Reform 1920–1950* (Oxford UP).

Grubb, Andrew (1999) "Commentary" *Medical Law Review* vol. 7 pp. 59–61.

Grunseit, A and Kippax, S (1994) *Effects of sex education on young people's sexual behaviour* (National Centre for HIV Social Research, Macquarie University Australia for WHO Global Program on AIDS).

Gupte, Manisha, Bandewar, Sunita and Pisal, Hemlata (1997) "Abortion Needs of Women in India: A Case Study of Rural Maharashta" *Reproductive Health Matters* vol. 9, pp. 77–86.

Gurdon, John (1962) "The Development capacity of nuclei taken from intestinal epithelial clees of feeding tadpoles" *Journal of Embryology and Experimental Morphology* vol. 10 pp. 622–40.

Guttmacher, Alan (1969) *Birth Control and Love: The Complete Guide to Contraception and Fertility* (London: Macmillan).

Guzman, Kathleen R (1997) "Property, Progeny, Body Part: Assisted Reproduction and the Transfer of Wealth" *University of California Davis Law Journal* vol. 31 no. 1 pp. 193–252.

Hadley, Janet (1997) *Abortion: Between Freedom and Necessity* (London: Virago).

Haimes, Erica (1992) "Gamete donation and the social management of genetic origins" in Stacey, Meg (ed.) *Changing Human Reproduction: Social Science Perspectives* (London: Sage) pp. 119–47.

—— (1998) "The making of 'the DI child': changing representations of people conceived through donor insemination" in Daniels, Ken and Haimes, Erica (eds.) *Donor Insemination. International Social Science Perspectives* (Cambridge UP) pp. 53–75.

—— and Daniels, Ken (1998) "International Social Science Perspectives on Donor Insemination: An Introduction" in Daniels, Ken and Haimes, Erica (eds.) *Donor Insemination: International Social Science Perspectives* (Cambridge UP) pp. 1–6.

—— and Timms, N (1985) *Adoption, Identity and Social Policy* (Aldershot: Gower).

Haines, Michael (1992) "Occupation and Social Class During Fertility Decline: Historical Perspectives" in Gillis, John, Tilly, Louise and Levine, David (eds.) *The European Experience of Declining Fertility 1850–1970: The Quiet Revolution* (Oxford: Blackwell) pp. 193–226.

Haldar, N, Cranston, D, Turner, E, Mackenzie, I and Guillebaud, J (2000) "How reliable is a vasectomy? Long-term follow-up of vasectomised men" *Lancet* vol. 356 p. 43.

Hall, Celia (1999) "Give Contraceptive Implants to Girls of 12 says Expert" *Electronic Telegraph www.telegraph.com* Issue 1349.

Haller, Mark (1963) *Eugenics: Hereditarian Attitudes in American Thought* (Brunswick, New Jersey: Rutgers UP).

Hanagan, Michael (1992) "Population Change, Labor Markets and Working-Class Militancy: The Regions around Birmingham and Saint-Etienne 1840–1880" in Gillis, John, Tilly, Louise and Levine, David (eds.) *The European Experience of Declining Fertility 1850–1970: The Quiet Revolution* (Oxford: Blackwell) pp. 127–145.

Handyside, AH, Knotogianni, EH, Hardy, K and Winston, RML (1990) "Pregnancies from Biopsied Human Preimplantation Embryos Sexed by Y-specific DNA Amplification" *Nature* vol. 244 pp. 768–70.

Hardon, Anita (1997) "Defining Quality of Care and Adherence to Reproductive Rights in Family Planning Programmes" in Hardon, Anita, Mutua, Ann, Kabir, Sandra and Engelkes, Elly (eds.) *Monitoring Family Planning and Reproductive Rights: A Manual for Empowerment* (London: Zed Books) pp. 7–22.

—— and Engelkes, Elly (1997) "Core Quality of Care Indicators" in Hardon, Anita, Mutua, Ann, Kabir, Sandra and Engelkes, Elly (eds.) *Monitoring Family Planning and Reproductive Rights: A Manual for Empowerment* (London: Zed Books) pp. 31–50.

Hardy, Ellen (1996) "Long-Acting Contraception in Brazil and the Dominican Republic" in Moskowitz, Ellen and Jennings, Bruce (eds.) *Coerced Contraception? Moral and Policy Challenges of Long-Acting Birth Control* (Washington DC: Georgetown UP) pp. 206–16.

342   *Bibliography*

Harper, P (1993) "Clinical consequences of isolating the gene for Huntington's Disease" *British Medical Journal* vol. 340 pp. 397–8.

Harris, John (1985) *The Value of Life* (London: Routledge).

—— (1989) "Should we Experiment on Embryos" in Lee, Robert and Morgan, Derek (eds.) *Birthrights: Law and Ethics at the Beginnings of Life* (London: Routledge) pp. 85–95.

—— (1998a) *Clones, Genes and Immortality: Ethics and the Genetic Revolution* (Oxford UP).

—— (1998b) "Rights and Reproductive Choice" in Harris, John and Holm, Søren (eds.) *The Future of Human Reproduction: Ethics, Choice and Regulation* (Oxford: Clarendon Press) pp. 5–37.

—— (1999a) "Clones, Genes and Human Rights" in Burley, Justine (ed.) *The Genetic Revolution and Human Rights* (Oxford UP) pp. 61–94.

—— (1999b) [1997] " 'Goodbye Dolly?' The Ethics of Human Cloning" in Kuhse, Helga and Singer, Peter (eds.) *Bioethics: An Anthology* (Oxford: Blackwell) pp. 143–52.

—— (1999c) "Doctor's orders, rationality and the good life: commentary on Savulescu" *Journal of Medical Ethics* vol. 25 pp. 127–9.

Hart, H.L.A. (1963) *Law, Liberty and Morality* (Oxford UP)

Hartmann, Betsy (1995) *Reproductive Rights and Wrongs: The Global Politics of Reproduction* (Boston, Mass: South End Press).

Heinsohn, Gunnar and Steiger, Otto (1982) "The Elimination of Medieval Birth Control and the Witch Trials of Modern Times" *International Journal of Women's Studies* vol. 5 pp. 193–215.

Heitman, Elizabeth (1995) "Infertility as a Public Health Problem: Why Assisted Reproductive Technologies are not the Answer" *Stanford Law and Policy Review* vol. 6 no. 2 pp. 89–102.

—— and Schlachtenhaufen, Mary (1996) "The Differential Effects of Race, Ethnicity and Socio-Economic Status on Infertility and its Treatment: Ethical and Policy Issues for Oocyte Donation" in Cohen, Cynthia (ed.) *New Ways of Making Babies: The Case of Egg Donation* (Bloomington and Indianapolis: Indiana UP) pp. 188–212.

Hellum, Anne (1993) "New Reproductive Technologies in an Ecological Perspective" in Anne Hellum (ed.) *Birth Law* (Oxford UP) pp. 125–135.

Henley, Madeleine (1993) "The Creation and Perpetuation of the Mother/Body Myth: Judicial and Legislative Enlistment of Norplant" *Buffalo Law Review* vol. 41 pp. 701–77.

Henshaw, Stanley and Singh, Sushella (1986) "Sterilisation Regret Among US Couples" *Family Planning Perspectives* vol. 18 no. 5 pp. 238–240.

Hertig, AT, Rock, J, Adams, EC (1956) "A Description of 34 human ova within the first 17 days of development" *American Journal of Anatomy* vol. 98 pp. 425–91.

Hervey, Tamara (1998) "Buy baby: the European Union and regulation of human reproduction *Oxford Journal of Legal Studies* vol. 18 no. 2 pp. 207–234.

Hindell, Juliet (1997) "Abortionists Prosper as Japan Keeps Ban on Pill" *Electronic Telegraph* Issue 744 8 June 1991 *www.telegraph.com*.

Hirsch, Eric (1999) "Negotiated Limits: Interviews in South-East England" in Edwards, Jeanette, Franklin, Sarah, Hirsch, Eric, Price, Frances and Strathern, Marilyn (eds.) *Technologies of Procreation: Kinship in the Age of Assisted Conception* 2nd edn. (London: Routledge) pp. 91–121.

Hoa, HT, Toan NV, Johansson A, Hoa VT, Höjer B and Persson LA (1996) "Child spacing and two child policy in practice in rural Vietnam: cross sectional survey" *British Medical Journal* vol. 313 pp. 1113–1116.

Hogben, Susan and Coupland, Justine (2000) "Egg seeks sperm. End of story. . .? Articulating gay parenting in small ads for reproductive partners" *Discourse and Society* vol. 11 no. 4 pp. 459–85.

Holm, Søren (1998a) "Ethical Issues in Pre-implantation Diagnosis" in Harris, John and Holm, Søren (eds.) *The Future of Human Reproduction: Ethics, Choice and Regulation* (Oxford: Clarendon Press) pp. 176–190.

—— (1998b) "A life in the shadow: one reason why we should not clone humans" *Cambridge Health Care Quarterly* vol. 7 pp. 160–2.

Holmes, Helen Bequaert (1995) "Choosing Children's Sex: Challenges to Feminist Ethics" in Callahan, Joan (ed.) *Reproduction, Ethics and the Law: Feminist Responses* (Bloomington and Indianapolis: Indiana UP) pp. 148–177.

——, Hoskyns, B and Gross, M (1981) *The Custom-Made Child? Women-Centred Perspectives* (New Jersey: Humana Press).

Holtzman, Neil and Shapiro, David (1998) "Genetic Testing and Public Policy" *British Medical Journal* vol. 316 pp. 852–856.

Horsburgh, Beverley (1996) "Schrodinger's Cat, Eugenics and the Compulsory Sterilisation of Welfare Mothers: Deconstructing an Old/New Rhetoric and Constructing the Reproductive Right to Natality for Low Income Women of Color" *Cardozo Law Review* vol. 17 pp. 531–82.

—— (1998) "Jewish Women, Black Women: Guarding Against the Oppression of Surrogacy" *Berkeley Women's Law Journal* vol. 8 pp. 29–62.

Hubbard, R and Lewontin, RC (1996) "Pitfalls of Genetic Testing" *New England Journal of Medicine* vol. 334 no. 18 pp. 1192–4.

Hughes, Bill (2000) "Medicine and the Aesthetic Invalidation of Disabled People" *Disability and Society* vol. 15 no. 4 pp. 555–68.

Hultman, CM, Sparén, P, Takei, N, Murray, RM, Cnattingius, S and Geddes, J (1999). "Prenatal and perinatal risk factors for schizophrenia, affective psychosis, and reactive psychosis of early onset: case-control study" *British Medical Journal* vol 318 pp. 421–6.

Human Fertilisation and Embryology Authority (1993) *Public Consultation on Sex Selection* (London: HFEA).

—— (1994) *Donated Ovarian Tissue in Embryo Research and Assisted Conception* (London: HFEA).

—— (1995) *Egg Donation* (London: HFEA).

—— (1998) *Code of Practice* 4th edition July 1998 (London: HFEA).

—— (1999) *Annual Report* (London: HFEA).

—— (2000a) *HFEA to permit the use of frozen eggs in fertility treatment* Press Release 25 January 2000 (London: HFEA).

—— (2000b) *National Data Statistics* (London: HFEA).

—— (2000c) *Annual Report* (London: HFEA).

—— and Advisory Committee on Genetic Testing (1999) *Consultation Document on Preimplantation Genetic Diagnosis* (London: HFEA).

Human Genetics Advisory Commission and the Human Fertilisation and Embryology Authority (1998) *Cloning Issues in Reproduction, Science and Medicine* (London: HGAC).

Huntington, Patricia (1995) "Toward a Dialectical Concept of Autonomy" *Philosophy and Social Criticism* vol. 21 no. 1 pp. 37–55.

Iberico, G, Navarro, J, Blasco, L, Simon, C, Pellicer, A and Remohi, J (2000) "Embryo reduction of multifetal pregnancies following assisted reproduction treatment: a modification of the transvaginal ultrasound-guided technique" *Human Reproduction* vol. 15 no. 10 pp. 2228–33.

Ikemoto, Lisa (1992) "The Code of Perfect Pregnancy: At the Intersection of the Ideology of Motherhood, the Practice of Defaulting to Science and the Interventionist Mindset of Law" *Ohio State Law Journal* vol. 53 no. 5, pp. 1205–1306.

Ikonomidis, Sharon and Singer, Peter (1999) "Autonomy, Liberalism and Advance Care Planning" *Journal of Medical Ethics* vol. 25 pp. 522–527.

Illman, John (1998) "Morning After Pill to go on Open Sale" *The Observer* 31 May p. 7.

Intercollegiate Working Party (1998) *Reducing Mother to Child Transmission of HIV Infection in the United Kingdom. Recommendations of an Intercollegiate Working Party for Enhancing Voluntry Confidential HIV Testing in Pregnancy* (London: Royal College of Paediatrics and Child Health).

IPPF (1999) "Nepal: Fighting to Change a Harsh Abortion Law" *Real Lives* issue 3 *www.ippf.org*.

Irvine, S, Cawood, E, Richardson, D, Macdonald, E and Aitken, J (1996) "Evidence of deteriorating semen quality in the United Kingdom: birth cohort study in 577 men in Scotland over 11 years" *British Medical Journal* vol. 312 pp. 467–71.

Jackson, Emily (1997) "Fractured Values: Law, Ideology and the Family" *Studies in Law, Politics and Society* (1997) vol. 17 pp. 99–119.

—— (2000) "Abortion, Autonomy and Prenatal Diagnosis" *Social and Legal Studies* vol. 9 pp. 467–94.

Jacobs, Sally (1992) "Norplant Draws Concern Over Risks and Coercion" *Boston Globe* 21 December 1992 at A1.

Jaggar, Alison (1983) *Feminist Politics and Human Nature* (Totowa, NJ: Rowman and Allenheld).

James, David (1998) "Recent Advances: Fetal Medicine", *British Medical Journal* vol. 316 pp. 1580–1583.

Joffe, Michael (2000) "Time trends in biological fertility in Britain" *Lancet* vol. 355 pp. 1961–5.

Johansson A, Nga NT, Huy TQ, Dat DD and Holmgren K (1998) "Population Policy, Son Preference and the Use of IUDs in North Vietnam" *Reproductive Health Matters*, vol. 6 no. 11 pp. 66–76.

Johnson, George (1998) "Soul Searching" in Nussbaum, Martha and Sunstein, Cass (eds.) *Clones and Clones: Facts and Fantasies about Human Cloning* (New York: Norton) pp. 67–70.

Jones, Owen (1993) "Reproductive Autonomy and Evolutionary Biology: A Regulatory Framework for Trait-Selection Technologies" *American Journal of Law and Medicine* vol. 19 no. 3 pp. 187–231.

Kan, AK, Abdalla, HI, Ogunyemi, BO, Korea, L and Latache, E (1998) "A survey of anonymous oocyte donots: demographics" *Human Reproduction* vol. 13 no. 10 pp. 2762–6.

Karlin, Elizabeth (1998), "We Called it Kindness: Establishing Feminist Abortion Practice" in Rickie Solinger (ed.) *Abortion Wars: A Half Century of Struggle 1950–2000* (Berkeley: University of California Press) pp. 273–289.

Kass, Leon (1972) "New Beginnings in Life" in Hamilton, MP (ed.) *The New Genetics and the Future of Man* (Grand Rapids, Mich: William B Eerdmans) pp. 14–63.

—— (1998) [1979] " 'Making Babies' Revisited" in Pence, Gregory E (ed.) *Classic Works in Medical Ethics* (Boston Mass.: McGraw Hill) pp. 93–117.

Kato Y, Tani T, Sotomaru Y, Kurokawa K, Kato J, Doguchi H, Yasue H and Tsunoda Y (1998) "Eight calves cloned from somatic cells of a single adult" *Science* vol. 282 pp. 2095–8.

Kay, Margarita (1982) *Anthropology of Human Birth* (Philadelphia: F.A. Davis).

Keane, Noel and Breo, Dennis (1983) *The Surrogate Mother* (New York: Everest House).

Kellmer-Pringle, ML (1977) *The Needs of Children* (London: Hutchinson).

Kennedy, Ian (1991) *Treat Me Right: Essays in Medical Law and Ethics* (Oxford UP).

—— (1998) "Commentary" *Medical Law Review* vol. 6 pp. 99–131.

—— and Grubb, Andrew (2000) *Medical Law*, 3rd edition (London: Butterworths).

Kenney, Sally J (1986) "Reproductive Hazards in the Workplace: the Law and Sexual Difference" *International Journal of the Sociology of Law* vol. 14 pp. 393–414.

Keown, John (1988) *Abortion, Doctors and the Law: Some Aspects of the Legal regulation of Abortion in England from 1803–1982* (Cambridge UP).

Kerr, Anne and Cunningham-Burley, Sarah (2000) "On Ambivalence and Risk: Reflexive Modernity and the New Human Genetics" *Sociology* vol. 34 no. pp. 283–304.

Kettle, Martin (1996) "In Cold Blood" *The Guardian* 23 November 1996 p. 23.

Kiernan, K (1995) *Transition to Parenthood: Young Mothers, Young Fathers—Associated Factors and Later Life Experiences* Welfare State Programme Discussion Paper WSP/113 LSE.

King, David (1999) "Preimplantation Genetic Diagnosis and the 'New' Eugenics" *Journal of Medical Ethics* vol. 25 pp. 176–82.

Kirby, Douglas and Wasbak, Cindy (1992) "School Based Clinics" in Miller, Brent (ed.) *Preventing Adolescent Pregnancy* (London: Sage) pp.185–219.

Kitcher, Philip (1997) *The Lives to Come: The Genetic Revolution and Human Possibilities* (London: Penguin).

Kitzinger, Sheila (1972) *The Experience of Childbirth* (Harmondsworth: Penguin).

Klaus, MH, Jerauld, R, Kreger, NC, McAlpine, W, Steffa, M, Kennel, JH (1972) "Maternal attachment: Importance of the first post-partum days" *New England Journal of Medicine* vol. 286, no. 9, pp. 460–3.

Klein, Nancy A, Sewall, Gretchen and Soules, Michael R (1996) "Donor Oocyte Program at University of Washington Medical Center" in Cohen, Cynthia (ed.) *New Ways of Making Babies: The Case of Egg Donation* (Bloomington and Indianapolis: Indiana UP) pp. 3–14.

Klein, Renate Duelli (1989) *Infertility: Women Speak Out about Their Experiences of Reproductive Medicine* (London: Pandora).

Klotzko, Arlene Judith (1997) "The Debate about Dolly" *Bioethics* vol. 11 no. 5 pp. 427–38.

Knopoff, Katherine (1991) "Can a Pregnant Woman Morally Refuse Fetal Surgery?" *California Law Review*, vol. 79 pp. 499–540.

Knoppers, Bartha Maria and Laberge, Claude (1991) "The Social Geography of Human Genome Mapping" in Bankowski, Z and Kapron, AM (eds.) *Genetics, Ethics and Human Values: Human Genome Mapping, Genetic Screening and Gene Therapy, Proceedings of the XXIVth CIOMS Round Table Conference* (Geneva: CIOMS) pp. 273–289.

Kokole, Omari (1994) "The Politics of Fertility in Africa" in Finkle, Jason and McIntosh, Alison (eds.) *The New Politics of Population: Conflict and Consensus in Family Planning* (Oxford UP) pp. 73–88.

Kolata, D (1990) "Rush is on to Capitalize on Testing for Gene Causing Cystic Fibrosis" *New York Times* 6 February 1990 C3 col. 1.

Kolata, Gina (1997) *Clone: The Road to Dolly and the Path Ahead* (London: Penguin).

Kolbert, Kathryn and Miller, Andrea (1998) "Legal Strategies for Abortion Rights in the Twenty First Century" in Solinger, Rickie (ed.) *Abortion Wars: A Half Century of Struggle 1950–2000* (Berkeley: University of California Press) pp. 95–110.

Kolker, Alicia and Burke, Meredith (1994) *Prenatal Testing: A Sociological Perspective* (London: Bergin & Garvey).

Kopp, Marie E (1936) "Legal and Medical Aspects of Eugenic Sterilization in Germany" *American Sociological Review* vol. 1 no. 5 pp. 761–770.

Krimmel, Herbert (1992) "Surrogate Arrangements from the Perspective of the Child" in Alpern, Kenneth (ed.) *The Ethics of Reproductive Technology* (Oxford UP) pp. 57–70.

Kulczycki, Andrzej (1999) *The Abortion Debate in the World Arena* (Basingstoke: Macmillan).

Kymlicka, Will (1989) *Liberalism, Community and Culture* (Oxford UP).

Lacey, Nicola and Wells, Celia (1998) *Reconstructing Criminal Law: Critical Perspectives on Crime and the Criminal Process* (London: Butterworths).

Lamb, Christina (1998) "Votes for Sterilisation Threaten Brazilian Tribe" *Electronic Telegraph* issue 1206 13 September *www.telegraph.com.*

—— (1999) "Peru Condemned over Mass Sterilisation Abuses" *Electronic Telegraph* Issue 3325 10 January *www.telegraph.com.*

Lane, Karen (1995) "The medical model of the body as a site of risk: a case study of childbirth" in Gabe, Jonathan (ed.) *Medicine, Health and Risk: Sociological Approaches* (Oxford: Blackwell) pp. 53–72.

Langton, James (1998) "Mothers-to-be who drink face detention" *Sunday Telegraph* 31 May 1998 p. 11.

Lasker, Judith N (1998) "The Users of Donor Insemination" in Daniels, Ken and Haimes, Erica (eds) *Donor Insemination: International Social Science Perspectives* (Cambridge UP) pp. 7–32.

Latham, Melanie (1998) "Regulating the New Reproductive Technologies: A Cross Channel Comparison" *Medical Law International* vol. 3 pp. 89–177.

Lattimer, Maxine (1998), "Dominant Ideas Versus Women's Reality: Hegemonic Discourse in British Abortion Law" in Lee, Ellie (ed.) *Abortion Law and Politics Today* (London: Macmillan) pp. 59–75.

Laughlin, Harry (1914) "The Legal, Legislative and Administrative Aspects of Sterilisation" *Eugenics Record: Official Bulletin* No. 10B 115–20.

Laurie, Graeme (1999) "In Defence of Ignorance: Genetic Information and the Right not to Know" *European Journal of Health Law* vol. 6 pp. 119–32.

Law, Sylvia (1994) "Silent No More: Physician's Legal and Ethical Obligations to Patients Seeking Abortions" *New York University Review of Law and Social Change* vol.21 no. 2, pp. 279–321.

Lazarus, Ellen (1984) "What do women want? Issues of choice, control and class in pregnancy and childbirth" *Medical Anthropology Quarterly* vol. 8 no. 1 pp. 25–46.

Lee, Ellie and Davey, Jenny (1998) *Attitudes to Abortion for Fetal Abnormality* (Canterbury: Pro-Choice Forum).

Lee, Ellie and Gilchrist, Anne (1997) "Abortion Psychological Sequelae: The Debate and the Research" in Lee, Ellie and Lattimer, Maxine (eds.) *Issues in Pregnancy Counselling: What do Women Need and Want?* (Canterbury: Pro-Choice Forum) pp. 37–46.

Lee, Robert and Morgan, Derek (1989) "Is Birth Important?" in Morgan, Derek and Lee, Robert (eds.) *Birthrights Law and Ethics at the Beginning of Life* (London: Routledge) pp. 1–16.

Leighton, Neil (1995) "The Family: Whose Construct is it Anyway" in Ulanowsky, Carol (ed.) *The Family in the Age of Biotechnology* (Aldershot: Avebury) pp. 91–104.

Leridon, Henri and Ferry, Benoit (1985) "Biological and Traditional Restraints on Fertility" in Cleland, John and Hobcraft, John (eds.) *Reproductive Change in Developing Countries: Insights from the World Fertility Survey* (Oxford UP) pp. 139–64.

Lewin, Tamar (1997) "New Procedure Makes Abortion Possible Days After Conception" *New York Times www.nytimes.com* 21 December 1997.

Lewis, T and Chamberlain, G (1990) *Obstetrics by Ten Teachers* 15th edn. (London: Edward Arnold).

LIFE (1984) *Warnock Dissected: A Commentary on the Report of the Committee of Inquiry into Human Fertilisation and Embryology* (Leamington Spa: LIFE).

Lindegren, ML, Byers, RH Jr, Thomas, P, Davis, SF, Caldwell, B, Rogers, M, Gwinn, M, Ward, JW and Fleming, PL (1999) "Trends in perinatal transmission of HIV/AIDS in the United States" *Journal of the American Medical Association* vol. 282 no. 6 pp. 531–8.

Lippman, Abby (1991) "Prenatal Genetic Testing and Screening: Constructing Needs and Reinforcing Inequities" *American Journal of Law and Medicine* vol. 17, pp. 15–50.

Little, George Bradbury (1997) "Comparing German and English Law on Non-Consensual Sterilisation: A Difference in Approach" *Medical Law Review* vol. 5 pp. 269–293.

Lockwood, Charles J (2000) "Prediction of pregnancy loss" *Lancet* vol. 255 pp. 1292–3.

Lombardo, Paul (1996) "Medicine, Eugenics and the Supreme Court: From Coercive Sterilisation to Reproductive Freedom" *Journal of Contemporary Health Law and Policy* vol. 13 pp. 1–25.

Lord Chancellor's Department (1999) *Making Decisions: The Government's proposals for making decisions on behalf of mentally incapacitated adults* Cm. 4465 (London: HMSO).

Lovell Banks, Tannya (1996) "Legal Challenges: State Intervention, Reproduction and HIV Infected Women" in Faden, Ruth and Kass, Nancy (eds.) *HIV, AIDS and Childbearing: Public Policy, Private Lives* (Oxford UP) pp. 143–77.

Low, Lawrence, King, Suzanne and Wilkie, Tom (1998) "Genetic Discrimination in Life Insurance: Empirical Evidence from a Cross Sectional Survey of Genetic Support Groups in the United Kingdom" *British Medical Journal* vol. 317, pp. 1632–5.

Low, Valentine (1998) "Lesbians Order Internet Baby" *Evening Standard* 9 July 1998, p. 1.

Lublin, Nancy (1998) *Pandora's Box: Feminism Confronts Reproductive Technology* (Oxford: Rowman and Littlefield).

Luker, Kristin (1984), *Abortion and the Politics of Motherhood* (Berkeley: University of California Press).

Lupton, Deborah (1993) "Risk as moral danger: the social and political functions of risk discourse in public health" *International Journal of Health Services* vol. 23 pp. 425–35.

Lupton, Deborah (1996) *Food, the Body and the Self* (London: Sage).

Lyall, H, Gould, GW and Cameron, IT (1998) "Should sperm donors be paid? A survey of the attitudes of the general public" *Human Reproduction* vol. 3 no. 3 pp. 771–5.

Lyndon Shanley, Mary (1995) "'Surrogate Mothering' and Women's Freedom: A Critique of Contracts for Human Reproduction" in Boling, Patricia (ed.) *Expecting Trouble: Surrogacy, Fetal Abuse and New Reproductive Technologies* (Oxford: Westview) pp. 156–67.

Macintyre, Alastair (1981) *After Virtue: A Study in Moral Theory* (London: Duckworth).

Mackinnon, Catharine (1987) *Feminism Unmodified* (Cambridge, Mass: Harvard UP).

Macklin, Ruth and Gaylin, Willard (1981) *Mental Retardation and Sterilisation: A Problem of Competency and Paternalism* (New York: Plenum Press).

—— (1996) "Cultural Difference and Long-Acting Contraception" in Moskowitz, Ellen and Jennings, Bruce *Coerced Contraception? Moral and Policy Challenges of Long-Acting Birth Control* (Washington DC: Georgetown UP) pp. 173–91.

—— (1996b) "What is Wrong with Commodification?" in Cohen, Cynthia (ed.) *New Ways of Making Babies: The Case of Egg Donation* (Bloomington and Indianapolis: Indiana UP) pp. 106–121.

Macpherson, G (ed.) (1995) *Black's Medical Dictionary* 38th edn. (London: A & C Black).

Mahlstedt, PP and Probasco, KA (1991) "Sperm donors: their attitudes toward providing medical and psychosocial information for recipient couples and donor offspring" *Fertility and Sterility* vol. 56 no. 4 pp. 747–53.

Mair, Jane (1996) "Maternal/Foetal Conflict: Defined or Defused" in McLean, Sheila *Contemporary Issues in Law, Medicine and Ethics* (Aldershot: Dartmouth) pp. 79–97.

Malinowski, Bronislaw (1937) "Foreword" to Montagu, MF Ashley *Coming into Being Among the Australian Aborigines: A Study of the Procreative Beliefs of the Native Tribes of Australia* (London: George Routledge & Sons) pp. xix–xxxv.

Malinowski, Michael (1994) "Coming into Being: Law, Ethics and the Practice of Prenatal Genetic Screening" *Hastings Law Journal* vol. 45 pp. 1435–1526.

Marteau, Theresa and Croyle, Robert (1998) "Psychological Responses to Genetic Testing" *British Medical Journal* vol. 316 pp. 693–696.

——, Plenicar, M and Kidd, J (1993) "Obstetricians presenting amniocentesis to pregnant women: practice observed" *Journal of Reproductive and Infant Psychology* vol. 12 pp. 121–32.

Martin, Emily (1987) *The Woman in the Body: A Cultural Analysis of Reproduction* (Boston: Beacon Press).

Maruyama, Hiromi (1995) "Abortion in Japan: A Feminist Critique" *Wisconsin Women's Law Journal*, vol. 10, pp. 131–160.

Mascarenhas, L (1998) "Insertion and Removal of Implanon" *Contraception* vol. 58 pp. 79–83.

Mason, JK and McCall Smith, RA (1994) *Law and Medical Ethics* 4th edn. (London: Butterworths).

Mathieu, Deborah (1991) "Mandating Treatment for Pregnant Substance Abusers: A Compromise" *Politics and the Life Sciences* vol. 14 pp. 199–208.

Mayersohn, Nettie (1997) "The 'Baby Aids' Bill" *Fordham Urban Law Journal* vol. 14 no. 4 pp. 721–7.

Mayor, Frederico (1998) "Devaluing the Human Factor" *The Times Higher Educational Supplement* 6 February 1998, p. 13.

Mayor, Susan (1999) "Department of Health Changes Advice on Third Generation Pills" *British Medical Journal* vol. 318 p. 1026.

Mawer, Caroline (1999) "Preventing Teenage Pregnancies, Supporting Teenage Mothers" *British Medical Journal* vol. 318 pp. 1713–1714.

Mazrui, Ali (1994) "Islamic Doctrine and the Politics of Induced Fertility Change: An African Perspective" in Finkle, Jason and McIntosh, Alison (eds.) *The New Politics of Population: Conflict and Consensus in Family Planning* (Oxford UP) pp. 121–134.

McCall Smith, Alexander (1995) "Fetal Medicine: Legal and Ethical Implications" in Barron, SL and Roberts, DF (eds.) *Issues in Fetal Medicine: Proceedings of the 29th Annual Symposium of the Galton Institute* (Basingstoke: Macmillan) pp. 163–71.

McHale, Jean and Fox, Marie with Murphy, John (1997) *Health Care Law: Text, Cases and Materials* (London: Sweet and Maxwell).

McLanahan, Sara and Sandefur, Gary (1994) *Growing up with a Single Parent: What Hurts, What Helps* (Cambridge, Mass: Harvard UP).

McLaren, Angus (1992) "The Sexual Politics of Reproduction in Britain" in Gillis, John, Tilly, Louise and Levine, David (eds.) *The European Experience of Declining Fertility 1850–1970: The Quiet Revolution* (Oxford: Blackwell) pp. 85–100.

—— and McLaren, Arlene Tigar (1997) *The Bedroom and the State: The Changing Practices and Politics of Contraception and Abortion in Canada 1880–1997* (Oxford UP).

McLean, Sheila (1997) *Consent and the Law: Review of the current provisions in the Human Fertilisation and Embryology Act 1990 for the UK Health Ministers* (London: HMSO).

—— (1999) *Old Law, New Medicine: Medical Ethics and Human Rights* (London: Pandora).

McMahan, Jeff (1999) "Cloning, Killing and Identity" *Journal of Medical Ethics*, vol. 25, pp. 77–86.

Mead, Rebecca (1999) "Eggs For Sale" *The New Yorker* 9 August 1999.

Medical Research Council (1995) *Principles in the assessment and conduct of medical research and publicising results* (London: Medical Research Council).

Meek, James and Barton, Laura (2000) "When does pain begin?" *The Guardian* 31 August 2000, G2 pp. 2–3.

Menon, N (1993) "Abortion and the Law: Questions for Feminism" *Canadian Journal of Women and Law* vol. 6, pp. 103–118.

Meyer, Cheryl L (1997) *The Wandering Uterus: Politics and the Reproductive Rights of Women* (New York UP).

Meyers, Diana T (1989) *Self, Society and Personal Choice* (New York: Columbia UP).

Michie, Helena and Cahn, Naomi R (1997) *Confinements: Fertility and Infertility in Contemporary Culture* (New Brunswick: Rutgers UP).

Michie, S, Bron F, Bobrow M, Marteau, TM (1997) "Nondirectiveness in Genetic Counselling: An Empirical Study" *American Journal of Human Genetics* vol. 60, pp. 40–47.

Mill, John Stuart (1859)[1975] *On Liberty* (Oxford UP).

—— (1874) [1969] "Nature" in *Essays on Ethics, Religion and Society: Collected Works of John Stuart Mill vol. X* (Toronto: University of Toronto Press) pp. 373–402.

Miller, Brent and Paikoff, Roberta (1997) "Comparing Adolescent Prevention Programs: Methods and Results" in Hardon, Anita, Mutua, Ann, Kabir, Sandra and Engelkes, Elly (eds.) *Monitoring Family Planning and Reproductive Rights: A Manual for Empowerment* (London: Zed Books).

Miller, John (1994) "A Political Review of Alternative Surrogacy Proposals" *University of San Francisco Law Review* vol. 28 no. 3 pp. 627–632.

Miller, William Ian (1998) "Sheep, Joking, Cloning and the Uncanny" in Nussbaum, Martha and Sunstein, Cass (eds.) *Clones and Clones: Facts and Fantasies about Human Cloning* (New York: Norton) pp. 78–87.

Miringoff, Marque-Luisa (1991) *The Social Costs of Genetic Welfare* (New Brunswick: Rutgers University Press).

Mishra, Raja (2000) "US approval expected for abortion pill" *Boston Globe* 28 September 2000 p. A01.

Modell, Bernadette (1994) "Screening for Fetal Abnormalities" in Bewley, Susan and Ward, Humphrey (eds.) *Ethics in Obstetrics and Gynaecology* (London: RCOG Press) pp. 215–224.

—— and Modell, Michael (1992) *Towards a Healthy Baby: Congenital Disorders and the New Genetics in Primary Health Care* (Oxford UP).

Montgomery, Jonathan (1991) "Rights, Restraints and Pragmatism: The Human Fertilisation and Embryology Act 1990" *Modern Law Review* vol. 54 pp. 524–34.

Moore, Adam D (2000) "Owning Genetic Information and Gene Enhancement Techniques: Why Privacy and Property Rights may Undermine Social Control of the Human Genome" *Bioethics* vol. 14 no. 2 pp. 97–119.

Morgan, Derek (1988) "Surrogacy: Giving it an Understood Name" *Journal of Social Welfare Law* vol. 10 pp. 216–239.

—— (1996a) "The troubled helix: legal aspects of the new genetics" in Marteau, Theresa and Richards, Martin (eds.) *The Troubled Helix: social and psychological implications of the new human genetics* (Cambridge UP) pp.187–210.

—— (1996b) "Health Rights, Ethics and Justice: The Opportunity Costs of Rhetoric" in McLean, Sheila *Contemporary Issues in Law, Medicine and Ethics* (Aldershot: Dartmouth) pp. 15–27.

—— and Lee, Robert (eds.) (1989) *Birthrights Law and Ethics at the Beginning of Life* (London: Routledge).

—— (1991) *Blackstone's Guide to the Human Fertilisation and Embryology Act 1990* (London: Blackstone).

—— (1997) "In the Name of the Father? *Ex parte Blood*: Dealing with Novelty and Anomaly" *Modern Law Review* vol. 60 pp. 840–56.

Morgan, Lynn M (1999) "Materializing the Fetal Body, or What are those Corpses doing in Biology's Basement" in Lynn M and Michaels, Meredith W (eds.) *Fetal Subjects: Feminist Positions Morgan* (Philadelphia: University of Pennsylvania Press) pp. 43–60.

Morris, Caroline (1997) "Technology and the Legal Discourse of Fetal Autonomy" *UCLA Women's Law Journal* vol. 8 no. 1 pp. 47–97.

Moskowitz, Ellen, Jennings, Bruce and Callahan, Daniel (1996) "Long Acting Contraceptives: Ethical Guidance for Policymakers and Health Care Providers" in Moskowitz, Ellen and Jennings, Bruce (eds.) *Coerced Contraception? Moral and Policy Challenges of Long-Acting Birth Control* (Washington DC: Georgetown UP) pp. 3–19.

Mudur, Ganapati (1999) "Indian Medical Authorities Act on Antenatal Sex Selection" *British Medical Journal* vol. 319 p. 401.

Mulkay, Michael (1997) *The Embryo Research Debate: Science and the Politics of Reproduction* (Cambridge UP).

Muller, HJ (1936) *Out of the Night: A Biologist's View of the Future* (London: Gollancz).

Munzer, Stephen (1990) *A Theory of Property* (Cambridge UP).

Murphy, Clare (1997) "Distance or Control: Abortion and Counselling in Germany" in Lee, Ellie and Lattimer, Maxine (eds.) in *Issues in Pregnancy Counselling: What do Women Need and Want?* (Canterbury: Pro-Choice Forum) pp. 54–57.

Murphy-Lawless, Jo (1998) *Reading Birth and Death: A History of Obstetric Thinking* (Cork UP).

Murray, Clare and Golombok, Susan (2000) "Oocyte and semen donation: a survey of UK licensed centres' technique" *Human Reproduction* vol. 15 no. 10 pp. 2133–9.

Murray, Thomas H (1996) "New Reproductive Technologies and the Family" in Cohen, Cynthia (ed.) *New Ways of Making Babies: The Case of Egg Donation* (Bloomington and Indianapolis: Indiana UP) pp. 51–69.

Nakayama, Don K (1995) "Fetal Surgery" in Barron, SL and Roberts, DF (eds.) *Issues in Fetal Medicine: Proceedings of the 29th Annual Symposium of the Galton Institute* (Basingstoke: Macmillan) pp. 94–104.

Narayan, Uma (1995a) "The Discriminatory Nature of Industrial Health-Hazard Policies and Some implications for Third World Workers" in Callahan, Joan (ed.) *Reproduction, Ethics and the Law: Feminist Responses* (Bloomington and Indianapolis: Indiana UP) pp. 398–409.

—— (1995b) "The 'Gift' of a child: Commercial Surrogacy, Gift Surrogacy and Motherhood" pp. 177–201 in Boling, Patricia (ed.) *Expecting Trouble: Surrogacy, Fetal Abuse and New Reproductive Technologie,* (Oxford: Westview) pp. 177–201.

Nathan, Adam (2001) "Under-age girls to be given morning-after pill at school" *The Sunday Times* 7 January p. A1.

National Bioethics Advisory Commission (1997) *Cloning Human Beings: Report and Recommendations* (Rockville, Maryland: NBAC).

National Institutes of Health Panel (1997) *Genetic Testing for Cystic Fibrosis: NIH Consensus Statement 14–16 April 1997.*

Nau, J-Y (1994) "Bioethics Laws in France" *Lancet* vol. 344 p. 48.

Naumberg, Estelle, Bellocco, Rino, Cnattingius, Sven, Hall, Per and Ekbom, Anders (2000) "Prenatal ultrasound examinations and risk of childhood leukaemia: case control study" *British Medical Journal* vol. 320 pp. 282–3.

Nedelsky, Jennifer (1989) "Reconceiving Autonomy" *Yale Journal of Law and Feminism* vol. 1 no. 1 pp. 7–36.

—— (1990) "Law, Boundaries and the Bounded Self" *Representations*, vol. 30 no. 1 pp. 162–89.

—— (1993) "Reconceiving Rights as Relationships" *Review of Constitutional Studies* vol. 1 no. 1 pp. 1–26.

—— (1995) "Meditations on Embodied Autonomy" *Graven Images* vol. 2 pp. 159–70.

Nelkin, Dorothy and Tancredi, Lawrence (1994) *Dangerous Diagnostics: The Social Power of Biological Information* (Chicago UP).

Nelson, Hilde and Nelson, James (1989) "Cutting Motherhood in Two: Some Suspicions Concerning Surrogacy" *Hypatia* vol. 4 pp. 3–96.

Nelson, Margaret (1983) "Working-class women, middle-class women and models of childbirth" *Social Problems* vol. 30 no. 3 pp. 284–97.

Newman, Karen (1996) *Fetal Positions: Individualism, Science, Visuality* (Stanford, Ca: Stanford UP).

Nielsen, Linda (1996) "Procreative Tourism, Genetic Testing and the Law" in Lowe, Nigel and Douglas, Gillian (eds.) *Families Across Frontiers* (Dordrecht, Netherlands: Kluwer) pp. 831–98.

Nolan, David (1998), "Abortion: Should Men Have a Say?" in Lee, Ellie (ed.) *Abortion Law and Politics Today* (London: Macmillan) pp. 216–231.

Norrie, Kenneth (1989) "Sterilisation of the Mentally Ill in English and Canadian Law" *International and Comparative Law Quarterly* vol. 38 pp. 387–395.

—— (1991) *Family Planning Practice and the Law* (Aldershot: Dartmouth).

North K, Golding J (2000) "A maternal vegetarian diet in pregnancy is associated with hypospadias" *British Journal of Urology International* vol. 85, no. 1, pp. 107–113.

Novaes, Simone Bateman (1998) "The Medical Management of Donor Insemination" in Daniels, Ken and Haimes, Erica (eds.) *Donor Insemination: International Social Science Perspectives* (Cambridge UP) pp. 105–130.

—— and Salem, Tania (1998) "Embedding the Embryo" in Harris, John and Holm, Søren (eds.) *The Future of Human Reproduction: Ethics, Choice and Regulation* (Oxford: Clarendon Press) pp. 101–126.

Nozick, Robert (1974) *Anarchy, State and Utopia* (New York: Basic Books)

Nussbaum, Martha (1999) *Sex and Social Justice* (Oxford UP).

Oakley, Ann (1980) *Women Confined: Towards a Sociology of Childbirth* (Oxford: Martin Robertson).

—— (1984) *The Captured Womb* (Oxford: Blackwell).

Oberman, Michelle (1992) "The Control of Pregnancy and the Criminalization of Femaleness" *Berkeley Women's Law Journal* vol. 7, pp. 1–12.

O'Brien, Mary (1981) *The Politics of Reproduction* (Boston: Routledge and Kegan Paul).

O'Donovan, Katherine (1989) " 'What shall we tell the Children?' Reflections on Children's Perspectives and the Reproduction Revolution" in Lee, Robert and Morgan, Derek (eds.) *Birthrights: Law and Ethics at the Beginnings of Life* (London: Routledge) pp. 96–114.

O'Morain, Padraig (2000) "Emergency contraceptive pill withdrawn" *The Irish Times* 17 November 2000.

Office for National Statistics (1997) *Abortion Statistics* Monitor AB 97/5 (Lodon: HMSO).

—— (1997) *Population Trends* (London: HMSO).

—— (2001) *Social Trends* vol. 31 (London: HMSO).

Oghoetuoma, JO, C McKeating, G Horne, DR Brison and BA Lieberman (2000) "Use of *in vitro* fertilisation embryo cryopreserved for 5 years or more" *Lancet* vol. 355: p. 1336.

Ojo, OA (1995) *Fertility Regulation in Developing Countries* (Ibadan UP).

Osakue, Grace and Martin-Hilber, Adriane (1998) "Women's Sexuality and Fertility in Nigeria: Breaking the Culture of Silence" in Petchesky, Rosalind and Judd, Karen (eds.) *Negotiating Reproductive Rights: Women's Perspectives Across Countries and Cultures* (London: Zed Books) pp. 180–216.

Otlowski (1999) "Re Evelyn: Reflections on Australia's First Litigated Surrogacy Case" *Medical Law Review* vol. 7 no. 1 pp. 38–57.

Overall, Christine (1995) "Frozen Embryos and 'Father's Rights': Parenthood and Decision-Making in the Cryopreservation of Embryos" in Callahan, Joan (ed.) *Reproduction, Ethics and the Law: Feminist Responses* (Bloomington and Indianapolis: Indiana UP) pp. 178–198.

Pai Panandiker, VA and Umashankar, PK (1994) "Fertility Control and Politics in India" in Finkle, Jason and McIntosh, Alison (eds.) *The New Politics of Population: Conflict and Consensus in Family Planning* (Oxford UP) pp. 89–104.

Paige, Richard (2000) "Post-mortem pregnancies: a legal analysis" *Dispatches* vol. 9 no. 3 pp. 2–5.

Paintin, David (1998) "A Medical View of Abortion in the 1960s" in Lee, Ellie (ed.) *Abortion Law and Politics Today* (London: Macmillan) pp. 12–19.

Panel on Human Artificial Insemination (1973) "Report" *British Medical Journal*, supplement i, pp. 3–5.

Parker, Phillip (1983) "Surrogate Mothers' Motivations: Initial Findings" *American Journal of Psychiatry* vol. 140 no. 1 pp. 117–8.

Parkinson, Judy, Tran, Wuong, Tan, Tih, Nelson, Jeffrey, Batzofin, Joel and Serafini, Paulo (1998) "Perinatal Outcome after *in vitro* fertilization-surrogacy" *Human Reproduction* vol. 14 no. 3 pp. 671–676.

Paterson-Brown, Sara (1998) "Should doctors perform an elective caesarean section on request?" *British Medical Journal* vol. 317 pp. 462–3.

Payne, Doug (1999) "Record numbers of Irish women visit Britain for abortion" *British Medical Journal* vol. 319 p. 593.

Pearce, Tola Olu (1996) "Ethical Issues in the Importation of Long-Acting Contraceptives to Nigeria" in Moskowitz, Ellen and Jennings, Bruce (eds.) *Coerced Contraception? Moral and Policy Challenges of Long-Acting Birth Control* (Washington DC: Georgetown UP) pp. 192–205.

Peckham, C and Gibb, D (1995) "Mother-to-child transmission of the human immunodeficiency virus" *New England Journal of Medicine* vol. 333 no. 5 pp. 298–302.

Pennings, Guido (2000) "The ethics of gamete donor anonymity". Paper presented at *Gamete privacy: should egg and sperm donors be anonymous?* Conference organised by Progress Educational Trust, The Royal Society, London 14 December 2000.

Persson, Ingmar (1999) "Equality and Selection for Existence" *Journal of Medical Ethics* vol. 25 pp.130–6.

Petchesky, Rosalind (1979) "Reproduction, Ethics and Public Policy: The Federal Sterilization Regulations" *Hastings Center Report* vol. 9 pp. 29–41.

—— (1984) *Abortion and Women's Choice* (London: Longman).

—— (1998) "Cross-Country Comparisons and Political Visions" in Petchesky, Rosalind and Judd, Karen (eds.) *Negotiating Reproductive Rights: Women's Perspectives Across Countries and Cultures* (London: Zed Books) pp.295–323.

Petersen, Alan and Lupton, Deborah (1996) *The New Public Health: Health and Self in the Age of Risk* (London: Sage).

Peterson, Ivor (1995) "The G.O.P.'s Family Cap has a Democratic History" *New York Times* 21 September 1995 at B10.

Peterson, Kerry (1996) "Private Decisions and Public Scrutiny: Sterilisation and Minors in Australia and England" in McLean, Sheila (ed.) *Contemporary Issues in Law, Medicine and Ethics* (Aldershot: Dartmouth) pp. 57–77.

Pfeffer, Naomi (1992) "From Private Patients to Privatization: A brief history of services for the treatment of infertility in England and Wales during the twentieth century" in Stacey, Meg (ed.) *Changing Human Reproduction: Social Science Perspectives* (London: Sage) pp. 48–74.

—— (1993) *The Stork and the Syringe: A Political History of Reproductive Medicine* (Cambridge: Polity).

Philadelphia Inquirer (1990) "Poverty and Norplant: Can Contraception reduce the Underclass?" 12 December 1990 at A18.

Phillimore, Jane (2000) "Special Delivery" *Evening Standard,* 18 February 2000 pp. 13–14.

Philp, T, Guillebano, J, Buoo, D (1984) "Complications of Vasectomy: review of 16,000 Patients" *British Journal of Urology* vol. 56 no. 6 pp. 745–8.

Polaneczky, M, Slap, G, Forke, C, Rappaport, A and Sondheimer, S (1994) "Use of Levonorgestrel Implants for Contraception in Adolescent Mothers" *New England Journal of Medicine* vol. 331 no. 18 pp. 1201–6.

Policy Studies Institute (1994) *Fourth National Survey of Ethnic Minorities* (London: PSI).

Polkinghorne, John (1989) *Review of the Guidance on the Research Use of Fetuses and Fetal Material* (London: HMSO), Cm 762.

Pollard, Irene (1994) *A Guide to Reproduction: Social Issues and Human Concerns* (Cambridge UP).

Pollitt, Katha (1995) *Reasonable Creatures: Essays on Women and Feminism* (New York: Vintage Books).

Potts, Malcolm (1999) "The population policy pendulum" *British Medical Journal* vol. 319 pp. 933–4.

Powderly, Kathleen (1996) "Contraceptive Policy and Ethics: Lessons from American History" in Moskowitz, Ellen and Jennings, Bruce (eds.) *Coerced Contraception? Moral and Policy Challenges of Long-Acting Birth Control* (Washington DC: Georgetown UP) pp. 23–33.

Pratten, Belinda (1990) *Power, Politics and Pregnancy* (London: Health Rights).

Price, Frances (1989) "Establishing Guidelines: Regulation and the Clinical Management of Infertility" in Lee, Robert and Morgan, Derek (eds.) *Birthrights: Law and Ethics at the Beginnings of Life* (London: Routledge) pp. 37–54.

—— (1992) "Having Triplets, Quads or Quins" Stacey, Meg (ed.) *Changing Human Reproduction: Social Science Perspectives* (London: Sage) pp. 92–118.

—— (1999) "Beyond Expectation: Clinical practices and clinical concerns, Solutions for Life and Growth? Collaborative conceptions in reproductive medicine" in Edwards, Jeanette, Franklin, Sarah, Hirsch, Eric, Price, Frances and Strathern, Marilyn *Technologies of Procreation: Kinship in the Age of Assisted Conception* 2nd edn. (London: Routledge) pp. 29–59.

Prothro, Gwendolyn (1997), "RU486 Examined: Impact of a New Technology on an Old Controversy" *University of Michigan Journal of Law Reform* vol. 30, pp. 715–741.

Purdy, Laura (1996) *Reproducing Persons: Issues in Feminist Bioethics* (Ithaca: Cornell UP).

Putnam, Hilary (1999) "Cloning People" in Burley, Justine (ed.) *The Genetic Revolution and Human Rights* (Oxford UP) pp.1–13.

Radford, Tim and Dodd, Vikram (1998) "First Dolly, now Missy . . . scientists get $5m to clone millionaire's dog" *The Guardian,* 25 August 1998 p. 2.

Radin, Margaret (1987) "Market Inalienability" *Harvard Law Review* vol. 100 pp. 1849–937.

Ragone, Helene (1994) *Surrogate Motherhood: Conception in the Heart* (Boulder: Westview Press).

Rajan, VG Julie (1996) "Will India's Ban on Prenatal Sex Determination Slow Abortion of Girls?" *Hinduism Today* vol. 18 no. 4 pp. 8–16.

Ramrakha, Sandhya, Caspi, Avshalom, Dickson, Nigel, Moffitt, Terrie E and Paul, Charlotte (2000) "Psychiatric disorders and risky sexual behaviour in young adulthood: cross sectional study in birth cohort" *British Medical Journal* vol. 321 pp. 263–6.

Ramsay, Sarah (2000) "Enforced Sterilisations in Sweden confirmed" *Lancet* vol. 355 p. 1250.

Rawls, John (1971) *A Theory of Justice* (Cambridge, Mass: Harvard UP).

Raymond, Janice (1993) *Women as Wombs: Reproductive Technologies and the Battle over Women's Freedom* (New York: Harper Collins).

Raz, Joseph (1986) *The Morality of Freedom* (Oxford UP).

Reece, EA (1999) "First trimester prenatal diagnosis: embryoscopy and fetoscopy" *Seminars in Perinatology* Volume 5 pp.424–33.

Reece, Helen (1996a) "Subverting the stigmatization argument" *Journal of Law and Society* vol. 23 no. 4 pp. 484–505.

—— (1996b) "The Paramountcy Principle: Consensus or Construct" *Current Legal Problems* vol. 49 pp. 267–304.

Reichlin, Massimo (1997) "The Argument from Potential: A Reappraisal" *Bioethics* vol. 11 no. 1 pp. 1–23.

Reilly, Philip (1986) "Involuntary Sterilisation in the United States: A Surgical Solution" *The Quarterly Review of Biology* vol. 62 no. 2 pp. 153–70.

Reiss, Michael, J (2000) "The Ethics of Genetic Research on Intelligence" *Bioethics* vol, 14 no. 1 pp.1–15.

Renard, Jean-Paul, Chastant, Sylvie, Chesné, Patrick, Richard, Christophe, Marchal, Jacques, Cordonnier, Nathalie, Chavatte, Pascal, Vignon, Xavier (1999) "Lymphoid hypoplasia and somatic cloning" *Lancet* vol. 353 pp. 1489—1491.

Report of the International Conference on Population and Development (1994) Cairo 5–13 September 1994 (New York: United Nations).

Reproductive Health Matters (1998) *Round Up of Law and Policy* vol. 6 no. 11 pp. 166–172.

Resnik, David, B (1998) "The Commodification of Human Reproductive Materials" *Journal of Medical Ethics* vol. 24 pp. 388–93.

Richards, M (1996) "Lay and Professional knowledge of genetics and inheritance" *Public Understanding of Science* vol. 5 pp. 217–230.

Riddle, John (1997) *Eve's Herbs: a History of Contraception and Abortion in the West* (Cambridge, Mass: Harvard UP).

Rigdon, Susan (1996) "Abortion Law and Practice in China: An Overview with Comparisons with the United States" *Social Science and Medicine* vol. 42 no. 4 pp. 543–560.

Roach Anleu, Sharyn L (1997) "Reproductive Autonomy and Reproductive Technology: Gender, Deviance and Infertility" in Petersen, Kerry (ed.) *Intersections: Women on Law, Medicine and Technology* (Aldershot: Ashgate Dartmouth).

Roberts, Christine, Tracy, Sally and Peat, Brian (2000) "Rates for obstetric intervention among private and public patients in Australia: population based descriptive study" *British Medical Journal* vol. 321 pp. 137–41.

Roberts, Dorothy (1993) "Crime, Race and Reproduction" *Tulane Law Review* vol. 67 pp. 1945–77.

Roberts, John (1996) "US is Short of Contraceptive Choices" *British Medical Journal* vol. 312 pp. 1631–1632.

Robertson, John (1990) "Surrogate Mothers: Not So Novel After All" in Hull, Richard (ed.) *Ethical Issues in the New Reproductive Technologies* (Belmont, Ca: Wadsworth) pp. 156–66.

—— (1994), *Children of Choice: Freedom and the New Reproductive Technologies* (New Jersey: Princeton University Press).

Robertson, John (1996) "Genetic Selection of Offspring Characteristics" *Boston University Law Review* vol. 76 no. 3 pp. 421–482.
—— (1998) "Liberty, Identity and Human Cloning" *Texas Law Review* vol. 76 no. 6 pp. 1371–1456.
Robertson, Stephen (1998) "The ethics of human cloning" *Journal of Medical Ethics* vol. 24 p. 282.
Rothenberg, Karen (1996) "Reproductive Choice and Reality: An Assessment of Tort Liability for Health Care Providers and Women with HIV/AIDS" in Faden, Ruth and Kass, Nancy (eds.) *HIV, AIDS and Childbearing: Public Policy, Private Lives* (Oxford UP) pp. 178–213.
—— (1997) "Breast Cancer, the Genetic 'Quick Fix' and the Jewish Community: Ethical, Legal and Social Challenges" *Health Matrix: Journal of Law and Medicine* vol. 7 pp. 97–124.
Rothman, Barbara Katz (1982) *Giving Birth: Alternatives in Childbirth* (Harmondsworth: Penguin).
—— (1989) *Recreating Motherhood: Ideology and Technology in a Patriarchal Society* (New York: Norton).
Rowland, Robyn (1992) *Living Laboratories: Women and Reproductive Technologies* (Bloomington and Indianapolis: Indiana UP).
—— (1999) "Human Embryo Research: A Global Social Experiment" in Kuhse, Helga and Singer, Peter (eds.) Bioethics: An Anthology (Oxford: Blackwell) pp. 95–9.
Royal College of Obstetricians and Gynaecologists (1996) *Supplement to A Consideration of the Law and Ethics in Relation To Court-Authorized Obstetric Intervention* (London: RCOG).
—— (1999) *Male and Female Sterilisation* (London: RCOG).
—— (2000a) *The Care of Women Requesting Induced Abortion: Guideline* (London: RCOG).
—— (2000b) *The Management of Infertility in Tertiary Care* (London: RCOG).
Royal Commission on New Reproductive Technologies (1993) *Proceed with Care: Final Report of the Royal Commission on New Reproductive Technologies* (Ottawa, Canada: Minister of Government Services).
Ruddick, Sara (1989) *Maternal Thinking: Toward a Politics of Peace* (New York: Ballantine Books).
Ruzek, Sheryl (1991) "Women's Reproductive Rights: The Impact of Technology" in Rodin, Judith and Collins, Aila (eds) *Women and New Reproductive Technologies: Medical, Psychosocial, Legal and Ethical Dilemmas* (Hillsdale NJ: Lawrence Erlbaum) pp. 65–87.
Salstanhall, R (1993) "Healthy bodies, social bodies: men's and women's concepts and practices of health in everyday life" *Social Science and Medicine* vol. 36 no. 1 pp. 7–14.
Samuels, Alec (1999) "The Doctor and the Lawyer: Medico-Legal Problems Today" *Medico-Legal Journal* vol. 67, no. 1 pp. 11–24.
Sandel, Michael (1982) *Liberalism and the Limits of Justice* (Cambridge UP).
Sandelowski, Margaret (1990) "Failure of Volition: Female Agency and Infertility in Historical Perspective" *Signs: A Journal of Women and Culture* vol. 15 no. 3 pp. 475–499.
—— (1993) *With Child in Mind: Studies of the Personal Encounter with Infertility* (Philadelphia UP).
Sander, W (1992) "Catholicism and the Politics of Fertility" *Population Studies* vol. 46 no. 3 pp. 477–89.

Sanders, Cheryl (1992) "Surrogate Motherhood and Reproductive Technologies: An African-American Perspective" *Creighton Law Review* vol. 25 no. 5 pp. 1707–1718.

Sargent, Carolyn and Stark, Nancy (1989) "Childbirth education and childbirth models: Parental perspectives on control, anaesthesia and technological intervention in the birth process" *Medical Anthropology Quarterly* vol. 3 no. 1 pp. 36–51.

Sauer, MV, Gorrill, MJ, Zeffer, KB and Bustillo, M (1989) "Attitudinal Survey of Sperm Donors to an AI clinic" *Journal of Reproductive Medicine* vol. 34 no. 5 pp. 362–4.

—— and Paulson, RJ (1992) "Understanding the Current Status of Oocyte Donation in the United States: What's Really Going On Out There?" *Fertility and Sterility*, vol. 58 pp. 16–18.

Savulescu, Julian (1999a) "Should doctors intentionally do less than the best?" *Journal of Medical Ethics* vol. 25 pp. 121–6.

—— (1999b) "Should we clone human beings? Cloning as a source of tissue for transplantation" *Journal of Medical Ethics* vol. 25 pp. 87–95.

Science and Technology Committee (1997) *The Cloning of Animals from Adult Cells* Fifth Report HC 373–1 (London: HMSO).

Schauer, Frederick (1985) "Slippery Slopes" *Harvard Law Review* vol. 99 pp. 361–83.

Schenker, Joseph G (1991) "The Rights of the Pre-embryo and Fetus to *In Vitro* and *In Vivo* Therapy" in Bromham, David, Dalton, Maureen, Jackson, Jennifer and Millican, Peter (eds.) *Ethics in Reproductive Medicine* (London: Springer Verlag) pp. 33–45.

—— (1997) "Assisted Reproduction Practice in Europe: legal and ethical aspects" *Human Reproduction Update* vol. 3 no. 2 pp. 173–84.

Schneider, Carl (1990) "Surrogate Motherhood from the Perspective of Family Law" *Harvard Journal of Law and Public Policy* vol. 13 no. 1 pp. 125–131.

Schrater, Angeline Faye (1995) "Immunization to Regulate Fertility: Biological and Cultural Frameworks" *Social Science and Medicine* vol. 41 no. 5 pp. 657–671.

Shuman, AN and Marteau, TM (1993) "Obstetricians' and midwives' contrasting perceptions of pregnancy" *Journal of Reproductive and Infant Psychology* vol. 11 pp. 115–8.

Schuster, Mark, Bell, Robert, Berry, Sandra and Kanouse, David (1998) "Impact of a High School Condom Availability Program on Sexual Attitudes and Behaviours" *Family Planning Perspectives* vol. 30 no. 2 pp. 67–72.

Sen, Amartya (1990) "More than One Million Women are Missing" *New York Review of Books* 20th December p. 61.

Seymour, John (2000) *Childbirth and the Law* (Oxford UP).

Shakespeare, Tom (1995) "Back to the Future? New Genetics and Disabled People" *Critical Social Policy* vol. 15 pp. 22–35.

—— (1999) " 'Losing the plot'? Medical and activist discourses of contemporary genetics and disability" in Conrad, Peter and Gabe, Jonathan (eds.) *Sociological Persepctives on the New Genetics* (Oxford: Blackwell) pp. 171–90.

Shalev, Carmel (1989) *Birth Power* (New Haven, Conn: Yale UP).

Shannon, Thomas (1988) *Surrogate Motherhood: The Ethics of Using Human Beings* (New York: Crossroad Publishing).

Shapiro, Michael H (1994) "How (Not) to Think About Surrogacy and other Reproductive Innovations" *University of San Francisco Law Review* vol. 28 no. 3 pp. 647–680.

Sheldon, Sally (1997a) *Beyond Control: Medical Power and Abortion Law* (London: Pluto).

Sheldon, Sally (1997b) "Multiple pregnancy and re(pro)ductive choice" *Feminist Legal Studies* vol. 5 pp. 99–106.

Shenfield, Francoise (2000) "UK and European legal context" Paper presented at *Gamete privacy: should egg and sperm donors be anonymous?* Conference organised by Progress Educational Trust, The Royal Society, London 14 December 2000.

Sherwin, S (1992) *No Longer Patient: Feminist Ethics and Health Care* (Philadelphia: Temple UP).

Shorter, Edward (1983) *A History of Women's Bodies* (London: Allen Lane).

Shultz, Marjorie (1990) "Reproductive Technology and Intention-based Parenthood: An Opportunity for Gender Neutrality" *Wisconsin Law Review* vol. 2 pp. 297–398.

—— (1994) "Legislative Regulation of Surrogacy and Reproductive Technology" *University of San Francisco Law Review* vol. 28 no. 3 pp. 613–625.

Sills, E Scott, Strider, William, Hyde and Henry J (1998) "Gynaecology, Forced Sterilisation and Asylum in the USA" *Lancet* vol. 351 6.June *www.lancet.com*.

Simpson, Audrey (1998) "Abortion in Northern Ireland: A Problem Exported" in Lee, Ellie (ed.) *Abortion Law and Politics Today* (London: Macmillan) pp. 99–109.

Simpson WM, Johnstone, FD, Boyd, FM, Goldberg, DJ, Hart, GJ and Prescott, RJ (1998) "Uptake and acceptability of antenatal HIV testing: randomised controlled trial of different methods of offering the test" *British Medical Journal* vol. 316 pp. 262–7.

Singer, Peter (1998) [1985] "The Moral Status of the Embryo" in Pence, Gregory E (ed.) *Classic Works in Medical Ethics* (Boston, Mass: McGraw Hill) pp. 83–92.

Skegg, David (2000) "Third generation oral contraceptives" *British Medical Journal* vol. 321 pp. 190–1.

Skene, Loane (1998) "Patients' Rights or Family Responsibilities? Two Approaches to Genetic Testing" *Medical Law Review* vol. 6 pp. 1–41.

Smart, Carol (1987) " 'There is of course the Distiction Dictated by Nature': Law and the Problem of Paternity", in Stanworth, M (ed.) *Reproductive Technologies: Gender Motherhood and Medicine* (Minneapolis: University of Minnesota Press) pp. 98–117.

Smith, Patricia (1995) "The Metamorphosis of Motherhood" in Callahan, Joan (ed.) *Reproduction, Ethics and the Law: Feminist Responses* (Bloomington and Indianapolis: Indiana UP) pp. 109–130.

Snow, Rachel, Garcia, Sandra and Kureshy, Nazo (1996) *Investigating Women's Preferences for Contraceptive technology: Focus Group Data from Seven Countries*, Working Paper May 1996 Harvard School of Public Health.

Snowden, Robert and Snowden, Elizabeth (1998) "Families Created Through Donor Insemination" in Daniels, Ken and Haimes, Erica (eds.) *Donor Insemination: International Social Science Perspectives* (Cambridge UP) pp. 33–52.

Social Exclusion Unit (1999) *Teenage Pregnancy* Cm 4342 (London: HMSO).

Solinger, Rickie (ed.) (1998) *Abortion Wars: A Half Century of Struggle 1950–2000* (Berkeley: California UP).

Soloway, Richard (1997) "The Galton Lecture 1996: Marie Stopes, Eugenics and the Birth Control Movement" in Peel, Robert (ed.) *Marie Stopes, Eugenics and the English Birth Control Movement* (London: The Galton Institute) pp. 49–76.

Spallone, Patricia (1989) *Beyond Conception: The New Politics of Reproduction* (Basingstoke: Macmillan).

Spitz, Stephen S (1993) "The Norplant Debate: Birth Control or Women Control" *Columbia Human Rights Law Review* vol. 25 pp. 131–69.

Spurgeon, David (2000) "Abortion doctor suffers second attack in six years" *British Medical Journal* vol. 321, p. 197.

Srinivason, K (1986) "Modernisation and Fertility Change: A Review of Theoretical Developments" in Mahadevan, K (ed.) *Fertility and Morality: Theory, Methodology and Empirical Issues* (London: Sage) pp. 171–83.

Stein, Edward (1998) "Choosing the Sexual Orientation of Children" *Bioethics* vol. 12 no. 1 pp. 1–24.

Stein, Zena and Susser, Mervyn (1998) "The risks of having children in later life" *British Medical Journal* vol. 320 pp. 1681–2.

Steinberg, Deborah Lynn (1997) *Bodies in Glass: Genetics, Eugenics, Embryo Ethics* (Manchester UP).

Steinbock, Bonnie (1990) "Surrogate Motherhood as Prenatal Adoption' in Gostin, Larry (ed.) *Surrogate Motherhood: Politics and Privacy* (Bloomington: University of Indiana Press) pp. 125–135.

—— (1991) "Maternal-Fetal Conflict: Pregnant Drug Addicts" in Bromham, David, Dalton, Maureen, Jackson, Jennifer and Millican, Peter (eds.) *Ethics in Reproductive Medicine* (London: Springer Verlag) pp. 49–58.

—— (1996) "The Concept of Coercion and Long-Term Contraceptives" in Moskowitz, Ellen and Jennings, Bruce (eds.) *Coerced Contraception? Moral and Policy Challenges of Long-Acting Birth Control* (Washington DC: Georgetown UP) pp. 53–78.

—— (1998) "Sperm as Property" in Harris, John and Holm, Søren (eds.) *The Future of Human Reproduction: Ethics, Choice and Regulation* (Oxford: Clarendon Press) pp. 150–161.

Stich, Denise (1993) "Alternative Sentencing or Reproduction Control: Should California Courts use Norplant to Protect Future Children from Child Abuse and Fetal Abuse?" *Santa Clara Law Review* vol. 33 nos. 3–4 pp. 1017–55.

Stockdale, Alan (1999) "Waiting for the cure: mapping the social relations of human gene therapy research" in Conrad, Peter and Gabe, Jonathan (eds.) *Sociological Persepctives on the New Genetics* (Oxford: Blackwell) pp. 79–96.

Strathern, Marilyn (1999a) "A Question of Context" in Edwards, Jeanette, Franklin, Sarah, Hirsch, Eric, Price, Frances and Strathern, Marilyn (eds.) *Technologies of Procreation: Kinship in the Age of Assisted Conception* 2nd edn. (London: Routledge) pp. 9–28.

—— (1999b) "Regulation, Substitution and Possibility, A relational view" in Edwards, Jeanette, Franklin, Sarah, Hirsch, Eric, Price, Frances and Strathern, Marilyn (eds.) *Technologies of Procreation: Kinship in the Age of Assisted Conception* 2nd edn. (London: Routledge) pp. 171–216.

Strong, Carson .(1996) "Genetic Screening in Oocyte Donation: Ethical and Legal Aspects" in Cohen, Cynthia (ed.) *New Ways of Making Babies: The Case of Egg Donation* (Bloomington and Indianapolis: Indiana UP) pp. 122–137.

Stumpf, Andrea E (1986) "Redefining Mother: A Legal Matrix for New Reproductive Technologies" *Yale Law Journal* vol. 96 pp. 187–208.

Tanne, Janice Hopkins (1999) "Dolly's other DNA came from donor egg" *British Medical Journal* vol. 319 p. 593.

Tännsjö, Torbjörn (1998) "Compulsory Sterilisation in Sweden" *Bioethics* vol. 12 no. 3 pp. 236–49.

Taub, Nadine (1990) "Surrogacy: A Preferred Treatment for Infertility" in Gostin, Larry (ed.) *Surrogate Motherhood: Politics and Privacy* (Bloomington and Indianapolis: Indiana UP) pp. 221–232.

Taylor, Charles (1979) "What's Wrong with Negative Liberty" in Ryan, Alan (ed.) *The Idea of Freedom* (Oxford UP) pp. 175–93.

—— (1985) *Philosophical Papers Volume Two: Philosophy and the Human Sciences* (Cambridge UP).

Taylor, Janelle S (1998) "Image of Contradiction: Obstetrical Ultrasound in American Culture" in Franklin, Sarah and Ragone, Helene *Reproducing Reproduction: Kinship, Power and Technological Innovation* (Pennsylvania UP) pp. 15–45.

Templeton, A and Morris, JK (1998) "Reducing the risk of multiple births by transfer of two embryos after *in vitro* fertilisation" *New England Journal of Medicine* vol. 339 pp. 573–7.

Te Velde, Eijkemans, R and Habbema, HDF (2000) "Variation in couple fecundity and time to pregnancy, an essential concept in human reproduction" *Lancet* vol. 355 pp. 1928–9.

Tew, Marjorie (1990) *Safer Childbirth? A Critical History of Maternity Care* (London: Chapman Hall).

Thom, Deborah and Jennings, Mary (1996) "Human pedigree and the 'best stock': from eugenics to genetics?" in Marteau, Theresa and Richards, Martin (eds.) *The Troubled Helix: social and psychological implications of the new human genetics* (Cambridge UP) pp.211–34.

Thomas, Richard (1998) "New born baby boy given life by frozen sperm is 'the image of his dead father' " *The Observer* 13 December 1998 p. 2.

Thomson, Judith Jarvis (1971) "A Defence of Abortion" *Philosophy and Public Affairs* vol. 1 no. 1 pp. 47–66.

Thomson, Michael (1998) *Reproducing Narrative: Gender, Reproduction, and Law* (Aldershot: Ashgate/Dartmouth).

Tighe, Margaret (1999) [1994] "A Pandora's Box of Social and Moral Problems" in Kuhse, Helga and Singer, Peter (eds) *Bioethics: An Anthology* (Oxford: Blackwell) pp. 91–3.

Titmuss, Richard (1970) *The Gift Relationship: From Human Blood to Social Policy* (London: Allen and Unwin).

Tizzard, Juliet (1998) "Jumping Through Hoops" *Progress in Reproduction* vol. 2 nos. 1/2 p. 3.

Todd, Dave (1991) "Expert Sounds Alarm on Indonesia Birth Control Program" *The Montreal Gazette* 26 November 1991 at A1.

Tomlinson, Suzanne (1998) "Genetic Testing for Cystic Fibrosis: A Personal Perspective" *Harvard Journal of Law and Technology* vol. 11 no. 3 pp. 551–564.

Tong, Rosemarie (1995) "Feminist Perspectives and Gestational Motherhood: The Search for a Unified Legal Focus" in Callahan, Joan (ed.) *Reproduction, Ethics and the Law: Feminist Responses* (Bloomington and Indianapolis: Indiana UP) pp. 55–79.

—— (1996) "Toward a Feminist Perspective on Gamete Donation and Reception" in Cohen, Cynthia (ed.) *New Ways of Making Babies: The Case of Egg Donation* (Bloomington and Indianapolis: Indiana UP) pp. 138–55.

—— (1997) *Feminist Approaches to Bioethics* (Boulder: Westview).

Tonti-Filippini, Nicholas (1999) [1994] "The Catholic Church and Reproductive Technology" in Kuhse, Helga and Singer, Peter (eds.) *Bioethics: An Anthology* (Oxford: Blackwell) pp. 93–5.

Torres, A and Forrest, JD (1988) "Why do Women have Abortions?" *Family Planning Perspectives* vol. 20, pp. 284–292.

Toumey, CP (1992) "The Moral Character of Mad Scientists: A Cultural Critique of Science" *Science, Technology and Human Values* vol. 17 pp. 411–37.

Townshend-Smith, Richard (1989) *Sex Discrimination in Employment: Law Practice and Policy* (London: Sweet and Maxwell).

Trindade, Francis and Cane, Peter (1999) *The Law of Torts in Australia* 3rd edn. (Melbourne: Oxford UP).

Trombley, Stephen (1988) *The Right to Reproduce: A History of Coercive Sterilization* (London: Weidenfeld & Nicholson).

Tudor, Andrew (1989) *Monsters and Mad Scientists: A Cultural History of the Horror Movie* (Oxford: Blackwell).

Turney, J (1995) "The public understanding of genetics—where next?" *European Journal of Genetics and Society* vol. 1 pp. 5–20.

—— (1998) *Frankenstein's Footsteps: Science, Genetics and Popular Culture* (New Haven, Ct: Yale UP).

Unger, Roberto (1983) *The Critical Legal Studies Movement* (Cambridge, Mass: Harvard UP).

Usher, J (1991) *Women's Madness: Misogyny or Mental Illness* (New York: Harvester Wheatsheaf)

Utian, WH, Sheean, L, Godfarb, JM and Kiwi, R (1985) "Successful pregnancy after *in vitro* fertilization-embryo transfer from an infertile woman to a surrogate" *New England Journal of Medicine* vol. 313 pp. 1351–2.

Van Den Akker, OBA (1999) "Organizational Selection and Assessment of Women entering a Surrogacy Agreement in the UK" *Human Reproduction* vol. 14 no. 1 pp. 262–299.

Van Hollen, Cecilia (1998) "Moving Targets: Routine IUD Insertion in Maternity Wards in Tamil Nadu" *Reproductive Health Matters*, vol. 6 no. 11 pp. 98–106.

Vance, Jeanne (1994) "Womb for Rent: Norplant and the Undoing of Poor Women, *Hastings Constitutional Law Quarterly* vol. 21 pp. 827–55.

Vaux, Kenneth (1989) *Birth Ethics: Religious and Cultural Values in the Genesis of Life* (New York: Crossroad Publishing).

Venn, Alison, Watson, Lyndsey, Bruinsma, Fiona, Giles, Graham, Healy, David (1999) "Risk of cancer after use of fertility drugs with in-vitro fertilisation" *Lancet* vol. 354 pp.1586–1590.

Wachbroit, Robert and Wassermen, David (1995) "Patient Autonomy and Value-Neutrality in Non-Directive Genetic Counseling" *Stanford Law and Policy Review* vol. 6 no. 2 pp. 103–111.

Walkinshaw, Stephen A (1995) "Clinical Methods of Prenatal Diagnosis" in Barron, SL and Roberts, DF (eds.) *Issues in Fetal Medicine: Proceedings of the 29th Annual Symposium of the Galton Institute* (Basingstoke: Macmillan) pp. 69–81.

Wallerstein, Claire (1998) "Pakistan Lags Behind in Reproductive Health" *British Medical Journal* vol. 317 p. 1546.

Wang, JX, Davies, M, Norman, RJ (2000) "Body mass and probability of pregnancy during assisted reproduction treatment: retrospective study" *British Medical Journal* vol. 321 pp. 1320–1.

Warnock, Mary (1984) *Report of the Inquiry into Human Fertilisation and Embryology* Cm 9314 (London: Department of Health and Social Security).

—— (1985) *A Question of Life : the Warnock report on human fertilisation and embryology* (Oxford : Blackwell).

Warnock, Mary (1987) "Do Human Cells Have Rights" *Bioethics* vol. 1 no. 1 pp. 1–14.
—— (1998) "Informed Consent: A Publisher's Duty" *British Medical Journal*, vol. 316, pp. 1002–3.
Warren, Mary Anne (1999) "Sex Selection: Individual Choice or Cultural Coercion?" in Helga Kuhse and Peter Singer (eds.) *Bioethics: An Anthology*, (Oxford: Blackwell) pp. 137–42,
Watson-Smyth, Kate (1997) "Paid Surrogacy should be legal in UK" Electronic Telegraph issue 619 *www.telegraph.com* 3 February.
Watts, Geoff (1999) "Fears that a rise in genetic testing will rule out insurance are 'paranoia' " *British Medical Journal* vol. 319 p. 273.
Webb, Anne (1999) "Emergency Contraception: Is it Time to Change Methods?" *British Medical Journal* vol. 318 pp. 343–3.
Weir, Tony (2000a) "The Unwanted Child" *Cambridge Law Journal* vol. 59 no. 2 pp. 238–41.
—— (2000b) *A Casebook on Tort* 9th edn. (London: Sweet and Maxwell).
Weiss, Rick (1996), "Anti-Girl Bias Rises in Asia" *Washington Post* 11 May 1996 at A1.
—— (1999) "Clone Defects Point to Need for Two Genetic Parents" *Washington Post* 10 May 1999 at A1.
Wellcome Trust (1998) *Public Perspectives on Human Cloning* (London: The Wellcome Trust).
Wertz, Dorothy and Wertz, Richard (1977) *Lying-In: A History of Childbirth in America* (New Haven: Uale UP).
Wertz, Dorothy (1997) "Society and the Not-So-New- Genetics: What are we Afraid Of? Some Future Predictions from a Social Scientist" *The Journal of Contemporary Health Law and Policy* vol. 13 no. 2 pp. 299–345.
West, Robin (1991) "Jurisprudence and Gender" in Bartlett, Katherine T and Kennedy, Rosanne *Feminist Legal Theory: Readings in Law and Gender* (Boulder, Colorado: Westview Press) pp. 201–34.
—— (1992) "The Difference in Women's Hedonic Lives: A Phenomenological Critique of Feminist Legal Theory" in Frug, Mary Joe (ed.) *Women and the Law* (Westbury, NY: The Foundation press) pp. 807–25.
Whetham, WCD and Whetham, CD (1909) *The Family and the Nation* (London: Longmans).
Whitbeck, Caroline (1991) "Ethical Issues Raised by the New Medical Technologies" in Rodin, Judith and Collins, Aila (eds.) *Women and New Reproductive Technologies: Medical, Psychological, Legal and Ethical Dilemmas* (Hillsdale, New Jersey, Lawrence Erlbaum) pp. 49–64.
White, Tyrene (1994) "Two Kinds of Production: The Evolution of China's Family Planning Policy in the 1980s" in Finkle, Jason and McIntosh, Alison (eds.) *The New Politics of Population: Conflict and Consensus in Family Planning* (Oxford UP) pp. 137–158.
WHO Task Force on Immunological Methods for Fertility Regulation (1978) "Evaluating the safety and efficacy of placental antigen vaccines for fertility regulation" *Clinical Experimental Immunology* vol. 33 pp. 360–375.
Widdett, Ceri and Thomson, Michael (1997) "'Justifying Treatment and Other Stories" *Feminist Legal Studies*, vol. 5 no. 1 pp. 77–89.
Widyantoro, Ninuk (1994) "The Story of Norplant Implant in Indonesia" *Reproductive Health Matters* no. 3 pp. 20–28.

Wikler, Daniel (1995) "Policy Issues in Donor Insemination" *Stanford Law and Policy Review* vol. 6 no. 2 pp. 47–56.

Wilder, Mary (1998) "The Rule of Law, The Rise of Violence and the Role of Morality: Reframing America's Abortion Debate" in Solinger, Rickie (ed.) *Abortion Wars: A Half Century of Struggle 1950–2000* (Berkeley: University of California Press) pp. 73–94.

Willan, P and Hawkes, N (1993) "White Baby Born to Black Mother" *The Times* 31 December 1993 p. 1.

Williams, Bernard (1973) *The Problem of the Self: Philosophical Papers 1956–1972* (Cambridge UP).

Williams, Gareth, Popay, Jennie and Bissell, Paul (1995) "Public heath risks in the material world: barriers to social movements in health" in Gabe, Jonathan (ed.) *Medicine, Health and Risk: Sociological Approaches* (Oxford: Blackwell) pp.113–132.

Williams, Glanville (1983) *Textbook of Criminal Law* 2nd edn. (London : Stevens and Sons).

Williamson, Robert (1999) "Human Reproductive Cloning is unethical because it undermines autonomy: commentary on Savulescu" *Journal of Medical Ethics* vol. 25, pp. 96–7.

Wilmut I, Schnieke, AE, McWhir, J, Kind, AJ and Campbell, KHS (1997) "Viable offspring derived from fetal and adult mammalian cells" *Nature* vol. 385 pp. 810–3.

Wilmut, Ian (1999) "Dolly: The Age of Biological Control' Eugenics and Human Rights" in Burley, Justine (ed.) *The Genetic Revolution and Human Rights* (Oxford UP) pp. 119–28.

Wilson, Elizabeth (1991) "Injectable Contraceptives" in London, Nancy and Baird, David (eds.) *Handbook of Family Planning* (Edinburgh: Churchill Livingston) pp. 143–158.

Wright, Daniel, Henderson, Marion, Raab, Gillain, Abraham, Charles, Buston, Katie, Scott, Sue and Hart, Graham (2000) "Extent of regretted sexual intercourse among young teenagers in Scotland: a cross sectional survey" *British Medical Journal* vol. 321 pp. 1243–4.

Wright, M (1986) "Surrogacy and Adoption: Problems and Possibilities" *Family Law* vol. 16 pp. 109–113.

Wolfenden Committee (1957) *Report of the Committee on Homosexual Offences and Prostitution* Cmnd 247 (London: HMSO)

Wood, Clive (1971) *Intrauterine Devices* (London: Butterworths).

World Health Organization (1978) *Risk Approach for Maternal and Child Health Care: a Managerial Strategy to Improve the Coverage and Quality of Maternal and Child Health/Family Planning Services Based on the Measurement of Individual and Community Risk* (Geneva: World Health Organisation).

Wyatt, John (2000) "Medical Paternalism and the Fetus" Paper presented at *The New Ethics of Abortion* BPAS 21 February 2000.

Yamey, Gavin (1999) "Sexual and reproductive health: what about boys and men?" *British Medical Journal* vol. 319 pp. 1315–6.

Young, Iris Marion (1997) *Intersecting Voices: Dilemmas of Gender, Political Philosophy and Policy* (Princeton UP).

Yoxen, Edward (1990) "Conflicting Concerns: The Political Context of Recent Embryo Research Policy in Great Britain" in McNeil, M, Varcoe, I and Yearley, S (eds.) *The New Reproductive Technologies* (Basingstoke: Macmillan) pp. 173–99.

Zabin, Laurie Schwab and Hayward, Sarah (1993) *Adolescent Sexual Behaviour and Childbearing* (London: Sage).

Zuhur, Sherifa (1992) "Of Milk-Mothers and Sacred Bonds: Islam, Patriarchy and New Reproductive Technologies" *Creighton Law Review* vol. 25 no. 5 pp. 1725–1736.

Index